1st Edition 2007

New York

The Complete **Residents'** Guide

Passionately Publishing...

EXPLORER

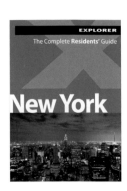

New York Explorer 1st Edition   ISBN 13 - 978-976-8182-80-7   ISBN 10 - 976-8182-80-6

Front Cover Photograph: Pamela Grist

Printed and bound by Emirates Printing Press, Dubai, United Arab Emirates.

Explorer Publishing & Distribution
PO Box 34275, Zomorrodah Bldg, Za'abeel Rd, Dubai
United Arab Emirates
Phone   (+971 4) 335 3520
Fax   (+971 4) 335 3529
Email   Info@Explorer-Publishing.com
Web   www.Explorer-Publishing.com

Welcome...

If you live in New York, you've picked up the right book. It's not meant for tourists who are only looking for the Hard Rock Café – it's meant for you, the smooth-talking, fast-walking, no-nonsense, fun-loving New Yorker who wants the inside track on slotting into the city's hectic pace.

Flick through the pages of **General Information** to brush up on your New York facts - handy for when you want to impress visitors with info on the city's geography, history, politics and more. The **Residents** chapter is your user's guide to everything life throws at you, from renting an apartment to getting a job, from finding a vet to getting married, and from passing your driving test to actually being able to find a parking spot when you do.

The **Exploring** chapter is like having your own personal tour guide, and steers you away from the tacky tourist traps into the really cool areas. **Activities** lists hundreds of things to do and will ensure you spend less time sitting on your own in Starbucks.

If money is burning a hole in your pocket, check out the **Shopping** chapter for some ideas on where you can blow your dough, whether you've got a dollar left until payday or your trust fund just kicked in. Finally, the **Going Out** chapter lists 200 restaurants, coffee shops, bars and nightclubs that have been personally recommended by our team of New York experts.

Phew! That's a lot of info packed into one book. If you're trying to figure out where to begin, turn to the **Maps** section at the back to get your bearings and start a new adventure in the Big Apple.

So there you have it – that covers just about everything. But if you find something you've missed (like your favourite naked yoga class?), then go to www.explorerpublishing.com, fill in the Reader Response Form, and share the knowledge with your fellow explorers.

The Explorer Team

Explorer online

Life can move pretty fast so make sure you keep up at www.explorerpublishing.com. Register for updates on the latest happenings in your city, or let us know if there's anything we've missed out with our reader response form. You can also check out city info on various destinations around the world - whether you're planning a holiday or making your next big move, we've got it covered. All our titles, from residents' guides to mini visitors' guides, mini maps to photography books are available to purchase online so you need never be without us!

Only 6 295 days till my first Volkswagen.

It gets me. I can't quite say why I'm so madly attracted to my Volkswagen. It's like we share an uncommon passion. Sure, it feels so safe and sound on the road, while also looking sleek and styled on the outside. It also feels nice and comfortable on the inside, too!

But it's really more than all that. It's another dimension. A real connection – it's like a soul mate. I guess I can say it's the ONE for me. So why do I always go for a Volkswagen? Because it simply gets me.

For the love of automobiles

Hashim MM
AKA: Speedy Gonzales

They don't come much faster than Hashim – he's so speedy with his mouse that scientists are struggling to create a computer that can keep up with him. His nimble fingers leave his keyboard smouldering (he gets through three a week), and his go-faster stripes make him almost invisible to the naked eye when he moves.

Jane Roberts
AKA: The Oracle

After working in an undisclosed role in the government, Jane brought her super sleuth skills to Explorer. Whatever the question, she knows what, where, who, how and when, but her encyclopaedic knowledge is only impressive until you realise she just makes things up randomly.

Helen Spearman
AKA: Little Miss Sunshine

With her bubbly laugh and permanent smile, Helen is a much-needed ray of sunshine in the office when we're all grumpy and facing harrowing deadlines. It's almost impossible to think that she ever loses her temper or shows a dark side... although put her behind the wheel of a car, and you've got instant road rage.

Jayde Fernandes
AKA: Pop Idol

Jayde's idol is Britney Spears, and he recently shaved his head to show solidarity with the troubled star. When he's not checking his dome for stubble, or practising the dance moves to 'Baby One More Time' in front of the bathroom mirror, he actually manages to get some designing done.

Henry Hilos
AKA: The Quiet Man

Henry can rarely be seen from behind his large obstructive screen but when you do catch a glimpse you'll be sure to get a smile. Lighthearted Henry keeps all those glossy pages filled with pretty pictures for something to look at when you can't be bothered to read.

Kate Fox
AKA: Contacts Collector

Kate swooped into the office like the UK equivalent of Wonderwoman, minus the tights of course (it's much too hot for that), but armed with a superhuman marketing brain. Even though she's just arrived, she is already a regular on the Dubai social scene - she is helping to blast Explorer into the stratosphere, one champagne-soaked networking party at a time.

Ieyad Charaf
AKA: Fashion Designer

When we hired Ieyad as a top designer, we didn't realise we'd be getting his designer tops too! By far the snappiest dresser in the office, you'd be hard-pressed to beat his impeccably ironed shirts.

Katie Drynan
AKA The Irish Deputy

Katie is a Jumeirah Jane in training, and has 35 sisters who take it in turns to work in the Explorer office while she enjoys testing all the beauty treatments available on the Beach Road. This Irish charmer met an oil tycoon in Paris, and they now spend the weekends digging very deep holes in their new garden.

Ingrid Cupido
AKA: The Karaoke Queen

Ingrid has a voice to match her starlet name. She'll put any Pop Idols to shame once behind the mike, and she's pretty nifty on a keyboard too. She keeps us all ticking over and was a very welcome relief for overworked staff. She certainly gets our vote if she decides to go pro; just remember you saw her here first.

Ivan Rodrigues
AKA: The Aviator

After making a mint in the airline market, Ivan came to Explorer where he works for pleasure, not money. That's his story, anyway. We know that he is actually a corporate spy from a rival company and that his multi-level spreadsheets are really elaborate codes designed to confuse us.

Kiran Melwani
AKA: Bow Selector

Like a modern-day Robin Hood (right down to the green tights and band of merry men), Kiran's mission in life is to distribute Explorer's wealth of knowledge to the fact-hungry readers of the world. Just make sure you never do anything to upset her – rumour has it she's a pretty mean shot with that bow and arrow.

Abdul Gafoor
AKA: Ace Circulator
After a successful stint on Ferrari's Formula One team Gafoor made a pitstop at our office and decided to stay. He has won our 'Most Cheerful Employee' award five years in a row – baffling, when you consider he spends so much time battling the traffic.

Andrea Fust
AKA: Mother Superior
By day Andrea is the most efficient manager in the world and by night she replaces the boardroom for her board and wows the pants off the dudes in Ski Dubai. Literally. Back in the office she definitely wears the trousers!

Ahmed Mainodin
AKA: Mystery Man
We can never recognise Ahmed because of his constantly changing facial hair. He waltzes in with big lambchop sideburns one day, a handlebar moustache the next, and a neatly trimmed goatee after that. So far we've had no objections to his hirsute chameleonisms, but we'll definitely draw the line at a monobrow.

Cherry Enriquez
AKA: Bean Counter
With the team's penchant for sweets and pastries, it's good to know we have Cherry on top of our accounting cake. The local confectioner is always paid on time, so we're guaranteed great gateaux for every special occasion.

Claire England
AKA: Whip Cracker
No longer able to freeload off the fact that she once appeared in a Robbie Williams video, Claire now puts her creative skills to better use – looking up rude words in the dictionary! A child of English nobility, Claire is quite the lady – unless she's down at Jimmy Dix.

Ajay Krishnan R
AKA: Web Wonder
Ajay's mum and dad knew he was going to be an IT genius when the found him reconfiguring his Commodore 64 at the tender age of 2. He went on to become the technology consultant on all three Matrix films, and counts Keanu as a close personal friend.

David Quinn
AKA: Sharp Shooter
After a short stint as a children's TV presenter was robbed from David because he developed an allergy to sticky back plastic, he made his way to sandier pastures. Now that he's thinking outside the box, nothing gets past the man with the sharpest pencil in town.

Alex Jeffries
AKA: Easy Rider
Alex is happiest when dressed in leather from head to toe with a humming machine between his thighs – just like any other motorbike enthusiast. Whenever he's not speeding along the Hatta Road at full throttle, he can be found at his beloved Mac, still dressed in leather.

Enrico Maullon
AKA: The Crooner
Frequently mistaken for his near-namesake Enrique Iglesias, Enrico decided to capitalise and is now a regular stand-in for the Latin heartthrob. If he's ever missing from the office, it usually means he's off performing for millions of adoring fans on another stadium tour of America.

Alistair MacKenzie
AKA: Media Mogul
If only Alistair could take the paperless office one step further and achieve the officeless office he would be the happiest publisher alive. Wireless access from a remote spot somewhere in the Hajar Mountains would suit this intrepid explorer – less traffic, lots of fresh air, and wearing sandals all day - the perfect work environment!

Firos Khan
AKA: Big Smiler
Previously a body double in kung fu movies, including several appearances in close up scenes for Steven Seagal's moustache. He also once tore down a restaurant with his bare hands after they served him a mild curry by mistake.

Erin Donnelly

You can take the girl out of Texas, but despite five years in New York, Erin can't shake her addiction to artery-clogging Tex-Mex food. Fortunately she's an NYC nightlife expert so she knows where to go to dance off the calories. Erin is currently blazing a trail around London's after-dark scene.

Jennifer Keeney Sendrow

Jennifer wasn't born in New York, but she got there as soon as she could. Ten years later, she's a freelance writer, editor and radio producer, and a licensed NYC tour guide on the side (five boroughs in one day? Easy peasy!).

Rania Adwan

This little firecracker has lived in New York on and off for the last six years, and still pops in from time to time, whenever she's not in London, Dubai, Cairo or Washington. She misses Polish pastries from Greenpoint Brooklyn and the buskers on the subway.

Dana Micheli

Despite the weather and lack of parking spaces, Dana flatly refuses to live anywhere but New York. After graduating law school and realising that it was nothing like LA Law, she decided to forgo a legal career for literary one. She is currently writing for a local newspaper in Brooklyn and co-authoring a novel. .

Samantha Debicki

Samantha Debicki moved to New York to attend Columbia, where she majored in English. Between acting and writing jobs, she loves yoga, singing, wine bars, drinking her weight in coffee, good books, and trashy magazines.

Amanda Scott

Amanda is proud to announce that she was finally cast as the lead in the school play. Sure she's 30, 'but take that Ramona Gilden!' Amanda would like to dedicate her shopping chapter to her mother, who taught her the most important phrases in the English language: '50% off' and 'final clearance.'

AnneLise Sorenson

Travel writer and editor AnneLise has penned (and wine-tasted) her way across four continents, writing for books, magazines and websites. She holds a special fondness for the New York, a metropolis that continually rewards her wanderlust (and her cravings for steak-frites at 3am).

Vadim Liberman

Russian-born Vadim has lived in New York since he was 3, but still swears allegiance to Vodka. He enjoys a balanced high-brow/low-brow lifestyle: while he loves browsing around museums and going to the theatre, he can't get enough of trashy reality TV.

Jennifer Kellas

Jennifer is a world expert on Titian's Mary Magdalene (in other words people, she's into art). She also hosts concerts in the city and attends a lot of glamorous rock-star parties. She has travelled from Istanbul to Inverness but has always called New York home.

Karim Farid

Karim freelances for various magazines and newspapers in New York – it gives him the money to support his addiction to outdoor sports. When he's not writing, you can find him snowboarding, fishing, or bungee jumping off the Statue of Liberty.

Leonard Jacobs

Leonard is a lifelong New Yorker and theatre lover, and has worked as a playwright, director, dramaturg and producer. He is the national theatre editor of Back Stage, a publication for American actors, and is the first-string critic for Back Stage as well as for the New York Press.

Thanks...

Authors aside, there are many friendly faces who worked behind the scenes to help us get this book published. A big thank you goes out to everyone who played a special role in the book, including: Marko Ferenc for his help at the beginning, Justin, Hannah and Lily for their support, Pam for company and cosmopolitans, Jen K for cherry beer and McSorley's, and Kevin Friedman for the final bagel at JFK! Thanks also to the Washington, DC Tourism Corporation, the Greater Philadelphia Tourism Marketing Corporation, and the Pocono Mountains Visitors Bureau for the images on p.242 and p.249. Last but not least, thanks to everybody in the Explorer office for their support. We can all be very proud of this book!

Rafi VP
AKA: Party Trickster
After developing a rare allergy to sunlight in his teens, Rafi started to lose a few centimeters of height every year. He now stands just 30cm tall, and does his best work in our dingy basement wearing a pair of infrared goggles. His favourite party trick is to fold himself into a briefcase, and he was once sick in his hat.

Shyrell Tamayo
AKA: Fashion Princess
We've never seen Shyrell wearing the same thing twice – her clothes collection is so large that her husband has to keep all his things in a shoebox. She runs Designlab like clockwork, because being late for deadlines is SO last season.

Sunita Lakhiani
AKA: Designlass
Initially suspicious of having a female in their midst, the boys in Designlab now treat Sunita like one of their own. A big shame for her, because they treat each other pretty damn bad!

Roshni Ahuja
AKA: Bright Spark
Never failing to brighten up the office with her colourful get-up, Roshni definitely puts the 'it' in the IT department. She's a perennially pleasant, profound programmer with peerless panache, and she does her job with plenty of pep and piles of pizzazz.

Tim Binks
AKA: Class Clown
El Binksmeisterooney is such a sharp wit, he often has fellow Explorers gushing tea from their noses in convulsions of mirth. Years spent hiking across the Middle East have given him an encyclopedic knowledge of rock formations and elaborate hair.

Sean Kearns
AKA: The Tall Guy
Big Sean, as he's affectionately known, is so laid back he actually spends most of his time lying down (unless he's on a camping trip, when his ridiculously small tent forces him to sleep on his hands and knees). Despite the rest of us constantly tripping over his lanky frame, when the job requires someone who will work flat out, he always rises to the editorial occasion.

Tissy Varghese
AKA: PC Whisperer
With her soft voice and gentle touch, Tissy can whip even the wildest of PCs into submission. No matter how many times we spill coffee on our keyboards she never loses her temper – a real mystery, especially as she wakes at 3am every day to beat the Sharjah traffic.

Shabsir M
AKA: Sticky Wicket
Shabsir is a valuable player on the Indian national cricket team, so instead of working you'll usually find him autographing cricket balls for crazed fans around the world. We don't mind though – if ever a retailer is stumped because they run out of stock, he knocks them for six with his speedy delivery.

Tom Jordan
AKA: The True Professional
Explorer's resident thesp, Tom delivers lines almost as well as he cuts them. His early promise on the pantomime circuit was rewarded with an all-action role in hit UK drama Heartbeat. He's still living off the royalties – and the fact he shared a sandwich with Kenneth Branagh.

Shefeeq M
AKA: Rapper in Disguise
So new he's still got the wrapper on, Shefeeq was dragged into the Explorer office, forced to pose in front of a camera, and put to work in the design department. The poor chap only stopped to ask for directions to Wadi Bih, but since we realised how efficient he is, we keep him chained to his desk.

Zainudheen Madathil
AKA: Map Master
Often confused with retired footballer Zinedine Zidane because of his dexterous displays and a bad head-butting habit, Zain tackles design with the mouse skills of a star striker. Maps are his goal and despite getting red-penned a few times, when he shoots, he scores.

Laura Zuffa
AKA: Travelling Salesgirl
Laura's passport is covered in more stamps than Kofi Annan's, and there isn't a city, country or continent that she won't travel to. With a smile that makes grown men weep, our girl on the frontlines always brings home the beef bacon.

Mohammed T
AKA: King of the Castle
T is Explorer's very own Bedouin warehouse dweller; under his caring charge all Explorer stock is kept in masterful order. Arrive uninvited and you'll find T, meditating on a pile of maps, amid an almost eerie sense of calm.

Mannie Lugtu
AKA: Distribution Demon
When the travelling circus rode into town, their master juggler Mannie decided to leave the Big Top and explore Dubai instead. He may have swapped his balls for our books but his juggling skills still come in handy.

Motaz Al Bunai
AKA: Car Salesman
Motaz starts every day with a tough decision, namely, which one of his fleet of exotic cars he's going to drive to work. If he ever takes a break from his delightful designing, he could always start his own second-hand car garage – Motaz's Motors.

Maricar Ong
AKA: Pocket Docket
A pint-sized dynamo of ruthless efficiency, Maricar gets the job done before anyone else notices it needed doing. If this most able assistant is absent for a moment, it sends a surge of blind panic through the Explorer ranks.

Noushad Madathil
AKA: Map Daddy
Where would Explorer be without the mercurial Madathil brothers? Lost in the Empty Quarter, that's where. Quieter than a mute dormouse, Noushad prefers to let his Photoshop layers, and brother Zain, do all the talking. A true Map Daddy.

Matt Farquharson
AKA: Hack Hunter
A career of tuppence-a-word hackery ended when Matt arrived in Dubai to cover a maggot wranglers' convention. He misguidedly thinks he's clever because he once wrote for some grown-up English papers.

Pamela Grist
AKA: Happy Snapper
If a picture can speak a thousand words then Pam's photos say a lot about her - through her lens she manages to find the beauty in everything – even this motley crew. And when the camera never lies, thankfully Photoshop can.

Mimi Stankova
AKA: Mind Controller
A master of mind control, Mimi's siren-like voice lulls people into doing whatever she asks. Her steely reserve and endless patience mean recalcitrant reporters and persistent PR people are putty in her hands, delivering whatever she wants, whenever she wants it.

Pete Maloney
AKA: Graphic Guru
Image conscious he may be, but when Pete has his designs on something you can bet he's gonna get it! He's the king of chat up lines, ladies – if he ever opens a conversation with 'D'you come here often?' then brace yourself for the Maloney magic.

Mohammed Sameer
AKA: Man in the Van
Known as MS, short for Microsoft, Sameer can pick apart a PC like a thief with a lock, which is why we keep him out of finance and pounding Dubai's roads in the unmissable Explorer van – so we can always spot him coming.

Rafi Jamal
AKA: Soap Star
After a walk on part in The Bold and the Beautiful, Rafi swapped the Hollywood Hills for the Hajar Mountains. Although he left the glitz behind, he still mingles with high society, moonlighting as a male gigolo and impressing Dubai's ladies with his fancy footwork.

"It's that Volkswagen feeling!"
It Gets Me.

I can't quite say why I'm so madly attracted to my Volkswagen. It's like we share an uncommon passion. Sure, it feels so safe and sound on the road, while also looking sleek and styled on the outside. It also feels nice and comfortable on the inside, too!

But it's really more than all that. It's another dimension. A real connection – it's like a soul mate. I guess I can say it's the ONE for me. So why do I always go for a Volkswagen? Because it simply gets me.

For the love of automobiles

Residents' Guides

All you need to know about living, working and enjoying life in these exciting destinations

* Covers not final. Titles available Winter 2007.

Activity Guides

Drive, trek, dive and swim... life will never be boring again

Mini Guides
The perfect pocket-sized
Visitors' Guides

＊ Covers not final. Titles available Winter 2007.

Mini Maps
Wherever you are,
never get lost again

＊ Covers not final. Titles available Winter 2007.

Photography Books
Beautiful cities caught through the lens

Contents

Contents

moving?

relax.
we carry the load.^{SM}

Door to door moving with Allied Pickfords

Allied Pickfords is one of the largest and most respected providers of moving services in the world, handling over 50,000 international moves every year.

We believe that nothing reduces stress more than trust, and each year thousands of families trust Allied Pickfords to move them. With over 800 offices in more than 40 countries, we're the specialists in international moving and have the ability to relocate you anywhere anytime. Move with Allied to Allied worldwide.

www.alliedpickfords.com

General Information

Geography

So good they named it twice? Not quite so. While New York State and New York City are synonymous for many people, they are not one and the same. The State of New York was one of the 13 original states of the United States of America and the country's capital until the honour was passed on to Philadelphia in 1790.

Nestled in the north-east nook of the United States, New York State is a mass of juxtapositions. Divided into upstate and downstate, you can breathe the fresh air of the green open landscapes of upstate New York or, just as easily, get lost in the dizzying subway system of the city, indulge in a killer hot dog at Nathan's on Coney Island or hide out in a log cabin in the Catskills. From the Great Lakes to the breathtaking Manhattan skyline, it's all here and it's all good.

With the Atlantic lapping on its eastern shores, the state boasts rolling green meadows, stunning forestry, over 6,500 natural ponds, 10 freshwater lakes, and of course Niagara Falls, which spills out 40 million gallons of water 55 metres downward every minute, across a ragged ledge nearly a kilometre wide.

New York City is the largest city in the United States and the most densely populated. Often referred to as the Big Apple (you'll find out why on p.6), Gotham, or 'The City that Never Sleeps', it is home to over 40% of the population of New York State.

The city itself is made up of five boroughs: the island of Manhattan, the Bronx, Staten Island, Brooklyn and Queens. Though much of the city is typical of any metropolis, Central Park, slap bang in the middle of Manhattan, was the first landscaped park in the country. Surprisingly, there are plenty of green bits in the city and the Hudson River, which runs for around 350km, separates Manhattan from the other boroughs as it runs into New York Bay.

History

From the indigenous tribes to the western European trials and tribulations of colonialism, from onions to apples, Amsterdam windmills to the British Duke of York, New York City arguably has a more interesting history than any other American city. It has been a bargain trade and a prized possession for many a European hotfooting it across the Atlantic.

What was it about Old World travellers and bad bearings? The 'discovery' of New York was an accident (twice!). The first jolly wanderer was Giovanni de Verrazzano, an Italian commissioned by the French to find the Orient. Instead, he sailed straight into the harbour in 1524 and named it New Angloueme, after the French King Francis I. And as soon as he realised his error, Verrazzano turned right around, never officially setting foot on the land. It wasn't until 85 years later that British explorer, Henry Hudson, commissioned by the Dutch this time and also in search of the elusive Orient, stumbled into the Hudson River (yes, he named it after himself), proclaimed New Angloueme for the Dutch and renamed it New Amsterdam.

USA Fact Box

Coordinates: 38 00 N, 97 00 W

Number of states: 50

Territories: 15

Borders: Canada to the north, Mexico to the south, Atlantic Ocean to the east and Pacific Ocean to the west.

Total Area: 9,826,675sq km (3,794,083sq mi)

Land only: 9,161,964sq km (3,537,438sq mi)

Water: 664,711sq km (256,645sq mi)

Total coastline: 19,924km

Highest point: Mount McKinley, Alaska (20,320ft)

Seattle

Ottawa

San Francisco

Boston
New York
Washington DC

Los Angeles

Hooston   New Orleans   *Atlantic Ocean*

Pacific Ocean

Mexico   *Gulf of Mexico*   Miami

La Habana

Cuba

Mexico City

Belize   Haiti
Jamaica

Guatemala

Alaska

New York Fact Box

Borders: The Canadian province of Ontario, Lake Ontario and Quebec to the north, the New England states of Vermont, Massachusetts and Connecticut to the east, the Atlantic ocean and New Jersey on the south-east, Pennsylvania to the south and Lake Erie to the west.

Total land area: 54,471,144 square miles

Total coastline: 127 miles of Atlantic Ocean coastline

Highest point: Mount Marcy, Essex County - 5,344ft (1,629 m)

But the story actually begins in Lenapehoking (the land of the Lenape). This was the very first name bestowed upon what is now New York. The indigenous Lenape tribe lived here for thousands of years, farming the land and living in relative comfort in a lush and unspoiled habitat right up until Europeans kept looking for the Orient in the wrong place.

Nevertheless, by 1613 the Dutch Fur Settlement was established, and the Dutch West India Company sent over 100 settlers to the southern tip of the Island (Mannahatta). The Lenape tribe defended their land and only conceded defeat after several courageous battles. In 1626 Peter Minuit, the first governor of New Amsterdam, decided to try a different tack with the locals and pulled off the city's first real estate scam by persuading the tribe to trade all of Manhattan and Staten Island for goods valued at the historical equivalent of $500.

Although this resulted in a short period of peaceful relations, Dutch West India still couldn't get people to move there willingly. Slaves, servants, prostitutes, orphans, thieves and other cast-outs were shipped off to the new land to put down roots and start a population. The population of 100 grew to 400 in the following 10 years. However, with the backgrounds of the immigrants and the fact that one in four structures was a tavern, New Amsterdam quickly became a capital for squalor, horrendous crime rates and general degeneracy.

In 1640, the city changed hands when Minuit passed it on to Peter Stuyvesant, the director of the Dutch West India Company. Peg-Leg Pete (as he was fondly known) was quite the party-pooper, and as a member of the Dutch Reform Church he imposed his puritanical attitudes on the city and its inhabitants. He came in and set about clearing up the mess that had accumulated before his time - first making peace (again) with the Lenape tribe, who were starting to realise just how badly they had been ripped off. Then he outlawed drinking on Sundays, closed down the taverns, established the first school, hospital, post office, prison and poor house, as well as inaugurating the first police force, made up of nine brave members. Despite his reputation as a killjoy, Stuyvesant's policies soon paid off and the population quadrupled in the decade that followed.

Newcomers came in voluntarily to work in the slave, fur or farm trades, and before you could click your New Amsterdam clogs, the city became a melting pot of ethnicities. Stuyvesant, a puritan through and through, started to get a little antsy at the different tongues and dialects that could be heard on the streets of lower Manhattan and took to turning people away. His aversion to immigration extended to the banning of the Sephardic Jews escaping the Spanish Inquisition, a move that angered the Dutch and resulted in him getting a stern telling off for his intolerance. His subsequent turnaround on the matter resulted in the first Jewish community settling in the New World.

New York City Fact Box

Borders: The Hudson River separates NYC from New Jersey and the East River separates the Bronx and Manhattan Long Island.

Total land area: 321sq mi (approximately 830km)

Total coastline: 578 miles, 17% of New York State's coastline

Highest point: Forte Washington/Bennett Park: 284ft

Highest Building: Empire State Building: 1,250ft (381m)

3

Along Came the British...

The British have always been keen to get in on the act with new settlements, and with things suddenly looking up in New Amsterdam, they wanted the whole pie, not just a piece. In 1664 they swooped in and got the lot. Stuyvesant didn't put up any kind of fight, unlike the Lenape (yep, still around) who fought some pretty ruthless battles. Thousands died, and those that survived were forced upstate. European settlers now numbered 3,000 and the city got a new British name: New York (after the Duke of York, who was the brother of King Charles II). New York became an important holding ground for Britain's political and military operations for the rest of America. Thanks to this and the slave trade, by 1740 New York was the third busiest port in the British Empire.

But all good empires must come to an end, and the series of wars that made up the American Revolution took place between 1775 and 1783. It was inevitable, given the ridiculous taxation and British pomp, so New York started its battle against the Red Coats on 26 August 1776. After seven bloody years, two major fires and thousands of lives lost, George Washington and his men marched victoriously down Broadway, reclaiming the city. On 13 September 1788 New York became the first capital of the Red Coat-free United States of America. Less than a year later (30 April 1789) General George Washington was inaugurated as the first president in the Federal Hall Building on Wall Street. New York remained the capital city until 1790 when the honour was bestowed to Philadelphia.

Onwards & Upwards

The country was free, the city's economy was booming, maritime commerce was on the up thanks in part to Robert Fulton and his steamboat escapades. Merchants introduced regularly scheduled routes between New York and Liverpool on what was called the Black Ball Line (the trans-Atlantic crossing) and the city was the American shipping epicentre. But as the city became richer and more successful, it also became more congested and so in 1807 Mayor DeWitt Clinton took action. He commissioned a city plan placed on a grid system, running 12 avenues from east to west and 220 streets running north to south, which turned out to be a great idea! Drunk on success and big dreams, Clinton proposed a canal to link the Hudson with Lake Erie in the North. Despite the protests of nay-sayers who thought it couldn't be done, in 1825 the Erie Canal became the longest in the world, spanning 27 miles and linking the Atlantic to the agriculturally rich Midwest and the lucrative markets of Canada.

The Melting Pot Steweth Over

By 1830 the population hit a staggering 170,000, with newcomers laying roots daily. Tensions ran high between old immigrants who could trace their lineage back two generations, and those fresh off the boat. The rich folk fled away from the port and southern tip of the island to fancier footings uptown, reducing certain areas of the city into slums. The most infamous was the Five Points neighbourhood, an intersection of three major streets (Park, Worth and Baxter). It was a lurid part of town under the control of some pretty nasty gangs (like the Dead Rabbits, the Whyos and the 40 Thieves), and was characterised by dilapidated tenement housing, gang wars, drunkenness, gambling, prostitution, extortion and political corruption.

Although it was one of the nastiest, Five Points was by no means the only slum in New York, with more and more immigrants flocking to the

Alexander Hamilton

Alexander Hamilton, the illegitimate son of a Scottish nobleman, played a key role in revolutionary history. The young man moved from the West Indies and enrolled in Kings College (now Columbia University), becoming politically active and angrily anti-British. He wrote, printed and distributed anti-colonial pamphlets that helped fuel the war. As Lieutenant Colonel in General George Washington's army, Hamilton was instrumental both before and after the war, playing a vital role in rebuilding the city. Once Washington was sworn in, Hamilton was given the job of Secretary of the Treasury. As such, he established the foundations for the New York Stock Exchange (1792), the first bank (1784) and the first newspaper, the Evening Post (still going today in the guise of Rupert Murdoch's New York Post).

A Bit of Greenery Does You Good

Immigrants were coming in by the boatload, factories were chugging, poverty was rife and the crisp, costly clothes of the rich upper set were being stained with the muck of the ordinary. Reluctant to give up aesthetics to house more immigrants, and inspired by the grand green open spaces of London and Paris, the Central Park Commission set up a design competition in 1853. The result: America's very first landscaped park. The winners, designer Federick Law Olmstead and architect Calvert Vaux, took the next four years to produce the lush Central Park, which stretched two and a half miles long and half a mile wide.

city in the hopes of a better life. The filth of Five Points was finally flushed out by a massive cholera outbreak in 1832 that killed thousands and sent thousands more fleeing from the downtown area.

The American Civil War (1861 to 1865) tested the city's strong commercial ties with the south. Anger about the forced army draft led to divided sympathies between the Confederacy and the Union. Being a city based entirely on immigration and a hodgepodge of colours, ethnicities and nationalities, New York tension was on the brink of eruption and in 1863 it finally exploded in one of the city's ugliest battles ever, the Draft Riots.

All men were forced to fight in the civil war, unless of course they could cough up the $300 exemption fee. This meant that the wealthy stayed safe and the poorest of the poor, predominantly the huge Irish community, were forced to take arms in a battle they wanted nothing to do with. On 13th July, an Irish mob of 15,000 took to the streets in bloody protest leaving a whirlwind of damage in their wake. They destroyed shops, homes, and then the riot took an even more ugly turn. Blaming the black community for the civil unrest (the American Civil War was fought for many reasons, superficially with the intention of freeing the black slaves) and fearing free slaves would mean stealing work from the white workforce, the mob turned against people of colour, vandalising their homes, burning down the Colored Orphan Asylum and even beating and lynching black people in the streets. Four days and 105 deaths later, peace was finally restored.

The Five Boroughs & the Birth of a Nation

By 1898 the population of New York had boomed to over three million, and the city limits had spread well beyond those laid out in the previous century. The five boroughs (the Bronx, Manhattan, Staten Island, Brooklyn and Queens) were bought together officially to make up New York City.

The height of European migration came in the 1920s, as thousands upon thousands came to America seeking a better, more prosperous life. Streaming through the processing centre on Ellis Island port, their first encounter with the new world would be the breathtaking sight of the Statue of Liberty and all that she stood for. Between 1892 and 1954, an estimated 15 million immigrants flowed through the harbour, prodded through the processing office, through health checks, inspections, interrogations and examinations. It is said that some 40% of all Americans have an ancestor that arrived at Ellis Island. Some moved on to pastures new, others (as many as five million) stayed in the sprawling metropolis.

The Statue of Liberty, originally called 'Liberty Enlightening the World', was a gift from the French to mark America's 100 years of independence from the British. Money was raised by the Franco-American Union for sculptor Frederic-Auguste Bartholdi to create the icon, which rises to 46 metres. Shipped in parts and assembled in New York, Lady Liberty had no base on which to stand. Money for her pedestal was raised by the affluent Hungarian

Rockefeller Center Sculpture

immigrant and publishing mogul, Joseph Pulitzer (publisher of *The World* daily newspaper), who encouraged Americans to dip into their pockets. And dip they did, finally unveiling the copper beauty in 1886. The Statue of Liberty stands a clear 305 feet high on her base, which is an 11 pointed star. The tallest statue in the world, it is probably one of the most iconic New York sights and a must-see tourist attraction. Land was fast becoming a rare commodity but the flow of people was not ebbing in the least. The economy was booming, as New York became the country's industrial capital, financial hub and headquarter haven for all kinds of companies from steel mills to cotton pickers. The race to grow upwards (instead of outwards) was on and by 1902 the city was able to boast a whopping 66 skyscrapers. And then came the growth below. In 1900 the underground transit system (or more commonly, the subway) tagged a $35 million spend and moved thousands of New Yorkers around the five boroughs less than a decade later.

Big Apple

The term 'The Big Apple' was coined by touring jazz musicians of the 1930s who used the slang expression 'apple' for any town or city. Therefore, to play New York City is to play the big time, or big apple. This is one theory anyway. Some say it originated in horse racing, and others say it relates to economic instability (Wall Street suits who had lost their jobs in the big crash of 1929 would supposedly sell apples, still in their suits, to make a living). Before any references of apples at all, the city was referred to as 'The Big Onion' for what seems like no particular reason.

The early 1900s saw a lot more firsts for the city. It was where the first labour and union organisations were formed, it was the first city to ratify the 19th amendment in 1920, giving women the right to vote, and it became the new world centre for publishing (an honour snatched from London) as Pulitzer and Hearst set up shop. New York was also the first city to defy prohibition, with over 30,000 illegal boozing establishments.

And For a While the Party Stalled…

They say that when New York sneezes the rest of the country gets a cold. On Tuesday 29th October 1929, the city gave an almighty 'atchoo' as the stock market crashed and the country plummeted into what came to be known as The Great Depression. Adding insult to injury, the corrupt dealings of Mayor James J Walker finally caught up with him and then the rest of the city as one million New Yorkers lost their jobs. It wasn't until tough talking, Jewish-Italian Fiorello LaGuardia (nicknamed 'the little flower') took office after Walker resigned (1932) that the place took a turn for the more prosperous. Over the course of his three terms, LaGuardia moved the city's economy through World War II (making the city's factories profitable contributors to the American war effort), streamlined the government, paid off some of the exorbitant debt racked up and rejuvenated the ailing infrastructure.

Rudi Rules

The city's 107th Mayor, Rudolph 'Rudi' Giuliani, was instrumental in New York's recovery after 9/11. His presence and hands-on involvement endeared him to even his harshest critics - so much so that *Time* magazine named him 'Man of the Year' for his hard work and efforts.

The Great Depression hit hard and president Herbert Hoover found himself in one almighty bind. Accepting that the ailing economy was beyond US control, Hoover felt that the key to recovery was trust in the economy. Americans blamed Hoover's passivity and felt that his initiatives to help were too late and too lame. New York native Franklin D. Roosevelt, next in line and 32nd president to the batting post, was ready for some radical experimentation in order to get the country out of the dark pit it currently found itself wallowing in. The New Deal was struck up, a series of programmes that included the Emergency Banking Act, the Federal Emergency Relief Administration and the Social Security Act. Some programmes worked and some didn't, but the country slowly crawled out of the depression and started on its bid to be one of the greatest economies of the world.

The Hip, the Trips and the Happenings

New York hurtled through the 20th century truly making the era its own. The art scene boomed as young hip things moved into the village (east and west) to make it home to all things bohemian. Andy Warhol and The Factory (his studio and its army of hangers-on) moved all things contemporary to the city, as he did with his protege, Brooklyn born Jean-Michel Basquiat. Everyone who was anyone would mingle at The Factory, from Mick Jagger and Salvador Dali to Bob Dylan and Allen Ginsberg. Ginsberg was also a Beatnik mover and shaker helping create the Beat movement that shot to fame such literary greats as Jack Kerouac's *On the Road* (1957), Ginsberg's own *Howl* (1956), and William S. Burroughs' *Naked Lunch* (1959). The literati were everywhere. A handful of intellectuals would get together at a round table at the Algonquin Hotel (p.32) to discuss culture, politics and propaganda and just like that, the *New Yorker* came into being.

Legendary club CBGB opened in the village and the music scene was the icing on the city's cake, with the likes of Bob Dylan and Joan Baez hanging around. Then came Woodstock, the sexual revolution, a proud gay community and everything in between. New York was the place to be, it was party central, intellectual haven, rock hangout and just downright cool!

New York is proud owner of the largest gay and lesbian scene in the world. This wasn't always the case. After years of being roughed up by a corrupt police force, the gay and lesbian community retaliated in 1969, resulting in the three-day Stonewall Riots at Stonewall Inn on Christopher Street. Stonewall Inn is considered sacred since the riot ended with the birth of the modern gay and lesbian rights movement. The original inn no longer exists, but the site and the movement is still very much alive and kicking.

On the 11th September 2001 New York faced one of its most fatal tragedies, as terrorist attacks destroyed the twin towers of the World Trade Center. That day, thousands of lives were lost and the entire nation was rocked to its foundation. The American economy was shattered, as was its 'you-can't-touch-us' resolve.

The world mourned as the entire country came to a complete standstill and New York fell to its knees. American foreign policy and sentiment changed after that fateful day and world history was about to get involved. George Bush Jnr, halfway through his controversial first term in office, took the country into war, only the second the US has ever instigated. Americans were fearful and untrusting as media outlets and government propaganda spewed paranoia, conspiracy theories, and an insistence that a war be heralded against an adjective and not a static thing, person or place. The 'war on terror' began and Afghanistan and Iraq felt the physical blows. Since then, world history has been marred and American freedoms have been massively infringed upon. Government scandals abounded, stern moves came into play including tighter security measures, the Judith Miller case and the leaking of anti-war secret agent files, infringements on freedom of information and freedom of speech, light shed on the infamous Guantanamo prison, the Patriot Act, and the right of the US Government to eavesdrop on anybody it chooses, including United Nations Secretary General Kofi Anan.

> ## CBGB & OMFUG
> This musical institution (Country Bluegrass Blues and Other Music for Uplifting Gormandizers) is famous as the birthplace of the American punk scene. In case you're wondering, a gormandizer is a 'hedonistic guzzler of music'. The club closed in October 2006 after a long and heated dispute with local residents.

World Trade Center Memorial

New York and its inhabitants have since recovered, licking their wounds as the foundations for the new Freedom Tower are set in place to stand on the ruins of what was. The rest of the world however, is still reeling from the day that never should have happened.

Live, Work, Play
If you're new to New York and are still trying to figure out which areas are cool, which are dangerous, or which are just miles out of your price range, check out the comprehensive guides to areas in this book. Find your ideal living space using the area guide in the Resident's chapter (starting on p.104), and discover where all the hipsters hangout in the Exploring chapter (starting on p.182).

Wall Street

Wall Street, the financial centre of the world, was so named because of a great big wooden wall built by the Dutch settlers to keep the indigenous Lenape out and guard lower Manhattan from further attacks. On the other side of the wall, slave owners used to bring their 'wares' for display and sale. The wall no longer exists, nor does the threat of attack from the Lenape, but Wall Street still stands as the world's most influential trading district.

New York Timeline

1524	Giovanni de Verrazzano sails into New York, renames it after a French king and sails right back out
1613	The Dutch Fur Settlement was established, and the Dutch West India Company sends over 100 settlers to try and fill the place. City renamed New Amsterdam
1626	First governor, Peter Minuit, trades land with the indigenous tribe, the Lenape
1664	The British take over and rename it New York
1783	George Washington reclaims New York
1788	New York becomes the first capital of the United States of America
1789	George Washington inaugurated first president in the Federal Hall Building on Wall Street
1853	Work on Central Park begins
1863	The Draft Riots ravage the city
1883	Construction of the Brooklyn Bridge is completed (after 13 years)
1886	The Statue of Liberty is unveiled
1898	The Bronx, Manhattan, Staten Island, Brooklyn and Queens are joined to form New York City
1892 - 1954	An estimated 15 million immigrants stream through Ellis Island
1904	The New York City Subway opens
1929	New York stock market crashes and the Great Depression begins
1931	Empire State Building is officially opened
1934	Fiorello La Guardia takes over as Mayor from the corrupt James J. Walker (resigned 1932)
1952	UN Headquarters is built
1977	The New York City Blackout lasts for two days and the subsequent riots and looting mark a lowpoint in New York's history
1980	John Lennon is murdered in front of his apartment near Central Park
2001	Terrorist attacks destroy the twin towers of the World Trade Center
2011	Freedom Tower is due to open in the place where the Trade Center towers stood

USA Overview

As the third largest country in both size (after Russia and China) and in population (following China and India), the US is considered a global superpower with the largest economy of scale. America has suffered a few crises of economy already this decade (the terrorist attacks of 9/11 and hurricanes Rita and Katrina have all had unprecedented bearing on the economy), but generally and despite the setbacks, the outlook is of continual growth and progressive development.

As a capitalist state, the private market predominates. There is a heavy 'two-tier labour market' where those at the bottom lack the skills and education appreciated and shared by those at the top. In due course, the bottom tier will fall behind professionally, spiralling into a continual failure to gain higher wages, decent health coverage and other benefits.

The 2001 terrorist attacks had a huge effect nationally as well as on the country's international economic prospects for growth, with risk factors running higher than normal. The government spend shifted considerably from what could be considered as immediate national well-being (infrastructure, housing developments, pension schemes and medical assistance) to anti-terrorist programmes and defence.

Much of the budget (left in almost $40 million surplus by the previous Clinton administration) was sapped into deficit by the war of 2003 and the US-led coalition in Iraq. The continued war efforts have increased economic risk and growth uncertainty. The United States is currently running on a $400 billion deficit. The budget for 2005 closed on revenues reaching some $2.119 trillion, while expenditures tallied $2.466 trillion.

Nationals vs Others

The country is suffering from astronomically high numbers of illegal immigrants particularly from Mexico and Latin America. Though the country's roots are entirely based upon a melting pot of ethnicities, the number of illegal migrant workers is registered at anything between 11.5 to 20 million, many of whom are Latino.

The situation reached boiling point in early 2006 when the media continued to highlight the appalling conditions these migrant workers were forced to endure. This, and a steady stream of criticism that has been building up, prompted the government to consider new laws to protect foreign workers.

The controversy wasn't so much that these people were supposedly taking American jobs - in fact they were making a valuable contribution to society by taking up badly

paid positions that Americans deemed 'unsuitable'. From taxi drivers to hot dog vendors to kitchen hands, the hard and often miserable work of the foreign labourer was what made the underbelly of economy tick and allowed the rest of the country to focus on bigger things.

The scandal was that these people were still paying taxes, living in atrocious conditions, and trying to survive on minimum wage. At the same time, they don't get essential benefits, such as health insurance, which is essential since free healthcare is non-existent.

The government passed a semblance of an immigration act that would allow Latino workers to come to the States on a valid one-year work visa with all the fringe benefits, including the much sought-after health coverage.

Gross Domestic Product

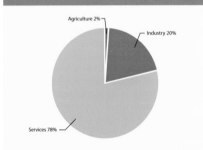

Agriculture 2%

Industry 20%

Services 78%

For white-collar immigrants, the situation is just as depressing. There is so much red tape surrounding the process of acquiring a work visa and the hoops that American employers have to go through are plentiful. For a start, an employer has to prove that an American citizen in unable to fulfil the requirements of the position, and the employer must show that they have adequately and sufficiently advertised the position nationally before seeking a foreign candidate. If that wasn't deterrent enough, the employer must pay an annual fee to sponsor the foreign national's work visa, which can be very expensive (see p.74).

Exports from the US total around $900 billion every year, and the main export partners are Canada, Mexico, Japan, China and the United Kingdom. The major products that are exported come from the agricultural, consumer goods, industrial supplies and capital goods sectors.

The US imports goods worth over $1.5 trillion each year, mainly from Canada, China, Mexico, Japan and Germany. Dependence on foreign oil is strong, with foreign oil making up two-thirds of total consumption.

While the economy is relatively stable, it's not all good news: around 5% of the labour force is unemployed, and an estimated 12% of the population lives below the poverty line.

New York Overview

The start of this decade came with a full swag-bag of bangs – from the pop of the dot-coms to the national recession and then of course 9/11. However, despite the adverse gloom, the city's economic cycle has surprisingly – and for the most part – stayed on track.

Growth

The Federal Bank recorded that as of May 2006, the labour market was looking considerably stronger, with both the rate of job creation and job return picking up. The rise in GDP can be put down to the technological advancements successfully garnered by the United States. New York, in the role of the country's epicentre for finance, commerce, IT and information, served to considerably influence the figures, well deserving its own standing ovation.

The city was touted the world's 25th fastest growing economy in 2005 with its own GDP of 3.3% (0.2% shy of the national number). That same year, the annual per capita personal income was little over $50,000, up 5.9% from the previous year, ranking fifth in the nation and eighth in the world.

Economy

Imports & Exports

Top exports: foodstuffs, commodities, minerals, manufactured goods, cut diamonds and car parts.
Top imports: oil, natural gas, electricity, gold, aluminium, rough diamonds and lumber.

Trade

Hub of the western world's banking, financial and communication sectors, New York is a beast unto itself trade-wise. The New York Stock Exchange (NYSE) sits proudly on Wall Street and the Bureau of Economic Analysis estimated that the gross state product for 2005 was $963.5 billion, third after California and Texas.

New York State is in the top five states for agriculture with outputs including dairy, cattle and livestock, and apples (of course!). Industrial outputs include printing and publishing, tourism, scientific instruments and chemical products.

The top five export markets in 2004 were Canada ($30.2 billion), UK ($3.3 billion), Japan ($2.6 billion), Israel ($2.4 billion), and Switzerland ($1.8 billion).

Employment

New York City experienced an unorthodox and unexpected employment growth for four consecutive years and ended the 90s on a considerable high. Even before the terrorist attacks, a slight dip in figures was starting to show and 9/11 merely accelerated a general slowing down in the job market. Immediately following the attacks, the private sector suffered continual employment drops that accumulated to a little over 7% in decline (that's around 225,000 jobs). The negative effects of the terrorist attacks have since shrunk, with economists citing little evidence of it causing a lasting effect.

New Developments

The city, renowned for not sleeping, is not about to rest on its laurels just yet, with more developments than you can shake a stick at.

The Empire State Building celebrated its 75th birthday in 2006 by opening a second observation deck, this time on the top floor as well as the traditional deck on the 86th floor. The views are the same, but from higher up. It should also help to relieve some of the frustrations of having to stand in long queues.

The city's Heritage Tourism Center recently opened and, partnering with the History Channel on cable TV, New York history has never been easier to discover. Cool tours, travel counsellors and specialised literature are all housed in the newly renovated version of one of New York's most historical sites, Federal Hall.

One of the trendiest neighbourhoods, the Meatpacking District, ups its street cred as it prepares to unveil the High Line Park (due to open in 2008). What was once a bustling railway 30 feet above street level, is now being turned into 'the nation's first urban water park' with 26 acres of wave pools, waterslides and an indoor beach club. The High Line will extend from the Meatpacking district through to West Chelsea and the Hudson Yards.

Coney Island, Brooklyn's south shore, is due for a refreshing nip/tuck job. A snip at $83 million, the shoreline, with creaking rollercoaster and the original Nathan's (best hot dogs in the world, ever!) will be turned into a year-round entertainment destination. Old charm and unique character will still prevail (fingers crossed).

The cheers will be louder as each of the five boroughs looks into getting some brand spanking new sporting facility. Having hit and run for 83 years at the 'House that Babe Ruth Built', the Yankees will be moving to an all new 51,800 capacity stadium, adjacent to where it is now in the Bronx. The Mets, never ones to be out-run, are breaking new ground for their new stadium in Queens, which will hold up to 45,000 screaming fans. Even the world's most famous sporting venue isn't taking a backseat. Madison Square Garden will be moving one block west to its new site on Ninth Avenue.

A world-class new golf course, designed by PGA champion Jack Nicklaus, is set to be a new jewel in New York's golfing crown. You can expect to tee off at Ferry Point in south-east Bronx from 2008 onwards.

The New York Film Festival, the Tribeca Film Festival, and now Sundance? That's right - Robert Redford is bringing his cooler-than-cool Sundance to the east coast - Brooklyn, to be exact. Closely collaborating with BAM (the Brooklyn Academy of Music) the Sundance Institute will host a series of performances, panel discussions and film screenings, including the best new dramatic and documentary feature films from the (real) January 2006 Sundance Film Festival.

The museum scene will also get a new lease of life in the coming year: some old (the National Cartoon Museum, formerly the International Museum of Cartoon Art, gets a new home), some new (the first ever sports museum will open in Spring 2008 in lower Manhattan) and some just because they can (the lower east side will welcome a new art museum, the first ever in the Downtown area) – the museum scene is workin' it baby, working it!

With CBGC gone for good (well, to Las Vegas, Nevada according to the rumours), music fans have been a little down and out, but the new Nokia Theatre might help fill that musical void. With 2,100 seats, the state-of-the-art venue opened late last year in the heart and soul of the city, Times Square. Also waiting to move into its new home is Cirque du Soleil. The group is looking forwarding to setting ground roots at a permanent theatre on 42nd Street.

Construction on the Freedom Tower, the 1,776 foot skyscraper that will sit where the World Trade Center twin towers used to be in downtown Manhattan, is due to open in 2011. Features include 2.6 million square feet of office space, a rooftop restaurant and an observation deck. The World Trade Center Memorial and Museum is also being worked on. Said to reflect 'absence', the designers are aiming for the two voids to represent the footprints of the twin towers. The structure will be surrounded by an oak forest, complete with cascading water falling into an illuminated reflecting pool.

Tourism

All visitors are welcome in New York, no matter what part of the world they are from or what their budget. According to the New York City Tourist Office, a record 43 million visitors enjoyed the city's many attractions in 2006, 7.2 million of which were international visitors. Being in such high demand places a strain on resources, however, but New York is rising to the challenge. There are currently around 70,000 hotel rooms in New York, with an additional 5,000 to be added during 2007.

The reasons to visit are endless, but here are just a few:

For starters, the many parades held throughout the year are the ultimate reason to party. From Gay Pride to St Patrick's Day, and from the Thanksgiving Day Parade to Puerto Rico Day, you're invited to participate. Make the most of it by dancing in the streets, waving your hands in the air. Then of course there are the various film and fashion festivals, the beach (it may only be

Radio City Music Hall

Coney Island, but the Hamptons are just around the corner), and the five 'S's: sights, sounds, skyline, smells and shopping.

International Relations

New York is home to a consulate of almost every country in the world (embassies tend to be located in the country's capital a few thousand miles away). Perhaps a more important indication of New York's importance in matters of international relations is that the world headquarters of the United Nations offices (p.181) are here, and the US is a voting key member of the UN Security Council.

Regional alliances are both well thought-out and economically solvent, and cover neighbours to the North (NAFTA – North American Free Trade Agreement, signed with Canada and Mexico to encourage trade) and to the South (CAFTA- of DR-CAFTA – Dominican Republic-Central American Free Trade Agreement, signed with the countries of Central America including Costa Rica, El Salvador, Guatemala, Honduras and Nicaragua).

Government & Politics

The founding fathers of American independence were so burnt by the British rule that they feared that if they had only one government branch it would become too powerful to be fair and balanced, and thus America's complex political system was born. The United States works on a federal presidential representative democratic republic. There are three main branches of government; the legislative, judicial and executive.

The legislative branch includes Congress (where bills are written and, if passed by the president, made into law) and government agencies. Congress also has the power to declare war and control inter-state trade. The two chambers of Congress are made up of the Senate and the House of Representatives.

Each of the 50 states elects two senators, and each senator has a six-year term with no limits placed on the seat. The Senate is responsible for conducting trials, approving treaties and confirming presidential nominations.

The House of Representatives is made up of 435 representatives, the number varies depending on the state since representation corresponds to population. Each representative is responsible for a congressional district – so the larger the state, the more the districts, the more representatives needed. Each representative serves a two-year term.

The judicial branch follows Article III of the Constitution and created the Supreme Court with the power of judicial review, interpreting laws and deciding how these same laws should be applied. The Supreme Court is the highest court in the country, it's set in place to keep a watchful eye on government ensuring that neither the president nor Congress step out of constitutional line. The nine members of the court are appointed by the president and hold the position for life, until they choose to resign or are impeached. The court also has the power to overturn laws and decisions made by lower courts.

The president, vice president and independent agencies make up the executive branch of government that concentrates on enforcing the laws passed by Congress. The president is, first and foremost, the head of the executive branch of the government. The powers of the president are stipulated in Article II of the Constitution and include: Commander-In-Chief, declaring war and overseeing treaties (with the approval of Congress), suggesting bills and then, once approved, signing them in as laws, and appointing judges and heads of government departments, among other things. The president serves a four-year term with a two-term maximum. His party, however, can stay in power as long as they are elected.

The Superpower
The US is considered the only world superpower, particularly since the end of the Cold War era and the demise of the former Soviet Union. The country plays a vital role in almost every aspect of foreign politics, from hosting peace talks between Israel and Palestine, to involvement in the Irish north/south unrest, to the peacekeeping forces the country sends abroad as and when is needed. A little further afield, relations are being tested. The invasion of Iraq and subsequent ongoing war has tugged at ties with the Middle East, and America's increased reliance on Middle Eastern Oil hasn't helped. Encounters with certain EU states have been met with mixed sentiment, again due to the war and the controversial justifications thereof.

13

New York Population Age Breakdown

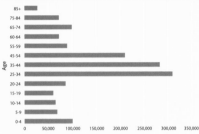

Population by Nationality

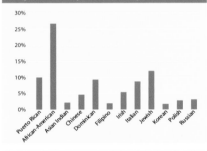

Population by Principal Language

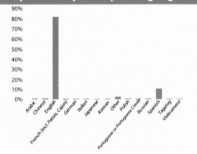

Education Levels

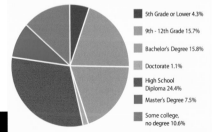

- 5th Grade or Lower 4.3%
- 9th - 12th Grade 15.7%
- Bachelor's Degree 15.8%
- Doctorate 1.1%
- High School Diploma 24.4%
- Master's Degree 7.5%
- Some college, no degree 10.6%

Population

The current recipe of the city's culture and population is an amalgamation drawn from a deep historical well. One-third of the people here can trace their lineage back to Europe, Hispanic immigrants make up another third and African-Americans account for a quarter of the population.

The 'Asian invasion' is said to be the fastest-growing component towards New York's immigration count, making up for almost one-tenth of the final figure.

The 20th century also saw a vast stream of Dominicans, Russians and Chinese relocating to New York. As a result, the New York of today is a complex stew of nationalities, ethnicities, religions and colours – it's what makes this place incredible – so tuck in and enjoy.

The last official census was conducted in 2000, with the next one scheduled for 2010. The 2000 census put the population of New York City at 8,008,278. The 2005 update put the population at 8,213,839. Staten Island had the largest increase in population (7.1%). Manhattan came in second with a 4.5% increase.

National Flag

There are three flags worth recognising. The first is the ubiquitous US flag flapping proudly on public buildings, outside corporate offices, up and down Fifth Avenue and on private residences. The flag is so well known internationally, but just in case you've just made your way off that deserted island, it is made up of 13 equally sized horizontal red and white alternating stripes (representing the first 13 states that defied the British and made up the Union) and a blue rectangle in the top left hand corner with 50 small, white, five-pointed stars - one for each state – arranged in nine offset rows of six and the five stars.

It is against the law to burn or defame the flag in any way. Since 9/11 in 2001, it has come to represent much more than just a flag. When it comes to symbolism, the global politics makes the flag even more potent with many New Yorkers and Americans generally holding the Star Spangled Banner in great esteem as a symbol of freedom, nationalism and patriotism.

New York State, as with the 49 other states, has its own individual flag. The state's coat of arms is emblazoned on a dark blue background. Lady Liberty stands with a pole in her hand. On top of the pole is a Phrygian cap, historically given to emancipated Roman slaves and adopted by French Revolutionaries: she, her pole and the cap stand for freedom. At her feet is a discarded crown, freedom from the British after the revolutionary war. On the right stands the goddess of Justice, blindfolded and aptly carrying the scales of impartial

New York Stock Exchange

justice for all. Beneath them on a white ribbon is the state's motto: Excelsior (meaning ever upwards), epitomising the idea of reaching up to high goals. Between with two ladies is the shield depicting an image of the sun rising over the Hudson highlands with two ships sailing the river, representing commerce. Above this grand affair rests an eagle on a globe, he faces right, a good omen.

Just when you thought you couldn't have another flag, there's the city's very own. A slightly less elaborate affair, it harks back to historical beginnings. For a start it's the same colours as the Kingdom of the Netherlands in the 1600s; blue, white and orange. In the middle, the seal of New York City, the shield flanked by a Native American to one side (representing the native population before euro invasion), on the other, a sailor (representing the settlement in the area). The shield they stand by encompasses an amalgamation of symbols and symbolism: the beaver represents the Dutch West Indian Company, the windmill, barrel and flower all symbolise early industry. And then of course there's the big '1625', which of course is the year Manhattan was established by the Dutch (see History on p.2) .

The Mayor's office has its own twist of this last flag, with an extra five-point star for the five boroughs of New York.

Local Time

New York is generally five hours behind UCT (Universal Central Time – formally known as GMT or Greenwich Mean Time). Remember, however, that the United States has daylight savings (an hour) that starts on the second Sunday in March and ends on the first Sunday of November.

Social & Business Hours

It's a work-hard-play-hard ethic that rules here. The standard office hours are either 08:00 to 17:00 or 09:00 to 18:00, Monday to Friday, with overtime and coming in on the weekends being pretty common practice if the job calls for it. New York is very competitive with quite a cut-throat working culture. That said, as soon as work is out, New Yorkers like nothing more than dressing up and heading out.

Public transportation runs 24 hours a day, with less frequent but still well-serviced subway and bus stops, so it's pretty normal to find folk about town even in the wee hours (hence being known as 'the city that never sleeps').

Shops and department stores tend to keep varying hours of business opening as early as 08:00 and shutting as late as 22:00. During major retailing seasons like Christmas or sale time, the hours may change to stay open for longer.

Weekend Hours

Weekends tend to be much busier in Manhattan with more borough dwellers coming in for a night of partying. But with the gentrification of Brooklyn and Harlem as well as certain neighbourhoods like the Meat Packing District, new bars, clubs and restaurants are popping up all the time so its well worth steering clear of the more touristy traps and finding out where the real New Yorkers chill (See Going Out, p.370).

Public Holidays

Public holidays here are based on either Christian construct (Christmas, Easter and St Patrick's Day among the more celebrated) as well as patriotic anniversaries such as Independence Day and the Thanksgiving Day parade, general patriotism with Dominican Day (celebrating the heritage of the Dominican Republic), the Puerto Rican Day Parade and West Indian Day Carnival Parade, which falls on the same weekend as Labour Day, among others. There are a couple of out-there, just-for-the-fun-of-it days like Gay Pride (a lot of fun, whatever your orientation), Groundhog Day and, of course, the world-famous Halloween Parade. See p.48 for more information.

Just because it's a holiday doesn't necessarily mean it's a holiday. Public and government bodies as well as banks are more likely to be closed during religious holidays as well as a few of the other (more general) patriotic anniversaries. But the private sector is more than likely to be toiling away through many of these, with workers joining in the fun after having punched in a full day's slog.

Public Holidays	
New Year's Day	Jan 1
Martin Luther King's Day	3rd Mon in Jan
President's Day	3rd Mon in Feb
Memorial Day	Last Mon in May
Independence Day	July 4
Labor Day	1st Mon in Sep
Columbus Day	2nd Mon in May
Veterans Day	Nov 11
Thanksgiving	4th Thu in Nov
Christmas Day	Dec 25

Photography

Clicking away with your camera is perfectly acceptable, though it will point you out as a shameless tourist if you're by a public monument.

Photography is prohibited inside government institutions, including parts of the airport, courthouses, the UN and other places such as art galleries. Look out for any signs up about photography, which will normally either pertain to security risks (government properties) or hazardous effects (art galleries, theatre houses and churches). Taking a tripod inside most government properties is prohibited, and in some cases you may not even be allowed to take your camera.

New Yorkers move far too quickly for you to try and snap them, but it shows bad manners to try and take pictures of people without their prior permission.

Times Square

Climate

New York's climate fits with its Mediterranean latitude, with humidity varying enough to notice throughout the year (the city is coastal, remember). In fact, its waterways ensure the place never gets as cold as it does further inland. The seasons here are well defined, with hot and sweaty summers (the chances of a cooling breeze are minimised by the city's enveloping concrete landscape, tall and congested) and chilly winters. White Christmases are common, drizzly rains even more so during the winter months. Spring and autumn are pleasant seasons, avoiding the extremes of the bits in between, with mild temperatures and low humidity levels.

New York functions well to its weather, unlike other large cities. The subways are well equipped to oppose whatever nastiness is going on outside, so expect blasting air conditioning to cool you down from the swelter and warm air to warm your cockles when they need warming. The same thing goes for the buses, though obviously not the bus shelters – so dress accordingly for the wait.

Because this is such a pedestrianised city and even if you're using public transport, it is always wise to check the weather online or on TV before you venture out. You can find the temperature on the bottom right-hand corner of the screen on the national terrestrial channels from the early hours to mid-morning. Weather conditions can change every few hours, but fortunately TV weather channels always seem to know what's coming.

Let it Snow

Figures vary from year to year, but February is usually the snowiest month. While you can't always count on there being a white Christmas, every year it snows enough to cover the ground. Snowfalls of 20 inches or more are not unheard of.

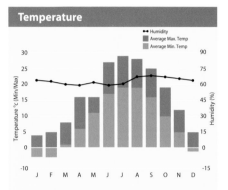

Temperature

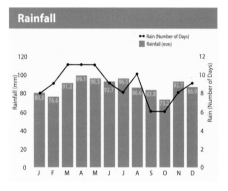

Rainfall

Flora & Fauna

With huge topographical and geographical contrasts, New York has a real mish-mash of natural wonders. What you see today owes much to the rapid changes as a consequence of urbanisation. Before that, the state was predominantly woodland, forestry and meadowlands, some of which still prevail, though the order and dominance has obviously changed.

Surrounded by water (the Atlantic and Lakes Erie and Ontario for the state and the Hudson River for the city) New York also boasts some 8,000 lakes and 10 major rivers, all adding to the bustling ecosystem, but trembling under the weight of the concrete garden of New York City. The most dominant characteristics of the plant life found in the city include the ability to survive against acid rain, thick polluted air and a lack of sunlight behind the heaven-bound skyscrapers that nestle a little too close for natural comfort.

The most prolific of the city's wildlife would have to be the cockroaches and rats that share the land with the thousands upon thousands of humans, a rather more grim testimony to European immigration!

There is still natural growth and better wildlife, an assortment of fish, a variety of birds, raccoons, the odd wild coyote and Central Park's very own kaleidoscope of squirrels. The boroughs of New York City, complete with sanctuaries, do well to maintain the menagerie of nature from the industrialisation of modern life, including the wildlife refuges in Alley Pond (Queens) and Staten Island's Jamaica Bay and Clove Lake.

Botanical Bonanza

One of the best ways of navigating the city and state's flora is a visit to one of the two botanical gardens, the first in the Bronx and the other in Brooklyn. Both are highly rated as excellent, state-of-the-art facilities and will extend your learning to American flora as well as New York's finest. Every borough in the city also has its own zoo, a perfect way to spend an afternoon and learn a thing or two in the process of languidly walking around the beautiful grounds (see p.232)

Flora

Despite the urban sprawl that has befallen the state for some 500 years, there exists in the state almost 150 different kinds of trees. Close to the Atlantic, you're likely to find willow oaks, sweet gums and laurel magnolias, with hickory and chestnuts nearer the Hudson and Mohawk valleys. Northern hardwoods dominate, namely beech, ash, cherry and birch. South-eastern New York is sheltered by a variety of oaks, while the eastern region takes care of the apple trees and other fruit bearers that make up much of the state's agricultural offerings.

The state flower happens to be the rose – and for good reason given the abundance and variety. Add in the more common meadow flowers, such as dandelion, Queen Anne's lace, and black-eyed Susan and you have yourself a real lush picking of natural beauty.

As of 2003, there are six endangered plant species and a list of protected plants that includes all species of fern, orchids and rhododendron.

Fauna

Cockroaches and rats aside for a minute – the state shows off other original inhabitants, from the very tiny deer mouse to the fluffy eastern cottontail, the snowshoe hare, the muskrat and racoons. Squirrels are also very common, very arrogant (they don't move out of the way, you do!) and vary from chestnut brown to grey. Bigger beasts to look out for include busy beavers, white-tailed deer and black bears. New York is also well known for its snakes, so keep a watchful eye out for the grass, garter, water and milk variety. Rattlesnakes did once inhabit the Adirondacks in great numbers but have since died out and are no longer a common sight.

Traipse around the city zoos if you're looking for a quick fix of animal life, or for a real slice of what the state has to offer, check out some of the hiking trails and outdoor fun (p.252).

Birds

Unfortunately, you can't appreciate the 260 species of birds prominent in New York while in the city. Don't expect any sweet chirping of the state's official bird, the bluebird, while you're snapping away in Times Square. But do make an effort to get out of the urban swell to catch a glimpse of the hawks and woodpeckers that inhabit the region. The wild turkey went missing at the end of the 18th century only to be brought back in the late 1970s. New York is invariably (due in part to its geographic location) a fantastic host to migratory birds, from the American goldfinch to the eastern bluebird, the bluejay to a variety of owls, hawks, ruffed grouse, mallard, and the common house sparrow (another European blessing, somewhat nicer than the 'roach).

Marine Life

There are over 200 different species of fish relative to New York, over 100 are in the Hudson alone and another 100 or so exclusive to the Ontario. Freshwater fish include species of bass, pike, and the good old trout, the official state fish.

Environment

Environmental Issues

New York takes its environmental issues very seriously. The New York State Department of Environmental Conservation exists to 'conserve, improve, and protect New York State's natural resources and environment, and control water, land and air pollution, in order to enhance the health, safety and welfare of the people of the state and their overall economic and social well being.'

With a tonne of programmes in place, every effort is made to roll back the dirty wheels of the industrialised urban sprawl in years past, but also to slow the effects of a city still growing.

Environmental Issues & the Ecosystem

As a global centre of economy, trade and industry, New York City goes to great efforts to keep itself clean. Mayor Bloomberg makes sure of it, being one of the 248 mayors from 41 states to sign 'the US Mayors Climate Protection Agreement'. The idea is to 'strive to meet or beat the Kyoto Protocol targets in their own communities', and so far so eco-friendly.

It is the law to recycle and every New Yorker is active to the point of obsessed with separating their trash. City dwellers will not tolerate litterbugs (especially since the city has a huge rat problem) and will happily, and not so kindly, take it upon themselves to tell you should you be so careless.

So focused are New Yorkers and those that govern them, the city has taken its environmental impact onto the streets by buying and running diesel-hybrid buses and even hybrid taxis. The city has also invested heavily in energy efficient equipment for city offices and public houses and ranks high on the charts for energy efficient 'green' offices.

Water Usage & Desalination

You wouldn't think scarcity would be an issue considering how water-locked parts of the city and generally the state are. And the issue isn't necessarily that New Yorkers are lacking in water, more that the consumption in correlation to the population is demanding at best. This is a legacy left behind from the turn of the century, as social reformers promoted heavy water use for hygiene and epidemic control. Studies show that per capita usage is higher in the United States than anywhere else in the world, with New York looming dangerously close to the top of the list of over-users. So much so that in the early 80s conservation policies were put in place and since then the city has seen a 28% decline in water usage. Cost is also being used as a curbing device, with water bills climbing higher, making it the most expensive utility.

According to the Environmental Protection Department of New York City, from June to June (2005 to 2006), the average daily consumption was in the region of one billion gallons – in a city with a population of 8.2 million – down 5.2% from 2002. *The New York Times* suggests this figure was the lowest recorded since 1951, when the city's population stood at 7.9 million.

Environmental Organisations

The state prides itself on its many conservation parks and programmes which include the Adirondack Forest Preserve, the Catskill Forest Preserve, as well as a handful of environmental education camps and centres. Many environmental organisations exist in New York, most of which are government organised and funded.

Greenpoint Oil Spill
Not so long ago the Brooklyn neighbourhood of Greenpoint, then home to many an oil refinery, experienced a 17 million gallon spill into nearby Newton Creek. The slippery mistake was considered the worst in the history of the United States, and for years afterwards oil continued to seep into the city's waterways. Long after the oil gang moved out, the folks of Greenpoint filed a lawsuit against ExxonMobil, the company responsible, for its slow cleanup of 50 acres worth of ruin caused by the accident.

Brooklyn Bridge

19

Culture

New York City is a celebration of culture – everyone's culture! It doesn't matter where you came from, once you step foot on the Apple, the only thing that matters is making a part of it yours. The fact that this is everybody's home makes the metropolis one of the most culturally rich and ethnically abundant in the world.

This is home to some of the world's cultural elite, from the Algonquin Round Table (humble beginnings of the renowned *New Yorker* magazine) to icons like Truman Capote, Jackson Pollack, Allen Ginsberg, John Lennon and Herman Melville – all have gravitated around the Big Apple and helped shape the global art scene.

The city's liberal attitude towards ethnic blending and acceptance of the unorthodox make it a fertile ground for creativity. Art galleries, museums, theatre and film are all here in an abundant tribute to all things cultural.

Race Relations

From its earliest days, the city has attracted a eclectic mix of people and has a larger range of ethnicities than most of other places on earth. Race relations in the city have twisted and turned along a turbulent timeline. However, considering the number of different cultures living together on one tiny island (and the boroughs), it's a relatively perfect example of how human beings can live in harmony despite their differences.

Of course there have been moments in history when racial tension has bubbled over into racially motivated violence. The Draft Riots led to the Mayor's Committee on Unity by Executive Order, which eventually became today's Commission on Human Rights. The Crown Heights Riots of August 1991 saw violence and general havoc as Jews and African Americans living in Crown Heights, Brooklyn, got a bit hot under the collar because of perceived discrimination issues.

Language

English is the official language in New York, though with the many dialects and heavy, heavy accents (good luck in Staten Island) it might not always seem it. The large Hispanic population has made Spanish the unofficial second language, and walking through any of the five boroughs, your ears will ring with so many different tongues it's like a linguistic fanfare to internationalism.

Though shop signs, restaurant awnings and the occasional menu may be written in a foreign transcript, English dominates the signposts. Chinatown is perhaps the only exception where some form of Chinese or Mandarin script accompanies the English.

Religion

Just as New York is the place where anyone is welcome, so is it the place where any religion is tolerated. At the start of its history, there was a predominant Roman Catholic population, thanks to the large number of Irish immigrants. Not long after, however, a large Jewish community started forming, and exists to this day.

Today, no one denomination or religion takes precedence. Whatever you believe in, you are free to practise your religion and the city has an exhaustive list of churches, temples, mosques and synagogues.

Places of Worship

Abyssinian Baptist Church	Harlem	212 862 7474
American Buddhist & Taoist Inc	Little Italy	212 227 8851
Bialystoker Synagogue	Lower East Side	212 475 0165
Cathedral of St John the Divine	Harlem	212 316 7490
Eastern States Buddhist Temple of America	Chinatown	212 966 6229
Fifth Avenue Presbyterian Church	Midtown	212 247 0490
Islamic Society	Midtown	212 888 7838
Lexington United Methodist Church	Upper East Side	212 838 6915
Mahayana Buddhist Temple	Chinatown	212 925 8787
Riverside Church	Harlem	212 870 6700
St John's Lutheran Church	Chelsea	212 242 5737
St Patrick's Cathedral Rectory	Midtown	212 753 2261
St. Paul's Chapel (Episcopalian)	Financial District	212 233 4164
Temple Emanu-El	Central Park & Fifth Ave	212 744 1400
Trinity Church	Financial District	212 602 0872

National Dress

No national dress prevails unless you consider jeans and Chuck Taylor High Tops a look worth maintaining. This is the style centre of the world, and it doesn't matter whether it's yellow footless tights or aviator sunglasses in the winter, as long as you've got the attitude you can make feathers fly. Every style and sensibility is catered for and one of the most popular pastimes here is people watching, so make sure you put on a good show. New York really is about group individuality – it's cool to stand out, as long as there's a gang of others who look exactly the same. Certain cliques have their own uniform and their own hip hangouts. But really anything goes. Wear it with your chest puffed out and your head held high, and make it look like you were born to parade with silver stilettos on your feet and fruit in your hair!

Food & Drink

Other options **Eating Out** p.371

New York may be the city that never sleeps, but it's also the city that always eats - no matter what time of day or night it is, you can get yourself a little bit of what you fancy. A cream cheese bagel at 05:30? Chinese food at midnight? It's all possible.

The jumble of ethnicities in the city certainly results in varied cuisine - Italian, Mexican, American, Jewish and French are some of the more common ones, but that doesn't mean you can't find a huge range of Vietnamese, Indian, Greek, Japanese and African specialities as well. You'll be able to eat your way around the world (just make sure you wear your stretchy pants).

Because of the frenetic pace of the working week, New Yorkers don't usually get the chance to take a lingering lunch. Enter the convenience of that great New York institution - the deli. Ready-cooked meals and a range of sandwiches are all just a pair of tongs away - just pile whatever you want into a plastic box, get it weighed at the till, and wolf it down on your way back to the office. Other 'hurry up' lunch options include hot dogs from street vendors or a gigantic slice of pizza, available at countless pizza places throughout the city - just follow your nose to find one. After you've chosen your slice, fold it in half lengthways and eat it using one hand only - while walking, if you want to look like an experienced New Yorker! Dinner is totally different, and usually involves no rushing around at all (unless of course you're an intern on Wall Street, in which case you can just repeat the five-minute lunch routine for all your meals). The evening meal is usually as much about socialising as it is about sustenance. Whether you decide to dress up for a fancy dinner at one of the city's top restaurants, or dress down for a casual meal with friends at a cafe or deli, you'll find plenty of venues where you can simply hang out for ages.

Bagels

21

Visas

Other options **Residence Visa** p.61, **Entry Visa** p.58

Visa requirements for entering the United States vary greatly between different nationalities, and regulations should always be checked before travelling, since details can change with little warning. The country essentially works on an 'open door, secure borders' policy, allowing foreign visitors to travel or live here permanently as long as they can navigate the miles of red tape and fit immigration requirements. In theory this is true, but in the wake of 9/11 and a massive influx of illegal workers, immigration has turned into a rather touchy subject. Still, it is not impossible to get in, as long as you do things right and don't mess around with the immigration laws.

Every foreign national needs a visa, whether it's to visit (non-immigrant visa for temporary stay) or to live in the States permanently (immigrant visa for permanent residence). Immigration law, your nationality and your reasons for being in the country will determine what kind of visa you will apply for.

Visa Waiver Programme (VWP)

The Visa Waiver Programme was established in 1986 to allow visitors from certain countries easy access to enter the States without actually having to go through the rigmarole of applying for a full-on visa. You can be here for tourism or business but your stay cannot exceed 90 days. It's only permitted for certain countries and requires visitors to carry machine-readable passports complete with integrated data chip and digital photograph.

Not all nationalities are privy to the VWP, and even if you are from a country that falls under the agreement, you may still not be eligible. You are screened before entry, and then included in the 'US-Visit' Programme spearheaded by the Department of Homeland Security.

There are two ways of getting a Visa Waiver; the first is to apply ahead of time to the US embassy or consulate in your home country. The second is to board your flight and fill out a green I-94 visa waiver form before you hit the customs desk. The official behind the desk will ask you a few questions about the length and purpose of your visit, before taking your photo and your fingerprint (everyone has to have this done). It is essential that you have an address of where you will be staying - if you don't fill out that section of the form you will be denied entry. It is best to be prepared. For more information you can check out the http://travel.state.gov website.

Other Temporary Visas

Travellers not on the VWP list are still able to apply for other temporary visas relating to the purpose of their travel. There are many different classifications of non-immigrant visas (temporary visas), and you can get a full list from www.unitedstatesvisas.gov. A few categories worth noting include Australian in Specialty Occupation, Border Crossing Card (for Mexican travellers, diplomats and government officials), Exchange Visitors, Fiancee to Marry US Citizen, International Organisations and NATO, Media & Journalists, Religious Workers, Students, Temporary Workers Overview, and Treaty Traders and Investors.

Renewing a Temporary Visa
Renewing a visa does not necessarily entail you travelling to your home country and can be done from within the borders of the US. However, it is not always a straightforward process and many categories of temporary visa holders are not permitted to apply for an extension. The golden rule is that you should always apply well before the time your existing visa is due to expire. And visit www.uscis.gov to check further regulations relevant to your visa category.

Costs of these temporary visas vary - some are even free of charge, and only require you to fill out the relevant forms in good time, while others require you to fill out an application and attend a quick interview at the American consulate or embassy in your home country.

VWP Countries
There are currently 27 countries that participate in the Visa Waiver Programme: Andorra, Austria, Australia, Belgium, Brunei, Denmark, Finland, France, Germany, Iceland, Ireland, Italy, Japan, Liechtenstein, Luxembourg, Monaco, the Netherlands, New Zealand, Norway, Portugal, San Marino, Singapore, Slovenia, Spain, Sweden, Switzerland and the United Kingdom.

Permanent Residence

If you are seeking permanent residence in the US, you have a whole new set of challenges to deal with. The regulations are convoluted at best, and finding a category that best fits your profile can take some serious research before you file for the paperwork.

Destination USA, a government-run body that aids the assessment of permanent immigration into the country highlights how the government has recently updated its policies due to increased security issues (yep, 9/11 all over again). They helpfully provide the warning that your visa will take much longer than it used to thanks to new security measures. You can find out more from their website (www.unitedstatesvisas.gov). If it's all too confusing for you to figure out on your own, you could always hire an immigration lawyer - this will save you the legwork, but also cost you an arm and a leg!

E-tickets and Electronic Check-in

Electronic tickets and check-ins are practically the norm when it comes to travelling within the United States. The process is incredibly simple and you can do it even if you have luggage to stow (as opposed to just having carry-on luggage). It saves you the hassle of queuing and queuing – and queuing some more. International travel is now more often e-ticketed (that means that you get an email confirmation with your flight details and at check-in you either present a copy of the email or just your passport). Because of customs, passport control and increased security regulations, international flights do not allow electronic check-in, so take a number and practise your patience while you stand in the check-in queue.

Airport Info
For more information about customs checks at your airport of arrival or destination, call ahead: JFK (718 553 1648), La Guardia (718 476 438), or Newark (973 645 3409).

Customs

Customs and border control is a pretty serious business in New York. The 9/11 terrorist attacks, the London bombings in July 2005, and the general heightened safety awareness that has arisen due to American foreign policy have made it pretty nerve-wracking going through any border post, even if the most contraband item in your suitcase is an extra carton of cigarettes.

Ports and airports are always on high alert, so you can expect customs and baggage screenings to be as meticulous as possible. The US Customs Service works in conjunction with the INS (Immigration and Naturalization Service), and the two forces control what and who comes in and out of the country.

Both tourists and citizens are required to fill out a customs form on the plane and submit it as you pass through the customs gate, whether you have items to declare or not. The forms will require you to declare whether you are bringing in items such as foodstuff, meats, money and so on.

Random inspections are common. If you get pulled over for your bags to be checked don't panic and think this means they have profiled you as a threat - these checks are totally random and are for everyone's safety. During the checks, you may be asked questions about your country of citizenship, the purpose of your visit, and any items you are bringing into the US. Even if you have just come off a nightmare long-haul flight, try to stay calm and pleasant during the checks, and answer all questions politely and as comprehensively as possible.

Find out more about the rules and regulations of the Customs and Excise Department at www.customs.gov.

Restricted & Banned Items

The list of restricted and banned items changes quite regularly, so always check before you travel what you can and cannot bring with you, particularly in your hand luggage. Almost every airline has banned obvious items like pocket knives, utility tools, scissors, lighter fluid and matches, as well as some less obvious ones like nail files and tweezers. There may be restrictions on certain cosmetics, medicines and liquids (please check with your airline before you pack these things, otherwise you may have to bid a sad farewell to your near-full bottle of perfume). Travellers to the US are not allowed to carry livestock, meats, birds, fruits or vegetables - this is to avoid agricultural disruption. Banned products include fruits, plants, food, insects, meats, animals (or animal products), cell cultures, snails and soil (and you should inform authorities if you have recently visited a farm outside of the US).

Duty Free Allowances

Each person may carry the following:
- $800 of duty-free purchases;
- One litre of alcohol (only for people over 21)
- One carton of cigarettes (200 cigarettes, and only for people over 18)
- 100 Cuban cigars (only for people over 18)

Travellers under the age of 21 may not carry alcohol into the country, even if it is intended as a gift for someone else. Travellers from certain countries (US Virgin Islands, certain Caribbean countries) may be permitted to carry more than one litre of alcohol. Additional quantities are permitted, although they will be subject to duty and IRS taxes. Duty is usually 3% of the value, and IRS tax is usually up to 31 cents per bottle of wine, 67 cents per bottle of champagne, and $2.14 per bottle of liquor. For more information, see the duty free shopping index (www.dutyfreeshoppingindex.com).

Emergency Services

Ambulance	911	Emergency services
Cabrini Medical Centre	212 995 6000	Hospital
Children's Hospital of New York	212 746 5454	Hospital
CVS (various 24 hr stores)	www.cvs.com	24 hour pharmacy
Duane Reade (various 24 hr stores)	www.duanereade.com	24 hour pharmacy
Fire	911	Emergency services
Mount Sinai Hospital	212 241 6500	Hospital
Neergaard Pharmacy	800 696 1107	24 hour pharmacy
Operator	0	Operator
Police Emergency	911	Emergency services
Police General Information	646 610 5000	Police services
Rite Aid	800 748 3243	24 hour pharmacy
St Luke's - Roosevelt Hospital	212 523 6800	Hospital
St Vincent's Hospital	212 604 7998	Hospital
Walgreen's Pharmacy	212 734 6076	24 hour pharmacy

In Emergency

Emergencies can strike at any time and the only way to deal with them is to be prepared. Make sure that you always have your emergency numbers handy, whether you need help from the police, the fire department, an ambulance or your embassy. Fortunately New York is one of the most developed cities in the world, with a host of emergency services at your fingertips. Your first job when you move to a new area should be to locate your nearest emergency hospital and NYPD precinct.

Health Insurance

Healthcare in the country is not free, and nor is it cheap, so it is highly advisable to take out some kind of insurance if you are travelling to the US. If you are immigrating to the US, medical insurance is often a prerequisite condition of your visa application. If the worst happens and you are in need of urgent medical attention, the only thing a hospital is obliged to do for free is save your life. The rest, including recovery after the life-saving treatment, is on your dime.

Health Requirements

At the time of going to print, no direct vaccinations were required for entering the United States. This may change depending on epidemic cases of Avian Influenza (Bird Flu) and any other medical nasties that are doing the rounds globally. Be sure to check the Centre for Disease Control website (www.cdc.gov) for updates and urgent warnings.

The only time you will need proof of immunisation will be for children applying to schools, in which case you will need to prove vaccinations against diphtheria, measles, poliomyelitis, and rubella. In addition, the school entry requirements of most states include immunisation against tetanus, pertussis, mumps, and hepatitis B.

Embassies & Consulates

Australia	212 351 6500	Israel	212 499 56 10
Austria	212 737 64 00	Italy	212 737 91 00
Bahamas	212 421 64 20	Jamaica	212 935 90 00
Bangladesh	212 599 67 67	Japan	212 371 82 22
Belgium	212 586 51 10	Jordan	212 355 93 42
Brazil	212 827 09 76	Malaysia	212 490 27 22
Canada	212 596 16 28	Mexico	212 217 64 00
Chile	212 980 37 07	Netherlands	212 246 14 30
China	212 244 94 56	New Zealand	212 832 40 38
Czech Republic	212 717 56 43	Norway	212 421 73 33
Denmark	212 223 45 45	Peru	212 481 74 10
Egypt	212 759 71 20	Philippines	212 764 13 30
Finland	212 750 44 00	Russia	212 348 06 26
France	212 606 36 88	Saudi Arabia	212 752 27 40
Germany	212 610 97 00	South Africa	212 213 48 80
Greece	212 988 55 00	Spain	212 355 40 80
Hong Kong	212 330 72 23	Sweden	212 563 25 50
Hungary	212 752 06 69	Switzerland	212 599 57 00
India	212 774 06 00	Thailand	212 754 17 70
Ireland	212 319 25 62	United Kingdom	212 745 02 00

Female Visitors

In the late 70s and 80s, New York had a reputation as one of the crime capitals of the world. Fortunately, its reputation today is vastly different, with it being ranked as the safest city in the USA (quite a feat considering it is also the most populated). This is something that New Yorkers are particularly proud of, and why shouldn't they be? To live in the city that never sleeps and to feel relatively safe while doing it is something that should not be taken for granted.

However, it would be foolish to have a false sense of security - it is a big city after all, and big cities harbour crime. If you are a woman travelling alone in New York, you should take the same precautions you would anywhere else in the world. There is not much in the way of public annoyances and harassment by male onlookers, but you should make sure you are always aware of what is going on around you and be street smart at all times. Hold your head up high and walk with confidence, as if you know where you're going. Stopping in the middle of a sidewalk to fumble about in your handbag for your phone may make you a target.

Even walking around at night is ok, as long as you stay in the well-populated areas where there is plenty of light. The subway operates around the clock, although trains become more infrequent in the wee hours. If you need to ride the subway and feel a bit nervous, try not to sit in an empty car (not difficult: this is the city that never sleeps, remember?). One bit of advice that you should probably follow is to avoid the parks late at night - but that's just common sense, of which you'll have plenty if you're used to travelling alone.

Clever Kids
Nurture those inquisitive little minds with trips to New York's child friendly museums: Children's Museum of the Arts (212 274 0986), Children's Museum of Manhattan (212 721 1234)and the Brooklyn Children's Museum (718 735 4400).

Travelling with Children

Despite what you may think about little kids and big cities, New York is a great place for children. There are beaches, theme parks, street fairs and even special museums just for kids, and then of course there's Central Park (p.233) - the best backyard ever. There's the carousel, Loeb Boathouse, Wollman Rink (p.267) and the zoo, plus lots of lawn for running about and a team of inquisitive squirrels to contend with.

Restaurants and hotels offer varying services when it comes to the little ones - posher places may not have an arms-wide-open-in-welcome attitude to your little ones, but there are plenty of venues where kids are part of the charm. Look out for the 'kids welcome' icon on restaurant listings in the Going Out chapter, p.370.

Physically Challenged Visitors

On the whole, the city is well prepared for people with special needs. The Mass Transit System (MTA) in particular has taken great steps to ensure that all passengers are taken care of, including those with physical challenges or special needs. There are Braille maps, large-print maps, elevators and ramps in many subway stops, and a door-to-door para-transit service. Visit www.mta.info or call 800 734 6772 for more info.

Many of the larger hotels, and some restaurants, are built with spacious doorways and corridors, ramps for wheelchair users, and extra services for people with special needs. Busy pedestrian walkways and impatient New Yorkers are perhaps the biggest hindrance, especially during rush hour when the sidewalks take on an 'every man for himself' aggression.

Telephone & Internet

Sure, there's a phone box on every corner, but finding one that works or is unoccupied when you need one... another story! Public phones take coins, but no pennies, so keep your copper in your pocket. They also take pre-paid calling cards, and sometimes credit cards, depending on the phone. Four minutes of talking will cost you around 25 cents for a local call, $1 for a national call, and a small fortune for an international call. It can work out cheaper when phoning internationally to buy a card from any bodega, deli or cornershop - just shop around, because some are cheaper than others for certain regions. This is America, and when you're in America you have rights - even if you're only using a public phone. You have the right to know how much a call will cost you (you can find out from the operator), and if you think you have been charged too much for a call, you have the right to make a complaint to the Federal Communications Commission (www.fcc.gov). Internet cafes are so last century - these days it's all about Wi-Fi. New York has plenty of Wi-Fi spots where all you have to do is turn up with your laptop and tap into the wireless connection. Many Wi-Fi spots are in coffee shops, so buy a cuppa if you plan to camp out for hours using their Wi-Fi - you'll enjoy your surfing more if you've got a clear conscience. You'll struggle to find a branch of Starbucks, Barnes & Noble or McDonalds that doesn't offer Wi-Fi (although in rare cases there may be a charge), but one of the coolest Wi-Fi spots has to be the Apple Store on Fifth Avenue - it's open 24 hours a day, with free Wi-Fi, and if you can't be bothered to lug your own laptop around you can just surf away on one of their display laptops.

Internet Pay Phones
There are 25 randomly located phone and internet units throughout Manhattan, installed and operated by an independent operator, TCC Teleplex (www.tccteleplex.com). The units work as an internet station that doubles as a pay phone, though costs vary depending on usage and time spent.

Area Codes & Useful Numbers

Brooklyn, Bronx, Queens, Staten Island	347 & 718
Crime Victims Hotline	212 577 7777
Directory assistance	411 or 800 555 1212
Government Information	212 639 9675
JFK Airport	718 244 4444
LaGuardia Airport	718 533 3400
Long Island	516
Manhattan	212 & 646
Medical emergencies	800 395 3400
Mobile & pager for Manhattan, Bronx, Queens, Staten Island, Brooklyn	917
Newark Airport	973 961 6000
Newark NJ	732
Non-emergency Services	311
Operator	0
Subway & Bus Information	718 330 1234
Toll free when dialled from US	800, 877, 888
USA Country Code	+1

Dress

It's one of the fashion capitals of the world and one of the best places to try out your 'anything goes' style experiments. Nothing is off limits, and nobody stares - New York is the land of the fashion-free!

Obviously if you are attending a religious service in a temple, church or mosque, it's only respectful to stick to conservative attire. Some restaurants have smart dress codes, and some venues may have wacky dress codes (Like The Eagle, p.430, which insists on leather on certain nights of the week).

Your greatest challenge will be dressing appropriately for the weather, which can change in an instant. Sometimes air conditioning can be a bit aggressive, especially in cinemas and on the subway during summer, so an emergency cardigan may come in handy.

Dos & Don'ts

Despite New York being fairly liberal, there are some laws you should definitely not cross. It is illegal to drink alcohol in public places, so if you must carry around a bottle of booze, you are required to have it covered or inside a brown bag (classy). Laws are

Extra Clean Water
The Safe Water Drinking Act has ensured that New Yorkers and visitors are supplied the best quality water facilities. It's safe to drink straight from the tap, but you're also dealing with a culture that finds swilling from schmancy bottles de rigueur, so it's your call.

Buy a Plug Converter

ConEdison Solutions is the local utility supplier, and before deregulations came into place it was the only energy supplier in the city. Not so much now, but it still happens to be the most popular. The United States runs on 110V at 60Hz, so you'll need a converter since the rest of the world runs much higher at 220/240 Volts 50 Cycles (50HZ). American plugs have two parallel flat blades above a circular grounding pin. The alternative is a plug that is just two parallel flat blades.

similarly strict when it comes to smoking - you are not allowed to smoke inside any building, except for your own home. Restaurants, bars and nightclubs are all smoke-free zones, although some may have little smoking balconies where the few remaining smokers can huddle outside for a quickie. And if you're really longing to see swirls of tobacco smoke inside, there are many cigar bars and lounges throughout the city where you can smoke cigars – although not cigarettes.

Why Cops?

Why are police officers called 'cops'? Before there was a uniform to distinguish police officers from civilians, police would just wear a badge on their normal clothes to show they were officers of the law. The badges were made of copper, earning police officers the nickname 'coppers'. It wasn't long before this was shortened to 'cops'. Find out more fascinating facts like this at the New York City Police Museum (212 480 3100).

Crime & Safety

Other options **In Emergency** p.25

For a big city, New York is pretty safe - thanks largely to a visible police presence, some groundbreaking reforms, and streets that are generally busy any time of day or night. Crime rates have dropped consistently over the last 10 years, which is good news especially when you consider that most other cities are battling against rising crime rates. However, crime has not been eliminated completely and you do need to keep your wits about you.

Walk with purpose and don't stop to dither over directions or to find your 'cellphone' in the depths of your handbag - if you need to stop to check your map, pop into a shop or cafe, get your bearings and head back out onto the street. If you love the bling, be careful about flashing loads of jewellery around. Keep a firm clutch on your handbag, and don't make life easy for pickpockets by carrying your wallet in your back pocket. All these suggestions form the basic common sense, or 'street smarts', that everybody should develop, especially if they're living in a big city.

One last word on crime: beware of scam artists. They say New Yorkers are rude but that's actually untrue. However, with so many scam artists on the prowl, it's best to just avoid eye contact with others and keep on walking if anybody tries to stop and talk to you in the street. Someone who pops out in front of you to ask the time could be distracting you while his mate pickpockets you, and that is just one of the millions of scams out there. So be vigilant and don't fall for any of their tricks.

If you do end up being one of the unlucky ones who falls victim to a crime, give the Crime Victims Hotline a call (212 577 7777).

Police

Endearingly referred to as 'New York's finest', the NYPD (New York Police Department) has come on leaps and bounds in an attempt to shirk some ugly stereotypes and generalisations such as corruption, racism and idleness. The NYPD has a history as colourful as the city itself and you can find out more at the New York City Police Museum (www.nycpolicemuseum.org). On the whole, NYPD officers are vigilant and happy to help,

whether you're lost and just need directions or if you have a genuine emergency. Dressed in dark blue uniforms and characteristic hats, you'll see police officers on almost every street corner, and even on the subway, which is now part of their patrol. They are armed and take their role seriously, aiming to make the city as safe as possible while still maintaining a friendly demeanour. The official website has lots of useful information, including details of all NYPD precincts, contact information, safety tips and some scary 'most wanted' photographs (www.nyc.gov/html/nypd).

Lost/Stolen Property

Rental Car Insurance
While they don't force it upon you, buying the additional car rental insurance when you're picking up your rental is highly advisable. In case of any unforeseen disasters this will cover all bases. Though basic insurance comes as part and parcel of the lease contract, this does not cover accidents, scratches and anything else that the rental company can jip you on.

If you have been the victim of a crime you must report the incident to the police as soon as possible. Either dial 911 (emergency service and ask for police department) or stop a cop, which is easy to do, as they are everywhere and super helpful. You will have to file a police report on anything that's been taken, especially if you're hoping to get some semblance of payback from your insurance company.

Should you lose your travel documents, the first thing to do is to file a police report. Then get in touch with your embassy or consulate as soon as possible. Don't panic! As a precaution though, you should always make sure you have easy access to copies of your important documents.

Tourist Information

You'll find plenty of kiosks throughout the city, doling out handy information on places to go and things to see. Whether or not you'll find them helpful when you get there, or worth standing in long queues for (as you will during busy seasons), is another matter. Cover all bases by checking out some of the excellent online resources first. Try www.nycvisit.com or www.NYCtourist.com for some excellent tips and tricks to making the most of your stay, or even just

Tourist Information	
Big Apple Visitors' Center	212 879 8905
Bronx Tourism Council	718 590 3518
Brooklyn Information & Culture	718 855 7882
Intours	718 888 1717
NYC and Co	212 484 1222
Staten Island Tourism Council	800 573 7469

your day, in New York. Or you could head for the Big Apple Visitors' Center on East 86th Street - they can help you plan your trip, come up with a suitable itinerary, and give you some excellent insider tips, whether you want front-row tickets on Broadway, get across town quicker, or experience the best of the city without spending a fortune.

Places to Stay

New York welcomes thousands of guests every day, from every corner of the world and with every size wallet – from the two-penny rubbers to the mightier clientele with deeper pockets. Hence the city's accommodation structure: you'll find all sorts here from five star to five in a room, and from bunk beds to boutique chic.

Waldorf=Astoria

Budget Accommodation

Doing New York on a shoestring is just as easy as booking the penthouse suite at the Waldorf=Astoria (p.35), and sometimes a lot more fun. There are so many options, from swanky hostels to shabby guesthouses - you just have to use your common sense and do your research. Astronomical apartment rent prices are bad news for residents but have a happy silver lining for visitors: often when New Yorkers head out of town they try to make some extra money by subletting their apartment to people looking for temporary accommodation. Have a browse through the entries on Craig's List (www.craigslist.org) - you can get some pretty decent places for around $100 per night. There are other options: www.priceline.com allows for an auction-style search, and www.hotels.com is another good resource for finding accommodation in your price range.

Hotels

Other options **Main Hotels** p.32

New York City certainly has its fair share of hotels. Most are in Manhattan, but it's just as easy, and usually much, much cheaper, to venture out into the boroughs. Certain neighbourhoods, like the theatre district and Times Square, tend to be cluttered. Expect to fork out a handsome sum for the more upscale hotels, and if you're adamant on staying in Manhattan, you'll find some fairly outrageous prices where the service and standards just don't seem to match. Just because you are paying a lot doesn't mean you are guaranteed luxury or even hygiene. Some places are poorly managed and unfortunately, due to high demand, there is no real incentive for these places to clean up their acts - with plane-loads of tourists arriving by the hour, these places know that they will always be busy, so why bother striving for excellence? If you do find yourself in a sorry hotel situation, speak up and don't settle for sub-standard accommodation.

However, there are also some real gems to look out for. Some of the more quirky boutique hotels (such as the Gershwin, p.32) double up as art galleries, so you can soak up some alternative culture while you're staying there. And even if you can't afford the penthouse at the Gansevoort (p.33), you can still get dressed up and have a drink at their ultra-hip, super cool bar.

For a basic bed and breakfast you're looking at around $150 per night - this can go up to $750 and well beyond if you are looking for real luxury. Some hotels have amenities straight out of a Hollywood fantasy, like in-room massage, chefs that will come to your room to prepare dinner, and free club entries.

One way to try getting more luxury for your dollar is to log onto travel deal websites like www.expedia.com or www.lastminute.com, where you can sometimes get fancy hotels at bargain prices (you have to have luck on your side though).

The gentrified neighbourhoods of Harlem, Brooklyn and Queens have some cheaper alternatives, and with some amazing art, culture and history – and these areas are also sometimes even more interesting than Manhattan.

Hotels

Five Star	Phone	Website
Best Western President Hotel	212 246 8800	www.bestwestern.com
Four Seasons New York	212 758 5700	www.fourseasons.com
Hilton Times Square	212 840 8222	www.hilton.com
Hotel Plaza Athenee	212 734 9100	www.plaza-athenee.com
Hotel QT	212 354 2323	www.hotelqt.com
Mandarin Oriental	212 805 8800	www.mandarin-oriental.com
Millennium Broadway Hotel - Times Square	212 768 4400	www.millenniumhotels.com
New York Marriott Marquis Times Square	212 398 1900	www.marriott.com
Night	212 835 9600	www.nighthotelny.com
Royalton Hotel	212 869 4400	www.royaltonhotel.com
Sheraton Hotel And Towers	212 581 1000	www.starwoodhotels.com
The Carlton Hotel on Madison Avenue	212 532 4100	www.carltonhotel.ny.com
W New York	212 755 1200	www.starwoodhotels.com
W New York Union Square Hotel	212 253 9119	www.starwoodhotels.com
Westin New York Times Square	212 201 2700	www.westinny.com
Four Star		
Crowne Plaza Hotel	212 977 4000	www.crowneplaza.com
Dream	212 247 2000	www.dreamny.com
Excelsior Hotel	212 362 9200	www.excelsiorhotelny.com
Grand Hyatt New York	212 883 1234	www.grandnewyork.hyatt.com
Inter-Continental The Barclay New York	212 755 5900	www.ichotelsgroup.com
Shelburne Murray Hill	212 689 5200	www.mesuite.com
The Alex Hotel	212 867 5100	www.thealexhotel.com
The Muse - A Kimpton Hotel	212 485 2400	www.themusehotel.com
The New York Palace	212 888 7000	www.newyorkpalace.com
Three Star		
City Club Hotel	212 912 5500	www.cityclubhotel.com
Holiday Inn Downtown	212 966 8898	www.holidayinn-nyc.com
Hotel 41 at Times Square	212 703 8600	www.hotel41.com
Milford Plaza	212 869 3600	www.milfordplaza.com
Park Central New York Hotel	212 247 8000	www.parkcentralny.com
Signature Suites Greenwich	888 511 5743	www.a1-discount-hotels.com
Wingate Inn Hotel	212 967 7500	www.wingateinnnyc.com
Two Star		
Americana Inn	800 555 7555	www.americanainnnewyork.com
Anchor Inn	718 428 8000	www.theanchorinn.com
Buckingham Hotel	212 246 1500	www.buckinghamhotel.com
Comfort Inn By The Javits Center	212 714 6699	www.choicehotels.com
Hotel Newton	212 678 6500	www.thehotelnewton.com
Regency Inn and Suites	212 947 5050	www.regencyinnandsuitesny.com
Sohotel	212 226 1482	www.sohotel-ny.com

Main Hotels

60 Thompson Street
Soho
Map 10-E2

60 Thompson

877 431 0400 | www.thompsonhotels.com

With only a hundred rooms, this Soho boutique hotel is tranquil and exclusive. It is also one of the most stylish hotels you'll find, with no expense spared in preparation. Hip hotel designer Thomas O'Brien has worked his magic here, with beautifully decorated rooms (complete with Fresh bath products and a Dean & Deluca pantry) and a breathtaking lobby that lends an air of sophistication and modern glamour. Amenities include two bars and well-known Thai restaurant Kittichai (p.385), as well as a fitness centre, event facilities and a 24 hour concierge.

59 West 44th Street
Midtown
Map 5-A4

The Algonquin

212 840 6800 | www.algonquinhotel.com

If these walls could talk... This hotel, located in the heart of New York, has a history that is as fascinating as it is long. It is perhaps most famous as the home of the Algonquin Round Table - a group of writers, comedians and critics who met daily for lunch during the 1920s. It encapsulates the heart and soul of old New York, from its 'old money' decor to the pampered house cat, Matilda. Package deals include Broadway tickets and are always a sure bet. The Algonquin also features a winning range of food and beverage outlets, and hosts passing music stars, such as Curtis Steiger.

Times Square
Midtown
Map 4-F4

Casablanca Hotel

212 869 1212 | www.casablancahotel.com

Escape from the madness of Times Square into this tranquil haven of Moroccan splendour. Based largely on the classic film of the same name, the Casablanca will take you back to a time when romance was a civilised, elegant affair. Each of the 48 newly refurbished rooms are decorated to theme. Wander into Rick's Café on the second floor to snuggle up near the fireplace or to enjoy the complimentary continental breakfast served every morning. Kids are very welcome here, and the hotel does a special 'Here's Looking at You, Kid' package that will make them feel right at home.

Gershwin Hotel

212 545 8000 | www.gershwinhotel.com

It's as striking on the inside as it is from the outside, not least because this trendy, very funky hotel doubles as an art gallery. The hotel welcomes guests of all financial standing: if you're on a budget you can grab a bunkbed for as little as $40 a night, or languish in the luxury of a suite from $249. Amenities are basic but for the beauty you'll find inside, and the amazing area of New York you'll be exploring outside, this is one hotel you'll want to linger

7 East 27th Street
Chelsea
Map 7-A3

in longer. The central location means that some of the city's most well-known sights are just a short walk away, but the area has plenty of 'off the beaten track' secrets too.

2 Lexington Avenue
Gramercy Park
Map 9-B1

Gramercy Park Hotel

212 920 3300 | *www.gramercyparkhotel.com*
If name-dropping is one of your hobbies, you'll love the Gramercy: Humphrey Bogart got married here, Babe Ruth used to drink here, and it's been revamped by the great Ian Schrager (of Studio 54 fame). The interior is full of oversized artworks and contemporary minimalism, making it one of the most stylish stopovers in the city. The 185 guest suites are individually decorated - no two are the same - and the penthouse is the last word in luxurious opulence. The private roof club is the 'it' place to be - if you can stroll in here without being questioned, you're probably famous!

222 West 23rd Street
Chelsea
Map 6-E4

The Hotel Chelsea

212 243 3700 | *www.hotelchelsea.com*
The Hotel Chelsea has attracted an assortment of the most interesting people in the world during its history, which is perhaps why it has chosen the strapline 'a rest stop for rare individuals'. Mark Twain, Thomas Wolfe, Dylan Thomas, Arthur C Clarke, Arthur Miller and Stanley Kubrick are just a few of the famous names to have lived at the Chelsea - it is also the place where Sid Vicious of the Sex Pistols allegedly murdered his girlfriend, Nancy Spungen. Murder aside, however, the privacy and tranquility of the hotel is a hotbed for creativity and a magnet for bohemia. Every room looks different, and a single room starts from $195.

18 Ninth Avenue
Meatpacking District
Map 8-C2

Hotel Gansevoort

212 206 6700 | *www.hotelgansevoort.com*
Stunning views, full-service luxury, stylish surroundings and a hot location in Manhattan's Meatpacking District make the Gansevoort a destination of choice for stylistas, the uber cool, celebrities and the wealthy (although various package rates do take the sting out of the prices somewhat). With its exclusive spa, temperature-controlled rooftop pool and hip Japanese restaurant 'Ono' (see p.396), you'll wish you could move in for good. The hotel is complemented perfectly by the neighbourhood's eclectic mix of fashion and fun.

365 Park Ave South
Midtown
Map 7-A4

Hotel Giraffe

212 685 7700 | *www.hotelgiraffe.com*
Return to the glamour of the 20s and 30s at this popular boutique hotel that is quirky and luxurious in equal measure. Its 73 guest rooms are all comfortable and beautifully decorated, and the lobby, with a baby grand piano as its centrepiece, is the kind of place you'll love to hang out - not least because there is a selection of complimentary refreshments served there throughout the day, including champagne from every weekday. Room rates are reasonable considering the high standards, and there is a range of extras such as champagne and long-stemmed roses, should you wish add that special touch.

33

107 Rivington Street
Lower East Side
Map 11-C1

Hotel on Rivington

212 475 2600 | *www.hotelonrivington.com*
Fancy lying in bed and having a panoramic view of the
Manhattan skyline? This award-winning hotel is basically a
21 storey glass tower on the Lower East Side, and nearly all
of the rooms feature floor-to-ceiling windows, giving you an
unobstructed view. Even some of the showers have views to
die for. Fall asleep surrounded by the billions of twinkling
lights that make Manhattan so beautiful at night, and wake
up to the fascinating hustle and bustle of the LES. State-of-
the-art amenities and renowned restaurant, Thor, complete the perfection.

160 Central Pk South
Central Park
Map 4-F1

Jumeirah Essex House

212 247 0300 | *www.jumeirahessexhouse.com*
This luxurious hotel was first built in the 1930s and bears
the distinction of being the first venue to offer Sunday
brunch to Central Park walkers. Since January 2006, the
hotel has been under new management. Its 515 rooms
and suites are spread over 44 floors, and offer amazing
views over Central Park and Manhattan. Apart from its
excellent in-house restaurant and lounge, and superb
range of fitness facilities (it has a health spa, a fitness
centre and a jogging track), the hotel is also conveniently close to major attractions like
Times Square, Lincoln Center, Museum Mile, Carnegie Hall, and (of course) Central Park.

147 Mercer Street
Soho
Map 10-F1

Mercer Hotel

212 966 6060 | *www.mercerhotel.com*
It's the understated luxury that makes this hotel special -
leave your shoes out overnight and they'll be returned in
the morning, hand-buffed to a gleaming shine; indulge in
an in-room beauty or massage treatment; or order steak
and fries at 03:00 from the 24 hour room-service menu.
The Mercer has 75 rooms over six floors, each decorated to
match its majestic Romanesque exterior. For the ultimate
in luxury, book the opulent penthouse suite - it will set you
back close to three grand, but you'll sure feel special.

237 Madison Ave
Midtown
Map 7-B2

Morgans Hotel

212 686 03 00 | *www.morganshotel.com*
Slap bang in the heart of swanky Manhattan, Morgans
strives to be a home away from home – but you'll wish
your home was like this! Chic yet welcoming decor
characterises all of the 113 rooms in this beautiful hotel,
credited as being New York's very first boutique hotel. With
20 successful years behind it, the hotel is a temple of
comfort and style, and is always in demand. The in-house
restaurant, Asia de Cuba, blends Asian and Latin cuisines
and is packed every night of the week.

34

Madison Avenue
Midtown
Map 5-B4

Roosevelt Hotel

212 661 9600 | *www.therooseveithotel.com*
It's over 80 years old and thanks to an extensive refurbishment, completed in 1997, it doesn't show its age at all. It is centrally located in the Midtown district of Manhattan, walking distance from the Rockefeller Center, the Metropolitan Museum and the Empire State Building, and is a huge draw for visitors who want to be where the action is. But the luxurious rooms (and there's over a thousand of them), and the legendary service levels are also good reasons to choose this landmark hotel.

310 West Broadway
Soho
Map 10-E2

Soho Grand

212 965 3000 | *www.sohogrand.com*
This hotel is modelled around the typical Soho-style lofts that are sought after by the wealthy, the arty and the glitterati. It has 363 rooms, each one redefining contemporary design. Huge windows give you great views of the New York skyline up close, while the comfort of the rooms provide a haven from the hustle and bustle, so you can enjoy the best of both worlds. Their attitude to service is perhaps best summed up by their strangest offering: if you feel lonely in your room, they can bring you a pet goldfish to lift your spirits (at no extra cost!).

1 Central Park West
Central Park
Map 4-E1

Trump International Hotel

212 299 1000 | *www.trumpintl.com*
The man, the comb-over, the catchphrase ('you're fired!'), the towers and now the hotel, Trump is big on everything including luxurious suites, stunning skyline views and of course, award-winning restaurant Jean Georges (p.389). It's geared towards the business traveller, and is particularly suited to long stays. Awesome views over Central Park will have you pressing your face against the huge windows for hours. The hotel is perfect for the well-heeled business traveller - in fact, they'll even press your suit for you on arrival.

301 Park Avenue
Central Park
Map 5-B3

Waldorf=Astoria

212 355 3000 | *www.waldorf.com*
Throw budget caution to the wind and step inside this tower of luxury - from the gorgeous art deco design to the seamless service, it's easy to see why this hotel has captured the hearts of guests for well over a hundred years. The rooms (a range of deluxe rooms, super-comfortable suites and stunning apartments) are beautifully furnished and come with all the luxuries you can imagine. It's a magnet for visiting dignitaries and US government officials, and it's very, very posh!

35

Hotel Apartments

Hotel apartments can be rented on a daily, weekly or monthly basis, and they range from teeny-tiny studios, to one-bedroom suites, to luxurious penthouses that cost a small fortune. Your budget will dictate where you stay, but don't cross the big names off your list for fear of high prices - some of the hotel chains like Hilton or Marriott have some excellent long-stay and corporate rates that can often be surprisingly reasonable. Amenities will differ, but one common factor in most hotel apartments is a kitchenette where you can make your own coffee and even prepare meals. Some of the

Hotel Apartments		
Metro Home	212 813 2244	www.metro-home.com
Mini Suites of Minetta	212 475 6952	www.minetta-suites.com
Morton Suites	212 475 6952	www.spnewyork.com
Radio City Apartments	212 730 0728	www.radiocityapts.com
Sherry-Netherland	212 355 2800	www.sherrynetherland.com
Signature Properties	212 475 4756	www.spnewyork.com
The Atrium Suites	212 475 6952	www.spnewyork.com

more expensive apartments will have a swimming pool in the building and may even be serviced daily, whereas the more basic places will come with clean sheets and towels, and little else.

Signature Properties (www.spnewyork.com) has hundreds of furnished hotel apartments available, and the Sherry-Netherland (www.sherrynetherland.com) is a Central Park hotel that offers five-star service for long-term guests.

Guest Houses

B&Bs and guesthouses are plentiful in the city, with the cosier options located in the Lower East Side, TriBeCa, Soho and Brooklyn. Many are no cheaper than hotels, but they are far more personal with fewer rooms, congenial staff and a family atmosphere. Almost all of them will offer basic amenities including free internet connection, cable TV and in-room telephone as well as continental breakfasts. New York guesthouses are usually small and often situated in old (but well-maintained) buildings - the Abingdon Guest House (www.abingdonhouse.com) takes up two adjoining brownstones in the West Village and is tastefully decorated and professionally run. The East Village Bed & Coffee (www.bedandcoffee.com) is a relaxed, eclectic guesthouse with individually themed rooms and some funky common areas.

Motels

Motels are really those roadside stopovers for motorists who need to catch a few hours' sleep before driving the next leg of a long journey. Therefore, you won't find any motels within New York City itself - they tend to be off major highways. If you're planning to make the most of the city, it's not worth checking into a motel, since you'll spend too much time commuting. But if you are merely passing through, the Howard Johnson (www.howardjohnson.com) and Holiday Inn Express

Motels		
Anchor Inn	718 428 8000	www.theanchorinn.com
Best Western City View Inn	718 392 8400	www.bestwestern.com
Commack Motor Inn	631 499 9060	www.thecommackmotorinn.com
Floral Park Motor Lodge	516 775 7777	www.floralparkmotorlodge.com
Off Soho Suites Hotel	212 353 0860	www.offsoho.com
Queens Motor Inn	718 457 7755	www.queensmotorinn.com

(www.ichotelsgroup.com) chains are good top-end motels, while Econo Lodges (www.choicehotels.com/ny) may provide more for your money, with rooms starting at around $65 per night.

Hostels

Hostels are not restricted to hard-up students or bearded travellers - if you look around you'll find some very decent, very safe and very clean hostels that offer dorm-style or even private rooms. Almost all hostels have shared bathrooms though - this can be off-putting for many people, but it is the only downside to some very funky little places. YMCA (www.ymcanyc.org) has a number of hostels throughout Manhattan, but the Vanderbilt hostel on the Upper East Side is particularly good - the location and price are phenomenal although you have to book well in advance as demand is high.

Hostels		
Americana Homestay Host Service	917 669 0579	www.americanahomestay.com
Broadway Hotel & Hostel	212 244 7827	www.broadwayhotelnyc.coma
Gershwin Hotel	212 545 8000	www.gershwinhotel.com
Greenpoint YMCA	718 389 3700	www.ymcanyc.org
Harlem YMCA	212 281 4100	www.ymcanyc.org
Hostelling International	212 932 2300	www.hinewyork.org
Hotel 31	212 685 3060	www.hotel31.com
The Portland Square Hotel	212 382 0600	www.portlandsquarehotel.com
Vanderbilt YMCA	212 912 2500	www.ymcanyc.org
Wanderers Inn West	212 222 5602	www.wanderersinn.com
West Side YMCA	212 875 4100	www.ymcanyc.org

Campsites

Other options **Camping** p.257

There's not much camping going on in the city, but if you venture further afield you will find some very beautiful places to pitch your tent. The NY Parks Department (www.nycgovparks.org) has set up a division called the Urban Park Rangers, who aim to help people get back to nature. During the summer months, they organise various camping trips to parks in the city. To find out more information, and reserve your place on a camping trip, all you have to do is call 311 and ask for the Urban Park Rangers. If you're a hardcore camper and you'd rather go it alone, the official New York State Tourism website (www.iloveny.com) lists various state parks where camping is permitted.

Campsites		
Battle Row Campground	516 572 8690	www.nassaucountyny.gov
Fla-Net Park Campgrounds	973 347 4467	www.beachcomber.com
Greenwood Lake & Campground	973 728 8505	na
KOA Campgrounds	212 869 8293	www.koa.com
Liberty Harbor Marina & RV Prk	201 386 7500	www.libertyharborrv.com
Mahlon Dickerson Reservation	973 663 0200	www.trails.com
NJ State of: Cheesequake State Park	732 566 2161	www.njparksandforests.org
Sports & Arts Center Island Lake	212 753 7777	www.islandlake.com
Sun-Air Lakeside Camp	973 697 3489	www.sunairlakesidecamp.com
Tower Trailer Park	732 969 2285	na

Getting Around
Other options **Maps** p.439, **Exploring** p.178

Once you find your bearings, New York is one of the easiest cities in the world to navigate, with a complex yet superlative network to get you from Avenue A to the Bronx. The grid system means that you should be able to find your way around (street numbers increase northwards, while avenues run east to west with the

numbers increasing westwards). With every street lined with great shops, interesting history and beautiful sights, New York is an amazing city to explore on foot - perhaps this is why over two-thirds of New Yorkers don't own cars (although a lack of free parking and traffic congestion both play a large role too - more on this later).

The public transport system is excellent, and consists of a network of public buses, the subway and overland trains that most residents depend upon. Public transport is operated by the MTA (Mass Transit Authority), and runs throughout the day and night in all areas of the city, including the boroughs.

Classic yellow New York taxi cabs are everywhere and very handy - although they are most prolific in Manhattan. They are cheap and hailing one is pretty easy once you've learnt a few tips and tricks (and as long as it's not raining, when it's nearly impossible to find an available cab).

The various bridges and tunnels connecting Manhattan to the other boroughs are part of a daily commute for hundreds of thousands of people heading into or out of the city. Apart from their necessity, many are also known for their history and archaeological significance. Brooklyn Bridge, which links lower Manhattan with Brooklyn, is probably the most iconic of the bridges, and has a heightened wooden walkway so that you can stroll over (or jog, ride or skate) without fear of getting snarled up in the traffic below. Along the way you'll find a few plaques detailing the history of this world-famous landmark, and once you get to the Brooklyn side there are some nice restaurants where you can refuel before you walk back over. The Williamsburg and Manhattan Bridges link Manhattan to Brooklyn as well, although both are further up the island. The Queensboro Bridge links Manhattan to Queens, and the Verrazzano Narrows Bridge links lower Brooklyn to Staten Island.

There are four major tunnels: the Lincoln Tunnel, which runs under the Hudson River between Manhattan and New Jersey, the Holland Tunnel, which also runs under the Hudson and connects Manhattan to New Jersey, the Queens Midtown Tunnel connects Queens to Manhattan, and the Brooklyn-Battery Tunnel runs under the East River and connects Manhattan to Brooklyn.

Air
New York City is currently served by three airports, although there is a plan for a fourth airport in the future (a study is being undertaken and Stewart International Airport, in the Hudson Valley, has been earmarked as a possibility). Two international airports – JFK

Airlines

Aer Lingus	866 886 8844	www.flyaerlingus.com
Air Canada	888 247 2262	www.aircanada.com
Air France	800 237 2747	www.airfrance.us
Alitalia	800 223 5730	www.alitaliausa.com
American Airlines	800 433 7300	www.aa.com
British Airways	800 247 9297	www.britishairways.com
Cathay Pacific	800 233 2742	www.cathaypacific.com
China Airlines	917 368 2000	www.china-airlines.com
Continental Airlines	800 523 3273	www.continental.com
Delta Airlines	800 221 1212	www.delta.com
Emirates Airlines	800 777 3999	www.emirates.com
Etihad Airways	888 838 4423	www.etihadairways.com
Gulf Air	888 359 4853	www.gulfairco.com
Lufthansa	800 645 3880	www.lufthansa.com
Malaysia Airlines	212 697 8994	www.malaysiaairlines.com
Northwest Airlines	800 225 2525	www.nwa.com
Qantas Airways	800 227 4500	www.qantas.com
Singapore Airlines	800 742 3333	www.singaporeair.com
South African Airways	800 722 9675	www.flysaa.com
Southwest Airlines	800 435 9792	www.southwest.com
United Airlines	800 864 8331	www.united.com
US Airways	800 428 4322	www.usairways.com
Virgin Atlantic	800 821 5438	www.virgin-atlantic.com

in Queens and Newark in New Jersey - and one dedicated to domestic flights only (La Guardia in Queens) currently handle the millions of air passengers that fly into New York every year.

JFK is seen as the major point of entry for international travellers. Everyone landing there must go through passport control, even if they are only there in transit. This involves a passport check, where you have to submit the relevant visa form (p.58) and answer a few security questions. You'll also be photographed (so smile!) and have your fingerprints taken.

Since 9/11, air travel has taken on a new level of seriousness and you should definitely allow extra time for various security checks before your flight. The Transport Security Administration (TSA) exists to make flying as safe and secure as possible. Before you travel, you should check out their website for the latest updates (www.tsa.gov).

Airport Bus

3-1-1

US airports have implemented the 3-1-1 system, allowing travellers a small (one-quart size) zip-lock transparent bag to carry on board the flight, that would contain whatever liquid or gel toiletries travellers may need in their hand luggage. The numbers relate to what travellers are allowed: three-ounce containers, in one quart transparent bag and only one per person, hence the 3-1-1! For exceptions and more information click on to www.tsa.gov

Public ground transportation connecting to either regional or light rail networks serve both major airports. You can just as easily catch a cab (although this is the most expensive option) or even a commuter bus. Different to public buses, these will pick you up from your gate within 20 minutes (or less) and deliver you straight to your home or hotel doorstep at a fraction of a cab price (an average cost for a one-way trip would be about $19 from JFK to Manhattan). You can book in advance or simply rock up to the free phone desk by the exit and pay the driver when he drops you off. These privately run companies will also move you the other way, picking you up at your doorstep and delivering you safely to your chosen airport.

Boat

The Staten Island Ferry is the busiest in the United States, carrying millions of people from Manhattan to Staten Island and back again. Since 1997, passage on the ferry has been free, making this one of the best bargains in New York. Even if you don't need to go to Staten Island, it's still worth getting on the ferry for amazing views of the Statue of Liberty and the breathtaking New York skyline. There are several other boat services, such as the Water Taxi (www.nywatertaxi.com), NY Waterway (www.nywaterway.com), and the Circle Line Ferry (www.circlelinedowntown.com).

Be Prepared

Get through security faster by being prepared. You will have to put all your belongings through the scanners, including your shoes - it will save time if you start taking these off while still in the queue. Laptops have to come out of laptop bags to be scanned separately. All jackets and scarves must also be scanned.

Bus

In addition to the subway system, a fleet of nearly 6,000 buses chug (on green energy, see environment p. 19) along the 300 bus routes (local and express), moving residents around the city. Both bus and subway stops are clearly marked and always within walking distance (bus stops are on every other street, and subway stops are predominantly the same in the city).

A one-way journey on the bus or subway will cost you $2.00 and on the bus you have to have the exact money since the driver will not be able to give you back any change. For fuss-free travel, pick up a MetroCard (pay for a daily, weekly or monthly pass) at any of the stations to allow you access to the subway and bus network.

The Port Authority Bus Terminal (625 Eighth Ave, between Eighth and Ninth Avenues and 40th to 42nd street) is the central stop for all the buses, including services that take you beyond the fabulous five (boroughs that is). You can catch the Greyhound and the Peter Pan from here. Both serve nationally.

Car

Other options **Transportation** p.168

New Yorkers are not particularly bothered about owning a car, what with few parking places in the more congested parts of the city and parking lots charging astronomical prices. In fact, the city is considered particularly car unfriendly, hence the excellent public transport network. Vehicle and driver insurance is pretty steep too, so most people are happy to let go of their 'behind-the-wheel' dreams in favour of public transport, cycling and especially walking.

Ask any New Yorker why they don't drive and most will give the same answer: parking is a nightmare! There are so many parking restrictions and anyone breaking them gets a hefty fine. You can't park within 15 feet of a fire hydrant. In many places you have to move your car before 08:00 so that street cleaning can commence. If you find a good parking spot, grab it! But before you walk away from your car, double check that there are not any signs about prohibiting parking for any reason - it is not unknown for parking to be temporarily prohibited in otherwise perfectly fine parking places.

Car Hire

So not many New Yorkers have wheels, but what happens when they need to take a road trip? Hiring a car is easy and all major international chains are represented, not only with depots at any (or all) of the airports, but also with various locations around the city. Dollar Car is a national company that often has great deals on long-term rentals.

With virtually all car hire companies, you can book your car online and pay using your credit card (in fact, most car hire companies will require credit card details as a

Lap of Luxury

Would you rather be zooming down Broadway in a Bentley than a basic saloon? Then you're in the right city. Flash motors and zippy numbers are rarely seen in the grub and grime of daily city life, but if you got the cash to flash then let loose and pick yourself a beauty. Gotham Dream Cars (www.gotham dreamcars.com) will lend you a must-have red Ferrari or silver-as-stars Aston Martin for a cool $4,500 a week. You can also rent their gems by the half-day if you just want to pretend like you can afford it.

Hired Hands

Too good to be steering? NYC Limousine (www.nyclimousine.com) can provide a stretch limo, complete with uniformed driver to open and close doors for you, for about $75 an hour. Manhattan Coach International (www.manhattancoach.com) makes sure you paint the town red in style - they specialise in weddings, proms, tours of the city and other special occasions - picture yourself in a stretch Hummer with 25 of your close friends ($210 per hour for two to five hours).

Car Rental Agencies

AAMCAR	212 927 7000	www.aamcar.com
Accessible Vans of America	800 282 8297	www.accessiblevans.com
Alamo	800 462 5266	www.alamo.com
Avis	800 331 1212	www.avis.com
Budget	800 527 0700	www.budgetrentacar.com
Dollar Rent A Car	800 800 4000	www.dollarcar.com
Enterprise Rent-A-Car	800 325 8007	www.enterprise.com
Hertz	800 654 3131	www.hertz.com
National Car Rental	800 227 7638	www.nationalcar.com
New York Rent-A-Car	212 799 1100	www.ny-car.com

Insure For Sure!
It's always a good idea to get extra insurance - even the tiniest scratch on a hire car will cost you big bucks.

guarantee, so have the plastic ready. Rates can start as low as $75 per week for a standard car, or you can treat yourself to something flashier for $50 per day and upwards.

When you pick up the car the tank is full of gas, and that's how you should return it (or pay a gas surcharge). Remember, all reputable car hire companies will do a thorough, multi-point check on the car, inside and out, while you are present - this is to check for existing damage and is for your own protection. The last thing you need is to be charged for a scratch that was on the car long before you got in it.

Make sure that you are permitted to take your hired car out of state - often the small print says otherwise. If you are planning an epic roadtrip, Kerouac-style, consider paying a bit extra to rent a global positioning system (GPS). Avis charges $10 per day.

Cycling

Other options **Cycling** p.259

Five Boro Bike Tour
If commuting on two wheels is not for you, perhaps you'd enjoy a more recreational approach to cycling. Last year's Five Boro Bike Tour saw around 300,000 riders taking on the 42 mile course. See p.41 for more details.

Over 100,000 New Yorkers travel around on two wheels every day, and it's a growing trend. Not only do you get to skip the traffic jams, but you can pat yourself on the back for being kind to the environment at the same time. There are around a hundred bike lanes throughout the city, with more on the cards. Cyclists can be fairly aggressive, especially if you are strolling along in a bike lane - but you can't blame them, given the hair-raising traffic conditions they take on every day.

Once you're brave enough to face cycling through the traffic, remember the following rules: stick to the right hand side of traffic, stick to bike lanes where they exist, watch out for parked-car doors opening suddenly, and never jump a red light (or try to make it on amber). You're going to want to make yourself visible so do whatever it takes - bright clothing, reflective neon body vests, bells, whistles... don't be shy.

You are allowed to take your bike on the subway, but only during off-peak hours and from stations where there is a gate (rather than just a turnstile). You can also take your bike on the Staten Island Ferry, but only if you stay on the lower deck. If you're going to be leaving your bike on the street while you pop into a shop or cafe, invest in a good lock, or you might be walking home!

Rickshaws (or pedicabs) are a growing method of public transport and there are now around 500 rickshaw drivers who pedal you from one place to the next. They are safe and can transport two people at the same time. See www.manhattanrickshaw.com for more information on how to hail one off the street or book one for a special occasion.

Taxi

Yellow cabs must be one of the top 10 most recognisable icons of New York. There are over 13,000 yellow cabs and over 40,000 other taxis (including mini cabs, limo services and other for-hire vehicles). Yellow cabs are licensed by the New York City Taxi and Limousine Commission, and drivers have to follow strict regulations. They are the only cabs permitted to pick up passengers hailing from the street, although others will try to do so. All yellow cabs are metered and a journey starts at $2.50, although this goes up to $3.00 after 20:00 and $3.50 during the peak hours between 16:00 and 20:00). The meter ticks up every one-fifth of a mile, or every two minutes if you're stuck in traffic. If you are hailing a cab from the street, make sure you only try to flag down the ones with their roof lights on - if the light is off it means that the cab is already occupied or the driver is off duty. A maximum of four passengers is allowed in standard cabs. If you're lucky you may be able to find a mini-bus sized cab that can accommodate more passengers, or you can call a car service ahead of time). All cabs are non-smoking. It is highly recommended (and required by law) to fasten your seatbelt during your journey. It is always a good idea to sort of know where you are going - most New Yorkers give the street or avenue number and the cross street, but if you know of a

particularly good route you should share it with your cabbie.

You should always, always tip the driver. There is no regulation or fixed guideline on how much the tip should be, but as a general rule you should tip $1 for a trip costing under $10, $2 for a trip costing $10 to $20, and so on. Catching a cab from any of New York's airports can be costly, since you have to pay a fixed fare (around $50) as well as road tolls.

Taxi Companies

1-877-Jet-Limo.com	877 538 5466	www.1-877-jet-limo.com
Andrea Town Car Taxi Service	718 392 9191	http://andreacarservice.com
Car 24 Transportation	212 677 7777	www.ctftransportation.com
Carmel Car & Limousine Service	212 666 6666	www.carmellimo.com
Executive Shuttle - VANS	718 968 3100	www.executiveshuttle.us
Nations Transportation	866 454 6687	www.nationslimo.com
New York Taxi & Limousine Commission	212 692 8294	www.nyc.gov/taxi
On Time Taxi	914 285 0505	www.ontimetaxi.net
SuperShuttle	800 258 3826	www.supershuttle.com
Tel-A-Car of New York	800 678 5466	www.telacar.com

Train

There are over 250 train stations in the tri-state area along some 20 railway lines. These form an essential part of the daily commute for over 150 million passengers in and out of New York City. The train network is formed by three main players: the Long Island Railroad and the Metro-North Railroad (both operated by the MTA), and New Jersey Transit.

Tram

The only tram in New York City is the aerial one that runs from Manhattan to Roosevelt Island. It climbs to nearly 80 metres over the East River, but is perfectly safe and used by hundreds of commuters daily. A one-way trip costs $2. The tram was featured in *Spiderman*, where the Green Goblin threw a tram filled with school kids down towards the river so that Spidey could perform a daring rescue. In real life there have been no such scares, although a loss of power in 2006 resulted in commuters being trapped in the tram for seven hours. The tramway was closed for six months while the Roosevelt Island Operating Corporation upgraded the safety and emergency features of the tram.

Subway Music

The MTA sponsors the 'Music Under New York' programme, where it sponsors over 100 musicians to perform at various locations each week. Musicians range from the extraordinarily talented to the just plain extraordinary - if you can find her, check out the 'Saw Lady' - Natalia Paruz plays a long bendy saw to create a melancholic yet beautiful song (www.sawlady.com).

Subway

The New York Subway is one of the largest underground train systems in the world, and is used by billions of people each year. It is safe, easy to navigate (once you get the hang of it), and it can be pretty entertaining, thanks to a large variety of 'travelling' musicians, poets and artists riding along with you, hoping for a bit of spare change. Even if there is no entertainment, a ride on the subway is a great way to get up close with the people of New York, who are an eclectic bunch!

The subway connects all the boroughs except for Staten Island. The PATH (Port Authority Trans-Hudson Railroad) subway system links New York to neighbouring New Jersey. The network may seem confusing to a newcomer at first, but before long you'll get to know the ins and outs of how to make your way around in the quickest possible time. See the subway map on the inside back cover.

To ride the subway, all you need to do is get yourself a ticket. Every subway station has a ticket office or a vending machine - the vending machines are a quick way to get your subway pass: you just pop in the amount required (some machines give change), follow the instructions on screen, and you'll get a plastic card with a magnetic strip that you can just swipe at the turnstiles. A one-way ride (no matter what distance) costs $2, but you can get a one-day pass giving you unlimited rides for $7. A seven-day unlimited ride pass costs $24 and a 30 day unlimited ride pass costs $76. Reduced fares are available for people over 65 and those with certain disabilities.

Be a Polite Pedestrian

If you're going to walk the walk, make sure you walk it right. Try to move at the same pace as everybody else, and learn to weave through the crowds to get past the slow coaches. Never stop abruptly: if you need to stop or slow down, move to the inside of the pavement (closer to the buildings than the street).

Walking

Other options **Hiking** p.264

Walking is one of the most popular ways to get around in the city, with millions of New Yorkers taking to the streets to get from A to B every day. Things can get pretty congested at times and there is a definite 'street code' to follow, so don't dawdle along or suddenly stop in the middle of the pavement to take a photo of something. But on the whole, walking around is not only healthier but it also helps you 'feel' more of the city - the sights, the sounds, the smells and the collective heartbeat of all the other New Yorkers on the streets. Before you buy that subway ticket, check on a map how far it really is between where you are and where you're going. In many cases, walking does not take that much longer than going underground. The grid system of the streets makes it really easy to figure out where you're walking to, until you get into Soho, and then things get more confusing. However, once you get below Houston Street and the grid system disappears, your feet are often the best mode of transport anyway, since the streets are congested and not even the most determined cab driver can beat the traffic in Soho and the Financial District.

Money

Cash may be king, but New York is one of the shopping capitals of the world, and as long as you can pay, you can pay any which way you like. Only a handful of smaller shops or market stalls won't accept cards, so it pays to keep a stash of cash on you, just in case. Some hotels require a credit card as guarantee, even if you intend to settle your final bill with cash. Nearly all restaurants accept cash or card, and you can even buy your subway Metrocard using your credit card.

Cheques and travellers' cheques are a bit more tricky - you won't find many places that accept cheques without asking questions, and travellers' cheques need to be converted, which can be time consuming. New York is one of the most international cities in the world, but don't go thinking that means your foreign currency is welcome - if you are paying cash then you'll need good old American dollars.

Local Currency

The monetary unit is the dollar ($), which is equal to 100 cents. All the notes are the same colour - green - no matter what the denomination. It is one of the world's most widely circulated currencies, along with the euro.

Each denomination note carries a portrait of previous US presidents, as follows: George Washington ($1), Thomas Jefferson ($2), Abraham Lincoln ($5), Alexander Hamilton ($10), Andrew Jackson ($20), Ulysses S Grant ($50) and Benjamin Franklin ($100).

Coins are available in denominations of one dollar, 25 cents (also called a quarter), 10 cents (a dime), five cents (a nickel) and one cent (a penny).

Exchange Rates

Foreign Currency (FC)	1 Unit FC = x $	$1 = x FC
Australia	0.789	1.268
Canada	0.846	1.182
China	0.129	7.778
Denmark	0.174	5.758
Euro	1.294	0.773
Hong Kong	0.128	7.802
India	0.023	44.20
Iraq	0.001	1,298
Japan	0.008	121.6
Kuwait	3.459	0.289
Mexico	0.091	10.94
Philippines	0.020	48.98
Saudi Arabia	0.267	3.751
Singapore	0.650	1.539
South Africa	0.141	7.120
Switzerland	0.801	1.249
United Arab Emirates	0.272	3.673
United Kingdom	1.978	0.506

Banks

A strong network of banks in New York includes all the major American and international names, each with several branches around the city. To find a particular bank's nearest branch, it is best to check on their website - not only will you find out branch locations, but also what services are available at each branch (like whether there is a customer service desk or an ATM). Without US residency and a social security number, you can't open a bank account. For more information on opening a bank account, please see p.80.

Banking hours vary from one to another, but they are generally 08:00 to 17:00, Monday to Friday. Most are closed on public holidays.

ATMs

You're never far away from an ATM (automatic teller machine) in New York - you'll find one in most banks but also in many delis, supermarkets, hotel lobbies, bodegas and even in some bars. ATMs in locations other than banks charge you a minimum of $1.50 for every transaction.

Every ATM will display symbols of the financial networks that are accepted, such as Cirrus, Visa, Visa Electron, Plus and MasterCard. Often, an ATM will only let you withdraw a minimum of $20, so bad luck if you are down to your last $10! Many also have maximum daily withdrawal amounts, and this varies from bank to bank. As a security measure you can usually instruct your bank to keep the maximum daily withdrawal at a lower amount - this way if your card is stolen and someone manages to withdraw money from your account, at least the damage is minimal. When withdrawing money from an ATM, make sure that no one is standing too close behind you and try to use your body to shield the keypad so that nobody can see what digits you are pressing. If someone tries talking to you while you are mid-transaction, press the 'cancel' button immediately, take your card and walk away - a common scam is to switch cards while you are distracted. Whenever you leave an ATM, make absolutely sure that your own card has been returned to you. Most ATMs will have an emergency number on them - if you suspect that you have been a victim of a scam, phone the number immediately. Wherever possible, try to use an ATM that is fitted with a camera. After your transaction is completed, take the time to put your money in your wallet and your wallet back in your handbag or pocket before you walk away - even if there is a long queue behind you.

Money Exchanges

Unfortunately money exchange is a fairly complicated affair, with many major banks only offering the service for their own customers. There are random exchange offices (or bureaux de change) around town, but these usually give lousy rates or charge high commission. One solution is to use your credit card or ATM card to withdraw dollars. If you do need to exchange money, try to do it at the airport or at well-known offices like Thomas Cook (at various locations).

Exchange Centres		
Thomas Cook	Financial District	212 363 6209
	Midtown	212 679 4365
	West Village	212 643 3620
Travelex	Financial District (Broadway)	212 753 2595
	Financial District (Vesey)	212 227 8156
	Midtown (32nd St)	212 679 4365
	Midtown (48th St)	212 265 6063

Credit Cards

All major retailers and some of the smaller shops, as well as hotels and restaurants will take your plastic, whether it's one of the main ones (Visa, MasterCard, American Express) or a lesser-known one (like Discovery, although you might want to check first). Most delis and bodegas will also accept cards, but in many cases there will be a minimum spend requirement (usually $10), or a surcharge (usually around $1.50). Otherwise, there are no other charges for using a credit card.

Markets and street vendors rarely accept cards, so keep some cash handy, just in case. If you lose your credit card, contact your bank as soon as you can so that they can block it. Once you've reported the loss, you will not be liable for any further transactions made on your card.

Tipping

Get used to tipping in New York - it is practically a crime not to tip for most services, even if the service was awful. Tip your taxi driver (see p.373), your restaurant waiter, your barman, hotel bellhops and maids, and the list goes on. In a pub or a bar, the rule is $1 to $2 per drink, or more if the drink involved some skillful mixing. You'll often see service deteriorate if your tip is deemed too small, so be prepared to part with the cash if you want your drinks with a dash of speed and a hint of a smile! You should tip your restaurant waiter anything from 15% to 20% (if your maths is bad, just double the tax). A bellhop will expect between $2 and $5 if he helps you with your bags or hails you a cab, and you should leave $2 or $3 per day for your hotel maid. If you are paying by credit card, you just add the tip to the final amount before signing.

The Whole World's Your Home

Explorer Residents' Guides are going global, with new titles for locations as far flung as Dublin and New Zealand in the pipeline. So if you fancy living abroad check out the complete list of current and upcoming Explorer guides on our website **www.explorer-publishing.com** Remember life's a trip...all you need to do is pick a destination.

EXPLORER London

45

Newspapers/Magazines

New York is a global hub for the publishing industry with some of the most famous newspapers and magazines in the world being published there. There are over 40 daily newspapers and over 300 consumer magazines in various languages. Tabloids and broadsheets are popular, and of course the commuter culture results in high newstand sales because, well, you've just got to have something to read on the subway. Many international news agencies have set up home in New York, and an estimated 10,000 journalists are based in the city.

Four major US newspapers are from New York: the *Wall Street Journal*, the *New York Times*, the *New York Daily News* and the *New York Post*. Some of the magazine giants in the city include Time Warner Publishing (*Time*, *People*, *Sports Illustrated*), Condé Nast (the *New Yorker*, *Vanity Fair*, *Vogue*) and the Hearst Corporation (*Cosmopolitan*, *Esquire*). There are several ways to get your daily news fix: newspapers can be bought at paper stands found on almost every street, from vending machines, bookshops or subway stations. You can also subscribe to your favourite papers and magazines and have them delivered straight to your doorstep. The average price of a broadsheet (like the *Wall Street Journal* and the *New York Times* is $1.25, although Sunday editions can cost a bit more ($2.00). Bookshops and larger paper stands sell international and foreign language newspapers and magazines.

Free Weeklies

There are several weekly papers that are packed with useful information for residents and visitors. The Village Voice *is a popular paper published every Wednesday and distributed free of charge from red boxes on street corners (www.villagevoice.com). Lookout also for* The L Magazine, *which features listings and news and has great coverage on Brooklyn (www.thelmaga zine.com).*

Books

Other options **Websites** p.46

There are countless books on New York – hardly surprising, considering it is such an inspiring and multi-faceted city. If it's New York info you're after, there are plenty of guidebooks to help you make the most of the city. Lonely Planet's *NYC*, the *Time Out Guide to New York*, and Fodor's *New York City* are all popular and useful. Shecky's (www.sheckys.com) publish a range of colourful nightlife and shopping guides to complement their website. And one of the most popular guides in the city is the *Zagat Guide*, which represents feedback received from thousands of New Yorkers on some of the best restaurants, bars and nightclubs in the city (www.zagat.com). If you've got little ones in tow, there are several guidebooks that expose the best the city has to offer for children: *Fun Places to go with Children in New York* by Randi Millman-Brown is recommended, although there are many others.

Photography books featuring the many beautiful sights of the city are also plentiful, and almost all are beautiful. *New York: 365 Days*, published by the *New York Times*, is a great coffee-table book featuring a selection of fascinating 'then and now' images.

In terms of history, there are a few books worth mentioning. EB White's essay *Here is New York* is a moving piece on what New York meant to one man in 1949 – it is quoted often and sparked new interest after the 2001 terrorist attacks, when White's musings that the city's towers could be burned by a single fleet of planes took on a chilling, prophetic accuracy. *How The Other Half Lives* by Jacob Riis is equally fascinating – it is a collection of photographs and text published in the late 1800s documenting the slums and poorhouses of the city, and the squalid conditions thereof. Although Riis faced some criticism over his intrusive methods of research, his book is widely believed to have been responsible for certain reforms.

Websites

In New York, websites are a huge resource of information and opinion, and you could spend hours – days – surfing the internet and finding out millions of random facts that you never knew. Some websites are helpful, some are entertaining, and some are just plain weird.

If you're looking for some tips on what to do or where to go, try www.nycvisit.com or www.nyc.gov. Both of these sites are excellent for tourist information. If you're trying to plan your social schedule, www.timeout.com/newyork or www.nymag.com (New York Magazine's online edition) have all the info on clubs, bars, restaurants, cinema, comedy and theatre, as well as reviews. The home page of the *New York Times* is also handy (www.nytimes.com). Craig's List (www.craigslist.org) is a hugely successful listings site, and useful whether you're looking for a flatmate, a job, a car or a threesome!

Blogs

When they first became popular, blogs were a great way to get the opinions of some very interesting people on a variety of topics. Nowadays, there are so many blogs out there that it is hard to find the really good ones. It's worth visiting www.nycbloggers.com, a site that hosts bloggers and lets you search them by borough. The ones you pick as your favourites will depend on your tastes, and you may have to sift through hundreds of random blogs before you find one that you think is worth reading on a regular basis. Try www.gothamist.com for comment, and www.overheardinnewyork.com for a hilarious peek into the everyday conversations of regular New Yorkers. Metroblogging New York City is an interesting collection of posts by a group of writers (http://nyc.metblogs.com).

Websites

New York Information	
www.10best.com	10 best parades and events
www.ci.nyc.ny.us	Official New York City site, with information on city agencies, programs and services
www.centralpark.com	Official site of the world's most famous city park
www.citidex.com	New York company and service listings
www.craigslist.org	Find a room mate, second-hand furniture and more
www.iloveny.com	The Official New York State Tourism Website
www.newyork.citysearch.com	New York restaurants, bars, night clubs, hotels, shops, spas, events, attractions, yellow page listings
www.newyork.com	New York hotels
www.ny.gov	New York State Government information and services
www.nyc.allinfoabout.com	Dining, accommodation, Entertainment
www.nyc.freecityevents.com	Free events
www.nymag.com	Daily coverage of New York's restaurants, nightlife, shopping, politics, and culture
www.nymtc.org	New York City Police Department
www.nytimes.com	Online edition of the newspaper
www.sheckys.com	Nightlife and shopping listings
www.TicketsNow.com	Concert tickets
www.visitnewyorkstate.net	Where to stay, shop, eat, etc
www.weather.noaa.gov	National Weather Service
www.zagat.com	Nightlife survey and listings
Business/Industry	
www.mtahq.org	Metropolitan Transportation Authority
www.nycvisit.com	New York City's official tourism marketing organization
www.nyse.com	Buy! Sell! Information on the New York Stock Exchange
www.nysdot.gov	New York State Department of Transportation
www.nyu.edu	Official website for New York University
www.panynj.gov	Port Authority
www.travelinfony.com	New York State Transit & Buses

New York Annual Events

Restaurant Week

Foodies on a budget wait anxiously for this event, which takes place during summer and winter each year. The city's finest restaurants serve their most lip-smacking specialities for just a fraction of the usual price. Over 150 restaurants are involved, including culinary greats such as Aureole (p.375), Nobu (p.395) and Union Square Cafe (p.379). Prices do go up a little bit each year, but you're looking at around $24 for the lunch menu and $35 for the dinner menu. It's a great way to sample food prepared by the city's top chefs without having to remortgage your home. Keep your eyes peeled on the local press for details, and make your reservations early!

Three Kings Parade
www.elmuseo.org

This cultural festival celebrates one of the most important days in the Latin American calendar – the day the three kings visited baby Jesus. The streets of Spanish Harlem are filled with adults, children and a variety of barnyard animals, accompanied by street music and a festive atmosphere. Prominent Latino figures dress up to play the three kings. The parade departs from 106th Street, just off Fifth Avenue.

Chinese New Year

The awesome Dragon Parade is only a small part of the celebrations – it is a period of fireworks, parades, dancing unicorns and other far eastern delights. Hang out at Mott and Bayard Street at noon and Market Street and East Broadway at 14:00 on the first day of the event to see some great firecracker displays, supposedly intended to ward off evil spirits.

New York Fashion Week

Twice a year the glitterati descends on New York in a frenzied torrent of tutus and cashmere, and twice a year the great city plays good host to these gurus of style for one whole week (actually eight days, from Friday to the following Friday) at a time. Bryant Park is converted into a temporary fashion arena complete with runways, lounges and air-conditioned tents. Limo-loads of celebrities turn out to drool over next seasons 'must-haves'.

Empire State Building Run-Up
www.esbnyc.com

Every year, the truly brave (or crazy) run, walk or crawl up the 1,576 steps of the Empire State Building to reach the Observatory Deck on the 86th floor. The event has been going for 30 years, and is organised by the New York Road Runners (www.nyrr.org). Entry to the race is by invitation only, so if you want to participate you should apply to the NYRR and they will invite you to take part based on your performance in other races throughout the year.

Westminster Kennel Club Dog Show
www.westminsterkennelclub.org

This is a howler of an event, with all breeds, and their owners, strutting around hoping to win 'best in show'. The show takes place over two full days, and while it is great fun for spectators, participants take it pretty seriously. But it's all for a good cause: all proceeds go to the 'Angel on a Leash' K9 therapy programme, where cute pooches are taken to visit poorly children for some much-needed cheering up.

February *The Armory Show*
www.thearmoryshow.com
Stimulate your senses at this contemporary art exhibition, which started in 1999 at the 69th Regiment Armory (hence the name). Today the exhibition is held at Pier 94 on Twelfth Avenue. It's a great opportunity to catch up with some cutting edge modern American art as well as work by various international artists.

17th March *St Patrick's Day*
The city turns green for a day to celebrate all things Irish, so paint your face and indulge in some green beer while you enjoy the festivities. Don't worry if you are not even slightly Irish, the atmosphere is electric and everybody is welcome. The grand St Patrick's Day Parade, which heads up Fifth Avenue, is a huge affair, with hundreds of thousands of people taking part.

March *Macy's Flower Show*
www.macys.com
This flower show has marked the start of spring in New York for over 30 years. A colourful selection of flowers and tropical plants are on display, so perhaps not the best place to go if you suffer from hayfever! Renowned horticulturists from around the world participate each year, and over half a million visitors stream in to see their handiwork.

First Week in May *Tribeca Film Festival*
www.tribecafilmfestival.org
The Tribeca Film Festival showcases an impressive range of international blockbusters, independent works, documentaries and family-friendly films during the first week of May. The film festival was founded in 2002 by Robert DeNiro and Jane Rosenthal, in an effort to inject some hope and regeneration into the Tribeca area after the 9/11 attacks. It gets bigger and more popular every year, and you have to book very early to get tickets.

May *The Great Five Boro Bike Tour*
www.bikenewyork.org
As the name suggests, this recreational bike race winds its way through all five boroughs along a 42 mile course. While some of the riders are competitive, many participants are just there to enjoy the great weather and friendly camaraderie with fellow cyclists. The roads are closed to normal traffic, there is free health food passed out along the route, and at the end of it all you get to boast that you lasted nearly a whole day in the saddle!

Last Week in May *Fleet Week*
Men in uniform, check! Booze, check! Men in uniform getting liquored up with the ladies, check and double check! This is fleet week, when troops of clean-cut navy boys take New York by storm. Girls (and guys): you've got seven full days to enjoy the best of what the boys in white have to offer. Expect lots of riotous, raunchy fun.

May *New York Aids Walk*
www.aidswalk.net/newyork
This 10km walk starts and ends at Central Park and aims to raise money through donations and sponsorships for 50 Aids charities. In 2006 over $250 million was raised, thanks to the participation of thousands of walkers. Apart from money, the walk is also crucial in educating the public on the ongoing problem of Aids.

Second Tuesday in June

Museum Mile Festival
www.museummilefestival.org
For one full day in June, 23 blocks along Fifth Avenue are cleared of traffic and filled with live musicians, street performers, dancing, and general fun. Entrance to nine different museums is totally free for that day, so you can wander in and out at will.

June

Gay and Lesbian Pride Parade
www.hopinc.org
This friendly, funny, flamboyant day out is the perfect example of summer bliss. For all the fun, however, there is also a serious side: the march was originally started to remember the Stonewall riots, and a moment of silence is held each year at 14:00. The march begins down Fifth Avenue and ends up on Christopher Street, which was once home to the infamous Stonewall Pub. June is Gay Pride month, and this is just one of the events celebrating the freedom to live your life the way you want to.

June

New York Jazz Festival
www.festivalproductions.net
The New York jazz scene is one of the best in the world, and thus the New York Jazz Festival is one of the most hotly anticipated events on the musical calendar. It takes over concert halls and cosy clubs, public parks and even street corners. It's a two-week celebration of everything that makes jazz cool. Previous headline acts include Ella Fitzgerald, Lauren Hill, Joao Gilberto and many, many more.

4th July

Independence Day
On the 4th July, America celebrates winning its independence from the British. Although it is a day of significant historical importance, festivities are a far less serious affair, with barbecues and brilliant fireworks. Try to bag yourself an invite to a rooftop house party for great views of the fireworks, or head for the Midtown area for the Macy's fireworks display. Bars and pubs usually have special events and prices on the day.

August/September

US Open Tennis Championships
www.usopen.org
This is the final event in the Grand Slam Tournament. It is played at the USTA Billie Jean King National Tennis Stadium in Flushing Meadows. All the big names turn out to fight for the champion's trophy, currently held by Roger Federer and Maria Sharapova. You have to be on the ball to get your tickets before they all sell out, but if you do manage to get courtside, you'll get to watch some heart-stopping tennis action.

September

Broadway on Broadway
www.broadwayonbroadway.com
Give your regards to Broadway every September during this festival, where you can see excerpts from the biggest shows in a free concert in Times Square. See performances from classics like *The Lion King*, *Les Miserables* and *Rent*, and get previews of new up-and-coming shows.

September/October

New York Film Festival
www.filmlinc.com
What sets this apart from other film festivals is that no prizes are awarded. The only winners are the audiences, who get to see a selection of 28 feature films and 12 short films selected by a committee of experts. The festival lasts for 17 days, and gives you the opportunity to view some memorable, groundbreaking films. Be smart: book your tickets online well in advance.

50

31st October

Halloween
www.halloween-nyc.com
At this scary time of year New Yorkers don freakishly weird and wonderful costumes and celebrate this pagan ritual. The Village Halloween Parade features ghouls, goblins, ghosts and other scary critters prancing through the streets of Greenwich Village, accompanied by marching bands, floats and giant puppets. The parade aside, the Halloween weekend is particularly memorable for all the costumes you see during a routine night on the town – so be prepared to find yourself sipping beer next to Indiana Jones or dancing with a devil.

First Sunday in November

New York Marathon
www.nycmarathon.org
Lace up your running shoes and dig out your headband to join thousands of other runners, joggers and walkers over this 26.2 mile course through the five boroughs of New York. It's the largest marathon in the world, with a whopping 90,000 athletes taking part in 2006. And various celebrities have taken part over the years, including Lance Armstrong, P Diddy and Van Halen's David Lee Roth - so even if you can't take part you can at least keep your eyes peeled for the fit and famous!

November

Veterans Day Parade
Since it began in 1929 the annual Veterans Day Parade has touched the lives of many people as New Yorkers gather to honour the brave men and women who fought in previous wars. It is also a day of tribute to those who are in the service currently. The parade begins with a wreath laying ceremony at the Eternal Flame in Madison Square Park, and then the thousands of marchers make their way up Fifth Avenue accompanied by marching bands and floats.

Fourth Thursday in November

Macy's Thanksgiving Day Parade
www.macys.com
Undoubtedly the city's biggest parade, the Macy's Thanksgiving Day Parade has pulled the crowds for over 80 years. Although the parade kicks off at 09:00, you need to find a good spot on the route from about 07:00. The route starts at Central Park and heads through Times Square and on to Macy's, and features giant helium-filled balloons in the shape of popular animated characters like Scooby Doo, Curious George, Garfield, Bugs Bunny, Superman and Snoopy. Dress warmly.

November

Christmas Tree Lighting Ceremony
www.rockefellercenter.com
The famous Christmas tree at the Rockefeller Center is lit at the end of November each year, marking the start of the holiday season. It is televised and features performances by the Radio City Rockettes. Each year thousands of people send in photos of trees they have grown in their gardens, hoping theirs will be selected as the tree used by Rockefeller – but this isn't just any old tree: the guideline dimensions are 65 feet tall and 35 feet wide!

December/January

New York National Boat Show
www.newyorkboatshow.com
Held annually at the Jacob Javits Convention Center, this phenomenal exhibition tickles the fancy of water lovers from all over. If it has anything to do with water, you're likely to find it on sale or at least on display here, from watersports gear and fishing equipment to stunning yachts and one-man canoes. There are also seminars, demonstrations, test dives in scuba tanks, and lots of fun stuff for kids. Put your name down for the contests, because there are loads of great prizes to be won.

51

December ◀ *John Lennon Vigil*

Every year fans of this great man gather together on Strawberry Fields in Central Park to pay tribute. Although rare, Yoko Ono has been known to join the mourners herself to remember her husband. Although you'll see your fair share of obsessed fans who appear a little bit crazy, the touching vigil is also attended by ordinary people who come to remember the man and his music, and lament the violent way he was taken too soon.

31st December ◀ *New Year's Eve*

The Times Square New Year's Eve celebrations are world famous and something you should do at least once in your New York lifetime! Gather with thousands of other shivering revellers to watch the crystal ball drop and ring in the new year. The Ball of Lights is raised to the top of the pole of the One Times Square building, and then 'dropped' after a raucous countdown. If you'd prefer to avoid the crowds, and the cold, New Year's Eve is big business in New York and there are numerous other celebrations to join in with instead.

Dry Cleaners p.74
Divorce Lawyers p.108

Written by residents, these unique guidebooks are packed with insider info, from arriving in a new destination to making it your home and everything in between.

Explorer Residents' Guides
We Know Where You Live

EXPLORER

AES INTERNATIONAL

Individual Solutions...

...for individual clients

- Savings and Investments
- Offshore Banking
- Foreign Exchange
- Financial Planning
- Tax and Legal Advice
- Corporate Services

info@aesfinance.com   www.aesfinance.com

14 Rue Maunoir, 1207 Geneva, Switzerland, TEL:+41 22 534 9474

Residents

Residents

Overview

The epicentre of global trends, the media and publishing hub, the core for the financial industry, the greatest city on earth and certainly up there with the most expensive – New York is the city that has inspired a thousand reputations. Call it what you will but you can't call it boring. There is so much going on all the time that it's hard keeping up – it's a rat race, with millions of fellow New Yorkers pounding the pavement, pushing for the A train, and competing for that better job or bigger apartment.

The aim of this chapter is to talk you through every imaginable aspect of living here – whether you are reading this in the comfort of your home country contemplating a sojourn abroad, already preparing to pack your bags, are fresh off a plane with your whole life in a suitcase, have lived in the city for months or even years, or are about to say your bittersweet farewells.

NYC Quick Facts
New York State has 1,300 museums and galleries, 64 performing arts centres, and 230 theatres. It is also home to over 400 golf courses and 55 ski areas. Apparently, the term 'The Big Apple' was first used in the 30s by touring jazz musicians who used the slang expression 'apple' for any town or city. Thus, to play in New York City is to play in the biggest apple of them all – The Big Apple.

Considering New York

It's one of those cities that you either love or hate, and despite being relatively small in terms of square miles, there is plenty to love, and plenty to hate, depending on your mood. For a start, the city never sleeps. This is a good thing if you fancy a bite to eat at 03:00, not so cool if you have an early morning meeting and happen to live in a busy neighbourhood. The city can get mighty pricey, what with astronomical rent prices and not so high wages. You'll bump into many a starving actor/singer/dancer. But budget right and take advantage of the city's many freebies, and not only will you get by, but you'll get to live a life of culture, excitement and community on a shoestring.

The cost of living in NYC is high and seems to always be creeping ever higher. Manhattan is often seen as a desirable neighbourhood, but it's worth considering moving to the boroughs since the gentrification process sweeping the city is turning certain areas into absolute gems. In fact, certain parts of Brooklyn and Harlem are already surpassing parts of Manhattan in terms of property prices and general standards of living. You'll need a job that pays well if you want to keep up. So before jumping on the first plane, test the job market by sending some emails to potential employers and monitoring the overseas appointments pages and recruitment websites (p. 78).

You also need to consider how you're going to enter the country and how long you can legally stay there. Residency in the US isn't that easy to come by (see p. 61 for details), but you can probably enter on a visitor's visa for a limited period and go from there (p. 22). Whatever you do, don't overstay your welcome, no matter how much you love the place. The penalty for overstaying your visa is severe with a ban of up to six years in place for serious offenders (see p. 22 for more information).

Before You Arrive

If you're coming to work in the city, you should have any qualification certificates and important documents (such as marriage certificates and children's birth certificates) attested in your home country. This can be a lengthy process and may involve solicitors and the US foreign embassy, so try to get the jump on this as early as possible.

If you are moving to New York from outside the US, the usual expatriate considerations should be made. If you own property in your home country, selling up before you move may not be the best option - consider renting it out for a year or so until you've found your feet in the US. You also need to get your financial affairs in order before you leave home, and that means informing your bank, your mortgage provider and the tax office. Speak to your pension company too – moving abroad could have implications on your contributions. If you've got kids you should start researching schools as soon as possible (see Education, p 163). Finding a place to live is one of the

Essential Documents
For many procedures, you'll
have to produce your 'essential
documents'. At the very least,
these are:
• Original passport
• Passport photocopies
(including photo page and
visa page, if appropriate)
• Passport photographs
Depending on the procedure,
you may also need to show a
copy of your employment offer,
a salary certificate and a
tenancy contract. It's also a
good idea to make copies of all
your original documents and
store them in a safe place.

most stressful and still most important tasks when moving to a new city, so if you can, you should take your time and explore the neighbourhoods you'd consider moving to (see p. 104). A good idea is to arrange temporary accommodation while you look for your perfect home - you can find a listing of apartment sublets on www.craigslist.org. If you have been employed from your home country some companies will even pay for this initial accommodation as well as cover relocation fees. When you do move it's likely you'll want to bring more than just your suitcase with you, so speak to shipping or relocation companies ahead of time and be sure to book well in advance (see p. 308).

If you're coming to look for employment, do your homework before you arrive. Contact recruitment agencies and sign up with online job sites as far in advance as possible. There may also be agencies in your home country that specialise in overseas recruitment. The Work section (p. 74) should provide some handy info.

When You Arrive

The list of things you'll have to deal with in the first few weeks can be a little daunting, and you may well be in for a lot of form filling, queuing, and coming and going. Try not to let it spoil things though, because you'll soon be a fully fledged resident enjoying your new life, and boring bureaucracy will be a distant memory. Here are some of the key issues you should be covering:

• Residency/visas – if you're on an employment or residency visa, you'll need to apply for a social security card as well as sign up with a health insurance provider (see p.148). If you're on a visit visa and land a job, be prepared to have to do a trip home to sort out the paperwork from your home country (see p.58 for more information).
• Furnish your new home and get connected – for advice on furnishing and how to get the water, electricity, phone and TV connected, see p.331 and p.140.
• Buy a car – for advice on what's available and whether it's even worth driving in the city as well as the registration process and so on, see Transportation on p.168.
• Licences – get your driving licence sorted as well as your parking permit (should you need it). See Licences on p.66.
• Register with your embassy – it is always worthwhile letting your embassy know you're living in a foreign country. See the table of embassies on p.25.
• Get acquainted – to help you settle in and find like-minded individuals, consider joining a social group. See p.283.

When You Leave

Rather than just jetting off, there are certain things that you have to wind up before you go, such as:

• Electricity and Water – be sure that all the bills have been paid and that your providers have a forwarding address for you in case they need to refund any deposits (p.140).
• Landlord – make sure the place is spick and span, otherwise you may lose some of your deposit.
• Shipping – just as with when you initially arrived, the more notice you can give the removal/relocation company, the better. For a list of companies, see p.132.
• Sell your home contents – sometimes easier (and cheaper) than shipping them. The thing about New York is that it's often just one big bargain bucket, so your trash is another person's treasure. Check out www.craigslist.org or eBay as a good way to shift your gear. If you've got some outdoor space and the weather is nice you can even make a day of it and have a yard sale - these are very popular and it's always fun to chat to people and tell them the stories behind your knick-knacks.

Documents

Millions of people immigrate to the United States each year, from all over the world. In 2004, over 18 million people arrived in the US, and that number grows each year. As a result, Immigration Law in the United States, which is controlled by the Immigration and Nationality Act, has grown into a daunting body of law. It is not for the faint of heart, but with some perseverance and a lot of patience, you will learn to navigate the system, as millions of others before you. And take some comfort in that fact that by choosing to enter the US through New York City, you will be surrounded by people who, at one time or another, were also from someplace else.

Entry Visa

Other options **Visas** p.22

There are several different ways that people from other countries can come to the United States, and often the procedure depends upon why they are coming, and how long they wish to stay.

Work Permits

If you are planning to come to the US for any significant length of time, chances are you will need to work in order to support yourself while you are here. In order to do this legally, you will need permission from the government, known as an employment authorisation document. As with all applications, you must first determine whether you are considered eligible under USCIS rules. You can apply for a permit to work in the US if you are a student, an applicant waiting for your petition for status as a lawful permanent resident to be processed, an applicant for temporary protected status, a fiancee of a US citizen, a dependant of a foreign government official, or if you are seeking asylum in the US. You do not need a work permit if you have obtained status of lawful permanent residence, or if you have arrived under a specific offer of employment (see below).
In terms of the procedure for getting a work permit, You must file Form I-765, along with the proper documentation and photographs, by mail, to the USCIS Regional Service Centre where you live.
If your application for a work permit is denied, you will receive a letter giving you the reasons why. You cannot appeal this decision, although you can file a 'motion to reopen' or a 'motion to reconsider' with the office that made the decision. If you file a motion to reopen, you must state new facts in your case, and you must include evidence. If you file a motion to reconsider, you are arguing that the decision was made on an erroneous application of US law or USCIS policy. You must show that the mistake was based on evidence that was in your file at the time the decision was made.

Visiting the United States

If you plan on visiting the US, in most cases you will need a non-immigrant visa. You must be planning to visit temporarily, for a pre-determined amount of time, for a specific purpose. While here, your activity will be confined to the parameters of your visa. In addition, you must have a valid passport and agree to leave the country at the end of the authorised time period. Most foreign nationals visiting under this provision must

Documents

Get a Lawyer
The information in this section is only a brief summary of some of the rules and procedures relating to immigration. It is not intended to be a substitute for conducting thorough research on your own, or consulting an immigration attorney.

keep a residence in another country, as well as proving financial support. Most importantly, they must be admissible, or have obtained a waiver, and they must agree to follow the terms of their visa.

Since 11 September 2001, the US government has changed some of the immigration rules and the agencies that determine these rules. As of 2003, the services and benefits functions of Immigration and Naturalization Services (INS) fall under the Department of Homeland Security as the United States Citizenship Immigration and Services (USCIS). The USCIS employs 15,000 federal workers and contractors in 250 headquarters and offices around the world, and it now determines who can enter the United States, and under what circumstances. It determines the policies and handles the adjudication of matters pertaining to immigration and naturalisation. Whether you are seeking a temporary or permanent residence visa, asylum in the US, or citizenship, you will have to become familiar with the policies and procedures of the USCIS.

Under the Immigration & Nationality Act, the government will operate under the presumption that everyone that enters this country intends to become an immigrant. Your responsibility, as a visitor, therefore, is to convince the government otherwise. You must show that your purpose is for the business, pleasure or the medical treatment stated on your visa application, as well as showing that you have obligations or interests outside the US to which you must return.

As in every immigration category, a visa does not guarantee admission into the US; the government can either limit the amount of time you may spend in the country, or deny the visit altogether.

Visas for Exchange Visitors

Working on J or Q
If you want to find out if you are permitted to work part-time while you are on a J-Visa or a Q-Visa, you should consult with the person at your school who counsels foreign students.

There are two types of visas for exchange visitors. J-Visas are governed by the Bureau of Consular Affairs of the Department of State, and are given for educational, cultural, arts or science purposes. The goal of these visas is to promote the exchange of culture and knowledge between the US and foreign nations. These visas typically apply to students, professors, medical personnel and researchers. If you receive a J-Visa, you must be able to prove that you have the money to cover all your expenses, or be receiving a stipend from your school.

To apply for a J-Visa, you must file form DS-2019 (Certificate of Eligibility for Exchange Visitor) with the Department of State. If you are there to receive medical training under a J-Visa, you must pass the Foreign Medical Graduate Examination in Medical Science, be able to speak English fluently and be able to stay for the duration of the medical residency period.

Q-Visas, which are governed by USCIS, are for people coming to the US under an international cultural exchange programme. The goal of these visas is to promote the exchange of history and culture. If you have this type of visa, you are paid during your visit by your employer (sponsor), at the same rate as local workers. To apply for a Q-Visa, you must file form I-129 (Petition for Non-Immigrant Worker), with the USCIS. Under both visas you must have a stamped record of your arrival and departure.

Non-Immigrants, Spouses or Children of US Permanent Residents

In the past, foreign nationals in this category had to petition from outside the US. Now, under the Legal Immigration Family Equity [LIFE] Act, a spouse (V-1) or child under 21 (V-2) of a legal permanent resident can live and work here as a non-immigrant while applying. The parent or spouse sponsoring you must have filed Form I-130 (Petition for Alien Relative), on or before December 21, 2000, and the person wanting to come to the US must have been waiting for at least three years for a visa that has not yet become available.

If the petitioner is in the country, they must file Form I-539 (Application for Non-Immigrant Status), and pay a fee. In addition, petitioners between the ages of 14 and 79 must be fingerprinted, at their own cost. Each must submit to a medical examination and send all appropriate forms and documents to US Citizenship and Immigration Services, PO Box 7216, Chicago, Il 60680-7216. There is no appeal available if this visa is denied. Just like people filing for other types of visas, V-1 and V-2 applicants are entitled to apply for a work permit (see procedure for getting a work permit on p.58).

If the petitioner is applying from outside the US, they must contact their local State Department Office or embassy.

> **Form I-94**
> Regardless of what kind of visa you apply for, you will have to have your Form I-94, 'Arrival/Departure Record', stamped by immigration officials, showing the length of the visit permitted. If you want to stay longer you must file form I-539, the application to extend status. The USCIS makes this decision.

Working on a K
People applying for K Visas can apply for a work permit while they are waiting. They are also permitted to travel outside the US, as long as the K-3 or K-4 visa has not expired. You should check with the USCIS office that has received your documents to check the status.

Visas for Non-Immigrants as a Spouse or Child of US Citizen

If you are married to a US citizen, you can apply for the K-3 visa. If you are the child of a US citizen or of an alien eligible for a K-3 visa (and you are under 21 and unmarried), you can apply for the K-4 visa. Both visas can be applied for while the petitioner is inside the US, and applicants can work while they are waiting for the visa to be processed.

To apply for a K Visa, the spouse must file Form I-130 (relative petition). In addition, Form I-129F (petition for alien fiancee) must be sent to the American Consulate in the country where the person wants to apply for the visa. The consulate must be in the country where the couple was married – if the marriage ceremony was held in the US then send it to the consulate with jurisdiction over where the alien spouse is presently living. When the USCIS has received Form I-130, it will send the US citizen Form I-797. It must be sent, with documents and a copy of Form I-129F, to the US Citizenship and Immigration Services, PO Box 7216, Chicago, Il 60680-7216. When the decision is made on the I-129F, the petition will then be sent on to the Department of State so the alien spouse can apply for K-3 and K-4 visas.

Humanitarian Parole

This basis for obtaining a Humanitarian Parole visa is at the discretion of the Secretary of the Department of Homeland Security. For complete information you should call 800 870 3676. The Secretary makes these decisions on a case-by-case basis. They are not given often, and when they are it is only in cases of humanitarian emergencies. It can not be used to get around standard visa procedures. It is important to remember that you must apply for this sort of visa from outside the United States. This kind of visa will be processed within 60 to 90 business days.

To apply for a Humanitarian Parole visa, you must send your application to the Department of Homeland Security, Attn: Parole & Humanitarian Assistant Branch, 425 I Street, NW, Washington, D.C. 20536. You can write to this address to check the status of your application as well. The maximum amount of time you can spend in the US under this visa category is one year, after which you can file for a renewal. However, if your application is denied, no appeals are permitted.

Extending Your Stay as a Non-Immigrant

Non-immigrant visitors are only allowed to stay in the country for the specified time. However, once they are in the US, they may be able to extend their visas. The most important thing is to apply for an extension before your visa expires (this is the date on your Form I-94 - Arrival/Departure Record) and you must keep your passport valid.

Documents

Victims of Trafficking

Trafficking is a global problem, and the US government is committed to helping its victims as well as apprehending its perpetrators. The Victims of Trafficking and Violence Protection Act of 2000 was enacted to provide relief for the victims of particular crimes, including crimes against women. To gain admission into the US under this law, you must prove that you have suffered extreme abuse. Victims of this kind of violence, if eligible, are allowed into the country on a temporary basis – however, this stay is sometimes extended. These people are eligible to receive federal and state aid.

If you miss the deadline, you must prove that the circumstances were beyond your control, that the length of time past the deadline was reasonable, that you did not violate your status in any other way, that you are still a non-immigrant, and that you have not been marked for deportation.

If your application to extend your visa is denied, you cannot appeal. You can, however, file a motion to reconsider or a motion to reopen (see the definition of these motions on p.58).

The procedure for applying for an extension depends on your reason for being in the US. You can either file Form I-539 (application to extend or change immigrant status), or your employer can file Form I-129 (petition for non-immigrant worker on your behalf).

Visa Waiver Program

The general rule is that every foreign national must have a visa before entering the United States, even those who are coming for a short visit. However, as with many of the immigration rules, there are exceptions. There are certain countries and adjacent islands from which visitors can come to the US for a short visit, without a visa. The list of countries and islands is determined by the Secretary of Homeland Security, and citizens of these countries can come to the US for 90 days or less, for business or pleasure.

You must have a valid passport from a country on the Visa Waiver list. The passport must be valid for at least six months beyond the end of your intended visit. You must be a national of the country from which you obtained the passport. In addition, you must have a return ticket to a non-US destination.

Visitors under the Visa Waiver Program must file Form I-94W (visa waiver arrival/departure record). As always, they must be admissible to the US.

The advantage of this programme is clear: you do not have to go through the inconvenience of getting a visa. The disadvantage is that you cannot extend or change your visit in any way. Also, you have no appeal if your application is denied; when you participate in this programme, you waive any right to appeal a denial of your application or to dispute your removal unless you are applying under the Convention Against Torture and Other Cruel, Inhuman, or Degrading Treatment or Punishment. You may travel outside the US while you are in the country under this programme - short trips to Canada, Mexico, or adjacent islands are acceptable. You must show that your visit has not expired, that you are prepared to leave the US on time, that your passport is valid, and that you continue to be eligible.

> **Visa Waiver List**
> Some of the countries currently on the list are Austria, Australia, the United Kingdom, Spain, France, Belgium, Germany, Switzerland, Portugal, Japan, and Norway. Although Mexico and Canada are not on the current list, you may cross the border under the Visa Waiver Program. For a complete list of countries and islands, check the US Department of State website (www.state.gov).

Residence Visa
Other options **Visas** p.22

Millions of people come to the US each year for a visit; many more come with the intention of making it their home. There are several ways you can go about becoming a permanent resident and ultimately a citizen of the US.

Lawful Permanent Resident Status (LPR)

People with this status, while not American citizens, have the right to live and work in the United States for as long as they wish to do so. They are issued 'Green Cards', and have no further need to obtain special permission to work or own property. If you are seeking LPR status, there are several different avenues you may take, depending upon your age, marital or employment status, and even the country in which you were born. The State Department regularly releases a bulletin informing petitioners what month and year it is currently processing, by country and preference category. This will allow you to approximate when you will receive your visa number.

Immigration through a Relative

Historically, it has been common to obtain a Green Card through a family member who is already a citizen or legal permanent resident of the United States. The procedure for obtaining a visa in this manner is fairly simple.

A relative willing to 'sponsor' you must fill out Form I-130 (petition for alien relative), and file it with the USCIS. Your relative must be able to prove, through proper documentation, their relationship to you, that they are in fact a US citizen or have LPR status, and that they can support you at 125% above the mandated poverty level.

If and when the USCIS approves the petition, the Department of State's National Visa Center will then notify you as to whether an immigrant visa number is available. When a number does become available, you must then apply to have a number assigned to you. How you apply depends on whether or not you are already in the United States. If you are, you must file Form I-485, which is the application to change your status to that of Legal Permanent Resident. If you are not in the United States, you must go to a US consulate servicing office where you live.

US Citizens can sponsor their children of any age, and their parents or siblings, as long as the citizen is at least 21. Those with LPR status (and not citizenship) may sponsor their spouses or unmarried children of any age.

In addition, visas in this category operate on the preference system. Immediate relatives of United States citizens, such as parents, spouses and unmarried children under the age of 21 do not have to wait for a visa number once the visa petition is approved by USCIS; the number will immediately become available. Other relatives, or relatives of sponsors with LPR status, must wait for a number according to a set of preferences. The first preference is for unmarried sons or daughters aged 21 or older. Second preference is spouses of people with LPR status, the couple's unmarried children under the age of 21, or the sponsor's unmarried children of any age. Third preference is married sons or daughters of US citizens, and fourth preference is the brothers or sisters of adult US citizens.

The USCIS will notify petitioners as to whether their petition has been approved. Approved visas are sent to the Department of State's National Visa Center, which will then notify the petitioner when the petition is received, and again when the number becomes available. The petitioner does not need to contact the National Visa Center unless there is an important change in information, such as the petitioner's address or a change in the age (reaching 21) or marital status of the petitioner or sponsor.

Immigration through Investment

Section 203(b)(5) of the Immigration and Nationality Act mandates that 10,000 immigrant visas be set aside each year to those seeking LPR status based on involvement in a 'new commercial enterprise'.

Under a pilot programme, 5,000 of these visas are reserved for those applicants in a designated 'regional centre'. A regional centre is a specific area that has been approved by the United States government. The programme's aim is to foster economic growth through increased export sales, improved regional productivity, the creation of new jobs, and increased capital investment.

Foreign investors must demonstrate that the investment is being made within an approved regional centre, and that it will achieve the goals of the programme. Under this programme, investors may come to the United States alone or with their spouses and unmarried children.

An Important Note

If you travel outside the US before you obtain LPR status under the Registry provision, you will not be able to return. The rule states that if you have been in the US illegally for over 180 days, once you leave you will not be admitted back in for a period of up to 10 years. Since you will have had to have lived in the US since 1972 to qualify under the Registry provision in the first place, you will automatically be prevented from returning. If you have to leave the country you must first get 'Advance Parole' by submitting Form I-131 for USCIS approval.

Investors must be able to prove that they are involved with a 'qualified' investment, and that this investment will benefit the US economy. A qualified investment may either be a new enterprise, or a pre-existing enterprise which the investor purchases and simultaneously reorganises so that it is essentially new, or that the investor has expanded an existing business by 140% (either in jobs or in net worth), or by preserving all existing jobs in a failing business that has lost 20% of its net worth in the last one or two years. The investor must invest $1 million (or at least $500,000 if the investment is being made in an area experiencing an unemployment rate of 150% and upwards).

To apply, the investor must file USCIS Form I-526 (immigrant petition by alien entrepreneur). The applicant must also provide documents proving that they meet all above requirements. Once the I-526 is approved, investors already living in the United States can file a I-485 (application to register permanent or adjust status, or Form I-829, petition by entrepreneur to remove conditions). These forms must be filed within 90 days before the second anniversary of the investor's admission to the country as a conditional resident.

Immigration through Employment

A foreign national may obtain LPR status through an offer of permanent employment in the United States. In cases such as this, the employer is the sponsor and petitioner and the foreign national is the applicant and beneficiary.

Firstly, the employer and the person seeking LPR status must check whether they are eligible for such status under USCIS guidelines. The employer should fill out Form ETA 750 (labour certification request), and submit it to the Department of Labor's Employment and Training Administration (qualified doctors who are practising in an area deemed 'underserved' by the Department of Health and Human Services are exempt from this requirement). Be sure to check with the Department of Labor to find out whether the employment category you are filing under requires this form.

The employer must then file visa petition Form I-140 (petition for alien worker). If it has been determined that you must file a Labor Certification Request, your employer should not file Form I-140 until the Labor Certification has been granted.

The Department of State then gives the applicant a visa number, even if the applicant is already in the US. As with the other categories, if the applicant is in the US, he or she must file form I-485 to adjust status – if he or she is not in the US, then he or she must go to the US consulate office in the area.

There are specific categories depending on what sort of work you do, and each category has its own rules for filing. You may check the UCSIS website to find out which category you fall into as well as the procedures your potential employer must follow.

Immigration through the Diversity Visa Lottery Program

Visa Lottery

Even if you have already applied for a visa in another category (such as employment), you can still apply for the visa lottery.

Yes it's true - you can actually win LPR status in the US through a lottery programme. Under the Immigration and Nationality Act, the US grants 55,000 visas every year to people from countries with low rates of immigration. Each year the Department of States releases a list of eligible countries (those which have sent less than 50,000 immigrants to the US within the last five years).

Applicants must follow Department of State's directions to the last detail. These directions are released in press releases and published in the Federal Register, usually each August – registration for the lottery of that fiscal year is usually in October. There is no fee to enter the lottery. However, if you win you will have to pay both a fee for the immigrant visa and a separate lottery surcharge.

63

The first thing you need to keep in mind is that only one entry per applicant may be submitted. Somebody else may apply on your behalf, but if the State Department receives more than one entry for you, you will be disqualified, even if one of those entries was sent in by someone else.

To apply, first make sure that you are a citizen of a country that meets the State Department's eligibility requirement – this means that the country of your birth has not sent more than 50,000 immigrants to the US within the last five years. If you are not from an eligible country but your spouse is, you can enter by claiming your spouse's country, as long as you are both included on the lottery entry, you are both issued visas, and you both enter the US at the same time.

Even if you were not born in an eligible country, you can still apply for the lottery if your parents were born in an eligible country but did not live there when you were born. To put it simply, if your parents were simply visiting, studying in or temporarily stationed in the ineligible country at the time of your birth, then they were not living there under the definition and you can 'claim' their country for the purposes of the lottery.

Entries by mail are not currently accepted and you must apply electronically through the website. The information you have to fill in on the electronic form includes your full name, your date of birth, your gender, the city and country of your birth, your country of eligibility, photos (of yourself, your spouse, and each unmarried child under 21), your mailing address, your current country of residence, the highest level of education that you have attained, your marital status, how many children you have (all of your unmarried children under 21, including adopted children), and detailed information on your spouse.

If you are selected, you must get your lottery visa, or adjust your status, by the end of the fiscal year. The death of a selected entrant disqualifies the application.

Finally, remember that selection of your application does not guarantee that you will get a visa. Applicants must be eligible for LPR under USCIS guidelines, must have a high school diploma (or equivalent), or at least two year's work experience within the last five years. For further details, please see the Department of Labor website (www.dol.gov).

Each year the Department of State randomly selects 110,000 applicants from all of the entries. However, there are only 55,000 visas available in total through this programme. Some of the applicants will be ineligible for immigration, and others may choose not to pursue a visa. The diversity visa programme year ends once all 55,000 visas have been issued.

LPR Under the Registry Provision of the Immigration & Nationality Act

If you have been living in the US since before January 1 1972, you may be able to get LPR status, even if you are living in the US illegally, or if you initially entered the country illegally. However, you must have lived in the US continuously since before that date in order to qualify. And, as always, you must otherwise qualify for LPR status under USCIS regulations. This includes showing that you are of 'good moral character', and that you are not and have never been involved in any terrorist activities or alien smuggling. In addition, if law enforcement has discovered that you are here illegally, and you fail to appear at your removal hearing or fail to leave the country after agreeing to do so, you will be ineligible for LPR under the registry provision for a period of 10 years.

More Lottery Info
For a detailed overview of the application procedure, check the website (www.dv.lottery.state.gov). This will give you the lottery deadlines for the year, and other information crucial to the acceptance of your entry. You can also get relevant information by contacting your nearest US embassy or consulate, or by calling the State Department Visa Lottery Info Center at 900 884 8840.

To apply under this provision, you need to submit Form I-485 with the filing fee, as well as Form G-325, with evidence that you have lived in the US continuously since before January 1 1972, to the USCIS office having jurisdiction where you live.

While your case is pending, you may apply for a work permit (by filing Form I-765) so that you can support yourself while you wait. Once you are awarded LPR status you will no longer need a work permit - your Green Card will prove that you are authorised to work in the US. The District Director of the USCIS will then determine your eligibility. There is no appeal from this decision, although you can petition to renew your application before an immigration judge.

In the seemingly endless list of forms you will have to fill out when applying for LPR status in the US, Form I-485 (application to register permanent resident or adjust status) is especially important, as you will have to use this form whenever you are applying while already in the United States. However, there is also other documentation that must be included when you are using Form I-485, such as two colour photos of yourself taken within the past 30 days, a medical examination sheet (Form I-693), and a biographic data sheet (Form G-325A). In addition, you must provide documents that support the underlying reason for using I-485. For example, if someone is sponsoring you, you must submit Form I-864 (Affidavit of Support). If you have been admitted as a fiance(e) of a US citizen, you must provide a copy of the fiance(e) petition approval notice and your marriage certificate.

Becoming a Citizen

As with all matters of immigration, becoming a US citizen is governed by the Immigration and Nationalization Act. This is only a brief overview of the seven major requirements – if you wish to become a citizen you should do so with the help of an immigration attorney.

Firstly, you need to live in the US, and be present there for an uninterrupted period of time. You must also have lived in a particular district of the USCIS before you file. Although the US does not have an official language, you must be able to read, write and speak English before becoming a citizen, and you must also know a certain amount about US history and the structure of its government. While these first four requirements are important, they may be waived under certain circumstances (for example, if you are applying for citizenship through your marriage to a US citizen). The following three, however, are never waived. You must show that you have good moral character, that you believe in the philosophies of the US Constitution, and that you are loyal to the US.

Health Insurance

Health insurance is not mandatory for expats living in the US, although with medical costs being so exorbitant, it is certainly desirable. Government healthcare, such as Medicaid and Medicare, is available for only those US citizens and expats that meet certain criteria (they have to make under a certain amount of money). Most people are not eligible to receive government healthcare, and are either insured through their employer or buy private healthcare insurance on their own). Employers are not obligated to provide health insurance, but most companies do provide some sort of health benefits for full-time employees. There are also several international insurance companies that provide insurance for expats around the world through which you may purchase a private policy. Please note that in general expats do not have to carry health insurance when coming to the US, although many colleges and universities require their students to have some sort of insurance when they enroll.

Driving Licence
Other options **Transportation** p.168

Other options **Transportation** p.168

Sweet Sixteen

First-time drivers must first get a learner's permit before being issued a licence. You must be at least 16 years old to get a permit, and if you are under 18 your parents must sign a consent form.

In New York, if you are a first time driver or coming from another country (except Canada), you must take a written test and a road test. These tests are not very difficult, however, you will need to know the rules of the road in New York, and you should study for it. If you fail either test, you can re-take them as many times as you want. After you are informed that you have failed the test you simply make a new appointment at the Department of Motor Vehicles. There are several DMV offices in New York City – to find locations, check out the website at www.nydmv.state.ny.us. When applying for a licence you will need to show valid forms of identification. There are several that are acceptable, including a foreign passport (translated into English if necessary), a work authorisation document, a visa, or a birth certificate. There is a complete list of acceptable forms of identification on the website.

Temporary Licence
A valid licence from another country is also valid in New York if you are just visiting – you do not need to get a New York State licence unless you become a resident of New York. Any visitors from other countries may use their licences from home. Please note that when you get your New York licence you will have to surrender your foreign licence and it will be destroyed within 60 days. If you plan on going back to your home country and using your licence, you can find out at the Department of Motor Vehicles about how to make sure it's not destroyed. When you leave New York to go home you will have to go back to that same location to get it.

In order to get your learner's permit, you must show identification and your social security card. If you are not eligible for a social security card, you must present a letter from the Social Security Administration (dated within 30 days of your application for the permit), stating that you are not eligible. In addition, you will also have to show the documents from the USCIS that the Social Security Administration used to decide that you are ineligible.

To get your permit, you must pass a written test, after studying the Driver's Manual and Study Guide, as well as a vision test administered at the Department of Motor Vehicles. While you have your learner's permit you must be supervised by a licensed driver over the age of 21.

Carry Your Licence!

You should carry your driving licence with you at all times. If you are caught driving without one, you will get a traffic ticket and will have to pay a fine. There are no spot checks to check your licence, but there are often roadblocks to check for drunk drivers and you may be asked to show your licence if you are stopped at one of these.

Permanent Licence
After getting your learner's permit, you must schedule a road test. You will be taken out with a driving instructor and required to demonstrate your skills in operating the car and show your understanding of the rules of the road. You will then be issued your driver's licence, which is valid for eight years. The fee for getting your driver's licence is $85.

Part of the penalty for getting certain moving traffic violations (not parking tickets) is points against your licence. If you get too many points, your licence can be revoked or suspended. Make sure you always pay fines associated with your ticket or appear at any court date that you are given when issued a violation. You can also lose your licence for driving while intoxicated.

Motorcycle Licence
You must have a separate licence to ride a motorcycle in New York. How you go about getting it depends upon whether you already have a driving licence and whether you have a motorcycle licence from another state. To find more details on obtaining this sort of licence check out the website for the Department of Motor Vehicles.

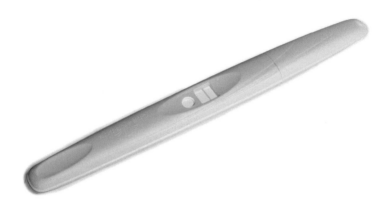

Written by residents, the London Explorer is packed with insider info, from arriving in a new destination to making it your home and everything in between.

London Explorer Residents' Guide
We Know Where You Live

Driving Schools in New York

Driving Schools in New York

There are literally hundreds of driving schools in the five boroughs of New York City – it is impossible to list them all here. To find a driving school closer to you, check out the Department of Motor Vehicles website (www.nydmv.state.ny.us), but in the meantime, check out the ones listed in the table.

Driving Schools

Ability Driving School	Harlem	212 865 4440	na
Auto School of America	Upper West Side	212 228 1100	na
Autocraft Driving School	Queens	718 575 1770	www.autocraftdrivingschool.com
Canal Driving School	Little Italy	212 334 9207	na
Ferrari Driving School	Queens	718 278 6679	www.FerrariDrivingSchool.com
Fox Auto Driving School	Brooklyn	718 854 7622	www.foxdriving.com
I Drive Safely	Various Locations	800 723 1955	www.idrivesafely.com
Pelham Auto Driving School	The Bronx	718 918 0035	na
Professional Driving School of the Americas	Gramercy Park	212 375 1111	www.prodriveny.com
Staten Island Defensive Driving Classes	Staten Island	718 608 9451	http://ddc58.tripod.com
Twenty-first Century Driving School	Lower East Side	212 674 6865	www.drivingschoolmanhattan.com
US Auto School	Brooklyn	212 865 8181	na

American as Apple Pie
Please note that under the Child Citizenship Act of 2000, a child who is born abroad but adopted by a US citizen has automatic US citizenship.

Birth Certificate & Registration

When you have a baby in the hospital, the staff will fill out the necessary paperwork and send it to the New York City Office of Vital Records, so the birth is then registered. If you chose to have your baby at home or in a birthing centre, the midwife will complete the paperwork and send it in to the city. You will then receive a copy of the birth certificate in the mail, usually within four weeks after the baby is born. You will also receive your child's social security number.

To obtain an extra copy of a birth certificate, you can request it from the Office of Vital Records by fax, telephone, mail, in person, or over the internet. The cost is $15 per certificate, plus a $5.50 mailing and service charge. Regardless of how you request it, you will have to provide the full name on the birth certificate, the baby's gender, the date, the hospital and the borough of birth, the mother's maiden name, the father's full name, if it is known, your relationship to the birth certificate owner, your mailing address, and the reason for the request.

Under the 14th Amendment of the US Constitution, a child born here is automatically a citizen. Therefore, if you are living in the US when you have your baby, no matter what your status is, you do not have to get a visa for your child. If you are in another country and have received a visa to come here, your child can enter the US as a derivative under your visa. For more information on this, please see the section on immigration (p.61), or check out the Department of State website (www.state.gov).

Passports

Each child, regardless of age, must have a passport in order to travel outside the US. The child must apply in person, with the parents, and there is a special procedure for children under the age of 14. First, the child and parents must have proof of the child's US citizenship and proof of relationship to the parents (the child's previous passport is not acceptable as proof of relationship). You must have a certified birth certificate, issued within one year of the child's birth, with a raised seal and signed by the registrar, as well as the date the certificate was filed with the registrar's office. If the birth certificate was filed more than a year after the child's birth you will have to list its supporting documentation, signed by the physician or midwife.

If you do not have a previous passport or a certified birth certificate to prove your citizenship, you will need a 'Letter of No Record'. This is a document, issued by the state, with the child's name, date of birth, the years searched in the database for the birth record, and a statement that there is no birth certificate on file, *and* as many of the following documents as possible: a baptismal certificate, a hospital (unofficial) birth certificate, a census record, early school record, a family bible record, and a doctor's record of post-natal care.

In regards to proof of relationship, you can provide any of the following documents with the parents' names: a certified birth certificate, a foreign birth certificate with translation if necessary, a report of birth abroad, a certificate of birth abroad, an adoption decree, or a court order establishing custody or guardianship.

For children under the age of 14, each parent must bring a proof of identification. Both parents must appear together and sign. If only one parent is able to be there, he or she must bring one of the following: the second parent's notarised statement of consent, a letter proving that the present parent has sole custody, the child's birth certificate listing only one parent, a court order granting sole custody, an adoptee decree listing only one parent, or the death certificate of the parent. The passport fee is $82. Phew!

Parent Support

There are many support groups to help prospective parents with this process, and to deal with issues that arrive after the adoption has been finalised. For a listing of these groups in your area, call 800 345 5437.

International Adoption

Each year more and more US citizens adopt children from other countries, partially due to a lack of children for adoption in the US. If you are a US citizen and would like to adopt a child from another country, you must be aware that the rules of that country will govern the adoption. You can call the US State Department for more information on 888 407 4747. However, the State Department cannot become involved, it can just advise you.

If you are a legal permanent resident of the US adopting a baby from another country, you may be in for an extremely frustrating experience. As mentioned in the immigration section, legal permanent residents and long-term non-immigrants may bring their spouses and children with them when they enter the country. However, the Immigration and Nationality Act does not provide for the situation when the legal permanent resident is already here and tries to bring a newly adopted child over. The INA recognises an adopted child after he/she has lived with the parent for at least two years. But the legal permanent resident cannot leave the US for two years to go live with the child abroad to fill that requirement. Therefore, it is advised that you become a citizen before trying to adopt abroad.

Naming Ceremonies

After the birth of a child, families often chose to have some sort of ceremony, usually according to their religious beliefs. For example, Christians have a christening, or baptism, where the child is officially brought into the religion and given a Christian name. Jews have a bris for male children, a ceremony at which the child is circumcised and is given his Hebrew name. Whatever your beliefs are, you can make arrangements at your chosen house of worship.

Adoption Within the US

Please note that adoption can be a lengthy and complex process: it may take six months or more from the time you apply until the child is placed in your home. And it may take three to 12 additional months before the adoption is finalised in court. The first step is to choose an adoption agency. You can get a list of New York City agencies by calling the Administration for Children's Services at 212 676 WISH (9474).

Once you have chosen an agency, you must submit your application, including your background information, the number of people already living in your house, a description of what your family is like, and what kind of child you would like to adopt. The agency will then conduct a criminal background check on anyone over 18 living in the home. After the application is submitted, the 'Homestudy' process will begin. This is a series of meetings and interviews in which the agency checks out the family. Then the parent training sessions begin. These are designed to let parents know what they are letting themselves in for by adopting a child. The agency and prospective parents then begin looking for a child in the Family Adoption Registry, which has a list of children eligible for adoption. After a child is chosen, the family begins visiting with the child either at the agency, the family's home, or the place where the child is currently living. If all goes well with these visits the child is then placed with the family, to be supervised by the agency for three months.

Finally, after this process is complete, the adoption can be finalised in court. The family should have an attorney, who will file the petition with the court. Once the parents formally agree to fill their legal obligation for the child's care, they have legally become the child's parents.

Marriage Certificate & Registration

Whether you get married in New York or attend the weddings of friends and family, you will find that there is nothing quite like a 'New York wedding'. They are often lavish affairs, sometimes with several hundred guests at a cost of well over $50,000. There is the ceremony itself, followed by a cocktail hour (where guests mingle while being served appetisers and alcoholic drinks), a formal dinner and dancing until late into the night to the tunes of a band, a disc jockey, or both. There is simply no end to the type of wedding you may have in New York City: people have their wedding receptions in hotel ballrooms, on the beach, in their homes, anywhere they wish. As with clothes and music, styles and tastes in weddings change with the times, and often couples hire a wedding planner to make sure their wedding is perfectly en vogue and that the day runs smoothly (for a list of wedding services and shops, see p.355)

Scared of Needles?
In some states, you must have a blood test before obtaining a marriage licence – however, in New York this is not necessary.

Paperwork

Getting married in New York City is a relatively simple procedure. Well, at least technically. In order for the marriage to be valid, the first thing you must do is obtain a marriage licence. Marriage licences are valid for 60 days, and the ceremony must be performed within this time period or you will have to apply for another one. Your licence will cost $35, which must be paid by money order. You can get a money order at any bank or one of the hundreds of cheque-cashing places in the city. (These are places where you can cash cheques without a bank account.)

The bride and groom must apply for the licence together, in person, at the Office of the City Clerk. There are City Clerk offices in each of New York City's five boroughs. To find the addresses and business hours of these offices, call 212 669 2778.

When applying for your licence, you must prove that there is nothing that should prevent you from legally marrying. For example, you must provide any information about any previous marriages, and you may be asked to provide a divorce decree.

You will receive your marriage licence on the day you apply for it. However, you must wait at least 24 hours before the marriage ceremony is performed. You must present the City Clerk with valid identification, which can include a driver's licence, or a non-driver's identification card, from the US or one of its territories (If you are using driving 'learner's permit', it must be from New York State. Please see driving licences, p.66), an active US military card, a valid passport, your US certification of naturalization (it must have been issued within the last 10 years), your permanent resident (Green) card, with valid expiration, and your work permit, also with valid expiration.

More Marriage Facts

If you are under 18 and wish to marry, you must have the consent of a parent. If you are under 16, you must have the consent of a parent and a judge. Also, be sure how you want to change your last name upon marrying. Once you list it on the marriage licence, it can't be changed, unless you get married again!

Visa Rules
If you are a foreign national marrying a US citizen you must be aware that if the wedding takes place outside the US, you will probably not be allowed into the country while you are waiting for your visa application to be processed. The government will assume that your goal is to be a permanent resident of the US and will not give you a visitor visa. If you do marry in the US, you will be allowed to stay in the country with your spouse until your status as a resident is determined.

Once you have obtained your marriage licence, the ceremony may be performed by any number of religious or civil individuals, according to your preferences and beliefs. This includes the mayor or former mayor of New York City, judges, priests and rabbis, as long as the person conducting the ceremony is registered with the City of New York. To check and see if the person you have chosen to marry you is registered, call the Office of the City Clerk at 212 669 2778. The cost of getting married by a religious official can be several hundred dollars or higher, depending on the house of worship and the particular person you ask to perform the ceremony.

You can choose to have a civil (non-religious) ceremony, performed by the City Clerk. Just go to an office in any one of the five boroughs during business hours and the clerk will marry you and provide you with your marriage certificate that day. All you will need is a $25 money order, at least one person over 18 to serve as a witness, and photo identification for the bride, groom, and witness.

If you have been married by someone other than the City Clerk, the person who performed the ceremony will fill out the certificate and mail it to the City Clerk's office within five days a copy will later be mailed to your home.

A foreign country's embassy or consulate, however, is considered a 'foreign jurisdiction'. Therefore, if you want to send a copy of your marriage certificate you will have to send one with a raised seal and original signature. You may request one from the Office of the City Clerk in Manhattan: there is a $35 fee, payable by money order. If you are basing your residency upon your marriage, you should send a copy to US Immigration or your native country's embassy.

If you are from another country and have married a US citizen, the good news is that your marriage is most likely valid anywhere in the world; the general rule is if the marriage is valid where the ceremony took place, it is valid everywhere.

Tax Implications

When you get married, your filing status changes for tax purposes. You must inform the IRS if your name or address changes. You must also choose whether you want to file a joint tax return with your spouse, or whether you want to file as 'married filing separately'. If you have changed your last name you must also inform the Social Security Administration.

It is strongly advised that you consult an accountant regarding the best way to deal with your taxes. (Please see Taxation, p.83)

Domestic Partnerships

Same-Sex Weddings
In New York, it illegal for same-sex couples to marry. However, New York City recognises 'Domestic Partnerships', which grants, to same-sex and other non-traditional couples, several of the rights afforded to married couples. This case is certainly not closed, so watch this space.

New York City law has created a relationship category protecting certain rights for same-sex and other non-traditional couples. In order to be eligible for a domestic partnership, either both people must be New York City residents, or at least one of them must be employed by the City of New York. Both partners must be 18 years or older, and they must be otherwise eligible. For example, neither can be married and they must not be related by blood. The partners must show that they are in a close, committed relationship and that they live together. Finally, neither partner can be involved in another domestic partnership, or have been in one in the past six months.

Paperwork

Registering for a domestic partnership is a very simple procedure. The partners must file a Domestic Partnership Affidavit, signed by both and notarised, with the Office of the City Clerk. The fee is $36, payable only by money order. Both partners have to show valid identification, including a driver's licence or a non-driver ID, an original birth certificate, a passport, an official school record, an immigration or employee authorisation card. The City Clerk will then issue a Certificate of Domestic Partnership.

71

While a domestic partnership does not confer the same legal status as a marriage, it does provide a few of the same benefits. Domestic partners who work for the City of New York can take bereavement leave or childcare leave. Domestic partners can visit each other in prison, and in hospitals that are run by the New York City Health and Hospital Corporation. And, as anyone who has braved the New York real estate market can appreciate, a domestic partner may be added to a lease for an apartment, as a family member, by the New York City Housing Authority. Domestic partners can also succeed to the tenancy if the other partner passes away. New York City employees can add their domestic partners to their healthcare policies. For a complete list of benefits, check with the City Clerk's office.

Termination of a Domestic Partnership

Dissolving the domestic partnership is even easier than registering it: one party files a termination statement with the Clerk's office. In addition, the partnership is automatically terminated if one of the partners marries.

Death Certificate & Registration

If a friend or family member passes away in New York, the circumstances of the death determine the steps you need to take. If the person dies alone, the moment the body is discovered you should call 911. (Please note that 911 should be called in the event of any emergency, for example, if you or someone you know is the victim of a crime, suffers from a heart attack or stroke, or has an accident that requires medical attention.) Explain to the 911 operator that someone has passed away, and the operator will immediately send the police and medical examiner to your home. After the investigation is completed, the medical examiner will release the body to be buried or cremated as the family sees fit.

If no investigation is necessary, the first call you need to make is to a funeral home. There are funeral homes of every religion and ethnicity in New York City, and they may be easily found by looking in the phone book directory or on the internet. If the person has died at home, the funeral home will pick up the body and bring it to their facility to prepare it for the burial service. If the person has died at the hospital, the family members can tell the hospital which funeral home they would like to use, and the hospital staff will make the call. You will also have to choose where you want the person to be buried. There are separate cemeteries for religious denominations, as well as non-denominational cemeteries, where people of all religions are interred.

Registering a Death

This procedure also depends on the circumstances of death. If the situation is such that the medical examiner must conduct an investigation, the Office of Medical Examiner will register the death with the New York City Office of Vital Records. If the body is going directly to a funeral home, the staff of the funeral home will collect the necessary information needed for the death certificate and will register the death. The deceased's next-of-kin will receive a copy. If the deceased held a life insurance policy, the beneficiary of the policy will have to present proof of death to the insurance company. This will include the death certificate and a copy of the insurance policy. The beneficiary will have to present valid identification as well. For specific requirements you must check with the particular life insurance company.

Getting a Copy of a Death Certificate

You can obtain a copy of a death certificate, either by mail or in person, from the New York City Office of Vital Records. The cost is $15, payable by cheque or money order, made out to the NYC Department of Health and Mental Hygiene. If you are mailing it, you must

Leading Causes of Death in the USA

The leading causes of death in the United States have consistently been heart disease, cancer, and vehicular accidents. Also making the list are diabetes and suicide.

include a request form or letter including the full name of the deceased, their gender, the date, place, and borough of death, their social Security Number, their mother's maiden name, father's name and spouse's name, their age at time of death, the purpose for which you are requesting the certificate, your mailing address, and your relationship to the deceased. You can download the request form from the www.nyc.gov website or pick one up at The New York City Office of Vital Records, 125 Worth Street Box 4, Room 133, New York, NY 10013.

Either way, you must show photo identification – bring it with you to the office or include a copy if you mail the request. In addition, a mailed request must include a self-addressed stamped envelope.

If you are requesting the certificate on behalf of someone else, you must include with your documentation a notarised letter from that person authorising you to collect the certificate.

Investigation and Autopsy

There are certain circumstances under which an investigation into the death, including an autopsy, will be performed. The New York City Office of the Medical Examiner will perform an autopsy when there is evidence of criminal violence or suicide, when the deceased appeared in good health but died suddenly, when the deceased was unattended by a physician, or if the deceased died in prison. In other words, any time the death seems suspicious to law enforcement. In addition, an autopsy will be performed when the executor of the deceased's will or next of kin applies for a cremation permit.

If the police conclude that the person died of natural causes, but you still have suspicions, you may hire a private investigator, and even a private pathologist, to check the matter out further.

Register with the Organ Donor Network Registry

Even if you have already opted to be a donor on your licence you should register with the Network as well, to make it extra clear. As the Network will request consent from the next-of-kin in the event of a donor's death, potential donors should make their family aware of their decision to participate in the registry programme.

Returning Deceased to the Country of Origin

Often when an immigrant or foreign-born citizen dies, his or her wishes include burial in the country of origin. In this case, many funeral homes will make the necessary arrangements. Please be aware that this involves several logistical issues. The procedure for this, including what documentation is needed, depends upon the rules of the country of origin. There will probably be consulate fees, special casket regulations, and air travel restrictions. Also, in addition to the already high cost of burials, you must be prepared to pay several thousand dollars more to have the deceased shipped for burial in another country. Make sure the funeral home you choose is experienced in this sort of procedure and is able to guide you through the process.

Organ Donation

Organ and tissue donors give an invaluable gift to thousands of sick individuals in need of a transplant every year. If you want to become an organ donor in New York, you must register with the New York Organ Donor Network. You can opt to be a donor on your driver's licence or non-driver identification card. When you fill out the paperwork for your licence at the Department of Motor Vehicles, you must indicate that you want to donate your organs in the event of your death. Your status as a donor will then be marked on your identification card.

73

Working in New York

America is a country built on the backs of immigrants, most of whom passed through the harbours of New York. Today, the ports of entry may have become more dispersed, but New York is still a major destination for those seeking employment from abroad. About 14 million workers in the United States are foreign, with an estimated five million of them 'undocumented', or illegal. The percentage of foreign workers in New York is split between the service industries and large overseas companies, particularly those in banking, finance and computers. Because New York is home to many different cultures, you will find that most religions and ethnicities are tolerated and embraced. Once employed in New York, you will most likely find that the job you worked so hard to get looks after you pretty well. An increasing number of companies have created casual Fridays and instituted programmes such as yoga classes and group field trips to museums. It is important to research the work environment of a company well before accepting a position. With work hours lengthening, you don't want to be stuck somewhere you hate to go every day.

Salaries

New York is an expensive city to live in and consequently, the salaries are generally higher. However, you will find that you will not necessarily save any of the money you earn. New Yorkers generally spend over half their salary on rent and then a large proportion on dinner and going out. Take this as par for the course.

Speaking English

English is not the official language of the United States, but even if it were, New York would be the exception to the rule. There are some neighbourhoods where one need never speak English, such as the ever growing Chinese community in lower Manhattan's Chinatown, or the burgeoning Spanish Harlem in the north. However, if you plan on ever leaving Harlem and Chinatown to seek employment, you will find it difficult if you do not have at least an intermediate grasp of English. Those who speak one or more languages fluently are at a great advantage. With record-breaking numbers of tourists visiting NYC, companies are always looking to hire those who speak anything from Hindi to Persian.

Types of Work Visas

B-1 Business Visitor Visa: Foreigners interested in visiting the United States for exploratory business purposes that do not involve receiving salary or payment are eligible to apply for a B-1 business visitor visa. Additional screening and interviews are required at most United States Embassies and Consulates in order to attain this type of visa. They are valid for six months at a time.

TN Visa: a temporary work visa available only to citizens of Mexico and Canada under the North American Free Trade Agreement (NAFTA).

H-1B Visa: this enables professionals in 'speciality occupations', who can prove they can make a valuable contribution to the American economy, to live in the US. Examples of these occupations include accounting, computer specialists, engineers, financial analysts, doctors, nurses, scientists, architects and lawyers. The H-1B visa generally only applies to those with a higher education and requires a labour attestation, issued by the Secretary of Labor, and a letter of petition from an employer. A maximum of 65,000 H-1B visas are issued every year, are good for three years, and can be extended to a maximum of six years. An H1-B visa holder can apply for a Green Card if a company wants to sponsor his application.

H-2B Visa: This allows people to come to the United States temporarily, mainly for non-agricultural jobs in skilled and unskilled professions for which the US has a short supply of workers. A higher education is not needed for this type of visa and up to 66,000 H-2B visas are issued every year.

E-3 Visa: This type of temporary work visa is only available to Australian citizens. It is usually issued for two years at a time and only for those going to the US to work in a 'specialty occupation.' The spouses and children of E-3 visa holders are entitled to E-3D (dependent) visas and work authorisation, and need not be Australian citizens. The annual quota for this is 10,500 - very high in relative terms and usually easier to attain than H-1B visas. They can also be renewed indefinitely in two-year increments.

L-1 Visa: This is for workers employed outside the United States but whose company wishes to transfer them to the United States, and who are in higher positions which require specialised knowledge. A petition and application must be made to the US embassy for this visa and can be done through your company, who must also prove that you have been employed with them for at least a year. There are no quota restrictions for this visa, making it easier to attain than an H-1B, and children and spouses can accompany you with an L-2 visa.

Setting Up a Business

There are a few complications involved in starting a business in America without full residency status. A foreign national is allowed to start a business on a B-1 visa – although you cannot then manage that business. To legally manage your own business in the US you will need employment authorisation, such as an H-1B visa. The H-1B visa also poses a problem however: while you can start a business with it, you cannot draw a salary from that business, since 'work authorization for H-1B foreign specialty workers is employer-specific (ie. limited to employment with the approved employer/petitioner).'

As an H1-B visa holder, you can apply for permanent residency status in the US, as 'H-1B foreign specialty workers are not required to maintain foreign residence and may seek permanent residence in the US.' Once you have obtained permanent residency status, you can start and operate your business without constraints.

Working Hours

New York is a city that lives and breathes the phrase, 'work hard, play hard.' General work hours are 09:00 to 17:00, 40 hours a week, but depending on what industry you are in, those hours could be doubled. For instance, it is not unheard of for new employees in the finance industry to clock 100 hour work weeks. However, the time spent on the job for hourly waged positions is much more regulated. Employees must be paid time and a half for any hours worked over the standard 40, and a meal time of at least half an hour is required – that is federal mandated law.

If you hold a nine to five position within a company or in any governmental position, you can expect all major federal holidays off, including Christmas and Thanksgiving. This does not apply to the service industry which, especially in New York, is generally open on all major holidays. With so many religions now represented in New York, some companies now offer what they call 'floater holidays' which can be used for the religious event of your choosing.

Finding Work

Finding a job bussing tables in NYC is easy, finding a job in your chosen field is another story. People from all over America and countries around the world come to NYC searching for their dream position. With so many employees for companies to choose from, competition can be tough, to say the least. Those with masters degrees, prior experience (always highly valued), and a knowledge of one or more languages (especially Arabic, German, Japanese, Mandarin and Hindi) are at a great advantage.

Need Some Direction?

The *Explorer Mini Maps* pack a whole city into your pocket and once unfolded are excellent navigational tools for exploring. Not only are they handy in size, with detailed information on the sights and sounds of the city, but also their fabulously affordable price mean they won't make a dent in your holiday fund. Wherever your travels take you, from the Middle East to Europe and beyond, grab a mini map and you'll never have to ask for directions.

Narrowing the Search
There are many other sites with specialised job listings, like www.mediabistro.com for media jobs and www.nyfa.org for jobs in the arts. A quick search on the internet should give you plenty more sites to choose from.

Finding Work Before You Come

Many internationals come to New York without employment, and though it is possible to find work and apply for a visa once you are already in the country, with the rivalry to find a job in New York, you might find this to be a difficult and expensive task. Searching for work beforehand will save you time and money. If you are able to afford it, set up interviews in NYC before you move. Remember, you will also need to ask interviewers whether their company sponsors foreign nationals to come to the US – some may not want to go through the hassle.

Finding work in New York while outside of the United States is the same as if you were in the country, as long as you have the internet. The four main sites to visit to begin your search are www.nytimes.com, www.newyork.craigslist.org, www.monster.com, and www.villagevoice.com. *The New York Times* and *Village Voice* list the same classifieds as their print versions and often have more up-to-date listings.

If you wish to sign up with a recruitment agency (see below), you can also do this while outside the country. For example, Adecco Staffing has an online assessment form for those unable to come into the office. You will also find that many larger companies have online application forms, such as Deutche Bank (www.db.com/careers), Universal Music (www.careers-umusic.com) and Time Warner (www.timewarner.com). NYTimes.com also has a pay feature on their site that will automatically fax your uploaded resume to the employers advertising on their site, making the process even simpler.

LIFEbeat: the Music Industry Fights AIDS
How would you like to turn your love for live music into some positive charity work? Check out www.lifebeat.com. This organisation is the music industry's way of both supporting and trying to reduce New York's HIV/AIDS population. Volunteers educate gig-goers by handing out pamphlets and free contraception at the city's hippest music events. They then get to enjoy the show themselves – for free.

Finding Work While You're Here

Going for daily interviews is of course easier if you already live in the city. The process for finding job openings is similar to the above search options, but you may also want to visit firms and set up appointments with their HR departments to discuss the company and any openings they may have in the future. This shows that you are interested in working for them and hopefully will give you an edge when a vacancy arises. If searching through newspapers for classifieds, be sure to pick up the Monday and Sunday editions, particularly *The New York Times*, as they will have the most jobs posted.

Networking in New York is an important skill: it is a city based on the concept that it's not what you know, but who you know. And remember, just because someone is wearing jeans and a ratty T-shirt, doesn't mean they don't own a house in the Hamptons as well as a loft in Soho. If you plan on finding a job using this method, a bit of research about the different areas where industry people hang out is in order. For example, bands and music people are in the Lower East Side bars, gallerists and artists are in Soho and Chelsea, and you'll find general business people in the bars all along Second Avenue from Midtown to the East Village.

Business Councils & Groups

American Australian Association	212 338 6860	www.americanaustralian.org
Austria Trade Commission	212 421 5250	www.austriantrade.org
Belguim Trade Commission	212 586 5110	www.belgium-emb.org/usa
Brazil Government Trade Bureau	212 827 0976	www.braziltradeny.com
British Trade & Investments Office	212 745 0495	www.britain-info.org
BritishAmerican Business Inc	212 661 4060	www.babinc.org
Colombia Trade Development Bureau	212 223 1120	www.proexport.com
Ecuador Government Trade Office	212 687 0484	na
Enterprise Ireland	212 371 3600	www.irish-trade.ie
France, Commercial Services	212 305 8800	na
German Information Center	212 610 9800	www.germany-info.org
Italy Trade Commissioner Office	212 980 1500	www.italtrade.com
Malaysia Commercial Section	212 682 0232	www.matrade.gov.my
Mexico, Foreign Trade Commission	212 826 2916	www.bancomex-nyc.com
Phillipppines Office of Foreign Trade Representative	212 575 7925	www.dti.gov.ph

Recruitment Agencies

Registering with recruitment, or temp, agencies is easy and usually requires simply a copy of your resume, your licence or passport (which will need the necessary visas since you will technically become an employee of the agency at first) and in most cases, a few exams to test your computer skills. Job competition in New York is tough and it is not a good idea to rely solely on recruitment agencies for employment. However, if going through an agency, it is important to keep close contact with them. In other words, annoy them. An agency can have thousands of applicants per week, but if you are the one person to call and make sure your name is remembered, they will want to get you a job as soon as possible – if only to stop you phoning.

Third Party Recruiters or Headhunters

If you wish to go the less stressful route of attaining work and a visa before arriving in the US, you may want to hire a headhunter. Headhunters work differently to recruitment agencies, they are people working just for you to find you a job while recruitment companies work for employers looking to fill openings. A headhunter's fee will come from your first year's salary, typically 20-30% of it. This may seem like a lot to ask, but headhunters are often very specialised in different fields and have connections that could land you the perfect job, or a job that pays much higher than expected. There are even some firms that specialise in computer and IT jobs that help employees gain an H-1B visa.

Voluntary & Charity Work

New York is home to an unceasing volume of volunteer opportunities, from museum docents to trash collectors to volunteer lawyers. Depending upon your interests, there will be an opportunity for you to volunteer in just about every field. You do not need a work visa to volunteer but it is a good idea to ask the organisation for which you are volunteering how long their waiting list is, just in case it exceeds your time in New York. Some organisations have lists so long that volunteers can wait months for a position, such as the American Museum of Natural History, whose volunteers wait up to a year to be placed.

Volunteer Organisations

Good places to start looking for work are sites that bring together opportunities from non-profits all over the city.

New York Cares organises non-profits according to industry and allows volunteers to search through their database for opportunities. You can search through their projects at www.nycares.org or call 212 228 5000.

Volunteer NYC sorts opportunities by neighbourhood and interest and has a searchable data base at www.volunteernyc.org (212 251 4016).

Street Project is a charity group catering to busy professionals looking to volunteer during their spare time to various charities (www.streetproject.org).

Working as a Freelancer/Contractor

It is the dream of every New Yorker to work freelance, and with so many companies looking to outsource their work instead of paying full-time employees, this dream is becoming a reality for more and more. If you are hired as a freelancer, it is possible to apply for a work visa, you will just need to be working full time and have a letter from your employer stating the length of your assignment. If starting work as a freelancer, you may want to become a member of The Freelancers' Union (www.freelancersunion.org). Other sources for employment are www.newyork.craigslist.org, www.freelancewriting.com and www.thehiredguns.com – which works as a sort of freelance recruitment agency.

Employment Contracts

New York's labour laws are pretty comprehensive and therefore it is not unusual to start a new job and not sign a contract. Your basic rights are outlined in the law, so in the case of a dispute, the courts will look to the law to settle the matter. However, some companies do request you sign a contract. If this happens, take due care to read and understand everything in it: if there is then a dispute between you and your employer, the courts will look to your contract, rather than to the labour law, to settle the dispute. If you have any doubts about a clause in your labour contract, it is worth getting a legal specialist to read through it and tell you if it contains anything out of the ordinary.

Labour Law

Wage

Because of the high cost of living in New York, the minimum wage is higher than the federal level ($5.15) at $7.15, and any hours worked over 40 must be paid at time and a half according to the Fair Labor Standards Act. If hired as a migrant or seasonal worker engaged in agriculture, you are protected by the Migrant and Seasonal Agricultural Worker Protection Act. This law requires that your wage cannot be less than the higher end of the applicable state minimum wage. Which means even if you are picking apples in Upstate New York, you must be paid at least $7.15 an hour.

Pension Plans

A pension plan is an employee benefit plan established or maintained by an employer or by an employee organisation (such as a union) that provides retirement income or defers income until termination of covered employment or beyond. There are a number of types of pension plans including the 401(k) and the traditional pension plan, known as a defined benefit plan. Pension plans are not guaranteed by law, but they do have laws governing them in case of termination or a company closure by the Employee Retirement Income Security Act.

Health Plans

A group health plan is established by an employer or union, and provides medical care for participants or their dependents directly or through insurance or reimbursement. Again, health care is not a guarantee in any position, though in most cases you will find the companies do have some sort of system set up for their employees to receive it. Health care in America is unfortunately not free and your company's health care plan may cost you $200 or more per month. If your firm does not provide health coverage, you may be eligible for the Health New York Plan, information on which can be

Recruitment Agencies		
Adecco Employment Services	212 682 3438	www.adecco.com
All Support Personnel	212 391 9889	www.allsupportpersonnel.com
Asset Staffing	212 430 1060	www.assetstaffing.com
Atrium	212 292 0550	www.atriumstaff.com
Career Blazers	212 719 3232	www.cblazers.com
CTI Personnel Group	212 697 4000	www.ctipersonnel@cti-group.com
Harper Group	2129 35- 3280	www.harpergroupllc.com
Staff Innovators	212 490 7788	www.edenstaffing.com
Staff Mark	212 271 3900	www.progressiveinfo.com
Tuttle Agency	212 499 0759	www.tuttleagency.com
Wall Street Services	212 509 7200	www.wallstservice.com

found at www.ins.state.ny.us. Upon termination of employment, some workers and their families will have the right to choose to continue their health benefits for limited periods of time – it is important to inquire about this at the time of dismissal.

Family and Medical Leave

The Family and Medical Leave Act provides up to 12 weeks of job-protected, unpaid leave during any 12 month period to eligible, covered employees for birth and care of a child (including adoption), care of an immediate family member (spouse, child, parent) who has a serious health condition, or care of the employee's own serious health condition. It also requires that the employee's health benefits continue during the leave.

Holiday Time

For employees working under certain government contracts, holidays and vacation benefits may be required. In other instances, however, there is no such requirement. In those cases, the extent of the leave and whether it is paid in whole, in part, or not at all is generally a matter of agreement between an employer and an employee. If working a 9 to 5, weekday job however, one can generally expect to be given all governmental holidays, including Thanksgiving and Christmas, off.

Unemployment Benefits

Workers who are unemployed through no fault of their own (does not include quitting, termination for stealing, etc), may be eligible to receive unemployment benefits. Unemployment is intended to provide temporary financial assistance to unemployed workers who meet the requirements of New York State law.

Equal Employment

Equal employment opportunity laws prohibit specific types of employment discrimination. Collectively, these laws prohibit discrimination in most workplaces on the basis of race, colour, religion, sex, age, national origin, and status as an individual with a disability or a protected veteran.

Unions

Certain industries may have unions which you can join. If employed in one of those industries (sanitation, police, fire, security, construction, transportation), you may be required to join the union or coerced to do so by your fellow employees. This is especially true in New York where unions have a long and complex history. For many unions, corruption goes hand in hand with support in your fight for higher wages and better benefits.

Many employers will most likely try and discourage their employees from joining a union, and with so many laws currently in practice to protect workers' rights, the days of the union might soon be gone. Any benefits negotiated on the part of a union will also be transferred onto you, even if you are not a member.

Company Closure

If your company closes, you may be owed a benefits package depending on how long you have worked there, and if you signed a contract with the company. This, however, is no guarantee. The Worker Adjustment and Retraining Notification Act, however, protects workers and their families by requiring employers with 100 or more employees (though generally not counting those who have worked for less than six months with the company or those who work less than 20 hours a week) to provide at least 60 days advance written notice of any foreseeable closing.

Work Visas

If you are not a citizen of the US, you need to get a work visa. The procedure can be complicated, depending on your circumstances. See p.74 for more information.

BankRate

Interest rates vary, depending on the institution and the type of account you open. To find the most current rates, check the website at www.bankrate.com. This website will provide you with the most current interest rates for bank accounts, mortgages and other loans. It also provides advice about the best account for you.

Bank Accounts

There are approximately 7,540 banks in the US, with 75,000 branches throughout the world. The US banking system is regulated by the Federal Reserve System, which is the central bank. It was created by Congress in 1913 in order to create a stable yet flexible financial structure. The Federal Reserve provides financial services to the US government, as well as the public and other financial institutions.

There are two kinds of banks in the US, the first being local banks. These banks conduct relatively simple traditional banking business, such as lending and deposit services. The second type of bank is the 'mega' bank: they have local braches but are based in global financial centres, such as New York, and conduct international transactions as well as regular banking business. The number of branches depends upon the bank. Whereas a small bank such as Richmond County Savings Bank has branches only on Staten Island, a mega bank such as Chase Manhattan has over 100 branches in New York City alone. Many banks offer 'one stop shopping' to the consumer, and therefore several different types of accounts. In addition to chequing accounts, there are also several types of savings accounts. For example, in addition to the traditional savings account, there are also different types of IRA accounts, some of which allow you to withdraw your money tax-free, without penalty. There are also retirement CDs (certificates of deposit), which allow you to deposit your money for a pre-determined period of time, from one month to 10 years, and offer a higher interest rate (your interest rate is determined by the amount of money you deposit). Many banks offer financial planning centres, in which you can create financial strategies for any facet of your life, business or personal. This includes taxes, buying or selling your home, and dealing with life's milestones, such as sending a child to college.

Most banks offer chequing and savings accounts, insurance and investment services, credit cards, ATM cards, debit cards, access to safety deposit boxes, loans, wire transfers, cheque cashing, accounts for children, and other services. You can conduct your banking at the branch, through an ATM, through the mail, over the phone or online. All banks charge fees for use of their services. For example, if you withdraw money from an ATM at your own bank, you may be charged a low fee ($1) or no fee at all. If, however, you take money out of the ATM of another bank or at a free-standing ATM machine (there is one in nearly every deli in New York City), you will be charged anywhere from $2-$5. In addition, your *own* bank will then charge you another fee (usually around $2) for taking money out elsewhere. In addition, you will be charged approximately $30 for bounced cheques, overdrafts, or if you stop payment on a cheque.

Most banks now offer free cheques, but you do have a choice. A chequing account in which you have to maintain a minimum balance usually offers more services, such as free overdraft protection, or a credit card with higher credit limit.

In order to open a bank account, you will usually need a driver's licence or state-issued non-driver identification, as well as a social security card and proof of address, such as a current electric bill. However, subject to bank approval, non-citizens and even non-residents can open a bank account in the US, with a valid passport (translated into English). Most banks will not allow non-residents to open an account online – you will have to go into the bank and provide the necessary documentation. An international bank, such as Chase Manhattan, has an international page with instructions for opening an account with them.

FDIC Protection

Whether you open a chequing, savings, or retirement account, your money will be protected against loss for an amount up to $100,000 by the Federal Deposit Insurance Corporation. The FDIC, which is an independent agency of the US government, was created in 1933 to address the failure of banking institutions during the Great Depression. Since the FDIC was created, no banking customer has lost funds due to the failure of a bank. The FDIC does not cover securities or mutual finds, however, and you should check the website at www.fdic.gov in order to make sure your accounts are properly protected. Please note that the FDIC also protects the victims of identity theft from financial loss.

Credit Unions

Please note that as an alternative to a bank, you may opt to conduct your financial business with a credit union. Credit unions are not-for-profit cooperatives, they are owned and controlled by their members, through an elected, volunteer board of directors. Only a member of the credit union can deposit or borrow money. Typically, credit unions pay higher interest rates on deposits and charge lower interest for loans.

Read Up On It

Two books that you may find helpful are the Price Waterhouse Cooper's Guide to Wealth Preservation *(a how-to on estate planning and passing wealth on to the next generation), and* Money Matters: Essential Tips and Tools for Building Financial Peace of Mind, *by Scott Hanson.*

Bank Opening Hours

Bank branches have different hours, but most banks are open from at least 09:00 to 17:00 Monday to Friday, and most are open on Saturdays until at least 13:00. Some branches will have a late night during the week, others may open early on a particular morning. ATM services are available 24 hours a day, every day.

Hoping For a Visit Visa?

Please be aware, if you open a US bank account from outside the US, it may cause a problem if you then apply for a visitation visa. Remember from the immigration section that when reviewing an application to come to the US for a visit, the US government assumes that you will want to remain here as an immigrant. Immigration will examine whether or not you have ties to the US which would indicate you wish to remain, and a bank account could show that you plan on staying here.

Financial Planning

A primary concern for most citizens in the US is saving for retirement. As the life expectancy increases, people have to work more years in order to support themselves in the lifestyle to which they have become accustomed.

New York City, for many people, is an exceedingly difficult place in which to save money. The high cost of living, coupled with the temptation of having literally everything at your fingertips, makes it hard to save for a rainy day. For example, it is too easy to jump in an expensive taxi rather than deal with the inconvenience of getting on a subway or bus. Don't feel like cooking dinner? Well, there are 24,000 restaurants in New York City, and several thousand of them deliver. Many people who live in Manhattan, in particular, find themselves with little money left over after the rent is paid. Therefore, many people choose to live in one of the four outer boroughs, where the rents are more reasonable. Many commute from Upstate New York, Connecticut or New Jersey.

The decision about whether to keep your savings in a US bank, a bank in your home country, or an off-shore account depends upon your particular situation. There are benefits and disadvantages to each choice, and you should consult a financial planner or accountant before making any big decisions.

Leading economists predict that the US dollar is going to get weaker in the next five years. They claim that the US consumer's desire for foreign goods (and the resulting flood of US dollars into the market), coupled with the growth of other countries, will contribute to the dollar's decline in coming years. These economists predict that the currency in up-and-coming countries like China and some Latin American nations will be on the rise. There are several different types of investments you can make, each with varying levels of risks and returns. You can invest in real estate, stocks (in which you are technically buying a piece of a company), gold, and mutual funds, to name but a few. Mutual funds collect money from thousands of small investors, and this money is then invested in a number of stocks, bonds and other securities. The mutual fund manager purchases these stocks and bonds, and monitors the investments on behalf of individuals. The benefit of this type of investment is that you can, with a relatively small amount of money, obtain a diversified portfolio with the added convenience of having someone else manage it for you.

Banking Comparison Table

Name	Phone	Web	Online Banking	Tele-Banking
Atlantic Bank of New York	800 535 2269	www.abny.com	yes	8005352269
Bank of America	212 836 5000	www.bankofamerica.com	yes	8008414000
Bank of New York	212 495 1784	www.bankofny.com	yes	na
Chase Bank	888 242 7324	www.chase.com	yes	na
Citibank	212 627 3999	www.citibank.com	yes	8003749700
Fleet	800 841 4000	www.fleet.com	yes	na
Washington Mutual	800 788 7000	www.wamu.com	yes	na

81

Whether or not to hire a financial planner is a personal choice, there is no right or wrong answer. If you do chose to work with a financial planner, experts recommend that you thoroughly interview at least three, and inquire about their education and licences. You should also get references from their other clients. A good planner will assess your goals by determining what you want and need, and balance those goals with the level of risk you are comfortable with. Financial planners are considered especially useful in terms of planning for sending your kids to college and your retirement.

If you decide to do without a financial planner, it does not mean you have to do it all on your own – many banks offer consulting services that can help you make the right decisions.

Expat Advice
Please note: it may be particularly important for foreigners working abroad to engage a financial planner. Foreign residents have unique tax and investment considerations that might be difficult to navigate without the help of a licensed professional.

Buying property in New York City is one of the best investments you can make. New York City neighbourhoods are constantly reinventing themselves: the lousy, low-cost area one year is the darling of real estate developers the next. Therefore, there is always the opportunity for the shrewd investor to buy cheap before the area becomes the next hip place. Also, people often buy two family homes, then live in one apartment and rent out the other for a price that can pay for the entire mortgage. For more information on property investment, check out the Buying Property section (p.100).

If you are interested in purchasing property as a foreign resident, there are several international real estate agents in New York City that can assist you. Two well-known firms are Halstead Property (www.halstead.com, 212 381 3263) and Coldwell Banker Hunt Kennedy Real Share International (www.cbhk.com, 212 877 1300). It might also be a good idea to check out the *International Real Estate Digest* website, www.ired.com. Buying property in a country you don't live in is a complex matter and should not be entered into lightly. You will have to deal with the laws and tax regulations of a foreign country, and each country varies significantly. For example, although land transactions in Mexico have typically been cash only, recently some companies have offered mortgage services, but they require a 30-40% deposit and carry high interest rates. Other countries have taxes specifically for vacation homes. In addition, the nation where you buy the property may have a treaty with the country in which you live that affects the taxes or other aspects of your real estate transaction. Therefore, it is highly suggested that you consult a real estate attorney or accountant experienced in these types of investments. Please note that in some countries non-residents also pay capitol gains tax at a different rate than residents when they sell the property.

Pensions

If you work for any government entity, such as the City of New York, you will receive a pension. Police officers, teachers, and other public servants can collect a pension after a certain amount of years on the job.

If you work for a private entity, there are other ways to prepare for the future through your place of employment. Many companies offer a 401(k) – a retirement plan to which employees contribute pre-tax income. This money is often invested in company stocks, some companies even *match* your contributions to a certain amount. However, some 401(k) plans will penalise you if you withdraw funds before a certain age.

Off-Shore Savings Accounts

An off-shore account is defined as one held outside your country of residence. It is usually in a low tax jurisdiction and therefore can be financially beneficial. For example, the interest on your account may be free of tax, therefore it may also be a good idea to transfer your existing savings and investments to an offshore account. Please be advised, however, if you are living in the US, you must declare all of your income to the government, even income derived from interest in your offshore account – it is considered taxable income. In addition, you will most likely have to make a sizeable deposit to open the account – maybe as high as $5,000.

Financial Advisors

Below are a few suggestions on where to begin your search for a financial planner, as well as contact information for the Financial Planning Association of New York, which can give you tips on how to find the planner that suits your needs.

Financial Advisors

Beck Mack & Oliver	212 661 2640	na
Charles Schwab	212 213 5313	www.schwab.com
Cowan Financial Group	212 536 6000	www.cowanfinancial.com
David Lipton CPA, PC	212 279 4747	na
Edelweiss Capital USA	212 564 1634	na
Fahnestock & Co.	212 668 8000	www.fahnestock.com
Financial Planning Association of New York	877 773 7269	www.fpany.org
Genworth Financial	888 436 9678	www.genworth.com
Goldman Sachs International	212 902 1000	www.gs.com
H & R Block	212 693 1680	www.hrblock.com
L. J. Altfest & Co.	212 406 0867	www.altfest.com
Merrill Lynch	212 449 1000	www.ml.com
Rohatyn Group	212 682 9777	na
Smith Affilitated Capital Corp.	212 644 9440	www.smithcapital.com
Thomson Financial	212 884 8200	www.thomson.com
Weiss Financial	212 697 7033	www.weissfinancial.biz

Taxation

Accountant Abundance

There are thousands of accountants in New York City, and you can find them either on the internet or by looking in a phone directory under 'certified public accountants.' There are also several large accounting companies with offices all over the city – one of the most well-known is H&R Block. To find an office location, call 800 472 5625, or go on their website at www.HRBlock.com.

According to the US Constitution, Congress has the power to 'lay and collect taxes…to pay debts and provide for the common defence and general welfare of the United States.' Therefore, although tax rates in the US are typically lower than in other similarly developed countries in Europe and Asia, nearly everyone in the United States must pay taxes, whether they are citizens or immigrants. Tax money supports the government, the military, social welfare programmes, maintenance of roads, and many other things necessary for the running of the country. (American citizens or legal permanent residents working abroad must also report their earnings to the US government – it will later be determined whether they will have to pay taxes on those earnings.)

Individual states, and cities, also levy their own taxes: if you live or work in New York City, you can expect to pay federal, state, and city taxes (subject to your status in the country). Taxes will be deducted directly from your pay cheque; the amount depends on what filing status you choose when filling out your initial paperwork as you start your job.

Each year, by April 15th, you must file a tax return with the Internal Revenue Service (IRS). Your tax return is a collection of forms in which you submit proof of your earnings from the previous year, as well as a list of any assets you have.

Your accountant will then assess whether or not you have overpaid what you owe the federal and state governments. If you have overpaid, you will be refunded the excess amount from the US government and/or the state in which you live. If you have underpaid your taxes, you will have to pay the government the difference. (If you cannot afford to pay the entire amount at once, the IRS will usually allow you to make a reasonable payment each month.) Please be aware that neglecting or evading paying your taxes can lead to financial penalties, and in some cases, a prison sentence.

There are many deductions that you may be eligible for when filing your tax return. If you have donated to a charity, for example, or if you own property, you may be eligible for a deduction in taxes. Also, the amount of money you earn determines the 'tax bracket' you fall in, and that may also determine the rate at which you pay your taxes. This is an extremely complicated area of law, and it is best explored with the help of an accountant or tax attorney.

If you are a legal permanent resident of the US, you are considered a 'tax resident' and are liable for taxes, even if you are absent from the US for an extended period of time. You must therefore report all of your earnings to the US government, even if you have earned the money *outside* the US. (Please note that even if you have left the US with the intention of giving up your status as a legal permanent resident, you are liable to pay US taxes until you receive official notice from USCIS that such status has been terminated) Green card holders must file Form 1040: green card holders who commit a tax crime may be deported.

Don't Do It Yourself

It is not a requirement that you hire an accountant to file your taxes for you: you can request the forms from the IRS directly. However, this is not recommended unless you are familiar with the tax laws and how they apply to you.

Other Taxes

In addition to the taxes you pay out of your salary, you will also pay a sales tax when you purchase any number of items. The amount of this tax depends upon the item, as well as where you live. For example, in an effort to reduce smoking, the state of New York has affixed a high sales tax on cigarettes. You will also pay taxes when you purchase alcohol, food, and books. For the last few years, New Yorkers have not had to pay sales tax on clothes and shoes that cost under $110. But you will pay taxes on any real estate you own and services you receive, such as electric and cable television in your apartment, even your cellular phone bill.

Cost of Living	
Bananas	$.30-$.50
Beer (six-pack)	$5
Bottle of House Wine	$20
Bread (loaf)	$3
Burger (takeaway)	$10
Bus	$4.50
Camera film	$7
Can of dog food	$1
Can of soft drink	$1
Cappuccino	$3
Car Rental (small car, per day)	$80
Carrots (per kg)	$.30
Chicken (fresh, per kg)	$2.99
Chocolate bar	$1.50
Cigarettes (pack of 20)	$6.50-8.00
Cinema ticket	$9-$11
DVD (new release)	$18
Eggs (dozen)	$1.50
Film developing	$10-15
Fresh beef (per kg)	$3-$5
Fresh fish (per kg)	$2-$10
Glass of House wine	$6
Local postage stamp	$.39
Milk	$2
Newspaper (international)	$4
Newspaper (local)	$.50-$1.50
Orange juice	$3
Pack of 24 aspirin	$4
Petrol (gallon)	$2.70
Pizza (large, takeaway)	$20
Postcard	$1
Potatoes (per kg)	$.75
Rice	$1
Salon haircut (female)	$10-$300
Salon haircut (male)	$10-$150
Strawberries	$2-$4
Sugar	$3
Text message	10c-25c
Tube of toothpaste	$2-$8
Water (restaurant)	$3
Water (supermarket)	$1.50

Legal Issues

The law in the United States is based on the Common Law, which was borrowed from the English system. Even after gaining its independence during the Revolutionary War, the United States continued to use the Common Law as a foundation for its own legal system. The US Constitution is the ultimate authority on every matter pertaining to law and government in the United States. Every statute, court decision or government action is held up to the Constitution – if it contradicts it, it will be struck down as contrary to the principles of the country.

The Constitution created three branches of the government: legislative, judicial and executive. The legislative branch creates law (or statutes), and the judicial branch interprets those laws. The executive branch is headed by the President of the United States, who is the Commander in Chief of the armed forces and oversees certain government agencies.

The Common Law system relies heavily on precedent: that is, decisions from courts that interpret statutes enacted by the legislative branch. Common Law also fills in any gaps not covered by statutes. The US also follows a federal system, which is a balance between state and federal law.

Child Support
This is a percentage of the combined income of the parents. It is set as 17% for one child, 25% for two children, 29% for three children, and 31% for four.

Legal Issues for Expats

Non-citizens living in the US enjoy the same legal rights as citizens. They are subject to the same laws and are entitled to the same protection from those laws. However, anyone who is not a citizen must be aware that many legal problems can have serious consequences regarding their ability to stay in the US. For example, a non-citizen accused of a crime may not only be sent to jail, but also deported. In addition, if your residency is based on marriage, your divorce many have serious consequences on that residency. Therefore, it is always best to consult an attorney experienced in immigration matters before proceeding with any legal issue.

Divorce

In the United States, divorce is governed by *state* law. There are six grounds for divorce in New York: cruel treatment, abandonment for one year or longer, imprisonment (of your spouse) for three years or longer, adultery, a court-granted legal separation for a year, or legal separation for a year through a signed agreement of the parties.

An uncontested divorce, in which the terms are agreed to by both parties and involves a simple division of property, can be completed in 30 days and will cost you anywhere between $250 and $2,500. In a contested divorce, however, your attorney will charge, which can cost between $175 and $450 an hour. In addition, your lawyer will probably ask for a down payment for his or her fees, also known as a retainer. You should also note that a complicated divorce, with lots of property or child custody issues to be settled, can take one to three years.

Tax Liable?
Non-immigrants may also be considered tax residents, depending on how much time they have spent in the US in a given year. If you have been in the US for 183 days of the tax year, you will have to pay taxes.

In order to obtain a divorce in New York, the state must have jurisdiction. You and your spouse must have married in New York *and* either of you must be a resident when the divorce proceeding starts, with one of you resident for one year immediately before. Alternatively, you and your spouse must have *lived* in New York as husband and wife, and live in New York when the divorce proceeding starts, as well as the year before. Lastly, you can also get a divorce in New York if either one of you has been a continuous New York resident for at least two years immediately before filing for divorce.

Legal Settlements

Child Support in New York is determined by its Domestic Relations law. Every parent is responsible for the support of their child until the child reaches 21 years of age. In determining custody and child support, the governing principal for the court is the best interest of the child. The court will calculate the basic child support and obligation, considering many factors, including the non-custodial parent's proportionate share. In terms of child custody, again the court will balance a number of factors, with the foremost priority being the best interest of the child.

For both custody and child support, parents are free to come up with their own reasonable agreement and waive the law. For example, if the parents agree that the child would be better off living with one parent most of the time and spending holidays with the other, that would be ok with the court, as long as it is in the child's best interests. Also, one parent may agree to pay more for the child's support based on the fact that that parent earns significantly more money than the other.

New York alimony laws are gender-neutral. The court will look at several factors when determining whether either party gets alimony and how much, including the standard of living during the marriage, the circumstances of the divorce, the duration of the marriage, and the age and health of the parties. They will also consider whether the potential recipient of the alimony was out of work while married, and what, if any, professional opportunities that person passed up in order to raise children, and so on.

Crime-Busting in Every Language
Although all court proceedings are conducted in English, translators are provided for participants who cannot speak English.

In terms of division of marital property, New York is an equitable distribution state. That means that the court, looking at the particular facts of the case, will divide the assets and debts acquired during the marriage according to the contributions of each spouse. The court will look to the length of the marriage here as well, usually when the marriage has been 20 years or longer, the court will divide the property 50/50, but again, this depends upon the specific facts.

Making a Will

While it is perfectly legal in New York to make your own will, as with all other areas of law, you should consult a lawyer – in this case you will need a probate lawyer.

A will in New York must be signed at the end by the testator (the person making the will). It must also be signed by two witnesses that have nothing to gain from the estate (there are exceptions to this rule, which your lawyer will explain to you). The testator must sign in the presence of the witnesses, and the will must be notarised. Please note that New York does not recognise handwritten wills. If you would like to change, add to or remove something from your will, you can draw up a *codicil*, which, like the original will, must be signed in the presence of witnesses.

Alimony Rules
Note that the recipient will not get more alimony if the paying partner was cruel to them, but the recipient may receive less if they were cruel to the paying partner.

Depending on the size of your estate, the beneficiaries may have to pay an estate tax. In New York, taxes must be paid if the estate is one million dollars or more. Again, you should consult an attorney when dealing with these tax issues.

Adoption

Adoption is quite common in the United States: thousands of children are adopted each year and brought to live in the US by citizens and immigrants. It involves a rather complex process and can be affected by your residency status in the US. See p.69.

Drinking & Driving

- **Driving While Ability Impaired:** (BAC of .05-.07). Carries a mandatory fine of $300 to $500, a maximum jail sentence of 15 days, and mandatory loss of licence for 90 days.
- **Driving While Intoxicated (DWI):** (BAC of .08 or higher).   Carries a mandatory fine of $500 to $1,000, maximum sentence of one year in jail, and mandatory loss of licence for at least six months.
- **Aggravated DWI:** (BAC of .18 or higher). Carries a mandatory fine of $1,000 to $1,500, maximum sentence of one year in jail, and mandatory loss of driver's licence for at least one year (If you get a second aggravated DWI within 10 years, the penalty increases to a mandatory fine of $1,000 to $5,000, a maximum of four years in jail and mandatory loss of licence for at least 18 months).

New York's DWI law also criminalises driving under the influence of drugs or a combination of drugs and alcohol. This includes otherwise legal medication prescribed by a doctor. You must pay attention to the warning labels on your medication regarding whether it is safe to drive and mix with alcohol while you are taking it. For the full list of offenses and penalties you can check out the website for the New York Department of Motor Vehicles website, www.nydmv.com.

Crime

The attitude toward crime in the US is a matter of perspective. Some feel that the punishments for crimes are too severe, and others feel they are not severe enough. Views on certain crimes also vary from state to state. For some crimes, people are expected to pay a fine, for others they may have to do community service, such as cleaning up public areas or working with those less fortunate. Some crimes, however, are considered severe enough to warrant incarceration.

People are sent to prison for a few different reasons. But prison is also seen as a potential deterrent (if people know they can be sent to prison perhaps they will rethink committing a crime), as well as rehabilitation. Finally, incarceration is used to keep dangerous, repeat offenders off the street in order to protect society.

The American legal system is a balancing act, that of weighing the rights of society with the rights of the individual accused to be treated fairly under the law.

Over the past 15 years, New York City has enjoyed a significant decrease in crime, and has been named, for the past several years, the safest large city in the United States. Indeed, with eight million people, New York is the largest city in the country, as well as the one with the most dense concentration of people in a geographic area.

Always Insure
Please note that in New York you must have car insurance for as long as the car is registered, even if you have it parked in your driveway and never use it.

Prisons

Life behind bars in the US, on paper, may not seem so bad. Prisoners, like everyone in the US, are entitled to a certain amount of rights: they receive three meals a day, medical care, and freedom to practise their religion. There are televisions and libraries. Prisoners can receive an education – some get a high school diploma, college degree, or even a law degree. Many write books in prison. And because the main goal of the prison system is rehabilitation of criminals, prisoners can also receive psychiatric treatment for whatever social or mental ills that may have contributed to their decision to commit a crime.

Of course, the reality is that these people have been sentenced to a period of incarceration, perhaps for the rest of their lives. They live on a strict schedule determined by the prison staff: they do not decide what time they wake up, when or what they eat, when or for how long they can exercise. Also, in New York, those convicted of a felony cannot vote while they are in prison or on parole.

Another reality of prison life is that no matter how many rules and regulations are set up by prison staff, there is a criminal subculture that exists in jails that cannot be completely controlled. Gangs flourish in jails and prisoners must often choose a gang in order to be protected. Rape is rampant in jails for both men and women, and prisoners are often attacked or killed by other inmates.

Law Firms		
Adam Leitman Bailey	212 825 0365	www.alblawfirm.com
Berkman Bottger & Rod	212 867 9123	www.berkbot.com
Chadbourne & Parke	212 408 5100	www.chadbourne.com
Coudert Brothers	212 626 4400	www.coudert.com/offices/newyork.htm
DeBevoise & Plimpton	212 909 6000	www.debevoise.com
Hochheiser & Hochheiser	212 689 4343	www.hochheiser.com
Pepper Hamilton	212 813 9668	www.pepperlaw.com
Russin & Vecchi	212 210 9543	www.russinvecchi.com
Skadden, Arps, Slate, Meagher & Flom	212 735 3000	www.sasmf.com
Slaughter & May	212 888 1112	www.slaughterandmay.com
Stephen B Kass	718 302 4000	www.sbkass.com
White & Case	212 819 8200	www.whitecase.com

87

If you are accused of a crime, you are not automatically put into prison (thank goodness!). There is a complex maze of procedural rules that law enforcement and courts must follow from arrest to, and throughout, the trial. Everyone is presumed innocent until proven guilty beyond a reasonable doubt . You would definitely, however, be subject to US law. You may or may not be entitled to bail before your trial: that will be determined by a judge at your arraignment (a hearing which takes place after your arrest). Whether you are granted bail depends on a number of factors, including what you are accused of, whether you have a previous criminal record, and whether you are a flight risk.

If you are an expat and have been accused or convicted of a crime, it may very well result in your deportation (unless you have become a US citizen). Therefore, your criminal record will follow you back to your home country. Likewise, if you have a criminal record in your home country, it will likely prevent you from coming to this country in the first place. In addition, even if you are admitted to the US, it may still affect your chances of finding work here. Many companies now do background checks, and your record will easily be discovered. Also, many work applications ask if you have ever been convicted of a crime: if the potential employer finds out that you have lied on your application, you will most certainly not get the job. You probably will eventually get some sort of work, but it will be more difficult to obtain a job, and it may not be the type of work you want to do.

Driving While Intoxicated

Each year, several thousand people are killed in the United States in alcohol-related accidents. DWI laws, therefore, have become very strict. Penalties include monetary fines, loss of your driver's licence, even time in jail. Laws vary from state to state, but currently you are legally intoxicated in every state if a breath, blood, urine or saliva test indicates that you have a blood alcohol content (BAC) of .08 or higher. (Please note that while you can refuse to take these tests, if you do you will most likely lose your driver's licence for at least a year and have to pay $500 to get a new one.)

Never take a DWI charge lightly: you should hire an experienced lawyer and, as with any criminal charge, be aware that a conviction or a guilty plea for any crime may be grounds for deportation if you are not a US citizen. In New York, legal precedent has established that lawyers and judges are not bound to tell you this before you plead guilty.

In New York, DWI offences are included in the Vehicle and Traffic Law. Section 1192-3 is a common law offence. This includes whatever a police officer observes after pulling you over: the smell of alcohol on your breath, if your eyes are bloodshot, if your speech is slurred, if you are driving erratically or are not able to walk a straight line. Section 1192-2 is 'statutory', which means your BAC is .08 or higher.

Drug Possession

In 1973, New York enacted the Rockefeller Laws, which include the harshest mandatory minimum sentences for drug possession in the country. These laws have been hotly protested in New York State as being brutally unfair, and there has been a movement to have them repealed. Opponents of these laws claim that they tie the judge's hands so that they are not able to take the individual circumstances into account when sentencing.

If you are arrested with possession of drugs, the severity of the charge often depends upon the weight of the substance you are carrying. If you are found with a small amount for personal use, then it would be a misdemeanour. If you are found with more, police can charge you with intent to sell, and then you will be charged with a felony, which is much more serious.

Say Goodbye to Your Wheels
Please note that if you drive while intoxicated in New York, you may also lose your car. The Police Property Clerk may return your car to you if your BAC was under 1.5, if it was your first offence, and if you did not cause an accident. You probably will have to be evaluated by an individual certified by the state to see whether you need treatment for alcohol abuse. In such cases, you have to complete the treatment programme before you get your car back.

Assault

Assault is defined as any harmful touching of another person. It encompasses threatening to injure a person, as well as striking or throwing something at them. If you actually strike the person, you have also committed battery. If someone accuses you of assaulting them and you plead guilty or are convicted at trial, you may very well go to prison. The length of your sentence will depend on several factors, such as the severity of the assault and whether this is your first offence.

Traffic Accidents

If you are in an accident and there are no injuries, you must stop and exchange insurance information. If you have destroyed a parked car, other property or have injured a pet, you must find the owner or call the police. If someone has been killed, you must call the police immediately. You and the police must file an accident report. It is illegal to leave the scene of an accident when someone is hurt or killed. If you are at fault for the accident and someone is hurt or killed you may be arrested, depending on the circumstances. For example, if you were drunk or driving recklessly at excessive speeds, you may be prosecuted for vehicular homicide.

Even if you are not convicted, the family of the deceased can sue you in civil court for wrongful death. If the court finds against you, you may have to pay a significant amount of money. Depending on the amount and the circumstances, your insurance may cover it, but you would have to check this with your individual insurance company.

Traffic & Parking Tickets

There are many rules or regulations concerning driving in the city of New York. Parking spaces are a rare commodity, and you must be diligent, and lucky, in your search for a spot. In addition, you must read posted street signs to be sure you are in a legal spot. If you do get a parking ticket, the penalty can be anywhere from $35 to over $100. If you get a ticket, you can follow the instructions on the ticket and pay with a cheque or money order – if you want to fight the ticket you can go to the traffic court listed on the ticket and argue the case on your own behalf.

Drunk & Disorderly Conduct
This crime is a misdemeanour, which is usually a pretty minor offence. If you are convicted of a misdemeanour, you can be sentenced to a maximum of 12 months in jail, a monetary penalty, probation or community service.

Dangerous Areas

As previously mentioned, New York is a fairly safe city: you'll find that staying safe here is, like everywhere else, 95% common sense. New Yorkers are known for being street smart: they are always aware of their surroundings, especially at night. If you are not familiar with the city, it is best not to venture out aimlessly by yourself at night. This does not mean you cannot run down to the corner deli for a pack of cigarettes, but it is not advisable to go wandering down an empty alleyway at 03:00, unless you are very sure of the neighbourhood, and yourself.

There is an endless list of neighbourhoods in each of the five boroughs, some safe, some not – it would be impossible to describe them all here. Since Manhattan is the centre of New York nightlife, as well as the place where most tourists and other new arrivals go, that is the most important area to cover. The first rule is to remain in places where there are a lot of people out and about – and luckily in Manhattan, these areas are not hard to find. Greenwich Village, for example, is packed with people, year round, until at least 04:00 when the bars close for the night. There are several cabs on every street waiting to take you where you need to go, so you don't have to walk round looking for transportation.

Play it Safe

Until you become familiar with the different neighbourhoods of New York, you should travel with others as much as possible. Whether you are alone or with others, always be aware of who else is around, whether it is a police officer who can help you, or someone that seems like they might cause trouble.

89

It is a fact of life that in New York, as in many other places, women have to be more careful in terms of personal safety. If possible, do not walk down deserted, dark streets alone, and avoid the subway late at night. And, very importantly, never leave a drink unattended in a bar, not even for a minute. There are many cases in which someone has drugged a woman's drink, and then attacked her when she is incapacitated. These drugs are known as 'date rape' drugs, and these crimes can be hard to prove. The drug often leaves the body very quickly, and the woman may not remember all of the attack.

Petty Crimes

Keeping your personal belongings safe, again, involves common sense. Hold tightly onto your purse, keep it zipped up, don't keep your wallet in your back pocket. When in a restaurant, don't hang your purse on the back of the chair – keep it on your lap or on the floor by your feet. If these things are taken, the chances of you getting them back are slim. But with a few small precautions, you can safely enjoy all that the city has to offer.

Getting Arrested

The Fourth Amendment of the US Constitution protects people from unreasonable search and seizure by authorities. Before police can even stop you for questioning, they must have a reasonable suspicion that you have committed, are committing, or about to commit a crime. You can ask if you are under arrest or if you are free to leave. If a police officer reasonably suspects that you are a danger to him or others, he can pat you down, over your clothing, to make sure you do not have any weapons. You are not in police custody at this point and you may leave at any time.

The standard for arrest is even higher: the police cannot arrest you unless they have probable cause. This is a legal standard defined as 'reasonable cause to believe such person has committed a crime.' If the police do not have probable cause the arrest is invalid. In many cases the police must have an arrest warrant: this is a document signed by a judge that sets out facts illustrating that probable cause exists. There are circumstances, however, when the arrest must be made immediately and the requirement for a warrant is waived, such as if police catch you in the act of robbing a store, or if they think you are going to dispose of the evidence of a crime.

If you are arrested, this means you are in police custody and are not free to leave. The police must tell you why you are being arrested and advise you of your Miranda Rights. These are rights set out in a US Supreme Court decision of the same name, and they are required in all 50 states. Miranda Rights include the right to remain silent, and therefore not incriminate yourself (the police must also advise you that anything you say can be used against you in a court of law), the right to an attorney (if you cannot afford an attorney, one will be appointed for you), and the right to legal representation, which is protected by the Constitution. If you get arrested, you do not have to answer any questions until you have spoken to your attorney. The moment you request an attorney, your right is said to have 'attached', and law enforcement must cease all interrogation. In addition, New York provides the added protection of the 'indelible right to counsel'. This means that you can waive your right to counsel, only in the presence of counsel.

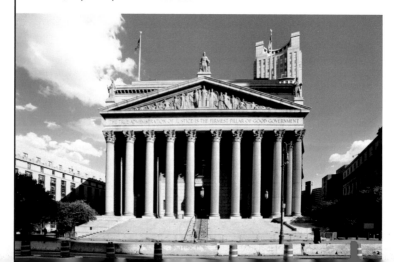

When you're lost what will you find in your pocket?

Item 71. The half-eaten chewing gum

When you reach into your pocket make sure you have one of these minature marvels to hand… far more use than a half-eaten stick of chewing gum when you're lost.

Explorer Mini Maps
Putting the city in your pocket

Housing

There is good news and bad news about the New York housing market. The bad news is that it is expensive and cut-throat. If you find a reasonably priced place that you can afford, you do not have time to dwell on whether or not to take it – in the blink of an eye it will be gone. The good news is that there is so much diversity in the five boroughs of New York City that whatever your needs or desires, there is a place for you here. Even if it doesn't seem to be your heart's desire when you choose your living space, it is sure to grow on you. Each neighbourhood is rich with its own flavour and tempo, and many New Yorkers, once used to their own neighbourhood, become so provincial that they are reluctant to stray to other areas of the city.

Housing Disputes ◀

Housing disputes, including eviction proceedings, are adjudicated by the New York Housing Court, which is part of New York State's civil court system. This court is one of the busiest in the world – nearly 300,000 landlord/tenant cases are filed with the Housing Court each year. For more information, check out the website (www.courts.state.ny.us).

Buying & Renting Property

If it is possible for you to buy property, it is preferable, in many ways, to renting. Property in New York City is an incredible investment; you are sure to make a profit when you sell. You will also have equity in your property, which you will be able to borrow against for home improvement loans or for sending your kids to college. In addition, many homes in New York are large enough for two or more families, so you would be able to pay your mortgage from the rent money you collect, and possibly make a profit each month. If you cannot or do not want to buy, you can rent or sublet a space. If you are the primary tenant, you and the landlord are legally bound to each other; if you are subletting from the primary tenant, you are legally bound with that tenant, and that tenant is still legally bound to the landlord.

Choosing an Area

If you are new to New York, there are many things to consider in choosing an area to live in. If money is an issue, price will probably be the most determinative factor in deciding on a neighbourhood. However, there are also many other factors, such as the neighbourhood's safety, its schools, perhaps its ethnic make-up, and nightlife. If money is no object, then you are very lucky indeed and you'll have a wonderful time choosing your residence.

There are several areas of New York City that are considered highly desirable, depending upon your particular needs. Maybe you want to live near your job: if you work on Wall Street, for example, you could look for a place in Battery Park City (at the southernmost tip of Manhattan) so you can walk to work. If it's nature you crave, and you can afford the price tag, you can live on Central Park West, and enjoy a splendid view of one of the largest and most famous city parks in the world.

If you cannot afford an apartment in Manhattan, there are several neighbourhoods in the outer boroughs that are also in high demand. Although living outside Manhattan is considered by many to be a 'step down', often people find these areas have many benefits to living in 'the City'. These areas are less expensive and less crowded, and have their own amenities. All of the outer boroughs have neighbourhoods that are suburban by New York City standards, and each has its own beaches.

Amenities

Depending on what sort of housing agreement you have, certain amenities may be included in your rent. For example, heat and hot water may be included, but usually electricity is not. Parking is not likely to be included either. First of all, parking in New York City is a commodity worth its weight in gold – relatively few buildings have their own parking garages. If there is parking, it will likely be something you have to opt for, and pay a lot for. Many buildings with parking also have waiting lists: you may be parking on the street until someone moves out of the building.

Typically, landlords are responsible for general maintenance of their rental properties and they must adhere to certain standards. For example, they must provide heat in the winter. But the tenant is also responsible for the upkeep of the apartment. For instance, the landlord is responsible for painting the building, but if the tenant punches holes in the wall he or she will be responsible for the damage. Some landlords are willing to deal with their tenants, for example, the tenant may be able to paint the apartment or rewire faulty electric and then deduct cost from the rent. This, however, depends on your individual lease and landlord.

Usually leases are signed on a year-to-year basis. If you sign a subletting agreement, it may be for a different, more informal, length of time, depending on your needs and those of the primary tenant. In addition, at the end of the initial lease period, a choice to renew the lease for one or two years is sometimes offered.

The standard lease usually dictates that the rent payment be made each month. While most landlords, especially with first-time tenants, would be reluctant to accept post-dated cheques, you may be able to negotiate paying a lump sum every few months. Any negotiations you may or may not be able to make depends largely on what neighbourhood you live in, and what type of building. For example, if you are living in a large, corporate-owned high-rise building in Manhattan, the rent and other conditions are not negotiable. However, if you move into a two family house in a Brooklyn neighbourhood, the landlord (who most likely lives in the other apartment) may be willing to make a mutually-beneficial deal with you.

Utilise Utility
Arrangements
If you are subletting from a primary tenant, you may be able to make arrangements to pay one fee which includes all of your utilities. This is likely if you are renting from someone who plans to return to the apartment in the future and is keeping all the utility services in their name.

New York Rents

Rents in New York City only seem to go in one direction: up. The average rent for a small studio in Manhattan is over $2,000 per month, and they keep on climbing. Even while the prices of real estate is plummeting in other parts of the US, Manhattan prices continue to sky rocket (which is why you can never go wrong in purchasing property there). The fact that the Manhattan market recovered so rapidly from the downturn experienced in the wake of the September 11 attacks is a testament to its strength.

You will most like have to pay a security deposit for your new apartment, unless you know the landlord. Most places require first and last month's rent as security. The landlord will hold these funds in escrow while you are living there, and if you have paid all of the rent owed and have not damaged the living space, these funds will be returned to you when you move out.

Finding a Home

Whether or not you engage a real estate agent is a personal choice, depending on your needs, and your wallet. While many people do engage agents in New York City, it is certainly common for people to find a place on their own. If you don't have a lot of money, it will be more economical to search yourself and avoid the often exorbitant realtor's fees. You can look for a place on your own in a number of ways: on the internet (www.craigslist.org has gained a lot of respect in the past few years), in the newspapers (*The New York Times* and *Village Voice* both have extensive real estate

93

Employment Contracts
Most permanent employment contracts do not include housing contracts or subsidies. If you are sent on temporary assignment in New York, your company may quite possibly pick up the tab, but once you settle here permanently, you are on your own. One reason that salaries are usually higher in New York City, particularly Manhattan, is to compensate for the higher cost of living.

sections), or through word of mouth. Simply tell people you know that you are looking for a place, and you will inevitably hear about several people seeking tenants, subletters, or roommates (even if you're not necessarily sharing a room, they're still known as 'roommates' in New York – rather than 'flatmates'). You may also see postings just walking down the street: 'for rent' notices are often posted on poles and buildings throughout the city. If, on the other hand, you don't mind paying the realtor's fees and you want to spare yourself the headache of braving the New York City real estate market, you can simply hire an

Housing Abbreviations

BA	Bathroom
BR	bedroom
D/D	Dishwasher and garbage disposal unit
DR	Doorman building
EIK	Eat-in kitchen
FDR	Formal dining room
FRPLC	Fireplace
GAR	Garage
HDW	Hardwood floors
HI CEILS	High Ceilings
HVAC	Heating/ventilation/air conditioning
OFC	Office
OSP	Off-street parking
RF	Roof
SPAC	Spacious
ST	Studio apartment (no bedroom)
VUS	Views
W/D	Washing machine and dryer
WIC	Walk-in closet

agent to do the looking for you. He or she will make appointments to show you the apartments and you then meet the agent at the property on the agreed date and at the agreed time. You do not pay the agent until you have chosen an apartment and the lease is signed.

Apartment Sharing

Because housing in New York is so expensive, many people find it is more economically sound to have one, or several, roommates. Indeed, one stereotype of Manhattan living is five people crammed into an apartment the size of a walk-in closet. While this may be a bit of an exaggeration, it is not actually that far from the truth.

The best way to find a roommate, whether for a space in which you are currently living or for a new apartment to share, is definitely word of mouth. It is safer to live with someone you know, or a friend of a friend, etc, as the other person may feel some sort of obligation to be more trustworthy if there is a mutual association (although, unfortunately, this is not always the case).

If you don't know anyone that needs a roommate, you must begin the arduous process of searching the vast city, or even worse, cyberspace, for someone suitable. You may advertise with one of the many New York papers, such as the *Village Voice*, the *New York Press*, *The New York Times*, or the *New York Daily News*, to name but a few. These papers all have sizeable classified sections, in print and online. Again, Craig's List (www.craigslist.org) is an excellent source. Once on the site, you can search by city, for jobs, apartments, shared living, and even personals.

Subsidised Housing

The biggest landlord in New York City is the City itself, and the City, State, and federal governments provide subsidised housing for low-income individuals and families, known as 'Section 8' – a federally-funded subsidy. The Public Housing Authority in New York applies to the US Department of Housing and Urban Development for Section 8 funds, which are then passed along to eligible families. Those given particular consideration are homeless families, victims of domestic violence, and individuals participating in witness protection programmes.

Real Estate Agents

Real estate agents serve as the liaison between landlords and potential tenants. They can provide an invaluable service in helping you find the perfect apartment. However there are some con-artists about. It's not unusual to go check out an apartment and find it's very different from how it was described in the ad: for example, a 'spacious two bedroom' may in fact be a room slightly bigger than a closet with a half-wall thrown up in the middle. If something sounds like it is too good to be true, it probably is, so keep looking and don't settle for something you are not comfortable with.

Real estate agents are easy to find online, in the phone book, or by simply walking down the street and seeing their signs posted on properties for sale or rent. The best way to find an agent is through a friend or business associate – then you will get an idea of who you are dealing with. Real estate agents must be licensed by the New York State Department of State Division of Licensing Services. When you find someone, you should contact the department to make sure they are listed and in good standing. You can check the listing of registrants online at www.dos.state.ny.us, or call 518 474 4429. In many cases, you will have to pay the real estate agent a fee equal to one month's rent. When a real estate agent advertises a 'no fee' apartment, that means the landlord has already paid the realtor. However, sometimes the landlord will work that fee into the rent, so be aware of exactly what you're paying for, and how much.

There are literally hundreds of real estate agents in New York City, but the table should help you get started.

Vacating Your Apartment
If you want to leave the premises, the common practice is to provide 30 days' written notice.

The Lease

A residential lease agreement is like any other contract between two parties: it sets out the obligations of the landlord and the tenant. The lease will give the specific address and apartment number of the property, as well as the rent amount and when it should be paid, usually monthly. It will also state the length of the lease, and whether you may renew it at the end of the term. The tenant(s) name(s) will be listed on the lease, along with a provision that no one else may reside in the apartment. Landlords do not want people who are not legally bound to them living in their properties, even if they are contributing to the rent.

The lease will also list any additional costs you are responsible for, such as utilities, and what you are allowed to do in terms of improving the premises. For example, many people living in small apartments or studios, particularly in Manhattan, erect walls to create separate rooms – this is usually illegal.

Write It Up!
If a dispute arises due to you subletting to another, the court will look to the written document, and not any arrangement made verbally between you and your landlord – so get it on paper.

Real Estate Agents

Name	Areas Covered	Phone	Web
A. J. Clarke Real Estate	New York City	212 541 5522	www.ajclarkenyc.com
Benjamin James	Manhattan	212 645 4477	www.benjaminjames.com
Century 21 Kevin B. Brown	Worldwide	212 872 2238	www.c21nyc.com
Chapin Group	Manhattan	212 751 1001	www.chapingroup.com
Coldwell Banker Hunt Kennedy & Garfield	Brooklyn	718 622 7600	www.garfieldrealtynyc.com
Cooper Square Realty Sales & Leasing	Manhattan	212 372 7335	www.abnyc.com
Douglas Elliman	Worldwide	212 891 7277	www.elliman.com
E&G Realty Group	Manhattan	646 435 0544	www.eandrealtygroup.com
Hecht Group	Manhattan	212 717 8484	www.Hechtgroup.com
Mary Jane Pastor Realty	Bronx	914 368 2006	www.maryjanepastor.com
MLBKaye International Realty	Manhattan	212 259 0400	www.mlbkayerealty.com
Neuhaus Realty	Staten Island	718 979 3400	www.neuhausrealestate.com
Raz Realty	Manhattan	212 865 2366	www.razrealty.com
Remax Realty Solution	Manhattan	718 884 3065	www.rrsny.com
Remax South Shore Realty	New York State	718 949 4848	www.remaxss.net
S. Goodstein Realty Commercial	Worldwide	212 750 5550	www.goodstein-realestate.com
Weichert Realtors-FH Realty	Queens	718 544 4000	www.weichert.com

Your lease will likely be a 'boiler-plate' contract, that is, a form lease with standard provisions according to New York law. They are, therefore, often 'pro-landlord'. Whether you have to adhere strictly to every provision depends upon your individual circumstances. For example, your lease may state that you cannot sublet the apartment to another party, but your landlord may tell you it is ok for you do so – although you need to get this in writing. Another common example is a clause stating that pets are not allowed. This is standard in many leases, but many New Yorkers have pets and it is overlooked as long as they do not menace other tenants or damage the premises.

Tenant Rights

Some of your rights as a tenant will also be listed, but not all of them. As stated above, the leases are often written in favour of the landlord, but that is not the whole story. Courts treat leases as contracts, rather than as a property conveyance, such as a deed or mortgage. Therefore there are implied covenants in the lease that will serve as protection for a tenant bringing a case in Housing Court. These include your right to live in peace in your apartment, and to basic amenities, such as heat and hot water. The landlord must keep common areas such as hallways and stairwells safe and maintained, as well as repair any dangerous conditions within the apartment. Your lease may also read as though the landlord can easily evict you, when in fact it is not so easy to get rid of a tenant – it must be adjudicated in court like any other case.

Signing Your Name

You must sign and initial your lease in the pertinent places, just as you would with any contract. You then give the lease to the landlord (or the real estate agent acting on the landlord's behalf), along with your security deposit (usually first and last month's rent). The landlord will sign and give you a copy, hand you the keys, and you are ready to move in.

Main Accommodation Options

Whether you are renting or buying a home, New York City offers a host of options. The price range is enormous, ranging from a rent of $1,000 a month to a purchase price of several million. And although the size and condition of a place does affect the cost, the most determinative factor is location. Ask any provincial New Yorker where the centre of the universe is, and they will undoubtedly say 'The City', as if it were the most ridiculous question in the world. To New Yorkers, 'The City' means Manhattan and the price of nearly every property is based on either its location in, or its *proximity* to, Manhattan. It is no coincidence that Brooklyn Heights, for example, is one of the costliest neighbourhoods in Brooklyn: it is one subway stop away from the Financial District of, you guessed it, Manhattan. The average price to rent an apartment in Manhattan is over $2,000 a month: the average purchase price of an apartment is over one million dollars.

The size of accommodations in New York, particularly Manhattan, can seem, at first, quite small, depending upon your frame of reference. They range from the tiny one-room apartment barely bigger than a closet, to the enormous loft of over 2,000 square feet. A respectable size by city standards is around 600-800 square feet. The issue then becomes how many people will be living in it!

The list of typical accommodations you will find in New York includes the studio, which is a living space typically smaller than a regular apartment (although some can be quite large by New York standards). A studio does not have a separate bedroom, but will have a tiny kitchen and a bathroom. Typically this type of apartment is less expensive, although, depending upon the neighbourhood and the size, it can still be quite pricey.

Then there is the standard apartment, which is, well, standard. It includes a living room, kitchen, bathroom and from one to several bedrooms. (The price goes up significantly with each bedroom).

Thinking of Buying?
It's all about location, so don't make a mistake. Check out the guides to each area in this chapter (starting on p.106), and also in Exploring (starting on p.184).

The loft apartment, once the bohemian, anti-establishment 'place to crash' for starving artists, is now one of the most fashionable types of accommodation in New York today. Unlike the cramped space of a studio, a loft is a large, open area, with a second-floor landing that can be used for storage or as a bedroom (as distinguished from a duplex apartment, which has two full floors). These apartments are usually very costly – expect a monthly rent of several thousand dollars, again depending on the size and neighbourhood.

The Perks

High rents sometimes come with perks as well. While you can by no means assume that you will have these amenities, you may be lucky enough to find a place with a doorman and laundry facilities, perhaps even a fitness centre. A doorman provides security for the building by screening guests, as well as collecting packages for tenants. The building may also have a laundry room to be shared by all tenants, or if you are really fortunate, a washer and dryer inside the apartment. These mean you can wash your clothes in your own place, on your own time – no dragging heavy bags back and forth to the launderette.

Other Rental Costs

When assessing how much you can spend on rent each month, bear in mind some other incidentals that can really add up. These include utilities such as electricity, mobile and landline telephones, cable television and internet services (some landlords include heat and hot water in the rent). While you will not have to put down a deposit on the utilities unless you have poor credit, you will have to put a security deposit down on the apartment itself (usually first and last month's rent). In addition, if you hire a real estate agent to help you find a place, you will most likely have to pay their fee (usually a month's rent). In some cases, however, the fee will be paid by the landlord.

Buying Property

In general, buying property is viewed as a wiser move than renting: home ownership is still very much a part of the 'American Dream'. If you buy, you will be making payments toward something you will eventually 'own', rather than 'throwing money away' on rent. And even before your property is paid off, you will be able to borrow against the equity in the property to pay for your child's education, start your own business, or buy a second piece of property.

The real estate market in New York City is both prohibitively expensive *and* a sound investment. Even though there are millions of people in New York who cannot afford to buy, there are many who can. If you can manage to buy an apartment or house, you will be able to sell it or rent at least part of it out, making it an incredible investment for your future.

Of course, buying isn't the right decision for everyone. Maybe you are not ready to commit to a particular home or city, or perhaps you cannot afford it. It is a personal decision and depends on your personal finances and desired lifestyle.

Currently, the housing market in the US is beginning to recover from a bit of a slump. It is still, however, a buyer's market, especially now that interest rates on mortgages are beginning to come down.

Buying Restrictions

In many areas of the US it is common for people to buy a piece of property and build a house to their specifications. In New York City, however, it is pretty rare to find a vacant lot, let alone one that is zoned for a single home. Not only is New York City the most densely populated in the US, but many areas are zoned for apartment buildings, condos, and businesses – you cannot just buy a vacant lot in Midtown Manhattan and build a single family home on it. Your best bet would be to buy a pre-existing home and, if you can afford it, knock it down and build what you want.

There are no restrictions on where you can buy property in New York City. If it's for sale and you can afford it, you can buy it.

Non-citizen Restrictions

Non-citizens are free to buy property in the United States. However, they may be subject to additional requirements when applying for a mortgage – it depends on the lender. For example, some lenders require non-citizens to show that the house they are buying in the US will be their primary residence, others require that they have a social security card or a permanent resident alien (Green) card. Still other lenders may require that the non-citizen put down an extra down payment on the property, plus have permission to work in the US for a lengthy amount of time. Therefore, while it is advisable for all potential homeowners to shop around before choosing a lender, it is especially important for non-citizens to do so.

Freehold and Leasehold Interests

In the United States, you can obtain a freehold or leasehold interest in property. Freehold property is that which you owe 'in fee', which means absolute ownership: it includes commercial or residential property. A leasehold interest is a tenancy for a pre-determined period of time. Many businesses acquire a leasehold interest for many decades.

The Process

Once you have decided to buy a house, it is highly recommended that you become very familiar with the housing market in the city: you want to know what you can get and for how much. This is the time to decide whether or not to use a real estate agent. If you want to forego the agent, you should start by looking on websites and in

Time It Right

The resale value of the property all depends upon the market when you sell. Although in New York City you are not likely to get less money than you spent on the apartment, it is best to sell when the prices are generally on an upswing so that you can get the biggest return on your investment.

newspapers for FSBO, or 'for sale by owner' notices. For more information, a helpful website is www.forsalebyowner.com.

If you do want to engage an agent, you should shop around for someone you feel comfortable with, who has listings in your price range and who will take the time to make sure you get what you want.

Purchase Agreement

Once the owner has agreed to sell to you, you will then sign a purchase agreement. This is a contract setting out your intention to buy and the seller's to sell. This agreement, however, does not give you any legal rights to the property: your rights as an owner do not vest until the *title closing*. The closing is a meeting between the parties, and their attorneys, to finalise the sale. The seller will pay off any mortgage (s)he is carrying on the home, and the buyer will pay for the house, using their down payment and funds loaned to them by the mortgage holder. The seller will then deliver the deed to the buyer, and any necessary documents will be signed. You will be expected to bring proof of your identification, and, if you are not a citizen, proof of your legal presence in the US.

Remember the Rules
Some lenders require non-citizens to live in the property. If you are planning to rent out the property and live elsewhere, be aware of your lender's requirements.

Where's Hot Right Now?

There are many popular areas in New York City, again, almost anywhere in Manhattan is desirable. Of course, some areas are constantly changing: today's run-down, dangerous, or industrial area may be tomorrow's renovated, up-and-coming hip 'hood. For example, a few years ago, Williamsburg, Brooklyn was not considered a desirable place to live. It was a dilapidated, seedy-looking area, and not the safest place to be after dark. But things changed, and it has now become a thriving residential area, with renovated loft apartments and a hopping nightlife (and, of course, rising prices). The key is to find out which areas are on the rise and buy early, before prices skyrocket. Currently, some of the most popular areas to live in Manhattan include Soho, Tribeca and Greenwich Village.

Title Insurance

Also present at the closing will be a representative of the title insurance company. Title companies provide title insurance to buyers to ensure that there are no problems with the property that prevent its legal sale. Deeds of ownership carry with them certain rights for buyers: for example, you have the right to buy a home that is free of tax liens. The title company will perform searches to make sure there are no bankruptcies or any other liens associated with the property. It will also make sure that the seller really is the legal owner of the property and therefore has the right to sell it, and that the property does not violate any City codes. In addition, the title company will perform a Patriot Search: after September 11, 2001, title companies became obligated to make sure no one involved in the transaction is or has been involved in any terrorist activities or has received funds in connection with terrorism. The buyer pays all closing costs.

Buying to Rent

Many people buy property as an investment: they may buy a two family house, rent one apartment to tenants and live in the other. This can be a very wise investment, as the rent paid by the tenants may cover your mortgage and perhaps some of the maintenance fee, depending on how much you can reasonably charge for the apartment.

New York City has stringent rules that landlords must adhere to. The City takes steps to ensure the safety of its residents, and this includes making sure that buildings comply with health and fire codes. If you buy a building with several apartments, you will have to get certain permits from the City. For example, you must get a Certificate of Occupancy from the New York City Department of Buildings, which sets out how many

99

people are occupying the building. In addition, if you want to add an apartment, you must obtain a building permit and amend the Certificate of Occupancy to reflect the change in the number of residents. Please note that even if you want to add another bathroom for your own use, you must obtain a building permit. For more information call the Department of Buildings at 718 520 3402.

The downside to renting property is the aggravation you may encounter in your role as landlord. You are responsible for fixing the plumbing, the windows and any number of other problems in the dwelling, as well as dealing with late rent payments (or none at all), and a whole host of other problems.

Housing Market

The housing market will determine whether you should make an offer as soon as you find a property you like. If it is a buyer's market, which means prices are down and there are a lot of properties available, you may be able to negotiate to see how low the owner is willing to go. On the other hand, if it is a seller's market, there will be fewer properties on the market and they will be more expensive. Then you may find yourself in a bidding war with other potential buyers and you'll have less negotiating power.

Selling

How you go about selling your property is completely up to you. You can sell it privately, by advertising in newspapers or on the internet, or you can engage a real estate agent – it all depends upon your needs. The first thing to do, either way, is to have your property appraised. An appraiser will survey your land and the house and, taking the location, size, and condition of the house into consideration, make a determination as to its value. This will help you decide your asking price. (Depending on the market, you may have to lower the price in order to sell, so it is always better to put it on the market for more than you expect to get.)

Once your house is on the market, you will have to make it available for showings to potential buyers. This means keeping your house in tip-top shape, and perfectly neat: no one wants to buy a messy house with too much furniture. You want the potential buyers to be able to picture the home with their own personal touch, and that is hard to do if it is too cluttered. If you have an agent, they will find potential buyers and make arrangements to show them the house. (You may have to give the agent the key so they can show it when you're not home, so you should keep valuable jewellery and cash out of sight.) Please note that if you do hire an agent, their commission will be 5-6% of your sales prices, which can add up to quite a lot of money.

Once you find a buyer, you will sign the contract for sale, and then wait for them to get the proper financing. At the closing you will get your money and turn over the deed to the new owners. At this time you will also have to repay any mortgage you still have for the property so that the new owners start fresh, with their own mortgage. This is known as selling property 'free of encumbrances', and it is every buyer's right to get property free of debt.

Capital Gains Tax

Please note that when you sell the property, you will most likely have to pay capital gains tax. Capital gain is the profit you have gained from selling the property at higher value than you originally paid for it. Capital gain is taxed at a lower rate than other types of income. Currently, if you sell the property more than a year after you bought it, you will have to pay 15% of your capital gain; if you sell one year or less after you bought it, you will be taxed at your normal tax rate. There are certain exemptions you can claim to avoid paying capital gains. For example, if you have realised capital losses in the same year, your losses may cancel out the gains.

Mortgages

Real estate professionals suggest that before seeking a mortgage, you check your credit and get pre-approved or pre-qualified to see firstly, if you can get a loan, and then how much you can get one for. Your credit score will range from 200 to 850, and the higher it is, the better. Credit agencies check whether you pay your bills on time, whether you are heavily in credit card debt, and whether you have been responsible with your credit over time. If your credit is not good enough, you will either not qualify for a mortgage, or more likely, you will get a mortgage with a high interest rate. Your mortgage payments will be hundreds of dollars more a month and you may not be able to afford the house you want. Experts recommend that you check your credit six months before you want to buy, so you have time to improve your credit before applying for the loan. This includes not opening up any more credit cards. Once a lender has assessed your credit, you will be given a letter of commitment stating the loan amount you have been pre-approved for. You can then bring this letter to a real estate agent so that they won't waste their time, or yours, taking you to see properties you cannot afford.

Down Payment

After you have ascertained the amount you qualify for, and found the property you want to buy, the next step is to figure out the amount of the down payment. The recommended amount is 20%: if you can put down this much you will be able to avoid private mortgage insurance. PMI protects the lender if you default, and also increases your monthly payment without adding to the equity of your home. While some lenders allow certain buyers to buy with no money down, please keep in mind that the less you put down in the beginning, the higher your mortgage payments will be each month. You must decide whether you want to spend that nest egg on a down payment or keep it in the bank and pay more in monthly bills.

Applying For a Mortgage

More and more banks are offering mortgages; which one you chose depends upon your particular needs. As with every other step in buying a home, it is advisable to shop around for the people or institution you feel comfortable with. Once you have shopped around and found a lender you feel comfortable with, you can then apply for your mortgage. You will be required to supply the following information for your loan application: pay stubs for the past two to three months, W2 forms for the past two years, information on long-term debts, recent bank statements, proof of any additional income, and the address and description of the property. In addition, mortgage lenders will also check whether you have declared bankruptcy, if there are any tax liens against your property, and your recent bank account activity.

Typically, most mortgages have had repayment terms of 30 years. Some people however chose to have 15 year mortgages. There is an Early Redemption Penalty for paying the entire amount off early – the amount depends upon the terms of your mortgage.

Mortgage Providers

Below is the contact information for several mortgage providers in New York City. Please note that most banks provide mortgage services, not only for the original mortgage, but for refinancing as well. Many people decide to use their own bank for their mortgages. In addition, many people are getting mortgages through online companies.

Mortgage Providers

Apple Mortgage Corp.	212 221 6666	www.applemortgage.com
NY Finance.com	212 628 9300	www.nyfinance.com
The Manhattan Mortgage Company	888 593 4343	www.manhattanmortgage.com

10

Other Purchasing Costs

In addition to your down payment and monthly mortgage, there are other expenses associated with home ownership. New York leads the country in title closing costs: the average is more than $3,000, and it is the buyer's responsibility. In addition, you will have to pay taxes on the mortgage itself, at a rate of 1.75% in New York. And finally, if you buy an apartment in New York City, you will have to pay a monthly maintenance charge in addition to your mortgage payments: these costs run, on average, between $600 and $1,000 a month.

Freehold & Leasehold

In the United States, freehold is absolute ownership of a piece of real property. Leasehold interest is a tenancy for a pre-determined period of time. In other words, it means simply 'to rent'. A corporation can obtain a leasehold interest in a building for a period of 20, 50, even 100 years, but they do not own the building.

Real Estate Law

Real estate law, like most areas of law in New York City, is quite complicated. For example, if you buy a 'co-op' instead of a regular apartment, there are a whole different set of rules. Co-ops are apartments owned by a non-profit corporation, which then grants the tenants occupancy rights. You would be purchasing shares in this corporation, to which you will pay real estate taxes, building maintenance and other overhead expenses. The benefit of this is that these expenses are tax-deductible. The building is governed by a co-op board, which must approve, not only new tenants before they can buy into the co-op, but also certain home improvements tenants wish to make. That said, the basic legal procedures are those mentioned above: procuring a mortgage, signing the purchase contract, and attending the closing.

Invite Your Lawyer

It is always advisable to have a real estate lawyer present at the closing. It is not required, but it gives you extra protection to have legal counsel to make sure the title company has performed all necessary searches (a patriot search, or searches for liens against the property, for example).

Inheritance

It is always advisable to have a will once you have acquired property, and buying a house is no different. Remember, though, that you do not have any ownership rights in the land until after the closing. In addition, once you have purchased the property, if you should die 'intestate', or without a will, New York intestacy laws will dictate that your spouse and/or you children will inherit all of your property. Therefore, while it is always better to have a will, whether you have one or not, your immediate family will inherit the house.

*MOTO*RAZR *maxx V6*

Move faster with 3.5G HSDPA high speed mobile broadband, external touch music keys and a 2 mega-pixel camera with flash. **The new MOTORAZR maxx V6. Cutting-edge speed for cutting-edge style.**

hellomoto.com

Residential Areas
Other options **Exploring** p.178

Other options **Exploring** p.178

Although Manhattan is covered in the most detail in the following section, remember that other boroughs have some great affordable neighbourhoods. Certain things are inevitable when you live in New York: parking spots are hard to find, housing prices are astronomical, and if you do find a bargain, gentrification will inevitably seep into your neighbourhood and inflate the prices of everything.

That said, every service you can imagine, from food and banks to dry cleaners and fitness centers, will be easily accessible, whatever neighbourhood you live in.

Each of the outer boroughs has its own distinctive characteristics, landmark, history and ethnic communities - you can often tell where someone lives just by their accent. When looking for a home in New York, don't forget to browse around the other boroughs... the extensive network of public transport options make commuting from home to work a piece of cake, no matter where you live. The following section covers the main residential areas.

© Explorer Group Ltd. 2007

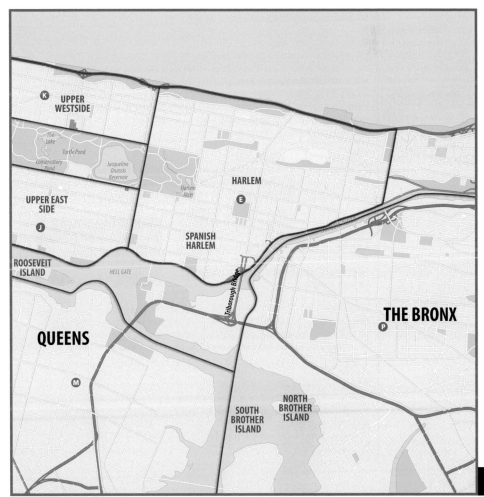

Maps 12 & 13 ◀

Battery Park City & Financial District

Located at the southern tip of Manhattan is arguably the centre of the financial world: Wall Street (p.218). Battery Park City (p.106), on the western tip of lower Manhattan, was originally built to be a convenient walk for the stockbrokers and bankers working in the area. It is known for its incredible views of the Hudson and East Rivers, as well as the Statue of Liberty (p.217). It has grown exponentially in recent years, and at 92 acres, has become a city unto itself. This area is now a wonderful family community with its own schools, shopping, restaurants and parks.

Battery Park City is literally next door to the World Trade Center site and one of the neighbourhoods hardest hit by the attacks of September 11, 2001. But the area has rebounded miraculously, and there is more community development going on there than ever before.

Best Points

The neighbourhood is quiet, good for families, with breathtaking views of the water. It is a very 'green' area of the city, with a lot of parks and places to sunbathe. It is also very convenient if you work in Tribeca or the Financial District.

Accommodation

Most of the living accommodations in Battery Park are housed in high-rise buildings, and the majority of apartments are one or two bedrooms (although you can certainly find both studios and larger apartments as well).

Shopping & Amenities

Worst Points ◀

This area is close to Ground Zero – therefore for the next several years there will be a lot of ongoing construction. It's also a tourist magnet as people from around the world come to pay their respects.

Like most places in Manhattan, if you live in Battery Park City everything is at your fingertips. It is home to a softball field, an enormous movie theatre, clothes shopping and a selection of restaurants featuring every type of food. But it is also a fairly quiet area by city standards – this is not a neighbourhood in which you'll have drunken club-goers howling outside your window at 05:00. Nearby is South Street Seaport (on the east side), which is home to a shopping mall and several waterfront bars that are packed with the after-work crowd every evening.

Entertainment & Leisure

It is already home to the Museum of Jewish Heritage and the Skyscraper Museum, and plans are under way to establish the Women's Museum and the World Hunger Center, as well as a branch of the New York Public Library. This is not the place to move if you are looking for a 24 hour party. While there are many restaurants and bars, it is mainly an after-work scene. Late at night it is a pretty desolate area. Also, by Manhattan standards, it is a bit out of the way from more populated areas, such as Greenwich Village or Midtown, which are more centrally located.

More Info

For more information about the neighbourhood, log on to www.batteryparkcity.org.

Education

There are several schools that serve Battery Park, including Public School 89 (the first to be built into the base of a residential building) and Stuyvesant High School (www.stuy.edu), which is regarded as one of the best high schools in the state.

Health

Battery Park City is within walking distance from New York Downtown Hospital (212 312 5000), which is the only hospital in lower Manhattan. It is located on 170 William Street. You can find out more information about the facility, as well as a list of neighbourhood doctors, at www.downtownhospital.com. In addition, a walk-in medical clinic, the Downtown Family Care Center, is located at 150 Essex Street (212 801 1730).

Traffic & Public Transport

Only the truly brave (or those who love being snarled up in traffic congestion) would drive around in this area on a daily basis. Fortunately, Battery Park City is easily accessible from the A, C, J, M, Z, 2, 3, 4 and 5 subways.

Safety & Annoyances

It's proximity to the World Trade Center site means it may be affected by new developments there. The area is always overrun with tourists, especially at weekends and over national holidays.

Maps 6 & 8

Chelsea & the Meatpacking District

The neighbourhood of Chelsea has a unique flavour. Sitting on the west side of Manhattan, it's boundaries are 15th Street to the south and 39th Street to the north, and it is within walking distance to Midtown West, the West Village and the Meatpacking District. Chelsea has been the heart of the gay community in New York City for many years, and has many community services addressing the specific concerns of gays and lesbians, including advocacy services and anti-violence groups. In addition, there are many gay bars and galleries featuring the works of gay artists.

Chelsea is within walking distance to another great neighbourhood: the Meatpacking District. Not long ago, this area was a wasteland of meatpacking plants and industrial buildings. But Manhattan is constantly re-inventing itself, and this area is no different: it has been completely renovated and is now home to several high-end shops, expensive clubs, and the luxurious Gansevoort Hotel. The MPD is now a true 24 hour Manhattan neighbourhood, and has Chelsea as its neighbour.

Best Points

It's a cultural capital where everyone is welcome. There's great shopping and plenty of recreational activities, as well as the city's hottest hotspots in the MPD.

Worst Points

There's not much to say about Chelsea's bad points, since there aren't any. Unless you're a family, in which case you might find it hard to integrate into this mainly single society.

Accommodation

Historically populated by townhouses and pre-war co-ops, Chelsea is now also home to newly built luxury apartments. You can expect to pay upwards of $2,500 for a studio, and upwards of $3,500 for a three-bedroom apartment. Have you got a cool million bucks just hanging around in your bank account? You'll need it (and then some) if you want to buy a place here. Once you get past 30th Street, prices do tend to be cheaper, but only by a bit.

Shopping & Amenities

Chelsea is home to the famous Chelsea Market (www.chelseamarket.com), located on Ninth Avenue between 15th and 16th Streets. This indoor marketplace is filled with gourmet shops selling assorted culinary delights. The brownies from Fat Witch Bakery (888 419 4824), situated inside the market, could be the most compelling reason to move into the neighbourhood.

Entertainment & Leisure

Chelsea has around 200 art galleries, some of which are located within Chelsea Market. The market also has a dance studio where tango lessons are given every Saturday. Chelsea Piers is a destination point for people from all five boroughs and beyond. Its enormous complex on the Hudson River offers sports of all kinds, from golf and basketball to rollerskating and rock climbing. It also has a fitness centre and a luxury spa (www.chelseapiers.com).

The Gansevoort Hotel is a slice of cool and a great place to head for cocktails – their in-house Japanese restaurant, Ono, is a magnet for beautiful people. The Gansevoort is also near the High Line, a now-defunct, elevated railway that was scheduled for demolition before a group of interested people started lobbying to have it turned into a community park (www.thehighline.org).

Health

St Vincent's Hospital, located right on the border of Chelsea and the West Village, has been providing excellent care to the residents of downtown Manhattan for many years. For further information about the hospital, or to find a doctor in the area, call 212 604 7000, or check out their website (www.svcmc.org).

Education

Chelsea is not a hugely popular area for families, so you won't find many schools there. Chelsea school (PS 33) is a popular option (212 244 6426), but there are more choices in neighbouring areas.

Traffic & Public Transport

The best way to get around this colourful area is on foot. Chelsea is a fascinating, varied neighbourhood with great architecture and a tangible character. Almost everything you need is just a short walk away. Trains to Chelsea include: A, C, E, 1, 2, 3, B, D, F, N, Q, R, V and W.

Safety & Annoyances

Although very rare, Chelsea has been the scene of a few hate crimes aimed at the gay community. So while you will certainly feel safe and free to be yourself most of the time here, keep your common sense handy to avoid getting into any danger.

Maps 7& 9

Flatiron District & Gramercy Park

One of New York's historically exclusive neighbourhoods, Gramercy Park is a slice of heaven to those who can afford it. Bordered at the south by 14th Street and at the north end by 30th, this eastside oasis surrounds a private park between 20th and 21st Streets. Only those who live in the 40 or so buildings that face the park are allowed entry.

The Flatiron District is a very small area neighbouring Gramercy, and is named for the famous triangular-shaped building at 23rd Street where Fifth Avenue intersects Broadway. It is mainly a commercial area, and is sometimes called the toy district thanks to the large number of toy manufacturers there. It is also sometimes referred to as Midtown South. The official Flatiron borders are 14th and 30th Streets, between Sixth Avenue and Park Avenue.

Best Points

Gramercy Park is quiet, safe and good for families. Flatiron is less expensive than SoHo and TriBeca, even though you can still get the same kind of bright, airy loft-type accommodation there.

Accommodation

Gramercy Park is a mixture of small and medium apartments, co-ops and brownstones, but good luck finding a vacant place – people tend to stick around here once they manage to get in. It's also very expensive to rent or buy property here. Some new residential accommodation is underway, although it is not clear when this will be completed.

Accommodation in the Flatiron District includes some lovely spacious, well-lit lofts, which are thankfully not as expensive as the ones you might find in SoHo or TriBeca. More recently, several high-rise apartment buildings have gone up in the area – these tend to be home to young professionals and medical students.

Worst Points

With only one train (the 6 train) serving the area, it can be hard to get to Gramercy Park. There's not much nightlife to speak of either. Flatiron is very commercial, and therefore residential amenities are thin on the ground.

Shopping & Amenities

There's plenty of shopping to be done in Gramercy Park, with an eclectic mix of luxurious food stores, art shops and boutiques. Flatiron is not set up to be a residential area, therefore residents will have to walk a bit to get food and other household items. In addition, there are no schools in Flatiron – children usually attend schools in neighbouring Gramercy. This is also true of hospitals and medical care.

Entertainment & Leisure

The park in Gramercy Park is an example of exclusivity: only residents of the buildings facing the park are allowed to have a key, and they have to pay $350 per year for the privilege. And don't go thinking you can 'accidentally' lose your key (by selling it off to one of your friends): the fee to replace a lost key is a whopping $1,000. The park is also governed by a very strict set of rules that can make it feel a bit like being back at school: you're forbidden to eat on the grass, jog anywhere but on the gravel path, or, heaven forbid, feed the birds or squirrels.

However, exclusivity and strict rules aside, this is where you'll see residents strolling along with their Burberry-coated dogs, enjoying the fresh air and the scenery of New York's only private park. If you can't afford a place on the park, you could always treat yourself to a night in the Gramercy Park Hotel (p.33) – they have a limited number of keys for guests to use. The Gramercy's rooftop bar is amazing – a few cocktails here, with its 'old New York' quaintness and breathtaking views of the city, and you'll feel like you're on top of the world.

There are plenty of recreational activities in the Gramercy Park area, especially for children and families, including parks, bowling and libraries with daily story readings for kids.

There are great restaurants around Flatiron, but not actually in it. One of note, however, is L'Express, a 24 hour eatery on Park Avenue South at E. 20th Street (212 254 5858). There are also several nightclubs in the area, such as the Cheetah Club (212 206 7770), where you can dance till dawn to the latest club, hip-hop and reggae tunes.

Health

Quality healthcare is not far away in the form of Cabrini Medical Center (www.cabrininy.org), and the Beth Israel Paediatric Association. This children's health centre offers excellent care for your youngsters, and is located in nearby Union Square, (212 844 8300). For more information or to find a doctor, check out their website at www.bethisraelpediatrics.yourmd.com.

Education

There are also several wonderful schools, including the renowned Friends Seminary (www.friendsseminary.org). Since 1786, Friends has combined a rigorous academic curriculum with the Quaker values of peaceful living and helping others.

Traffic & Public Transport

If you're taking the train to Gramercy Park, you'll need to get on the number 6 to 23rd Street. Trains to Flatiron include: R, W, N, and 6.

Safety & Annoyances

Gramercy Park is not easily accessible by train, and it's expensive and exclusive (or so the 'have-nots' who can't afford to live there will tell you). It is very safe though. In Flatiron you need to be a fraction more concerned about personal safety, particularly in the areas bordering the Garment District.

Maps 8, 9 & 11

Greenwich Village & the Lower East Side

Located between 14th and Houston Streets, Greenwich Village and the West Village
are some of the most desirable spots in New York City. The quiet tree-lined blocks
frame the cosy brownstones of the Village and West Village and are just blocks away
from some of the best nightlife in the city. The Village, which has been historically
known as a bohemian refuge for musicians, writers and artists, is now a melting pot.
People from every walk of life work, live and play here, from corporate lawyers to
actors to entrepreneurs. It is also a destination for tourists from all over the country,
and the world.

The East Village is a prime example of the gentrification that New York City is so
famous for. A few short years ago, the East Village was run down, inexpensive, and
fairly neglected by almost everyone except those who lived there. But not anymore:
while it has always been a haven for artists, it is now a trendy spot for professionals
craving the culture of its boutiques and the tiny, yet oh-so trendy, eateries serving
food of every ethnicity.

The Lower East Side is located south of East Houston and is bounded by the East River.
Although its exact boundaries, like so many other Manhattan neighbourhoods, are
constantly changing, the Lower East Side is bordered by Chinatown, Nolita and the East
Village. The Lower East Side used to be considered one of the seedier parts of town,
although it is becoming more popular with the middle class. Historically, the area was
home mainly to Eastern European Jewish immigrants. More recently however, many
artists, writers and professionals of every ethnicity have moved into the area, adding to
the sizeable Latino and Chinese populations.

Best Points
*Culture, architecture,
nightlife, everything! It
is also close to
everything you might
need, such as the
offerings of Downtown
and the restaurants of
Chinatown and Little
Italy, and home to a
rich community of
artists. For now, the
Lower East Side is one
of the few Manhattan
areas where you can
still find a good bargain
on your apartment.*

Worst Points
*Crowding can be a
problem, and the main
streets can turn a little
seedy when the sun
goes down. Parts of
the area are a little
isolated in terms of
public transport.*

Accommodation

Prices have gone up substantially in
all these areas – it's an inevitable side
effect of gentrification. While the East
Village is still cheaper than the West
Village, it is no longer the place
where you can find a great bargain.
And although it is cheaper, it is also
not as upscale as the West Village.
There are some great real estate
bargains to be found on the Lower
East Side, particularly among the
walk-up tenement buildings, co-ops
and conversions. You can buy a two-
bedroom apartment on the Lower
East Side for around $700,000: a hard
offer to beat elsewhere in the city.

Entertainment & Leisure

This neighbourhood literally never
stops. While some other areas of the
city clear out during the summer
months (when anyone who can
afford to leaves for their summer
homes), the streets of the Village are
always crowded. Sixth Avenue, West
4th Street and the famous Bleeker
Street are jam-packed with

restaurants, bars, lounges, comedy clubs, small theatres and tattoo parlours. In fact, with all the places to hang out (with most of them being open until 04:00), and the various street vendors selling jewellery, hats and sunglasses, the Village can at times seem like one big street fair.

The nightlife on the Lower East Side is legendary. Head for Clinton Street or Ludlow Street (between Rivington and Stanton), where you'll find several live music venues, including the Bowery Ballroom (www.boweryballroom.com). This area is also the site of the original McSorley's Old Ale House (p.418), a famous Irish pub established in 1854.

Nightlife aside, there is plenty to keep you busy on the Lower East Side. Residents take part in recreational activities in East River Park, which has baseball fields, walking trails and an amphitheatre. Another popular activity is walking along the footpath of the Williamsburg Bridge.

Health

St. Vincent's Hospital (212 604 7000) is located in the heart of the Village on Seventh Avenue. In addition, there is an evening and weekend walk-in clinic in the East Village, at 540 E. 13th Street, between Avenues A and B (212 238 7129).

The East Village is close to both St. Vincent's Hospital and Cabrini Medical Center, which is located at 227 E. 19th Street (212 222 7464). To find more information about the Center or to get in touch with local doctors, check out the website at www.cabrininy.org. In addition, there is Cabrini East Village Family Medical Practice, located at 97 E. Fourth Street, between First and Second Avenues (212 979 3200).

Hospital and clinics serving the Lower East Side include the Lower East Side Service Center (46 E. Broadway), the Lower East Side Health Center (92 Ludlow Street), and Beth Abraham Hospital (337 Broome Street).

Education

The Village is the location of the number one dream school of most college-bound students in the US: New York University (www.nyu.edu). The enormous campus, which spreads out over several blocks, includes a law school, dental and medical schools, and the famous film school.

There are also several schools for children, including PS 41 and the Greenwich Village School (212 675 2756), which are both considered to be among the finest schools in the city.

Lower East Side Schools include PS 110, located at 285 Delancey Street, for children aged 3 to 12 (212 674 2690), and the Lower East Side Prep School (212 505 6366), also known as High School 515. Many children living on the Lower East Side also attend schools in Greenwich Village, Gramercy Park and Chinatown.

Traffic & Public Transport

The general theme of New York City traffic congestion continues through the villages and the Lower East Side. So leave the car at home and make use of the comprehensive train network. Trains to Greenwich Village include: 1, 9, A, B, C, D, E, F, V, N, R. Trains to the East Village include: 6, F. Trains to the Lower East Side include: B, D, F, V, J, M, Z and 6.

Safety & Annoyances

The gentrification has brought with it a burgeoning night scene, bringing noise to a formerly quiet residential area. Parts of the Lower East Side can still be quite seedy, and it is not considered as safe as some other areas.

Harlem & Spanish Harlem

Harlem, located between 110th and 155th Streets from the East River to the Hudson River, is the centre of African-American culture in New York, and arguably, the country. It is made up of several smaller neighbourhoods, including Hamilton Heights, Manhattanville, Striver's Row and Sugar Hill.

Spanish Harlem is located between 96th and 141st Streets, from the East River to Fifth Avenue. Many of the residents are Puerto Rican, and it has become one of the largest Hispanic communities in New York City. Spanish Harlem, however, is by no means a homogenous area – it is alive with the cultures of immigrants from all over the world. Formerly known as Italian Harlem, the area now has few Italian residents.

Best Points ◀

This area is culturally rich and increasingly diverse. It is also filled with great restaurants, art galleries and museums, and is fairly close to the northern tip of Central Park.

Worst Points ◀

It has a higher crime rate than many other parts of Manhattan. It is also not centrally located, so you'll have a longer commute if you work in lower Manhattan.

Accommodation

For some years now Harlem has been undergoing rigorous gentrification and revitalisation, which has done wonders for crime rates but unfortunately housing prices in this area have tripled in the past few years. The streets of Harlem are home to some of New York's best architecture and classic brownstones. There are several condos and co-ops under construction, and these will possibly be available within 2007. Striver's Row features some upscale (and very expensive) homes, but if you have a good look around north of that, you may get lucky and find a brownstone at a great price (but it will be a fixer-upper). Housing in Spanish Harlem is architecturally much the same as that of Harlem, with slightly lower prices.

Shopping & Amenities

The neighbourhood features some great shopping and services, with plenty of specialist stores carrying items that will remind its multi-cultural residents of home. On West 116th Street there is an enormous open-air market called the Malcolm Shabazz Harlem Market (p.364), a great place to find African artefacts and clothing.

Entertainment & Leisure

There is much to see and do in Harlem. The Studio Museum of Harlem (www.studiomuseum.org) showcases some amazing African-American art, and the Schomberg Center for Research in Black Culture (212 491 2200) has a collection of five million books and documents on black history. Check out some traditional gospel music at a Sunday service in one of Harlem's 400 churches. Like Harlem, Spanish Harlem is also the location of several houses of worship, including Catholic churches, mosques, Greek Orthodox churches and a Russian Orthodox church.

Harlem is also the location of the historical Apollo Theater (www.apollotheater.com), which hosts a televised amateur night. The Hue-man Bookstore and Café (www.huemanbookstore.com) features a huge selection of children's books and hosts book readings and other special events almost every evening. And Sylvia's Soul Food, located at 328 Lenox Avenue (p.379), is a famous tourist stop serving some of the best soul food in New York.

In Spanish Harlem there is a thriving art community, featured at museums such as El Museo del Barrio (www.elmuseo.org), which displays the works of Latin American and Caribbean artists.

Health

Hospitals serving the residents of Harlem include Harlem Hospital at 506 Lenox Avenue (www.harleminternalmedicine.org) and North General Hospital at 1879 Madison Avenue (www.northgeneral.org). The closest hospital for residents for Spanish Harlem is Mount Sinai Hospital, located at 1190 Fifth Avenue. The phone number is 212 241 6500, and the website is www.mountsinai.org.

Education

There are several schools in Harlem, including PS 30, PS 154, All Saint's School (Pre-Kindergarten to the Eighth grade) and the Rice High School (for boys). Harlem is also known for its large number of charter schools. These schools are publicly funded elementary and secondary schools that do not have to follow all of the rules and regulations of other public schools. They instead must adhere to their own charters in order to continue to receive funding. Schools in Spanish Harlem include mostly public schools, including PS 108 and PS 50. However, The Harlem School of the Arts is also located here (www.harlemschoolofthearts.org).

Traffic & Public Transport

Harlem is easily accessible by train. Trains to Harlem include: A, B, C, D, 2 and 3. Trains to Spanish Harlem include: 4, 5, 6.

Safety & Annoyances

Crime rates in parts of Harlem top those in most other areas of Manhattan, although there has been significant improvement in recent years.

Maps 9 & 11

Little Italy & Chinatown

Once one of the largest Italian neighbourhoods on the east coast, Manhattan's Little Italy, located on Mulberry Street between Broome and Canal Streets, has now shrunk to a mere few blocks of Italian restaurants and street vendors. Chinatown has encompassed most of the area, and you will rarely hear Italian spoken in the street or offered in area churches and schools. Still, it is a great place to experience some of the Italian culture, or at least the food.

Bordered by Canal Street to the north, Chambers Street to the south, Broadway to the west and the Manhattan Bridge to the east, Chinatown has grown in leaps and bounds in the past few decades, gradually encroaching upon neighbouring areas such as Little Italy and the Lower East Side.

Best Points

Many restaurant and street vendors keep Little Italy and Chinatown exciting and a great destination point in terms of shopping and dining.

Worst Points

Both are overrun with restaurants, which attracts crowds. Canal Street, in particular, is often difficult to traverse, either by car or on foot.

Accommodation

There is not a lot of new construction in Little Italy, and most of the housing consists of older, tenement-style apartments inhabited by old-timers. In comparison to the rest of Manhattan, the limited housing available in this area has been a bit less expensive than others, but it is really hard to find. People looking for housing have instead been moving to an area a little bit north of Little Italy, or Nolita. This area is fairly reasonable now, but promises to eventually become the next Soho or Tribeca, and prices will surely rise. Upscale shops have moved into the area, and some new high-end apartment buildings are being built, with units costing about $2 million.

Housing in Chinatown remains mostly crowded, tenement-style buildings. There is virtually no new building presently going on in Chinatown and it remains one of the most densely populated areas in New York City. It is also one of the least diverse: the residents are almost exclusively Chinese, and many speak only Chinese.

Shopping & Amenities

Little Italy and Nolita are home to some well-known, upscale shops, whereas walking through Chinatown is like walking through a gigantic open-air market. Hundreds of vendors line Canal Street every day, selling various wares from jewellery and perfumes to clothes and DVDs. In addition, Chinatown is host to 200 Chinese restaurants and fruit, vegetable and fish markets.

Entertainment & Leisure

Some restaurants of note in Little Italy include the famous Umberto's Clam House (www.umbertosclamhouse.com), as well as Da Nico (212 343 1212) and Il Cortile (212 226 6060). And the neighbourhood still celebrates the Feast of San Gennaro for 11 days each September. The entire street closes to vehicular traffic and pedestrians are free to stroll from one food vendor to another, sampling the sausage and peppers, calzones, pastas and tiramisu while listening to live bands and playing games for prizes.

Of course, Chinatown is where to head if you've got a craving for genuine Chinese food. You can't go wrong with Jing Fong (p.380) and Ping's Seafood (p.381).

Health

The hospital most easily accessible to residents is Downtown Hospital (212 312 5000). Hospitals in or near Chinatown include the St. Vincent's Hospital Chinatown Clinic (212 431 5501), located at 25 Elizabeth Street.

Education

Schools near Little Italy include the Little Red School House and Elisabeth Irwin High School, both located at 196 Bleeker Street (the website for both is www.lrei.org). Children in this area often attend schools in Greenwich Village, the East Village or Gramercy Park.

Educational institutions in Chinatown include the Chinatown Martial Arts and Fitness Center (212 566 2200), the YMCA of Greater New York (www.ymcanyc.org), PS 124 (212 966 7237) and Shuang Wen School (212 602 9700), a dual language elementary school.

Traffic & Public Transport

The following trains will get you down to Little Italy and Chinatown: R, N, W, Q, D, B, J, M, Z. The roads are congested, made even worse by the fact that these areas are popular stops on the routes of New York's many open-top bus tours.

Safety & Annoyances

In Chinatown the sheer number of people is bound to annoy, while in Little Italy the high prices might.

Maps 4, 5, 6 & 7

Midtown, Hell's Kitchen & Sutton Place

If you ask someone what streets make up Midtown Manhattan, you will probably get several different answers. Some will say Midtown is from 40th Street to 59th Street (the base of Central Park) between Fifth and Eighth Avenues. Those people would say that Midtown *proper* is flanked by Hell's Kitchen to the west and Sutton Place to the east. Others would say that Midtown is the entirety of the 30s, 40s, and 50s, from river to river. Hell's Kitchen (also known as Clinton or Midtown West), has such a colourful history that it stands out even in New York City. Nowadays the neighbourhood (once infamous for its organised crime, violent gangs and tenements) is more likely to feature artists, actors, and luxury apartments than criminals. It lies from 40th Street to 59th Street, between the Hudson River and Eighth Avenue, and is bordered by Chelsea, the Upper West Side and Midtown.

Midtown East, or Sutton Place, is wedged in between Gramercy Park and the Upper East Side and lies between 42nd and 59th Street, and between Fifth Avenue and the East River. It is known for its 'old New York' charm. More recently, some younger people, usually those who work in Midtown, have moved in, but it is still generally a neighbourhood suited more to older residents than young families. This is partly due to a relatively small number of schools and a greater distance to the subway.

Best Points

Parts of Midtown, particularly Hell's Kitchen, are more affordable than other areas of Manhattan. Plus there are some great restaurants, and a bustling vibe.

Worst Points

Some areas are a little bit shady once the sun goes down, and other areas are just too busy once it comes up.

Accommodation

Central Midtown is a commercial hub, and most of the residential areas lie to the east and the west, in Sutton Place and Hell's Kitchen. Hell's Kitchen has undergone major gentrification in the past several years, and is now considered a desirable area to live. The area used to be known for its cheap rents, but this is changing fast. Since September 11, 2001, there has been a major building boom in this area – zoning laws throughout Manhattan were relaxed to assist recovery and redevelopment after 9/11. New projects, such as the Hearst Tower (56th Street and Eighth Avenue) and the Time Warner Center on Columbus Circle (p.357), both feature luxury apartments at prices to match. Still, there are parts of Hell's Kitchen that are more reasonably priced than other areas of the city, and the further west you go, the less you will spend. With perseverance and a little luck, you may be able to find a studio or one bedroom for under $2,000 per month.

Shopping & Amenities

And if you want to 'shop till you drop', this is the place to do it – the flagship stores of Bergdorf Goodman (p.358), Bloomingdales (p.359), Macy's (p.361), and Tiffany's (p.336) are in Midtown, in addition to Saks Fifth Avenue (p.362) and the world-famous Diamond District on 47th Street.

Entertainment & Leisure

Midtown is a commercial area, with lot sof hotels and some of the most famous tourist attractions, including the Empire State Building (p.216), St. Patrick's Cathedral (p.21), and Times Square (p.217). There is a burgeoning 'Koreatown', mainly around West 32nd Street, featuring some great Korean restaurants, supermarkets and Karaoke bars.

In Hell's Kitchen there are several parks, art galleries, and the recently completed Pier 84, which has a boat house, a classroom, a dog run, a garden, and a playground for children. Hell's Kitchenis also home to the famous Restaurant Row, on West 46th Street between Eighth and Ninth Avenues. Here you can sample food from around the world: New York's usual suspects are there, such as Italian, Chinese, American and French, but you can also try food inspired by the cuisine of Afghanistan, Argentina, Turkey, Ethiopia and Vietnam. Ninth Avenue is also known for its affordable and diverse culinary offerings.

In Sutton Place you can find any sort of entertainment without straying far from the neighbourhood. There are two public parks, one at 57th Street and another at 53rd. Sutton Place also boasts a thriving nightlife for the college crowd.

Health

More Info
For a great listings website featuring a range of services and hotspots in Hell's Kitchen, check out www.hellskitchen.bz.

There is no shortage of medical care in this area: the neighbourhood is served by St. Vincent's Midtown Hospital (www.stvincentsmidtown.org) and St. Luke's Roosevelt Hospital (www.slred.org). There are numerous hospitals on or near Sutton Place, including the American Hospital of Paris (212 605 0380), the Hospital for Special Surgery (212 988 6732), the Children's Hospital of New York (212 746 5437), and New York Presbyterian (www.nyp.org).

Education

Hell's Kitchen has some famous schools, including the famous John Jay College of Criminal Justice (www.jjay.cuny.edu). There are several specialist high schools, including the Professional Performing Arts High School (www.ppasinfo.org) and the High School for Environmental Studies (http://envirostudies.org). Schools on Sutton Place include the Garden House School, a pre-school (www.gardenhouseschool.org), and the Montessori School of New York (www.mmsny.org), which is a school for children from pre-school to the eighth grade. Many children in this neighbourhood travel to other areas of the city to attend private schools.

Traffic & Public Transport

Hell's Kitchen is a transportation hub. In addition to the numerous subways that go to this area, you can catch a bus to countless destinations at the enormous Port Authority, located between 40th and 42nd Streets, and between Eighth and Ninth Avenues. Trains to Hell's Kitchen include: A, C, E (to its eastern border) and the 2, 3, 7, 9, N, Q, R, S, and W (to Times Square). Trains to Sutton Place are not so comprehensive, but you can take the 6, the E or the V.

Safety & Annoyances

During the day the Midtown area is busy, busy, busy, but after dark parts of it become quite desolate and you may feel a little insecure walking around on your own. Parts of Hell's Kitchen can be a bit seedy too, so use your common sense when venturing out alone at night. All of the Midtown area can get retty crowded during the daytime, especially during holidays.

Maps 10 & 11 ◀

Tribeca & Soho

Slightly north and west of Battery Park City are two of the hottest neighbourhoods in Manhattan. 'Tribeca', which stands for the 'Triangle Below Canal Street', and 'Soho', which stands for 'South of Houston Street', are both famous for their gothic architecture, cobble-stoned streets, fabulous shopping, and great restaurants.

Best Points ◀
Access to shopping and all the artistic culture and nightlife that New York City is famous for.

Worst Points ◀
These neighbourhoods are extremely expensive and street parking is extremely difficult to find, as on many of the streets parking is not allowed before 18:00. In addition, because of Soho's great shopping, on the weekends the crowds can be extremely annoying.

More Info ◀
For more information on living in Tribeca, check out www.tribeca.org, and for more information on Soho, check out www.sohonyc.com.

Accommodation

Tribeca and Soho have become famous for the enormous lofts you can rent there. Both neighbourhoods have unfortunately become extremely expensive over the past several years, with those lofts going for several thousand dollars a month and upwards.

Shopping & Amenities

Shopping in Soho is literally a potpourri of delights: just walking up and down Broadway between Canal and Houston Streets you will find anything your heart desires, from MAC to Banana Republic to Armani Exchange, as well as a host of street vendors and boutiques where you will find that unique dress or pair of shoes.

Entertainment & Leisure

Tribeca is known more for its quiet streets and amazing restaurants, while Soho is filled with art galleries, sumptuous shopping and several of the hippest bars and lounges around. Head for Tribeca if you want to eat out – no matter what you are in the mood for or how much you want to spend, there are several choices for you. Whether it is reasonably-priced but tasty diner food at the Gee Whiz Diner at 295 Greenwich Street or fine dining at City Hall on Duane Street, you are sure to leave happy. Soho is also known for its cutting-edge artistic community. It is home to several art galleries, as well as a branch of the Guggenheim Museum.

Health

Tribeca and Soho are in between two of the city's hospitals, New York Downtown Hospital (p.153), and St. Vincent's Hospital on 12th Street and Seventh Avenue in Greenwich Village (www.svcmc.org). Both healthcare facilities are only minutes away.

Education

Tribeca has plenty of schools for people of all ages, from the Buckle My Shoe nursery (www.bucklemyshoe.org) to the Manhattan School of Sailing (www.sailmanhattan.com). In addition, since it borders Battery Park City, Stuyvesant High School, PS 89 and PS 234 are all easily accessible from Tribeca as well.

Traffic & Public Transport

If you drive, good luck finding a parking spot. These neighbourhoods are made for walking, and you'll discover much more about the areas on foot. And if you've got your new stilettos on or it's pouring with rain, both areas are accessible using public transport. Trains to Tribeca include: 1, 2, A, C, E, R, W, and N (to Canal Street), and trains to Soho include: F, V, R, C, and E.

Safety & Annoyances

While some side streets in Soho and Tribeca can be desolate and dark late at night, these areas are both considered safe, trendy and upscale.

Maps 6 & 7

Union Square

It's a small area in size, but it's a huge part of daily life and the colourful history of the city. Centrally located between 14th and 17th Streets near Broadway, it's where you'll find some of New York's best restaurants and an enormous market bringing fresh produce to agriculturally starved urban dwellers. It is also a hub for public transport.

Best Points
The easy accessibility of the market and the park, as well as to the multiple subway lines. This neighbourhood also features some of the best eateries in the city.

Accommodation

Most of the housing in Union Square serves as dormitories for students of New York University. However, there are two luxury buildings for potential homeowners. The Zeckendorf Towers, located slightly east of the square, will set you back around $2 million for a two-bedroom apartment. Union Square South is the other building, and a one-bedroom rents for around $4,500 and sells for up to $1 million. You'll find a scattering of converted lofts and older buildings, but unfortunately you can't escape the high property prices in this area.

Worst Points
The expensive, limited housing makes this a difficult place to buy property. Rents are pretty high too.

Shopping & Amenities

The Green Market is a year-round venue for small regional family farmers, open every Monday, Wednesday, Friday and Saturday, between 08:00 and 18:00. The staggering variety of fresh produce at reasonable prices draws large crowds from morning till night. Virtually anything you need is located on the periphery of the square – this includes the designer shoe warehouse DSW, as well as the Virgin Megastore, which is an endless collection of music and movies. Down the street is the Regal Union Square Stadium 14, featuring the latest movies.

Entertainment & Leisure

Union Square Park is home to statues of several historical figures, including George Washington, Abraham Lincoln and Gandhi, paying tribute to the areas rich history. In the centre of Union Square Park, near the dog runs and walking tracks, is Luna Park, an outdoor restaurant and bar, open from April to October (212 475 8464). The queue can be quite long, since once people sit down among the fairy-lit trees, they don't want to leave.. Other restaurants in the area include the Union Square Café (p.379), Barocco Kitchen (212 254 6777), the Blue Water Grill (212 675 9500), Chat 'n' Chew (212 243 1616) and the super-trendy Coffee Shop (p.397).

Health

Part of the Beth Israel Medical Center (www.wehealnewyork.org) is located at the bottom of Zeckendorf Towers.

Education

There are no schools in Union Square, so families send their children to schools in surrounding neighbourhoods. Residents also travel to hospitals in nearby Gramercy Park or Chelsea (but the area is so small that this is not a far trip – merely a matter of a few blocks).

Traffic & Public Transport

With the area being so small, walking is the most obvious mode of transport. But trains through Union Square include 4, 5, 6, L, N, Q, R and W.

Safety & Annoyances

Probably the biggest annoyance in this area (apart from the high property prices) is the fact that it's so hard to get into your favourite restaurants! Still, it's a small price to pay for living in the same neighbourhood as some of the city's best eateries.

123

Maps 3 & 5

Upper East Side

Nestled between Central Park and the East River, the Upper East Side comprises two square miles of some of the most expensive real estate in the US, as well as the nation's highest concentration of individual wealth. While it is similar in many ways to the Upper West Side (which is considered more culturally diverse and arty), the Upper East Side is seen as more conservative and politically motivated.

Best Points
Madison Avenue shopping and easy access to museums and Central Park.

Accommodation

Mansions and enormous pre-war homes are part of everyday life for the fabulously wealthy residents of the Upper East Side. If you go east of Lexington you can still find some fairly reasonable townhouses and co-ops. It's worth noting, however, that if you do find a reasonably priced home, it will probably be a 'fixer-upper'. The area along Central Park has a collection of tall apartment buildings and formerly private mansions of old New York families. Most homes were built between 1900 and 1930 and have doormen, working fireplaces, patios and terraces. It also features plenty of luxurious serviced apartments that serve as temporary housing for the wealthy.

Worst Points
Some areas will be exceedingly crowded due to the proximity of the museums and other attractions.

Shopping & Amenities

Two words: Fifth Avenue. The street buzzes with the sound of thousands of cash registers and it's where you'll find the flagship stores of some of the world's most famous brands. Madison Avenue rivals sections of Fifth Avenue in terms of shopping. Presided over by legendary department store Barneys (p.358), Madison Avenue offers thousands of ways to part with your money.

Where the Other Half Lives
The area alongside Central Park this is one of the most expensive streets in the world, and is often called 'Millionaire's Mile' (although calling it 'Billionaire's Mile would be more correct).

Entertainment & Leisure

The Upper East Side has no shortage of cultural institutions, including 'Museum Mile', which is home to the Guggenheim (p.220), the Met (p.221) and the Jewish Museum (p.221). Excellent restaurants such as Daniel (p.388) and Café Boulud (p.387) live here.

Health

Nearby hospitals include Lenox Hill Hospital (www.lenoxhillhospital.org) and New York Presbyterian (www.nyp.org). Alternatively, Mount Sinai Medical Center, on 100th Street, is close enough (www.mountsinai.org).

Education

This area is also known for an exhaustive list of some of the most elite schools in the nation, including the nationally recognised Regis (www.regis-nyc.org).

Traffic & Public Transport

It's easy to get around the area on foot or by bicycle, and of course you'll find plenty of yellow cabs looking for tipping passengers. Trains to the Upper East Side include 4, 5, and 6. Trains to Central Park include A, C, B, D, R, N and 9.

Safety & Annoyances

Overcrowding, particularly on Madison Avenue and along Museum Mile during touristy times of the year. Watch out for the accompanying pickpockets and bag-snatchers. The proximity to Central Park and all the great shopping make this area a tourist magnet, and expect plenty of congestion over the holidays or in summer.

Maps 2 & 4 ◀

Upper West Side

This is one of the most famous areas in the city, if not the world. It is bordered by Central Park West, an avenue which runs for 51 blocks along Central Park's west side, from 59th to 110th Street. Every time you have watched a movie featuring scenes of Central Park, with its supple greenery bordered by some of the most luxurious apartment buildings you can imagine – you are looking at the Upper West Side.

Best Points ◀
Stunning views, easy access to Central Park and Midtown, rich cultural life.

Accommodation

Its pre-war loft apartments, luxury condos and four-storey brownstones are an integral part of the city's architectural character. Nearly all the accommodation in this area is on the fancy side – this is where Charlotte and Miranda (of *Sex and the City*) had their posh pads.

Worst Points ◀
Some parts of this area border Midtown and are very crowded, particularly in the summer months and during the holiday season.

Shopping & Amenities

The area has plenty of good neighbourhood shopping, including a good collection of supermarkets, delis and pharmacies that are open around the clock.

Entertainment & Leisure

The focal point of this area is, of course, Central Park. This breathtaking haven reaches from Midtown to Harlem and provides millions of New Yorkers with a daily dose of natural beauty. When you are strolling over its rolling hills and past its ponds, over its bridges and through its gardens, you feel like you are no longer in the city but in a fanciful forest. The park features recreational activities for people of all ages and tastes, including the Central Park Zoo (p.233), ice skating rinks (p.267), and the Delacorte Theater, where Shakespeare is performed each summer. For more information on what the park has to offer, go to www.centralpark.com. But there is much more to this area besides the park. The Upper West Side is also home to several historical and cultural institutions, including the world-famous Julliard School of Music, Grant's Tomb, Lincoln Center, and Columbia University. The Upper West Side has typically been home to several famous artists, writers and dancers.

Some of the city's most famous restaurants are found in the area, including Per Se (p.389), Jean Georges (p.389) and Tavern on the Green (p.379).

Health

There are several healthcare facilities close to the Upper West Side. Lenox Hill Hospital is located at 100 East 77th Street (212 535 6273, www.lenoxhillhospital.org). New York Presbyterian/Weill Cornell Medical Center is located at 525 East 68th Street (www.nyp.org). Weill Cornell Medical Associates is located at 12 West 72nd Street, between Columbus Circle and Central Park West (212 746 7800, www.cornellphysicians.com).

Education

The two big names in Upper West Side education are the Juilliard School of Music (www.juilliard.edu) and Columbia University (www.columbia.edu). Both these institutions have educated people who have gone on to become rich and famous: Jamie Foxx, Kelsey Grammer and Robin Williams are all graduates of Juilliard, and Columbia counts Jack Kerouac, Madeleine Albright and Art Garfunkel among its many alumni. Being an area that is popular with families, there are also plenty of schools and pre-schools around.

Traffic & Public Transport
It's a great area to walk around, with relatively quiet streets and good sidewalks. It's also popular with cyclists, who can make use of an extensive network of cycle paths (although drivers using cycle paths as parking spaces can cause problems). Trains to the Upper West Side include: A, C, B, D, 1, 2 and 3.

Safety & Annoyances
This is a pretty ideal area to live in, and perhaps the biggest annoyance is not being able to afford it.

Brooklyn

Known by many as New York City's favourite and most well-known borough (after Manhattan), Brooklyn has been the subject of so many books and movies that even if you've never been there, you could probably recognise it. With its 2.5 million residents, Brooklyn is the most populous borough in the city. In fact, if it was not part of New York City, Brooklyn, by itself, would be the fourth largest city in the US.

Brooklyn is connected to Manhattan by the Brooklyn, Manhattan and Williamsburg Bridges, as well as the Brooklyn Battery Tunnel, and several of its most popular and upscale neighbourhoods are just one or two subway stops away from the Financial District. Some of these areas, known collectively as Downtown Brooklyn, include Brooklyn Heights, Cobble Hill, Clinton Hills, Carroll Gardens, Boerum Hill, and DUMBO, an acronym for an artistic community known as 'down under the Manhattan Bridge Overpass'. DUMBO has become home to many artists, writers, and several upscale shops and restaurants. These areas have become exceedingly expensive, with the apartments and breathtaking brownstones costing millions of dollars. Downtown Brooklyn is also the third-largest central business district in New York City, after Midtown and Lower Manhattan.

Best Points

Its proximity to Manhattan, and occasionally lower housing prices. Also, the non-stop entertainment options and strong sense of community.

Worst Points

Unfortunately, the housing market has also noted its proximity to Manhattan, and most property prices have risen accordingly. Some areas are still best avoided at night or when alone.

Up and Coming

Gentrification has claimed many areas of Brooklyn. In 2005, the Brooklyn waterfront was rezoned, making the construction of several luxury high rises possible. In addition, the New Jersey Nets basketball team has recently decided to move to Brooklyn and a multi-billion dollar stadium will be built to house them, bringing more revitalisation to the area.

Accommodation

The areas nearer to Manhattan feature a range of housing options but the fact that these neighbourhoods are just one or two subway stops from the financial district mean that accommodation is expensive – almost as expensive as Manhattan itself. Further away from Manhattan are many less expensive areas, and each is known for its distinct ethnic flavour. Brooklyn residents identify strongly with their particular neighbourhood, almost as much as with the borough itself. Some of these areas include Bensonhurst, with a large Italian population, Brighton Beach, where a large community of Russians and Pakistanis live, and Borough Park, with its large group of Orthodox Jewish residents. Similarly, Bedford-Stuyvesant is home to many African Americans, Bay Ridge has large Italian, Irish and Arab groups, and Sunset Park is where you'll find Hispanic and Chinese communities. The housing in these areas includes everything from mansions costing millions of dollars to crowded apartment buildings, co-ops and condos for several hundred thousand.

Shopping & Amenities

Throughout Brooklyn you'll find many fine shopping opportunities, from independent stores and 'mom-and-pop' shops to gigantic malls and farmers' markets. Bargain hunters can head for the Atlantic Terminal Center Mall for Target and Daffy's (be warned, parking there is problematic). Fulton Street Mall (www.fultonstreet.org) has Macy's, Forever 21, Radio Shack, Toys R Us, and hundreds of other outlets along Fulton Street. The Park Slope Farmers' Market takes place every Sunday from June to November, from 11:00 to 17:00 – here you can stock up on delicious baked goods, fresh produce, health food and fresh flowers.

Entertainment & Leisure

You need never be bored in Brooklyn. Whether you are riding the waves at Coney Island (p.227), smelling the flowers at Brooklyn Botanical Gardens (p.231) or strolling along the Promenade near the base of the Brooklyn Bridge (p.216), there is always something to keep you occupied. There are also 60 branches of the Brooklyn Public Library, which is separate from the New York City Public Library in Manhattan (www.brooklynpubliclibrary.org). Brooklyn has a vibrant music and nightlife scene. Popular local bands include Akron Family, Animal Collective, Scumbo, Sufjan Stevens and Clap Your Hands Say Yeah. Parts of Brooklyn rival Manhattan in terms of nightlife, although there are more places with a friendly neighbourhood feel where everyone is welcome, as opposed to some of Manhattan's snooty 'you're not coming in unless you're somebody' venues. For relaxation, take a nice slow stroll around the very beautiful Prospect Park (p.233).

12

Health

There are many hospitals that are easily accessible for Brooklyn residents. These include Lutheran Medical Center (718 630 7000), Maimondes Medical Center (718 283 6000, www.maimonidesmed.org), New York Methodist Hospital (718 768 3158, www.nym.org), Downstate Medical Center (718 270 1000), Interfaith Medical Center (718 613 4000, www.interfaithmedical.com), and the Long Island College Hospital (718 780 1000).

Education

There is just as much of a variety in Brooklyn's educational institutions. Brooklyn Technical High School (www.bths.edu) is competitive with Bronx Science in terms of academic excellence, and the private Packer Collegiate Institute (www.packer.edu) is one of the most elite in the city. In addition, there are many Catholic Schools, run by the Roman Catholic Diocese of Brooklyn, and Jewish schools, owned and operated by the Satmar Jewish Community. Brooklyn also has several institutions of higher learning, including Brooklyn Law School (www.brooklaw.edu), Brooklyn College (www.brooklyn.cuny.edu), SUNY Downstate Medical Center (www.hscbklyn.edu), and the Pratt Institute (www.pratt.edu), one of the leading art schools in the US.

Traffic & Public Transport

Trains to Brooklyn include: 2, 3, 4, 5, A, C, D, F, J, M, N, R, L, and G. The Long Island Railroad, an above-ground commuter train, also makes several stops in Brooklyn.

Queens

The borough of Queens, wedged in between Manhattan and Long Island, is both the largest borough geographically and the most ethnically diverse. Nearly half of its residents are immigrants. Queens is also the location of two of the world's busiest airports: John F. Kennedy and LaGuardia. Queens is connected to Manhattan by the Triborough and Queensboro Bridges, as well as the Queens Midtown Tunnel, and is a short commute for those working in Midtown.

Queens is made up of five towns, including Long Island City, Jamaica, Flushing, Far Rockaway, and Floral Park. Each of these towns has its own smaller neighbourhoods, such as Howard Beach and Middle Village, where residents are mainly Italian, Astoria, which is primarily Greek but where there is also an influx of young professionals of all backgrounds, and Jamaica, which has a largely African-American and Caribbean population.

Accommodation

Housing in Queens mostly consists of two and three family brick homes, in addition to private homes and apartment buildings. The type of housing you'll find depends on the neighbourhood. They range in price from about $300,000 to several million for a mansion in Bayside.

Shopping & Amenities

Each neighbourhood in Queens has its own community of shops and services. Unlike in Manhattan, in Queens you'll find larger shopping complexes, such as the Queens Center in Elmhurst (www.shopqueenscenter.com), which houses over 70 stores. Bargain hunters head for the smaller Queens Place on Queens Boulevard, for a good browse in Target (p.323) and Best Buy (p.324).

Entertainment & Leisure

Things to see in Queens include the Queens Botanical Garden (p.231), the Queens Museum of Art, and the New York Hall of Science. In addition, the third-largest park in New York City, Flushing Meadows Park, is in Queens (p.272). The home of the New York Mets baseball team, Shea Stadium, is also in Queens.

Health

There are numerous hospitals in Queens, including Mount Sinai Hospital of Queens (718 932 1000), New York Hospital of Queens (718 670 1231), Queens Hospital Center (718 883 3000) and Elmhurst Hospital Center (718 334 4000).

Education

Schools include the highly rated Benjamin N. Cardozo High School in Bayside (www.cardozohigh.com), which is known for its DaVinci Science and Math Institute, the Mentor for Law and Humanities Program and the Performing Dance Program. In addition, there are 11 Catholic schools, seven highly-rated, non-religious private schools, and countless public schools.

Traffic & Public Transport

Trains to Queens include: A, E, F, G, J, M, R, N, V, 7, Z. The Long Island Railroad makes several stops in Queens as well.

12

Staten Island

Staten Island is the smallest borough of the City of New York, both in geographical size and population. It is also the furthest away from Manhattan and the least accessible by public transportation and therefore often referred to as the 'forgotten borough'. It is connected to Brooklyn by the Verrazzano-Narrows Bridge and to New Jersey by the Bayonne, Goethals and Outer Bridges.

Nearly half of Staten Island residents are Italian - in fact, Staten Island has the largest Italian population of any county in the US. Most of its inhabitants are also Catholic, although there is a Jewish community (fairly small as compared with the rest of New York City), as well as other Christian denominations.

Accommodation

Staten Island is by far the most suburban of all the boroughs, and its available housing reflects that fact. While there are some apartments, condos and co-ops, these are relatively sparse in comparison to other boroughs. Most people live in private homes and townhouses. Staten Island is relatively inexpensive compared with other boroughs - you can still buy a house here for $500,000, although there are many homes for millions of dollars to be found, especially in the upscale neighbourhood of Todt Hill.

Shopping & Amenities

Mall rats will make a beeline for the Staten Island Mall on Richmond Avenue (www.statenisland-mall.com). This retail behemoth is packed with well-known retailers like Macy's, Sears, Gap, Banana Republic, Old Navy, Borders, the Disney Store and Apple Computers.

Entertainment & Leisure

There are several museums on Staten Island, including the Alice Austen House Museum Conference House, the Garibaldi-Meucci Museum, Historic Richmond Town, the Snug Harbor Cultural Center, and the Staten Island Children's Museum.

The nightlife isn't going to set your stilettos on fire, but if you're after good Italian food, this is the place to be. Try the mouthwatering pizza pie at Denino's (p.392), Nunzio's (718 667 9647) or Joe and Pat's (718 981 0887).

Health

The two major hospitals on Staten Island are Staten Island University Hospital (www.siuh.edu), which has two locations, and St Vincent's Catholic Hospital (www.svcmc.org).

Education

Although there are several public schools on Staten Island, it is very common for children to attend one of the numerous Catholic private schools. Colleges on the island include Wagner College, the College of Staten Island, and St. John's, whose main campus is in Queens.

Traffic & Public Transport

Staten Island is not accessible by any of the subway lines. Those working in other boroughs must drive, take a bus, or ride the Staten Island Ferry, which runs from the Bay Street area to the Financial District in Manhattan. There is one train on Staten Island, but it runs only from the neighbourhood of Stapelton to the ferry station.

The Bronx

Just north of Manhattan, The Bronx is the only borough of New York City that is on the mainland. Nearly half of the population in The Bronx is Latino, and it has the largest number of Puerto Ricans of any other county in the US. Some famous areas of The Bronx include Arthur Avenue (The Bronx's 'Little Italy'), Fordham, where you'll find Fordham University and the Yankee Stadium, Riverdale, an upscale enclave with homes costing millions of dollars, and the South Bronx. The South Bronx used to be best known for its exceptionally high crime rate. It is now a gentrification project: the influx of artists started a few years back, and the price increases soon followed - since 2002 housing prices have quadrupled.

Accommodation

Housing in the Bronx is as varied as the neighbourhoods. There are private homes, whether one, two or three family, large apartment buildings, condos and co-ops. The prices range from a few hundred thousand to several million dollars, depending, of course, on the area. Co-op City, the largest cooperative housing development in the world, is located in the Bronx's Baychester section. With its 15,000 residential units, three shopping centres, schools, movie theatres and supermarkets, it is a city unto itself.

Shopping & Amenities

Shopping is varied. The multi-cultural history of The Bronx means that you can shop your way around the world. Arthur Avenue Retail Market, in particular, is where you'll be able to stock up on some authentic Italian goodies like cheese, sausage, pasta and olive oil.

Entertainment & Leisure

There are several things to do and see in the Bronx, including the Bronx Botanical Gardens (p.231), the Bronx Zoo (p.232) and the Bronx Museum of the Arts (www.bronxmuseum.org). Two of the city's largest parks are here: Pelham Bay Park and Van Cortlandt Park. One of the most famous landmarks in the Bronx is Yankee Stadium, the home of the New York Yankees baseball team (p.290).

Health

If you live in The Bronx, your closest hospitals are Bronx Lebanon (www.bronx-leb.org), Calvary Hospital (www.calvaryhospital.org), Jacobi Medical Center (718 918 5000), Montefiore Medical Center (www.montefiore.org), Our Lady of Mercy (www.ourladyofmercy.com), and St. Barnabas (www.stbarnabashospital.org).

Education

Some of the finest schools are in The Bronx, such as Bronx Science (www.bxscience.edu), one of three specialised science high schools in the city. Other highly recognised schools, such as Walton, DeWitt Clinton High School, and the High School of American Studies are in the Bronx. In addition, three of New York City's most elite private schools are located in The Bronx: Fieldston (www.ecfs.org), Horace Mann (www.horacemann.org), and the Riverdale Country School (www.riverdale.edu).

Traffic & Public Transport

Trains to the Bronx include: B, D, 2, 4, 5, 6 subways. In addition, the Harlem and Hudson lines of the Metro North (above-ground commuter trains) make stops in the Bronx.

Safety & Annoyances

The Bronx is still known as the most dangerous 'hood in New York. Despite recent getrification, you should always check out any area before deciding to lay your hat there.

Best Points
It's on the mainland, and therefore just a skip and hop into Manhattan, and the surge of arriving artists indicate 'SoBro' is going to be the next hip spot.

Worse Points
Crime rates are still relatively high, as are more recent house prices now that the trendsetters are beginning to deem the borough habitable.

City Island
Located just beyond Pelham Bay Park, City Island is surrounded by the waters of Long Island Sound and Eastchester Bay. Crossing over the bridge to City Island you feel like you are leaving New York City for New England. The small area is populated by several famous seafood restaurants, as well as upscale condos, co-ops and private homes. In the summer you will be hard-pressed to find a time when the tiny island is not swarming with crowds of New Yorkers and tourists alike on a short escape from the sweltering city.

Setting up Home

So, you've found a place to live in crazy, lovable New York City, and you've got everything in order: your electricity has been turned on, your cable and internet service has been installed and maybe you've even got your dog and cat acclimatised without too much yapping and mewing. Take a breath and explore your neighbourhood, from supermarkets, parks, and local eateries, to the nearest movie theatres and homeware stores, or perhaps locate your nearest public library, one of the Big Apple's best free assets. After that, you'll not be far off becoming a real local.

Moving With Finesse
• Get at least three quotes, preferably getting movers to visually inspect your belongings.
• Ask about the mover's liability insurance and how you can purchase additional insurance.
• Create a thorough inventory of all your belongings, including numbering all boxes.
• Ask the mover if they provide boxes and/or cardboard 'wardrobes' for clothing.
• Photograph the packing/loading process for evidence in case of a problem.
• Contact your local consulate about 'customs-restricted' goods, and pack these separately

Moving Services

Moving to – or within – New York City can be a frazzled disaster or an easy journey. Given the city's manic housing scene, you might have to move quickly, and sharp thinking always pays off.

First, beware: hundreds of companies want to move you – *Yellow Pages* listings alone run dozens of pages. Thus, word of mouth is essential: talk to your friends, your apartment broker, even your new neighbours. Visit websites like Craigslist.com, send exploratory emails, make phone calls. Ask about hourly and daily fees ($30-50/hr. and up, and per mover), liability insurance, advance notice, and special fees – some movers charge fees per flight of steps. If you have lots of boxes and furniture, perhaps pick an established company for the broadest overall protection, whereas a 'man with a van' for small moves might make more sense. Either way, never assume a cheap quote yields the best move. If you're moving from outside New York City but within the US, exercise your right to receive a copy of a mover's 'Annual Performance Report': if a mover is sued often, avoid them. A do's and don'ts list from the New York State Dept. of Transportation (www.dot.state.ny.us/ts/consumer_info.html) and various watchdog websites (www.movingscam.com) offer helpful hints.

Narrow your list to three movers and call the 'DOT' at 800 786 5368 to verify that they are all properly licensed. Now call the three movers again and request estimates based on a detailed inventory, including number of boxes and all furniture. Ask if the estimate is 'binding,' meaning the mover guarantees the fee. And read the *New York Better Business Bureau Moving Guide* (www.newyork.bbb.org, then click on Research/Publications/For Consumers/Moving, Storage & Transportation/Moving and Storage) for last-minute tips. If you're moving to New York City from abroad, consider your budget. If your furniture is of high sentimental value, move it, but know that you'll be socked with exorbitant fees for transportation and storage. Also, ask your local consulate about item restrictions, including pets. And consider making your new start in New York totally fresh by refurnishing – since furniture stores are aplenty.

Relocation & Removal Companies

A Poppi & Regal Relocation System Inc	212 427 4600	www.coolestcity.com
AAA Moving, Inc	800 884 4784	www.movingaaa.com
AAA on Time Express	718 851 0777	www.aaaontime.com
Above & Beyond Moving	212 721 1200	www.NYCmover.com
Aaron's Relocations	212 980 6190	www.aaronsrelocations.com
Asure Moving Relocation	212 316 5300	www.asuremovingrelocation.com
Allied Pickfords ▶ p.xvi	800 823 0755	www.alliedpickfords.com
Cross It Off Your List	212 725 0122	www.crossitoffyourlist.com
Divine Moving & Storage Limited	917 493 1300	www.divinemoving.com
Hudson Moving & Storage	212 678 4862	www.moving-storage.com
Mayflower	800 325 3863	www.mayflower.com
Meyer's Moving and Storage	212 688 8888	www.meyers-moving.com
Omega Shipping Co., Inc.	718 937 9797	www.omegashipping.com
Scanio Moving & Storage	212 722 6850	www.uppereast.com
U-Haul	212 491 7722	www.uhaul.com

Furnishing Your Home

Most New York City apartments – even those in the outer boroughs carved out of private homes – come empty, allowing you a blank canvas to fulfil your design dreams. New York City offers a myriad of furnishing options. Before exploring, measure your living space – and remember the older an apartment is, the more likely you'll find odd-shaped angles or uneven flooring.

Next, shop! Start with one of Manhattan's legendary, moderately priced department stores, like Macy's (www.macys.com) and Bloomingdale's (www.bloomingdales.com), then try specialty shops like Bed Bath & Beyond (www.bedbathandbeyond.com), Crate & Barrel (www.crateandbarrel.com), Gracious Home (www.gracioushome.com), Pottery Barn (www.potterybarn.com), and Pier 1 Imports (www.pier1.com). Even if just for inspiration, visit high-end retailers like ABC Carpet & Home (www.abchome.com), Maurice Villency, (www.mauricevillency.com) and Restoration Hardware (www.restorationhardware.com) or bargain-oriented venues like Fishs Eddy (www.fishseddy.com), and branches of the Salvation Army (www.satruck.com/FindStore.asp). Spend lots of time in mini-districts focused on furniture, like East 58th Street between Second and Third avenues, all of Soho, and Lafayette Street from Astor Place to Canal Street for retro items.

If your job requires you to log lots of hours and you really need to get some basics out of the way, it is possible to hire a carpenter to create new furniture for you. Be smart about it: instead of spending thousands to hire individual carpenters, visit Gotham Cabinet Craft (www.gothiccabinetcraft.com), which custom builds furniture at a fraction of the normal cost. You'll settle for predetermined styles, but the convenience and craftsmanship will last forever.

Second-Hand Items

A city of eight million means a tremendous second-hand market for everything you can possibly think of. Yes, the web has changed things: it's not unusual to buy that second-hand cabinet or couch on eBay. It does, however, take the fun out of strolling the city – visiting, say, a flea market so large it happens in three locations – West 39th Street near Times Square, and in two spots in the West 20s in Chelsea (www.hellskitchenfleamarket.com). The city also offers myriad thrift and consignment shops (see www.thensome.com/thrift.htm and www.bestconsignmentshopsoftware.com for lists), and the ultra-cool Olde Good Things (www.oldegoodthings.com), which specialises in architectural salvage. Don't assume prices are bargains. Some thrift stores, like those run by Housing Works (www.housingworksauctions.com), do offer major savings, but flea market vendors are noted for breathtaking mark-ups. Learn to haggle.

Tailors

For handcrafted tailoring, New York City can be a wonderland – provided you have the funds. Still, note that tailors do operate as independent contractors inside dry cleaning establishments, meaning they'll be handy for custom alterations. For high-end Manhattan tailoring, visit La Rukiko Custom Tailor (www.hongkongcustomtailor.com), Bermini Custom Tailors and Designers (www.bermini.com), or chains like Aphrodite (www.aphroditedrycleaners.com). There are also distinctions between tailors and upholsterers. Always call up first for an estimate before bringing in your furniture. Virtually no upholsterers make house calls, unfortunately.

Other People's Stuff

Occasionally, places to rent will be advertised as 'semi-furnished,' which may mean the soon-to-be-former occupant wants to get rid of furniture (always negotiate a fair price) or the apartment is in a cooperative or a condominium building that the owner is subletting. If so, see if the furniture suits you – if not, you may lack room for your own items. Furnished quarters are typically good for business travellers, not for those planning to stay.

Tailors		
Citiclean Carpet & Upholstery	Midtown	212 947 6866
Crosstown Shade and Glass	Upper West Side	212 787 8040
Elite Window Treatment	Chelsea	212 807 8674
Forsyth Decorations	Chinatown	212 226 3624
Marc Tash Interiors	Brooklyn	718 336 3326
Upholstery Unlimited, Inc.	Chelsea	212 924 1230
V2K Window Fashions	Brooklyn	718 522 7245

133

Household Insurance

While New York City is safer than 10 or 20 years ago – the government considers it America's safest major city – household insurance is a good idea. For renters, average policies run $15-20/month for $30,000 property coverage and $100,000 liability coverage, although this varies by the inventory of your belongings. Read the fine print to ensure policies cover disasters beyond fire and theft (such as flooding), and assume a rule of thumb: the higher your deductible, the lower your premium. Master terms like ACV (actual cash value) and RCC (replacement cost coverage) before signing paperwork. Renters' insurance isn't mandatory but homeowners' insurance is. Given New York City's amazingly high-priced real estate market, insurance can be a whopper – build your premiums into the same budget as your mortgage. Virtually no one buys property without real estate brokers and attorneys, so use their expertise to pick the policy best for you and your home.

Household Insurance		
AIG	212 944 7017	www.aig.com
Gotham	212 406 7300	na
Liberty Mutual Group	212 221 0199	www.libertymutual.com
Prudential	212 966 7333	www.prudential.com

Laundry Services

Few residences have washer/dryers, but most blocks have laundromats (launderettes) – many open 24/7. Whether you buy detergent or bring your own, bring coins: $1-2/wash; 25-50c /per 15 minutes in the dryer.

Many laundromats also wash clothes: outer-borough sites run $8-10 for the first 5-10 pounds, $1-2 per additional, Manhattan venues can be pricier. By law, lost-goods policies must be posted. There are usually reimbursement caps. In new/luxury buildings, launderettes may be in basements or by floor. These are convenient – just respect sharing machines with others.

Laundry Services		
Hallak & Sons Inc	Upper East Side	212 879 4694
Madame Paulette	Upper East Side	212 838 6827
Madame Paulette Dry Cleaners	Upper East Side	212 838 6827
Midnight Express Cleaners	Long Island City	718 392 9200
Mrs. Roles Private Laundry	Upper East Side	212 744 6620
Neighborhood Laundry & Dry	Upper East Side	212 831 2807
New Supreme Cleaners Inc	The Bronx	212 234 3202
River Parkway Laundry	Brooklyn	718 437 5554

Domestic Help

Other options **Entry Visa** p.58

Domestic help in New York City is largely for the economically privileged, but not uncommon. Indeed, housekeepers, maids, au pairs and nannies are a New York growth industry.

No matter what help you seek, personal recommendations and references offer invaluable insights. Beyond that, professional agencies are an impeccable resource. To find the right person for your needs, you'll pay a princely sum – several thousand dollars, sometimes a percentage of a gross annual salary – to interview and conduct background checks on candidates. But you'll get a keen look at your potential domestic, from their credit record, driving report, and any evidence of federal, state or local misconduct to their special skills: medical knowledge, academic prowess, culinary wizardry and overall demeanour.

Rates vary wildly. For maids, live-out can be far costlier than live-in: rates of $12-30/hour, $700-2,000/week and $2,000-5,000/month are not unheard of, again depending on specific requirements. Average work-weeks are five to six days/45-55 hours per week; overtime, vacation, holidays and insurance are usually contractual matters negotiated through agencies or, in rare cases, directly with the help. While domestics are one of the few employment types not covered under the legal minimum wage, for the most highly prized individuals, you'll need to compensate by whatever the market will bear. It is extremely important that employer and employee report all domestics' compensation to the government and that the employee is legally permitted to work in the US. For more information, visit www.4nannytaxes.com (for satisfying tax requirements), and obtain a New York State Department of Taxation and Finance publication, *What You Need to Know if You Hire Domestic Help* (www.tax.state.ny.us). In 2003, the New York City Council passed a bill requiring agencies and employers to inform domestics of their rights. You must sign a document affirming your understanding of the law before anyone begins their duties.

Domestic Help Agencies

Absolute Best Care, Inc.	212 481 5705	www.absolutebestcare.com
Maids Unlimited	212 369 9100	na
Manhattan Feather Dusters	212 406 7024	na
McMaid.com	212 371 5555	www.mcmaid.com
New York Domestics, Inc.	212 714 3519	www.newyorkdomestics.com
Oxford Maids	212 532 0308	www.oxfordmaids.com
Pavillion	212 889 6609	www.pavillionagency.com
White Glove Elite	212 594 2830	www.whitegloveelite.com

Spot the Nannies
Only 4% of the children of employed parents nationwide are cared for by a nanny or babysitter. In New York, home to more affluent couples, the figure is roughly 5%. Not surprisingly, two-income higher-earning families are the most likely to enlist nannies.

Babysitting & Childcare

There are different ways to acquire a babysitter in New York City – a place which, its low crime rate notwithstanding, can still be a scary place to rear a child. The first, most preferable method is word of mouth. Starting with your obstetrician and continuing with anyone you meet – other mothers, nurses and caretakers, mothers' groups (take a visit to www.babybites.nyc, www.clubmom.com and www.cafemom.com, for example), friendly neighbours, and family and personal friends – always ask for personal, direct references and then take the time to interview the person, asking carefully developed questions. Ideally, babysitters should be able to offer references that you can check out by phone. Babysitting is by far the most popular method for young people to make a little extra non-allowance income if they aren't yet old enough to get a part-time job. Usually, these are junior high school-age girls.

Or you may feel like you want to take your newborn or toddler wherever you go. Fortunately, certain amenities like baby-changing stations are very popular and not hard to find. Not every retail store or restaurant will have one – always ask – but their presence is increasing all the time. Other kinds of heavily-trafficked public establishments, like gyms, may offer short-term oversee services, so always ask about those as well.

Meanwhile, here are some additional ways to procure a babysitter. For one, examine the listings on craigslist.org, but just know that you'll be reading each advertisement and then determining who to call from there. A terrific website, sittercity.com, is one of the more well-constructed databases out there: a sample search using the zip code 10036 (representing Midtown) yields more than 100 immediate possibilities, and there are mini-bios to help you separate the wheat from the chaff. There's also a perennial favourite, the Baby Sitters Guild (www.babysittersguild.com), founded in 1940.

Daycare centres aren't hard to find in New York, although one should note that very few companies offer them on-site as opposed to many suburban offices, where they are frequently more de rigueur. The local government of New York City, under the auspices of the Department of Health, offers a list of daycare facilities at www.nyc.gov. This is broken down by borough – the table for the borough of Queens, for example, has more than 400 alone – and is often updated. If you click on the 'more info' tab next

135

Babysitting & Childcare

Babysitters Guild	212 687 4660	www.babysittersguild.citysearch.com
Barnard College Babysitting Service	212 854 2035	na
Chiquin In Home Babysitting Services	646 379 5562	www.maxpages.com/chiquin
Domestically Yours Agency Inc.	212 986 1900	na
Gentle Hands	718 252 7252	www.gentlehandschildcare.com
International Agency	212 687 7722	na
Pinch Sitters	212 260 6005	na

to each listing, you can also learn about any recent violations of the city health code and whether (and when and how) they were corrected. The age of the children that each daycare centre accepts can vary, always make inquiries and pay appropriate visits before making a choice.

According to the city's classification protocol, there are four kinds of licensed daycare facilities: group childcare facilities ('seven or more children located in an institutional setting'), group family daycare ('homes of six to 12 children in the home of an unrelated family'), family daycare ('child care homes of no more than three to six children in the home of an unrelated family') and school-age programme ('care provided on a regular basis to seven or more school-age children under 13 years of age'). Different governmental structures oversee each of these types.

For daycare centres that charge fees (most do), expect to pay a healthy sum – between $800 and $1200 a month, or more in some cases, depending on location, services, amenities, community stature, reputation and other factors. By comparison, nannies, which are rarely chosen by typical New Yorkers – that is, except by the comparatively wealthy – can run $9-12 an hour or up to $20 an hour, varying according to what's expected of them and the number of hours they must put in. Up to 40 hours is standard, but in some families, 60 hours or more each week is the norm. Obviously, this can add up.

Save Money
Homeowners save by contracting vendors: terms can vary by trade, frequency of service and occasionally geography. pest control firm may expect one rate for a mid-Manhattan high-rise, one for a century-old Bronx tenement, and one for a private home on the Nassau County outskirts. Even vendors' travel time can affect pricing.

Domestic Services

Household repairs are unavoidable, so it's handy if simple problems don't faze you or if you're into preventative maintenance. However, many of the city's thousands of rental buildings pay to house on-premises superintendents and will outsource (at owners' expense) any issue a 'super' can't fix. A more modest building might find the landlord actually changing that rusty valve. Always ask what's what long before signing a lease. Homeowners, meanwhile, wish for such advantages. Plumbers, electricians, painters – even those zapping termites, vermin and roaches – are so abundant that rip-offs are common and vetting them requires patience, even audacity. Gotham's supersonic lifestyle has consigned many trades to the web, especially Craigslist.com. Still, be

Domestic Services

Name	Area	Phone	Type of Service
ABCO Termite & Pest Control	Hell's Kitchen	212 354 0763	Pest Control
Air Care	Upper East Side	718 894 8313	AC repairs
AKA Pest Control Inc	Flatiron District	212 255 6470	Pest Control
Exterminare	East Village	212 254 4444	Pest Control
HandyDandy	Soho	718 858 4725	Handyman
Irwin Electrical	Chinatown	212 431 9886	Electrician
Jay Ell Plumbing & Heating Inc	West Village	212 989 6670	Plumbers
Kapnag Heating and Plumbing	Chelsea	212 929 7111	Plumbing & Heating
Solomonic Couture For Home	Chelsea	212 929 8718	Plumbers & Heating
T.E.C.I.	Harlem	212 564 2128	Electrician
Techline Studio	Chelsea	212 674 1813	Carpenters
Wood-O-Rama, Inc.	Upper West Side	212 749 6438	Carpenters

136

specific and assertive in your emails and calls – asking not only about fees, but for professional guarantees, years in the field, reachable references. By law, a realtor cannot recommend specific vendors, but generally they'll have lists to furnish and may also confide who, in their home, they've used for what.

DVD & Video Rental

Do you browse online or in person? It's a question you'll need to answer for in-home entertainment. After all, video/DVD rental shops are ubiquitous — and it's not just the national chain Blockbuster, either. Indeed, Blockbuster's detractors in liberal (and libertarian) New York City claim the mammoth chain's puritanical politics prevents many from viewing the complete range of films and DVDs issued every year, so independent chains dot the scene, like Kim's Video & Music (www.mondokims.com), Champagne Video

DVD & Video Rental			
DVD New York	Midtown	212 686 5860	na
J & R Music & Computer World	Financial District	212 238 9000	www.jr.com
Sam Goody	Brooklyn	718 253 6701	www.samgoody.com
Top CD Hits	No Area Listed	888 509 1964	www.topCDhits.com
Virgin Megastore Incredibly	West Village	2125 984 666	na

(www.champagnevideo.com), Cinema Classics (www.cinemaclassics.com) and TLA Video (www.tlavideo) in Manhattan, and outfits like Reel Life Video (www.reellifenyc.com) in Brooklyn. Each company has its own rules regarding deposits (via credit card), rental lengths (one to three days usually) and late fees (if applicable). It's a low margin, high-volume business, so competition is tight for your dollars. But again, this all assumes you prefer to browse in person. The hot trend is signing up with NetFlix (www.netflix.com) which delivers DVDs through the mail for famously low, flat fees, charges no late fees, offers a colossal selection, and saves customers incalculable time and bother. You choose!

Pets

New York City is pet country! Take a look at any major avenue or minor street and you'll see, day or night, an impressive array of dogs and owners: sometimes you'll wonder just who is walking who. If the regular walk-and-poop schedule doesn't fit your lifestyle – or when it's -10°C outside in the winter – you'll find New York City is also the land of the hip, and more low maintenance, cat. Nor is it exactly odd to hear parakeets, canaries, or cockatoos crooning their songs in the morning, or even to learn that your neighbour down the hall is the proud parent of a rabbit or fish. The thing is, the more exotic the potential pet – lions, tigers, or bears! – the more likely you may be in violation of the city's health code. To find out what the laws are, you can always read through it (www.nycacc.org/researchtools.htm?nychealthcode). If that's a slog, call 311, the city's one-stop-shopping phone number for governmental inquiries. Here, in the meantime, are some basics: ferrets are illegal, rabbits are not; some turtles are legal, crocodiles are not.

New York State law requires all owned dogs to be licensed (renewable annually – visit www.agmkt.state.ny.us and look at dog licence under the A-Z Index). In addition, the city's health code requires all dog owners to place tags on collars whenever the pooch is paraded in public (you can download a terrific guideline at www.nyc.gov by searching for 'dog', 'collar and 'tag').

Pet Rescue

Popular cable TV programmes like Animal Precinct, which frequently focuses on New York City, is a bizarrely popular way to have your heartstrings pulled and may have you marching into the nearest animal shelter to rescue a cute little pooch. The programme has dramatically raised the profile of the ASPCA (www.aspca.org), which maintains a constantly updated database of adoptable pets. Another excellent charitable organisation, Animal Care & Control of New York City (www.nycacc.org), updates its list five times a day. A search on www.1-800-save-a-pet.com reveals more than 300 shelter and rescue groups, and www.petfinder.com explains the distinctions between foster-care situations, shelters and humane societies.

No matter what you do, don't play dead: fines for violators can be steep, and prison time is not unheard of for those convicted of animal cruelty. Always remember the city's 'pooper-scooper' and leash laws (see www.doglaw.com), or else consider cats, birds or fish, for which rules are less strict.

Unless you plan to shell out thousands for purebred dogs – and plenty do just that, or they attend world-class events like the Westminster Dog Show (www.westminsterkennelclub.org), usually held at Madison Square Garden in late winter – there are plenty of ways for you to adopt a pet.

Before acquiring your pet, consult your landlord (and re-read your lease) to ensure you can have the little fellow: each housing development and even some individual buildings may place restrictions on what you can have or how much, for example, it might weigh. People who own private homes can do as they wish, but obviously you'll

Pet Boarding & Sitting

A Kitty Vacations	–	212 679 0991	Boarding and sitting
A. G. Services	Brooklyn	917 747 0291	Pet-sitting and Dog-walking
Capipets Grooming & Daycare		718 432 8091	Grooming, Daycare and Boarding
Chien Doggie Daycare	West Village	212 924 5864	Dog daycare and walkers, pet boarding, parrot boarding, dog behaviorist
Down Town Pet Service, A	West Village	212 647 0634	Dog walking and training
Pet Pals	Gramercy Park	917 715 7869	We tailor our services to your specific needs
Petaholics	Midtown	212 560 6593	Dog boarding, sitting, care
Peters Pets	Upper East Side	212 288 5712	Cat and dog boarding, sitting and day care.

need to ensure, through proper leashes, that Fido doesn't tear up the flowerbed next door. One good thing to do is to investigate local dog runs: the Parks Department (www.nycgovparks.org; search for 'dog' and 'runs') lists 19 in the borough of Manhattan alone, not including sections of Central Park. You'll have to observe all the expected dog-run courtesies, keeping your dog leashed, cleaning up after it and stopping any dog-eat-dog pugilism.

From time to time, like all New Yorkers, you may choose to jet out of town, and there's no shortage of dog kennels (visit www.citidex.com for just one list). To give your dog a day at the spa or to get it its regular grooming, visit Biscuits & Bath Doggy Gym (www.biscuitsandbath.com), New York Dog Spa & Hotel (www.nydogspa.com) or, if you're a cat owner, maybe check out Peters Pets (www.peterspets.com), which caters to cats as well as dogs. Aquatic Creations in Williamsburg (www.aquaticcreationsinc.com) is where you'll want to go when investing in fish – they can design and construct the watery abode of any fish's dreams. Again, you'll want to consult with city authorities regarding any fish you cannot have as pets, but you can assume piranhas are probably a no-go.

Veterinary Clinics

Animal Clinic of New York	Upper East Side	212 628 5580
Ansonia Veterinary Center	Upper West Side	212 496 2100
Carnegie Hill Veterinarians	Upper East Side	212 369 5665
Center For Veterinary Care	Upper East Side	212 734 7480
East Village Veterinarian	East Village	212 674 8640
Eastside Veterinary Center	Chelsea	212 751 5176
Lenox Hill Veterinarians	Upper East Side	212 879 1320
Metropolitan Animal Clinic	Upper East Side	212 831 0410
Thomas De Vincentis	Upper East Side	212 535 3250
VCA Manhattan Veterinary Group	Upper East Side	212 988 1000

Birds, too, are a thorny issue – there's been tremendous media attention paid in the last few years to the illegal trade in certain endangered species, so whether you've adopted a parakeet, a cockatiel or an African Grey, you'll want to be sure the feathery flapper has some kind of official paperwork to go with all those squawks and charming mimicry. Finally, there are hundreds of veterinarians and veterinary clinics in the five boroughs; www.thecityofnewyorkcity.com/veterinarian offers a pretty comprehensive list.

Pet Shops

As the saying goes, caveat emptor: let the buyer beware. Check out up-to-date sources like the pet issues of *Time Out New York* and *New York Magazine* that come out every few years, and use your instincts. If the parakeets sound like they have emphysema, don't buy them there. Also see if the pet store offers a complete selection of food items, toys, and other necessities. Always read up on any pet before you buy one.

Pets Grooming/Training

A Cut Above Grooming Salon	Upper West Side	212 799 8746	Grooming
Canine Styles	Upper East Side	212 751 4549	Grooming
Doggie Do and Pussycats Too	Midtown	212 661 2204	Grooming and day care
Downtown Doghouse	Chelsea	212 924 5300	Grooming
Natural Heights	Brooklyn	347 750 5870	Grooming
Ritzy Canine Carriage House	Midtown	212 949 1818	Grooming, training, day care and overnight boarding
Sutton Dog Parlour	Upper East Side	212 355 2850	Gentle grooming, boarding and day care
Tomy Maugeri Dog Salons	Upper East Side	212 861 6700	Grooming, door to door service
Whiskers Holistic Petcare	East Village	212 979 2532	Grooming

Pet Theft

According to the non-profit In Defence of Animals (www.idausa.org), five million pets are stolen in the US each year. So, be aware that the problem clearly exists, and don't be reckless in terms of your animal. That said, don't worry too much: in the urban thicket of New York City, animal thefts are relatively rare, although it can happen.

Bringing Your Pet to New York City

The Centers for Disease Control and Prevention, which is part of the Federal Department of Health and Human Services, oversees national rules for 'importing' your pet into the US. For an overview, visit the CDC's website at www.cdc.gov, and searching for 'import' and 'pets'. Here, however, is a version from the horse's mouth, as it were: 'The CDC does not require general certificates of health for pets for entry into the United States. However, health certificates may be required for entry into some states, or may be required by airlines for pets. You should check with officials in your state of destination and with your airline prior to your travel date.' For a complete list of restricted, banned or embargoed animals, visit www.cdc.gov again, and searching for 'restricted' and 'animals'. To ship your pet out of the US, contact the embassy or consulate of the country you are planning to visit.

Electricity & Water

The Choice is Yours ◀

By law, finally, the Consolidated Edison Company of New York must offer customers opportunities to select alternative and complementary power suppliers. It operates a website, www.power yourway.com, to expedite this obligation. Details of how this works – and sometimes how much money you'll save – will be attached to your bills.

There's an urban myth, perpetuated not just through years but across generations, that New York City's water is free. It's understandable: as detailed in Diane Galusha's book *Liquid Assets: A History of New York City's Water System*, the web of upstate reservoirs supplying the city's water – over a billion gallons a day – is largely delivered through gravity. Still, it's time to dispel the myth: homeowners pay water bills. Or at least they're supposed to. According to an expose in *The New York Times* in December 2006, millions of dollars in water bills go unpaid annually, the by-product of a colossally ineffective revenue-collection system. Now, with renewed attention being paid to this untapped (ahem) source of revenue, get ready for city government to crack down. Renters, rest easy: your water-bill share is almost certainly built into your monthly rent. But homeowners, if you're not paying and the local government gets its act together, you might need to pay up.

The body that oversees this is the New York City Department of Environmental Protection (www.nyc.gov/html/dep), which thankfully does a great job otherwise in protecting and servicing the city's precious water supply.

In addition to water, you'll need electricity. The Consolidated Edison Company of New York, a regulated utility known as ConEd (www.coned.com), provides it. While the company's antecedents go back some 180 years, today it brings electricity – partly through 91,000 miles of underground cables and another 35,000 miles of overheard wires – to all five boroughs (minus a sliver of Queens) and most of Westchester County, which is just north of the Bronx. ConEd also delivers natural gas to Manhattan, the Bronx and much of Queens and Westchester, and it also oversees what it calls the world's largest steam system, all of which services Manhattan.

Blackouts ◀

On August 14, 2003, the entire US northeast and a huge part of eastern Canada experienced the largest blackout in North American history, affecting 50 million people. For New York, it was the third blackout in the last 50 years – the others were in 1965 and 1977. The causes were investigated extensively in the media, and while there remains an ongoing concern about the age and stability of the interdependent power grids servicing the US and Canada, the odds of another such event remain remote. In 2006, a blackout in Queens was far smaller in scale, although the 100,000 residents affected weren't very happy about it.

Electricity

To get your electricity running, call ConEd on 1-800-75-CONED (800 752 6633). It is toll-free, open 24/7. All information needed to start your account can be taken over the phone. There are Spanish-speaking and English-speaking operators. If you're more comfortable in a different language, translators can be provided. Alternatively, visit www.coned.com/customercentral, and be sure to read your customers' rights. Your electricity should be turned on before you move in – all you need is your address. Sometimes ConEd asks for a copy of your lease, personal ID or a deposit, but these are rare exceptions and usually based on prior billing records that are less than satisfactory. If your request for electricity turn-on goes unfulfilled, ConEd tries to fix things in 24 hours. If you're home relies on gas, you'll need to give the technician entrance to your home. If you're in transit, ask your landlord, a neighbour or a friend to help.

Electricity bills vary, naturally, by usage. In a one-bedroom apartment, a good winter bill is $50-80 a month – assuming you don't use electric heat. If you do, your bill might climb another 50-100%. In summertime, air conditioning may be necessary; a monthly bill of $150 is pretty good. For each additional room, figure an additional $20-30 a month, or more during hot months. Private homes can be costly in terms of electricity, hence the benefits of conservation. Depending on your situation, you can strike a deal with ConEd to pay the expected average bill each month, regardless of your meter reading. While ConEd will want to read your meter monthly, if it's located in a hard-to-access place like a basement, someone may need to physically let the ConEd employee in to take the reading.

Electricity 101
- AC, or alternating current, is the US standard.
- Virtually all appliances, with the possible exception of those from Europe or Asia, have the plugs needed to run in a U.S. household.
- Most sockets are three-prong.

Water

Unless you're building a private home from the ground up, you can operate under the assumption that water lines are already connected to your residence. Certainly if you're moving into any kind of pre-existing structure – a rental, cooperative or condominium – you'll find the water ready to run. If, however, you're one of the very few New Yorkers creating a house on an untouched patch of land, your architect (to say nothing of your builders) will work with the city's Department of Environmental Protection (www.nyc.gov/html/dep) to tap your tap. According to a *New York Times* expose published in December 2006, millions of dollars in water bills are going unpaid every year. It's a governmental revenue-collection issue that you can expect will be dealt with in the next few years. It's also why the New York City Water Board raised 2007 water-use rates 9.4%. The info box below also provides some figures based on a rate of $4.68 per 100 cubic feet of water use. Again, these are averages. The heights and types of buildings vary in New York City, and again, if you're renting, these charges are already part of your rent. If you're paying your water bill, send payments to: NYC Water Board, PO BOX 410, Church Street Station, New York, NY 10008-0410 (making the cheque payable to: NYC Water Board).

Wash it Down
New York City's water is among the safest and tastiest in the world. It is slightly chlorinated but absolutely safe to drink, cook with or use any way you like.

Sewerage

As befitting a metropolis of eight million, New York City's sewer system is one of the world's largest, with over 6,600 miles of pipes and mains – twice the width of the continental US. It's also one of the world's oldest: the rudiments were started during the 17th century Dutch colonisation and formalised in the 20th century. Today, the city's 14 plants treat 1.3 billion waste-water gallons daily, and all paid for with your taxes! Recently, the city has upgraded its treatment plants to meet the standards of the federal Clean Water Act, thus encouraging certain kinds of fish and plant life to return to the Hudson and East Rivers, Long Island Sound, and other vital bodies of water. And no, alligators don't live in the sewer. At least, it hasn't been proven yet…

Rubbish Disposal and Recycling

Five boroughs, tens of thousands of buildings, homes, families, institutions and businesses – can you imagine how much garbage there is? According to the New York City Department of Sanitation, there's at least 25,000 tonnes of garbage (that's 50 million pounds) every day, picked up by a staff of nearly 10,000, operating more than 3,000 different vehicles. All residences and buildings have regular schedules for garbage pick-up, usually two or three times a week. And that's where you come in: recycling is the law in New York City. To read all about it, you can visit www.nyc.gov, but some of the basics should be second-nature to you. For example, you'll want to separate your paper items, like newspapers, from the rest of your garbage, and you'll also want to set aside glass objects and plastic items, like soda bottles, as well. Soon you won't think twice about it.

Where you physically put your garbage varies by residence. You may have large tubs outside your building, usually labelled to indicate

Average Water Costs

Type of Dwelling	Average Water Rate (annualised)
Single-family	$705 ($58.75/month)
Two-family	$1,094 ($91.16/month)
Walk-Up Building	$3351 ($504 per dwelling)
Elevator Building:	$37,710 ($571 per apartment)

141

which items go where. (You'll also want to be sure all garbage goes into garbage bags.) You may, however, live in a building with an incinerator or a compactor, or a central storage facility that gets emptied by your superintendent on certain days.

Telephone

Until the 80s, AT&T pretty much dominated the entire US telephone industry. But then the federal government decided to break it up, creating a large group of 'baby bells' – smaller telephone companies that ushered in an era of competition which continues until this day. It has also coincided with the growth of the computer industry, the invention of the cell phone, and the popularity of a long list of advanced types of telephony, from PDFs to Bluetooth and beyond. In New York City, the nation's media capital, the breadth of options for something as simple as a telephone can be pretty bracing. Verizon Communications (www.verizon.com), formerly known as Bell Atlantic (and NYNEX before that), is perhaps the largest landline provider to the five boroughs. But no one ever thinks of purely landline connection in the digital 21st century. You should also be thinking about internet and cable service, for example, as part of the equation. Almost all telephone companies offer packages that feature high-speed web access and cable. One particular upstart that's growing in popularity is RCN (www.rcn.com). Many residents are eschewing landlines entirely, relying instead on cell phones exclusively.

Telephone Companies		
AT&T	212 789 6400	www.att.com
Rosenman & Colin LLP	212 940 8624	na
Staples Communications	212 907 0211	www.staplescom.com
Teligent	800 799 7746	www.teligent.com

Imagine you've left home for the day without your cell phone and you've got to make that call. You're in luck! New York City's public telephones are still around, and while they aren't really booths anymore (sorry, Superman!), they're about as ubiquitous as curbs, manhole covers and street signs. For a quarter, you can call anywhere in the five boroughs. They do break down – about one in five public phones are 'on the fritz', some say – but they're a good resource in a squeeze. Some take phone cards, some take just coins; just look at the front of the phone to find out what's what.

The period before you move into your home is a great time to engage in that time-honoured American practice: comparison shopping. Speak to your landlord and your neighbours about which telephone provider they use, and visit their websites for packages and promotions. While the communications universe in town is diverse, the competition really is fierce, and loyalty may sometimes bring rewards like discounts and special offers. Always ask about peak hours and long-distance providers, but the days of special night time hours being drastically discounted are fast fading away – typically, these days, you'll get an unlimited amount of domestic calls for a specific flat fee. You'll also be offered all kinds of frills, from call waiting and call forwarded to three-way calling and speed dialling, and some of these will cost extra at times. The same goes for voicemail, which can be a nice thing if you don't want to set up an old-fashioned answering machine. You can also learn about blocking your phone from unwanted harassment, as well as how to join the federal 'Do Not Call' list (www.donotcall.gov), which prevents telemarketers from hawking their wares at all hours of the day and night. As you walk around the more middle-class neighbourhoods of New York - especially below 14th Street or above 96th Street in Manhattan, and

Mobile Service Providers		
AT&T	212 789 6400	www.att.com
Cingular Wireless	212 598 4180	www.cingular.com
International Cellular Services, Inc.	800 897 5788	www.internationalcellular.com
Omnipoint Center	212 687 4800	www.omnipoint.com
Omnipoint Communications	212 358 6300	na
Sprint PCS	800 818 0961	www.sprint.com
Verizon Wireless	212 206 7587	www.verizonwireless.com

The Big Card Con
If you're trying to find the cheapest way to call overseas, the worst bet, alas, is phone cards. They're marketed as inexpensive, but they are really profit-generating devices for autonomous sellers of phone time and rarely save customers money.

almost everywhere you look in the Bronx, Queens, Brooklyn and Staten Island – you'll find groceries and delis and bodegas offering phone cards for international calls. As the core of the nation's melting pot, immigrants from more than 100 different countries are living in New York, and they call home as much as possible. Here and there, you'll see stores full of nothing but small private booths where these calls can often be made. Sure, the rates on these calls can be outrageous – take a trip on the subway and you'll see advertisements touting a $5 fee to talk to Malaysia for five minutes and things of that ilk. If at all possible, make these calls from your home phone, or your cell phone if your plan allows for it. Phone cards are designed to be enormously profitable to the seller and unfathomably expensive for the purchaser.

Cheap Overseas Calls

Making overseas calls will always be financially challenging. Certain phone companies will run discounts from time to time, and you'll even find that on the subway, international-call discounts may be touted from time to time. At the time you set up your phone service, you'll be asked to choose your long-distance provider, and this is a good time to visit the websites of different companies to assess which one, potentially, might be the best bet. One avenue to investigate is internet telephony

Cheap Overseas Calls		
Acculinq		www.acculinq.port5.com
Cingular Wireless	888 333 6651	www.cingular.com
Sprint	800 877 7746	www.sprint.com

or Voice over Internet Protocol (VoIP): check out websites such as www.tmcnet.com, www.gizmoproject.com, and www.skype.com.

Internet

Other options **Websites** p.46, **Internet Cafes** p.406

All Wired Up
You'll quickly find most New Yorkers connecting to the web at home and at work. It's an immensely well-wired town. And the internet, despite political wrangling to the contrary, remains one of the most beautiful expressions of the First Amendment – the freedom of speech – the US has ever known.

Before the US was wired for broadband – today, 95% of all US zip codes have at least some high-speed web subscribers – dialing-up was the way to go. It was the era when America Online ruled it all. Today, especially in New York, connecting to the internet is a race to the financial bottom: more and more you can bundle – cheaply – your web connection with your cable or telephone service, or independently. You can log on via AOL ($5.99 a month is a great deal), but behold the competition: Road Runner (via Time Warner Cable), rcn.com (plus phone and cable service), gmail.com (through Google), earthlink.net (as low as $12.95 per month for the first six months), yahoo.com, msn.com, mac.com, hotmail.com, Comcast.net – the list goes on and on. Some offer web access, some just email, some a blizzard of options. The point is: the web is getting cheaper to hook onto, and is one of the few things in New York that is genuinely inexpensive!

Fortunately, all of New York City is increasingly being wired for Wi-Fi hotspots. No, it's not on the urban agenda the way it is in Philadelphia – which has pledged to make the whole city Wi-Fi friendly – but there are literally hundreds of free wireless-access sites. There are 85 public library branches, for example, as well as FedEx Kinko's stories and scores of Starbuck's branches.

So why would you want to visit an internet cafe? Good question – it's one reason they're starting to disappear from the landscape. Still, it's hard to print something out while sunning yourself on a Central Park lawn. CyberCafe Times Square (www.cyber-cafe.com), opened in 1995, is a good

Internet Service Providers		
A1 Terabit Net	212 344 4443	www.terabit.net
Digital Fusion	973 285 2600	www.digitalfusion.com
Galaxy Internet Services	888 334 2529	www.gis.net
Grand Central Networks	888 426 0010	www.grand-central.net
New York Internet Company	212 696 3822	www.nyi.net
New York Internet Services	212 414 4638	www.newyorknet.net
Smartweb Inc.	212 692 0074	www.smartweb.net
Web Express, Inc.	888 932 4736	www.webex.net

one with two Midtown branches, although it's expensive: $6.40 per half-hour minimum, $3.20 per each 15 minutes thereafter. Consider their prepay deals to lower costs. In Greenwich Village and elsewhere, check out Web2Zone (54 Cooper Sq, other locations, www.web2zone.com), which offers customers videogame access, an internet entry point, and a small business owner unit all in one shop. For $60, you can browse the web for the day, or opt for smaller deals, like $3 per 15 minutes or $12 an hour.

Bill Payment

Just as it is elsewhere in the US, your phone, cable, and web access charges, whether billed all in one or separately, must be paid each month. Credit cards are also billed monthly. Your electric bill (if you pay one) is due each month. It's hard to think of any bill that isn't available to be transacted or satisfied on the internet. Indeed, many corporations, in the spirit of thinking environmentally, now offer financial inducements to customers who opt not to receive paper bills through the mail. In the richly capitalistic society that we live in, late fees are ubiquitous, so you should always try paying your bills on time. Sometimes penalties are meagre: 1.5% for late ConEd charges, for example. Sometimes they're borderline illegal – as if loan sharks are running your credit cards.

Post & Courier Services

Courier Services

There are many non-governmental courier services. Federal Express (www.fedex.com) is one that is domestically popular; while DHL (www.dhl.com) tends to be more global in scope. Fees and delivery times vary, of course.

The US Postal Service was created in 1775. It delivers billions of items annually, including 23 million pieces daily to New York City, and is a phenomenally efficient enterprise. The post office, as it's called, offers myriad ways to mail letters or send packages – visit www.usps.com to learn about them. Aside from typical letters and postcards, there's Express Mail, Priority Mail, Parcel Post and Media Mail (with varying arrival times and fees) and at least five variably-priced overseas mailing methods (add 'global' to the prior-mentioned terms, plus Global Airmail, Global Economy). US mail is delivered every day except Sunday. Domestically, a letter can arrive in one to three days. International mail can take two to four days or longer, depending on the country of origin. Packages will always take longer.

Through post offices, you can buy stamps (or buy them online and print them), track mailed items, ensure items are signed for, and insure the items. You can calculate postage at any post office or online. Mail can be stopped or started at different addresses (arranged via the web), and you can also receive your passport, make Social Security changes, buy money orders and rent on-site post office boxes where available. Mailboxes are everywhere in New York City – you'll never walk two blocks to find one. And unless you rent a post office box away from home, your mail will come to your door or to a mailbox suite in your building lobby.

Radio

Roughly half the New York radio stations are broadcast from within New York City, but that can change from year to year. For example, Clear Channel Communications, owner of more than 1200 radio stations nationwide, announced plans in 2006 to divest certain specific properties. For talk and a chance to phone in with your two cents worth, AM channels like WOR (710 on your dial), WABC (770) and WNYC (820) offer a good range of current affairs, local, national and international news and talk shows (Right-Winger Rush Limbaugh gets opinionated on his controversial show between 12:00 and 15:00 on WABC). Tweak your knob to FM stations for more music and mayhem as you'll hear on WHTZ

Courier Services		
Aramex	718 553 8740	www.aramex.com
Dart Courier	212 947 7777	www.dartcourier.com
DHL	800 225 5345	www.dhl-usa.com
Direct Rush	800 980 7874	www.directrush.com
JFX Direct	877 312 3339	www.jefex.com
Quik-Trak Messenger Service	212 463 7070	www.quik-trak.com
RDS Delivery Service	212 260 5800	www.rdsdelivery.com
UPS	800 742 5877	www.ups.com

Reality TV Rules

Reality TV rules the US airwaves at the moment, with shows like American Idol, Dancing With the Stars, Biggest Loser and Survivor dominating the ratings. However, there are also several non-reality shows that also perform consistently well. If you're not addicted to Lost, House, Prison Break or Desperate Housewives, you probably don't have your own TV!

(100.3) - otherwise lovingly known as 'Z-100' – with madcap competitions, prizes, phone-ins and a lot of DJ banter. For more of a Hip Hop and R&B tip, swing on by to 97.1, home to WQHT or 'Hot 97'. Commercial radio does tend to get a bit same-old-same-old but college radio is on the up and offers a bit more of an alternative. Try WNYU (89.1) and WKCR (89.9) coming out of NYU (New York University) and Columbia University, respectively. Fordham University airs the coolest blues, folk and Irish music (WFUV – 90.7). The infamous Howard Stern does his thing 06:00 to 10:00 daily on WXRK (92.3) where he mixes sleaze with alternative music.

Television

As the media capital of the US, New York City offers an overwhelming array of television stations, typically as part of larger national networks. WCBS-TV, WNBC, WNYW-TV, WABC-TV, WWOR-TV and WPIX, for example, all present local newscasts on weekday and usually on weekend evenings, but also participate in the national programming of their network owners (CBS, NBS, ABC, Fox, etc.) during other times of the day. WNET (known as 'Channel 13'), on the other hand, is an affiliation of the Public Broadcasting Service, which is commercial-free yet handsomely subsists on contributions from hundreds of thousands of members in the tri-state (New York/New Jersey/Connecticut) area. If a few television stations are genuinely independent, they are almost always affiliated in some way with other networks and organisations. NY1 (pronounced 'New York One') is the city's beloved all-news channel, offered by Time Warner Cable. Virtually all TV stations in the US are in English, but there are Spanish-language stations available for viewing in New York City through virtually all cable providers. Most television programming is digital-ready, and censorship – or at least restrictions on content and language – is the provenance of in-house standards and practices departments as well as overseen by the Federal Communications Commission. When sufficiently provoked, the FCC has been known to levy hefty fines for acceptability violations. It can also revoke a station's licence.

Satellite TV & Radio

TV History

The Museum of Television and Radio (25 West 52nd Street, www.mtr.org, 212 621 6800) is a neat way to while away a few hours. You can check out your favourite golden oldies and flick through their collection of 50,000 American TV and Radio programmes from across the ages.

Given Gotham's immense focus on media, it's perhaps surprising that satellite TV hasn't properly caught on until fairly recently. Possibly one reason is the dominance and ubiquity of cable television, which began fully wiring the city more than 25 years ago. However, with NYC's enduring historical status as the worldwide intersection of media, finance and geopolitics – satellite television is definitely on the rise. The Dish Network and Direct TV are two main providers, with packages that start at $29.99 a month. Through satellite TV service, you'll be able to see all programmes available via cable television, as well as hundreds of shows on thousands of broadcast stations around the globe. Another satellite-programming trend is radio. For example, American 'shock-jock' Howard Stern, for many years a fixture on syndicated FM radio nationwide, began to broadcast on Sirius Satellite Radio (www.sirius.com) in January 2006. Sirius, just like its primary competitor XM Radio (www.xmradio.com), sports nearly 200 additional 'channels,' encompassing every conceivable kind of music and talk, available for listening and downloading. Sirius fees currently include a 'lifetime' subscription for $499.99, a one-year subscription (plus one month free) for $142.45, a two-year subscription (plus three months free) for $271.95, and month-to-month service for $12.95. Fees for XM Radio come in yearly packages – $142.45 for one year, $271.95 for two years, $359.64 for three years, $479.52 for four years (sense a trend here?), and $599.40 for five years. There's also a $12.95 monthly rate.

Satellite/Cable Providers

DirecTV	800 494 4388	www.directv.com
Dish Network	888 825 2557	www.dishnetwork.com
Time Warner	212 567 3833	www.twcnyc.com

145

General Medical Care

New York offers some of the best hospitals and health care centres in the world, but the United States government does not guarantee its citizens regular access to medical care. Hospitals maintain emergency rooms which are required by federal law to treat individuals in need of emergency attention, regardless of their ability to pay. However, outside of emergencies, most individuals rely upon private health insurance plans (often subsidised by their employers) to help manage the extremely high costs of health care, as no universal government health plan exists.

The majority of healthcare occurs in privately run outpatient treatment centres, where people see a primary care physician for regular check-ups, prescriptions, and treatment for common illnesses. Private health insurance companies generally maintain lists of doctors whose fees they will subsidise, and New Yorkers often rely upon word of mouth to choose doctors from the lists which their insurance companies provide them. Maternity care is also important, and tends to be covered under medical insurance plans. Pregnant women have regular visits with their obstetrician-gynecologists ('OBGYNs') during their pregnancies and in the months after giving birth.

Dental care is also a priority for most residents, who, on average, visit the dentist twice a year for cleanings and check-ups. Dental health care insurance is generally available separately from primary medical health insurance.

New York is a major centre for cosmetic surgery in the United States, but cosmetic surgery does not tend to be covered by health insurance plans, unless it is the direct result of a disfiguring accident or illness.

Government Healthcare

The primary sources of government-funded health insurance are Medicare (for individuals 65 and older or with long-term disabilities), Medicaid (for the underprivileged), and the State Children's Insurance Program (for low-income children of the 'working class poor' whose parents are not eligible for Medicaid). However, in order to be eligible for government-funded health care programmes, most legal, non-citizen residents of the United States must first reside in the country for five years.

Private Healthcare

The standard of private health care in New York is high, as it is a major centre for privately run 'teaching hospitals' that maintain affiliations with prominent universities. Where to go depends on what you are seeking treatment for. Memorial Sloan Kettering Cancer Center, for example, is the city's pre-eminent cancer treatment facility, while New York-Presbyterian Hospital at the Columbia University Medical Center offers the best care for stroke victims, according to a November 2006 survey of doctors performed by *New York Magazine*. Other prestigious private hospital centres include the Hospital for Special Surgery (renowned for its orthopedic care), Mount Sinai Medical Center, NYU Medical Center, Bellevue Hospital Center, New York-Presbyterian Hospital at Weill-Cornell Medical Center, Beth Israel Medical Center, and Lenox Hill Hospital.

It is virtually essential to obtain medical insurance in order to diffuse the increasingly high costs of health care in New York and throughout the United States. Many employers subsidise health insurance as a perk of employment (including for non-citizen residents), but generally only for full-time employees. The various types of health insurance plans available in the United States tend to utilise some form of 'managed care' – policies designed to cut down on health care costs by placing

Fit to Work?
Employers do not generally require health checkups, although some may require their employees to pass drug tests as a condition of employment.

Can't Breathe? Can't Hear?
Air and noise pollution can pose health risks for New Yorkers. As a result, city law bans smoking in enclosed, public spaces and limits the number of new bars or clubs that can be opened in primarily residential areas. Some New York residents rely upon machines to produce 'white noise' in their homes to help block out loud outdoor noises, and use ear plugs to protect their ears against loud underground subway traffic.

146

restrictions on the services an insurance company will subsidise, and often requiring patients to obtain approval in advance of receiving specialised care.

The major types of insurance plans are: 'fee-for-service' plans, health maintenance organisations ('HMOs'), and preferred provider organisations ('PPOs'). With fee-for-service plans, individuals pay a monthly premium and, after they have hit a specified 'deductible' (minimum amount, usually $200 or more, they must pay out-of-pocket before their insurance kicks in), their insurance pays a percentage of their healthcare costs (usually 60-80%) and they pay the balance. However, there is often an annual cap placed upon the amount the individual will be required to pay himself. Once this pre-specified limit is reached, the insurance company will pay the remainder of all fees and expenses in full, although the individual will still be required to pay the monthly premium. Although they tend to be more expensive, a major advantage of fee-for-service plans is that they allow individuals to utilise any doctor or hospital they wish. HMOs, by contrast, are less expensive but are also more restrictive. Consequently, they tend to attract the young and healthy, who may only need to visit the doctor once or twice per year. With an HMO, you pay a monthly premium (around $350) and have no deductible to hit; you simply make a standard co-payment, depending upon the type of treatment you receive. However, you must use doctors and treatment facilities on the insurance company's pre-approved list. The co-payment for a visit to a primary care physician is around $15, an emergency room visit will cost you around $50-100, and the co-payment for prescription drugs can range from anywhere to $10-$100, depending upon the type of drug and whether it is available in a generic (non-brand name) variety. PPOs offer a compromise between standard HMO care and Fee-for-Service Plans. Like HMOs, they require you to pay a monthly premium of around $350. When you use a doctor on their list of 'preferred providers,' you make a standard co-payment, along the lines of what you would pay through an HMO. If you see a doctor who is not on the list, they will still cover a portion of your fees, although less than if you had seen a preferred provider.

Emergency Services

Get Help

If you have an illness or accident that prevents you from being able to transport yourself to the emergency room, dial 911 and an operator will confirm your address and immediately dispatch an ambulance with paramedics. Response times vary, but an ambulance will generally arrive within 10-15 minutes, as they are stationed in multiple locations throughout the five boroughs of New York City.

Many New York City hospitals offer 24 hour emergency care, and are required by law to treat emergency care patients, regardless of their ability to pay. In an emergency, you can go directly to the hospital's emergency ward, where patients are prioritised according to the urgency of care needed. Bellevue Hospital Center, New York-Presbyterian Hospital, Mount Sinai Medical Center, and NYU Medical Center offer particularly excellent emergency care, as reported in a 2006 *New York Magazine* survey.

Pharmacies

Most pharmacies in New York are located within grocery stories or 'drug stores' (such as Duane Reade, CVS, Rite Aid, or Walgreen's) that carry basic food and household items. Most pharmacies tend to be open at least 12 hours from Monday to Friday (generally from 09:00 to 21:00), with shorter Saturday hours (10:00 to 18:00 or so), and they remain closed on Sundays. However, 24 hour pharmacies do exist at certain branch locations, such as Walgreen's (145 Fourth Avenue at 14th Street), Duane Reade (1279 Third Avenue at 72nd Street), and CVS (1622 Third Avenue at 91st Street). These pharmacies supply prescription medication around the clock, such as birth control pills, antibiotics, or strong pain relievers. Drugs available 'over the counter' (without a prescription) include aspirin, acetaminophen, and mild cold and allergy relief medications. These medications can be purchased in drug stores, grocery stores, or at kiosks located throughout the city, even when pharmacies are closed.

For a list of pharmacies, see the table on p.339. It's always a good idea to call a few pharmacies in your area to find out where your nearest 24 hour pharmacy is.

147

Health Check-Ups

Most New Yorkers rely on their primary care physicians for regular medical check-ups. However, many non-profit organisations throughout the city offer free or low-cost health services for those who cannot afford regular doctor visits but may not qualify for Medicare or Medicaid. The New York City Free Clinic, affiliated with New York University and located at 16 East 16th Street, offers comprehensive free healthcare. The Planned Parenthood of New York, which offers free family planning services, also provides free health check-ups. The City of New York periodically promotes preventative health care screenings. For example, the city government's 'Take Care New York' health initiative (www.nyc.gov, search for 'Take Care New York') offered free walk-in health screenings at public hospitals in all five boroughs every Tuesday in October 2006. Available screenings included diabetes, high blood pressure, cholesterol, asthma, depression, and cancer.

Health Insurance Companies

Alnic Inc	212 787 3405	www.alnicinc.com
CIGNA	212 618 5500	www.cigna.com
Group Health Incorporated	212 615 0000	www.ghi.com
Principal Insurance	212 687 5858	www.principal.com

Donor Cards

The New York State Organ and Tissue Donor Registry maintains a list of people who want to donate their organs and tissues after death. You can enrol by checking the donor box on a driving licence or identification card application, obtained from the New York State Department of Motor Vehicles (DMV). It is also possible to enroll in the donation programme through the State Health Department's website (www.health.state.ny.us), which will send donor cards to registered individuals to carry in their wallets. Whether or not you are registered as a donor, it is still necessary for your family to provide their consent to organ and tissue donation in the event of your death.

Blood Drives

For additional information on blood drives throughout the city and collection centres, visit the websites of the New York Blood Center (www.nybloodcenter.org) or the American Red Cross (www.givelife.org).

Giving Blood

Blood donation is a common practice throughout the United States, and blood drives are sponsored by local and state governments, hospitals, schools, and employers virtually every day of the year. Hospitals and treatment centres are desperately in need of donations from individuals of all blood types, but individuals with 'O-negative' blood are in particularly high demand, as they are the 'universal donors.'

Giving Up Smoking

The 'Take Care New York' initiative sponsors a Smoker's Quitline. By dialling 311 on a landline, smokers can receive free help quitting. Many hospitals run 'Smoking Cessation' clinics, which provide some combination of individual, group, telephone, and online support. The Directory of Health and Hospitals Corporation (HHC) Smoking Cessation Clinics, organised by borough, is available online (www.nyc.gov). The New York State Smoker's Quitsite (www.nysmokefree.com, or 1 866 NY QUITS) offers a compendium of educational and resource links, and a free starter kit of nicotine patches, gum, or lozenges for eligible New York State smokers. Alternative approaches like hypnotherapy or acupuncture are also readily available (see p.159).

Main Government Hospitals

Most hospitals in New York are structured as privately owned, non-profit organisations, although there are some public hospitals in the area. These have higher occupancy rates, and although they don't always receive the same degree of accolades as privately owned hospitals with larger endowments, the standard of care is still high.

Public Hospitals

Bellevue Hospital Center	Gramercy Park	212 562 4141
Coler-Goldwater Memorial	Roosevelt Island	212 848 6054
Harlem Hospital Center	Harlem	212 939 1000
Metropolitan Hospital Center	Harlem	212 423 6262

148

Main Private Hospitals

First Ave
At East 16th St
Gramercy Park

Beth Israel Medical Center

212 420 2000 | *www.wehealnewyork.org*

The Beth Israel is one of the five hospitals included in the Continuum Health Partners non-profit hospital system of New York City. It is a teaching hospital, and has been helping patients from its Lower East Side location since the early 1900s. Services available include deliveries, care of newborns, drug abuse treatment, and psychiatry. Beth Israel has been recognised within New York State for excellence in cardiology and orthopaedics. The hospital welcomes volunteers who wish to help in any area, from assisting elderly patients, to caring for children or those with cancer.

535 East 70th St
Upper East Side

Hospital for Special Surgery

212 606 1930 | *www.hss.edu*

The Hospital for Special Surgery is a smaller hospital which, true to its name, provides exceptional specialised care. Their orthopaedic surgery is among the best in the world, and they perform over 17,000 procedures annually. HSS is also a pioneer in many treatments, including the first total knee replacement, and some of the best and most cutting edge anaesthesia techniques. Dr. James Knight, along with just 20 prominent New Yorkers, founded the hospital in 1863. Its relatively long history makes it a particularly desirable institution to score a place on a residency programme.

1275 York Ave
Upper East Side

Memorial Sloan-Kettering

212 639 2000 | *www.mskcc.org*

Sloan-Kettering, the nation's oldest cancer hospital, is also considered by many to be the best cancer treatment hospital in the whole of the United States, and treats more than 400 different subtypes of cancer every year. The hospital offers some of the best patient care, research facilities and education programmes available anywhere. Other nationally ranked departments include gynaecology, urology, otolaryngology (ear/nose/throat) and gastroenterology.

1 Gustave L Levy Pl
Upper East Side

Mount Sinai Hospital

212 241 6500 | *www.mountsinai.org*

One of the country's biggest voluntary teaching hospitals, Mount Sinai has received national attention for its geriatrics, gastroenterology, otolaryngology, rehabilitation, and psychiatry departments. Treating since 1852, the hospital is also one of the country's oldest teaching hospitals, with very high standards of clinical care, education, and scientific research in most types of medicine. Facilities include the Guggenheim Pavilion, designed by architect I.M. Pei, who used natural light and space to encourage positive healing and feelings in patients.

Dermatologists

Abrahams, Irving, MD - Dept of Dermatology, Columbia Presby	Gramercy Park	212 305 5301
American Dermatology Center	Hell's Kitchen	212 245 8123
Bickers, David, MD - Columbia Presbyterian Association	Central Park & Fifth Avenue	212 326 8465
Buchness, Mary Ruth, MD - St Vincents Hospital & Med Center	Flatiron District	212 647 6400
Deleo Vincent MD	Hell's Kitchen	212 523 6003
Franks, Andrew G., Jr., MD - Gramercy Park Dermatology Assoc	Gramercy Park	212 475 2312
Gordon, Marsha MD - Mt Sinai Dermatology Assoc	Central Park & Fifth Avenue	212 831 4119
Hatcher Virgil a MD	Chelsea	212 675 4244
Katz Bruce MD	Midtown	212 688 5882
Lombardo, Peter C, MD - Sutton Place Dermatology	Midtown	212 838 0270
Orlow, Seth, MD - Dermatologic associates	Gramercy Park	212 263 5889
Spencer, James M., MD	Upper East Side	212 241 6189

149

622 West 168th St
Btn Fort Washington
Ave & Broadway
Harlem

New York Presbyterian Hospital -Columbia Presbyterian Medical Center

212 305 2500 | *www.nypsystem.org*

The New York-Presbyterian Healthcare System is a monster organisation that includes a network of hospitals, specialist institutes, and care centres, all serving both New Jersey and Connecticut as well as New York. Its nationally recognised departments including neurology, neurosurgery, psychiatry, gynaecology, paediatrics, urology, cardiology, cardiac surgery, and orthopaedics. With an aim to change the way healthcare is delivered to the community, its website also has a very handy interactive guide to various diseases and conditions.

550 First Ave
Midtown

New York University Hospitals Center – Tisch Hospital

212 263 7300 | *www.med.nyu.edu*

Run by the Mount Sinai-NYU Medical Center and Health System, the Tisch Hospital is nationally renowned for its rehabilitation, rheumatology, orthopaedic, oncology, and cardiac care. The New York University School of Medicine itself is over 150 years old, and its students have helped shape American medicine throughout its history. For example, the school had the first department of physical medicine and rehabilitation, and the first outpatient clinic in the United States.

525 E 68th St
Upper East Side

New York Weill Cornell Med Center

212 746 5454 | *www.med.cornell.edu*

Affiliated with NewYork-Presbyterian Hospital, Memorial Sloan-Kettering Cancer Center, and the Hospital for Special Surgery, New York Weill Cornell Med Center has been up and running since 1898, and offers degree and PhD opportunities in areas such as clinical medicine or maternity care. It has nationally ranked specialties including psychiatry, neurology and neurosurgery, urology, gynaecology, gastroenterology, rheumatology, and cancer treatment.

1111 Amsterdam Ave
Harlem

St. Luke's – Roosevelt Hospital Center

212 523 4000 | *www.wehealny.org*

St. Luke's – Roosevelt is part of Continuum Health Partners, a nonprofit hospital system that also runs Beth Israel Hospital. St. Luke's – Roosevelt maintains two divisions at separate locations: St.Luke's next to Columbia University on Amsterdam Avenue, and the Roosevelt Hospital, two blocks west at Tenth Avenue at 59th Street (212 523 6800). The two hospitals joined in 1979 to offer excellent community care and cutting edge medical research.

Health Centres/Clinics

Bedford Stuyvesant Family Health Center Inc	Brooklyn	718 857 4268	Private
East New York Diganostic & Treatment Center	Brooklyn	718 240 0400	Government
Gouverneur Healthcare Services	Midtown	212 238 7000	Government
Greenpoint Family Health Center	Brooklyn	718 349 8500	Private
Lenox Hill Radiology & Medical	Upper East Side	212 772 3111	Private
Lincoln Medical and Mental Health Center	Brooklyn	718 579 4337	Government
Morrisania Diagnostic & Treatment Center	na	718 960 2777	Government
Park Slope Family Health Center	Brooklyn	718 832 5986	Private
Renaissance Diagnostic & Treatment Center	Harlem	212 932 6500	Government
Rtech Healthcare	Midtown	212 792 4389	Private
The Mount Sinai Medical Centre	Central Park & Fifth Avenue	212 241 6756	Private
Woodhull Medical Center	Brooklyn	718 963 8000	Government

Maternity

The standard of maternity care in the United States, including in New York, is quite high. As a result, many non-citizens elect to give birth in the States, where they have access to a wide range of birthing options. These options include giving birth at a hospital, at an independent 'birth centre' (which may offer the option of a 'water birth,' in which the mother delivers her child in a tub of water), or at home. While home births and water births are legal options, they must be attended by a doctor or certified nurse midwife. It should be noted that most doctors and midwives are not willing to perform home births, because in the event of delivery complications, there is generally not enough time to transport mother and child to a nearby facility to perform emergency procedures.

Although the vast majority of women in the United States give birth in hospitals, an increasing number of women who have experienced normal pregnancies and do not anticipate complications are choosing to give birth outside of the traditional hospital setting. As alternative birthing methods have increased in popularity, many hospitals have responded by constructing maternity care wards designed to evoke a 'more homely' and less institutional atmosphere.

Treatment and Care Options

The process of having a baby is fairly standardised across the United States, although there are a number of decisions to be made along the way. It is up to each woman to determine what kind of health care provider will monitor her regularly throughout her pregnancy, preside over the delivery, and monitor her health in the months following the birth. Most expectant mothers in the United States rely upon obstetrician-gynaecologists (OBGYNs), medical doctors who have received specialised training in providing medical and surgical care to females. In the case of normal pregnancies, family practitioners (medical doctors certified to perform standard vaginal births) or certified nurse midwives (licensed nurses with special training in midwifery) are also viable options. Family practitioners and midwives cannot perform Caesarean sections and generally refer complicated pregnancies to OBGYNs.

Other decisions to be made in collaboration with a health care professional include where to give birth, what kind of delivery to have (vaginal vs. Caesarean), when to induce labour (if necessary), and what techniques or drugs may be employed to relieve pain. Since 'customised' births are popular among New Yorkers, some elect to develop written birth plans that detail in writing their labour and delivery procedural preferences. While these plans are not legally binding, most doctors will adhere to them to the extent that it is medically advisable to do so.

Maternity Care Insurance Coverage

Most health insurance policies cover maternity costs, which includes prenatal care, delivery, and postnatal care. In New York, state law mandates that inpatient insurance coverage be provided for mother and newborn for at least 48 hours after vaginal childbirth and for at least 96 hours after delivery via Caesarean section. Hospitals are also legally obligated to provide education, assistance, and training in breastfeeding or bottle-feeding newborn infants. Beyond that, insurance coverage varies by company and policy.

Post-Natal Depression

Post-natal depression, also called post-partum depression, can occur up to a year after giving birth. Symptoms may include feelings of worthlessness or hopelessness, prolonged and high levels of anxiety, poor levels of bonding with the new baby, issues with eating, sleep difficulties, and a general sense of being 'out of control,' which may be accompanied by thoughts of harming yourself or your baby. Post-natal depression affects 10-15% of new mothers and is highly treatable through therapy and antidepressant medication. If you experience any of these symptoms for more than two weeks, contact your doctor immediately. For additional information on postpartum depression support resources in and around New York City, contact the Postpartum Resource Center of New York (www.postpartumny.org or 631 422 2255), the Mental Health Association of New York City hotline (800 273 8255), or any area hospital.

151

Older Mothers
Pregnant women 35 and over are more likely to have difficult labours or children with Down's Syndrome or birth defects. Because these women are in a higher risk category, their doctors may recommend that they undergo additional prenatal testing, such as extra blood tests or amniocentesis, which would identify certain conditions or potential developmental problems in the foetus.

Pain Management in Labour & Delivery

New York health care providers employ a number of approaches to alleviate some of the pain and stress of giving birth, through both 'natural' and medicinal methods. Natural techniques include focused breathing, massage, soothing imagery, and playing music during labour. Some parents employ doulas: these individuals are trained to provide practical and emotional support in the months preceding the birth and during labour, but are not certified to perform deliveries. Epidural anaesthesia, an 'ongoing injection of pain medication into the epidural space around the spinal cord (that) partially or fully numbs the lower body' is a common procedure, although some mothers opt to avoid this procedure because of certain risks involved.

Caesarean Sections

New York City has recently been at the centre of controversy regarding its disproportionately high level of Caesarean section deliveries and the failure of its hospitals to comply with the New York State Maternity Information Act, a law that requires hospitals to supply data regarding the number of c-section deliveries they perform. In 2004, nearly 29% of New York City births occurred via c-section, a rate that is significantly above the World Health Organisation's recommended 15%. Although elective caesarean sections do occur, an increasing number of doctors feel a responsibility to discourage them, as they pose more risks to mother and child than vaginal birth.

Antenatal Hospital Care

Once a baby is born, it receives a full physical examination. A blood test is administered to screen for hereditary diseases, HIV, and phenylketunoria. Although the initial physical examination cannot be delayed, some hospitals allow mothers to delay certain procedures (such as the blood test) in order to smooth the infant's transition into the world and to provide the parents with the opportunity to bond with the child, uninterrupted, for at least an hour after the birth. After the child's birth, a hospital liaison will generally coordinate the processing of the necessary paperwork, which includes filing a birth certificate and an application for a social security number (see 'Birth Certificate and Registration' section above). All individuals born in the United States, with the exception of children of foreign diplomats, are considered US citizens.

Choosing a Doctor

In New York, most women choose a maternity care doctor before choosing a hospital to deliver in, often through a general practitioner's referral or word-of-mouth recommendations. Each maternity care doctor is affiliated with a specific hospital or hospitals, which in turn narrows the field of hospitals from which to choose. New York's Maternity Care Information Act requires hospitals to provide written information to the public regarding the practices and procedures available, and specific data about the degree of frequency at which these services are performed. There are not specific hospitals for maternity – instead, maternal care units exist within the context of larger hospitals.

Classes and Support Groups

Many hospitals run prenatal and antenatal classes. Mount Sinai's Lauder Center for Maternity Care, for example, offers classes in the Lamaze technique (a popular breathing technique that can be used during labour and delivery), breastfeeding, sibling preparation, and infant care. Similarly, Columbia University's Department of Obstetrics offers childbirth and parenting classes, breast-feeding classes, and runs a phone line to provide support and to respond to childcare questions. It is best to check with individual hospitals to see what services and support they offer. The hospital resources available should be taken into consideration when deciding where to have your baby.

In addition to hospital support programmes, many gyms, yoga studios, and community centres offer classes and support for expectant mothers. New York Sports Club (212 246 6700) offers a fitness class entitled 'Preparing for the Marathon of Labour.' Many yoga studios, including Yoga Effects in midtown (212 754 5600) and SoHo Sanctuary (212 625 9353) offer neonatal yoga classes. The 92nd Street Y (www.92y.org) maintains a Parenting Center, where course offerings include Lamaze classes, a breastfeeding workshop, and a newborn care course.

Hospital Stay

Women who have uncomplicated deliveries generally stay in the hospital for two days, whereas those who deliver via c-section tend to stay for three or four days.

Maternity Care in Government Hospitals

Nearly all of the public hospitals in New York City offer Labour & Delivery services, as maternity care is one of the services they most frequently provide. Costs vary from hospital to hospital, depending upon the types of services selected and the complications that arise during the course of pregnancy or delivery. 'Birthing suites,' which offer a more comfortable, home-like atmosphere than standard labour and delivery rooms, are also more expensive. Epidurals are an option, although these are only offered in standard labour & delivery rooms. Birthing rooms may offer other methods of pain relief, but typically are used for uncomplicated deliveries that do not involve epidurals. Private rooms may be an option, but their availability is generally limited in public hospitals, and the cost will be higher than that of a double occupancy room. Although a woman in labour will not be turned away from a hospital that provides maternity services, it is recommended that each woman 'pre-register' at the hospital where she plans to give birth. At a minimum, patients can expect to be charged $5,000 - $8,000 for prenatal and delivery care. The extent to which these charges are subsidised by insurance varies tremendously.

Maternity Care in Private Hospitals

Like public hospitals, private hospitals in New York City offer a range of options for giving birth. Pre-natal, delivery, and ante-natal care are generally billed separately. Caesarean sections, epidurals, and treatment of any complications that arise will increase fees. As discussed above, birth plans are an option, and will usually be observed to the extent medically possible. The birthing suites described under the 'Government Hospitals' section are also available at private hospitals. These suites are generally more accommodating of special requests (e.g., candles or music) and tend to offer luxurious surroundings designed to camouflage medical equipment. Labour and delivery wards, by contrast, offer standard hospital accommodations at lower costs than the specialised birthing suites.

Delivery Room Guests

Allowing multiple people in the delivery room has become increasingly common throughout the United States. Policies vary across different hospitals, but the number of guests allowed is generally dictated by the constraints of the space. Birthing suites tend to be larger and can accommodate more guests. At St. Luke's Roosevelt Hospital Birthing Center, for example, there are no restrictions on the number of guests allowed. In the case of a Caesarean section, generally only one person is allowed in the operating room. Many hospitals offer patients the option, for an additional fee, of

Maternity Hospitals & Clinics

Childbirth Education Associates	Flatiron District	212 645 4911
NYU Downtown Hospital: Maternity Center	Flatiron District	212 312 5815
Saint Vincents Catholic Medical Ctrs of New York: Maternity Education	Chelsea	212 604 7946

153

working with a doula, an individual trained to provide emotional support to parents during pregnancy and delivery. Independent doulas, chosen and paid for directly by the individual, are also permissible.

Giving Birth in Your Home Country

United States airlines do not permit women 36 weeks or more pregnant to fly, so if you intend to give birth in your home country, you should plan on being there for at least the last four weeks of your pregnancy. If it is absolutely essential that you travel within four weeks of your due date, you must be examined within 48 hours of your departure time by an obstetrician and certified as 'medically stable for flight.' Also, if you are visibly pregnant, some airlines require a signed note from your doctor stating your estimated due date.

When you return from your home country with your infant, keep in mind that your infant will need a passport and visa. Healthy newborns are considered physically fit to fly; however, many airlines still require a certified doctor's note for newborns less than a week old. An infant under two years of age can sit on the lap of an accompanying adult for no extra charge. However, government-approved car-seats are generally recommended for air travel. It is important to check with the airline in advance to see if they have car-seats available or if you should bring your own. Many airlines offer discounted seats for infants under the age of 2.

Before you head to your home country to give birth, you should obtain copies of your prenatal medical records to give to your doctor in your home country. Similarly, when you return to the United States, you should bring copies of all medical records of pre-natal, labour and delivery, and post-natal care obtained in your home country. You should also have with you a copy of your child's birth certificate.

Antenatal Care

Antenatal care in the United States is generally excellent. Many women rely upon their regular OBGYN to see them through labour and delivery. However, if they are older or anticipate complications, they may want to see a doctor with special training/focus in handling complicated pregnancies. Most OBGYNs maintain relationships with specific hospitals, so your choice of OBGYN will likely affect where you can give birth. If you are committed to giving birth at a specific hospital, it is best to at least consider their staff OBGYNs, who will be most familiar with the equipment and services they provide.

Post-Natal Care

In the hospital, your baby will receive a full physical examination. At one minute and five minutes after birth, it will receive an Apgar score, which rates skin colour, heart rate, muscle tone, breathing, and reflexes to evaluate overall health. The baby will also be screened for deafness, blindness, HIV, and other potential physical ailments.

Once discharged from the hospital, newborns should be taken to the paediatrician at two weeks, while mothers should visit their OBGYNs for a check-up six weeks after giving birth. All hospitals provide breastfeeding training to mothers before they are discharged. In addition, many hospitals and private organisations sponsor breastfeeding support groups, hotlines, and classes (see 'Classes & Support Groups' above). Certified lactation consultants are widely available throughout New York. For example, the Manhattan Lactation Group (www.manhattanlactationgroup.com) offers one-on-one sessions, breastfeeding classes, and breastfeeding support groups. The New York Lactation Consultant Association (www.nylca.org) contains a listing of certified lactation consultants in the New York area as well as a compendium of breastfeeding resources and information.

Breastfeeding Buys

The Upper Breast Side (www.upperbreastside.com), on Manhattan's Upper West Side, sells a full range of nursing bras and clothing, and offers both sales and rentals of breast pump equipment.

154

Although breastfeeding in public is a topic of ongoing debate in the United States, New Yorkers have fairly liberal attitudes. New York has always been at the forefront of breastfeeding legislation in the United States, and state law protects the right of mothers to breastfeed in public. However, discretion is always appreciated, particularly in fancier restaurants, clubs, and lounges.

Maternity Leave

Paid maternity leave in the United States is rare. The Family and Medical Leave Act (FMLA) guarantees up to twelve weeks of unpaid leave, with health insurance, to new parents (male or female), following an adoption or birth. In order to be eligible for coverage under FMLA, you must be employed by the government or by a private company with 50 or more employees that you have worked at for at least a year. If you decide not to return to your job after taking leave under FMLA, your employer may require you to reimburse them for the cost of maintaining your health insurance while you were on leave. For additional information on the FMLA, contact the US Department of Labour at 866 487 9243.

New York State requires employers to have temporary disability programmes that pay benefits and partial salary to any expectant mother whose pregnancy is characterised as a 'disability' by her doctor.

Beyond these legal minimums, the amount of paid or unpaid leave provided to an employee is up to the individual employer. Many require their employees to use a combination of vacation and sick days to cover the remainder of their time off.

Gynaecology & Obstetrics

As with most doctors in New York, the best way to find a good gynaecologist is through word-of-mouth referrals from other patients. Male and female gynaecologists are available.

The major methods of contraception that can be obtained by prescription only are: birth control pills (oral contraceptives), the birth control patch (which releases hormones through the skin), the ring (inserted into the vagina for a month at a time and releases hormones), the shot (an injection of hormone), the implant (a newer method, whereby a small plastic implant is inserted underneath the skin of the upper arm), diagrams/caps/shields (physical inserts into the vagina), and intrauterine devices ('IUDs', inserted by a doctor into the uterus).

'Barrier' methods of birth control are available in pharmacies, drug stores, and grocery stores without a prescription. The most common are the 'male' condom (worn over the penis), vaginal inserts such as the female condom or the sponge, and spermicide (suppositories, jellies, or creams designed to release chemicals that immobilise sperm; may be used in conjunction with other barrier methods).

For women over the age of 18, emergency contraception is available over the counter in the form of 'Plan B' hormone pills that can reduce the risk of pregnancy when taken within five days of unprotected sex. Women under the age of 18 will need a prescription to obtain these pills.

For additional information on contraception and reproductive rights, contact the New York City chapter of the Planned Parenthood (www.ppnyc.org), a national

Breast Cancer & Mammograms

Women over 40 and those with a family history of breast cancer should receive regular mammograms (every one to two years). It is estimated that as many as one in eight women get breast cancer at some stage, yet one out of every four women in New York City does not receive regular mammograms. The Health and Hospitals Corporation (HHC) provides low-cost mammogram screenings at six locations throughout the city. For more information, dial 311 and ask about mammograms. Free mammograms are available to qualified individuals without insurance. For a complete listing of sites offering free mammogram services throughout New York, visit www.health.state.ny.us, or browse www.nyc.gov for additional information about breast cancer prevention and mammograms.

155

Gynaecology & Obstetrics

Gruss Leslie Dr	Soho	212 966 7600
Jacobs Allan J MD	Midtown	212 263 2353
Rehnstrom Jaana MD	Flatiron District	212 366 4765
Rodke Gae MD	Upper West Side	212 496 9800
Sadarangani Balvinder B MD	Gramercy Park	212 982 4100
Sailon Peter MD	Upper East Side	212 879 9191
Steadman E Thomas MD PC	Upper East Side	212 628 1500
Strongin Michael Jay MD	Upper East Side	212 535 4611
Yale Suzanne MD	Upper East Side	212 744 9300

organisation dedicated to providing family planning services and education re: sexual and reproductive rights to all individuals, irrespective of age or income.

Abortions

New York City is sometimes referred to as the 'Abortion Capital of America,' due to its historically liberal abortion laws and the unusually high rate of abortions performed throughout the city (as compared to the rest of the country). In the United States, a woman can legally elect to have an abortion during the first trimester of her pregnancy, without restriction. 'Medication abortion' is available during days 49-63 of pregnancy, involves administering medication to terminate the pregnancy, and can take place mostly at home. 'Vacuum aspiration' can be performed at any point during the first trimester (the first 14 weeks), and the foetus is removed from the vagina via suction. This procedure must take place at a hospital or in a doctor's office, and may require anaesthesia. Second trimester abortions are less widely performed, and after the 24th week of pregnancy, abortions are permitted in situations of serious health problems only (when the mother's life would be endangered by carrying the foetus to term). It is legal to have an abortion if early birth defects are detected in the foetus, although this is a controversial social and cultural issue.

Paediatrics

Hospitals and private clinics in New York City both offer excellent paediatric care. It is generally advisable to choose a doctor first, rather than focusing upon where they provide their services. By paying an additional monthly premium to your health insurance company, you can obtain insurance coverage for your dependents. Word of mouth and doctors' recommendations are generally the best way to find a good paediatrician, although online publications can also provide helpful suggestions. New York Magazine publishes a listing of the best doctors in the New York metropolitan area (http://nymag.com) and the website 'The City of New York City' sorts its listing of area paediatricians by borough (www.thecityofnewyorkcity.com, under 'physician'). The popular website www.newyork.citysearch.com publishes a 'yellow pages' listing of area doctors which can be sorted by specialty, including paediatrics.

Children with Disabilities

The New York State Department of Education provides free programmes and services for parents or families of children with disabilities. It maintains four 'parent resource centres' in New York City, three of which have Spanish language assistance available. It also runs Special Education Training and Research Centers, which provide coaching and technical assistance to school districts with special needs students. Public schools are required to work with parents to provide support services to those students, and many private schools do as well. For additional information on support services for special needs children, visit the state-run 'Lifelong Services Network' (www.vesid.nysed.gov). For additional information on psychologists who can work with learning disabled children, see the Counsellors/Psychologists table provided. Many non-profit organisations also provide free support, such as the Learning Disabilities Association of New York City (www.ldanyc.org), which maintains the Learning Disabilities Helpline (212 645 6730), a free phone referral and information service.

Paediatrics

N.Y.Foundling Hospital	–	718 784 4422	Hospital
Natan Schleider, MD - New York House Call Physicians	Midtown	646 957 5444	Clinic
New York Presbyterian Hospital	Upper East Side	212 452 5121	Hospital
New York Weill Cornell Med Center	Upper East Side	212 746 5454	Hospital
Pediatric Associates-New York	Gramercy Park	212 725 6300	Clinic
Schneider, Joyce - Global Pediatrics	Upper East Side	212 585 3329	Clinic
Tisch Hospital	Chelsea	212 263 7300	Hospital

If your baby is assigned to a paediatrician at the hospital where it is born, you are under no obligation to stay with that paediatrician for ongoing care. Most parents choose a paediatrician in advance of their child's birth, so that they have ample time to meet with several prospective doctors in order to determine the best fit.

Vaccinations

The recommended immunisation schedule is standard across the United States. In the first year of life, infants should receive Hepatitis B, Diptheria/Tetanus/Pertussis, Haemophilias Influenza Type B, Polio, and Pneumococcal vaccinations. These vaccinations, along with the MMR (Measles, Mumps, and Rubella) and Chicken Pox vaccination, are required for entrance in New York schools. The complete recommended immunisation schedule is available at www.cdc.gov, the website of the Center for Disease Control and Prevention, and the immunisation requirements for school entrance are available at www.health.state.ny.us/prevention/immunization/. Annual flu shots, although optional, are strongly recommended, particularly for children with asthma or other chronic medical conditions.

One-Dollar Smile

Individuals seeking less expensive dental treatment may want to consider seeing a dental student at a university (NYU College of Dentistry), as their fees are less expensive and they remain under the supervision of certified dentists.

Dentists/Orthodontists

Corrective and cosmetic dentistry is popular in New York City. Orthodontics (teeth straightening) tends to be at least partially covered by insurance companies, while procedures considered primarily cosmetic (teeth whitening or veneers) are less likely to be covered under a dental insurance plan.

Opticians & Opthamologists

Many opticians and ophthalmologists in New York can be found 'in residence' at stores that sell prescription eyeglasses and sunglasses, although seeing a store's resident doctor does not obligate you to purchase their products. Once you receive a prescription for corrective lenses, you can purchase eyeglasses, contact lenses, or prescription sunglasses through your doctor's office, online, or at any vision care store throughout the city. Drug stores and grocery stores sell contact lens cases, contact

Dentists/Orthodontists

Dentistry for Children	Upper West Side	212 496 9600
DownTown Dental Studio	Financial District	212 964 3337
Hennessey, Dr. N. Patrick	Midtown	212 683 6470
Jack Schwartz, D.D.S.	Midtown	212 582 6617
Levingart & Levingart	Central Park & Fifth Avenue	212 581 0707
Mark, Dr. Joel	Midtown	212 697 1094
Metropolitan Dental Associates	Financial District	212 732 7400
Mid-Manhattan Dental, P.C.	Midtown	212 581 0986
New York University - College of Dentistry	Gramercy Park	212 998 9856
Park Avenue Dental Arts	Midtown	212 286 0716
Westside Dental Center	Upper West Side	212 496 2260

lens solution, and eyeglass lens cleaners. Basic magnifying 'reading' glasses can be purchased at drug stores or grocery stores without a prescription.

Newborn infants are screened for vision problems before they are released from the hospital, but if you suspect your baby has vision problems, contact your child's paediatrician immediately. He or she will likely refer your child to an optometrist or ophthalmologist for further assessment. All children should receive comprehensive eye exams at 6 months of age, 3 years of age, and 5 years of age. After that, they should be examined annually.

Can You Read That Number Plate?

In order to obtain a driving licence, you must pass a basic vision test at the Department of Motor Vehicles (DMV), the state-run agency that supplies driving licences. If you are unable to pass the DMV test, you must have an eye test report from any certified eye care practitioner, which indicates that you can meet basic vision requirements.

Cosmetic Treatment & Surgery

New York City is an internationally prominent centre for plastic surgery. Some of the most renowned plastic surgeons in the city are affiliated with Manhattan Eye, Ear, and Throat Hospital and NYU Medical Center. Popular procedures include breast augmentation and reduction, liposuction, abdominoplasty (tummy tucks), eye and face lifts, and rhinoplasty (nose jobs). Botox® is among the most common non-surgical alternatives. Patients receive injections of botulinum toxin that temporarily reduces lines on the face by paralysing facial muscles. The results last for up to four months. (Recent research has also suggested that Botox® injections can be helpful in relieving migraine headaches.) Other popular non-surgical cosmetic procedures include chemical facial peels, laser hair removal, and microdermabrasion.

Laser Eye Surgery

New York City is a major centre for laser eye surgery and research, and laser eye procedures are available at hospitals and vision care centres throughout the city. The procedure lasts only 15 minutes, and after a day or two, most patients are able to resume their normal routines. Costs range from $2,000 to $5,500, and because it is an elective procedure, it is not usually covered by insurance. For other specialist eye treatment, two of the best places to go are Mount Sinai Hospital (p.149)vand the New York Eye and Ear Infirmary (www.nyee.edu).

Alternative Therapies

Alternative therapies abound, and are particularly popular with New York City's sizable population of yoga-practising, organic food-purchasing 'health nuts.' The city's large community of visual artists, musicians, actors, dancers, and other creatives also tend to gravitate towards these treatments, which include acupuncture/acupressure, meditation, homeopathy, and the Alexander Technique.

Alexander Technique

Individuals studying the Alexander Technique usually work privately with a certified

Latest Cosmetic Treatments

In recent years, non-surgical facial procedures have become 'hot' in the world of plastic surgery. Injections of Botox, Restylane, and Hylaform are frequently used to 'fill in' the lines of the face. Individuals are seeking these anti-aging treatments at increasingly younger ages (as young as in their 20s!) and mothers and daughters or couples sometimes undergo the procedure as a joint venture. Talk about family bonding.

Cosmetic Treatment & Surgery		
Beraka George MD	Upper East Side	212 288 1122
Colen Helen MD	Upper East Side	212 772 1300
Ginsberg Gerald MD	Central Park & Fifth Avenue	212 452 3421
Herman Steven MD	Central Park & Fifth Avenue	212 249 7000
Lesesne Cap MD - International Cosmetic Surgery	Upper East Side	212 570 6318
McCarthy Joseph G., MD	Gramercy Park	212 263 5208
Millman, Arthur MD - Manhattan Center for Facial Plastic Surgery	Midtown	212 697 9797
Ofodile Ferdinand MD	Upper East Side	212 861 9000
Park Plaza Plastic and Reconstructive Surgery	Upper East Side	212 750 9494
Pitman Gerald MD	Upper East Side	212 517 2600
Profiles & Contours	Central Park & Fifth Avenue	212 861 4100

instructor to learn to recognise and release unhealthy patterns of tension and movement in the body and to move and speak with greater ease. This technique is especially popular among performers, and it is taught at all major fine arts conservatories. It is also helpful for individuals suffering from chronic pain or restricted movement. Teaching sessions usually take place in private studios, although a few practitioners are willing to make house calls. To find a certified teacher in the New York area, see the American Society for the Alexander Technique listing at www.alexandertech.com.

Acupressure/Acupuncture

Acupressure and acupuncture treatments are usually administered at private clinics, although some acupuncture practitioners will make house calls for an additional charge. Some of the best acupuncture centres are located in the Chinatown neighbourhood, on and around Canal Street.

Addiction Counselling & Rehabilition

Hundreds of rehabilitation centres offer both inpatient and outpatient addiction treatment in New York City. Some are affiliated with area hospitals, while others are privately run, and many insurance companies will subsidise treatment. Alcoholics Anonymous, Al-Anon (for relatives and friends of addicts), Cocaine Anonymous, Co-Anon (also for relatives and friends), Co-Dependents Anonymous, Debtors Anonymous, Gambler's Anonymous, Narcotics Anonymous, Overeaters Anonymous, and Pills Anonymous are just a few of the non-profit organisations that run hotlines,

Acupressure/Acupuncture

Acupuncture by Dr David PJ Hung	Midtown	212 752 9227
Acupuncture Healthcare Service	West Village	917 582 6216
Acupuncture, Facelifts, Shiatsu & Nutrition	Central Park & Fifth Avenue	212 242 4217
Asclepius Acupuncture	East Village	212 677 6969
Manhattan Acupuncture	Chelsea	718 208 3641
New York Center-Acupuncture	Midtown	212 399 3575
New York PhD's Acupuncture & Chinese Herbal Medicine Center	Midtown	212 920 4528

resource centres, and weekly group support meetings. The five area hospitals run by Continuum Health Partners - Beth Israel Medical Center, St. Luke's Hospital, Roosevelt Hospital, Long Island College Hospital, and the New York Eye and Ear Infirmary – offer treatment in conjunction with the Addiction Institute of New York, the Stuyvesant Square Chemical Dependency Treatment Program, and the Department of Psychiatry. For females, the Women's Health Project and Research Center at St. Luke's – Roosevelt Hospital Center (www.whpnyc.org) offers cutting edge research and care for substance addictions and abuse.

Rehabilitation & Physiotherapy

Many New York residents lead active lifestyles, working hard and then playing hard. But accidents and injuries do happen, so whether you pulled something in the gym or just sprained your ankle by tripping in the subway, you'll be pleased to hear that the city has some excellent facilities to help you on the road to recovery.

Rehabilitation & Physiotherapy

Midtown Therapy	Flatiron District	212 216 9060
MRPT Physical Therapy	Midtown	212 661 2933
Spine & Sports Medicine	Midtown	212 986 3888
University Physical Therapy	Greenwich Village	212 604 1316

159

Aromatherapy		
Aromatherapy	Midtown	212 279 0504
Aromatixs & Aromatherapy	Upper East Side	212 838 9196
Aveda Aromatherapy Esthetique	Midtown	212 832 2416
Bed Bath & Beyond	Flatiron District	212 255 3550
Cosmetology & Aromatherapy	Midtown	718 263 5850
Enfleurage Inc	West Village	212 691 1610
Ki-Touch Beauty Center	Midtown	212 682 1166
Standard Aromatics	Upper East Side	212 926 2000

Aromatherapy

Aromatherapy treatments are available at holistic health centres and spas throughout New York. They are sometimes offered in conjunction with other treatments, such as aromatherapy massages, or as part of meditation. Boutiques, spas, and salons also sell aromatherapy products for home use.

Healing Meditation

Meditation has become increasingly popular among New Yorkers seeking refuge from stressful jobs and the often hectic pace of life in the city. Meditation classes are offered at gyms, yoga studios, and holistic wellness centres around the city.

Homeopathy

Some New Yorkers turn to homeopathy when traditional medicine fails to relieve chronic aches and pains, while others use it as a supplement to standard medical treatment. For those individuals interested in becoming certified homeopaths, many wellness centres offer training and certification courses.

Reflexology/Massage Therapy

Other options **Massage** p.298

Reflexology/Massage Therapy		
Dharma NYC	Brooklyn	917 923 1114
Equinox Spa	Upper East Side	212 750 4671
Holistic Center of NY	Midtown	212 752 1060
Kneaded Bodyworks	Midtown	212 465 7245
Madison Towers Health Spa	Midtown	212 685 7155
Manhattan Massage Therapy	Midtown	212 203 2215
MassageSpaceNYC	Chelsea	212 229 1529
Maternal Massage and More	Flatiron District	212 533 3188
New York Institute For Massage	Gramercy Park	212 213 3595
Physical Advantage	Midtown	212 460 1879
Space for Wellness	Upper East Side	212 570 2700

Reflexology and massage therapy are perhaps the most popular alternative therapies among stressed-out New Yorkers, and are offered at gyms, salons, spas, wellness centres, and studios. Athletes may prefer the 'sports massage' offered at many gyms, and individuals with chronic aches and pains gravitate towards therapeutic massage. For those seeking to relax or to indulge, traditional spa massages are available at various salons and spas. Couples' massages are also popular, and many masseuses will come to your home for an additional charge.

Back Treatment

In the United States, the distinction between chiropractors and osteopaths is more clearly defined than in the rest of the world. Osteopaths are considered medical practitioners, and the training and certification procedures for Doctors of Osteopathy (DOs) is very similar to that of Medical Doctors (MDs). Doctors of Osteopathy utilise a more holistic approach to medicine and receive special musculoskeletal training, but manual therapy is only one component of their practice. Chiropractors, by contrast, are not doctors and focus exclusively on making manual adjustments to realign the spine. Osteopaths can be found through any listing of area doctors, and visits are generally covered by insurance. Chiropractors can be found in private practices and at alternative medicine or holistic wellness centres. Repeated visits are usually necessary, and the cost of diagnostic x-rays and multiple visits can add up to hundreds or even thousands of dollars. Furthermore, chiropractor visits are less likely to be covered by insurance.

Back Treatment

Advanced Sports Medicine & Rehabilitation	Flatiron District	212 414 8508
Fazzari Patrick MD	Midtown	212 376 3184
Functional Restoration	Midtown	212 319 5888
Goldberg Robert DO	Meatpacking District	212 929 9009
Midtown Therapy	Midtown	212 216 9060
Rehabilitation Medicine Associates	–	212 305 4818
Steven Shoshany DC	West Village	212 645 8151
Village Chiropractic Associates	Flatiron District	212 673 4331

Craniosacral Therapy
Craniosacral therapy is available through DOs or through non-medical practitioners at spas or holistic wellness centres. However, aside from DOs, craniosacral therapists do not necessarily have special certification and are not regulated by the government.
Back Treatment

Nutritionists & Slimming

If you are seeking treatment for a digestive disorder or want to lose weight, you should first consult your primary care doctor. He or she may be able to treat your disorder or supervise weight loss. If for some reason you require additional support or treatment, your general practitioner may refer you to a gastrointestinal doctor or to a nutritionist. According to *New York Magazine*, the top three hospitals for treatment of digestive disorders are, in descending order, Mount Sinai, New York-Presbyterian, and NYU Medical Center. Certified nutritionists often run private practices, as is the case with Nu-Train (www.nutrain.com), a particularly excellent facility that teaches athletes as well as people seeking to lose or gain weight how to eat healthfully. Some people also use acupuncture or hypnotherapy to treat digestive disorders and to aid in weight loss. Many health and wellness centres integrate traditional and alternative services for 'one-stop shopping.' For example, The Mind Body Digestive Center in Manhattan (www.mindbodydigestive.com) has a staff which includes a gastroenterologist doctor, a clinical psychologist, a nutritionist, and an acupuncturist.

Nutritionists & Slimming

Diet Center	Midtown	212 759 8118	www.mayemusk.com
Head to Health Nutrition	Midtown	646 226 1745	headtohealth.com
Journey to Nutrition	Midtown	917 572 3683	na
Living Proof Nutrition	Midtown	212 308 2990	na
Musk Maye MS Rd Nutrition International	Gramercy Park	212 673 8766	mayemusk.com
Nourish	Chelsea	646 784 6865	na
Nu-Train	Upper East Side	212 769 3200	nu-train.com

Fitness Centres
Gyms, yoga studios, and Pilates centers are all extremely popular with New Yorkers. Many gyms, such as New York Sports Club, New York Health & Racquet, and Equinox, offer free classes in addition to the use of workout machines and weightlifting equipment, for a monthly membership fee. These gyms also keep trainers on staff, and for an extra charge, you can book private sessions with these trainers. Some private trainers or fitness instructors will make house calls, but these are less common, due to the relatively small size of most New York apartments. Many excellent yoga studios are available that teach a number of different styles. Among the best is Yoga Effects (www.yogaeffects.com), a smaller studio in midtown with a personal touch, that offers over 60 drop-in Vinyasa yoga classes per week to students of all ages and levels. Visit www.newyork.citysearch.com for a listing of the top ten gyms, yoga studios, Pilates studios, personal trainers, and nutritionists, chosen by popular vote.

Counselling & Therapy

Nearly all hospitals maintain psychiatric units (in-patient care treatment is generally geared towards the treatment of severe psychiatric problems), and New York-Presbyterian Hospital, Bellevue Hospital Center, and Mount Sinai Medical are considered three of the best. Psychiatrists, psychologists, and clinical social workers offer private counselling, and some specialise in group therapy, family therapy, or marriage

161

Counsellors/Psychologists

Affinity Zone.com	212 737 8538
Alcoholics Anonymous Inter-Group Association	212 647 1680
Depressive and Bipolar Support	917 445 2399
Linda Brierty, LCSW	212 228 7090
Manhattan Psychotherapy	212 724 8767
The Mood Disorders Support Group	212 533 6374
Network Inc The	212 260 8868
Nicotine Anonymous	212 941 0094
NYC Self Help Center	212 586 5770
Overeaters Anonymous	718 266 1160
Saint Vincents	212 604 8068
Shari Heller Rev	212 982 8835
Single Parent Resource Center	212 951 7030

counselling. Many hospitals run treatment and research centres for specific mental disorders (Mount Sinai's Eating and Weight Disorders Program is excellent), and private treatment clinics exist inside and outside the city. Mental health care for children is also fairly common, and psychiatrists, psychologists, and learning disability specialists with specific training in treating children or adolescents are widespread. The NYU Child Study Center (www.aboutourkids.org) offers many therapeutic services and educational resources. Their specialised clinical programmes include Anxiety and Mood Disorders, ADHD and Behavioural Disorders, Family Studies, Eating Disorders, and Autism Spectrum Disorders.

Social Groups

To help new residents settle in and meet new people, New York has a number of social groups and societies, some of which cater to people of a shared nationality. For more information, see Social Groups on p.283.

Support Groups

The fast pace and vibrant energy of New York City make it an exciting but challenging place to live. Moving to New York can be an especially difficult adjustment for expats who have relocated from smaller suburban or rural communities, and homesickness and culture shock are common at first (even for Americans who have moved from smaller cities in the United States). Fortunately, however, New York offers every kind of support group imaginable, including general expat groups as well as expat groups designed for specific nationalities, ethnicities, cultures, or religions. A sampling of other support groups available includes mother to mother, bereavement, physical and mental illness, separation and divorce, crime victim, gay-lesbian-bisexual-transgender (GLBT), and holiday support groups.

Although there are too many support groups to describe in detail, a few deserve special mention. Gilda's Club of New York City (www.gildasclubnyc.org) maintains headquarters in Manhattan and Brooklyn, and offers free support and networking groups, lectures, workshops, and social events for people whose lives have been affected by cancer. The Gay Men's Health Crisis (www.gmhc.org) provides services, counselling, support groups, education, and public advocacy for people living with HIV or AIDS.

For details on support groups, any branch of the New York City Public Library is an excellent resource. Its most famous branch, the Humanities and Social Sciences Library, is located at 455 Fifth Avenue (at 42nd Street) and offers free internet access along with a large collection of reference books. Hospitals or community centres (such as the 92nd Street Y) are also excellent places to check for support group listings.

Culture Shock

Culture shock can be expected when moving to a foreign country - you will often experience a natural period of adjustment and strong feelings (such as disorientation, anxiety, or homesickness) associated with that adjustment. However, in extreme cases, when symptoms of culture shock do not improve and appear to be worsening over time, depression may have developed. In this situation, it is important that you consult your primary care physician, who can prescribe antidepressants or may refer you to a mental health professional for specialised care. Joining support groups (p.162) or participating in community activities, such as religious groups, volunteer groups, or sports leagues (see Activities, p.252) are non-medical alternatives that may relieve symptoms of culture shock. They can give you the opportunity to feel part of a community of people with shared values and interests.

Psychiatrists

Brooklyn Psychiatric Center	718 453 2277
Gracie Square Hospital	212 988 4400
Kings County Hospital	718 240 0600
Kingsborough Psychiatric Center	718 574 1515
New York State Psychiatric Institute	212 543 5000
Payne Whitney Psychiatric Clinic	212 746 3800

62

Education

After-School Clubs
For students whose parents work, many schools offer after-school activities or give parents the option of enrolling their children in 'extended day' supervision programmes. These programmes vary by school, but popular after-school activities include sports teams, music groups, student government, special interest clubs, and, for non-native English speakers, ESL (English as a Second Language) instructional programmes.

The educational system in the United States is quite good, and free public education is available to legal residents between the ages of 5 and 21. Non-resident enrolment in public schools is subject to school district approval and may require the payment of annual tuition. Public schools designed for the 'gifted and talented' present a challenging alternative for students who can satisfy rigorous standards of admission. For those with money to spare, New York City's competitive private school system offers excellent single sex and co-educational schooling.

If you plan to move to New York City with school-age children, you will need to supply your child's school with immunisation records, proof of your child's age, and proof of legal residency. Assuming you can provide the first two, your child will be admitted to school immediately, even if you cannot demonstrate legal residency. You are not required to provide proof of your own immigration status or that of your child. If your child does not speak English, he or she still has the legal right to attend public school and may have the option of attending free bilingual education courses or English as a Second Language (ESL) classes.

Local public schools are required to accept all students who reside within their neighbourhood zones, as determined by the city government, but private schools and selective public magnet schools are not required to admit all students and often maintain 'wait lists' of students not initially admitted. Average public school class sizes range from 20 to 30, while private or selective public school classes tend to be smaller. Mandatory education begins at age 6 and lasts until age 16 or 17. New York City public schools adhere to state-wide curriculum standards that require students to receive instruction in language arts (reading and writing), social studies (history, geography, economics, civics, citizenship, and government), mathematics, science, technology, and physical education. Initial diagnostic testing is used to place students within appropriate levels of instruction, and city-wide and state-wide standardised assessment tests are administered periodically throughout a student's academic career. In high school (grades 9-12), students must pass New York State Regent exams in various subjects in order to graduate. For a complete schedule of required exams, see http://schools.nyc.gov.

Nurseries & Pre-Schools

New York City has both public and private pre-schools, and they usually accept children between the ages of 2 and 5. The city's private nursery school admissions process is fiercely competitive, and these schools often have long waiting lists. While public school education is free, annual tuition at private nursery schools can range from $7,000 to $20,000 per year. Half-day and full-day programmes are available, and some parents choose to enrol their students for only two, three, or four mornings per week. Drop-off daycare programmes or playgroups (structured more like childcare facilities) offer parents greater flexibility and the option of paying 'per use' on a weekly or monthly basis.

Unlike elementary and secondary school educators, who are required to have at least a bachelor's degree from a university, pre-school teachers are not subject to standardised certification requirements. Some have only high school diplomas, but at expensive private nursery schools, most teachers have university degrees along with special training in early childhood development and education. Schools that utilise specific educational techniques (such as Monetessori or Reggio Emilia) ensure that their teachers have received training in these modes of education. The 92nd Street Y (www.92y.org) and the Toddler Center at Barnard College (www.barnard.edu/toddlers) are two of the strongest and most popular pre-school programmes in New York City.

163

Primary & Secondary Schools

The School Year

Schools are generally in session Monday to Friday for approximately seven hours per day. The typical school day begins around 8:20 and lasts until 14:40, with a midday break for lunch. The school year runs from late August or early September until May or June, and students have a break during the summer months (from May or June to August). Breaks occur around Thanksgiving (late November) and Christmas (late December through New Year), and a week-long spring break is given around Easter.

Private schools and selective public schools require entrance exams and student interviews as part of the admissions process, and some require family interviews as well – particularly for programmes that admit students at a young age. Slots at these schools are highly coveted, and the selection process is therefore extremely competitive. As a result, many students wind up on waiting lists at their first or second choice schools. The curriculum in private schools adheres to state-imposed standards, but frequently expands to include foreign language, community service, and fine arts requirements. Some schools have specific areas of focus, such as the four specialised public high schools. Of these, the 'science schools' (which emphasise science and mathematics courses) are Stuyvesant High School, Bronx High School of Science, and Brooklyn Technical High School. Fiorello H. LaGuardia High School of Music and Art and the Performing Arts provide performance training to young musicians, dancers, and actors, and require prospective students to audition.

The standards of teaching vary from school to school, but are generally quite high, and many teachers take advantage of the immense cultural resources available throughout the city. Classroom facilities also vary, but all schools provide computer and internet access for students. Outside space in Manhattan tends to be cramped, and playgrounds are often squeezed onto rooftops or adjacent lots. Space constraints prompt some schools to lease sports facilities at locations separate from the main campus.

As discussed above, public school education is free, and students are loaned textbooks and supplies free of charge. Private school tuition can range from $10,000 to $30,000 annually, and additional expenses (books, transportation, lunch, and activity fees) may range from several hundred to several thousand dollars.

In addition to the selective public schools cited above, some of the most highly regarded New York City primary and secondary schools are Collegiate School (www.collegiateschool.org), Horace Mann (www.horacemann.org), the Dalton School (www.dalton.org), the Dwight School (www.dwight.edu), Lycee Francais (www.lfny.org), and Regis High School (www.regis-nyc.org).

University & Higher Education

The United States has many excellent universities that attract students from all over the world, and several of these prestigious institutions are located in New York City. They include Columbia University, New York University, and Fordham University, as well as specialist institutes like the Juilliard School for performing arts and the Pratt Institute for art and design. Many expat students choose the United States especially to take advantage of its internationally renowned colleges and universities.

Entrance Requirements

Undergraduate students must apply for admission to universities by submitting secondary school transcripts, letters of recommendation, activities and awards resumes, personal statements, and standardised test scores. Most undergraduate institutions require students to take the SAT Reasoning Test: a standardised exam that measures critical reasoning skills, which comprises three sections: writing, critical reading, and mathematics. Additionally, universities often require students to take several SAT Subject Tests, includingEnglish Literature, History and Social Studies, Mathematics, Sciences, or Languages. Most universities charge a non-refundable application fee of $50-$100, but they will usually waive the fee for prospective students who can demonstrate an inability to pay.

Post-graduate students seeking a Masters of the Arts or Science also have hoops to jump through, including biographical essays, various tests, successful course, school

Greek Town

Fraternities and sororities, commonplace in schools across North America, are social organisations for higher education students. The Greek system uses Greek letters to make up the names of these groups as a cloak of secrecy, such as the literary group, Kappa Alpha Theta and Phi Sigma Kappa. Though founded with the intention of excelled learning, community service, sound leadership qualities, 'frat' houses and sorority sisters have a reputation for having more of a good time then anything else. Many students join as a quick way to build a social network, organise housing (you live in a fraternity or sorority delegated house) and establish connections for the future.

and TOEFL exams (for students coming in from non-native English speaking countries) and GRE (Graduate Record Examination) scores. Similar to SATs, the GREs test verbal, quantitative (math), and analytical reasoning skills.

Student Visas

In order to apply for a student visa, you will need to go for an interview at a US Consulate or Embassy, and you must supply them with an I-20 Certificate of Eligibility. Most accredited universities can issue you this form. You will also need to be able to provide evidence that you have the funds available to pay for tuition and living expenses. It can take anywhere from several days to several months to obtain an interview appointment, and visas take time to process, so it is best to get the ball rolling as quickly as possible.

Further Education

For adults seeking to advance or switch their careers, New York offers a number of vocational training institutes and continuing education programmes. Computer training, technical skills courses, culinary schools, and real estate certification programmes are only a few examples of non-liberal arts options. Admissions requirements for these programmes are usually much less stringent than at traditional universities.

Anyone who can provide proof of residency in New York can get a New York Public Library (NYPL) card, and any branch of the library is a good place to start researching course offerings. The NYPL maintains a website called the Training Resources and Information Network (TRAIN), an excellent information and referral site that can be accessed by anyone with a valid library card. The Learning Annex (www.learningannex.com), Craig's List (www.craigslist.org), and the continuing education programmes run by schools such as Columbia University, New York University, and the City University of New York (CUNY) are also good places to check.

Universities

41 West 42nd St
Midtown

City University

800 286 9937 | www.cuny.edu

A public university that serves some 400,000 students at 23 colleges dotted around the city, CUNY (as it's lovingly known) happens to be the largest urban university in the country. Founded in 1847 as the Free Academy by Townsend Harris, the purpose of the school has always been to offer the highest standards of education to anyone seeking it. With its own cable TV service, CUNY-TV (channel 75 on Time Warner), 11 senior colleges, six community colleges, a graduate school, a journalism school and a law school, CUNY is well known for offering top-notch higher education.

2960 Broadway
Harlem

Columbia University

212 854 1754 | www.columbia.edu

Established in 1754, this private university is one of the eight Ivy League universities in the country and leads the world in Nobel Prize affiliations. Initially named King's College, these grounds have seen many great thinkers pass through, including Alexander Hamilton, Robert Livingston and John Jay. The university is renowned for its graduate schools, among which the most notable are the School of Journalism (CJS), which also collaborates and shares office space with the Columbia Journalism Review (a publication for the media by the media industry), the School of International and Public Affairs (SIPA) and the Columbia Law School. The University's affiliations extend to nearby Barnard College (BC), an undergraduate liberal arts college for women and one of the Seven Sisters (seven liberal arts colleges for women).

441 East Fordham Rd
The Bronx

Fordham University

718 817 4000 | www.fordham.edu

Originally founded as St. John's College by the Catholic Church in 1841, Fordham has since established itself as a private, independent institution still following the Jesuit tradition. In fact, the university is one of the 28 member institutions in the Association of Jesuit Colleges and Universities and its motto, 'Sapientia et Doctrina' (wisdom and learning), is still its fundamental principle. With three residential campuses (one in the Bronx, one in the Lincoln Center in Manhattan and the third in Tarrytown, New York), the school has become synonymous with excellence and accommodates some 8,500 undergraduate students and 7,500 postgraduate students.

60 Lincoln Center Pl
Upper West Side

The Juliard School

212 799 5000 | www.juilliard.edu

Initially founded as the Institute of Musical Art back in 1905, the school has since become the bedrock in performing arts and one of the best-known schools in the world, with a glittering reputation and alumni. The admissions process is very difficult and prospective students are expected to have some form of professional training before attempting admittance into this renowned school of drama, music and dance. Look out for regular performances by the orchestral group and the occasional theatrical show.

22 Washington
Square North
West Village

New York University (NYU)

212 998 4500 | www.nyu.edu

One of the largest private universities in the country, NYU was established in 1831 under the vision of Albert Gallatin, secretary of the treasury serving President Thomas Jefferson to build a 'system of rational and practical education' for one and all. From only 158 students in its first semester of business, enrolment now reaches a staggering 40,000 students attending 14 schools and colleges at one of the five major Manhattan locations, or in one of the 25 countries around the world that the university extends to. NYU is based in the heart of Greenwich Village, where the creative buzz is louder than the non-stop traffic.

Pratt Institute

200 Willoughby Ave
Brooklyn

718 636 3669 | *www.pratt.edu*
This place is part legacy and part world famous school of art. The very first art classes started up in 1887. Now with two campuses – one in Manhattan and the main school in Brooklyn – the school's motto 'be true to your work and your work will be true to you' still stands as a declaration of excellence. Programmes on offer include art, architecture, fashion design, design, illustration and creative writing among many others. The school has a broadcasting radio station that is internet based (www.prattradio.com), as well as a closed television station available only on campus, Pratt TV.

Special Needs Education

Public schools are required to provide support services to children with special needs. Advocates for Children of New York, Inc. (www.advocatesforchildren.org) works to support and to advance the rights of special needs children in New York City public schools. Independently run private schools are not obligated to admit special needs students, but if they have the necessary resources, some will work to accommodate students with learning or developmental disabilities. Some parents opt to teach children with special needs at home, which they are legally permitted to do, assuming they can demonstrate compliance with New York State educational standards. To obtain additional information on special needs resources, support groups, and referrals available in the New York City area, the website of Resources for Children with Special Needs (www.resourcesnyc.org) is a good starting point. Many schools and programmes specifically for children with special needs are also available.

The Gateway School of New York

236 Second Ave
Btn 14th & 15th St
Gramercy Park

212 777 5966 | *www.gatewayschool.org*
The Gateway School enrols children aged 5 to 12 years, and seeks to help and eventually reintroduce children with mild to severe learning disabilities to mainstream schools by both improving their academic skills and learning strategies, and helping to increase their self confidence.

The Quest Program at the Dwight School

291 Central Pk West
Upper West Side

212 724 2146 ext 212
Dwight primarily enrols mainstream students from nursery school to 12th grade, but it runs a small programme for students with minor learning disabilities who require additional classroom support and resources. The programme has the flexibility to accommodate a spectrum of needs, from those students who need help in only one or two subjects to those who require assistance across the board.

West End Day School

255 West 71st St
Upper West Side

212 873 5708 | *www.westenddayschool.org*
This school accepts students with a wide variety of special needs, including those with social and emotional difficulties. It works closely with children from age 5 to 13, as well as their families, and aims to prepare students for entry into mainstream schools whenever possible. Classes are not sorted by grade, but instead children get put into whichever group (usually made up of 10 pupils) that will work best academically and socially for them.

187

Transportation

Other options **Car** p.40, **Getting Around** p.38

There are five main methods of transportation within New York City: taxi, bus, train, subway and the good old sidewalk (or pavement, if you're not American). Because New York is home to people from all walks of life and financial situations, no one method of transportation is used above the other – you will find it just as difficult to find a taxi during rush hour as you will to find a seat on the subway. The high use of public transportation goes for commuters coming into the city as well. Commuter trains leave midtown rail stations, Grand Central and Penn, for destinations within the tri-state area (Long Island, Westchester, Connecticut and New Jersey) at least every hour and even more frequently during rush hour.

Subway

The subway is a quick, cheap and easy way to get to and from most any spot in the five boroughs. A one-way fare between any two locations, no matter what the distance, is $2. Subway fares are no longer given in token form – instead, you can buy a metro card at the machines located outside the subway turnstiles or from the booth operator. The metro card machines take both cash and credit cards. You may find that purchasing a metro card that gives you unlimited rides is a worthwhile investment. Unlimited cards are available for one day, one week or one month and range from $7 to $76. Additionally, you can simply add money onto any existing metro card. That money on your card will not expire and works like a subway debit card. By purchasing a card for $10 or more, a 20% bonus is added to your card for free; thus a $10 card would become $12 and a $20 card, $24.

Driving in New York

If you do decide to drive into Manhattan, there are a few things you should keep in mind if you want your commute to be as smooth as possible.

Rush Hour

Morning rush hour starts promptly at 06:00 and lasts until 11:00. Evening rush hour begins at 15:00 and lasts roughly until 20:00. Many of the major roadways are on a rotating construction schedule, so it is best to check out traffic websites, such as www.traffic.com or www.metrocommute.com, or AM radio stations, such as 880 or 1010 WINS, before heading out. It is not unheard of to wait for more than an hour in standstill traffic during construction at all times of the night but this can easily be avoided by taking alternative routes.

Bridges and Tunnels

Toll charges fluctuate regularly. An easy way to receive a small discount on tolls, not to mention save you some time, is to buy an EZPass. An EZPass attaches to your windshield and automatically deducts funds from a pre-paid account. Visit www.ezpass.com to order one.

The **George Washington Bridge** is free from New York to New Jersey, connects West 178th Street and Fort Lee, New Jersey, and forms part of Interstate Highway I-95.

The **Third Avenue Bridge** is free in both directions, connects Third Avenue, East 135th Street, Bruckner Boulevard, and Lincoln Avenue in the Bronx, to East 128th Street, East 129th Street, Lexington Avenue, and the Harlem River Drive in Manhattan.

The **Willis Avenue Bridge** is free in both directions, connects First Avenue and East 124th Street in Manhattan to Willis Avenue and East 134th Street in the Bronx.

The **Triborough Bridge** (leads into the Grand Central Parkway) has a toll in both directions. The Triborough is actually an amalgamation of three bridges, a viaduct and 14 miles of approach road. The three bridges meet on Randall's island where a tollway sorts out the traffic. It runs from the north-western tip of Queens to 125th St in Manhattan, with an off ramp leading into the Bronx. From Queens, you can reach it via the Grand Central Parkway, which will get you from LaGuardia Airport to Manhattan. You can reach the bridge in Manhattan via the FDR Drive and in the Bronx via the Major Deegan Expressway.

The **Queensborough Bridge** (or 59th Street Bridge) is free in both directions and connects Long Island City Queens, via Queen Boulevard or the Long Island Expressway, with Second Ave and 59th Street.

The **Queens Midtown Tunnel** has a toll in both directions, and connects the Long Island Expressway (Queens) with Second Ave and 34th St.

The **Lincoln Tunnel** is free from New York to New Jersey, and connects West 42nd Street south to West 30th Street at Tenth Ave with U.S. Routes 1 and 9, 3 and the New Jersey Turnpike.

The **Williamsburgh Bridge** is free in both directions, connects Brooklyn with Lower Manhattan, and is accessible from the Brooklyn Queen Expressway, I-278, or Delancey Street in Manhattan.

The **Holland Tunnel** is free from New York to New Jersey, and connects west Canal Street in Manhattan to eastern New Jersey.

The **Manhattan Bridge** is free in both directions, and connects Canal Street in lower Manhattan to Flatbush Avenue in Brooklyn.

The **Brooklyn Bridge** is free in both directions, and connects the Brooklyn Queens Expressway or Tillary St in Brooklyn with Franklin and Pearl St in Manhattan's Financial District.

The **Brooklyn Battery Tunnel** has a toll in both directions, and connects the Brooklyn-Queens Expressway to Manhattan via the FDR Drive near Wall St.

Petrol Stations

Petrol stations are few and far between on the island of Manhattan. Be sure to fill up before you cross over. Often there are reasonably priced petrol stations right before the bridges. For instance, the Queensborough (or 59th St) Bridge has about five fuelling spots clustered around it and none have gauged prices. In the other four boroughs stations are more frequent. If you desperately need petrol, head towards East Houston, where you will find a well lit and busy BP station, The Eastside service station on East Houston and 2nd St, and the few taxi service stations in Chelsea along Eleventh Avenue. Expect petrol to be more expensive in the city, but not astronomically.

Carpooling

Unfortunately, not enough people commuting into New York City choose to carpool. However, those who do are rewarded by the Long Island Expressway with a High Occupancy Vehicle Lane, or HOV lane. In the suburbs around New York City, there are commuter lots where you can leave your car in a safe location for free while you carpool. For a list of carpoolers in your area, try www.commuterlink.com, www.carpoolworld.com or http://newyork.craigslist.org.

169

Park with Caution
Wherever you park, always check the nearest parking sign. Tickets may run as high as $150 and towing is nearly triple that. It is also illegal to park in front of fire hydrants. If parking near one, make sure your car is at least 15 feet away.

Parking

There are two ways to park in New York City - either on the street or in a garage. There are no street parking permits in New York City. When finding parking, look for spots with either a meter or a sign that indicates a non-commercial vehicle may park there during the hours you need. Meters in NYC take quarters, though it is now possible to use a pre-paid parking card in some of the new meters around the city – specifically in Midtown. Parking cards may be purchased at The City Store (Municipal Building, 1 Centre Street, North Plaza, Tribeca: open Monday to Friday, 09:00 to 16:30). To order a card by phone, call the City Store on the NYC information helpline, 311, or 212 NEW YORK (639 9675) if outside the city. Be careful, metered parking around the city often has a one or two-hour time limit and police will chalk the ground around your tyres to make sure you have moved.

Some areas of Manhattan are easier to find street parking in than in others. Neighbourhoods to avoid during the day are Midtown, Hell's Kitchen and anywhere south of Canal Street (Tribeca, Financial, South Street Seaport). Easier places to find parking before 18:00 are the Lower East Side, East Village, Murray Hill and Harlem. Generally, during week day evenings parking is not an impossible task, but on Friday or Saturday nights, the city can get crowded with weekend partiers, otherwise known as the 'bridge and tunnel' crowd, driving in (via bridge or tunnel, you see?) for a night out. If you want a safe and easy place to park your car when heading into Manhattan, head for a parking garage. However renting a parking space in New York is nearly as expensive as renting a studio apartment: even for an hour, tolls can run as high as $40 in Midtown. To help avoid a hefty bill, search www.nycgarages.com before you head out. NYC Garages is a wonderful site that allows drivers to compare both daily and monthly rates of parking garages all over Manhattan, even breaking down the locations by attraction. With over a hundred garages in a single neighbourhood offering a variety of prices, it is definitely worth checking ahead of time to avoid wasting petrol by cruising around for a space.

International Driving Permit
Remember, an International Driving Permit is not a licence. It is not required to have an IDP, but it may come in handy if pulled over by an officer since the permit states in several languages that you have a valid licence. Always carry your licence - it is illegal to drive without it.

Driving Licence

As long as you have a valid driving licence from your home country, you do not need to apply for a New York State licence. That is unless you plan on becoming a state resident. If you become a resident of NYS, you must exchange your foreign driving licence for an NYS licence within 30 days. In order to obtain an NYS driving licence, you must pass a written test, complete a five-hour driving course and pass a road test. All of this can be done at your local Department of Motor Vehicles (www.nydmv.state.ny.us). You will also need a Social Security Card, or, if you are not eligible for an SSC, you must provide the form SSA-L676 from the United States Social Security Administration that states you are not eligible along with your US Citizenship and Immigration Services documents. After you have passed your road test, you will be asked to hand in your foreign licence to the examiner. Your

Driving Habits

According to New York State's Department of Motor Vehicles (www.nydmv.state.ny.us), in 2005 there were 45,954 car accidents within New York City. It is not an easy city to drive in, even for the most experienced of motorists. The speed limit within the city is 30mph but signs for this are scarcely posted and vehicles often reach speeds of over 50mph, especially cab drivers. Lanes are taken as more of a suggestion than the law, so when driving it is important to be aware of your surroundings at all times. Be on the look out for cabs quickly changing direction to pick up a fare, bike messengers swerving in and out of lanes and rogue pedestrians running across the street. Driving in NYC can be an exciting, draining and exhilarating experience, but it is definitely not for the faint of heart.

local Department of Motor Vehicle will hold your licence and destroy it after 60 days. If you want to use your licence upon returning to your country, simply ask the road test examiner not to destroy it and you may return anytime to retrieve it from the DMV.

Vehicle Leasing

There are advantages and disadvantages to both buying and leasing a car for new citizens or long-term visitors to the United States. Buying a car means better prices and ownership of your car at the end of your payments. However, it also means that those monthly payments will be higher and that you will be required to complete them before you leave the country.

Depending on the length of your stay, leasing a car might be a more flexible option. It is like renting an apartment – you can just give it up and move out when you are through. Talk honestly, however, to any car dealer and they will tell you that leasing a car is almost never the smart choice. Monthly payments are lower than when buying, but at the end you do not own the car and it must be given back to the dealer.

Whichever option you choose, both require a passport with a valid United States work visa along with proof of employment. You will also need to be credit approved, which car companies can do to a certain degree even if you are not an American citizen. Finance and loan options for buying can be for as little as one year. Leasing can also be for 12 months, although monthly payments will be higher with this option.

Vehicle Leasing Agents

AAMCAR	212 927 7000	www.aamcar.com
Avis	212 593 8469	www.avis.com
Budget	212 807 8700	www.budgetrentacar.com
Dollar	212 399 3590	www.dollarcar.com
Drive Master Co	973 908 9709	na
Enterprise Rent-A-Car	212 581 8883	www.enterprise.com
Hertz	212 486 5912	www.hertz.com
National	212 875 8362	www.nationalcar.com
New York Rent-A-Car	212 799 1100	www.ny-car.com

Short-Term Lease Programmes

More and more car companies are initiating short-term lease programmes. Many foreign car companies operating within the US (such as Audi or Volkswagen) have a Foreign Business Professional programme, that allows customers to lease a vehicle for exactly the amount of time they will be in the country. To register for this programme you will need several things. Firstly, you need a letter from your employer stating your position, hire date, income and length of stay in the United States, as well as a copy of your United States social security card or documentation from the Social Security Administration confirming your social security number. To determine your specific finance terms, you will need a copy of your visa with expiration date (or for extended stays, the date on your employment letter), with your employment contract, your permanent resident card, or your I-94 form. You'll also need three personal references from individuals residing in the United States, and verification of your residence and phone number. Finally, your monthly payment must not exceed 25% of your gross monthly income – and your minimum gross income must be at least $45,000 per year. These requirements can be transferred to any other car company.

Buying a Vehicle

When they say that you can buy just about anything in New York, they mean it. So when looking for a car, whether it be a Rolls or a Rover, the sky's the limit. As long as you hold a valid work permit and licence, you may purchase a vehicle as soon as you arrive in New York.

The cheapest new cars run from $8-20,000 and you can expect to save up to $9,000 off of the new price if you buy the car used. Financing will be more expensive for a used vehicle and depending on the condition of your car, the insurance may be slightly

New Car Dealers

BMW	BMW of Manhattan	212 586 2269	www.bmwofmanhattan.com
Cadillac, Chevrolet, Buick	Potamkin Buick/Cadillac/Chevrolet	212 399 4400	na
Ford, Lincoln Mercury	Manhattan Ford	212 581 7800	www.nycford.com
Honda	Martin's Manhattan Honda	212 974 1010	www.martinshonda.com
Jaguar	Manhattan Jaguar	212 459 9400	www.jaguarnyc.com
Lexus	Lexus of Manhattan	212 977 4400	www.lexusdealer.com/manhattan
Mercedes	Mercedes-Benz Manhattan	800 626 9191	www.mb-manhattan.com
Nissan	Nissan Autotech Services	212 977 9540	www.nissanusa.com
Saab, Land Rover, Isuzu	Zumbach Sports Cars	212 247 1444	na
Toyota	Toyota of Manhattan	212 399 9600	www.toyota.com
Volvo	Martin's Manhattan Volvo	212 586 0780	www.martinsvolvo.com

higher, but the overall price will be significantly lower. When purchasing a used car, there are a few places to look before settling: franchise and independent dealers located all over the city (newyork.citysearch.com has a complete listing of them), rental car companies selling their used cars, leasing companies, used car superstores (such as Car Max) and even the internet. Before buying from a used car company, you may want to call the Better Business Bureau of New York (www.newyork.bbb.org) to research any unsettled disputes between the dealership and customers.

Used Car Dealers

Acura Of Manhattan	Hell's Kitchen	212 459 9200
Auto AAA	Financial District	917 595 3681
Auto All City	Chelsea	917 595 3043
BMW of Manhattan	Hell's Kitchen	212 586 2269
Exclusive Euro Auto Sales	Chelsea	212 727 0115
Freedom Man Auto	Lower East Side	212 965 1513
Manhattan Jeep Chrysler Dodge	Hell's Kitchen	212 765 6633
Sports & Classics	Tribeca	212 226 7602

Vehicle Finance

Check with your bank about auto loan rates. It is common for the new or used car dealer to assist you with finance - many have agreements with banks or finance companies.

Registering a Vehicle

It is required by law to have your vehicle registered with the Department of Motor Vehicles (www.nydmv.state.ny.us). To do so, there are several items you will need. To start with, you need proof of ownership. If your vehicle was purchased through a dealership, they will most likely fill out the paperwork required for registration and send it to the DMV for you. In case they do not, the proof of ownership for a new vehicle is the manufacturer's certificate of origin (MCO) or the manufacturer's statement of origin (MSO) and form MV-50 (dealer's bill of sale). The proof of ownership for a used vehicle is the title certificate that the previous owner signed to transfer the ownership to the dealer and a form MV-50 that the dealer signs to transfer ownership to you. When purchasing a vehicle from another person you will need a bill of sale and a title certificate as proof of purchase. Make sure the bill of sale includes the year and make of the vehicle, the vehicle identification number, the date of sale, the purchase price and the names and signatures of the buyer and the seller. The seller takes responsibility for applying the title certificate. You'll also need the odometer and damage disclosure statements, which are on the title certificate and should be filled out by the seller, as well as a New York State insurance identification card (given to you by your insurance agent), some proof of identity and age in the form of a birth certificate, driving licence, or passport, and the Form MV-82 – the vehicle registration form, which is available at the DMV. Finally, don't forget proof of your sales tax payment (found on the bill of sale), and of course – the payment. This depends on the weight of the vehicle

Vehicle Insurance

GEICO Auto Insurance	212 461 3301	www.geico.com
GGI Insurance Brokerage	347 589 1662	www.GGIBrokerage.com
Gotham	212 406 7300	na
Multi-Line Insurance Agency	212 927 4595	na
Nationwide Insurance Agent Emmanuel Osuyah	212 568 5700	na

and can run from $20.50 to $112 for two years. There is also a vehicle use tax which is $30 for two years. If you need a licence plate, you can also purchase that for $15.

Traffic Fines & Offences

Speed limits are not well posted in New York City. Unless you are driving at an excessive speed, say over 60mph, you will most likely not be pulled over. Going through red lights, however, is a big no-no. There are red light cameras set up all over the city which will capture an image of you and your licence plate if you breeze through one. Also, making a right on a red light is illegal across the five boroughs and you will be ticketed for doing so. All moving violations are issued on the spot and don't come cheap: expect to pay upwards of $150 for even minor offences. It is also important to note that in New York and New Jersey, the use of a mobile phone while driving is illegal and this offence is being cracked down upon all over the tri-state area. Buying a hands-free phone kit is a worthwhile investment. If you are pulled over for any of these offences, make sure your seatbelt – and your passengers' – are buckled. A $50 fine is added for each person not wearing a seatbelt.

If you receive a parking ticket, you are required to respond within 30 days. Failure to do so will result in added penalty fees. There are detailed instructions on the back of tickets with instructions about where to send your payments (locations differ within the city) and what to do if you want to dispute the fine. If you fail to respond to a ticket, a suspension may be put on your licence, but a $35 fee will take this off.

Towing Charges

The Department of Consumer Affairs has instituted a maximum charge for towing in New York City:
• Tow: $80.00 (This is for vehicles under 10,000 lbs, and includes flatbed towing and the first day of storage. It does not include tolls and 8.25% tax).

• Tow: $125.00 (This is for vehicles in excess of 10,000 lbs, and includes flatbed towing and the first day of storage. It does not include tolls and 8.25% tax).

• Mileage: $4.00 per mile.

• Labour at scene: $12.00 per 15 minutes per truck.

• Storage: $15.00 per day for the second and third day. $17.00 per day from day four and every day thereafter (storage days are counted by calendar days).

Be Patient! Towing is a long, gruelling process and if it happens to you, make sure you give yourself three hours' free time before arriving at the towing facility - perhaps you should bring a book.

Towing

If you think your vehicle has been towed, call 311, or 212 New York (639 9675) outside of the city. You will need your licence plate number to navigate the automated phone system, as without that it will be nearly impossible to locate your vehicle – strange as that may sound. If your car has been towed because of a parking violation and you have unpaid tickets over the amount of $101, then you will be required to pay all of the fines before your car can be released. The fastest way to pay your fines is at the Finance Business Centres, of which there is one located in each borough. Once you have taken care of any outstanding debt, request a vehicle release form and take this with you to redeem your vehicle at the NYPD impound lot.

Other documents you will need to release your vehicle are: your valid driving licence (or someone else who has one), the original vehicle registration stub (or the title), the vehicle's valid insurance card and a vehicle release form if necessary. If any of these things are in your car, you may request a property release form at the site, and then you will be allowed into the lot accompanied by a guard. If you do not retrieve your vehicle the day it is towed, there will be a storage fee of $10 the first two days and $15 each additional. The tow fee is currently $185 plus $70 for the execution fee (whatever that is). Add the fine from your ticket and you are looking at half your month's rent down the drain.

Breakdowns

If your car breaks down on a major roadway, highway, bridge or tunnel, you may call the police at 911 for assistance. The police will then send a licensed towing firm that works under the Directed Accident Response Program. By law, the towing firm must take your car wherever you specify. Make sure that the authorisation you sign states that it is for towing only and not for repairs – a towing company may try and convince you to let them bring your car to a specific repair shop. If a towing company appears at your accident that does not have a DARP sticker, they are working illegally and may charge you inflated rates to tow your car.

Recovery Services/Towing (24 hour)	
AAA Automobile Club of New York	212 757 2000
Advanced Tow & Recovery	212 996 2885
City Wide Towing	212 924 8104
JDS Towing	212 947 2749
Mid Up Towing	212 947 9025
Oz Towing	212 247 0445

Any other time you need towing assistance, you may call a licensed DCA (The NYC Department of Consumer Affairs) towing company of your choice. It is best to call around for rates though, as towing can be expensive, and there are over 2,000 car towing companies in and around New York City. If you need a list of licensed towing companies in your area, call the city information line at 311. You will need to sign papers that allow the towing company to take possession of your vehicle. Make sure that these papers say authorisation to tow and not to repair. The towing company must also give you a consumer bill of rights regarding towing, which states that you have the right to choose your own repair shop. Your insurance company may cover the towing cost, so make sure you get an itemised bill before your car is taken away.

Traffic Accidents

Other options **Car** p.40

Car Insurance
Remember, driving without insurance is illegal in the United States and you could face hefty fines or jail time if caught without it you also will not be able to retrieve your vehicle if impounded.

If you have an accident, it is important to call the police immediately. You must have your insurance card, registration and driving licence ready to show the officer once they arrive on the scene. Even if you, or the person who hits you, wants to settle the damages without your insurance companies, having a police report will ensure that you are paid. Be sure to always call your insurance company directly after the accident occurs again, even if not pursuing claims through the agency. This will ensure that the other party cannot counter sue you for unwarranted damages. The police report will not include the other driver's phone number – you must obtain that information on your own before leaving the scene. If you require a copy of the accident report for insurance reasons, you may call or visit the local police agency or precinct where the accident occurred. There may be a small charge for obtaining this. If possible, move off the road after your accident occurs. Accidents account for the majority of traffic in and around the city and your fellow motorists won't take well to you blocking the middle lane.

Repairs (Vehicle)

There are countless auto repair shops in New York City. The best advice is to just shop around and if possible, use a repair shop that has been recommended to you. If you need repairs due to an accident, your insurance company will pay for the work. However, before you have the repairs done, talk to your insurance company. Often, you will need to pay for the repairs and then be reimbursed. The table lists some of the highest rated auto-repair shops in New York according to customer rating.

Repairs (Vehicle)		
Auto Care East	Lower East Side	646 237 1466
Auto Repair 24 Towing	Gramercy Park	646 237 1490
Cybert Tire & Car Care	Hell's Kitchen	212 265 1178
Jake's Auto Repair	Upper West Side	212 307 7940
Manhatan East Auto Repair	Upper East Side	212 831 4300
Manhattan Auto Collison	Lower East Side	212 353 0125
Montero & Chino Auto Repair Shop	Hell's Kitchen	212 564 6760
One Stop Auto Center	Chelsea	212 695 6808

I  beautiful music

Music now looks as beautiful as it sounds. The new W880i
Walkman® phone with up to 900 songs, it's just as
beautiful on the inside.

sonyericsson.com/walkman

Sony Ericsson

Raw power, refined.

The new Chevrolet Tahoe refines the raw power of a 355 horsepower Vortec V8 engine and couples it with smooth handling and a quiet ride. Examine Tahoe's luxuriously appointed interior and you'll find refinement in every detail.

CHEVROLET

Tahoe 2007

Exploring

Exploring

Exploring

The City that Never Sleeps. The Big Apple. Gotham. The Capital of the World. Does New York City need an introduction? No, although a brief history lesson might be useful. In 2009, the city will celebrate the 500th anniversary of Henry Hudson's arrival, the event that put the small European settlement (to become New Amsterdam) on the map for the first time. The Dutch colony became British New York in 1664, and by 1789 it was the short-term capital of the new United States of America. Its current incarnation as a metropolis of five boroughs is the product of the great consolidation of 1898, that then made New York second only to London in size. A few years later in 1904, the subway system opened and forever changed the way New Yorkers travelled. Throughout the 19th and early 20th centuries, New York became an international centre of both culture and commerce, embracing new immigrants from abroad as well as ambitious men and women from all over America. Lean years in the 1970s and 1980s have now given way to an innovative 21st century city with a growing economy, a dynamic population, and the means to secure its position as one of the world's leading cities well into the future. From subways to sidewalks, New York gets crowded. The largest city in America, and one of the largest in the world, it has a population of 8.2 million and growing. Add the surrounding suburbs, and the metropolitan area population climbs to 22.1 million, a significant percentage of which travel into Manhattan for work every weekday. On top of residents and commuters, an astonishing 44 million tourists came to the city in 2005, and current Mayor Michael Bloomberg would like to see the number reach 50 million in the next few years.

Though most famous for its skyscrapers, this city of islands also has about 578 miles of waterfront including 14 miles of public beach. There are 6,375 miles of streets to wander and 753 bridges and tunnels to traverse. If local landmarks look familiar, it's not deja vu: last year alone more than 100 television programmes and 250 films were made in New York, beaming images of the city to audiences around the globe. It is the undisputed centre of American media, with two national newspapers, all four major American television networks, a dozen cable networks, and several film studios based in town. Hundreds of museums, art galleries, and performance venues flourish, supported both by patrons and the city's arts budget, a sum larger than the federal National Endowment for the Arts.

The city's population is also exceptionally diverse. Socio-economic classes mix freely, and you will find multi-millionaire bankers living in proximity to waiters working for minimum wage. About 36% of residents were born abroad, so in addition to the four major daily newspapers, one can find immigrant publications in no less than 42 languages.

People of all ages are drawn to New York. One might call it America's largest college town, with dozens of colleges and universities enrolling nearly 600,000 students. Since plummeting crime rates have made it the safest large city in America, families and older adults are making homes in the city, filling playgrounds with children and contributing to the growth of new retirement communities.

New York can be overwhelming, and this chapter is designed to help you get acquainted with the very best sightseeing it has to offer. The checklist is a perfect place to get started, outlining everything you will definitely want to see and do before leaving the city. Next, the neighbourhoods of greatest interest to visitors are described in brief alongside some suggested activities for visitors. Sections describing the major art galleries, heritage sites, museums, beaches, and parks follow, as well as detailed information about sightseeing tours. At the end of the chapter, you will find suggestions for short trips outside the city to suit every taste and budget.

Size is Everything

New York is home to many 'World's Largests' - the New York Stock Exchange trades the most volume at $3 billion daily, while the NASDAQ (National Association of Securities Dealers Automated Quotations) is tops in listings. The Cathedral of St. John the Divine is the biggest gothic cathedral, and Macy's 2.1 million square feet of shopping space beats all other stores. The Panorama of the City of New York is the largest architectural model with 895,000 structures built to scale, and the city's subway system surpasses all others in mileage with 656 miles of track. Show-off.

Art Museums

New York is one of the most important and thriving art centres in the world, and therefore boasts some of the very best art galleries and museums in existence. A mooch around either the spiral-shaped Guggenheim (p.220), the epic Metropolitan Museum of Art (p.221) or the recently renovated Musuem of Modern Art, p.222 is candy for the eyes and soul.

Empire State Building & Top of the Rock

The Empire State Building (p.216) is New York's most popular tourist attraction, and for good reason. Both the building's sky-high view over the city and its art deco interior are awe-inspiring. Those in the know, however, dodge the hefty queues and zoom up to the recently renovated observation deck of 30 Rockefeller Plaza (Top of the Rock) for an equally dazzling panorama of the city (www.topoftherocknyc.com).

Shopping on Fifth Avenue

Imagine you're Audrey Hepburn and sashay around Tiffany's in the Diamond District, or play a manicured Fifth Avenue princess and simply march down the sidewalk with an army of designer bags hanging off your arm. If your budget doesn't quite stretch to Prada, there are plenty of mid-range stores too (p.366).

Grand Central Terminal

At Grand Central, the last thing you want to do is catch a train. The transport hub boasts breathtaking beaux arts features, such as the giant clock and zodiac ceiling mural (with dark splodge purposefully left to reveal recent maintenance work), as well as shops, events, stylish bars, and an underground floor of food options. Check out one of the twice-weekly free tours (www.grandcentralterminal.com), or just wander in and soak up the vibrant atmosphere.

Statue of Liberty from the Staten Island Ferry

Lady Liberty would be positively insulted if you came to New York and didn't pay her a visit. Either catch a ferry over to the statue itself and climb inside, or, if you want to save a few dollars, relax on the free half-hour ride over to Staten Island, from which you can catch ample views of the famous 1886 statue (p.217).

Central Park

Central Park (p.233) is the eye in the middle of New York's hectic storm, a place people go to escape the rat race and catch a glimpse of green. Join the jogging army doing a lap, hire bikes and explore your own routes, or act like a tourist and do it by romantic horse-drawn carriage. During summer, catch free concerts or theatre, or practise your pirouettes on one of two winter ice rinks. Whatever outdoor activity you fancy, it's happening in Central Park.

Times Square

For many, Times Square epitomises New York. It is the neon-lit, pulsating heart of the city, where gigantic moving advertisements and fantastic architecture overwhelm the senses from every angle. It's busy and noisy, but it's a great place to visit as soon as you arrive, or whenever you want to remind yourself you're in the city that never sleeps.

Eat at a Deli

Nearly every street in New York has a deli, where delicious food is freshly prepared with trigger-quick service and a long list of customisation options. Try the cheesecake at Carnegie Deli (p.381), or pop into Katz's Deli (pictured, p.381) for a pastrami on rye - Katz's is one of the oldest delis in NY, and also the most famous thanks to Meg Ryan's classic faking scene in *When Harry Met Sally*.

Score a Bargain at Century 21 or Loehmann's

Not everyone's a fan, perhaps because of the crowds and the seemingly random sizes available. But if you're feeling scrappy and you have some time on your hands, a good rummage through the piles of designer labels at Century 21 (p.360) or Loehmann's (p.322) can net you some amazing, unbeatable bargains.

Walk Across Brooklyn Bridge

It's not that far – really. March, amble or cycle the 6,016 feet from Manhattan to Brooklyn and you get to enjoy sigh-inducing views of the city and lower East River. And the bridge itself is a beauty, with unforgettable late 19th century Gothic towers and swirls of super strong cables. Head over towards Brooklyn at around sunset for some memorable views of the Manhattan skyline.

Sip a Cosmopolitan in the Meatpacking District

New York's trendiest bars and areas change as fast as the cab drivers sail down the avenues, but the meatpacking district seems to have hung onto its hip for longer than normal. APT (p.423) offers slick DJs and a laidback vibe in a pseudo apartment, while at Gin Lane (p416) you can sup swanky cocktails and soak up the sophisticated, speakeasy vibe.

Ground Zero and St Paul's Chapel

Pay tribute to the victims and celebrate the tenacity of the survivors at the site where the World Trade Center towers once stood (p.218). A visit here is made all the more moving by a gallery of photos and a timeline of 9/11. The memorial in nearby St Paul's Chapel (p.217) is also unmissable, not just because it was the only structure in the area to suffer no damage in the attacks, but also because it was home for the brave volunteers who helped out during the aftermath.

Helicopter Tour

Add some daredevil excitement to your stay with a quick chopper-ride over the city. With most companies you have to book the trip a day in advance and arrive half an hour early, but the admin is all worth it when you find yourself sailing over the Statue of Liberty, with your stomach still somewhere at ground level.

Magnolia Bakery Cupcakes

Ah, but this is no ordinary cupcake. This is the kind of baked, sugary marvel that gets people queuing around the block in sub-zero temperatures. The West Village's favourite bakery (p.327) ferries out all manner of sweet treats well into the night, but it's the multi-coloured cupcakes that everyone (perhaps, most famously, the *Sex and the City* ladies) can't get enough of.

Catch Some Live Jazz

New York wouldn't be New York without its army of pork pie hats and smoky jazz rooms. The flashy new Lincoln Center (p.xxx) offers pricier jazz with a stunning view over Central Park, the West Village's Blue Note (www.bluenotejazz.com) is a world famous jazz institution, and there is always fresh talent at Village Vanguard (www.villagevanguard.com) and Smoke (www.smokejazz.com).

UN Headquarters

Technically, you can leave New York while still in Manhattan. Step into international territory by visiting the influential 18 acre UN headquarters (p.xxx). Soak up the history on one of the frequent 45 minute tours around the 83 acre site, and see where international leaders meet and world-changing decisions are made.

Reading Room at the New York Public Library

In a city positively scraping the sky with amazing architecture, the New York Public Library is one particularly good-looking building. Keeping New Yorkers well-read since 1911, entrance to the Beaux-Arts building is free, and the enormous reading room is the perfect place to spend a few reflective moments. While you're there, don't forget to look up at the dreamy mural on the ceiling.

Splurge on Dinner at One of New York's Top Restaurants

One-dollar hot dogs and deli sandwiches serve their purpose, but while in one of the world's top restaurant destinations it would be crazy not to treat your tastebuds to some fabulously fine dining. If your wallet's full and your stomach's empty, dine at the much-praised Babbo (p.392), Daniel (p.388), Bouley (p.387) or Per Se (p.389).

Wall Street and the NYSE

Wander around the financial district on a weekday morning and you can just smell money being made. Although the New York Stock Exchange is not open for tours, the exterior facade deserves a photo, and if you listen hard enough you can hear the bell launching the daily stock scrum every morning at 09:30.

Get a Slice of Genuine New York Pizza

Forget Italy, New York is home to the most delicious slices of tomato and cheese topped bread in the world – or at least, that's what the guys at Brooklyn-based Grimaldi's Pizzeria (p.393) or Lombardi's (pictured, p.394) will tell you. And once you've chowed down one of the gigantic slices they serve, you'll be saying the same.

Ice Skating

Ice skating (p.267) is a real social event in New York – and great exercise too. Obviously only an option during the winter months (rinks are typically open from October to April), pick from gliding around Central Park, Rockefeller Center and now Bryant Park.

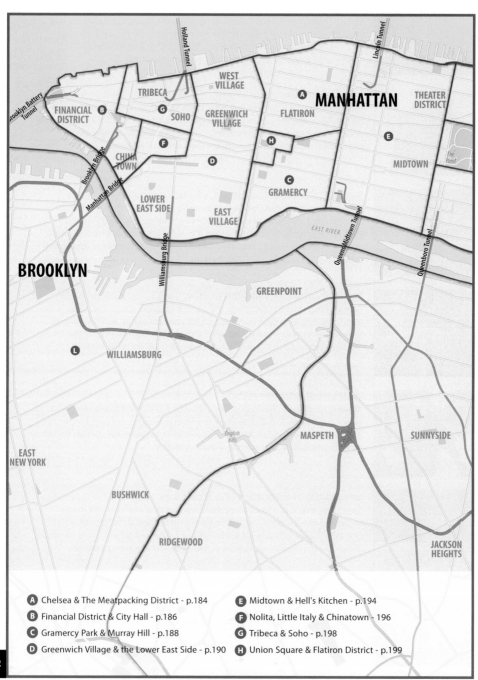

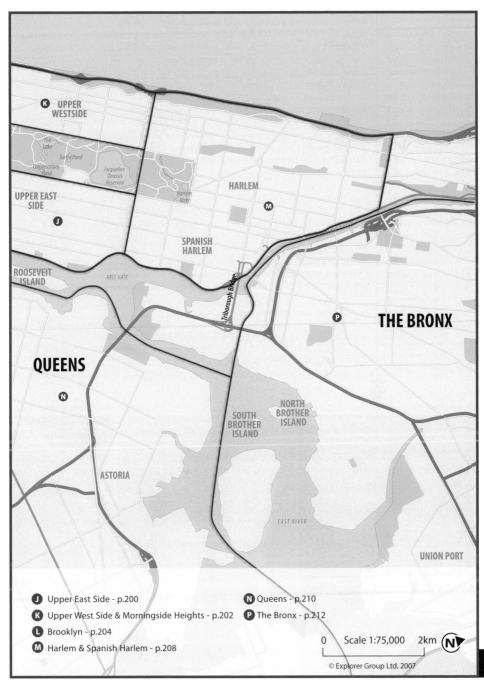

K UPPER WESTSIDE

The Lake

Turtle Pond

Conservatory Pond

Jacqueline Onassis Reservoir

UPPER EAST SIDE

J

Harlem Meer

HARLEM

M

SPANISH HARLEM

ROOSEVELT ISLAND

HELL GATE

Triborough Bridge

P

THE BRONX

QUEENS

N

SOUTH BROTHER ISLAND

NORTH BROTHER ISLAND

ASTORIA

EAST RIVER

UNION PORT

J Upper East Side - p.200
K Upper West Side & Morningside Heights - p.202
L Brooklyn - p.204
M Harlem & Spanish Harlem - p.208
N Queens - p.210
P The Bronx - p.212

0   Scale 1:75,000   2km   N

© Explorer Group Ltd. 2007

Maps 6 & 8 ◀

Chelsea & The Meatpacking District

In the 1990s the Meatpacking District was transformed from a collection of dingy butcher shops to a trendsetting neighbourhood… with a few remaining butcher shops. There are plenty of upscale bars, restaurants, and shops ready to contain the crowds of 30-something singles ready to mingle every Saturday night. Those rusty old railroad tracks overhead are the remnants of the long-defunct High Line, soon to become a public park. There is no completion date set, but the plan has already inspired a boom in condo construction and attracted the attention of a few cultural institutions eager to move.

Neighbourhood fixture Florent (69 Gansevoort Street at Washington Street, 212 989 5779) has been around for many years now, and it's still a great place to eat and drink 24/7. Bistro Pastis on Ninth Avenue at Little West 12th Street (p.385), while overrun on weekend evenings, is great for weekday breakfast or lunch or for the more exotic, Fatty Crab (643 Hudson Street at Gansevoort Street, 212 352 3590) has great Asian-fusion plates, as does Spice Market on West 13th Street at Ninth Avenue (p.386).

Chelsea was long a gay enclave, but now it is best known for its 200 art galleries and cluster of high profile nightclubs like Crobar (530 West 28th Street at Tenth Avenue, 212 629 9000), Marquee on Tenth Avenue at West 27th Street (p.426) and Bungalow 8, also on Tenth Avenue (p.424). To work out, ice skate, hit golf balls, and otherwise engage in a bit of athleticism, visit the vast sports complex at Chelsea Piers (Pier 60, www.chelseapiers.com).

The city's best place to buy art books is Printed Matter (195 Tenth Avenue at 22nd Street), and all things photo-related should come from the vast inventory of B&H Photo (420 Ninth Avenue at 33rd Street). Edible treats are for sale at Chelsea Market (75 Ninth Avenue at 16th Street) and blossoms by the bushel can be found in the Flower District on 28th Street between Sixth and Seventh Avenues.

As for refreshments and re-energising, Cookshop (156 Tenth Avenue at 20th Street, 212 924 4440) is a wonderful place for cocktails and large portions of well-prepared, seasonal comfort food, La Luncheonette (130 Tenth Avenue at 18th Street, 212 675 0342) and The Red Cat (227 Tenth Avenue at 23rd Street, 212 242 1122) are local standbys, and RUB BBQ (208 West 23rd Street at Seventh Avenue, 212 524 4300) can be counted on for hearty, all-American grub.

Hotel Chic ◀

This area has a couple of famous hotels that are worth hanging around at: the notorious Chelsea Hotel (p. 33) has hosted Jimi Hendrix, Janis Joplin, Andy Warhol and Tennessee Williams, among others. The architecturally intriguing Maritime Hotel (363 West 16th Street) has a fabulous facade and a couple of restaurants and bars that draw crowds to party on its spacious terrace. And then of course there's the Gansevoort (p.33), where you'll find all the pretty people and bucketloads of celebrities.

Chelsea Market

Derek Eller Gallery

Meatpacking Butcher

Is getting lost your usual excuse?

Whether you're a map person or not, this pocket-sized marvel will help you get to know the city like the back of your hand… so you won't feel the back of someone else's.

New York Mini Map
Putting the city in your pocket

Maps 12 & 13

Financial District & City Hall

As the oldest part of the city, the Financial District is packed with landmarks, the most notable being Battery Park - the site of first European settlement and today a park with a collection of monuments and several ferry terminals. The Staten Island Ferry Terminal is just east of the park, and the ferry to Governor's Island leaves from the Battery Maritime Terminal next door. Moving north along the river from the park, Battery Park City is a complex of residential and commercial buildings built on landfill produced by the construction of the original World Trade Center. Among the winding riverfront pathways sits the Museum of Jewish Heritage (36 Battery Place, 212 968 1800, www.mjhnyc.org) and several monuments. Moving south and east along the waterfront from the Battery eventually leads to the South Street Seaport (South and Fulton Streets), a complex that includes several ship museums, boat launches, indoor and outdoor shopping, and several restaurants.

Bowling Green (Broadway and State Street) is the city's oldest park and supposedly the site of the world's most unfair real estate deal; the transfer of Manhattan from the Native Americans to the Dutch in exchange for trinkets worth about $24. The large building behind the park is the turn of the century Beaux-Arts Customs House, now home to the Museum of the American Indian (1 Bowling Green at State Street), with statues on the front representing the four continents that traded with America. Grab the Charging Bull statue by the horns and make it happen over at the New York Stock Exchange (20 Broad Street at Exchange Place) and while you're on Wall Street, visit landmark Trinity Church (Broadway and Wall Street) and Federal Hall (26 Wall Street at Broad Street).

Walking up Broadway, notice the plaques in the sidewalk that displays the names of all the people who have been honoured with a ticker tape parade through the Canyon of Heroes (Broadway from Bowling Green to City Hall Park). St. Paul's Chapel (Broadway and Fulton Street) had been standing since colonial times, surviving the attacks of September 11, 2001 to become an informal memorial site. The World Trade Center Site (Church and Vesey Streets) sits just behind the churchyard and you'll find a city shopping landmark just around the corner; discount department store Century 21 (22 Cortlandt Street at Broadway).

Drinking and eating establishments downtown generally cater to a business crowd, closing in the early evening and remaining shuttered on weekends but as more residential buildings go up, more services are adding extended hours. If none of the pubs along pedestrian-only Stone Street off Hanover Square look appealing, try classic Irish bar, Killarney Rose (180 Beaver Street at Pearl Street, 212 422 1486) or expect the staff to mention that 'George Washington ate here' at Fraunces Tavern on Pearl Street at Broad Street (p.416), which has been serving food and drink since 1762. The area's best fine dining is Bayard's (1 Hanover Square at Pearl Street, 212 514 9454) inside the beautiful India House building.

City Hall Park recently underwent a complete restoration and now it looks worthy of hosting its two small but lovely buildings; City Hall and Tweed Courthouse. Some New Yorkers do not realize that the vast Municipal Building (1 Centre Street at Chambers Street) is not actually City Hall but a rather large city office building. The Official New York City Store in the building is a great place to buy souvenirs and gifts, located at the North Entrance on Centre Street.

There is no mistaking the Brooklyn Bridge, nor the gothic tower of the Woolworth Building (233 Broadway at Park Place). New York's storied 'Cathedral of Commerce' has a gorgeous lobby as well as a friendly cafe, restaurant, and bar called Woolworth Kitchen that is worth checking out.

It All Happens Here

Catch a ferry to Staten Island (even if you're only doing it for the views of Lady Liberty), visit Ground Zero (p.218), take a stroll around Battery Park (p.106), buy discount Broadway tickets from TKTS in South Street Sea Port, or just get caught up in the madness of wall street - some of the city's most memorable activities begin here.

Charging Bull

The Bridge Café (279 Water Street at Dover Street, 212 227 3344) and the Paris Café (119 South Street at Peck Slip, 212 240 9797) are two of the city's oldest restaurants but to just pick up coffee and a bagel, get to Blue Spoon Coffee (76 Chambers Street at Broadway, 212 619 7230) or Bits, Bites & Baguettes (22 Park Place at Broadway, 212 374 1111). Shopping is not terribly exciting in these parts; J&R Music World (33 Park Row at Beekman Place) for sonic electronics and Tent & Trails (21 Park Place at Church Street) for camping gear are the exceptions.

Brooklyn Bridge

Battery Park Pier

Trade Center Memorial

World Trade Center Site

Maps 7 & 9

Gramercy Park & Murray Hill

These two residential neighbourhoods are fairly quiet, with Gramercy Park retaining an air of exclusivity and Murray Hill catering to the post-collegiate, shared-apartment set. Gramercy Park, though owned by the city, is locked and accessible only to those that live in the stunning townhouses on its border. It's a long-standing tradition unlikely to change, so buy in or forever lack a key. For a brief peek, visit on Gramercy Day; it is the one day a year – usually the first Saturday in May – when the gates are opened to the public. Alternatively, fork out the $500 or so that it will cost you to spend the night at the Gramercy Park Hotel (p.33) - the hotel has 12 keys to the park that are available to guests. Even if you don't manage to get the key to the door, you can still enjoy the leafy tranquility of this area (from outside the park's fence) and mingle with lavender-rinse ladies and their Burberry-coated lapdogs.

Privileged for a Day
Mark the first Saturday in May in your diary: this is usually Gramercy Day, when the supremely exclusive park is open to the masses.

If you're hankering for a great vindaloo, head for Murray Hill - its plethora of authentic Indian restaurants has earned it the nickname 'Curry Hill'. Shoppers in search of spices should head to Kalustyan's (123 Lexington Avenue at 28th Street), a shop that also sells all matter of nuts, dried fruit, Middle Eastern-style breads, imported groceries, and some of the best home-made dips and sauces to be found in town. Get cheese, or a good cheese-based meal, at Artisanal on Park Avenue at 33rd Street (p.386), both a shop and a bistro, or for something a bit meatier, Blue Smoke (116 East 27th Street at Park Avenue) sells upscale barbecue, Sarge's Deli (548 Third Avenue at 37th Street, 212 679 0442) serves a mean pastrami sandwich which you can enjoy with a beer should you wish, and Penelope (159 Lexington Avenue at 30th Street, 212 481 3800) makes the best BBLT around – that's double bacon by the way.

On the whole, this area has a great 'best of both worlds' feeling about it. On the one hand, you're just a short walk away from some of the real gems of New York, such as the Chrysler Building, Grand Central Terminal and the shopping mecca of Fifth Avenue, but on the other hand you'll find yourself on quiet, beautiful streets with distinctive architecture, plenty of greenery and an air of refinement.

Not big, but very clever…

Perfectly proportioned to fit in your pocket, this marvellous mini guidebook makes sure you don't just get the holiday you paid for but rather the one that you dreamed of.

London Mini Visitors' Guide
Maximising your holiday, minimising your hand luggage

EXPLORER

Maps 8, 9 & 11

Greenwich Village & the Lower East Side

The Lower East Side

A century ago, the Lower East Side was filled with newly arrived immigrants, many of them Jewish, all crowding into small apartments and dreaming of a better life. See the past come to life at the Tenement Museum (90 Orchard Street at Broome Street) or one of its most historic houses of worship, the Eldridge Street Synagogue (12 Eldridge Street at Division Street). People still come to the Lower East Side in the hopes of a better life, but they are as likely to be living in a luxury loft conversion as in a tenement. Note that Third and Fourth Avenues merge to become Bowery downtown, a street that was once the site of Dutch farms (bouwerie), later a stretch of squatters' flats and homeless shelters where you'd see the 'Bowery Bums', and now home to trendy bars and a restaurant supply district.

Past and present collide in the old neighbourhood shops, many selling the best versions of Jewish speciality foods that have become iconic New York eats. Four generations have stood behind the counter at Russ and Daughters (179 East Houston Street at Orchard Street), selling great smoked fish since 1914, but Yonah Schimmel's Knishery (137 East Houston Street at Forsyth Street) had already been in business for four years by then, and they still bake far and away the best knishes in town. The original Guss is long gone, but Guss' Pickles (85 Orchard Street at Broome Street) continues to use the same recipe that has been selling for over a century. Kossar's Bialys (367 Grand Street at Essex Street) is only about seven decades old, but they do make the best bialy (a breakfast roll a bit like a bagel) in America. Another local legend is Economy Candy (108 Rivington Street at Essex Street) which was one of many penny candy shops in the 1930s, but is now one of the last in the city. Follow in the footsteps of 60 years of shoppers at Essex Street Market (120 Essex Street at Rivington Street), where a fishmonger, butcher, baker, kosher wine merchant, two cheesemongers, and several grocers supply the neighbourhood cooks.

A fun place to eat that represents the new immigrants on the Lower East Side is the Chinese porridge specialists at Congee Village (100 Allen Street at Delancey Street, 212 941 1818) or for fine dining, wd-50, on Clinton at Stanton Street (p.401), has one of the most creative menus in town.

Have What She Had

Katz's Deli on Houston at Ludlow Street (p.381), opened in 1888, is the oldest in town - everyone should eat here at least once, if not once a month. Come hungry, and order a pastrami on rye, potato pancakes, and a Dr. Brown's Cel-Ray soda – and don't forget to tip the man behind the counter when you place your order to get the best cuts of meat. Sit back and enjoy the photos of famous visitors and the memorabilia from When Harry Met Sally, *the film that made the place even more famous.*

Washington Square Park

The Lower East Side bustles at night, with lots of bars and music venues in a relatively small area. The places to see new bands play are Bowery Ballroom (6 Delancey Street at Bowery, 212 533 2111), Mercury Lounge on Houston at Essex Street (p.418), and Tonic (107 Norfolk Street at Delancey Street, 212 358 7501). To be the one onstage, try punk rock karaoke night at former bodega-turned bar Arlene's Grocery on Stanton at Ludlow Street (p.411). Dive bar lovers should visit Bar 169 (169 East Broadway at Rutgers Street, 212 473 8866), those who prefer an upscale cocktail will like Les Enfants Terribles (37 Canal Street at Ludlow Street, 212 777 7518), and everybody likes Good World (3 Orchard Street at Canal Street, 212 925 9975.).

The West Village

The street grid that covers most of Manhattan disappears in the West Village, but it's a beautiful place to get lost. Everything here is on a smaller, more humane scale than in other city neighbourhoods. Think of Hudson River Park's manageable stretch of bike path, the many narrow, tree-lined streets, rows of stately brownstones, tiny boutiques, and cosy restaurants. Everything is small, except property prices. This famously bohemian neighbourhood has gone upscale in recent years, but there is still plenty of old-fashioned charm to be found. Keep an eye on the houses while strolling by, as plaques mark the facades of historic homes that once belonged to the likes of Theodore Dreiser, Willa Cather and EE Cummings.

New York University keeps a constant flow of young people in the area, for better or worse, with Washington Square Park serving as its unofficial quad. Check out one of the city's loveliest streets, Washington Mews, just a half block north of Washington Square North. The Lucille Lortel Theatre (121 Christopher Street at Bedford Street) has been around since 1955 under different names, always a respected Off-Broadway house. Foot-tapping culture vultures need to visit The Village Vanguard (178 Seventh Avenue South at Perry Street, www.villagevanguard.com), one of the world's most famous jazz clubs, open for more than 70 years and run today by founder Max Gordon's widow, Lorraine Gordon. While The Knicks are not always fun to watch, the street ballers at West 4 Street Courts at Sixth Avenue never disappoint.

If you're in the mood to have a stronger drink than a coffee, pay tribute to Dylan Thomas' demise at the White Horse Tavern (567 Hudson Street at 11th Street, 212 243 9260), slip through the back door at one-time speakeasy Chumley's (86 Bedford Street at Barrow Street, 212 675 4449), hunker down like an old sailor at one of the oldest bars in the city, The Ear Inn (326 Spring Street at Greenwich Avenue, 212 226 9060), or throw some darts with NYU co-eds at Kettle of Fish (59 Christopher Street at Seventh Avenue, 212 414 2278). There are endless dining options in the West Village. Grab a quick bite at hole-in-the-wall Mamoun's Falafel (119 MacDougal Street at West 3rd Street), where the pita sandwiches really are not half bad – and very, very cheap.

Shopaholics Love the Village!

Shopping opportunities abound, with chain stores and boutiques alike. Broadway Panhandler (65 East 8th Street at Broadway) sells everything a home chef needs. Equip a cocktail party with bottles from one of New York's best booze shops, Astor Wine & Spirits (399 Lafayette Street at 4th Street), and hunks of prime dairy from Murray's Cheese Shop (254 Bleecker Street at Leroy Street). CO Bigelow Chemists (414 Sixth Avenue at 9th Street) will fill the bathroom cabinets, while Other Music (14 East 4th Street at Lafayette Street) takes care of the iPod. Flight 001 (96 Greenwich Avenue at Jane Street) has the goods for a stylish traveller, and neighbouring Mxyplyzyk (125 Greenwich Avenue at 13th Street) has jewellery, housewares, and gifts that make up for the tongue-twister name - it's pronounced Mix-ee-pliz-ik by the way.

19

'Gastropub' Spotted Pig (314 West 11th Street at Greenwich Avenue, 212 620 0393) is overrun with customers on the weekends, hungry for the Michelin-starred British and Italian fare – weekday evenings are typically quieter. Blue Hill (75 Washington Place at MacDougal Street, 212 539 1776), Five Points (31 Great Jones Street at Lafayette Street, 212 253 5700), and Home (20 Cornelia Street at West 4th Street, 212 243 9579) all serve stellar seasonal menus while Blue Ribbon Bakery (33 Downing Street at Bedford Street, 212 337 0404) is great for groups. There is often a line out the door at Tomoe Sushi (172 Thompson Street at Houston Street, 212 777 9346) and burger joint Corner Bistro on West 4th at Horatio Street(p.414) so time your visit wisely. Lupa (170 Thompson Street at Houston Street, 212 982 5089) wins with hearty Italian meals, Tea & Sympathy on Greenwich Avenue at 13th Street (p.406) has mastered cosy English comfort food, (especially with the fish and chip shop A Salt & Battery next door) and Pearl Oyster Bar (18 Cornelia Street at West 4th Street, 212 691 8211) is the best place to get a New England lobster roll outside of Boston.

The East Village

Bar Crawling

There are so many bars in the East Village that residents trying to prevent any more from opening up. Skip the Johnny-come-latelys and go to McSorley's on 7th Street at Third Avenue (p.418) - it has been in business since 1854, making it the city's oldest continuously operating saloon. There is sawdust on the floor and the drink options are 'dark' or 'light' draft beer, both served two mugs at a time. Women had to sue to gain entry in 1970, and you don't have a hope of getting in on St. Patrick's Day. For a comfortable dive bar, try Blue & Gold (212 473 8918) or Grassroots (212 475 9443). For an uncomfortable punk rock bar, try Mars Bar (212 473 9842).

The East Village is much more recently gentrified, so it still has a bit of an edge to it - or maybe that's just old graffiti that the locals left up on the walls for old times' sake. Tompkins Square Park is the local hub for dog walking, people gawking, and any other outdoor pursuit. Historic St.-Mark's-in-the-Bowery Church (131 East 10th Street at Second Avenue) is a community centre of sorts, hosting lectures, poetry readings, and local meetings and New York Theatre Workshop (79 East 4th Street at Second Avenue) and The Public Theatre (425 Lafayette Street at Astor Place) are two of the best places in the city to see staged works. Cinephiles must not skip the Anthology Film Archives (32 Second Avenue at 2nd Street). KGB Bar (85 East 4th Street at First Avenue) has a Soviet theme and a renowned reading series. Many believe that the Nuyorican Poets Café (236 East 3rd Street at Avenue C) is the birthplace of slam poetry, and it is certainly a great place to experience performances by local artists. The honest-to-goodness landmark here is the fully restored home at Merchant's House (29 East 4th Street at Lafayette Street).

Vegans and vegetarians will find many options here, including long time favourites Angelica Kitchen (300 East 12th Street at Second Avenue, 212 228 2909) and Kate's Joint (58 Avenue B at 4th Street, 212 777 7059). Café Mogador (101 St. Mark's Place at First Avenue, 212 677 2226) is a cosy place with simple Moroccan food, especially nice for breakfasts. Candlelit Italian bistro Il Bagatto (192 East 2nd Street at Avenue B, 212 228 3703) is great for a date, and Momofuku (163 First Avenue at 10th Street, www.momofuku.com) is a delicious choice for nights that run late but if it gets really late, Ukranian/Polish diner Velselka (144 Second Avenue at 9th Street, 212 228 9682) is open 24 hours for eastern European snacks and pancakes for breakfast. Aside from the garish gift kiosks on St. Mark's Place, the East Village has become a pleasant place to boutique shop, with plenty of vintage and new clothing for sale. Used book buyers must hit The Strand (828 Broadway at 12th Street), while all the latest academic publications find their way to St. Mark's Bookshop (31 Third Avenue at Stuyvesant Place). Veniero's (342 East 11th Street at Second Avenue, 212 674 7070) has been churning out noteworthy cannoli since 1894, not a bad buy if Brooklyn's Italian neighbourhoods are just too far away. Venerable bath and body shop Kiehl's (109 Third Avenue at 13th Street) has its flagship store here, so stop in and ask for plenty of free samples. That pear tree out front is a historic reproduction of sorts; a tree stood on that spot from the days when this land was Dutch Colonial Governor Peter Stuyvesant's farm, only to be destroyed by an errant carriage in the 19th century. Kiehl's planted a new one in 2003, and hopefully modern drivers will be more careful.

193

Maps 4, 5, 6 & 7 ◄

Midtown & Hell's Kitchen

Both major train stations are in Midtown, with national Amtrak trains and regional trains headed for Long Island and New Jersey departing from Penn Station (34th Street and Seventh Avenue), and regional trains headed to the Hudson Valley and Connecticut departing from Grand Central (42nd Street and Park Avenue). The former has nothing to recommend it, but the latter is a spectacular building with a collection of shops and a foodcourt worth visiting anytime.

Outdoor spaces of note include Times Square (42nd to 48th Streets between Broadway and Eighth Avenue) and Bryant Park, home of the New York Public Library (42nd Street and Fifth Avenue). New York's two most beloved skyscrapers are here; the Empire State Building (34th Street and Fifth Avenue) and the Chrysler Building (42nd Street and Lexington Avenue) and you'll also find St. Patrick's Cathedral (Fifth Avenue and 50th Street) and Central Synagogue (East 55th Street at Lexington Avenue) two of the most impressive houses of worship in the city. The queues to get up to the top of the Empire State Building are always huge, unless you go early in the morning (from 08:00 onwards), or late in the evening.

Tours of the United Nations (First Avenue between 42nd and 48th Streets) can be fun, but the traffic when the General Assembly is in session is definitely not. Do not leave town without taking in a concert at Carnegie Hall (West 57th Street at Seventh Avenue). If culture is your thing, MoMA (the Museum of Modern Art, p.222) lives up to its hype, and both the American Folk Art Museum (p.219) and the Museum of Television and Radio (p.223) are worth a visit.

The world's largest department store, Macy's at Herald Square (p.361), anchors the bustling shopping corridor along 34th Street between Fifth and Ninth Avenues. If you're feeling inspired and making clothes at home appeals, all the fabric and trimmings can be found in the Garment District between Fifth and Ninth Avenues in the 30s. Shopping is an art form on Fifth Avenue; department stores include Lord & Taylor, Saks Fifth Avenue, Takashimaya, and Bergdorf Goodman. FAO Schwartz is the place for toys, Henri Bendel supplies the party dresses, and for jewels that arrive in an iconic blue box, go and see Tiffany & Co.

Power lunching should ideally happen in the Grill Room at the Four Seasons (East 52nd at Lexington Avenue, 212 754 9494), or maybe at the 21 Club (West 52nd Street at Fifth Avenue, 212 582 7200), but elegant dinners belong to the incomparable Le Bernadin on 51st Street at Seventh Avenue (p.398). Aquavit (West 54th Street at Fifth Avenue, 212 307 7311) gives Scandinavian cuisine a toehold in the city while KunJip (West 32nd at Fifth Avenue, 212 216 9487) is the best of the many Korean diners on 32nd Street. Locals and visitors alike get drinks in the shadow of the Empire State Building on the rooftop patio of Me Bar at La Quinta (West 32nd Street at Fifth Avenue, 212 290 2460).

The gritty streets of Hells' Kitchen, a subsection of Midtown that runs from the Hudson River to Ninth Avenue in the 40s and 50s, were allegedly the inspiration for the rough neighbourhood depicted in the musical *West Side Story*. Gentrification has brought housing prices up, but plenty of areas still look run down, especially around the Port Authority Bus Terminal (42nd Street and Eighth Avenue). Rudy's (Ninth Avenue at 44th Street) will provide a free hot dog with every pint of beer purchased, but Hallo Berlin (10th Avenue at 45th Street, 212 977 1944) does a much better job with its sausages. Daisy May's BBQ USA (11th Avenue at 46th Street, 212 977 1500) makes some great slow-cooked pork – you might spot some of their carts on the city streets. Tony Luke's (576 Ninth Avenue at 42nd Street, 212 967 3055) sells the finest cheesesteak sandwich this side of Philadelphia while Don't Tell Mama (343 West 46th Street at Eighth Avenue, 212 757 0788) is a classic piano bar and a New York institution so you'll feel like a well-fed local in no time.

Best Views

Visiting Depression-era gem Rockefeller Center (48th to 51st Street between Fifth and Seventh Avenues) just got better with the new and improved three observation decks at the Top of the Rock (www.topof therocknyc.com) on the 70th floor; its Radio City Music Hall, America's largest indoor theatre, is the home of the world's most popular Christmas show, starring the high-kicking Rockettes.

Insider Secrets

The area's worst-kept secret for low cost dining: the locally famous halal cart at 53rd Street and Sixth Avenues, boasting round-the-block lines every night. The 1950s chic Burger Joint (212 245 5000), hidden inside the Parker Meridien Hotel on West 56th Street, is somewhat secret, very cheap, and incredibly good.

New York Public Library

THE WORLD'S LARGEST STORE

macy's ★macy's

Maps 9 & 11

Nolita, Little Italy & Chinatown

Nolita, an abbreviation for 'North of Little Italy,' is best known as a boutique shopping destination; a sort of low-key extension of Soho. There are many small shops along Mulberry, Mott, Prince and Elizabeth Streets, the majority selling women's clothing and accessories. Sigerson Morrison (28 Prince Street at Mott Street) and Otto Tootsi Plohound (273 Lafayette Street at Prince Street) are paradise for shoe fanatics while Francophiles might try Pylones (69 Spring Street at Lafayette Street) for colourful toys, accessories, and housewares from Paris, and everyone should head to Lunettes et Chocolat (25 Prince Street at Mott Street) for an unlikely mix of eyewear and candies. Just the across the street from the 1815 landmark Old St. Patrick's Church (260 Mulberry Street at Prince Street) is Café Gitane on Mott Street (p.391), a great place for coffee, especially when the sidewalk patio is open while the focus is on after-dinner treats at innovative wine and dessert bar Room 4 Dessert (17 Cleveland Place at Kenmare Street). Little Italy was once a proper neighbourhood, but it is now little more than the strip of shops and restaurants on Mulberry Street. The Bronx's Arthur Avenue or Brooklyn's Bensonhurst and Bay Ridge neighbourhoods are much better places to find Italian-American food, but a few of the tourist spots here are better than average. Da Nico (164 Mulberry Street at Grand Street) is a great restaurant for groups, Ferrara Pasticceria (108 Mulberry Street at Canal Street) is good for coffee and a pastry on the go, and Di Palo Fine Italian Foods (206 Grand Street at Mott Street) will happily stock your pantry with imported treats.

For many visitors, Chinatown is the collection of stalls lining Canal Street between Bowery and West Broadway, half of them selling counterfeit designer handbags, sunglasses, watches, perfume, and jewellery, and the other half selling cheap souvenirs and Chinese novelties. Look beyond the $20 'Prada' purses and the plastic dragons to find a pair of the city's best shops, Pearl River Mart and Pearl Paint.

Pearl River Mart (477 Broadway at Broome Street) moved from its original Canal Street location to nearby Soho, but the inventory is still strictly Chinatown. This department store has a wide selection of clothes, slippers, bags, housewares, gifts, food, and novelties of better quality than can be found on the street, at prices not much higher. A great spot for gift shopping, it is the place to go for Asian-inflected silk jackets and purses, unusual tableware, and all types of Chinese cookware. Pearl Paint (308 Canal Street at Mercer Street) is another gem, billing itself as 'The World's Largest Discount Art Supplier.' They have everything needed to get creative, with an entire building filled with all kinds of supplies for drawing, painting, etching, and sculpture, plus three additional storefronts out back selling craft supplies, frames, and home decor.

It is worth stocking the pantry with Asian ingredients while strolling in Chinatown, Canal Street and on the side streets just below it, street stalls sell a mix of local and imported produce while open storefronts sell meats and seafood. Vendors do not always speak English, but watching the other customers usually indicates what is fresh and in season. It is worth buying a pre-cooked peking duck from a shop window at least once, if only to watch the person behind the counter unceremoniously chop it up to fit the takeaway box. For both prepared foods and a full selection of groceries, Kam Man Food Products (200 Canal Street at Mulberry Street) is the best choice. The freshly made noodles sold in the refrigerated section are delicious, and they sell for under $1 per bag. Competent Thai takeout is ubiquitous throughout this city, but Bangkok Center Grocery (104 Mosco Street at Mulberry Street) still stocks everything necessary to cook a great curry at home or find candy and snacks both familiar and truly exotic – while trying free samples of everything on offer – at Japanese shop Aji Ichiban (167 Hester Street at Mott Street).

If you would prefer someone else to do the cooking, there are plenty of options here. Dumpling and noodle shops abound, and a simple meal can often be had for under $5.

San Gennaro

The best time, some would say the worst time, to visit Little Italy is during San Gennaro. This street festival has been held in honour of the patron saint of Sicily each year since 1927, and it seems to get bigger every year. For 10 days in September, over a million people pack themselves into just a few blocks of Mulberry Street to eat, drink, be merry, and buy schlocky souvenirs. It is something to see, but the crowds easily become overwhelming.

After Chinese...

Fortune cookies don't count as dessert; get a cone at Chinatown Ice Cream Factory (65 Bayard Street at Mott Street) or pick up some sweets at one of many local bakeries.

Check out the clientele to judge whether the cuisine served is authentic or tailored to American tastes, and choose accordingly. If the latter appeals, wait in line for the soup dumplings at Joe's Shanghai (9 Pell Street at Bowery) or make a table reservation for the elegantly served bird at Peking Duck House (28 Mott Street at Mosco Street). At lunchtime, Wah Fung (79 Chrystie Street at Hester Street) has good Fujianese buffet options and Saigon Banh Mi Bakery (138 Mott Street at the Manhattan Bridge) will supply Vietnamese sandwiches to go. Dim sum lovers will enjoy checking out the carts at Jing Fong on Elizabeth Street at Canal Street (p.380) or ordering off the menu at Dim Sum Go Go (5 East Broadway at Chatham Square).

Most restaurants in Chinatown specialize in Cantonese dishes, and Danny Ng (34 Pell Street at Mott Street) and NY Noodletown (28 Bowery at Bayard Street) might be the best around right now. For Shanghai plates in a no-frills room, try New Green Bo (66 Bayard at Mott Street). For a nightcap, try the dive-karaoke joint Winnie's (104 Bayard Street at Mulberry Street) or the busy lounge Double Happiness (173 Mott Street at Broome Street).

Maps 10 & 11

Tribeca & Soho

Tribeca is an abbreviation for 'Triangle Below Canal,' a neighbourhood bounded by the river and Broadway. Until just a few decades ago it was an unremarkable industrial district, but now luxury loft conversions abound, as do upmarket restaurants and bars. One of the best is Bouley on West Broadway at Duane Street (p.387), with an honourable mention for Danube (30 Hudson Street at Duane Street, 212 791 3771) which is owned by the same chef.

New York Film Academy

Capsouto Freres (451 Washington Street at Watts Street, 212 966 4900) is a classic French bistro, while City Hall (131 Duane Street at Church Street, 212 227 7777) does it American style with a New York theme. If you have little ones in the Big Apple then head to Bubby's on Hudson Street at North Moore Street (p.375) which is ideal for children, with a menu of American comfort food appealing to all ages and plenty of crayons on the table for entertainment.

Art in Soho

There is a tiny branch of the mighty Guggenheim in Soho, on the corner of Broadway and Prince St. It may be small, but admission is free and Andy Warhol's The Last Supper is one of the permanent exhibits.

For a quick bite on the go, try a veggie combo at Pakistan Tea House (176 Church Street at Reade Street, 212 240 9800), a gourmet sandwich at 'Wichcraft (397 Greenwich Street and Beach Street, www.wichcraftnyc.com), or a Cubano at Columbine (229 West Broadway at White Street, 212 965 0909). Drinks are cosy at bar and bistro Lucky Strike (59 Grand Street at West Broadway, 212 941 0772), see a scene at the bar inside the Soho Grand Hotel on West Broadway at Canal Street (p.35), and there are no frills at Nancy Whisky Pub on Lispenard Street at West Broadway (p.419).

Soho is the area 'South of Houston,' north of Canal Street, and between Crosby Street and West Broadway. Remember that it's pronounced HOWS-ton, never HEWS-ton. The dozens of handsome cast iron buildings were first industrial sites, then they became artists' lofts, and now they have become luxury lofts. You can't throw a credit card without hitting a shop in Soho, and it's possible to purchase anything from $5 vintage dresses to $500,000 couture gowns. Bloomingdale's (504 Broadway at Broome Street) downtown branch is in the midst of a packed shopping corridor on Broadway, a run of commercial storefronts that actually begins near Union Square and continues past Canal Street. Clothes and shoes dominate, but there are other gems to be found. Kate's Paperie (561 Broadway at Prince Street) is great for stationery, gift-wrap, and greeting cards. Local gourmands pay up for the fine foods at Dean & Deluca on Broadway at Prince Street (p.401), and get bottles from New York State's often surprising good vineyards at Vintage New York on Broome Street at Wooster Street (p.310). Everything is good at Jacques Torres Chocolate (350 Hudson Street at Charleton Street, www.mrchocolate.com), but the hot chocolate is to die for. Moss (146 Greene Street at Prince Street) has housewares that approach fine art, while Evolution's (130 Spring Street at Mercer Street) selection of

Balthazar

taxidermy, fossils, rocks, and shells would look at home in the Museum of Natural History.

Everything is fresh from the sea at Aquagrill (210 Spring Street at Sullivan Street, 212 274 0505), and the bar is a great place to get cocktails and oysters. Balthazar on Spring Street (p.387) has been a trendy spot for years, but the food also lives up to its hype and be sure to order the breadbasket at brunch, or stock the pantry with a box to go from Balthazar Bakery next door. For drinks, Fanelli's (94 Prince Street at Mercer Street, 212 226 9412) is a cafe and bar with old-fashioned appeal, while Milady's (160 Prince Street at Thompson Street, 212 226 9340) bar draws a younger crowd from nearby NYU.

Maps 6 & 7 ◀

Union Square & Flatiron District

Many assume that Union Square commemorates the Union's victory in the American Civil War, but it was actually named years before the war in reference to its location at the intersection of several major streets. It has long been a spot for political rallies and public events, most notably the site of America's first Labour Day celebration in 1882 and a large informal memorial after the World Trade Center attacks on September 11th, 2001. Today the park is home to the city's largest greenmarket, where local farmers, dairy producers, fishermen, and butchers sell their wares to discerning urban chefs. From late November to Christmas, the Union Square Holiday Market pops up with stalls selling all types of gifts and crafts while in summer, the park has an outdoor cafe and bar on its northern border. The park's equestrian statue of George Washington is a popular spot for meeting friends – or blind dates.

Flatiron Building ◀

The Flatiron Building (175 Fifth Avenue at 22nd Street) is one of the city's most recognisable structures and legendary as the site of Marilyn Monroe's skirt-lifting scene in The Seven Year Itch.

You can learn more about one of America's most beloved Presidents at the Theodore Roosevelt Birthplace (28 East 20th Street at Broadway). Music publishers and songwriters once congregated on the street nicknamed 'Tin Pan Alley,' 28th Street between Sixth Avenue and Broadway, from the 1880s to the 1930s.

Inside Madison Square, Shake Shack (212 889 6600) serves up delicious burgers and milkshakes but for fine dining in this area, head to Union Square Café on 16th Street (p.379), Eleven Madison Park (at 24th Street, 212 889 0905), Craft (43 East 19th Street at Broadway, 212 780 0880), or Gramercy Tavern (42 East 20th Street at Broadway, 212 477 0777), all serving American cuisine with style. For sweets, try City Bakery on 18th Street (p.401).

Large chain stores now line the stretch of lower Fifth Avenue once called 'Ladies' Mile' for its many dressmakers, but there are still a few unique shopping experiences nearby. ABC Carpet & Home (888 Broadway at 19th Street) has several floors of furniture, carpets, and home accessories, both new and antique. Fishs Eddy (889 Broadway at 19th Street) sells vintage tableware along with lines of their own design, including the popular '212' pattern depicting the New York City skyline, while for clothing bargains, Loehmann's (101 Seventh Avenue at 16th Street) is the place to be.

Union Square Market

Flatiron Building

Maps 3 & 5

Upper East Side

The Upper East Side is home to many of the wealthiest New Yorkers, replete with the grand architecture they inhabit, the famous prep schools they attend, the cultural institutions they support, and the upscale shops and restaurants they patronise. When people speak of having 'the right address' they mean right here on Fifth and Park Avenues. Central Park is the reason that New York society moved to the Upper East Side en masse in the late 19th century. The terraces above the tree line are the cream of local real estate and the park is the place to take the kids to play, walk the dog or go for a jog. Over on the river, Carl Schurz Park is the preferred recreation spot for the east side of the neighbourhood, and the home of the mayor's official residence, Gracie Mansion. For great views, hop on the aerial tram to Roosevelt Island at 59th Street and walk its waterfront promenade and park.

The 92nd Street Y (92nd Street at Lexington Avenue) is more than just a community centre; it is a city treasure offering hundreds of affordable classes plus a lecture and readings series that draws the world's brightest minds in politics, literature, and the arts.

Museum Mile is here, with the Met (p.221), the Whitney (p.224), the Guggenheim (p.220), the Neue Galerie (P.223), the Museum of the City of New York (p.223), the Cooper-Hewitt (p.220), the Jewish Museum (p.221), the Asia Society (725 Park Avenue at 71st Street), and the Frick Collection (1 East 70th Street at Fifth Avenue) all within walking distance.

Every designer worth their threads has a shop on Madison or Fifth Avenues, keeping the neighbourhood awash in posh labels and stylish couture. A small-scale shopping excursion can be had at boutiques like Cantaloup (1036 Lexington Avenue at 74th Street) and Scoop (1275 Third Avenue 73rd Street). Zitomer (969 Madison Avenue at 76th Street) is a good bet for beauty products. When it comes to edibles, Agata & Valentina (1505 First Avenue at 79th Street) is the best of the gourmet bunch. Old time butcher Schaller & Weber (1654 Second Avenue at 86th Street) churns out the best sausages, while Glaser's Bake Shop (87th Street and First Avenue) sells cookies like grandma used to make – both relics of the days when this area was still nicknamed 'Germantown'.

The Brooklyn Blackout cake at Two Little Red Hens (1652 Second Avenue at 86th Street) will make a birthday happy, as will the treats for sale at Dylan's Candy Bar (1011 Third Avenue at 60th Street) which is a dentist's nightmare – and a sweet lover's dream. The venerable Sherry-Lehman (679 Madison Avenue at 62nd Street) is one of the city's top wine shops, with bottles from around the world and eminently knowledgeable staff if your vices lean towards liquor instead of liquorice.

The best place to get a cocktail in this part of town is Bemelman's Bar inside the legendary Carlyle Hotel (35 East 76th Street at Madison Avenue, www.thecarlyle.com), especially now that The Plaza (768 Fifth Avenue at 58th Street) has gone condo. Some of the city's best restaurants are here, including Daniel on 65th Street at Park Avenue (p.388) and Davidburke & Donatella (133 East 61st Street at Lexington Avenue, 212 813 2121). Elaine's (1703 Second Avenue at 88th Street, 212 534 8103) and Swifty's (1007 Lexington Avenue at 72nd Street, 212 535 6000) are popular with writers, socialites, and other local notables. Fans of low key dining should try diner breakfasts at Eat Here Now (839 Lexington Avenue at 64th Street, 212 751 0724), blue-plate specials at EJ's Luncheonette (1271 Third Avenue at 73rd Street, 212 873 3444), and burgers in the basement at Jackson Hole (232 East 64th Street at Third Avenue, 212 371 7187).

The Three Bs

For department store shopping, remember the three Bs: Bloomingdale's (1000 Third Avenue at 59th Street), Barneys (660 Madison Avenue at 61st Street), and Bergdorf Goodman (754 Fifth Avenue at 57th Street).

Upper Sweet Side

Generations of kids have clamoured for frozen hot chocolate and ice cream sundaes at Serendipity 3 (212 838 3531). If you suffer from a more adult sweet tooth get pastries at Payard (212 717 5252), chocolate malts at Lexington Candy Shop (212 288 0057) and frozen sweets at Ciao Bella Gelato (212 431 3591).

Political Prowess

The national government is in Washington DC, but New Yorkers might be pulling the strings. The residents of postal code 10021 on the Upper East Side of Manhattan give more money to political campaigns – both Democratic and Republican – than any other place in the country.

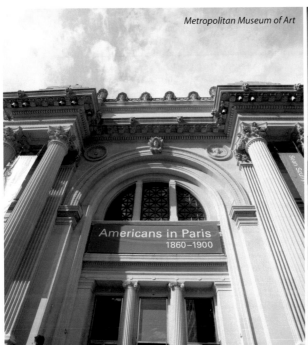

Metropolitan Museum of Art

Guggenheim

Central Park

The Complete **Residents'** Guide

Maps 2 & 4

Upper West Side & Morningside Heights

The Upper West Side is the highest-density residential area in the entire country, so this residential neighbourhood is filled with families and the everyday businesses that serve them. No surprise that its landmarks are historic co-op buildings: on Central Park West, the Majestic (at 71st Street), the Dakota (at 72nd Street), and the San Remo (at 74th Street); on Broadway: the Dorilton (at 71st Street) and the Ansonia (at 73rd Street). Central Park is very much the neighbourhood's backyard but Riverside Park, from 59th Street all the way to 158th Street, gives it a run for its money, especially for the biking and jogging set. Paths are wide and clean, and the view of the Hudson River and the New Jersey Palisades beyond is stunning. From spring until autumn, the cafe at the 79th Street Boat Basin inside the park is a great place for drinks and dinner. Find the answer to the old joke 'Who's buried in Grant's Tomb?' in upper part of the park, where the former president's grave is a national monument.

With more than a dozen arts organisations including the Metropolitan Opera, the New York City Ballet, and the New York Philharmonic in residence at the complex, there is always something going on at Lincoln Center (Broadway from 62nd to 65th Streets) and the nearby Beacon Theatre (2124 Broadway at 74th Street) is also a great concert and event venue. Visit dinosaurs at the American Museum of Natural History (at 79th Street), learn about America's oldest Jewish community at the 1654 Society (8 West 70th Street at Central Park West), and look into the city's past at the New York Historical Society (2 West 77th Street at Central Park West). Further uptown, the enormous and hauntingly beautiful Cathedral of Saint John the Divine (Amsterdam Avenue at 112th Street) is a must-see, and Riverside Church (Riverside Drive and 122nd Street) is worth a stop when in the area. Columbia University (Main campus between 114th and 120th Streets and Broadway and Amsterdam Avenues) is New York's entry in the Ivy League, while picturesque City College (138th Street and Convent Avenue) in nearby western Harlem is a public university with a storied past.

The main shopping corridors here are Amsterdam Avenue and Broadway. The two best-known shops on the Upper West Side are supermarkets: Zabar's (2245 Broadway at 80th Street) and Fairway (2127 Broadway at 74th Street); the former is famous for its lox and Jewish baked goods, and the latter has a cafe upstairs that serves a great brunch. Gracious Home (1992 Broadway at 67th Street) has housewares galore, and Labyrinth Books (536 West 112th Street at Amsterdam Avenue) will keep the shelves stocked. For one of Manhattan's few proper mall experiences, visit the swanky new Time Warner Center (p.357).

Two of the city's best restaurants are right on Columbus Circle: Jean Georges at 1 Central Park West (p.233) and Per Se inside the Time Warner Center (p.357), both with three Michelin stars. Ouest (2315 Broadway at 84th Street, 212 580 8700) serves French bistro fare that is better than most. The area is known for its brunch offerings, where patrons are known to wait upwards of an hour for the first meal of the day. Barney Greengrass (541 Amsterdam Avenue at 86th Street, 212 724 4707) is the granddaddy of them all, but nearby Popover Café (551 Amsterdam Avenue at 87th Street, 212 595 8555) is not too shabby either, or skip all the fuss, get a bag of the best at H&H Bagels (2239 Broadway at 80th Street), and eat at home. For a classic New York hot dog that is rumoured to be a favourite of Lauren Bacall, head to Gray's Papaya at 71st and Broadway.

The recent closing of the old P&G Bar (279 Amsterdam Avenue at 73rd Street) caused an outcry among locals because most local pubs are forgettable, so head uptown to Ding Dong Lounge (929 Columbus Avenue at 101st Street, 212 663 2600) for a bar with some character and some great happy hour deals. Columbia students get drinks at The Heights (2867 Broadway at 113th Street, 212 866 7035), and recover in the morning with pastries and coffee at Hungarian Pastry Shop (1030 Amsterdam Avenue at 111th Street, 212 866 4230).

You Know it so Well

This is a popular area of the city, especially among the more 'arty' set (you'll find the more conservative set across the park on the Upper East Side). Most movies and TV programmes set in New York will feature sweeping views of Central Park and the surrounding area - this is the Upper West Side, so even if you've never been there, you'll feel like you have!

Brooklyn

If being perceived as cool by fellow New Yorkers is important to you, be sure to live in the County of Kings (a reference to England's Charles II), the land that the Dutch named for their city of Breukelen - the place we call Brooklyn. With about 2.5 million residents, it is the city's most populous borough. Despite waves of gentrification that have 'Manattanised' many Brooklyn neighbourhoods, this borough retains a distinctive character.

The Great Mistake

As many a lifelong Brooklynite is quick to point out, Brooklyn would be America's fourth largest city if it were not for 'The Great Mistake of 1898' –the year that New York City became the five-borough conglomerate it is today, subsuming what was then a thriving independent city across the East River.

Greenpoint is the northernmost neighbourhood on Brooklyn's East River side, long an enclave of Polish immigrants and more recently an area popular with young people priced out of nearby Williamsburg. Manhattan and Greenpoint Avenues are its main commercial thoroughfares, packed with shops and restaurants. You can still experience a Polish night out: get drinks at the laid-back Pencil Factory (Franklin Street, 718 609 5858), see a band at Warsaw (Driggs Avenue, 718 387 0505), and sample the grub at Lomzynianka (718 389 9439) and Christina's (718 383 4382), both on Manhattan Avenue. Once a mix of industrial sites, Italian immigrants and Hasidic Jews, Williamsburg got an influx of artists in the 1980s that soon made it the place to move to after college graduation. The entire East Village basically picked up and moved across the East River to find cheaper rents and more space for studios and performance venues. By the late 1990s, the concentration of art galleries, quaint boutiques, slick restaurants, and deliberately divey bars around the L train stops at Bedford and Metropolitan Avenues had reached a critical mass. Now luxury towers are replacing old loft buildings everywhere, and weekends bring huge crowds to local bars and restaurants.

Brave the hordes and see what the scene is all about at gallery/performance space Galapagos (North 6th Street, 718 782 5188) and music venue Northsix (North 6th Street, 718 599 5103). Visit Brooklyn Brewery (www.brooklynbrewery.com) to see how your brew gets made, or skip the tour and just get a pint at Mugs Ale House (www.mugsalehouse.com) or East River Bar (718 302 0511).

Karaoke night at gay hangout Metropolitan (p.431) is fun for all. Roebling Tea Room (p.404) is great for casual eating and drinking at any time of day, but the nicest places for dinner are probably Aurora (Grand Street, 718 388 5100), DuMont (Union Avenue, 718 486 7717), or Miss Williamsburg Diner (Kent Avenue, 718 963 0802). For an old-school steakhouse experience, don't go anywhere but the famous Peter Luger Steakhouse (p.378).

DUMBO is an acronym for Down Under the Manhattan Bridge Overpass - and a decidedly unglamorous name for a very upmarket neighbourhood. Amid pricey residential buildings sit many home design shops and a handful of bars and restaurants, with Water Street being the main retail area. Waterfront Fulton Ferry Park has not only spectacular views of the Manhattan skyline and the two bridges, but a great playground for kids as well. The concerts and plays put on at St. Ann's Warehouse (38 Water Street at the Brooklyn Bridge) are well worth crossing the river to see.

Brooklyn's elite has long made its home in stately Brooklyn Heights; easily one of the city's most beautiful places to simply stroll and enjoy the architecture. The Brooklyn Heights Promenade has the best views of the downtown Manhattan skyline, which can be enjoyed along with a wonderful meal at waterfront River Café (1 Water Street at Old Fulton Street, 718 522 5200). The three nearby residential neighbourhoods of Boerum Hill, Cobble Hill, and Carroll Gardens have recently gentrified to resemble the Heights. Now they, too, are filled with brownstone blocks, quiet parks, and studded with small-scale commercial pockets. Destination shopping and dining is clustered on Atlantic Avenue, with Middle Eastern importer Sahadi's (187 Atlantic Avenue at Court Street) being the most famous of the shops, and along Smith Street, justly renowned as a shopping and dining destination. The most upscale of all the restaurants there is The Grocery (288 Smith Street at Sackett Street, 718 596 3335).

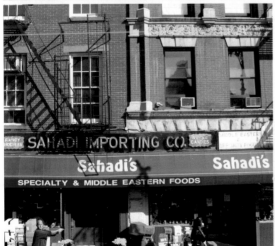

Nearby Downtown Brooklyn is a world away, filled with office buildings and cramped shops. The New York Transit Museum (Boerum Place and Schermerhorn Street) is here, as are the 230 shops of Fulton Street Mall (Fulton Street between Adams Street and Flatbush Avenue), plus a clutch of shops and restaurants along Court Street. Nearby, Junior's on Flatbush Avenue at DeKalb Avenue (p.377) is a landmark diner that is justly famous for its cheesecake and opens at 07:00 in case you wake up needing dessert breakfast.

Fort Greene is centred around Fort Greene Park, a favourite haunt of famous 19th century Brooklynite Walt Whitman. Here you will find The Brooklyn Academy of Music, usually referred to as BAM (30 Lafayette Avenue at Ashland Place), which was founded back in 1861 when Brooklyn was still independent. Today the complex of theatres is a great place to see music, dance, plays and movies, especially during the Next Wave Festival that brings artists from around the world to BAM's stages.

For local shopping, Myrtle Avenue has boutiques and the mall at Atlantic Terminal (Flatbush and Atlantic Avenues) has the chain stores but, if you prefer to support the independents, Cake Man Raven (708 Fulton Street at Hanson Place) sells great cakes, and the bath and body products at Carol's Daughter (1 S Elliot Place at DeKalb Avenue) merit a stop.

Prospect Park

Who needs Central Park? Brooklyn's Prospect Park is a huge expanse of well-maintained greenery in Brooklyn. It's the perfect place to spend a sunny afternoon just lying on the grass, but numerous activities are available for the more energetic. For more info, visit www.prospect park.org.

Park Slope and Prospect Heights sit along Prospect Park, a grand public space that hosts the Brooklyn Botanic Garden (p.231) and the Brooklyn Museum of Art (p.224). The main branch of the Brooklyn Public Library sits on the edge of the park in Grand Army Plaza, which is also the location of a large weekly greenmarket. If the offerings there are not enough to fill the kitchen, join the Park Slope Food Co-op (782 Union Street at 7th Avenue) to buy organic produce for less than supermarket prices. Just about the entire lengths of 5th and 7th Avenues between Flatbush Avenue and the Prospect Expressway are lined with independent boutiques, coffee shops, bars and restaurants so it's a great area for a stroll.

For drinks, Barbes (376 9th Street at 6th Avenue, 718 965 9177) and Great Lakes (284 5th Avenue at 1st Street, 718 499 3710) are among the best. A few of the city's finest restaurants are here, including Italian trattoria Al Di La (248 5th Avenue at Carroll Street, 718 636 8888) and seasonal-ingredient focused Applewood (501 11th Street at 7th Avenue, 718 768 2044). Chip Shop (383 5th Avenue at 6th Street, 718 832 7701) is the place to get a British expat's fix of all things fried, while Franny's (295 Flatbush Avenue at Prospect Place, 718 230 0221) turns out excellent pizzas with a great wine and cocktail list.

Inaccessible by subway and cut off from surrounding neighbourhoods by a web of highways, Red Hook might be forgotten if it wasn't by the water. Luckily it is, and places like Valentino Pier (Coffey Street on the waterfront) and the Beard Street Pier (Beard Street on the waterfront) let everyone take in the expansive harbour view. Street vendors crowd the border of Red Hook Ballfields to sell tasty Central and South

American food to soccer spectators from spring through to autumn and when in the area, eat at Hope & Anchor (347 Van Brunt Street at Wolcott Street, 718 237 0276) or The Good Fork (391 Van Brunt Street at Coffey Street, 718 643 6636), grab coffee and a cookie at Baked (359 Van Brunt Street at Dikeman Street, 718 222 0345), have drinks at Sunny's (253 Conover Street at Reed Street, 718 625 8211), bring home a pie from Steve's Authentic Key Lime Pies (204 Van Dyke Street inside Pier 41), and shop the well-edited selections of liquors at LeNell's (416 Van Brunt Street at Coffey Street). The young and mobile types who can no longer

afford Williamsburg are stretching into the industrial hinterlands of Bushwick and shabby-historic Bedford-Stuyvesant, a predominantly African-American community where the price of a brownstone is just now climbing over a million dollars. Sunset Park has one vibrant commercial corridor on 8th Avenue dominated by Asian businesses, and another on 5th Avenue dominated by Latino businesses. Victorian-era Green-Wood Cemetery sits here on the highest point in Brooklyn, and it has the views to prove it. It is the final resting place of many a famous New Yorker, and the site of the Battle of Brooklyn fought during the American Revolution.

Most of the businesses in the south Brooklyn neighbourhoods of Bay Ridge, Dyker Heights and Bensonhurst reflect Italian immigration, though long-gone Scandinavian residents and more recent Middle Eastern arrivals have made their mark as well. Stroll along the commercial corridors of 3rd, 4th, 5th, and 18th Avenues and 86th Street, pick up all things Norse at Nordic Delicacies (6909 3rd Avenue at Bay Ridge Avenue) and get the best cannoli in town at Villabate Bakery (7117 18th Avenue at 71st Street). Middle Eastern meals at Tanoreen (7704 3rd Avenue at 77th Street, 718 748 5600) are great, and Tommaso's (1464 86th Street at Bay 8th, 718 236 9883) matches its old school Italian-American dishes with an excellent selection of Italian wine and after that you might want to burn off the calories and take in a great view of the majestic Verrazano-Narrows Bridge, with a walk along the bay.

Beach Life

The three beach communities on New York Bay in eastern Brooklyn are Manhattan Beach, Brighton Beach and Coney Island. All three are crowded in summertime, but only the Russian community in Brighton Beach keeps the party going all year round and you can shop for clothing, furs, and other imports along Brighton Beach Avenue.

Crown Heights is a neighbourhood divided into Caribbean-American and Hasidic Jewish communities - and they are most definitely divided. When on the Caribbean side, try Jamaica's cuisine at Cheffy's (707 Nostrand Avenue at Sterling Place, 718 363 9515). Other Hasidic and Ultra-Orthodox Jewish areas in Brooklyn include the southern part of Williamsburg and the neighbourhoods of Borough Park, Midwood, and Ocean Parkway. The shops on 13th Avenue in Borough Park sell all things Jewish; kosher groceries and prepared foods, religious articles, modest fashions, and plenty of Yiddish and Hebrew books and movies. When visiting, respect local custom by dressing modestly. In Midwood, seek out some of the best pizza in the city at legendary hole-in-the-wall Di Fara's (1424 Avenue J at 15th Street, 718 258 1367). M&I International Foods (249 Brighton Beach Avenue at 3rd Street) and La Brioche Espresso (1073 Brighton Beach Avenue at 12th Street) are great for takeaway food, and vodka-fuelled parties run all night long at dinner clubs like Rasputin (2670 Coney Island Avenue at Avenue X, 718 332 8111) and The National (273 Brighton Beach Avenue at 2nd Street, 718 646 1225). Be prepared to pay anywhere from $50 to $100 per person for a prix fixe meal with drinks, and don't even bother going before midnight.

Beyond the beaches and neighbourhoods of western Brooklyn, in places like Gravesend, Sheepshead Bay, Canarsie, and Marine Park, it's possible to find old timers who have not bothered to go into 'the city' in years. Some of these self-sufficient neighbourhoods hold on to long-established identities based on ethnicity, religion, or geography, while others are home to insular immigrant enclaves. With a car, or patience for a long subway ride, exploring these off-the-beaten-track corners of the city can be very rewarding.

207

Harlem & Spanish Harlem

As its Dutch name suggests, Harlem was founded by colonists from the Netherlands city of Haarlem in the mid-17th century. It was a country village ringed by farm estates for years, only becoming part of rapidly expanding New York City in the 1870s. Large numbers of African-Americans began moving to the neighbourhood in the early years of the 20th century, soon earning Harlem its reputation as a centre of black culture as artists, performers, and intellectuals like Langston Hughes, Duke Ellington, Marcus Garvey, WEB DuBois, and Asa Philip Randolph set up shop there. Gentrification began in earnest in the 1990s, and now housing prices are high, shiny new stores line 125th Street and even former president Bill Clinton has his main office here.

It is worth nothing that several numbered streets and avenues in Harlem are marked with additional names honouring famous African-American leaders: 125th Street is also called Martin Luther King, Jr. Boulevard, Eighth Avenue is Frederick Douglass Boulevard, Seventh Avenue is Adam Clayton Powell, Jr. Boulevard, and Sixth Avenue is both Lenox Avenue and Malcolm X Boulevard. Historic homes abound in Harlem, especially near St. Nicholas Park. The best known are the townhouses that make up Striver's Row on 139th and 138th Streets between Adam Clayton Powell and Frederick Douglass Boulevards, so called because they once housed Harlem's best and brightest young professionals. Astor Row on 130th Street between Fifth and Lenox Avenues is remarkable for the Southern-style porches and front yards attached to each home. To see art and cultural exhibits relating to Harlem's history and black culture in general, visit the Schomburg Center for Research in Black Culture (515 Lenox Avenue at 136th Street) and the Studio Museum in Harlem (144 West 125th Street at Lenox Avenue).

Many famous black performers launched their careers in Harlem's nightclubs in the first half of the 20th century. The world famous Apollo Theater on 125th Street at Frederick Douglass Boulevard (p.436) was one of dozens of performance venues in the neighbourhood back in 1934, surviving where others failed with performances by stars including Ella Fitzgerald, Sarah Vaughan, James Brown, and Michael Jackson. Having hosted a well-known Amateur Night since it first opened, today the Apollo is known across the country for its televised program Showtime at the Apollo. The re-opened Cotton Club (656 West 125th Street at St Clair Place, 212 663 7980) hosted such greats as Dorothy Dandridge, Lena Horne, Duke Ellington and Cab Calloway on stage during its heyday in the 20s and 30s, but only allowed whites in the audience; that policy has obviously changed today. Bessie Smith, Ferdinand 'Jelly Roll' Morton, and Billie Holiday worked the Alhambra Ballroom (2116 Adam Clayton Powell, Jr. Boulevard at 121st Street, www.alhambraballroom.com) when it opened in 1926, and now it hosts weddings and special events.

Sing Hallelujah!
Of the hundreds of churches that dot the streets of Harlem, the Abyssinian Baptist Church (West 138th Street at Malcolm X Boulevard) is probably the most famous – held up as an example for racial equality when its congregation protested segregated seating. Its parish was founded in 1808, moving to Harlem in 1923 and all are welcome to take in a Sunday service and enjoy the full gospel choir – just remember to dress modestly and well.

For chain store shopping in the neighbourhood, look to the length of 125th Street and, in particular, to the large Harlem USA retail complex at Frederick Douglass Boulevard or get something more unique at the Malcolm Shabazz Harlem Market at 116th and Malcolm X Boulevard, open daily and filled with vendors selling African crafts, textiles, hair products, and sundry items. Two outstanding clothing and accessory boutiques with a local focus are Harlemade (174 Lenox Avenue at 119th Street) and SOH – Straight out of Harlem (704 St Nicolas Avenue at 145th Street) then get cakes to go at Wimp's Southern Style Bakery (29 West 125th Street at Fifth Avenue, 212 410 2296) if all the shopping has left you feeling in need of a sugar boost.

When in Harlem, be sure to sample some authentic soul food. Sylvia's on Lenox Avenue at 126th Street (p.379) is the most famous place around, and worth a Sunday brunch visit just for the convivial atmosphere. Other great eats include Amy Ruth's (113 West 116th Street at Lenox Avenue, 212 280 8779), Miss Maude's (547 Lenox Avenue at 138th Street, 212 690 3100), and Sugar Shack (2611 Frederick Douglass Boulevard at 139th Street, 212 491 4422). The friendly servers at Miss Mamie's Spoonbread Too (366 West 110th Street at Manhattan Avenue, 212 865 6744) might dish out the best fried chicken in town, but save some room for a piece of red velvet cake for dessert. If you're feeling inspired by the local music scene and fancy a buffet with a side of jazz, go to Copeland's (547 West 145th Street at Amsterdam Avenue, www.copelandsrestaurant.com) where you'll find southern cuisine and a Sunday brunch complete with gospel choir.

East Harlem – also known as Spanish Harlem, El Barrio, or, in recent real estate speak, 'SpaHa' – was an Italian enclave in the early 20th century. Only a few stalwarts from that era remain, including unlikely celebrity hangout Rao's (455 East 114th Street at First Avenue, 212 269 0151) and the original branch of local pizza empire Patsy's (2287 First Avenue at 118th Street, 212 534 9783). The neighbourhood is now home to a large community of Spanish speaking immigrants from Puerto Rico, Central and South America, and the Caribbean, plus a growing number of young professionals in search of low rents.

To learn more about local culture, check out El Museo del Barrio on Fifth Avenue at 140th Street (p.220). Two of the best local restaurants are Puerto Rican La Fonda Boricua (169 East 106th Street at Lexington Avenue, 212 410 7292) and Mexican El Paso Taqueria (1642 Lexington Avenue at 104th Street, 212 831 9831). One piece of offbeat public art worth a visit is the famed Keith Haring mural (Second Avenue and 127th Street) titled 'Crack is Wack'.

Queens

Named for the wife of England's King Charles II, Queens was just a collection of small towns and farms until being incorporated into the city of New York in 1898. To this day, postal addresses in Queens differ greatly from those in the rest of the city; street numbers are hyphenated, with the first number indicating the cross street number and the second number referring to the house. For example, 35-05 36th Street would be on 36th Street near 35th Avenue and the second line of a Queens address uses the old village and town names – Long Island City, NY, Astoria, NY, etc. – rather than the borough's names.

Both of the airports are here, as is the city's only horse racing track, the Aqueduct (Pitkin Avenue and Woodhaven Boulevard). The western and central parts of Queens encompass urban, heavily populated residential and business districts, while the eastern parts tend to look more like the Long Island suburbs they border.

> **The Importance of Maps**
>
> The street system of Queens reflects its haphazard development, and it is notoriously difficult for outsiders to understand the maze of numbered streets, avenues, roads, and places. It's worth investing in a Hagstrom Map showing all local streets before driving anywhere in the borough.

Astoria and Long Island City are two long-established neighbourhoods on the western border of Queens that have recently experienced an influx of young artists and professionals seeking lower rents than can be found in Manhattan and Brooklyn. There are beautiful waterfront views of the Manhattan skyline from Gantry State Park, and of the Triborough Bridge from Astoria Park and Pool. Art lovers must make a few trips to see some of the city's best museums; P.S. 1 (22-25 Jackson Avenue at 46th Avenue), the Fisher Landau Center (38-27 30th Street at 38th Avenue), the Museum of the Moving Image (36-01 35th Avenue at 36th Street), the Noguchi Museum (9-01 33rd Road at Vernon Boulevard), Socrates Sculpture Park (on Vernon Boulevard at Broadway), and SculptureCenter (44-19 Purves Street at Jackson Avenue).

The main commercial thoroughfares in these neighbourhoods are Vernon Boulevard between 51st and 45th Avenues for boutique shopping, Steinway Street between Northern and Astoria Boulevards for chain stores and more, and the stretches of 30th and 31st Avenues, Broadway, and Ditmars Boulevard between 29th and Steinway Streets for local services.

Get great baked goods worth the long subway ride at Laziza of New York Pastries (25-78 Steinway Street at 28th Avenue) for Middle Eastern specialities, Martha's Country Bakery (36-21 Ditmars Boulevard at 36th Street) for the best pound cake around, and Thessalikon Pastry Shop (33-21 31st Avenue at 33rd Street) for spinach pie that is almost too good to be true. For restaurant meals, excellent options are plentiful, spanning cuisine from around the world. Eat Greek at Aliada (29-19 Broadway at 29th Street, 718 932 2240), Egyptian-fusion at Kabab Café (25-12 Steinway Street at 25th Avenue, 718 728 9858), Brazilian at Sabor Tropical (36-18 30th Avenue at 36th Street, 718 777 8506), Italian at Trattoria L'Incontro (21-76 31st Street at Ditmars Boulevard, 718 721 3532), and French at Tournesol (50-12 Vernon Boulevard at 50th Avenue, 718 472 4355). There are many Irish pubs and Greek nightclubs around, plus two unique places that are great for groups; the city's last remaining outdoor beer garden is at old time Bohemian Hall on 24th Avenue at 29th Street (p.413), and a brand new place to sip out on the sand is on the East River at Water Taxi Beach (between 2nd Street and Borden Avenue, www.watertaxibeach.com). Getting beyond Astoria and Long Island City, there are many more neighbourhoods worth exploring, with restaurants and shops representing cultures from around the globe. All the neighbourhoods that line the 7 train – nicknamed the 'International Express' – are immigrant enclaves; try Mexican meals at De Mole (45-02 48th Avenue at

45th Street) in Sunnyside or drink a pint of Guinness with Irish locals at Sean Og's (60-02 Woodside Avenue at 60th Street, 718 899 3499) in Woodside. Indian businesses including Patel Brothers (37-27 74th Street) and Butala Emporium 37-46 74th Street) line 74th Street in Jackson Heights, a diverse neighbourhood that is also home to one of the city's large gay and lesbian communities.

Immigrants from all parts of Asia come to Elmhurst, so expect a vast array of grocery stores, restaurants, and shops on Broadway between Roosevelt Avenue and Queens Boulevard. The best of the bunch are Indonesian at Minangasli (86-10 Whitney Avenue at Broadway, 718 429 8207.), Indian-Chinese at Tangra Masala (87-09 Grand Avenue at Queens Boulevard, 718 803 2298), and Malaysian at Taste Good (82-18 45th Avenue at 82nd Street, 718 898 8001).

Corona's 103rd Street and Junction Boulevard are lined with shops, and an always-crowded outpost of the Latino chicken chain Pollo Campero (103-16 Roosevelt Avenue at 103rd Street, www.pollocampero.com) is nearby. Old Italian sandwich shop Leo's Latticini, also known as Mama's, (46-02 104th Street at 46th Street, 718 898 6069) and the famed frozen sweets vendor the Lemon Ice King of Corona (52-02 108th Street at 52nd Street) are required visits, as is the excellent Louis Armstrong Museum (34-56 107th Street at 34th Avenue). For some outdoor sightseeing, Flushing Meadows-Corona Park has hosted two World's Fairs and it is still the home of the New York Mets at Shea Stadium, late summer's US Open tennis championships at Arthur Ashe Stadium, the Queens Museum of Art, and the New York Hall of Science, among other facilities.

There are a few other Queens neighbourhoods that are off the 7 train track, but still easily accessible by subway and worth a visit. Forest Hills is known for its stately Tudor-style mansions located in the private community of Forest Hills Gardens, and the main commercial strips are in the area of Austin Street and Queens Boulevard. Try a pizza at Nick's (108-26 Ascan Avenue at Austin Street) or delicious dishes from Uzbekistan at Salut (63-42 108th Street at 63rd Drive, 718 275 6860), which sits amid a mall of shops selling goods imported from Eastern Europe. In contrast, the Rockaways are quiet, working class residential communities bordering the Atlantic Ocean, and neighbouring island Broad Channel in Jamaica Bay is even quieter. Jamaica Bay is known for the retail area along Jamaica Avenue, ('The Ave') where hip hop-influenced clothing, shoes, jewellery, and music shops are plentiful alongside immigrant businesses.

Exploring New York... Venture off the Beaten Track

All five boroughs have that special something and deserve to be explored. If you're looking for the motivation to venture off Manhattan (or indeed, onto Manhattan if you live in one of the other boroughs), try starting at the following spots:

The Bronx: Historic Van Cortlandt Park (Broadway to Jerome Avenue, Van Cortlandt Park South to City Line) is the site of America's first public golf course, one of the city's oldest houses, and a beautiful freshwater lake. Alternatively, Pelham Bay Park (on the Long Island Sound) is the city's largest, with 2,700 acres encompassing wooded trails, beaches, wildlife sanctuaries, and many athletic facilities.

Brooklyn: Sit and take in the downtown Manhattan skyline at Empire-Fulton Ferry State Park (Brooklyn, East River between Brooklyn and Manhattan Bridges), where kids can play in a nautical-theme playground.

Manhattan: Head down to Tompkins Square (Avenue A to Avenue B, 7th to 10th Streets) or Union Square (Broadway to 4th Avenue, 14th to 17th Streets). Both locations have long been sites for political activism, and the latter is best known today for hosting the city's largest Greenmarket.

Queens: Flushing Meadows-Corona Park (111th Street to Van Wyck Expressway, Northern Boulevard to Grand Central Parkway) has hosted two World's Fairs, and is now home to the New York Mets at Shea Stadium, the US Open at Arthur Ashe Stadium, the Queens Museum of Art, the New York Hall of Science, the World's Fair Skating Rink, and much more.

Staten Island: Get away from it all in the Greenbelt, with 2,800 wooded acres at the centre of the island laced with hiking trails. The city's Urban Park Rangers offer guided tours and the Greenbelt Nature Center provides maps for hikers.

A Touch of Romance

*Taking the ferry at sunset
is a great romantic date,
but why not leave a little
early and watch the sky
change from the
promenade at St. George?*

Staten Island

Staten Island is largely suburban, both the least populous and the most remote borough of the city; accessible only via car or bus over the Verrazzano-Narrows Bridge from Brooklyn, the Staten Island Ferry from lower Manhattan, and a single train line that runs along its eastern shore from top to bottom. It is also the least ethnically diverse part of New York, with almost half the residents being Italian and nearly 80% being white.

There is a lot to love about Staten Island. Heaped plates of traditional red sauce spaghetti and meatballs can be found in every neighbourhood and pizzerias like Lee's Tavern (718 667 9749) and Denino's (p.392), are among the best in the city, while Ralph's Famous Italian Ices (www.ralphsices.com) has served superior cups of the sweet stuff since 1928. Parks are plentiful here, with beaches along the eastern shore and the Greenbelt filling the island's centre with hiking trails. At the lovely Clove Lakes Park you'll find a spacious lake with rowboats for rent which is a far less crowded alternative to the same in Central Park. Historic houses of note include the Victorian era Alice Austen House, home of the famed photographer, and the 17th century Conference House, so named for the famous failed peace conference between the Americans and the British on the eve of the American Revolution.

Three museums on Staten Island are particularly worthy of a visit. The Museum of Tibetan Art (718 987 3500) houses the largest collection outside of Tibet in a stunning, Himalayan-style house, while local history comes to life at Historic Richmond Town (718 351 1611), where costumed guides occupy historic buildings. The Snug Harbor Cultural Center (718 448 2500) is a complex of buildings that was once a home for retired sailors and now houses several museums, art galleries, performance spaces, and gardens. The best-known attractions on site are the Chinese Scholar's Garden inside the Staten Island Botanical Garden, the seafaring memorabilia in the Noble Maritime Collection, and the family-friendly exhibits at the Staten Island Children's Museum.

Enjoy the Outdoors

*The Bronx has two
notable parks: Pelham
Bay, the city's largest, and
Van Cortlandt, one of its
more historic. Other
outdoor spaces in the
borough that draw
crowds are the Bronx Zoo
(2300 Southern Boulevard
at Garden Street), the
New York Botanical
Garden (Bronx River
Parkway and Fordham
Road), and Wave Hill
(West 249th Street and
Independence Avenue).*

The Bronx

The Bronx – which always keeps its 'the' – takes its name from the Bronx River, itself named after a former landowner, Jonas Bronck. It was part of neighbouring Westchester County until New York City annexed the land in two parcels in 1874 and 1895, and today the bulk of the borough is urban. Although some New Yorkers try to avoid the place entirely, it is no longer the notoriously impoverished, crime-ridden place that it was in the 1970s and 80s. In some ways, it never was: there have always been wealthy communities in Riverdale and Fieldston, and middle class families have long been the norm in neighbourhoods like Pelham Parkway, Co-op City, and Parkchester. Now new immigrants from Africa, Central and South America, and the Caribbean have breathed new life into many once-decaying neighbourhoods in the South Bronx, and rising real estate prices city wide mean that things are looking up all over.

The most famous landmark by far is Yankee Stadium (161st Street and River Avenue) and taking in a game with the Bronx Bombers is a must, preferably when you should be at work on an early summer afternoon.

Two neighbourhoods of interest in the Bronx are Belmont/Arthur Avenue and City Island. The former is a busy stretch with shops and restaurants, where locals get food to go at the Arthur Avenue Retail Market (2344 Arthur Avenue at 184th Street) or sit down for a meal at Dominick's (2335 Arthur Avenue at 184th Street, 718 723 2807). City Island is a community accessible via a bridge from Pelham Bay Park, with clapboard homes and a small shop-lined main street that looks more like New England than New York. Get excellent no-frills fried seafood with other fish fans at Johnny's Reef (2 City Island Avenue at the waterfront, 718 885 2086) or shop for art and antiques with other visitors along Coney Island Avenue.

Work Visas p.54
Weekend Breaks p.155

Written by residents, the Hong Kong Explorer is packed with insider info, from arriving in a new destination to making it your home and everything in between.

Hong Kong Explorer Residents' Guide
We Know Where You Live

Museums, Heritage & Culture

New York City is the cultural capital of the United States, and possibly the world... or so New Yorkers like to think! The facts are on their side: there are more than 500 art galleries, over 100 museums, and dozens of landmarks to visit here. Throw in all the theatre, dance, and musical performances, and it would take a lifetime to see it all. Get started with these suggested destinations, and be sure to check out the city's official tourism website at www.nycvisit.com to find out more about cultural institutions and special events around town.

Art Galleries

Other options **Art & Craft Supplies** p.311, **Art** p.311

With so many artists, art dealers, and collectors living in New York City, it is no wonder that there are hundreds of galleries here. Ancient to contemporary, primitive to post-modern, 'made in Brooklyn' to 'made in Borneo', decorative to downright offensive, there is something for every taste, if not every budget. Openings and closings happen every week, so before heading out, visit www.galleryguide.com to find out what is hanging where.

Other Galleries

There are many galleries scattered throughout Chinatown and the West Village, and a few dozen in Tribeca. The most notable of the lot are Deitch Projects (76 Grand Street) and the MELA Foundation (275 Church Street).

To see and be seen, and enjoy a bit of wine and cheese, remember that gallery shows typically open on Thursday evenings. The season for art, as with performing arts, is autumn through to spring. All the most anticipated shows happen in season, while summer offers younger artists and curators a chance to experiment while the establishment takes a vacation. Most galleries close their shows on Saturdays, and will remain closed for several days after to mount their next exhibition.

There are hundreds of galleries scattered throughout Manhattan, a few dozen in Brooklyn, and a handful in Queens. Chelsea is the undisputed centre of the city's art world, with other significant concentrations of galleries in Midtown, the Upper East Side, and Williamsburg, Brooklyn.

Chelsea Galleries

With more than 200 galleries occupying an area less than one square mile in size, Chelsea has the world's highest concentration of art dealers. It is the place to see the biggest shows of work by established artists from around the world - and be there when the latest trends hit. Any given Thursday evening in season begets an impromptu street party as openings spill onto sidewalks, with well-dressed patrons strolling from door to door with wine and beer in hand.

The majority of galleries can be found between 20th and 26th Streets from Tenth to Eleventh Avenues, with the most crowded streets being 22nd, 24th, and 25th Streets. Some notable local galleries are Andrea Rosen (525 West 24th Street), Exit Art (475 Tenth Avenue), Friedrich Petzel (535 West 22nd Street), Bellwether (134 Tenth Avenue), Gagosian Gallery (555 West 24th Street), Mary Boone (541 West 24th Street), Matthew Marks (522 West 22nd Street), and Dia: Chelsea (548 West 22nd Street). To visit many galleries in one place, try the Starrett-Lehigh Building (601 West 26th Street) or 529 West 20th Street. Plan ahead by visiting www.chelseaartgalleries.com, which offers show and special event listings, links to reviews, and a printable map of all area galleries.

The Armory Show

The biggest art event in the city is the annual Armory Show, held on Pier 94 at 12th Avenue and 55th Street. More than 150 galleries bring contemporary art to an international audience of connoisseurs and collectors during the four-day event, which takes its name from the famous Armory Show of 1913 that launched the modern art movement. Visit www.thearmoryshow.com for dates, location, and other information.

214

Midtown and Upper East Side Galleries

There are over 200 galleries spread throughout Midtown and the Upper East Side, where many art collectors live and work. There is not much in the way of cutting edge art here: expect decorative pieces, antiques, and the kind of work a dowager aunt would hang in her Park Avenue penthouse. The New York branches of Christie's (20 Rockefeller Plaza) and Sotheby's (1334 York Avenue) host the biggest art auctions in America here. Many galleries have congregated on 57th Street, and the best known are probably PaceWildenstein (32 East 57th Street) and Marlborough (40 West 57th Street).

Soho Galleries

Soho, once the place to shop for art, is now just an all-around shopping district. Between all the clothing boutiques and housewares shops, there are still several dozen galleries, mainly along Broadway, Prince, and Wooster Streets. Good bets in Soho and the immediate area include Bond Gallery (5 Rivington Street), Rivington Arms (102 Rivington Street), Louis K Meisel (141 Prince Street), Deitch Projects (18 Wooster Street) and Wooster Arts Space (147 Wooster Street). Visit www.artseensoho.com for show listings and a printable map of area galleries.

Brooklyn and Queens Galleries

Rents in Brooklyn's DUMBO neighbourhood have climbed so high that artists' studios have been replaced by art collectors' studio apartments, but there are still enough galleries to keep the neighbourhood's artsy reputation intact. Two multi-gallery spots are the DUMBO Arts Center (30 Washington Street) and 111 Front Street. The Under the Bridge Arts Festival in October is a perfect time to visit. For more information, go to www.dumboartscenter.org/festival.

Williamsburg's relatively low rents have meant that artists and art galleries can continue to grow. The Brooklyn neighbourhood is home to more than 20 galleries, several of which host performance events in addition to hanging art. Two of the many worth visiting are Lunarbase (197 Grand Street) and McCaig-Welles (129 Roebling Street). Visit www.williamsburggalleryassociation.com for a printable map of all the galleries.

To scout out as-yet-undiscovered talent, head to Long Island City in Queens. Though galleries are few, artist studios are many. The annual Open Studios weekend in October has more than 25 locations welcoming visitors, including P.S. 1's neighbour Crane Street Studios (Jackson Avenue and Crane Street) and LIC Artlofts (37-06 36th Street). Check out www.licartists.org for more information. One local gallery well worth a look: SculptureCenter (44-19 Purves Street).

Heritage Sites – City
Other options **Art** p.311, **Museums – City** p.218

New York has less than 500 years of history under its belt, but those were some eventful years. Culling from a long list of landmarks, here are a few of the city's most famous historic spots.

Broadway
At Whitehall &
State Streets
Financial District
Map 12-E3

Bowling Green and The Battery
This is where it all began. The Dutch founded their settlement of New Amsterdam down on the southwestern tip of Manhattan, establishing a fortification on the site of what is now Battery Park. When Peter Minuit purchased the island from its native inhabitants back in 1624, legend has it that the meeting took place on the site of Bowling Green, which later became the city's first public park.

Linking Manhattan
With Brooklyn
Map 13-B1

Brooklyn Bridge
A National Historic Landmark, the Brooklyn Bridge is one of the city's most recognisable structures. It was the longest suspension bridge in the world when it began carrying traffic between Manhattan and Brooklyn in 1883. Designer John Roebling made the structure six times stronger than he thought it needed to be, so it has stood the test of time when other bridges of its age have long been replaced. Don't leave New York without admiring this engineering marvel up close with a sunset stroll over the pedestrian walkway. History buffs will love the series of plaques that tell the remarkable story of its construction, and everyone will be impressed by the sweeping skyline view.

Ellis Island

Ellis Island National Monument
212 269 5755 | *www.nps.gov/ellis*
From 1892 to 1954, more than 12 million people passed through the Ellis Island Immigration Center on their way to new lives as Americans. According to the National Park Service, which operates the American Family Immigration History Center on the site today, more than 40% of Americans have an ancestor recorded here.

Fifth Avenue
At 34th Street
Midtown
Map 6-E1

Empire State Building
www.esbnyc.com
The tallest building in the world when it opened in 1931, the 1,454 foot tall Empire State Building once again became the city's top skyscraper after the destruction of the World Trade Center. The view from the observation deck stretches for 80 miles on a clear day and is well worth the price of admission. It is a safe bet that no other office building in the world has been featured in more than 100 films. The viewing deck is open daily from 08:00 to midnight, although at certain times of the year hours are extended to 02:00. A visit to the 86th floor viewing deck costs $18 for adults, $16 for teens, and $12 for kids. Kids under 5 and military

personnel in uniform go up for free. When you get up there, you can get a headset that gives you an audio tour for an extra $7. If you want to go all the way up to the viewing deck on the 102nd floor, it will cost you an additional $15.

Five Points

Intersection of Baxter, Worth & Park Streets
Chinatown
Map 11-A4

Today's Chinatown was once the site of America's most notorious slum; you can get the idea by watching Martin Scorcese's film Gangs of New York. Before construction of the Foley Square courthouse complex, Baxter, Worth and Park Streets intersected at five corners, forming the Five Points. Home to Irish immigrants and African-American migrants in the mid-19th century, the rough neighbourhood is credited with giving birth to tap dancing as a blend of African stepping and the Irish jig.

St. Paul's Chapel (Episcopalian)

209 Broadway
Financial District
Map 12-E1

212 233 4164

St Paul's Chapel was completed in 1766 and is Manhattan's oldest public building in continuous use. George Washington worshipped here, as did England's King William IV. After the WTC Towers collapsed in 2001 it was one of the few buildings in the vicinity to suffer no structural damage. The church became a refuge for those involved in the 9/11 aftermath, and it now hosts a moving memorial display in its chapel.

Statue of Liberty National Monument

Liberty Island

212 363 3200 | *www.nps.gov/stli*

This New York icon has stood watch over the harbour since October 28, 1886; a symbol of freedom for the millions of immigrants arriving at nearby Ellis Island. Take a ferry from Battery Park to visit Lady Liberty, or join the crowd getting a good look from afar by taking the Staten Island Ferry (free of charge) and snagging a seat on the west-facing deck. See p.217 for more information on the history of this iconic landmark.

Times Square

42nd St to 48th St
Btn Broadway & 8th Ave
Midtown
Map 4-E4

If it's time to give regards to Broadway, join the 31 million annual visitors and more that come to the bright lights of Times Square. One of the city's most recognisable streetscapes, its by-ways are packed with pedestrians nearly every day of the year. It's one of New York's tourism meccas, so apart from being busy nearly all the time, it's also where you'll find touristy hangouts like the Bubba Gump Shrimp Company! Fortunately, there are some classier food outlets to go to like The Living Room at the W Hotel (www.midnightoilbars.com), or Marquis at the top of the JW Marriott (1535 Broadway, 212 398 1900) where you can have a martini in the revolving restaurant. Times Square, named for its famous tenant, The New York Times, runs from 42nd Street to 48th Streets between Broadway and Eighth Avenue and its centre is, in fact, a triangle. Every New Year's Eve, all of America gets a live television broadcast of the celebration here, attended by hundreds of thousands of spectators who brave often subfreezing temperatures to join the party.

Btn Broadway &
South St
Financial District
Map 12-F2

Wall Street

Wall Street is so named because it was once the northern boundary of the colonial city, but today it is synonymous with the world's most powerful financial institutions. Step back in time at brownstone Trinity Church (74 Trinity Place, www.trinitywallstreet.org), home to one of the city's oldest parishes, founded in 1697. The New York Stock Exchange (11 Wall Street, www.nyse.com) is not open for tours, but the oft-photographed facade is always there for the gazing. Across the street, Federal Hall (26 Wall Street, 212-845-6888,

www.nps.gov/feha) marks the birthplace of American government. Now a museum, the original building was the site of President George Washington's inauguration as well as the first office of the president and chambers for Congress and the Supreme Court.

Financial District
Map 12-D1

World Trade Center Site

The expanse between West and Church Streets from Vesey to Liberty Streets was once occupied by the World Trade Center. All seven buildings in the complex, including the 110 storey 'Twin Towers' were destroyed by a terrorist attack on September 11, 2001. Competing interests in state and city government, transit authorities, and private developers have slowed the rebuilding process, and to date only one building – 7 World Trade – has been rebuilt. Plans include several new office towers, a new transit centre designed by architect Santiago Calatrava, and a memorial to those that died in the 9/11 attack. For more information on rebuilding plans, visit the Lower Manhattan Development Corporation website at www.renewnyc.com.

For the time being, the site is a cross between a giant construction yard and a very moving tribute to those who lost their lives in the attack. The feelings of New Yorkers and visitors alike can be felt here, whether it's through the person staring through the fence with tears in their eyes, or the graffiti messages scrawled on the boardings. Some of the photos taken at the time of the attacks have been enlarged and posted at the site, and there is also a fascinating timeline of how events unfolded on the day. Each year on the anniversary of 9/11 there is a memorial service, usually with lights beamed upwards to represent where the towers once stood.

Museums – City

Other options **Heritage Sites – City** p.216, **Art** p.311

New York is home to dozens of museums dedicated to art, history, science, and culture, and several of them are world-renowned institutions. Many are completely free, such as the Museum of American Folk Art and the Guggenheim Museum SoHo, while others ask for a suggested contribution or offer days when admission is free or at a reduced cost. Most museums offer free entry on Friday evenings, including MoMa, the Met and the Guggenheim, so even starving artists can soak up some culture - expect to queue for around half an hour to get in though. Check with individual museums for more information.

American Folk Art Museum

45 West 53rd Street
Midtown
Map 5-A4

212 265 1040 | *www.folkartmuseum.org*
The American Folk Art Museum opens a window onto folk culture from over 300 years ago. Adults and children alike enjoy well-curated displays of homespun drawings, paintings, sculptures, textiles, and photographs by self-taught artists from all parts of the country. The hand-made textile collection is a highlight, including the 9/11 National Tribute Quilt. Don't miss their gift shop, which sells an excellent and ever-changing selection of contemporary arts and crafts, all made by hand. The museum sponsors two popular annual events in January: The American Antiques Show and Outsider Art Week (in conjunction with the Outsider Art Fair). Tours, craft workshops, classes for children and adults, lectures, and symposia are held on an ongoing basis. Admission is $9 for adults, $7 for seniors and students, and free for children under 12.

American Museum of Natural History

Central Park West
At 79th Street
Upper West Side
Map 2-F2

212 769 5100 | *www.amnh.org*
A world of scientific discovery awaits you within this palatial 1877 building designed by Central Park co-creator Calvert Vaux and partner Jacob Wrey Mould. Visitors of all ages come for the displays of taxidermy animals, preserved plants, and, of course, dinosaur skeletons and fossils. The life-size whale in the Hall of Ocean Life has long been a crowd favourite, and a recent renovation has left the gallery better than ever. The collections of artefacts from 'primitive' cultures are extensive and colourful, though many have a whiff of being quaintly outdated. The Rose Center's space exhibits are equipped with the latest technology, and the Hayden Planetarium doubles as an IMAX theatre when it's not seeing stars.

Seeing all that AMNH has to offer can easily fill a day, but the highlights can be toured in three hours, not including special exhibits or planetarium shows. There are several places to eat in the museum, including a foodcourt, cafe, and juice bar. Look for fun menu selections inspired by current exhibitions. Several gift kiosks are scattered throughout the halls in addition to the main gift shop. Parents are advised to avoid the shop entirely unless they plan to purchase, as kids will be unable to resist the huge selection of dinosaur memorabilia and colourful educational toys. The admission suggested is $14 for adults, $10.50 for students and seniors, and $8 for children, plus fees for special exhibitions.

219

2 East 91st Street ◄
Upper East Side

Cooper-Hewitt National Design Museum

212 849 8400 | www.ndm.si.edu

America's only design museum holds 250,000 objects, including industrial products, home furnishings, textiles, and graphic designs from around the world. There are temporary exhibitions in addition to the permanent collection, and the National Design Triennial has become a renowned event for the newest, best work in American design. The museum has daily tours and a number of educational programmes for children and adults are held weekly. The museum's Summer Sessions, held every Friday from 18:00 to 21:00 from June until September are also wildly popular. Different DJs play in the gorgeous outdoor space behind the museum, and food and drink is served. The event is typically free with regular museum admission which is $12 for adults, $9 for students and seniors, and free for children under 12.

1230 Fifth Avenue ◄
Spanish Harlem

El Museo del Barrio

212 831 7272 | www.elmuseo.org

This museum in Spanish Harlem, also known as El Barrio, displays both permanent and temporary exhibitions devoted to the cultures of Spanish-speaking immigrants from Puerto Rico, the Caribbean, and the Americas. The permanent collection includes artefacts from pre-Columbian indigenous cultures and an array of traditional arts and crafts, as well as painting, drawing, sculpture, photography, and film by Latino artists. Tours and hands-on workshops are available by appointment. Many educational programmes and special events celebrating Latino culture occur throughout the year, the most popular being the Three Kings Day Parade in early January.
Admission is $4 for adults, seniors and students, and free for children under 12.

1071 Fifth Avenue ◄
Upper East Side

Guggenheim Museum

212 423 3500 | www.guggenheim.org

The Guggenheim's Frank Lloyd Wright building is an attraction in itself, sometimes more interesting than the art inside. Founded to showcase modern paintings, the museum now focuses on large temporary exhibitions of art from ancient to modern, architecture, and design. Adults will probably spend about an hour and a half looking around, depending on what is on display, just long enough for children to lose interest in the gallery's swooping spiralled pathway. There is a museum cafe on site, as well as a gift shop. Tours are given regularly and audio tours are available at all times. Admission is $18 for adults, $15 for seniors and students, and free for children under 12.
The Guggenheim SoHo (212 423 3500) is a tiny segment of the mighty Guggenheim located on Broadway and Prince. It is open from 11:00 to 18:00 every day except for Tuesdays and Wednesdays, when it is closed. Admission is free.

Various Locations ◄

Historic House Trust Museums

www.historichousetrust.org

The Historic House Trust operates 22 family-friendly museums located in parks throughout the five boroughs of New York City. Among the restored houses spanning four centuries of local history, you can find colonial Dutch farmhouses, sites relating to the American Revolution, and the homes of wealthy and famous New Yorkers. All can be seen in their entirety in well under an hour. Tours and special events are often held on site, often with a seasonal theme. Admission prices vary, but generally are under $5. All the houses are well worth a visit. In Manhattan, the museums include the 1832 Merchant's House (29 East 4th Street at Bowery, 212 777 1089), 1660s Dyckman Farmhouse (4881 Broadway at 204th Street, 212 304 9422), 1765 Morris-Jumel Mansion (65 Jumel Terrace at 160th Street, 212 923 8008), and 1799 Gracie Mansion, official residence of the mayor (Carl Schurz Park at 88th Street, 212 570 4773). HHT also maintains The Little Red Lighthouse, Manhattan's last remaining lighthouse and co-star of the popular children's book The Little Red Lighthouse and The Great Grey Bridge (Hudson River at 178th Street). Brooklyn's Wyckoff Farmhouse, built in 1652, deserves mention as the city's oldest house and a National Historic Landmark (5816 Clarendon Road at Ralph Avenue, Brooklyn, 718 629 5400).

1109 Fifth Avenue
Upper East Side

Jewish Museum

212 423 3200 | *www.thejewishmuseum.org*

This museum displays a collection of art, design, and religious objects created by Jewish artists from all parts of the world, from antiquity to the present. Temporary exhibits at the museum relate to the art, literature, and history of the Jewish diaspora culture. An hour would suffice for a walk through the galleries but more time would be needed to cover special exhibitions. Special events and educational programmes are plentiful, especially around the time of Jewish holidays, and tours are conducted regularly. Café Weissman (212 423 3307) serves creative glatt kosher meals on the museum's lower level. The museum has two gift shops; one offering books and souvenirs with a Jewish theme, and the other selling religious objects designed by contemporary artists.

Admission is $12 for adults, $10 for seniors, $7.50 for students, and free for children under 12.

90 Orchard Street
Lower East Side
Map 11-C2

Lower East Side Tenement Museum

212 431 0233 | *www.tenement.org*

This wonderful museum consists of a set of fully furnished family apartments recreating working class immigrant life in a typical New York tenement building from 1863 to 1935. Visitors are required to take a guided tour, choosing from several options; each one deals with particular aspects of the building's history and the lives of the families who once lived there. All tours take about one hour, and advance booking is recommended.

The museum also offers 90 minute walking tours of the Lower East Side from spring through to autumn, and a variety of educational programmes year round. The Visitor's Center screens a film about the lives of New York's immigrants and houses the museum's gift shop, selling many unique Lower East Side souvenirs.

Admission is $15 for adults, $11 for seniors and students, and free for children under 12. Call to inquire about tours appropriate for children under 5.

The Metropolitan Museum of Art

212 535 7710 | *www.metmuseum.org*

1000 Fifth Avenue
Upper East Side

The Met is one of the world's great museums; an art history textbook come to life in Central Park, with a collection of over two million pieces spanning 5,000 years of human history – all viewed by more than five million visitors each year.

The permanent collection includes vast holdings of American and European art, plus galleries devoted to art and objects from Asia, Africa, Oceania, Ancient Greece and Rome, Ancient Egypt, and the Islamic world. The Costume Institute holds 700 years of fashion from all parts of the world, and occasionally hosts crowd-pleasing exhibitions devoted to accomplished designers, historic fashion trends, or the personal wardrobes of famous individuals. Other collections at the Met include medieval weaponry, antique home furnishings, and musical instruments.

At any given time, there will be several temporary exhibitions on view. These could be anything from a major retrospective of an individual artist making its New York stop on international tour, to a small thematic show curated in-house. Art lovers could easily spend days exploring every gallery, but it is possible, with careful use of a museum map, to hit all the highlights in about three to four hours. Keep kids entertained with a stop in the Arms & Armor Gallery and – a classic New York childhood rite of passage – a romp though the Egyptian Temple of Dendur.

The Met has two bars, two members-only dining rooms, two cafes, and one cafeteria on the premises. Spring through to autumn, the Roof Garden Café is one of the city's best places to enjoy a cocktail with a view over Central Park. Gift kiosks are attached to exhibits throughout the museum, and the main shop is located off of the Great Hall. Both general and exhibition-specific tours are conducted several times daily, and audio tours are available at all times. Special events are held throughout the year, including lecture series, symposia, adult and children's classes, film screenings, jazz and classical concerts, and more.

The Met also has an uptown branch called The Cloisters (inside Fort Tryon Park, 212 923 3700). A collection of medieval art, including the world famous Unicorn Tapestries, is displayed in a stunning collection of cloisters imported from France. It is well worth the trip, especially during spring, when flowers are blooming in picturesque Fort Tryon Park. Admission is $20 for adults, $10 for students and seniors, and free for children under 12.

36 Battery Place
Battery Park
Map 12-D3

Museum of Jewish Heritage

646 437 4200 | www.mjhnyc.org

This museum tells the story of Jewish life before, during, and after the Holocaust, with special exhibitions relating to those themes displayed throughout the year. Educational programmes for children and adults are scheduled regularly, and activity books are available for young visitors. There is a cafe on site as well as a shop selling Judaica and educational books. Admission is $10 for adults, $7 for seniors, $5 for students, and free for children under 12.

11 West 53rd Street
Midtown
Map 5-A3

Museum of Modern Art

212 708 9400 | www.moma.org

MoMA began with just nine paintings back in 1929 and today holds over 150,000 works of art, 22,000 films, and a library of more than 300,000 volumes. One of the world's great modern art museums, it moved into a very modish new building designed by Yoshio Taniguchi in 2004, allowing the curators to display more of the

permanent collection and creating more space for educational programming. Highlights from MoMA's permanent collection of painting and sculpture reside on the fourth and fifth floors, including work by Monet, Van Gogh, Picasso, Matisse, Pollack, Warhol and Cezanne, but the photography and drawing exhibits on the third floor are also recommended. Temporary exhibition galleries are located on the third and sixth floors. Adults will want to see it all, which takes a minimum of two to three hours. Children who have not yet learned to appreciate Pollack can still enjoy the outdoor sculpture garden and the gadgets and toys on display in the gallery of design objects. Both general and exhibition-specific tours are conducted daily, and audio tours are available at all times. Special events include classes for children and adults, film screenings, and lectures, all listed on the museum's website. MoMA has informal cafe dining on the second and fifth floors, and an upscale restaurant called The Modern (p.389) on the ground floor. There is a small gift kiosk on the top floor, but shop at the main gift shop on the ground floor or the MoMA Design Store directly across the street from the museum's 53rd Street entrance. Well stocked with gifts for all ages at all price points, it is always a great place to shop for art books, housewares, jewellery, and gifts. Museum admission is not required for entry. Admission is $20 for adults, $16 for seniors, $12 for students, and free for children under 16.

25 West 52nd Street
Midtown
Map 5-A3

Museum of Television and Radio
212 621 6800 | *www.mtr.org*
The name says it all. If it went out over the airwaves, and it was worth watching, it is probably archived here and available for viewing by appointment. It's a great way to watch rare episodes of classic programmes. Visitors simply drop in for public screenings or watch their selections in a private console. One tip: when watching early television shows, the commercial breaks are often as fun as the shows themselves! Admission is $10 for adults, $8 for seniors and students, and $5 for children under 14.

1220 Fifth Avenue
Upper East Side

The Museum of the City of New York
212 534 1672 | *www.mcny.org*
This museum cares about all things New York; its 450 plus years of history, current events, and the shape the city might take in the future. Exhibitions cover all aspects of city life, with something for everyone; from children's toys, domestic interiors, and restaurant menus to professional sports, transit systems, and economic trends. It would take about three or four hours to see it all, but a quick spin is possible in two. The museum is especially kid-friendly and even hosts birthday parties on site and family events on a regular basis. Admission is $9 for adults, $5 for seniors and students, and free for children under 12.

1048 Fifth Avenue
Upper East Side

Neue Galerie Museum for German and Austrian Art
212 628 6200 | *www.neuegalerie.org*
The Neue Galerie, housed in an elegant 1914 Carrere and Hastings-designed building, focuses on early 20th-century art and design from Germany and Austria. Highlights from the permanent collection include work by Gustav Klimt, Egon Schiele, Paul Klee, Vasily Kandinsky, Marcel Breuer, and Mies van der Rohe. Two hours is enough time to see everything, however briefly. The museum's upscale restaurant, Café Sabarksy (212 352 2300), serves authentic Viennese cuisine, with some of the best pastry to be found anywhere in New York. The Design Shop sells high quality reproductions of objects found in the permanent collection. Tours are held only once daily on weekends or by prior arrangement, but audio tours are available at all times.
Admission is $15 for adults, $10 for seniors and students, and children under 12 are not admitted.

223

515 Lenox Avenue
(Malcolm X Boulevard)
Harlem

Schomburg Center for Research in Black Culture
212 491 2200 | *www.nypl.org/research/sc*
This branch of the New York Public Library is not a museum, but rather a cultural centre built around an archive of 10 million items relating to the history and culture of the worldwide African diaspora. The collection includes books, manuscripts, art, artefacts, films, audio recordings, photographs, and prints, available for research and displayed in special exhibitions curated by the library. Tours are available by appointment, and audio tours for specific exhibitions are available any time. Public programmes include classes, lectures, readings, symposia, musical performances, and film screenings. The Schomburg Shop on site sells a selection of books and gifts related to the African migration. Admission is free.

945 Madison Avenue
Upper East Side
Map 3-C2

Whitney Museum of American Art
212 570 3676 | *www.whitney.org*
The Whitney holds one of the world's largest collections of American art created from 1900 to the present, with over 12,000 pieces in total, only 1% of which is on display at any given time. The museum has long outgrown its current Marcel Breuer-designed home, so it is now in the process of expanding. Expect a larger Whitney to emerge in the coming years, most likely in a new downtown location. Highlights from the permanent collection include work by Edward Hopper, Georgia O'Keeffe, Alexander Calder, Willem de Kooning, and Jasper Johns. Curators keep the collection fresh and up to date by acquiring new work from artists shown at the Whitney Biennial, a survey of pretty much anything and everything of note in the contemporary American art scene.

Adults could easily spend two hours just browsing the galleries, while kids who are too young to enjoy paintings are likely to grow bored quickly.

The Whitney is best known for the Biennial, and it seems that every New Yorker with even a passing interest in art typically attends. Critics dispense sheaves of love-it-or-hate-it opinions, and there are always a few pieces that spark controversy. Ignore it at the peril of being excluded from dinner party chat for weeks after the opening.

The Whitney has a branch of the uptown institution Sarabeth's on site serving brunch and lunch; museum admission not required. The gift shop is small, but worth a look, filled as it is with quirky gifts and souvenirs for kids and adults. Tours are given daily and audio tours are available at all times.

Admission is $15 for adults, $10 for seniors and students, and free for children under 12.

Museums – Out of City
Other options **Tours & Sightseeing** p.234

200 Eastern Parkway
Brooklyn

Brooklyn Museum of Art
718 638 5000 | *www.brooklynmuseum.org*
It is often said that if the BMA were not in museum-saturated New York, it would be considered a major museum. One of the oldest and largest museums in America, it has a vast permanent collection including art and design that spans the ancient and modern history of the Americas, Europe, Asia, Africa, and the Middle East. Their temporary exhibitions are world class, competing with likes of the Met and MoMA for art lovers' attention.

It would take hours to see everything, but the highlights can be condensed into two well-planned hours. Tours are regularly available and audio tours are offered at all times. There is a cafe and a shop on site, the latter selling a wide array of gifts that include crafts by local artists. Admission is $8 for adults, $4 for seniors and students, and free for children under 12.

Fisher Landau Center

38-27 30th Street
Long Island City
Queens

718 937 0727 | *www.flcart.org*
This small, often overlooked museum has an impressive collection of contemporary art from 1960 to the present, including work by Frank Gehry, Jenny Holzer, Robert Rauschenberg, Kiki Smith, Cy Twombly, and Andy Warhol. An hour is enough to see everything, including temporary exhibits. It is open every day from midday until 17:00, except on Tuesdays and Wednesdays when it is closed. Admission is free.

Historic Richmondtown

441 Clark Avenue
Staten Island

718 351 1611 | *www.historicrichmondtown.org*
Historic Richmondtown is a living history museum where costumed guides inhabit a complex of 15 buildings, depicting life in New York from the colonial era to the present. A mix of demonstrations and hands-on activities is designed to appeal to visitors of all ages. There are tours daily, and guides are stationed inside most of the buildings. Educational programmes, including a children's camp, are held on site throughout the year. The M. Bennett Café serves breakfast and lunch daily, and homemade baked goods are for sale when available. Admission is $5 for adults, $4 for seniors, $3.50 for students, and free for children under 5.

Museum of the Moving Image

36-01 35th Ave
Astoria
Queens

718 784 4520 | *www.movingimage.us*
This museum is dedicated to films, videos, digital media, and the technology behind making them, with hands-on displays showing how moving images are made. Kids will love the exhibit that allows visitors to create their own flipbook, made available for purchase in the gift shop. There is a cafe on site across from the gift shop. Screenings of classic films are held several times a week, as are top-notch festivals dedicated to the work of individual directors, actors, and writers that last several weeks. Previews and premieres of new films, and talks by the people who make them, are a regular treat. At $65, an annual membership will pay for itself in just a few screenings. Admission is $10 for adults, $7.50 for seniors and students, $5 for children under 18, free for children under 5.

New York Hall of Science

47-01 111th St
Corona
Queens

718 699 0005 | *www.nyscience.org*
With hands-on exhibits designed to teach kids about everything from microbes to rocket science, this museum is a must for the primary school set. Audio tours are available at all times, and specialised tours and workshops are regularly scheduled. The museum has a cafe, a fantastic gift shop, and a science-themed playground on site, making it a great place for a budding physicist's birthday party. Admission is $11 for adults, $8 for students and seniors, and free for children under 2.

New York Transit Museum

Boerum Place
At Schermerhorn St
Brooklyn

718 694 1600 | *www.mta.info/mta/museum*
The Metropolitan Transportation Authority's museum is dedicated to the city's transportation networks, with exhibits of artefacts, photographs, posters, and art designed to appeal to both kids and adults. The whole thing can be seen in about an hour and a half. The gift shop has tonnes of fun New York souvenirs, with a branch on site here and another conveniently located inside Grand Central Terminal. If you're worried that the umbrella or T-shirt will brand you a tourist, you could always go for something more subtle, like a mousepad or a shower curtain featuring an exact replica of the Subway map! Admission is $5 for adults, $3 for students and seniors, and free for children under 3.

9-01 33rd Road
Astoria
Queens

The Noguchi Museum

718 204 7088 | *www.noguchi.org*

This museum is dedicated to the work of Japanese-American artist Isamu Noguchi, housing a permanent collection of his sculptures and home designs in a beautifully restored factory site. The whole museum can be seen in about an hour, but visitors often linger in the serene courtyard. Tours are given daily, and a number of educational programmes are held on a regular basis. Admission is $10 for adults, $5 for seniors and students, and free for children under 12.

22-25 Jackson Ave
Long Island City
Queens

P.S.1

718 784 2084 | *www.ps1.org*

Think of P.S.1 as MoMA's younger, hipper sister. While its famous sibling shows the work of the 20th century's greatest artists, P.S.1 shows new art that has not made it onto a postcard yet. Its name refers to the building that houses the museum, a creatively renovated public school where classrooms have now become a network of galleries. All exhibitions are temporary and they change frequently, so check with the museum to see what is on view. It can take several hours to visit every room in P.S.1 and the sprawling floor plan demands the use of a map. Do not skip stairwells, hallways, and bathrooms, which are also fair game for curators to place art.

During summer, P.S.1 hosts Warm Up every Saturday: a series of dance parties that attract world-famous DJs and huge crowds to the museum's courtyard. The museum recently came up with its answer to the Whitney Biennial: Greater New

York. It is a survey of art made in the five boroughs of New York City that takes place every five years, and so far the 2000 and 2005 shows have met critical and popular success.

Lectures and special events are held regularly, and tours are available by prior arrangement. The small but well-stocked shop, artbook@P.S.1, is a great place to pick up the latest tomes on the market. Same goes for the LeRosier Café, if the goal is to pick up the latest art student.

Admission is $5 for adults, $2 for seniors and students, and free for children under 12 or with a MoMA ticket dated in the past 30 days.

Flushing Meadows
Corona Park
Queens

Queens Museum of Art

718 592 9700 | *www.queensmuseum.org*

The QMA's quirky permanent collection includes materials from the two World's Fairs held on its site, crime scene photographs from the New York Daily News archives, and artist William Sharps' drawings of New York streetscapes. Temporary exhibitions of contemporary art are held throughout the year, often with a focus on immigrant communities in Queens. The gift shop is well worth a stop, selling Queens souvenirs including both original and reproduction pieces relating to the World's Fairs. Everything can be seen in about an hour and a half.

The museum's most famous attraction, a delight for adults and children alike, is the Panorama of the City of New York. Built for the 1964 World's Fair, it's an architectural model of the entire city, to scale, with 895,000 distinct structures. It was updated in the 1990s, and is currently undergoing another round of the revisions to reflect the current landscape. Don't leave the city without paying a visit. Admission is $5 for adults, $2.50 for seniors and students, and free for children under 5.

Parks & Beaches

Living in New York is the ultimate way to experience real city living: the skyscrapers, the grid system, the subway - everything you need is just a block or two away. But there's a country mouse hidden inside everyone, and no matter how much you love city life, every now and then it's essential to kick off your shoes and feel the sand, or grass, between your toes. Fortunately, despite being such a bustling metropolis, New York has plenty of grassy parks where you can get back to nature for an hour or two. And as for beaches, there are some pretty great ones - if you know where to find them.

Beaches

Other options **Parks** p.228, **Swimming** p.284

From West 37th Street
To Corbin Place
Brooklyn

Coney Island & Brighton Beach

718 946 1350 | www.coneyislandusa.com

Coney Island is New York's most famous – and crowded – beach. Although its glory days as a seaside resort for the masses are long gone, a renaissance is in the making. Redevelopment plans have been percolating for decades, and some are due to break ground as early as 2008. In the meantime, there are still honky-tonk attractions galore. No visit is complete without a stop at Nathan's Famous Hot Dogs, host of the nationally-televised July 4th Hot Dog Eating Contest, and a ride on the landmark wooden roller coaster, The Cyclone. The newest arrivals are a minor league baseball team affiliated with the Mets, the Brooklyn Cyclones, playing from June through to September at Keyspan Park. Visitors of all ages will enjoy the displays at the New York State Aquarium. For a view of all the action, ride the giant Wonder Wheel.

For a more relaxing day by the sea, stroll down to Brighton Beach. The neighbourhood's large Russian population has earned it the nickname 'Little Odessa,' so expect sunbathers to include svelte ice blonds and babushka-wearing grannies alike. Boardwalk restaurants serve traditional Russian meals, complete with vodka by the bottle.

Attractions at Coney Island and Brighton Beach include a boardwalk with shops, food concessions, amusements, an aquarium and a professional baseball stadium. Bathrooms, showers, changing areas, playgrounds, basketball courts and an indoor ice skating rink are also on site. Coney Island hosts several free annual events, including the colorful Mermaid Parade in June, the Siren Music Festival in July, and City Beach Volleyball Tournament in August.

Oriental Boulevard
From Ocean Avenue to
Mackenzie Street
Brooklyn

Manhattan Beach

718 946 1373

This small beach isn't far from the action at Coney Island, but it feels a world away. It has a large picnic area shaded by trees, making it a popular spot for families with young children looking to celebrate special occasions by the sea. Facilities include baseball fields, basketball and tennis courts, barbecue grills, food concessions, bathrooms, showers and changing areas.

Long Island Sound
Pelham Bay Park
The Bronx

Orchard Beach

718 885 2275

Built in the 1930s, 'The Bronx Riviera' has always been popular with local residents. Weekend crowds can be large, but weekdays are usually quiet. Facilities include a promenade, central pavilion with shops and food concessions, bathrooms, showers and changing areas, playgrounds, basketball, volleyball and handball courts, picnic areas, and parking. They also run free events for kids, such as owl watching, searching for songbirds and watching for waterfowl.

22⁹

Beach 1st St
To Beach 149th St
Queens

Rockaway Beach
718 318 4000
Rockaway is the city's largest beach at about seven miles long, and on its east side neighbours a National Park Service beach at Jacob Riis Park. Immortalised in The Ramones' hit song Rockaway Beach, it is best known for having the only designated surfing area in New York. The sand gets crowded near subway stops, but remains fairly quiet elsewhere, even on the weekends. Birdwatchers won't want to miss the chance to visit the nearby Rockaway Arverne Shorebird Preserve and the Rockaway Beach Endangered Species Nesting Area. Facilities include a small boardwalk with shops and food concessions, playgrounds, basketball and handball courts, and bathrooms, showers and changing areas.

Lower New York Bay
From Fort Wadsworth
To Miller Field
Staten Island

South & Midland Beaches
718 816 6804
This clean and well-maintained beach is far less crowded than others around town, with calm waters ideal for young swimmers. Facilities in the recently renovated park include a small boardwalk/promenade, playgrounds, baseball fields, handball, shuffleboard, bocce, and basketball courts, checker tables, a skateboard park, a roller hockey rink, a fishing pier, food concessions, bathrooms, a ramp for wheelchair accessibility, and parking.

Raritan Bay
Staten Island

Wolfe's Pond Beach
718 984 8266
This beach is almost always calm and quiet, surrounded by a Forever Wild Nature Preserve. A perfect place to hike and swim in a single afternoon, with plenty of wildlife, such as hermit and blue crabs and blue mussels. Facilities include playgrounds, picnic areas, bathrooms, ramps for wheelchair accessibility, and parking. The beach is located on Raritan and Prince's Bays, from Holton to Cornelia Avenues.

Parks
Other options **Beaches** p.227

I Tree Wed
Want to get married in Central Park? Call the Central Park Weddings Office at 212 360 2766 for information.

New York City maintains more than 1,700 parks, encompassing 28,000 acres across the city that include nearly 1,000 playgrounds, more than 600 ball fields, 36 recreational centres, 48 nature preserves and 22 historic houses. In addition to these, there are seven New York State parks and 11 sites operated by the National Park Service within city limits.
Facilities vary widely from park to park, with some smaller sites providing no more than a shady spot to picnic and larger ones offering up dozens of recreational opportunities. For a picnic or a fishing expedition with a good look at Midtown, try Gantry Plaza State Park (Queens, East River between 50th and 48th Avenues).
It is easy to get active with facilities available for baseball, softball, basketball, soccer, football, volleyball, handball, tennis, ice and roller hockey, cricket, rugby, Gaelic games, ice skating, swimming, running, bocce, skateboarding, kayaking, canoeing, boating, horseback riding, golf, bicycling, in-line skating, hiking, fishing, and more.
Most parks, especially those in Manhattan, are very well maintained, and the majority of them are officially open to the public from dawn to dusk. Riverside Park (Hudson River, 59th Street to Clair Place) is the uptown spot to walk, jog, bike, or in-line skate along the Hudson, downtown Hudson River State Park (Manhattan, Hudson River between 59th Street and Chambers Street) takes over the job. It matches a river view pathway with facilities for baseball, basketball, boating, golf, ice skating, rock climbing, soccer, swimming, trapeze, tennis, and volleyball. If the East River appeals, the mayor's residence sits on the other side of Manhattan in elegant Carl Schurz Park (East River from 84th to 90th Streets).

Use of all public parks is free of charge, with a few exceptions. Some National Park Service historic museums require a nominal admission fee, and charges for special activities such as ice skating or horseback riding vary. All year long there are free special events going taking place, from bird watching tours and basketball tournaments to Shakespeare in the Park and the Easter Eggs-stravaganza. Regulations are posted at park entrances. Alcohol is forbidden at all times, unless sold by a licensed concessionaire, and barbecues are permitted only in designated areas. Playgrounds are open only to children and their caretakers. Dogs are welcome in parks, but they must be kept on a leash. Brooklyn's Prospect Park has a dog beach where furry friends can swim off-leash, and there are fenced off-leash dog runs located in parks in all five boroughs.

For information on locations, facilities, upcoming events, and more, visit www.nycgovparks.org for city parks, www.nysparks.com/regions/nycity.asp for state parks, and www.nps.gov/npnh for national parks.

Get a Permit
Though most activities in city parks are free of charge, you must obtain a permit to hold an event for more than 20 guests, reserve time on a tennis court, or run a team sports league. Call 311 (or 212 NEW YORK) for more information.

Island Parks

The Gateway National Recreation Area stretches from Sandy Hook, New Jersey across Staten Island to the islands of Jamaica Bay, Queens, with natural preserves and areas for fishing, swimming, hiking, biking, boating, and team sports.

Cross the bridge from Manhattan over to Randall's Island (East River) for an athlete's paradise: teams from around the city head to its facilities for track and field, baseball, soccer, tennis, basketball, football and more.

In summer, ferries from Lower Manhattan sail to historic Governors Island National Monument, a long time military base whose stately, leafy campus is now open to the public. One year-round ferry gets visitors up close and personal with New York's most famous lady, the Statue of Liberty National Monument, while another travels to the famous hub of immigration, the Ellis Island National Monument.

60th St - 110th St
Btn Fifth Ave & Central Park West
Maps 2, 3, 4 & 5

Central Park

212 310 6600 | www.centralparknyc.org

The most visited park in the United States, the 834 acres is an oasis in the NYC urban jungle and a real gem in the city's historical crown. Drawing some 25 million visitors each year, 'New York's backyard' is still the perfect place to escape the madding crowd. Strolling on wooded paths, crossing elegant bridges, and sitting by The Lake is a sure way to diffuse workday stress. Skate on Wollman and Lasker Rinks (p.267) in winter, and play a few innings at Heckscher Ballfields in the lazy summer months. Kids flock to the zoo, while fans of The Beatles pay tribute to John Lennon at Strawberry Fields. There are free events in the park all year long, including concerts, theatre, readings, and athletic events.

Battery Park

State & Whitehall St
Financial District
Map 12-E4

212 267 9700 | www.bpcparks.org
Made by landfill in the 19th century, the 21 acres of this lush city escape occupies the southern tip of Manhattan, with incredible harbour views and doubles as the site of the original Dutch settlement. Though languid afternoons spent soaking up the sun is the perfect way to enjoy Battery Park, few people are aware of the buzz beneath it. Battery Park hides a lot of the city's southern side infrastructure, including the Brooklyn-Battery tunnel, the Battery Park Underpass and the South Ferry Subway stop. In 2005, while digging beneath the park to further the transportation network, authorities discovered the remains of a 200 year-old stone wall, believed to be part of the gun batteries that once protected the city and possibly even gave the park its name.

Washington Square Park

Waverly Place
West 4th St &
University Pl
MacDougal St
West Village
Map 8-F3

www.washingtonsquarepark.org
Once a potter's field (a graveyard for the poor) and a military parade ground, today Washington Square is the centre of New York University's campus and a prime place to people-watch. Its longstanding tradition of non-conformity fits in perfectly with the neighbourhood's bohemian do-as-you-please feel and the fountain is a major attraction for visitors big and small during the sticky summer months. The arch was erected first out of plaster and wood in 1888 to celebrate the centennial of George Washington's inauguration as the first president of the United States. The arch was then rebuilt in 1892 out of marble and stands a grand 77 feet (23 metres) high. The park is currently under hot debate regarding its reconstruction.

Bryant Park

Fifth & Sixth Ave
40th - 42nd St
Midtown
Map 7-A1

212 768 4242 | www.bryantpark.org
Seeped in history, conflict and controversy, Bryant Park is a slice of New York unto itself. First designated as a public space in 1686, George Washington and his troops then marched across it retreating from the Battle of Long Island in 1776. From 1823 to 1840, the Park was better known as a potter's field until the bodies were finally moved making way for the park proper in 1847, which was then named Reservoir Square. During the American Civil War, the area was used for military drills and then became the gruesome site of the New York Draft Riots in 1863 (see History p. 2). Now calmer, Bryant Park offers visitors a large sitting area, free wireless internet, and famous outdoor movie series in summer.

Prospect Park

Parkside Ave
To Eastern Parkway
Brooklyn

718 965 8951 | www.prospectpark.org
This is Brooklyn's answer to Central Park, quite literally, since the 585 acre space was created by the same duo that designed and made Central Park. Built in 1867 the park has since grown to encompass plenty of meadows, forests, and trails, plus a lake, a skating rink, a zoo, and a large farmers' market on the weekends. The park has always been considered a work of art, from its very inception and revolutionary style to the colourful creatures that wander the small plot of wilderness, slap bang in the heart of Brooklyn.

Amusement Parks

Other options **Amusement Parks** p.231

Other options **Amusement Parks** p.231

Views and Thrills
Demo's Wonder Wheel Park (3059 Denos Vourderis Place, West 12th St. 718 372 2592) is named for a New York City landmark. The 150 foot high Wonder Wheel has been spinning since 1920, and on a clear day the panoramic view from the top includes New York Harbour, the Manhattan skyline, and the New Jersey shore.

There are no true amusement parks in New York City, but if a cheap thrill will do, and you don't mind a little urban grittiness, head to Coney Island. Dozens of privately owned rides and games line the boardwalk, open on weekends from Easter to Labor Day (first weekend in September), daily from Memorial Day (last weekend in May) to Labor Day. There are kiddie rides and arcades for the little ones and games of skill and thrill rides for adults. Admission to the amusement areas is free, and the rides cost between $2.50 and $6 per ride with unlimited day passes on sale from individual vendors. Several redevelopment plans for Coney Island are in the works, so expect major changes in the near future.

For now, Astroland (1000 Surf Avenue, 718 372 0275) is still the place to find dozens of carnival rides, and it's the proud home of Coney Island's number one attraction since 1927, The Cyclone roller coaster. A New York City landmark and a site on the National Register of Historic Place, it is not to be missed.

Other attractions nearby include the New York State Aquarium, Brooklyn Cyclones baseball games at Keyspan Park, and Coney Island USA's Museum and Circus Sideshow. Don't forget to grab a bite at Nathan's Famous Hot Dogs (1310 Surf Avenue, 718 946 2202), a local institution since 1916, or sit down for an authentic New York pie at the famous Totonno Pizzeria Napolitano (1524 Neptune Ave, 718 372 8606). For more info about local attractions and special events in Coney Island, visit www.coneyisland.com.

Botanical Gardens

900 Washington Ave
Brooklyn

Brooklyn Botanic Garden

718 623 7200 | *www.bbg.org*

This garden in Prospect Park is a worthy alternative to the New York Botanic Garden, with a stunning Japanese hill and pond, charming Children's Garden, and unique Fragrance Garden among many excellent plant collections. Visitors come from all over the city for the annual Sakura Matsuri (Cherry Blossom Festival) each spring, when artists and performers from Japan entertain and educate alongside more than 200 cherry trees in glorious bloom. It is open throughout the year, except for Mondays. Admission is free on Tuesdays, Saturdays before noon, and daily mid-November through February. All other times admission is $5 for adults, $3 for student and seniors and free for children under 12.

Bronx River Pkway
& Fordham Road
The Bronx

New York Botanic Garden

718 817 8700 | *www.nybg.org*

The city's premier botanical garden has been growing since 1891. Its 250 acres are a National Historic Landmark housing 50 garden and plant collections, America's largest Victorian glass house, and several historic buildings. Popular annual events at the garden include the world class Orchid Show in early spring, and the Holiday Train Show in December, when city streetscapes are reproduced in foliage. It is open throughout the year, every day except Mondays. Admission prices vary.

43-50 Main Street
Queens

Queens Botanical Garden

718 886 3800 | *www.queensbotanical.org*

This garden began as a display for the 1939 World's Fair, and today its focus is on connecting horticulture with the diverse ethnic cultures of Queens. Major renovations are scheduled for completion in spring 2007 and will yield a number of innovative landscapes and buildings designed with environmental preservation in mind. Open year round, it is closed Mondays. Parking is available and admission is free.

1000 Richmond Ter
Staten Island

The Staten Island Botanical Garden

718 273 8200 | *www.sibg.org*

This garden boasts several unique attractions, including the Sensory Garden designed for the physically challenged, the Tuscan Garden, modelled on traditional Italian landscaping, and the Connie Gretz Secret Garden - a reproduction of an 18th century European garden maze. The highlight is the New York Chinese Scholar's Garden; a classical painting brought to life in a series of landscaped walkways and pavilions encircling a pond. Designed and built by Chinese artisans, it is the only garden of its kind in America.

Located within the Harbor Cultural Center, a former sailors' home repurposed as complex of artist studios, galleries, and performance spaces, the garden is open year round. Admission is free for the Botanical Garden, $5 for the Chinese Scholar's Garden and Secret Garden ($4 for children, students, and seniors), and $2 for the Secret Garden alone but children and adults accompanying children are free.

West 249th St
& Independence Ave
The Bronx

Wave Hill

718 549 3200 | *www.wavehill.org*

Built as a private estate in 1843, Wave Hill is set in one of the city's most beautiful landscapes. Famous former residents include President Theodore Roosevelt, novelist Mark Twain, and conductor Arturo Toscanini; all drawn to its breathtaking views of the Hudson River and the Palisades. The gardens and cultural centre are open year round, but closed on Mondays. Admission is free on Tuesdays, Saturdays before noon, and daily December through February. Parking is available. All other times admission is $4 for adults, $2 for student and seniors, free for children under 6.

Nature Knowledge

Urban Park Rangers are excellent guides, and run tours & workshops in 10 nature centres located in city parks. Learn more about nature reserves and activities by visiting www.nycgovparks.org.

Nature Reserves

The New York City Department of Parks & Recreation takes ecological conservation seriously, maintaining 48 Forever Wild Nature Preserves that cover 8,700 acres within the city. In addition to protecting native plant life, these forest, marshlands, and meadows provide habitats for an array of wildlife and birds.

The National Park Service's Gateway National Recreation Area also has several natural preserves, most notably the 9,155 acre Jamaica Bay Wildlife Refuge. This diverse coastal landscape is world-renowned for bird watching with over 325 species identified. Its trails are open from dawn to dusk daily, and parking is available.

Zoos & Wildlife Parks

New York has five zoos and one aquarium. All except the Staten Island Zoo are run by the public-private partnership non-profit Wildlife Conservation Society. The Society has a three-pronged mission to study animals, educate the public and protect wildlife, and they strive to house animals in environments that mimic their natural habitats.

2300 Southern Blvd
The Bronx

The Bronx Zoo

718 367 1010 | *www.bronxzoo.com*

This world-famous zoo first opened its gates in 1899. A pioneer in the use of natural habitats in the 1940s, today it houses more than 4,000 animals from around the world in specially designed exhibitions. Highlights include interacting with friendly primates in the 6.5 acre Congo Gorilla Forest, watching the Siberian cats on Tiger Mountain, seeing the small primates swing through the vines of Jungle World's recreation of an Asian rainforest, and finding the snow leopards and red pandas hiding in the Himalayan Highlands.

Open daily year round. Parking is available. Admission is $14 for adults, $12 for seniors, $10 for children 2-12, free for children under 2, and free for all on Wednesdays. There is an additional fee for the carousel and Congo Gorilla Forest.

Central Park ◀
Nr East 64th St
Upper East Side
Map 5-A1

Central Park Wildlife Center & Tisch Children's Zoo

212 439 6500 | *www.nyzoosandaquarium.com*
Central Park's small zoo is a popular family destination, welcoming about a million visitors each year. The Wildlife Center's most prominent residents are its sea lions, penguins, and polar bear, while the Children's Zoo focuses on animals for petting. Open year round, daily. Admission is $8 for adults, $4 for seniors, $3 for children 3-12, and free for children under 3.

Surf Ave & West 8th St ◀
Brooklyn

The New York Aquarium

718 265 3474 | *www.nyaquarium.com*
The city's only aquarium displays 350 different species housed in a variety of indoor and outdoor displays. Look inside for colourful Caribbean fish, eerily beautiful jellyfish and menacing sharks then head outside to watch the playful antics of the walrus, otters, sea lions, and penguins. There is an indoor cafe and several food carts should you get the munchies while you visit this fascinating attraction. Log onto the website for information about special tours and educational programmes throughout the year. The aquarium is open daily all year round. Admission is $12 for adults, $8 for seniors, $8 for children 2-12, and free for children under 2.

450 Flatbush Avenue ◀
Prospect Park
Brooklyn

Prospect Park Zoo

718 399 7339 | *www.nyzoosandaquarium.com*
Brooklyn's small zoo has three exhibition areas specially designed for kids, where young visitors can pet farm animals, get up close with some wild species, and learn about zoology and wildlife conservation. If you live in Brooklyn and have some time on your hands, you could always become a zoo volunteer - after a 12 week training programme you can become a valuable member of the team that looks after the animals and helps to educate the public. Prospect Park Zoo is open daily all year round. Admission is $6 for adults, $2.25 for seniors, $2 for children up to 3-12, and free for children under 3.

53-51 111th Street ◀
Flushing Meadows-
Corona Park
Queens

Queens Zoo

718 271 1500 | *www.nyzoosandaquarium.com*
This zoo has a unique collection consisting only of animals native to north and south America. This is the place to come if you want to catch up with the animals that feature in American heritage, like the American bison, the American bald eagle, and the Roosevelt elk. Long-time New Yorkers will remember Otis, the coyote that hid out in Central Park in 1999 - after his safe capture he was taken to the Queens Zoo, where you can still see him today. While the animals inhabit natural landscapes, the birds are housed in a geodesic dome designed by Buckminster Fuller for the 1964 World's Fair. Queens Zoo is open daily all year round. Admission is $6 for adults, $2.25 for seniors, $2 for children 3-12 and free for children under 3.

614 Broadway ◀
Staten Island

Staten Island Zoo

718 442 3100 | *www.statenislandzoo.org*
This small zoo won't impress adults, but it has lots of activities for families. There is a great variety of fish, amphibians and reptiles on display, but look elsewhere for large animals, and expect a limited collection of birds and mammals, such as meerkats, leopards, red pandas, bushbabies and groundhogs. They also offer a fantastic range of educational programmes, so if your little darling wants to be a zookeeper when they grow up, head for the Staten Island Zoo. It is open daily throughout the year, and has plenty of parking. Admission is $7 for adults, $5 for seniors, $4 for children 3-14, and free for children under 3.

Tours & Sightseeing

Other options **Out of New York** p.241,
Activity Tours p.235

Tour Right
There are more than 1,400 individuals licensed by New York City's Department of Consumer Affairs to give public tours. Each one had to pass a computerised exam covering local landmarks, history, and geography, provide character references, and pay an annual fee. Only tour with licensed guides!

With so much to see and do in New York City, there are sightseeing tours to suit every need. Short-term visitors pressed for time will benefit from organised tours that hit many popular sights all in one day, while even long time residents can appreciate the in-depth knowledge that professional guides share on specialised tours focused on particular neighbourhoods. Local tours can involve walking, riding the subway, taking a bus, being driven in a private car, or even travelling by helicopter. Information on local tours and tour operators can be found on the city's official tourism site, www.nycvisit.com.

Sightseeing & Shopping Tours

For an in-depth, personal approach to sightseeing, walking tours are the way to go. Various tour operators offer walking tours all around the city, and there are even a few tours that you can go on for free. It's a great way to get up close and personal with some of the city's monuments, plus there's the advantage of safety in numbers - if you're nervous about brandishing your hugely expensive camera while out and about on your own, you may feel more comfortable doing so on a walking tour where you're part of a group.

As for shopping tours, the rationale is simple; when you're in the city where people would rather shop than sleep, and there is the widest choice of retailers that you may ever see in your lifetime, it's best to call in the professionals. They'll steer you away from the tackiest places and take you to some hidden gems where you'll probably run yourself into financial ruin, but have fun doing so!

Many non-profit organisations in the city offer free walking tours of the neighbourhoods that they serve. The table includes a few of the most popular. Be sure to contact the office to get a schedule of upcoming tours before heading out, as departures may be infrequent.

Free Walking Tours

34th Street Partnership	500 Fifth Avenue, Suite 1120,	212-719-3434	www.34thstreet.org
Central Park Conservancy	14 East 60th Street, 8th floor,	212-794-6564	www.centralparknyc.org
Grand Central Partnership	122 East 42nd Street, Suite 601,	212-883-2420	www.grandcentralpartnership.org
Times Square Alliance	1560 Broadway, Suite 800,	212-768-1560	www.timessquarenyc.org
Union Square Partnership	4 Irving Place, Room 1148-S,	212-460-1200	www.unionsquarenyc.org

Various Locations

Big Onion Walking Tours

212 439 1090 | www.bigonion.com

Big Onion Walking Tours offer tours all over the city, covering dozens of different themes, led by guides who hold graduate degrees in fields like history, architecture, and literature. They even partner with the New York Historical Society. Tours include the Financial District, Central Park, a walk over the Brooklyn Bridge, and Chinatown. They also offer some particularly interesting 'special' tours, such as a Gangs of New York tour, a Gay & Lesbian History tour, a tour of Greenwood Cemetary (especially recommended for the Halloween week!), and a 'New York in War & Peace' tour.

Various Locations

Bridge & Tunnel Club Tours

347 323 4321 | *www.bridgeandtunnelclub.com*

A historian and a travel writer share their passion for exploring their city on tours to locations in all five boroughs. Get there like a local, by foot and public transportation. All itineraries are customised and can include stops for sightseeing, shopping, athletics, and dining.

Various Locations

Elegant Tightwad Shopping Excursions

516 735 2085 | *www.theeleganttightwad.com*

This experienced guide and former fashion industry pro offers tours of designer showrooms and sample sales in the Garment District, the Upper East Side, and downtown. Personalised tours are also available. Shopping 'treks' cost between $45 and $145 per person, depending on how many people are in your group and what the itinerary is. But in general, you can expect four hours of shopping, a copy of The Elegant Tightwad's book full of tips on how to dress to the nines on a budget, as well as a list of other shops and sales to discover once the tour is over.

Various Locations

Shop Gotham

866 795 4200 | *www.shopgotham.com*

This highly recommended company offers both pre-planned shopping routes and custom itineraries. Neighbourhoods covered include Nolita, Soho, the Garment District, and Fifth Avenue. Prices vary from tour to tour, but as an example, the Soho tour costs $38 and the Garment District comes in at around $65 - but this gets you into some wholesale showrooms that are open exclusively to tour members, as well as some of the most sought-after (and hard to find) sample sales. For $125, Shop Gotham will give you their 'Shopping List' treatment, which is a little like life coaching for shopaholics. Just tell them what you need (for example: your high school reunion is coming up and you need to look younger, slimmer and more successful), and they will sort it all out for you.

Activity Tours

Other options **Tours & Sightseeing** p.234

A Unique View

To really escape city life for a while, why not bubble away your stress under water? Captain Mike's Diving Services (www.captain mikesdiving.com) are scuba diving excursions run by a veteran of the NYPD Scuba Team. Options include lessons for beginners, group adventures for advanced divers, and diving trips outside the city.

Those who instantly imagine busybodies with clipboards and guides with irritating voices whenever they think of organised tours will think again when they try out one of New York's quirkier activity tours. A city made up of so many different aspects and cultures should be looked at via a number of different angles. Hush Tours (www.hushtours.com) which focuses on hip hop culture in Harlem and Queensbridge, and includes DJ and rap lessons, and even occasional celebrity guides. If Easter egg hunts happen far too infrequently for your liking, you could always go on a City Hunt Urban Adventure (www.cityhunt.org) and enjoy a private or public scavenger hunt across the city. Alternatively, other city-based activity tours include NYC Run (www.nycrun.com), which involves participants running anywhere from 1.5 to over 8 miles with a tour guide narrating the landscape as it passes by (don't worry – routes can be customised to fit individual interests and fitness levels), or On Location Tours Inc (www.sceneontv.com), a bus tour around locations seen on NYC-based films and popular television shows such as Sex and the City, The Sopranos, Friends, Seinfeld, and more, or Phototrek Tours (www.phototrektours.com), a small group walking tour accompanied by both a guide and photographer, during which participants choose from scheduled or customised two to four-hour itineraries – each receiving a CD of photos from their trip within 48 hours.

Bicycle Tours

1306 Second Avenue
Upper East Side

Bike The Big Apple
201 837 1133 | *www.bikethebigapple.com*
These bike tours entail about four to five hours of riding on routes in Manhattan, Brooklyn, Queens, and the Bronx. Guides ride at the front and back of the group, and both bikes and helmets are provided.

2 Columbus Circle
Central Park & Fifth
Avenue
Map 4-E1

Central Park Bicycle Tours/Rentals
212 541 8759 | *www.centralparkbiketour.com*
This company offers a two hour bike tour of Central Park. Bikes are provided, and bike rentals for personal use are available as well.

Boat & Yacht Charters
Dinner Cruises p.382

Various Locations

Caliber Yacht Charters
212 248 3800 | *www.caliberyachtcharters.com*
New York's iconic skyline has been reproduced on posters, mugs and T-shirts around the world, as well as featured in countless films and TV shows. Experience it first-hand by sailing past it (preferably armed with a cosmopolitan and a designer handbag, for full effect!) on a luxury yacht. If you're still saving up for your own yacht, try a cruise with Caliber Yacht Charters - whether you climb aboard one of their yachts, sailboats or paddlewheel boats, the experience is a memorable one from setting sail to the time you disembark. Any of their vessels can be hired for dinner cruises, birthday parties or corporate outings.

Various Locations

NY Boat Charters
212 496 8625 | *www.nyboat.com*
Escape the city and take to the seas on one of NY Boat Charter's luxury yachts or sailboats. Boasting 'the largest fleet of yachts in the New York City area', this charter company can accommodate groups of any size, be it a romantic dinner cruise for two or a huge corporate gathering of 1,000. They can also arrange catering. The company is owned by husband and wife team, Captain Rob and Lezlee, and Lezlee has been ordained as a priestess, allowing her to conduct marriages on board. Boats can be hired by the hour, the day, or even by the week if you really are planning on sailing off into the sunset.

Boat Tours
New York City is surrounded by water – the Hudson and East Rivers, several bays, the Long Island Sound, and the Atlantic Ocean – so boat tours are a popular way to enjoy the city skyline. They are also the only way to get to places like the Statue of Liberty and Ellis Island. Many companies offer boats for charter hire, and there are four major providers offering regularly scheduled public tours.

Chelsea Piers, Pier 62
Chelsea
Map 8-B1

Adirondack Sailing Excursions
646 336 5270 | *www.sail-nyc.com*
This company sails a luxury yacht five times daily from May to October. Options include sightseeing tours as well as cruises with brunch, sunset cocktails, or dinner. Charters are available.

Circle Line

Pier 83
West 42nd St
Hell's Kitchen
Map 4-B4

Circle Line

212 269 5755 | *www.circleline42.com*

This company has been running sightseeing cruises since 1945. Downtown harbour routes leave from the South Street Seaport (see www.circlelinedowntown.com), while ferries headed for Liberty and Ellis Islands depart from Battery Park. From the West Side, tour options include a three-hour circumnavigation of Manhattan and a two-hour semi-circle around lower Manhattan. Speedboat thrill rides are on offer at both locations. Charters are available.

Various Locations

New York Water Taxi

212 742 1969 | *www.nywatertaxi.com*

This company's yellow-chequered boats zip through the harbour, ferrying both commuters and sightseers alike. In addition to guided sightseeing and bird watching tours, passengers can purchase two-day passes that allow them to hop on and hop off at terminals in Midtown and the Financial District, Williamsburg and Red Hook, Brooklyn, and Hunter's Point (Long Island City), Queens. When travelling in summer, be sure to check out the bar at the Hunter's Point terminal, Water Taxi Beach. Charters are available.

Various Locations

NY Waterway

201 902 8700 | *www.nywaterway.com*

This company caters to both residents and tourists, with routes between Manhattan and New Jersey and a number of tour options. It is best known for its 90 minute Happy Hour cruises and two hour Party Tours, where the skyline becomes a backdrop for drinks and dancing. Charters are available.

Bus Tours

Other options **Walking Tours** p.240

Bus tours are a great way to get your bearings if you're new to the city, and if you make the most of them they can be great value for money too. Your tour guide will usually either be a fascinating native New Yorker who spews out little-known facts about the history, heritage, architecture, and movie trivia associated with the city, or an annoying, disillusioned tip merchant. If you stick to the better-known bus tour companies, you should hopefully get the former. Many of the buses are open at the top, and nabbing a seat up there will definitely give you the better views. It can also give you frostbite during the colder months, so be warned. Some enterprising vendors have cottoned on to a gap in the market and sell scarves and sweatshirts right near the bus stops. Still, if you don't like being chilly, play it safe and sit downstairs.

777 Eighth Ave
Btn 47th & 48th Sts
Midtown
Map 4-E3

Gray Line New York

212 445 0848 | *www.newyorksightseeing.com*

There's not much you won't see on this tour. You can take the Downtown loop, which will take you past the Empire State Building, the Flatiron Building, Greenwich Village, Soho, Washington Square Park, through Little Italy and Chinatown, past City Hall, down Wall Street, up through the East Village, past the UN Headquarters and the

Rockefeller Center, around Madison Square Garden and into Times Square. Alternatively, take the Uptown loop and head for the Lincoln Center, Central Park, the posh Upper West Side, Harlem Market, the Guggenheim, the Met and the Apollo Theater. Pay a special price and you can ride both loops for up to three days, hopping on and off at will. There's also a Brooklyn loop, leaving every 30 minutes from the South Street Seaport.

Culinary Tours

Various Locations ◀ Enthusiastic Gourmet
646 209 4724 | www.enthusiasticgourmet.com
These three-hour walking tours are led by a trained chef. Itineraries include tasting local specialities in Chinatown, the Lower East Side, and Little Italy.

Various Locations ◀ Foods of New York Tours
www.foodsofny.com
Eating and walking, walking and eating - these tours take you on a stroll through some of the city's most characteristic neighbourhoods and show you how to treat your tummy to some delicious local fare. Find all the best eateries in Greenwich Village, the Chelsea Market and the MeatPacking District, and Soho, with plenty of tasting along the way.

Various Locations ◀ New York Chocolate Tours
917 292 0680 | www.sweetwalks.com
Candy lovers can choose from one of two routes: one exploring a few upscale chocolate shops and another that stops in the newest local boutiques. Fortunately, all the walking purges any guilt and burns off at least a few of the calories.

Various Locations ◀ Savory Sojourns
212 691 7314 | www.savorysojourns.com
This company has 20 tour itineraries, covering more than a dozen neighbourhoods in Manhattan plus Atlantic Avenue and DUMBO in Brooklyn and Arthur Avenue in the Bronx. Custom tours are available.

Various Locations ◀ We Ate New York Foods of New York Tours
917 608 4235 | www.weatenewyork.com
This company offers tours of some of the city's best restaurants. You'll get a guided tour of the restaurant itself, as well as an exclusive visit to the kitchen where you can check out the culinary secrets of the head chef. Afterwards you can sample some of the restaurant's specialities. Expect to pay around $75 for a tour.

Helicopter & Plane Tours
Other options **Flying** p.263

If the view available from the airplane windows left you wanting more, try a helicopter ride with one of the two main companies offering tours to the public. Flights depart

from the Downtown Manhattan heliport on Pier 6 at South Street and the East River or the VIP Heliport at Twelfth Avenue and West 30th Street. Prices vary according to the length of the tour, but expect to pay about $120 per person for a 15 minute ride above the city. Be sure to call ahead to make arrangements, and remember that security concerns occasionally demand cancellation of all air travel over Manhattan.

Pier 6 & East River
Downtown Manhattan
Heliport

Helicopter Flight Services Inc
212 355 0801 | www.heliny.com
This company has sightseeing tours over Manhattan and the harbour that run from 15 to 30 minutes, as well as 30 minute private charters that begin at $1,350 for up to six passengers. They also offer additional services, such as airport transfers, flight training and aerial photography.

424 West 33rd Street
Suite 510
Hell's Kitchen

Liberty Helicopters Inc.
212 967 2099 | libertyhelicopters.com
These helicopter tours over Manhattan and the harbour run up to 17 minutes long. Tours cost as little as $30 for the shortest tour, which lasts just two minutes - it simply goes up and comes down again. Additional tours depart from Paulus Hook Pier on the waterfront in Jersey City, New Jersey. Contact the company for private charter information.

Heritage Tours

104 Malcolm X Blvd
Harlem

Harlem Heritage Tours
212 280 7888 | www.harlemheritage.com
Local residents lead tours of Harlem that focus on the African-American community's history, with special tours focused on jazz, hip hop, gospel, art, and more.

690 Eighth Avenue
Midtown

Harlem Spirituals/New York Visions
212 391 0900 | www.harlemspirituals.com
This company specialises in heritage bus tours of African-American communities in Harlem, Brooklyn, and the Bronx. Some itineraries offer a special focus on jazz and gospel music, soul food restaurants, or historic landmarks.

141 West 17th Street
Chelsea

Joyce Gold History Tours of NY
212 242 5762 | www.nyctours.com
An author and professor at New York University and the New School gives walking tours focusing on the history of various Manhattan neighbourhoods. Tours last around two and a half hours, and cost around $15, depending on the tour.

48-21 40th Street
Long Island City

Patriot Tours
718 717 0963 | www.patriottoursnyc.com
This company offers two and a half hour walking tours that visit Revolutionary War era landmarks throughout lower Manhattan. Groups are limited to 10 or 15 people, and private tours are also available.

2015 Kings Highway
Brooklyn

Timeline Touring
718 339 2302
This company offers public and private walking tours that focus exclusively on the Jewish history of the Lower East Side. Stops include kosher food shops, a historic tenement, and a landmark synagogue. Note that no tours are given on Saturdays.

Private Tours
Though most small tour companies offer the option of customised tours, some companies focus exclusively on private tours arranged through advance reservations. While groups can get a discount on a pre-scheduled itinerary, customised tours obviously tend to cost more. Be sure to do some research to find the right guide with the perfect itinerary.

239

Peck Slip Station
Financial District

Amazing New York Tours

212 587 0321 | *www.amazenyc.com*

This company features walking tours that last about three to four hours, tailored to participants' schedule and interests, and all for only $10 per person. All tours are guided by Howard (Howie) Levy, a licensed tour guide, native New Yorker, historian, and general showman.

205 West 57th Street
Midtown

V.I.P. Tours of New York

212 247 0366 | *www.viptoursny.com*

In addition to offering personalised tours of Manhattan neighbourhoods and landmark buildings, this company can arrange behind-the-scenes visits and meetings with the people who work in local museums, theatres, artist studios, and other tour locations.

Tours Outside New York

There are many tour companies that launch short escorted trips to the greater New York area. For more information about touring in New York State, visit www.iloveny.com. For New Jersey trips, try www.state.nj.us/travel. For visits to Connecticut, contact www.ctvisit.com; and for Pennsylvania, go to www.visitpa.com.

555 Eighth Avenue
Midtown

Get America Tours LLC

212 594 0888 | *www.getamericatours.com*

This national tour company offers short trips from New York City to Niagara Falls, Boston, Toronto, Washington DC, San Francisco, Los Angeles, Las Vegas, and more. Check the website for one-off deals, as well as special hotel rates. They also offer private sightseeing tours of New York City.

1644 Madison
Avenue
Upper East Side

Hines Tours – Eco Tours

646 403 5653 | *www.hinestours.com*

Tours offered include day trips to the Catskills and the Poconos, focused on hiking and visiting scenic landmarks. No trips are taken during the winter. The organisation is run by a group of nature-loving conservationists who want to educate city-slicker New Yorkers about the natural beauty to be found just a short car journey from the buzzing built-up metropolis.

Long Island

LI Wine Tours

516 546 6737 | *www.liwinetours.com*

This limo company picks up in the city and takes groups on an itinerary of their choice in Long Island's wine region. Trips to Foxwoods and casinos in Atlantic City are also available.

New Paltz

River Valley Tours

800 836 2128 | *www.rivervalleytours.com*

This company offers multi-night cruises on the Hudson River, stopping at riverside towns between New York City and Albany. For the best scenery, go during fall foliage season.

Travel Agencies		
Albo Tours & Travel Inc	718 786 2539	www.albotours.com
Ecovoyager	800 326 7088	www.ecovoyager.com
Intours	718 888 1717	www.intours.com
Liberty Travel	212 363 2320	www.libertytravel.com
Millennium Worldwide Travel, Inc	718 613 1300	www.mwwtravel.com
Now Voyage	212 431 1616	www.nowvoyagetravel.com
Pacific Asia Leisure	212 661 3270	www.pacificasialeisure.com

Out of New York

New York City certainly has enough to keep anyone busy for a lifetime, but that's no excuse not to get out of town every once in a while. There are a number of great destinations within short travel time that every New Yorker should visit at least once.

Philadelphia

Get to Know Philly
For information about Philadelphia hotels, restaurants, and attractions, visit www.gophila.com.

Just two hours south by train or car, Philadelphia is America's 'cradle of liberty'. History buffs will want to tour Independence Hall and the Constitution Center, see the Liberty Bell, and trace the steps of the Founding Fathers through the Olde City. Don't stop there, as the city has a vibrant arts scene, several must-see museums, more than a few notable restaurants, plenty of boutique shopping, and diverse nightlife options. The Philadelphia Museum of Art, the Pennsylvania Academy of Fine Arts, and the Rodin Museum have world-class collections for discerning grownups, while kids will be thrilled with the hands-on science exhibits at the Franklin Institute and the bizarre medical oddities displayed at the Mutter Museum. Grab grub from the local vendors at the Reading Terminal Market, perhaps an Amish soft pretzel, a cup of Bassett's ice cream, and classic Philly cheesesteak for a well-balanced meal. By night, follow a mix of rockers, rappers, and suburbanites to raucous South Street, order a martini with the yuppie set in upmarket Olde City, and or mingle with artistic types in Northern Liberties.

Book Early
Be sure to plan well in advance if you want to visit Philadelphia over the July 4 weekend, because 'America's Birthday' draws huge crowds and things get booked up months in advance.

Boston

More on Boston
Find more information for your trip to Boston at www.bostonusa.com.

Another historic city sits three hours north of New York by train or car. Boston attracts visitors eager to explore the history of the American Revolution on the Freedom Trail, stroll the campus of America's most famous university at Harvard Yard, and take in a Red Sox game the old fashioned way at Fenway Park. The Isabella Stewart Gardiner Museum will delight art lovers, and outdoorsy types will want to explore the Harbor Islands by water taxi. Cambridge and Somerville are the neighbourhoods to get a drink or see a band. Leaving town without trying some New England clam chowder, a traditional lobster roll, and a cone from one of Boston's homemade ice cream parlours would be a sin. Plan ahead if you want to visit in mid to late May, as the families and friends of Boston's large university population come into town to attend graduation ceremonies.

Washington DC

Capital Knowledge
Learn more about Washington DC at www.washington.org.

The nation's capital is about three and a half hours south of New York by train or car. Obvious attractions in "The District" are the Capitol, the White House, the museums of the Smithsonian Institute, and the assortment of national monuments filling the Mall and beyond. When all the sightseeing is done, neighbourhoods like Georgetown, Adams-Morgan, and Dupont Circle are great places to take a walk to visit shops, restaurants, and bars. If you plan to visit during the springtime Cherry Blossom Festival or around the time of a presidential inauguration, be sure to make your plans early.

Baltimore

Even More Baltimore
Get more information at www.baltimore.org.

Baltimore is just three hours south by car or train, close to Washington, D.C. Most tourists stick to the Inner Harbor area, visiting the world-famous National Aquarium, touring the ships, shopping along the water, and dining on Chesapeake Bay seafood, but this quirky city has much more to offer. For an offbeat tour, check out the work of self-taught artists at the American Visionary Art Museum, learn about oral health at National Museum of Dentistry, see likenesses of famous African-Americans at the National Great Blacks in Wax Museum, or watch potato chips get fried at the Herr's Factory.

Weekend Breaks

Whether it's just a day excursion, a weekend at a seaside hotel, or a season-long summer rental - a trip to the beach is a must in the summertime. All local beaches are busy during the season, so plan well in advance, especially on holiday weekends. To really get away from it all, nothing beats heading for the hills. There are three mountainous areas close to New York City, and each offers getaway options that range from primitive back-country camping to deluxe spa vacations, with plenty in between. Cooler temperatures beckon in summer, breathtaking foliage is the attraction in autumn, winter snowfalls draw sports enthusiasts, and spring is a time to relax and watch the flowers bloom.

Buses will take visitors into larger towns, but travel is definitely easier with a car. Traffic heading toward the countryside is never as heavy as it is towards the beaches.

There are many destinations that merit a weekend's visit so take a look at the regional tourism information online to plan the perfect trip.

Travel Bargains

Long Island Railroad (www.lirr.org) and Metro North Railroad (www.mta.info/mnr) routinely offer package deals that include transportation and admission to beaches, museums, and other attractions. Check their websites or the kiosks in main stations for more information.

Rent Some Wheels
If you are renting a car, shop online for the best price and remember that airport rentals are always the cheapest option. Try www.hotwire.com for a quick comparison of the lowest rates.

Travel Planning

Travel agents in the city typically deal exclusively with business travel, package trips and holidays abroad, so short weekend breaks are strictly a do-it-yourself affair. The internet makes planning easy, as each of the websites listed offers a wealth of detailed information about local accommodations, dining and attractions. Sites like www.tripadvisor.com can be very useful as well, featuring comparisons of hotels and attractions in tourist destinations throughout the US, alongside capsule reviews written by travellers themselves.

The first step is getting there, so here are the major car rental, rail, and bus companies for trips within the New York City area. Be aware that there are dozens more bus carriers on the road, running both regional routes and charter routes dedicated to transporting travellers to and from one specific point of cultural and commercial interest. The Port Authority Bus Terminal at 625 8th Avenue in Manhattan is a major hub for more than 20 bus companies, some travelling to destinations throughout North America. Information for all carriers and routes is available online at www.panynj.gov.

At 4211 Broadway, the George Washington Bridge Terminal is a secondary hub with many routes heading north and west of the city. Information is online at www.panynj.gov. To find out more about bus services at either terminal, call 800 221 9903 or 212 564 8484.

A number of bus companies, collectively referred to as the 'Chinatown Buses' will take you from Chinatown neighbourhoods in Manhattan, Brooklyn, and Queens to those in Boston, Philadelphia, Baltimore, and Washington DC for as little as $15 each way (though don't expect luxury, or the most savoury of travel companions). To see all the bus companies at a glance or make reservations online, visit www.gotobus.com.

Various Locations

Atlantic City & Foxwoods

There are two main destinations for gamblers in the New York City area, each about two and a half hours' drive from Manhattan. To participate in the growing American phenomenon known as 'Indian Gaming', visit Foxwoods, (www.foxwoods.com) a casino complex owned and operated by Mashantucket Pequot Tribal Nation on their sovereign land in south eastern Connecticut.

To see what happens when a classic seaside resort collides with the Las Vegas Strip, Atlantic City is the place to be. All casinos are open 24 hours, seven days a week, and

243

are open to gamblers age 21 and over. Parking is ample at both resorts, and many charter buses travel from stops in the city to the casinos for less than $20 a ticket. Atlantic City (www.atlanticcitynj.com) has been a beach resort since the mid-19th century; its streets immortalised in the American version of the popular board game Monopoly and its attractions portrayed in dozens of movies, plays, and television shows. All the Victorian era hotels are long gone today, the victims of 20th century urban blight that still taints much of the city beyond the glittering waterfront. There are some entertainment and shopping venues and even a handful of fine restaurants, but this is really a gambling town. Gaming was legalised in 1976 to rejuvenate the local economy, and the 11 towering casinos open today attracted the vast majority of the 35 million visitors that arrived in 2005. Amenities vary from place to place, but expect to see retirees lining the slot machines by day and a younger crowd around the card tables by night. The Borgata Hotel is the hottest game in town, snatching up high rollers and hip urbanites who might otherwise head to Vegas with luxury accommodation, upscale shopping and dining, and posh cocktails served by sexy 'Borgata Babes'.

Beyond the casinos, the beach is still wide and clean, but the world's first boardwalk offers little these days, especially with the last remaining amusement pier, The Steel Pier, now closed for redevelopment. The truly nostalgic can shell out a few bucks to ride a rolling chair; a quaint rickshaw-type conveyance that has long been used to whisk travellers up and down the boardwalk since 1887.

Foxy Gambling

At 4.7 million square feet, Foxwoods is the world's largest casino, and it's scheduled for further expansion by summer 2008. It's not all gaming of course: hotels, restaurants, shops, bars, nightclubs, a spa and salon, a golf course, a concert venue, and a museum and research centre devoted to native culture are also on site.

Massachusetts

The Berkshires
www.berkshires.org

The mountains of Western Massachusetts are part of the Appalachian Chain that stretches along the eastern seaboard from Alabama to Quebec. Mount Greylock, the area's highest peak, has summit views over five states on a clear day. City dwellers have long headed to the Berkshires for cooler air in the summer and snowy slopes in winter, but today there are plenty of cultural attractions on the agenda as well. Several famous arts festivals take place here in summer, including the Williamstown Theatre Festival (Williamstown), Jacob's Pillow Dance Festival (Becket), Berkshire Theatre Festival (Stockbridge), and Tanglewood (Lenox), the series of summer concerts by the Boston Symphony Orchestra held on the grounds on an estate once home to author Nathaniel Hawthorne. Great Barrington is the place to shop, eat, see a movie, and meet fellow weekenders.

In North Adams, the Massachusetts Museum of Contemporary Art (MassMoCA) demands attention with ambitious exhibitions in a restored industrial site. In addition to Tanglewood, Lenox is home to Edith Wharton's restored mansion, The Mount, and the well-known Kripalu Center for Yoga & Health. If Stockbridge looks like the ideal American town as painted by Norman Rockwell, that's because it is; the iconic artist lived and worked there, and he is honoured by a museum in town today. Pittsfield, the farmhouse where Herman Melville wrote Moby Dick, is now a museum to the author, and just outside town, Hancock Shaker Village opens a window onto the life and work of an early American religious sect famous for the sturdy, well-designed furniture that members designed and sold.

West of Hudson River

The Catskills
www.catskillvacation.net

Technically, the Catskills aren't mountains – they are the remnants of a broken plateau that runs west of the Hudson River between New York City and Albany. That makes no difference at all to the visitors who arrive each weekend to get active in the outdoors and explore historic villages. Outside the New York area, this region is best known in

American culture as the place where many 20th century comedians got their start on a Jewish resort circuit known as the 'Borscht Belt.' George Burns, Joan Rivers, Rodney Dangerfield, Woody Allen, Mel Brooks and Jerry Lewis are just a few of the famous names. New York State has regulated development in the Catskills, so picturesque vistas dominate the landscape. Great rewards await hikers who take to the trails: lookout points that offer views over the Hudson Valley and sights like Kaaterskill Falls, the highest waterfall in the state. Wear a bathing suit in summer for the occasional swimming hole, and pack snowshoes when the winter comes. Cross-country skiers will find trails in abundance, while the downhill ski and snowboard crowd heads to Hunter Mountain, two and a half hours from Manhattan by charter bus. Woodstock, site of the famous 1969 concert, is now an haute hippie paradise, all adorable bungalows and a main street lined with upscale, quirky boutiques and restaurants. Nearby Saugerties is a bit more down-to-earth, with a scenic lighthouse on the river that's worth a trip in itself.

Various Locations ◄

Finger Lakes & the North Fork

Winemakers are scattered all over New York State, but there are two regions where the concentration is high and the quality of the bottles remarkable. Both the Finger Lakes across central New York and the North Fork of Long Island can claim to have some the state's most scenic vistas, and it's easy to pair wine tasting excursions with hiking, bicycling, water sports, and cultural events.

The Finger Lakes are each lined with vineyards along their coasts, and it is possible to travel up one side of one lake and down the other in two days. Many varietals have made their way here, but the climate and soil is best suited to just a few grapes. Riesling is the star of the show, but there are good bottles of chardonnay, vidal blanc, and even an occasional cabernet franc to be found. Many vineyards also make excellent ice wines; sweet dessert wines made with grapes left to freeze on the vine. Seneca Lake has more than 50 wineries, with a few standouts being Lamoreaux Landing (Lodi), Standing Stone (Hector), and Hermann J. Wiemer (Dundee). Knapp (Romulus) and Sheldrake Point (Ovid) are the best of Cayuga Lake's 25 vineyards. Relatively tiny Keuka Lake has only 18 vineyards, among them the region's best: Dr. Konstanin Frank's Vinefera Wine Cellars (Hammondsport).

The North Fork of Long Island is home to 30 wineries. The climate and soil is compared to Bordeaux, so look for merlot, cabernet, or chardonnay to dominate. Bedell Cellars (Cutchogue), Sherwood House (Mattituck), and Shinn Vineyards (Mattituck) are the best of the bunch. Farm stands offer excellent local produce on the roadside, so stop often. The best place to stay overnight in North Fork is the historic whaling village of Greenport, where excellent lodging, dining and shopping fills a pedestrian-friendly town centre.

Along Hudson River ◄

The Hudson Valley

www.travelhudsonvalley.org

Thanks to the efforts of dedicated preservationists over the years, many places along the shore of the Hudson River remain as beautiful today as they were centuries ago. There are a number of beautiful parks to hike and camp, several small towns to stroll, and even a few museums and historic landmarks to visit. A car is not necessary for a day trip, but might be useful for more. The east side of the river is accessible via a stunning ride on the Metro North Railroad, which runs right along the river. On the west side, there are no scenic options, so just take one of several local bus lines. Hudson Highlands State Park has the best hikes in the area, notably the Breakneck Ridge Trail leading to the top of Beacon Mountain. Clarence Fahnestock Memorial State Park is a great place to cross-country ski in winter, with the most affordable ski rentals and trail passes around, and trails that can serve beginners and experts alike. Historic sites in the area include the spectacular Rockefeller family estate, Kykuit;

author Washington Irving's riverside home, Sunnyside; the restored colonial farm, Philipsburg Manor; and Union Church, a chapel with windows by Henri Matisse and Marc Chagall. Heading north, Dia: Beacon displays its collection of contemporary art from world-famous artists in a restored factory just across the road from the Beacon train station. Hudson Valley Shakespeare mounts productions outdoors at the riverside Boscobel Restoration near Cold Spring every summer. Need a big meal after all that? The Culinary Institute of America in Hyde Park has several restaurants on campus where tomorrow's top chefs are cooking today.

East of NYC

Long Island

Long Island's coastline is beautiful and easy to reach, attracting day-trippers, weekenders, and seasonal residents alike. Exclusivity increases the further one travels from the city, and the southern beaches on the Atlantic Ocean are far more popular than the northern beaches on the Long Island Sound. Buses and trains travel to most beach towns, but schedules vary widely. Drivers should expect serious, headache-inducing traffic during prime travel times on summer weekends.

These are just a few suggested destinations. For information about all the towns on Long Island's coast, visit www.longislandtourism.com.

Jones Beach

Only 33 miles from Manhattan, this state park has 6.5 miles of clean, well-maintained beach. It attracts big summer crowds with swimming, fishing, boating, performances at the outdoor Jones Beach Theater, and educational programming at the Theodore Roosevelt Nature Center. Admission is free. Parking is available and Long Island Bus offers routes that stop nearby. Find out more at http://nysparks.state.ny.us.

Long Beach

This is the best beach that is easily accessible from New York City without a car. The Long Island Railroad takes about an hour to arrive within blocks of the seashore, with a wide, clean beach and a small boardwalk with food concessions and shops. Beach passes cost $7 per day or $70 per season for non-resident adults. Parking is available in lots or in metered spaces. Find out more by visiting www.longbeachny.org.

Fire Island

A barrier island off Long Island's southern coast, Fire Island is 80% public parkland. Residential communities make up the remainder, catering to laid-back vacationers. The Pines and Cherry Grove are famous gay communities, while Ocean Beach is known for nightlife and hotels. Several private beaches exist, but most beaches are free and open to the public. Note that there are no cars on Fire Island, so visitors must arrive by ferry, water taxi, and private boat. Find out more at www.fireisland.com.

Hampton Jitney

Trains to the Hamptons run infrequently, so Hampton Jitney is the way to go without a car (or helicopter). These clean, air-conditioned buses serve many stops in Manhattan (www.hampton jitney.com).

The Hamptons

'The Hamptons' refers to a collection of towns on South Fork at the far eastern end of Long Island, including Southhampton, Easthampton, Bridgehampton, Sag Harbor, and Sagaponack. They have long been the favoured summer retreats of the rich, the famous, the rich and famous, and those aspiring to become one or both. Top-notch beaches and upmarket shopping and dining options abound, but hotels of any kind are scarce. Dress up for a night on the town, because this is no barefoot beach party. Most visitors tend to own or rent for the season, or stay with someone who does. Summer shares, houses where many people contribute to rent on a large house in exchange for use of one bedroom, are popular. Beaches are free, but parking nearby is often restricted. For more information, see www.hamptons.com.

Celebrity Montauk ◀

Andy Warhol once had an estate here, and the Rolling Stones wrote Memory Motel *about a local hotel bar.*

Montauk

If the Hamptons feel too much like Manhattan-by-the-Sea, try Montauk. Long Island's easternmost hamlet is perched at the very tip of the South Fork, earning its nickname 'The End.' Just follow the Sunrise Highway to Montauk Point State Park and the famous Lighthouse, guiding ships to port since 1796. From the top it's possible to see coasts of Connecticut, Rhode Island and Block Island on a clear day.

Though this is still a wealthy community, the vibe in town is decidedly younger and more creative than the rest of the East End. Surfers abound, especially at the Ditch Plains beach, chasing the best waves around these parts. Beaches are free. There are plenty of hotels for short-term stays, and campsites sit right on the beach at Hither Hills State Park. Visit www.onmontauk.com for more information.

Delaware River ◀

New Hope and Lambertville

www.newhopepa.com

New Hope and Lambertville sit on either side of the Delaware River about 90 minutes by car from Manhattan, linked by a car and pedestrian bridge. Both have small town centres lined with art galleries, antique shops, and an assortment of small boutiques, restaurants, bars, and historic inns. Just five miles from New Hope in Lahaska, Peddler's Village is another walkable shopping district with more than 75 shops and restaurants and a great country inn. The towns welcome visitors throughout the year, but from late November to New Year's Day, holiday lights illuminate the streets, and shoppers come out in full force. Every Tuesday and Saturday, Rice's Market brings vendors selling everything from farm produce to Chinese antiques to 30 acres near New Hope, just as it has for over a century.

South of New York ◀

New Jersey

www.state.nj.us/travel

Some New Yorkers will crack jokes about the Jersey Shore. It's true that many towns there are more crowded and commercialised than those on Long Island, but with 127 miles of coastline, the state still boasts plenty of wonderful beaches that even the most jaded city dweller will enjoy. New Jersey Transit gets visitors there without a car: northern beach towns are accessible by train, the southern towns by bus. These are just a few popular vacation spots.

The Stone Pony ◀

The must-see in Asbury Park for music fans is the favourite hometown haunt of the likes of Bruce Springsteen and Jon Bon Jovi, The Stone Pony (www.stonepony online.com).

Asbury Park

Asbury Park is definitely not to everyone's taste: not just rough around the edges, the place is downright gritty. Full-scale urban renewal is years away, but a renaissance led by a vibrant gay community and an army of the young and tattooed is well underway. After all, clean, free, nearly empty beaches this close to the city can't go unnoticed for long. The boardwalk is largely vacant, but a few shops and a breezy Tiki Bar near the water take a look. Main Street's bistros and shops channel the atmosphere of Park Slope, while Asbury Lanes (www.asburylanes.com) and Wonder Bar (www.thewonderbarnj.com) might look right at home in Williamsburg. The Empress Hotel's bar (www.asburyempress.com) – and the boys who frequent it – is downright sleek, but friendly dives like Georgie's (www.myspace.com/georgiesbar) party without pretence. There aren't very many places to stay overnight in town at present, but nearby Ocean Grove presents a good walking-distance alternative. See www.cityofasburypark.com for more info.

Cape May

Charming Cape May is not just another beach town, it is a National Historic Landmark community with a concentration of well-preserved Victorian homes second only to San Francisco. The Cape May Bird Observatory (www.njaudubon.org) is world famous, and most active during autumn migration season. Besides sunbathing and swimming, the most popular activity on Sunset Beach is searching for 'Cape May Diamonds,' small quartz pebbles that get polished by sea and sand to mimic a more precious stone. Beach passes cost $4 a day or $25 a season. There is no boardwalk, but the small commercial area in the centre of town should satisfy all shopping and dining needs. Hotels don't fit the atmosphere here, but there are a number of lovely inns and bed and breakfasts. See www.capemay.com for more information.

Ocean City

The island town that calls itself 'America's Greatest Family Resort' has eight miles of beautiful beaches and a tidy boardwalk that offers a mix of gift shops, quirky boutiques, family-run fast food shops, and a few small amusement parks. Don't leave town without trying Steel's fudge, Fralinger's salt water taffy, and Mack & Manco's pizza, all long time local favourites. Serious shoppers should check out Asbury Avenue, where everything from nautical antiques and original art to tie-dye sarongs and inflatable rafts are for sale. Beach passes cost $5 a day or $18 a season. There are a large number of hotels in Ocean City, though many families own or rent for a week or more. To find out more, visit www.oceancityvacation.com.

Dry City
A former Methodist retreat, the town of Ocean City has chosen to remain alcohol free. Public drinking is against the rules, but bars and liquor stores are plentiful just across town borders.

Ocean Grove

A trip to Ocean Grove feels like time travel. This picture-perfect village is owned and operated by a Methodist religious group, and a neighbourly vibe permeates the quaint, tree-lined streets and the meticulously maintained Victorian homes. Though church activities are ever-present in town, all are most welcome here and there is no attempt to convert visitors. Beaches are closed on Sunday mornings in deference to churchgoers. Beach passes cost $7 a day or $70 a season, with weekend and weekly tickets for sale as well. There are plenty of places to stay overnight, all of them clean, comfortable, and just blocks from the beach. The Starving Artist (732 988 1007) serves up excellent, creative cuisine, and Nagle's, an old-fashioned icecream shop and diner, is the place for a quick bite or a towering milkshake. There are no bars or liquor stores, but guests are welcome to bring their own bottle to restaurants in town. For bars and clubs, take a short walk or cab ride to Asbury Park right next door. See www.oceangrovenj.com for more information.

Sandy Hook

The Sandy Hook peninsula's seven miles of pristine beaches are part of the Gateway National Recreation Area. In summer, swimming and surfing are the main draws, but the park offers hiking, biking, and birding opportunities all year long. Don't miss the Sandy Hook Lighthouse, the oldest in America, built in 1764 and still in use today. Climb to the top to see the Manhattan skyline. Beaches are free, but parking usually incurs a fee. The most direct route to Sandy Hook is over water. SeaStreak (www.seastreak.com) runs a high-speed ferry from Lower Manhattan daily all year long, while NY Waterway (www.nywaterway.com) runs only on the weekend during the summer. The trip on either boat will take about 30 minutes. See www.nps.gov for more info on Sandy Hook.

Wildwoods Kids
Kids will love the Wildwoods for its many carnival games, arcades, souvenir shops, fast food, and five large amusement piers.

The Wildwoods

To many minds, the Wildwoods are the Jersey Shore. These three communities share lovely beaches, kitschy 1950s 'Doo Wop' architecture, and a long, loud, overcrowded boardwalk.
Beaches are free. There are dozens of hotels in the Wildwoods, and most are close to the beach. Luckily, many of the neon-bedecked motels have recently undergone renovations to bring their amenities up to date while preserving their retro charm. For more information on what the Wildwoods have to offer, see www.wildwoodsnj.com.

Pennsylvania ◄

The Poconos

www.800poconos.com

Like the Catskills, the mountains of north-eastern Pennsylvania are really just a broken plateau. The Poconos keep it simple: the only thing to do is to head outdoors for hiking, fishing, hunting, camping, boating, skiing, snowshoeing, and, of course, relaxing. It's not all log cabins and tents, though. The area has been popular with couples and honeymooners for decades, and some hotels and resorts even offer

cheeky amenities like heart-shaped or champagne glass-shaped hot tubs. The Delaware Water Gap National Recreation Area, marking the Pennsylvania-New Jersey border, is a perfect welcome for visitors, with stunning views of ridge and river. There are more than 25 parks, two rivers, and well over a hundred lakes to be found in the area beyond. Lake Wallenpaupack is the largest by far at over 5,600 acres, with plenty of places to stay and swim on its coast. Hawk Mountain is a famous site to watch migrating raptors, most active in autumn, and winter ski resorts include Camelback, Jack Frost, and Blue Mountain, among others. Shopping opportunities are slim, unless roadside fireworks stands and cigarette outlets are counted, but there are the Crossings Premium Outlets in Tannersville for a designer label fix.

Jackson ◄
New Jersey

Six Flags – Great Adventure

732 928 1821 | *www.sixflags.com*

Even the most coaster-phobic parents will be hard pressed to avoid at least one trip to New York's nearest amusement park. Six Flags actually encompasses three parks on one site. The Great Adventure theme park has kiddie and thrill rides, live entertainment, and carnival games galore; Hurricane Harbor is a water park with pools, float rivers, and slides; and the Wild Safari is the largest drive-through safari outside of Africa with 52 species on view. Park hours vary by season, and all three are closed in winter. Expect mobs of families and teens in spring and summer, especially on the weekends. Autumn is the best time to avoid crowds, and weekdays are usually quieter than weekends, as long as there aren't too many school groups.

One-day ticket prices range from $30 online for the theme park only, to $99 at the gate for an 'all-inclusive' pass to the three parks and coupons for food and merchandise. Season pass prices start at $80. There are almost always promotions going on that involve discounts or even 2 for 1 admission, so check online before heading to the park. Parking fees are additional and they vary by day and season.

498 Red Apple Court ◄
Central Valley

Woodbury Common

845 928 4000 | *www.premiumoutlets.com*

Serious shoppers will want to visit Woodbury Common Premium Outlets, where top designer labels go on sale as low as wholesale prices. From Adidas to Zegna, there are 220 stores in all selling clothes, shoes, food, jewellery, homewares, and gifts. The clientele is global: both currency exchange and international shipping can be done on site. The mall is an hour north of the city in Central Valley, accessible by car, Gray Line and Shortline buses, and Metro North Railroad. Woodbury also offers limousine and helicopter travel options, but that would cut in to the savings, wouldn't it?

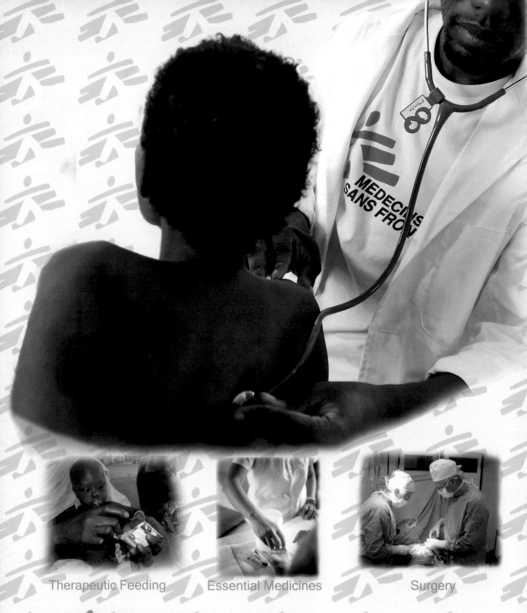

Therapeutic Feeding   Essential Medicines   Surgery

MEDECINS SANS FRONTIERES
أطبــاء بــلا حـدود

Providing emergency medical
relief in over 70 countries.

help us help the helpless

Activities

Sports & Activities

New York offers a wide variety of sports and activities. Not only can you find a host of outdoor activities, but there are also numerous indoor sports to be enjoyed. With each season, you will notice that the emphasis on a particular sport will shift according to temperature. During the winter you can ice skate in Rockefeller Center or Bryant Park, while summertime brings bicycle races and marathons. In spring you can enjoy boating trips along the Long Island Sound, and fall marks the beginning of baseball season.

If you enjoy the more conventional sports, like basketball, football, or baseball, then you won't have any trouble finding an available court or field. On the other hand, if you're more of an extreme athlete who enjoys jumping out of aeroplanes or Jetskiing, then you will find plenty of resources.

When most people think of New York, they picture skyscrapers and billboards, but this isn't necessarily the case. Out of Manhattan, New York also has mountains for skiers and snowboarders, wooded trails for bikers and hikers, and plenty of water for the avid angler or kayaker. There is also a wide range of indoor sports to be enjoyed. You can find at least one bowling alley in each borough, and plenty of gyms and sporting centres where you can play racquetball or lift weights. There are also numerous pools for aqua aerobics, swimming, or waterpolo.

The world meets in New York: many cultures bring their sports to the city and set up clubs that welcome new members. Some of these clubs are unofficial, and may meet in parks whenever members can find the time, while others require membership fees, have team uniforms and rigorous training schedules. Most sports also have various websites, magazines and online communities dedicated to them – this is a good way to meet like-minded people or find new members.

Fitness Facilities

Whether you want somewhere swanky to get sweaty, or you'd rather lift weights somewhere laid back, New York has the perfect place for you. See p.293 for a rundown of various sports and leisure facilities in the city.

Expand Your Horizons

They say that the key to happiness is to keep on learning, and New York offers plenty of hobbies and classes to keep you out of the 'all work and no play' mindset. Everyone has an inner artist of some kind, so indulge yours by taking art classes (p.254), learning to dance (p.260), mastering a musical instrument (p.274) or creating a pottery masterpiece (p.277).

Activity Finder

Aerobics & Fitness Classes

Body sculpting, spinning, Pilates, and step aerobics are just a few of the classes you can find in the health clubs and gyms throughout New York. There are also new and innovative aerobics classes that may involve chanting or breathing techniques, pole dancing, karaoke and even excercising alongside your dog (this is New York, people!). Classes are often categorised by fitness level, so look for a beginner's class if you're starting a new fitness regime. Class types and times change frequently so it is always best to call ahead for a full schedule of class offerings.

Aerobics & Fitness Classes

Name	Area	Website	Type of Class
Bally Total Fitness	Various Locations	www.ballyfitness.com	Step, Reaction Cycling, Boot Camp, Kwando, Low Impact, Rebounding & many more
Crunch Fitness	Various Locations	www.crunch.com	Step, Pilates, Reps, Spinning, Funk, Cardio Striptease, Cardio Dance & many more
Manhattan Pl. Health Club	Hell's Kitchen	www.mphc.com	Spin, Pilates, Tai Chi, Stretch, Power Yoga Bosu Bar, Hip Hop Cardio, and many more

American Football

If you're looking for some gridiron action, you may want to consider joining a flag football league. Since it can be difficult to round up the right amount of players, as well as playing fields, flag football leagues are an easy and fun way to enjoy the sport without having to look for pick-up games. There are plenty of organisations to choose from – for both youth and adult programmes – and joining a league can be as easy as signing up and paying a membership fee. For more information you can visit www.nycflag.com. There is also an amateur football league that covers New York State. The New York Amateur Football League (www.nyafl.org) started back in 1997 and is currently made up of eight charter member teams.

American Handball

Pulled a Muscle?

If your hamstring has gone, or your tennis elbow is back, it may be time for a little physio. Don't push yourself too hard as sports injures are all too common and can sometimes lead to long-term physical problems. Check out the physiotherapists listed on p.159.

American Handball is a competitive game, with thousands of fans in the New York area. Either hand can be used to hit the ball, and the objective is to win each rally by serving or returning the ball in such a way that your opponent cannot keep the ball in play. Points can only be scored while you are serving, and losing the serve is known as an 'Out'. Although handball requires endurance, agility, and a good sense of timing, it is still simple enough to be enjoyed by anyone. If you plan on playing, just be prepared to have a swollen palm the first few times out.

There are handball courts all over New York, and during the summer they can get to be pretty crowded. It is always best to get to a court with the expectation that you will have to wait for a few minutes before playing. One of the larger facilities in the area can be found in Central Park, where there are 12 regulation-size courts to play on. And of course there's also the West 4th Street courts in the West Village (also known as 'The Cage'), which are available for American Handball players – if you can persuade the basketball players to give you some court time, that is. There is also the Mayor's Cup Handball Tournament which takes place each year in New York, so if you get good enough you may just want to sign up. The tournament is one of the largest in the city, and attracts hundreds of players of all different ages and abilities.

For more information about the sport and where you can play it, visit the website of the US Handball Association (www.ushandball.org).

Art Classes

Other options **Art & Craft Supplies** p.311,
Art Galleries p.214

New York definitely sees itself as an epicentre of global creativity. Whether your artistic streak leads you to sculpture, ceramics, pottery or painting, there is a group or class that will allow you to practise the basic skills so that you can enjoy your hobby more, or use it to find fame and fortune. Alternatively, they'll also just allow you to relax and muck around with some paintbrushes or sticky-back plastic.

The Art Studio NY

West 96th St
Upper West Side

212 932 8484 | www.rebeccarts.com

The Art Studio NY offers classes for students of all ages, abilities, and artistic backgrounds. There's no need to fear condescending attitudes or snooty art teachers here: all classes are conducted in a positive and secure environment, so you can just let your creative juices flow freely. Classes focus on artistic communication, technique, and self-empowering creativity. There are never more than six students in a class, so you'll get plenty of attention from the teacher. Individual lessons are also available, as well as specialised workshops and international retreats.

Painting in the Park

Various Locations
Central Park &
Union Square Park

646 595 5979 | www.newyorkartworld.com

This outdoor landscape painting class meets in Central Park and Union Square Park where artists get the chance to work as a group, while being instructed by David Pena, a contemporary New York artist. Mediums explored include graphite, watercolours, oils, and acrylics. During the winter months these classes are moved to an indoor studio, but the focus on landscape painting remains the same. Private classes are available upon request, as well as an advanced master's class for those artists that have surpassed the beginner's mark. Classes take part in various locations, including Central Park at Bethesda Fountain, the Boat House, the Conservatory Garden or the Secret Garden, Union Square Park

Spring Studio

64 Spring St
Soho
Map 11-A2

212 226 7240

Considered by many artists to be one of the best places to draw in New York City, the Spring Studio attracts students from all over the world. Classes offered at the studio include daily life drawing sessions, as well as anatomy and portrait instruction. Figure drawing sessions are also available, and the models used at the studio are considered to be top class. Mediums include watercolours, pen and ink, and charcoal.

The Stevenson Academy of Fine Arts

20 Audrey Ave
Oyster Bay
Long Island

516 922 8011 | www.thestevensonacademy.com

This academy is an expansion of the renowned Stevenson Academy of Traditional Painting, which was established in 1960. This facility offers training by professional artists that are highly respected in their fields. Classes are based on classical art education, and teach many of the same techniques of the European art academies of the 19th century. Instruction is geared towards artists of all abilities, so even if

254

your rendition of the Mona Lisa looks more like Ozzy Osbourne, you don't need to be ashamed about being a beginner. And if you ever start thinking about turning your hobby into a career, the academy has extensive programmes that will help you along.

Ballet Classes
Other options **Dance Classes** p.260

Broadway Dance Center

322 West 45th St
At Eighth Ave
Midtown
Map 4-E4

212 582 9304 | www.bwydance.com

Whether you're a beginner or a career dancer, the teachers at the Broadway Dance Center are committed to helping you explore and discover the art of ballet. The classes are conducted by professional instructors and dancers that bring their field knowledge into the classroom. There are programmes for children as young as 4, as well as numerous workshops, masters classes, and an Absolute Beginners class for those with two left feet. The BDC moved from its old location (221 West 57th St) in December 2006, and reopens on West 45th Street in May 2007. In the interim, classes are being held at various locations in the Midtown area. Check the website for details.

Great Neck School of Dance

770 Middle Neck Rd
Great Neck
Queens

516 466 3515 | www.gnschoolofdance.com

The Great Neck School of Dance offers a variety of ballet classes for both adults and children in their Long Island studio. Adult classes include Ballet Body Exercise for beginners and Ballet Technique for advanced dancers. The beginners' class requires no previous ballet training, and is made up of a mix of breathing exercises, stretching, and training on the barre. Tutus are optional! Children can enjoy instruction in classical ballet, as well as combination classes like ballet-jazz or ballet-tap.

Rebecca Kelly Ballet Studio

579 Broadway
Nolita
Map 10-F1

212 431 8489 | www.rebeccakellyballet.com

This studio conducts a variety of ballet workshops, professional classes, teen classes, and intensive coaching sessions for serious dancers. The contemporary ballet class offers modern ballet instruction, and is available for both adults and children between the ages of 13 and 19. Classes are small, and designed to boost your abilities in partnering, contemporary, and other variations. Private classes can also be arranged by calling the studio and scheduling an appointment.

Baseball

The New York City Metro Baseball League

142-03 Oak Ave
Queens

718 366 2122 | www.leaguelineup.com

The New York City Metro Baseball League, formed in November of 2005, is a non-profit organisation for adults that enjoy playing America's traditional pastime. The league provides some of the best playing fields throughout New York, and is made up of players of all different skill levels. No matter how well you throw, hit, or catch, there is sure to be a spot for you on one of their many teams. Registration forms can be found online, as well as a full listing of league rules, eligibility information, and cost to the players.

Basketball

If you're into hoops, bringing the ball up court, driving to the lane, or even hanging out around the arc and shooting three-pointers, then your biggest problem is choosing which court to play on. There are numerous outdoor courts all throughout New York, including the semi-famous West 3rd Street courts on the corner of Sixth Avenue. During the winter you can play with The NY Urban Professionals Winter Basketball League, which welcomes both teams and individuals. The cost for this league is approximately ☒$1,700 per team, or ☒$170 per player. The fee includes one scrimmage (where your team will be ranked and placed in the appropriate division), 12 games throughout the season, and the divisional and interdivisional play-offs (if you get that far!). For more info on the league, have a look at their website (www.nyurban.com).

Bowling

From 16th-23rd St
Chelsea
Map 6-D3

AMF Chelsea Piers Bowl

212 835 2695 | *www.chelseapiers.com*

The Chelsea Piers sports centre offers a 40 lane bowling alley with automatic scoring, and an arcade featuring video games as well as air hockey and mini basketball. There is bumper bowling for the young bowler and Xtreme Bowling on weekend evenings, which incorporates black lights, fog machines and Day-Glo painted pins. Lane side table service is available, as well as a full service sports bar. Game fees are $6.25 per person per game Monday to Thursday, and $7.00 per person per game Friday to Sunday. Shoe rental is $4.00 per pair.

110 University Place
Btn 12th & 13th St
West Village
Map 9-A2

Bowlmor Lanes

212 255 8188 | *www.bowlmor.com*

Although the alley space fills up quickly, Bowlmor's 44 lanes offers an excellent bowling experience. On Monday nights Bowlmor hosts Night Strike, which features glow in the dark bowling and a live DJ spinning the latest house and techno music. Game fees are $5.95 per person per game during daytime hours Monday to Thursday, and $6.95 during the evenings, weekends and holidays. Shoe rental is $4.00 per pair.

Btn Eighth & Ninth Ave
40th-42nd St
Hell's Kitchen
Map 6-E1

Leisure Time Bowling Center

212 268 6909 | *www.leisuretimebowl.com*

This state-of-the-art bowling alley features 30 lanes with automatic scoring. There is also a cocktail lounge where you can enjoy drinks alongside a full bistro menu. There are two separate arcades for video game enthusiasts, and Leisure Time can host parties and events for all age groups. Game fees are $5.25 per person per game, and $3.50 for shoe rental.

Boxing

Over the past few years boxing has gained a reputation as an exercise program which promotes stamina, self confidence and ultimate fitness. Boxing is also a great way to release tension (just imagine your manager's/boyfriend's/mother-in-law's face on that punching bag), as well as being a pretty handy form of self defence, should you ever find yourself in a prickly situation. But with all the jabbing, bobbing and weaving you'll be doing, the best benefit of following a boxing regime is getting a hot body!

25 Park Place
Nr Church Street
Tribeca
Map 12-E1

Church Street Boxing Gym

212 571 1333 | *www.nyboxinggym.com*

Established in 1997, Church Street is now considered to be a leader in both the boxing and fitness industries. The coaching staff is exclusively made up of athletes who are

256

currently competing, or who have competed in the past, and can cater to all skill levels. They offer a special programme for children aged 12 to15, and you can even have a birthday party there. Monthly memberships are available for those who are not sure whether a full year of dodging jabs, hooks and southpaws is for them. Please note, however, that all activities at Church Street Boxing, including sparring, are carried out under the strictest safety regulations and procedures.

Fit 2 Fight Club

147 West 25th St
8th Floor
Chelsea
Map 6-E4

646 413 0535 | *www.fit2fightclub.com*

Fit 2 Fight Club is a modern facility offering both group classes and private training. All ages, sexes, and skill levels are welcome, and the first class is free. Training programmes cover cardiovascular fitness, resistance training and flexibility. You will learn the basics of boxing, tai chi, kung fu and kickboxing, depending on your goals and preferences. Fit 2 Fight can also give you some guidelines on following the right eating plan to help your body cope with the demands of the sport.

Nicco Boxing

Various Locations

646 387 9769 | *www.niccoboxing.com*

Nicco Boxing provides training programmes at various locations around the city, and they will even come to your existing gym to train you there, if necessary. Forget those bloody fights you've seen on the TV: boxing is, at heart, a much more complex sport that will get you into excellent shape. You can do boxing without even having to get into the ring with a sparring partner (but why deny yourself the fun part?). Paul Nicholas, the owner, used to fight in the heavyweight division, and although he has retired from competitive boxing, he can still share the secrets of making the most of a boxing programme with his clients. Nicco Boxing offers lessons and training at the following locations: Mendez Boxing (25 West 26th Street), Undisputed (34 East 23rd Street) and Club Normandie (225 East 95th Street).

Camping

If you're a camping enthusiast, and thought that camping in New York meant sleeping on one of the benches in Central Park, then you'll be glad to know that there are some fantastic campgrounds within easy reach of the city. Although a car is required to reach these campgrounds, the ride is well worth it, and the remoteness of some of these areas will leave you wondering as to whether or not you've crossed over the state line.

Preparation is important for just about every outdoor activity. By making sure that you have the necessary supplies and equipment, you will guarantee that your camping trip is an enjoyable and stress-free adventure. Your checklist may vary depending on the activities that you have planned, as well as the time of year and duration of your trip, but here are some general guidelines: For shelter, you will probably need a tent, a tarpaulin (or groundsheet), some extra stakes and rope (for those windy days!). You'll need a sleeping bag, with extra blankets if it is during a colder season, a pillow, and for the ultimate in camping luxury, an air mattress – just beware of punctures.

Be Prepared

Include these items on your camping checklist whenever you head off into the wilderness: sunscreen, a lantern, batteries (and extra batteries!), insect repellent, torches, a utility tool or penknife, an axe or a hammer, a shovel, a cellphone, a first aid kit, enough food and water (and extra water, just in case), and garbage bags.

257

County Rd 14
Red Tavern Rd
Duane Center

Deer River Campsite

518 483 0060 | www.deerrivercampsite.com

Located along New York's largest mountain range, the Deer River Campsite offers great views, as well as freshwater fishing, miles of hiking trails, and plenty of streams, lakes and ponds. There are 84 wooded sites with ample space around each, or five camping cabins to choose from. Onsite amenities include restrooms, a laundromat, and a playground for the kids. There is also a general store in case you run out of supplies, as well as boat and canoe rentals. So you see? It is possible to be a happy camper!

Route 8, Old Forge
Adirondack Park

Old Forge Camping Resort

800 226 7464 | www.oldforgecamping.com

The Old Forge Camping Resort, located in the heart of Adirondack Park, is open for all four seasons. The scenic campgrounds offer awe-inspiring views of the Adirondack Mountains and the private lake will ensure that your stay is both peaceful and memorable. There are 400 camping sites, and local attractions include the Enchanted Forest and Water Safari, both of which can be reached by shuttle bus. Onsite amenities include heated restrooms and shower facilities, camping kitchens, and utility sinks.

Canoeing
Other options **Kayaking** p.268

Brayton Park
Ossining

Champaign Canoeing Ltd

914 762 5121 | www.bestweb.net/~cc

Champaign Canoeing is a whitewater open canoe paddling school, which organises various canoeing trips throughout the year. Their trips include a week-long base camp wilderness trip, the Allagash Waterway wilderness trip, and weekend whitewater instructional trips for beginners. Private instructional classes are also available, as well as corporate outings to help get you and your colleagues away from the hustle and bustle of the office.

1123 Route 28
Warrensburg

Wild Waters Outdoor Center

800 8672 3353 | www.wildwaters.net

Wild Waters offers rafting courses between April and October each year. An experienced instructor can transform you from a whimpering, water-shy coward into a lean, mean rafting machine who can tame any rapid. You get to choose how many days you'll need to do this! If you're not sure about all the rushing water and Eskimo rolls, you could take the more sedate 'Introduction to Kayaking' course. Wild Waters also organises trips to various whitewater locations such as the Hudson River Gorge and the Sacandaga River. Check the website for more information and to request prices.

Chess

It may get a bad rap as 'a game for geeks', but the image of elderly gentlemen doing battle over a chessboard is as New York as Cosmopolitans and pastrami on rye. Central Park is home to the Chess & Checkers House, where you can pull up a chair at one of 24 outdoor chess tables. It is located a little to the south west of the Dairy, on 65th Street. You can hire a set of chess pieces for a refundable deposit of $20 (bring photo ID with you), or you can just bring your own. Indoor tables are also available, just in case the chilly weather starts to affect your strategic master-minding.

NY Chess

If you are really serious about your kings, queens and knights, get in touch with the New York State Chess Association (www.nysca.net) - apart from offering assistance to those wishing to improve their game, they also publish the quarterly chess magazine, *Empire*.

The Marshall Chess Club

23 West 10th St
Flatiron District
Map 8-F3

212 477 3716 | www.marshallchessclub.org

Membership in this club includes grandmaster lectures, chess classes for all levels of play, as well as tournaments that are rated by the United States Chess Federation. Weekend classes are available for children, as well as summer chess camps and social events. Exhibitions and casual games are arranged at this club, so regardless of your skill level, you're bound to find a way to flex your moves.

Cookery Classes

Miette Culinary Studio

109 MacDougal St
Chelsea
Map 8-E4

212 460 9322 | www.mietteculinarystudio.com

If you'd rather be a Bree Van De Kamp than a Susan Mayer, you may need some cookery lessons. Miette Culinary Studio has classes for adults and children, all taught by professional chefs who will not only teach you the basics, but also let you in on some of the secret techniques used in famous restaurants. Their weekend workshops team you up with your child (over 5s only) to learn how to create a simple but delicious meal. Other options are also available, depending on your needs. For example, you could get your whole company to do a big cooking class corporate event, or have Chef Paul give you a private lesson in the delicate art of fine cuisine.

Natural Gourmet Institute

48 West 21st St
Midtown
Map 8-F1

866 580 1797 | www.naturalgourmetschool.com

The problem with learning how to cook a gourmet meal from scratch is often the richness of the food: a few test runs of chicken baked in champagne, butter and cream and your apron's going to start getting tight. Not so at the Natural Gourmet Institute, where they'll teach you how to whip up a delectable feast that is also healthy (and vegetarian). Professional chefs will show you the ropes and let you participate in the cooking process (although you can just choose to observe if you want). After a few lessons with Natural Gourmet, you'll be able to prove that the old adage 'never trust a skinny chef' is no longer true.

The Wooden Spoon

Various Locations

917 627 5289 | www.thewooden-spoon.com

Of course it's easy to learn to cook in one of those professional cooking studios – they are all kitted out with gleaming stainless steel gadgets, pans with just the right kind of heavy bottom, powerful ovens and miles of work surface. But the chefs from Wooden Spoon will come to your house and teach you how to cook in your very own kitchen – even if it's the size of a suitcase. Book a single class if you want to learn how to cook a specific menu (say, if you've got a dinner party coming up), or have a few classes to learn different cooking techniques. Small groups can be accommodated too, so call in some of your friends to help you chop, steam and bake (and wash up afterwards).

Cycling

Other options **Sporting Goods** p.349, **Mountain Biking** p.273, **Cycling** p.290

New York is home to thousands of cyclists of all different ages and skill levels. Not only are there numerous cycling tours throughout the year, there are also dozens of clubs that meet to discuss cycling-related topics and organise cycling events. If you'd rather strike out on your own, then you will find that there are plenty of public parks to ride in, as the streets can be considered somewhat risky terrain – especially during rush hour. For some advice on cycling as a mode of transport, see p.41.

891 Amsterdam Ave
Upper West Side

Bike New York

212 932 2453 | www.bikenewyork.org

Although it was formed in 2000 to promote cycling both for transport and recreation, Bike New York is probably best known for its organisation of the Five Boro Bike Tour, which has taken place every year since 1976. This amazing, yet arduous, tour of all five boroughs of New York is an unforgettable experience, and the 2007 FBBT will take place in May (see p.48 or the website for more information).

Bike New York also offers various cycling education programmes, such as 'Teach Your Child to Ride a Bike' for parents, 'Bike Street Smarts' (essential if you are going to try and navigate the traffic on New York's main roads), and 'Share the Road', which aims to educate drivers about how to safely handle cyclists on the road.

Hostelling Intl
891 Amsterdam Ave
Upper West Side

Five Borough Bicycle Club

212 932 2300 | www.5bbc.org

The Five Borough Bicycle Club organises free day rides throughout the year within New York City. You can download a detailed schedule of rides planned for the current month, as well as detailed descriptions of meeting places. Although these rides are free, the club does encourage you to become a member for just $20 per year. They also organise some trips outside of the city (although there are charges involved to cover the costs of these longer trips). These trips range from a two-day trip to Montauk (about 140 miles one way) to the amazing seven-day trip to Martha's Vineyard and Nantucket. Becoming a member of the FBBC is a great way to increase your cycling activity, improve your fitness levels, and meet some friendly, like-minded people.

161 West 23rd St
Chelsea
Map 6-D3

New York Cycle Club

212 828 5711 | www.nycc.org

With nearly 2,000 members, this is one of the most active cycle clubs in the city. Apart from being an important community for cyclists, the club organises a variety of rides throughout the week and training programmes for all skill levels. Weekend trips are also offered – and if you're in need of a vacation a cycling trip is one sure-fire way to ensure you get plenty of fresh air. All members get a monthly bulletin with listings of upcoming rides and club events.

Various Locations

The Weekday Cyclists in NYC

212 838 2141 | http://members.aol.com/trudyth

The Weekday Cyclists is not a club – not a formal one anyway. It is just a group of cyclists who meet twice a week, on Tuesdays and Thursdays, to explore the city on two wheels. The meeting place is at the Loeb Boathouse in Central Park, and all are welcome. The rules for participating in a ride are simple: you have to wear a helmet, carry a spare inner tube, and bring your own water bottle. Rides are usually cancelled if there is more than a 50% chance of rain.

Dance Classes

Other options **Salsa Dancing** p.282

It's all about moving here and whether it's to the beat of your own drum or someone else's, this is as good a place as any to shake your groove thing to whichever rhythm you prefer. There are some incredibly hip classes to look out for. The Dance Factory New York (www.dancefactorynewyork.com) offers Hip Hop to Ballroom, while the Hawaiian Dance and Cultural Arts Group will show you what to do with a grass skirt (169 Mercer Street, 212 226 4467). Some forms of dance come and go in popularity but the classes still prevail, so if your hips can't stop shimmying it might be worth getting down to Serena Studio (www.serenastudios.com, 939 Eighth Ave (btw. 55th St. & 56th St., 212 247 1051) for tips on the exotic. The folks at www.partypop.com (333 W 52nd Street, 212.315.9299) will show you how to groove your thing up and down a pole (it's apparently a wonderful workout, just ask Kate Moss). West African dance is quite hot at the moment and a wonderful way to work off some of that left over angst from a hard day at the office. Check out www.westafricandance.com with Youssouf Koumbassa for a variety of classes.

Dance Manhattan Ballroom, Swing & Latin Studio

39 West 19th St
Flatiron District
Map 8-F1

212 807 0802 | www.dancemanhattan.com

Whether you've got two left feet or you glide across the floor like Fred and Ginger, Dance Manhattan has a class suited to you. Dance styles taught here include ballroom dancing, argentine tango, swing dancing and salsa, among others. Private classes are available, or you can sign up for group classes (a great way to meet fellow dance enthusiasts). If you've got a special event coming up and you want to wow people on the dancefloor, you can take one of their special weekend one-day crash courses.

Harkness Dance Center

1395 Lexington Ave
Upper East Side

212 415 5500 | www.92y.org

The Harkness Center offers a large variety of classes for students of all ages and abilities. There are also specialised classes that centre around dance techniques for senior citizens, dance educators, and even children looking to take their first steps on the dancefloor. If you're looking to swing with the best of them, or even practise some of those old jitterbug moves, then this may be the place for you. Other offerings include workshops for those interested in pursuing a career in dancing, and the opportunity to work with young choreographers in the area.

Peridance Center

890 Broadway
Flatiron District
Map 9-A2

212 505 0886 | www.peridance.com

For a well-rounded dance experience, the Peridance Center offers classes for various different dance forms, as well as classes on related subjects such as choreography and notation. Dancers of all abilities are welcome at the Center, and there are even child and teen programmes to help get the youngsters out onto the dancefloor. Frequent workshops are offered at Peridance, hosted by guest instructors on an ongoing basis. If you're looking to get those feet moving, but would also like to learn about what goes on behind the scenes, this may be the right place for you.

Drama Groups

Nearly everyone in New York fancies themselves as a bit of a thespian, some dedicating their lives to it, others waiting tables until they get their big break, and then there's the grown-ups who are happy to just have a go and be a horse's rear-end on stage. No matter, drama – in all its forms and glory – is the lifeblood of New Yorkers, and there are many acting schools set up to help lead you to where you want to get to, whether it's TV ads or Hollywood. Nothing is just for fun, but there are a lot of workshops and seminars for those who'd like to try their hand for a bit. The Transport Group (www.transportgroup.org) boasts that its aim is to develop and produce work by American playwrights and composers, and offers Diva Masterclasses as well as Monologue Intensive Sessions. The Blue Coyote Theater Group (www.bluecoyote.org) hosts regular competitions and interesting projects for playwrights, as well as the occasional workshop. Check out the American Association for Community Theatre (AACT) at www.aact.org or look in local press for details of amateur dramatic theatre groups and performances.

261

244 West 54th St
Broadway & 8th Ave
Midtown
Map 4-E2

The Acting Studio, Inc

212 580 6600 | www.actingstudio.com

The Acting Studio offers students the opportunity to take their acting and directing skills to the next level. Their numerous course offerings include instructional programmes for serious actors looking to make the move from college theatres to the big lights of Broadway. Other classes include advanced workshops for working actors aiming to stay fresh while between roles, or those who just want to make progress in their art while they have some downtime. One of the advantages of this studio is that they have a resident theatre company, the Chelsea Repertory Company, which puts on performances throughout the year.

61 Fourth Ave
East Village

Bruce Ornstein Acting Workshop

212 802 4955 | www.actingclassnyc.com

If you'd rather further your acting skills in small group sessions, where you receive individual attention and coaching, then you may find yourself interviewing with the Bruce Ornstein Acting Workshop. Classes combine a range of acting exercises, and students are encouraged to participate in each class. Students are also required to show a certain level of commitment to their art, so make sure that you're ready to take the plunge before signing up.

Fishing

When it comes to fishing in New York, you'll be pleased to know that there are over 7,500 lakes and ponds, and 50,000 miles of rivers and streams, where anglers can enjoy some of the best fishing in the country. A wide variety of freshwater and saltwater fish can be caught all across the state, and quite a few record books list New York as home to some of the country's largest fish. Charter boats for saltwater fishing trips can be found all across Long Island, to Sheepshead Bay in Brooklyn, and most of them will supply all the gear and bait that you will need. The charter boat schedules change according to season so it's always best to walk along the docks in order to get a feel for what's being caught. If you're more of a freshwater angler, then it may be a good idea to employ a guide to get some insider information as to which fishing holes are producing the big catches.

New York Game and Fish Magazine

New York Game and Fish Magazine is a publication for both hunters and anglers, and includes fishing information for both freshwater and saltwater species. This magazine has up-to-date fishing reports, as well as feature stories, and tips to help you bag the big one. Their website also has a tool that allows you to find relevant information about specific species of fish, including size regulations, season dates, and the best gear to use (www.newyorkgameandfish.com).

Noreast Saltwater Magazine

Noreast Saltwater is a fishing publication that can be picked up free of charge in almost any tackle shop. This magazine contains weekly fishing reports and tide charts, lists tackle shops, and contains special feature stories about what's hot in the world of fishing. Their website allows anglers to post and read daily reports, as well as receive reports for certain areas via email (www.noreast.com).

Flying

Despite the aviation disasters that seem to befall the city (9/11 was certainly the most terrifying and memorable, but in late 2006, Yankees Pitcher Cory Lidle crashed a small plane into a 50-storey condo on Manhattan's Upper East side), getting into the air is still an activity worth pursuing. Air traffic control is super stringent and getting your licence means navigating some heavy-duty paperwork, once you've mastered the lessons inside and out. But if you love being in the air, then it's well worth it. Flying tours (helicopter or small plane) of New York are also available and good fun if you don't mind being out of the captain's seat. There are no flying schools in the city itself, but you only need to move out a little to find a reputable school that is certified and safe.

Penn Yan Flying Club (www.pennyanflyingclub.com) provides lessons and merchandise and they also rent hangar space if you have your own jet (and why wouldn't you?!). Century Air (www.centuryair.com) is located a mere 20 minutes from New York City in Essex County Airport (also known as Caldwell Airport – CDW) in Northern New Jersey, and they offer a range of flying lesson options. The school is owned and operated by an airline captain with over 45 years of experience.

Courses at Air Fleet Training Systems (www.airfleettraining.com) include a full range of ground and instructional flight courses, as well as private pilot, transport pilot and flight instructor certifications. Super-serious aviators should check out the American Academy of Aeronautics (www.americanacademy.net), which has information on flying across the country.

Frisbee

Pick-Up Games

If you're looking for a pick-up game in your area, log onto the website of the Ultimate Players' Association (www.upa.org) and look for their pick-up listings.

Whether you're into a quick game of catch, or you're interested in meeting other Frisbee enthusiasts, head over to Central Park on a sunny day and you're bound to find what you're looking for. Central Park is large enough to house plenty of games so there's no need to worry about any unidentified flying objects, and you will usually find quite a few games in progress during the weekends. Another option is Washington Square Park, although the park is generally crowded, and finding the space could be difficult. Ultimate Frisbee is a non-contact team sport that has been gaining in popularity over the past few years. This sport has been described as a mixture of soccer, basketball, American football and netball, with a Frisbee! A regulation game consists of two teams, with seven players per team, and can be a great workout. There are regular pick-up games in Central Park, and most of them are geared to all skill levels of play.

Golf

If you're interested in playing on the same course as some of the world's top professionals, then you're in luck. Or if you just happen to be looking for the largest public golf facility in the world, well you're in luck too! You can find a little bit of everything- from tricky terrain to long, flat greens – on any one of the dozens of golf courses in New York. A great resource for golfers is www.teetimeking.com. This is where you can find a full list of golf courses and rates, and where you can even book a tee time at the various different courses in your area. There are also plenty of golf clinics, academies, and trainers listed on the site, to help you take a few strokes off your game.

Clearview Golf Course

202-12 Willets Pt Blvd
Bayside
Queens

718 229 2570 | www.americangolf.com

The Clearview Golf Course is a mix of flat greens and straight fairways, and a great course for both beginners and intermediates. This course offers 18 holes of golf, on 6,232 yards of green, and is conveniently located just south of the Throgs Neck Bridge. Since this course is known as a great place for beginners, experienced players may find themselves waiting on the group ahead of them. No malicious swings allowed.

Forest Park Golf Course

101 Forest Park Drive
Woodhaven
Brooklyn

718 296 0999 | http://forestpark.e-golf.net

The Forest Park Golf Course covers an area of 6,000 yards, and will test the skill levels of just about any golfer. This course was remodelled in 1995, and is said to be one of the top courses in the metro area. Not only will you find plenty of green and sand traps, this course has all the amenities you need, including a pro shop and renovated tee boxes.

The Golf Academy at Chelsea Piers

Pier 59
23rd St & Hudson River
Chelsea
Map 6-B4

212 336 6444 | www.chelseapiers.com

If you just need a few pointers, or have never even swung a club, then you may want to spend some time at The Golf Academy before heading out to the golf course. The Golf Academy is a training complex with all the right equipment to help you lower your score, while picking up some of the finer points of the game. Classes are available for all skill levels, as well as personal trainers for private instruction.

Kissena Golf Course

Booth Memorial Ave
Flushing
Queens

718 939 4594 | http://kissena.e-golf.net

The Kissena Golf Course is located in Kissena Park, and offers a hilly course spread out over 4,727 yards. Although this course may look easy to play, golfers will find that there are quite a few holes that won't allow for any mistakes, as well as several hills to provide a good up and downhill challenge. One of the attractions of this course is the breathtaking views of Manhattan that you can enjoy in between holes.

The Metropolitan Golf Association

49 Knollwood Rd
Elmsford

914 347 4653 | www.mgagolf.org

For some of the most up-to-date information on multi-level tournaments, the newest gear, and much, much more, become a member of The Metropolitan Golf Association. Membership includes a computerised handicap service to help you take a few strokes of your game, as well as tournaments and programmes for golfers of all skill levels.

Hiking

Just past the hustle and bustle of Manhattan, you'll find that there are some fantastic hiking areas in New York. The three major regions for hiking are the Finger Lakes, the Adirondacks, and southern New York. Each of these areas offers challenging terrain for the hardcore hiker, while still having plenty of trails for the weekend warrior. There are also quite a few state parks on Long Island where you can enjoy a quick nature walk through wooded areas with marked off trails. Whether you're looking for a half-day hike, or a week-long expedition, you're sure to find it along the footpaths and mountain regions of New York.

Chelsea Piers

Hiking with ADK

Sports & Activities

The Adirondack Mountain Club (ADK)
518 668 4447 | www.adk.org

This non-profit membership organisation offers its 30,000 members some unique outdoor experiences, while strongly maintaining its ethos to protect wild lands and waters through smart conservation. The activities list is pretty substantial with everything from camping to adventurous exploring trips on offer, as well as lectures, seminars and workshops on environmental issues.

Various Locations

The New York Ramblers
212 260 4879 | www.nyramblers.org

Founded way back in 1923 this slow moving (literally) group is creative about its hiking programmes making sure to try out new and interesting locations whenever they get together and go out (which is generally every Sunday, with an occasional Saturday thrown in for good measure). Destinations vary in strenuousness but are always within a two-hour radius of Manhattan by car, bus or train.

Various Locations

The Urban Trail Conference
212 924 7486 | www.urbantrail.org

This group is slightly different in that it sponsors walks and hikes through urban and natural environments. You can walk through historical neighbourhoods or hike your way across nature reserves, depending on the schedule. Membership is very cheap ($10 annually per adult) and ensures you receive a printed schedule to keep you up to date with what's going on.

Horse Riding

Adirondacks

Adventure Horse Riding in NYS
315 942 4769 | www.ridenys.com

If you'd like to spend some time on horseback through the Adirondack Mountains, then you may want to book an 'Adventure'. This ranch offers privacy and comfort in a setting that feels like the old west. Accommodations include a one bedroom cabin, and although you won't find electricity, you'll still be provided with all the creature comforts of home. Parties of up to four riders can be accommodated, and the ranch only hosts one party at a time so you can expect special attention.

9 Shore Rd
The Bronx

Bronx Equestrian Center
718 885 0551 | www.bronxequestriancenter.com

Lessons for different riding styles are available for all levels of experience and interest, as well as pony and hay wagon rides. Boarding is available, as well as trailer service to and from shows. The Bronx Equestrian Center also hosts special events throughout the year, including shows and training sessions. Another service offered by this Center is carriage rentals, which can help you make a memorable entrance and exit to your special event.

Peekskill Hollow Rd
Putnam Valley

Hollow Brook Riding Academy
845 526 8357 | www.hollowbrookriding.com

Pony rides, trail lessons for all ages, horse training and boarding are just some of the services at the Hollow Brook Riding Academy. For children above the age of 10 years old, there is a Cowboy Camp that runs throughout the summer, teaching the little ones how to work on a real dude ranch. Horses are also available to buy at the Academy, so if you're looking for your very own stallion, they're the ones to call.

The Complete **Residents'** Guide

38 White Hawk Trail
& Patterson

Inner Circle Farm

845 278 7395 | www.innercirclefarm.com

For professional training, and specialised instruction, call the Inner Circle Farm, where you will receive individual attention from trainers with many years of experience. The farm is set on 54 acres, with plenty of trails, and other services include grooming, stall cleaning, and even holistic horse care to make sure that your horse is in top form.

Allegheny Mountains

R&R Dude Ranch

716 257 5663 | www.recreationranch.com

Situated on 300 acres of privately owned land, The R & R Dude Ranch offers riding lessons, summer camps for children, and unforgettable thrills for adults. Amenities include country style meals, fishing sites, and even access to local ski areas. The R & R Dude Ranch is considered to be a 'working horse ranch,' so you can expect an authentic experience right out of the old west. By the end of your stay you'll be lassoing your steed with authority, and wearing your stetson like a pro.

Van Cortlandt Park
West 254th St &
Broadway
Riverdale

Riverdale Equestrian Center

718 548 4848 | www.riverdaleriding.com

Lessons and afternoon programmes for both children and adults can be scheduled at the Riverdale Equestrian Center, where you will find yourself deceptively surrounded by the beautiful country while still in the middle of the metropolitan area. The Equestrian Center is located on 21 acres in scenic Van Cortlandt Park, and is made up of 62 separate stalls, so you're guaranteed plenty of room for your four-legged friend.

Ice Hockey

Other options **Ice Skating** p.267

63 Fields Lane
Brewster

Brewster Ice Arena

845 279 2229 | www.brewstericearena.com

This arena offers open hockey sessions throughout the week for a $10 admission charge, unless, of course, you're a goalie – goalies get in for free. Safety gear is required, so make sure that you've got all your pads before heading over to one of their open sessions. The Brewster Ice Arena also hosts an adult hockey league, which is split up into separate divisions, and can accommodate players of all skill levels.

Pier 61
Hudson River
Chelsea
Map 6-B4

Chelsea Piers Summer Ice Hockey Camp

212 336 6100

The Chelsea Piers Summer Ice Hockey Camp accepts boys and girls, of all abilities, between 6 and 17 years of age. The camp includes individualised instruction and even video analysis to help improve every hockey skill. There is also an adult hockey league that is made up of three seasons: fall (autumn), spring, and the four-on-four summer tournament, as well as a spring women's league. Twelve-week instructional programs are available for players who are new to the game, but require that you have the basic skating skills needed to stay in control while on the ice.

PO Box 723
East Northport
Long Island

Island Ice Hockey

631 262 0543 | www.islandicehockey.com

This adult hockey league, located on Long Island, is divided into 15 different divisions, so there's a team for just about every level of player. Games are played in rinks all across Long Island, including the famous Nassau Coliseum, and arrangements can be made to fit almost any schedule. There is also a beginner's programme that takes place during the winter, and accepts both groups as well as individuals. Tournament players can take part in holiday and travel tournaments, and real aficionados may want to join in the hockey trips that are scheduled by Island Ice Hockey, which give you the chance to travel to other parts of the world and meet other players .

Rockefeller Plaza

Ice Skating

Other options **Ice Hockey** p.267

Bryant Park
Midtown

The Pond at Bryant Park

866 221 5157 | www.bryantpark.org

Skaters of all levels are welcome at this relatively new rink at Bryant Park (p.267), where the admission is free, and the sights are spectacular. Rental skates are available, as well as skating classes with both private and group instruction. There are also numerous skating shows that take place during the winter, so you may want to check their calendar of events before heading over. Admission is free of charge. Skate rentals are available for $7.50.

50th St
Btn Fifth & Sixth Ave
Midtown
Map 5-A3

The Rink at Rockefeller Plaza

212 332 7654 | www.therinkatrockcenter.com

This is one of the most picturesque rinks in New York, especially when the huge Christmas tree is lit. However, expect a crowd both on the ice and spectator side. Since this rink is such a popular spot for tourists, it may be best to skate outside holiday periods, when there are considerably fewer sightseers. Admission costs $10 for adults, $7.50 for children Monday to Thursday, and $14 for adults, $8.50 for children Friday to Sunday. Skate rentals are available for $7.50.

Central Park
Upper East Side
Map 5-A1

Trump Lasker Skating Rink

www.wollmanskatingrink.com

For the unforgettable experience of Central Park in the winter, head over to Trump Lasker Skating. The rink is smaller than it's big brother, the Wollman, so may be better for beginners, although there are fewer public skate times than at the larger rink. It's also very well maintained, so you can expect the ice to be in pretty good condition, with lots of expert supervisors gliding around. Lessons are available for group and private instruction, as well as a holiday youth skating camp for the kids, ice hockey lessons for all levels, and private events and parties. Admission starts from $4.50 for adults and $2.25 for children. Skate rentals are available for $4.75.

Central Park
Upper East Side
Map 5-A1

Wollman Rink

212 439 6900 | www.wollmanskatingrink.com

This large outdoor rink offers some of the toughest ice in the city so it may be a good idea to get your blades sharpened before skating. Walkmans are not allowed on the rink, but there are outdoor speakers that play music to help you keep your rhythm on the ice. It's quite the place to be during weekends in winter. The rink also runs skating lessons and courses, such as social ice dancing and figure skating, and customised parties and events. Admission costs $9.50 for adults, $4.75 for children Monday through Thursday, and $12 for adults, $5 for children Thursday through Sunday. Skate rentals are available for $5. Check the website for public skating times.

Jetskiing

Jetskis are becoming more popular with each passing summer. These personal watercrafts are fast, manoeuvrable and can be a lot of fun to ride when the conditions are right. Jetskis operate best in shallow water, on calm lakes and inlets, but advanced riders should have no trouble skimming through the waves of the Long Island Sound (an estuary between Connecticut and Long Island). Although there has been some controversy over the past few years regarding the safety of Jetski operation, these watercrafts tend to be a safe form of recreation, as long as the rider is responsible and follows the rules of the waterway. If you are unfamiliar with these basic rules, make sure that you ask your guide or rental facility for a quick briefing before heading out. It is also important to keep in mind that some rental facilities will require that you have a boater's licence before they rent Jetskis to you. If you aren't licensed, but still want to go Jetskiing, be sure to call the rental facility ahead of time to find out whether they will still allow you to rent one of their watercrafts.

91 Foster Ave
Hampton Bays

East End Jet Ski

631 728 8060

This rental facility comes with 25 years of experience, and offers safety instructions to make sure that your time on the water doesn't wind up being spent in traction. One of the advantages of this rental facility is that there is a section of private beach where you can enjoy your ride without having to worry about party boats or other water traffic. If you've never been on a Jetski before, then East End may prove to be a great place for you to learn.

West Lake Drive Ext
Montauk

Uihlein's Marina and Boat Rental

631 668 3799 | www.hamptonsweb.com/uihleins

Uihlein's offers many services to its customers, including guided tours on the water, and comprehensive Jetski instruction for those first time riders looking to get their feet wet. If you've never ridden a Jetski before, then it's always a good idea to take a lesson before going out on your first ride. You can better guarantee not only your safety, but also the safety of others on the water.

101 Whitehaven Rd
Grand Island

Waikiki WaterCraft Rental

716 773 5862 | www.waikikiwatercraft.com

This rental facility offers Jetski rentals to riders who are 18 years of age and older. Although a boater's licenceisn't needed to rent from Waikiki, you should make sure that they brief you on the rules of the waterway if you aren't licensed. Reservations are strongly recommended as the Jetskis are in heavy demand during the summer months – when the weather is cooperating.

Kayaking

Other options **Canoeing** p.258

New York's kayaking community is surprisingly large and enthusiastic about the sport. There are many kayaking clubs, and plenty of great places to paddle all across the state, as well as in the heart of the city. If you're more of a do-it-yourself kind of person, then all you really need is a kayak, pleasant weather, and a copy of the tide chart for your area. It's a great way to get away from it all, and build a killer upper body at the same time. If you don't have a kayak, there's no need to worry. Almost any sporting goods store in the city will either have kayaks in stock, or will help you order one from their distributor. If you are looking for a specific kayak, then you may want to consider ordering directly from the manufacturer. The best way to do this is by finding the

268

manufacturers website. Although this is probably the best way to get the kayak of your dreams, you should expect to pay a pretty hefty shipping fee.

Manhattan Kayak Company

Pier 63 Maritime
Hudson River
Chelsea
Map 6-F4

212 924 1788 | www.manhattankayak.com

The Manhattan Kayak Company is set on the Hudson River, which is home to some of the heaviest water traffic in New York. If you're looking for a real paddling experience, then you may want to consider signing up for one of their tours or instructional sessions. Membership at the Manhattan Kayak Company will cost you $2,000, but they also offer non-member private tours, as well as memorable sunset excursions at reasonable rates.

Kids' Activities

New York is a veritable playground for the big kid and the small, the child at heart or your regular energetic, sugar-fuelled bag of joy. Despite what you may think, there is plenty set up and fully stocked for the little ones. Warmer months are great in terms of entertaining the kids, since parks and outdoor activities are aplenty. But even during the winter season, NYC turns into a wonderland with ice-skating, twinkling lights and window displays, and the visits to Santa's Grotto in all the major department stores. The only downfall to this otherwise child-friendly city is the lack of stroller support on public transportation. Expect to rely heavily on the patience of your brood as you walk from spot to spot, or on taxis, which, though faster and more efficient, are slightly more expensive than other means of public transport.

Brooklyn Children's Museum

145 Brooklyn Ave
Brooklyn

718 735 4400 | www.brooklynkids.org

Founded in 1899 with a view to creating a space solely for the entertainment, education and creative inspiration of children, this is an exceptionally well organised, well-crafted approach to learning through play. Whether you go for a special exhibition, or just fancy messing about in their regular spaces, it's all an innovative experience that makes for a great day out. The award-winning, state-of-the-art facilities available at this venue also tour globally to other children's museums.

Children's Museum of Manhattan

The Tisch Bld
212 West 83rd St
Upper West Side
Map 2-E1

212 721 1223 | www.cmom.org

The museum has some cool and nifty parts to it, like 'Brain Games' for 5 years and up and an interactive exhibition called 'Playworks for Early Learning' for teeny babies to 4 year olds. There are programmes, workshops and classes that will keep the kids busy for hours if not days and then there are random playrooms like the 'Dora the Explorer' area, where your children can have adventures as neat as the little Latina heroine. There is a fabulous outreach programme here that makes every effort to include the city's disadvantaged children and their families, so donations are welcome.

Kids at Art

1349 Lexington Ave
Upper East Side

212 410 9780 | www.kidsatartnyc.com

Fancy your littl'un as a mini-Picasso? Head down to Kids at Art, a well-equipped art studio that caters for the creative, the mucky, and the downright messy. Kids aged 11 down to as young as 2 can toddle in (with parent or care-giver in tow). As long as they are prepared to pull up their sleeves and get dirty in the name of fun and art, they will be challenged and have their imaginations well exercised. There's even a gallery on the premises to display the works of genius that they create.

269

Manhattan Children's Theatre

52 White St
Btn Broadway & Church St
Tribeca
Map 10-F3

212 226 4085 | www.manhattanchildrenstheatre.org

This not-for-profit organisation was set up with the sole intention of developing affordable, high-quality theatre to entertain children and their families, particularly in the fields of classical and contemporary literature. There are classes and workshops available for mini-divas and their adoring parents, with the focus less on hissy tantrums and far more on fun. Stage performances are held regularly and clearly target certain age groups, so check beforehand to ensure that the production is suitable for your kids.

Paper Bag Players

25 West 99th St
Upper West Side

212 663 0390 | www.thepaperbagplayers.org

Founded in 1958, this company of kookie adults create and perform original theatre for children between 4 and 9 years of age. Their repertoire includes short plays and dances, and plenty of audience participation (followed by fits of giggles), with painting on stage and some super cool live ragtime music at every performance. Be prepared for a no inhibitions get-down-and-groove-on afternoon of fun.

Riverside Park

Riverside Drive
Btn 72nd & 153rd St
Upper West Side

212 360 1316 | www.riversideparkfund.org

Stretching some 81 blocks, from the river to the houseboats on the harbour, this is considered one of the cleanest and safest parks in the city with some spectacular views and super cool animal-themed activity spots. The Elephant Playground (76th Street) has a sandbox, swings and climbing frame and in the summer the elephants blast cooling water from their trunks. The Hippo Playground (91st Street) is fully equipped with playground facilities and hippo sprinklers. Don't miss The Dinosaur Playground on 97th, with one of the biggest sprinkler areas. Needless to say, you'll need a change of clothing.

Libraries

Other options **Books** p.314

New York City is home to over 80 different libraries, including four world-acclaimed research libraries, many branch libraries, four central libraries and a library for the blind and physically handicapped – so you won't have any trouble finding a quiet place to work, do some research, or seek out that hard-to-find book. Some libraries offer wireless internet access for laptop users, as well as computers for public use. If you are looking for a particular title, then it may be a good idea to call your local branch and ask them if they carry the book before heading over. If they don't have the title, then they may be able to direct you to the branch that does have it, saving you some legwork. Some libraries also offer programmes for children and teens, ranging from help with homework, to literary events involving authors of young-adult books. Libraries will also host events and exhibitions with free admittance (more often then not) that make for an interesting and fun day out for all the family. There are various ongoing adult classes offered free of charge, including computer training, English and literacy courses, help with research tools, and many others. Branch libraries also sometimes sell old book copies for a fraction of the price. For a full list of library branches, phone numbers, programmes, and available resources, visit the New York Public Library website at www.nypl.org.

A library card will allow you to do so much more than just check out materials. An NYPL card gives you online access to databases from home, plus you can reserve books and renew rentals from the comfort of your own swivel chair. There are two types of cards to choose from. A branch library card gives you access to databases as well as borrow items. The alternative is an access card, primarily used to request materials in any of the research library reading rooms. Research libraries are far more specialised with incredible collections to browse through. Both cards are free to residents and taxpayers of the state of New York. A branch card will cost non-residents $100 a year. Replacing a lost or stolen access card will also cost researchers (check with your local library for details of fines and penalties).

You can apply online or by mail (allow about a month for this method) and you'll need a photocopy of identification that shows your signature and current address, though not necessarily on the same document.

455 Fifth Ave
At 40th St
Midtown
Map 7-A1

Mid-Manhattan Library
212 340 0833 | www.nypl.org

You'll probably pass this structure a hundred times (it's the one with the big lions flanking the stairs) and you'd be really missing out if you didn't go in at least once. This is the largest library in the city with five floors stacked with all kinds of fabulous books covering thousands of subjects. The picture collection on the third floor is the largest of its kind with more than a million reference and circulating images, and the reading room is the perfect place to while away a cold afternoon.

Martial Arts

43 Park Place
Tribeca
Map 10-E4

Anderson's Martial Arts Academy
877 740 8132 | www.andersonsmartialarts.com

Pity the fool that messes with you once you've been to Anderson's. This is where you can learn how to protect yourself in almost any situation. Anderson's Martial Arts Academy offers classes in various different fighting styles, and is open to men and women of all skill levels. Students of the academy receive instruction from world-renowned instructors in various disciplines, and a selection of training videos will help them to sharpen their skills outside of the classroom.

385 Broadway
Tribeca
Map 10-F3

Bo Law Kung Fu Federation
212925 33 39 | www.bolawkungfu.com

If you don't have much experience with martial arts, but are eager to learn, then sign up for an introductory class at the Bo Law Kung Fu Federation. The introductory classes help gauge your level of ability, and will let you know whether or not you're ready to start working towards that black belt. If your skills are beyond the introductory level, then you'll be happy to know that Bo Law also offers programmes geared towards experienced students, as well as a masters programme for those students ready to take their skills to an even higher level.

147 Woodbury Rd
Huntington
Long Island

New York Martial Arts Hombu
631 549 9612 | www.newyorkmartialartshombu.com

For children who are interested in learning the martial arts, the New York Martial Arts Hombu provides instruction on the basic forms of karate, while maintaining an environment that is fun enough to stop the little ones losing interest. There are also programmes in women's self-defence, so this may be a good place for a mother and child looking to train as a crime fighting team.

271

The Sambo Combat Center

Sheepshead Bay Rd
Brooklyn

718 303 2632 | www.sambocenter.com

The Sambo Center is the place to learn a mixture of fighting styles without the use of weapons, such as staffs or swords. Their course offerings include judo, kickboxing, and many other styles focused on hand to hand combat (after all, if you get mugged down a dark alleyway, you might not always have your nunchakus immediately to hand). If you're looking to pick up some self defence training, but aren't interested in the hardware that goes along with some of the fighting forms, this is the place for you.

Mini Golf

Other options **Golf** p.263

Possibly the oddest game in the city, miniature golf (also called crazy golf or Putt-Putt) is the same as regular golf, although not really. Not only are the distances between the holes much shorter on a mini-golf course, but on a regular golf course you never have to aim for a clown's mouth or navigate your ball past the windmill – it's only in mini golf that such obstacles can make your game more challenging and a lot more boisterous. It makes for fabulous family fun and is highly entertaining, even after hours and hours of trying to get out of the bunkers. Try Coney Island's Go-Kart City (718 449 1200) and Staten Island Golf & Hockey (215 Schmidts Lane, 718 982 7660).

Flushing Meadows Golf Center

100 Fl. Meadows Park
Flushing
Queens

718 271 8182

The mini-golf course at the Flushing Meadows Golf Center is considered to be one of the best in Queens. The course is fully lit, and features 18 magnificently landscaped holes surrounded by streams, waterfalls, and other entertaining obstacles. It's fun for the whole family, no matter what age: The course is fun enough for children, yet challenging enough to keep adults entertained.

Jones Beach

Long Island
Queens

516 785 1600

Before you think this is too far out of the way for most New Yorkers, Jones Beach is just 33 miles from Manhattan, and makes for a nice weekend away or full day out during the summer months. The 18 hole pitch-putt course is just one of the amenities; others include shuffleboard courts, picnic and barbecue areas and, of course, the beach.

Mother & Toddler Activities

More and more New York parents are trying to veer away from constant nanny and care providers to try and raise their own kids themselves, or at least fit in more quality time with them. This is remarkably difficult in a city that is not only expensive but also massively cut-throat in almost every industry. It's not that easy to juggle work and family, but for those who do get to swing it, or for care-providers looking to broaden the horizons of their little charges, the city offers a varied array of programmes and classes aimed at toddlers and their accompanying adults.

A-Ha! Play and Learning Center

1624 First Ave
Upper East Side
Map 3-E1

212 517 8292 | www.ahalearning.com

Parent-child workshops are specifically crafted to incorporate foundational skills for infants using good old-fashioned fun. And it seems to work. Structured at Harvard, Play Labs are set up for little ones as young as 3 months to about 3 years, with programmes that are both themed and entirely immersive, pulling more from a child's individual drive and initiative than by any more forced methods.

202 East 86th St
Btn Second & Third Ave
Upper East Side
Map 3-D1

Just Wee Two

800 404 2204 | www.justweetwo.com

This is a programme perfect for children from 14 months to 3 years and their respective big folk, that combines developmental play with lots of interaction. Toddlers get to explore their surroundings through music, arts, crafts and story time – all solid, personality-building stuff. There are three sessions per year, each one lasting 11 weeks (one in fall, one in winter and one in spring), as well as a six-week mini-camp summer session. There are further locations throughout the tri-state area.

1059 Second Ave
Midtown
Map 5-D3

Moonsoup

212 319 3222 | www.moonsoup.net

Moonsoup is a whole bundle of fun rolled into one neat package. Walk in to the retail outlet and browse the shelves before stepping further inside to the play space and then a couple more steps before you reach the classes. It's a free-for-all with certain classes open to all ages (from teeny-tiny babies to 4 year olds) and the range of programmes includes Messy Art Mix, Romp and Music, Art, and Creativity and Play, each with an age suitability tag to match. Parents and caregivers are expected to stick around and join in with the party.

Mountain Biking

Other options **Cycling** p.259

Get the Best Gear
There are plenty of bike shops in every borough of the city, so you shouldn't have any trouble replacing those bent rims after a hard day's riding. See p.313 in Shopping for more information.

While some biking enthusiasts enjoy the parks and streets of New York, others are strictly trail riders looking for the adrenalin rush of zipping through wooded areas, nailing jumps, and catching some air. If you happen to be one of the latter, and are wondering where to go to get your bike muddy, then your biggest problem will be choosing where to ride. New York offers plenty of areas for mountain biking, and the trails cover a wide range of difficulty levels and length. Some trails are five miles long and ideal for beginners, while other trails have been measured at over 100 miles long, and will test even the best trail rider. If you're looking for other trail riders, there are plenty of organisations in New York that schedule group trail rides, as well informative sessions on all aspects of mountain biking.

Babylon

Belmont Lake State Park

631 667 5055 | www.nysparks.state.ny.us

Although the riding trail is only about five miles in length, the Belmont Lake Park offers a little bit of everything for trail riders. Biking through this park you'll find that there are many different types of paths and roads, and you may even encounter some puddles to splash through after heavy rain. Overall, the terrain is geared towards both experts and beginners, but it may be a good idea to ride through some of the paved roads at first until you're sure which of the gnarlier trails are best suited to your bike and your skill level.

273

Farmingdale ◀ Bethpage State Park
516 249 0701 | http://nysparks.state.ny.us
This park is where you can ride over 100 miles of marked terrain, so you won't find yourself making the same boring loops, and covering the same ground over and over again. The trails are well marked and maintained, and there are trails suited to all skill levels and abilities. Whether you're looking for sheer downgrades, or twisting paths, this park will have the terrain that you've been craving to bump over.

Huntington ◀ Caumsett State Park
631 423 1770 | http://nysparks.state.ny.us
If you're interested in a day of single track riding, then you may want to head over to the Caumsett State Park where you'll find almost 20 miles of these kinds of trails. The park offers a mix of wide turns that can be taken at your leisure, but there are also some difficult areas that require you to be at the top of your game. Since the majority of the trails in the park are single track, you should be cautious of other riders, especially around some of the sharper turns, and if you're just getting out on your bike for the first time.

Various Locations ◀ Concerned Long Island Mountain Bikers
212 271 6527 | www.climbonline.org
Concerned Long Island Mountain Bikers (CLIMB) is a group devoted to protecting the mountain bike trails on Long Island. Membership is for riders of all skill levels, and members can take classes which show them the proper way to construct and care for trails of their own. Great for bikers with a conscience.

Music Lessons

Some say that inside everyone there's a funky musician dying to get out. Music lessons can be the perfect way to unleash your inner rock god, and thankfully New York is the place to do it. No matter what instrument you want to learn, you can search for a teacher in your area on www.privatelessons.com. Just select your instrument, fill in your area, and the site will give you a selection of suitable options.

251 West 30th St
Chelsea
Map 6-E3 ◀ New York City Guitar School
646 485 7244 | www.nycguitarschool.com
No matter what you want to get out of your guitar lessons, the New York City Guitar School can do it for you – if you're a beginner, they'll teach you the basics, and if you're already an advanced player, they'll teach you how to rock your socks off. A block of 10 one-hour sessions will cost you $289 – this is for a group lesson with a maximum of five students. They can also do private lessons, either in your own home or in their studio.

321 East 69th St
Upper East Side
Map 3-D4 ◀ New York Conservatory of Music
212 717 9590 | www.nyconservatoryofmusic.com
Located on the Upper East Side of Manhattan, this school offers a wide variety of music classes for students of all ages and abilities. Classes are focused on the development of a student's potential, and incorporate numerous lectures and conferences throughout the semester. The lectures cover topics such as music theory, history, and appreciation. Individual and group lessons are available, and include instruction for violin, flute, guitar, keyboard, and many other instruments. Students are also given the opportunity to perform in recitals and competitions arranged by the Conservatory.

Orchestras/Bands

Other options **Music Lessons** p.274

American Composers Orchestra

240 West 35th St
Suite 405
Midtown
Map 4-F2

212 977 8495 | www.americancomposers.org
This is the only orchestra in the world purely devoted to music created by American artists. Performances are given in Carnegie Hall, and artists such as Michael Tilson have been known to make guest appearances with the orchestra. Other offerings include music reading lessons to help you appreciate your favourite songs on a deeper level, and their own radio broadcasts, which introduce you to some of the greatest American performers and composers of all time.

American Symphony Orchestra

333 West 39th St
Suite 1101
Hell's Kitchen
Map 6-D1

212 868 9276 | www.americansymphony.org
The American Symphony Orchestra performs in Avery Fisher Hall and their music can be appreciated by audiences of all types. This orchestra also performs at the Bard Music Festival (www.bard.edu/bmf, a festival to promote new ways of understanding the history of music to a contemporary audience, held in August at the Bard College campus, and in October at the Lincoln Center), as well as other venues in the metropolitan area. Their concert schedule showcases music by many of today's great composers, as well as the music that has been created by master musicians of the past. It's an excellent stop for lovers of classical music.

The Bronx Symphony Orchestra

2141 Muliner Ave
The Bronx

718 601 9151 | www.bronxsymphony.org
The Bronx Symphony Orchestra has been dedicated to performing free concerts throughout the metropolitan area for more than 50 years. The orchestra members come from various different backgrounds, and range from skilled artists to teachers and other non-professional musicians. Guest performers include youth groups from the area, and their concerts are made possible by grants and donations. For some of the brightest young voices in New York, check out one of the many concerts which The Bronx Symphony Orchestra performs throughout the year.

New York Philharmonic

Avery Fisher Hall
10 Lincoln Center Plaza
Upper West Side
Map 2-E4

212 875 5900 | www.nyphil.org
One of the most respected and listened-to orchestras in the world, the New York Philharmonic performs more than 150 concerts each year. Their many programmes include the Young People's Concerts, and their musical recordings make great gifts for just about any music lover. Even though they're called the New York Philharmonic, this orchestra doesn't only perform in the city but tours all over the world, bringing beautiful music to the ears of international audiences.

Paintballing

Cousins Paintball

Various Locations

800 352 4007 | www.cousinspaintball.com
With three locations in the New York area, you're sure to find an opening with Cousins Paintball. All players must be over 10 years of age to play at Cousins, and anyone under the age of 18 must fill out a Release of Liability form. If you've never played paintball before, make sure you pay attention to equipment instructions, as well as the safety rules prior to your first game so that you can ensure your safety on the colourful (and messy) battlefield.

Patterson

Liberty Paintball Games

845 878 6300 | www.libertypaintball-ny.com

In under an hour's drive from Manhattan, you can find yourself racing through the terrain and blasting away at opposing teams at Liberty Paintball. The minimum age to play is 10, and anyone under 18 will need parental consent forms to be signed before they are allowed on the field. Paintballs purchased outside of Liberty cannot be used on their facility, so expect to stock up on some when you get to their gaming centre.

Locke

Summerhill Paintball

607 898 4256 | www.summerhillpaintball.com

Summerhill Paintball's large field has plenty of obstacles to test your paintball skills. Gift certificates are available and make great presents for the paintball enthusiast, as are season passes for the diehard paintballer. If you plan on becoming a regular yourself, then a season pass could save you a good amount of money over the course of the season. Summerhill is closed on Sundays.

Photography

Photography is perhaps one of the most accessible art forms available today. Even if art was not your thing in high school, it's hard not to get excited when you get lucky and snap an amazing picture – even if it is only on your point and shoot camera. However, once your initial interest is sparked and you start trying to learn more about photography, you quickly learn just how much there is to learn, which is what makes photography such a rewarding, but often frustrating, hobby.

One of the best ways to accelerate your knowledge of photography is to join a photography club – apart from being able to tap into the knowledge of fellow members, you'll get the opportunity to go out on photo shoots as a group. Manhattan's International Center of Photography (www.icp.org) incorporates a highly regarded photography school that offers community programmes, continuing education programmes, and full-time courses.

Flatlands Ref. Church
3940 Kings Highway
Brooklyn

Brooklyn Camera Club

www.brooklyncameraclub.org

This super-friendly club welcomes all budding photographers, with no stipulations as to how experienced you are or how fancy your camera is. Every week they meet up for a different purpose: it could be a field trip or a workshop, a critique session (which is much more constructive than it sounds!) or a talk by a famous photographer. Surrounding yourself with like-minded photographers is one sure way to give your own pictures a bit more of the wow factor, so consider joining the club if you're open to plenty of face-to-face interaction and constructive discussion of your pics.

53 Broadway
2nd Floor
Financial District
Map 9-A2

Camera Club of New York

212 260 9927 | www.cameraclubofnewyork.org

$1,400 for an annual membership of this club may seem a bit steep, but once you have paid the fee you get to use their darkrooms (they have seven) for three four-hour sessions each week, at no further cost. You also get free admission to the many lectures hosted by the CCNY, which usually feature talks by prominent photographers and photojournalists. And you get discounts on the prices for their classes, should you wish to improve your skills (you can download a full class schedule from their website).

Online Learning

Don't forget online resources – they are a great way to improve your photography skills. BetterPhoto (www.betterphoto.com) is an excellent site with loads of free tips and tricks, a very popular monthly competition, and a series of highly recommended photography courses with an online instructor.

51 West 14th St
Meatpacking District
Map 8-F2

PhotoManhattan
212 929 3302 |
www.photomanhattan.com

PhotoManhattan is the place to go for both beginner picture takers and professional photographers alike. Darkroom rental is available to help you get those pictures developed, and one of their teaching techniques includes travelling through the boroughs in New York where you can snap away at some new scenery. Classes are open to everybody looking to learn some of the finer points of photography, and exhibitions are hosted to showcase student's work.

Pottery

120-33 83rd Ave
Kew Gardens
Queens

The Potter's Wheel
718 441 6614 | www.potterswheelny.com

This is an ideal workspace, complete with experienced teachers dedicated to you and your artistic expression. Classes are offered for many different forms of pottery, and include everything from ceramics to glazing. Instruction is given in relation to each student's skill level, so you can learn at your own comfortable pace.

2744 Broadway
Btn105th & 106th St
Upper West Side

Supermud Pottery Studio
212 865 9190 | www.supermudpotterystudio.com

Supermud is one of the best pottery studios in town, perhaps because of their somewhat unconventional approach to ensuring that pottery is as accessible to as many people as possible. First of all there's the classes: if you're a total beginner there's classes for you; similarly if you're an expert on the wheel they can still teach you some pretty nifty tricks. There are special classes for kids and for teens, and the parent & child classes offer a great way to get creative with your little one without having to worry about splattering clay all over your pale cream leather sofa at home. If classes are not for you, you could indulge your inner artist by simply painting a ready-made creation at the paint bar. Just select a 'naked' item (cups, salad bowls, plates, etc) and paint your own design on it – afterwards they will fire it for you in the oven and you can take it home. Or you could throw a 'mud party' for all your friends – you'll be given a project to make (like a mug or a windchime) and some time for refreshments. All materials are included.

Racquetball

Lexington Ave
At 92nd St
Upper East Side

The 92nd Street Y
212 415 5714 | www.92y.org

This facility features three racquetball courts, and even allows you to reserve a court online through their website. One-on-one lessons are available, given by professional players, to both help you sharpen your skills and to progress at your own pace. Group racquetball workshops are also offered at the Y, which can be a fun way to learn the game while enjoying the company of a few friends.

International Center of Photography

277

Various Locations

New York Health & Racquet Club
212 593 1500 | www.hrcbest.com

This gym offers three separate locations in the Metropolitan area with racquetball courts, so you get to decide where you play. Whether you're interested in a relaxed game, or you're itching to compete against others, you're sure to find what you're looking for. League matches are arranged through the club, and there are also tournaments scheduled throughout the year.

Rollerblading & Rollerskating

Various Locations

Inline Skate Classes And Tours for Everyone (ISCATE)
212 731 4805 | www.iscate.com

If you're looking for a place to rent inline skates, or if you need some lessons, then this is the place. ISCATE offers lessons for everyone, no matter how good or bad your skating is. Outdoor group lessons are available during the warmer months of the year so that you can enjoy those skates without having to wear gloves or a woolly hat. ISCATE also hosts The Lower Manhattan Skate Tour, which is a one-hour tour through some of the most scenic areas of New York (if you have good enough balance to look around).

Various Locations

NY Skate
212 486 1919 | www.nyskate.com

For some of the most cutting edge rollerblading and skating programs, call NY Skate and sign up for one of their many classes, tours, or social events. Classes will allow you to become the great skater you've always dreamed of being, while their tours will let you take in some of the wonderful sights around the city. There is also a Sunday Skate programme where you can meet other skaters from the area, while enjoying yourself along the Hudson River path.

515 West 18 St
Chelsea

The Roxy Rollerskating Rink
212 645 5156 | www.roxynyc.com

This indoor rink is open year round and offers both rollerskate and rollerblade rentals. One of the novelties of this rink is their Roller Disco that takes place on Wednesday nights and comes complete with all the trimmings to transport you back to the disco age. You must be at least 21 years old to take part in the Roller Disco, and a full bar is available onsite just in case you get thirsty. Instructional classes are available, so you may want to sign up for one before going to your first roller disco (and embarrassing yourself mid dance move).

Rowing

Various Locations

Floating the Apple
212 564 5412 | www.floatingtheapple.org

Floating the Apple sponsors frequent events for rowers during the summer time in New York. This organisation works to promote the rewards of rowing to the metropolitan community, and their events are held along New York's majestic waters. Perfect if you're looking to row in historic waterways and meet other rowers.

Pelham

The New York Athletic Club

914 738 9803 | www.nyacrowing.net

The New York Athletic Club Rowing team, with several championship titles, is one of most renowned rowing teams you can find. This club is targeted towards competitive rowers, and membership is for serious athletes looking to compete against other world class paddlers. Membership requires familiarity with racing, and applicants are assessed based on their skill level and track record. If you consider yourself to be at the top of your game, and are able to undertake an intensive training programme, then fill out an application form for this club.

Glenwood Landing

Sagamore Rowing Association (SRA)

631 673 8304 | www.sagamorerowing.org

The Sagamore Rowing Association is one of the most famous rowing clubs in America. They have hundreds of members and their initiation of numerous rowing related programmes has helped to make them one of the most distinguished clubs in the world. Club services include free coaching for beginners, launches, and much more. The club also hosts three regattas over the course of the year, and provides boat storage for both members and non-members.

Running

Whether you're a casual jogger who enjoys running through the park on Saturday mornings, or a professional runner looking to compete in marathons and races, New York has got what you're looking for. You can find everything from training centres with indoor tracks, to more than 1,700 parks in all the five boroughs, many with designated paths set aside for joggers, so there's a facility for just about every type of runner. New York is also home to dozens of marathons each year, with runners of every age and ability participating. If you're interested in meeting other runners, or taking part in group runs, then you'll be happy to know that there are plenty of running communities all throughout the city. Since both street and sidewalk traffic can get pretty dense in Manhattan, it's recommended that you run in one of the many parks or gyms, rather than dodging tourists and taxi cabs. Most parks will have tracks or running paths, and the majority of gyms in Manhattan feature specially sprung indoor tracks.

If you're looking for a running club to join, log on to the Running Network where you'll find a list of clubs by area (www.runningnetwork.com).

Montgomery St
To East 12th St & FDR Drive East Village
Map 11-F2

East River Park

www.nycgovparks.org

This park is the place to go to run in just about any type of weather, and features the amazing scenery of the East River. The quarter-mile track that can be found in this park is coated with rubber and offers superior grip for those rainy days. If you aren't into running laps, then you can enjoy jogging through the park grounds, which span over 57 acres.

The New York City Marathon

Anyone who is 18 years of age or older can apply to participate in this marathon, which is considered to be one of the largest marathons in the world. Approximately 90,000 runners from around the globe apply each year for the chance to compete in this race, which offers over $60,000 in prize money. With the starting line at the Verrazzano Narrows Bridge, and the finish line in Central Park, the course for this marathon spans five bridges, and all five boroughs of New York City. It's definitely not easy, but if you manage to finish it you've just had yourself a once-in-a-lifetime experience. For more info, see www.nycmarathon.org.

279

Various Locations

New York Flyers
www.nyflyers.org

With over 600 members and a non-competitive attitude, this is one of the largest, and friendliest, clubs in the city. Apart from their regular group runs (around the beautiful Central Park), they also take part in numerous social and charitable runs throughout the year. Annual membership costs just $25. For an extra $100, you can take part in the running classes held on Tuesday evenings.

9 East 89th St
Upper East Side

New York Road Runners
212 860 4455 | www.nyrrc.org

This extremely active club organises the New York City Marathon every year, which is one of the biggest annual events in the city, never mind the running community. As if that wasn't a big enough job, they spend the rest of the year promoting running as a sport, and offering support to nearly half a million runners around the country. Membership has countless benefits, including guaranteed entry into the NYC Marathon (if you are eligible), running workshops throughout the year, group runs, and member discounts on race fees and at certain retailers. Basic membership costs $40 per year.

Various Locations

The Reservoir Dogs
www.thereservoirdogs.com

The amusing name comes from their meeting place: most of the time, the meeting place for runs is at the bridge on the reservoir in Central Park. There are four group runs each week: on Monday, Wednesday and Thursday evenings, and then early on a Saturday morning, followed by brunch. Each group run focuses on a different aspect of training: some are more social, some are speed training runs, and others are recovery runs (surely the best way to recover from running too much… is to run again!). You can get a detailed schedule from their website.

461 Central Park West
Upper West Side

The Running Center
212 362 3779

The Running Center is a training facility for runners and offers programmes led by certified instructors. Training programmes range from beginner classes to marathon training. Other services provided at the Running Center include sports massage to help loosen up your muscles after a hard workout, and nutritional counselling to help keep you in top running condition.

Sailing
Other options **Boat & Yacht Charters** p.236

417 Hunter Ave
City Island
The Bronx

The Harlem Yacht Club
718 885 3078 | www.hyc.org

This club dates back to the late 1800s and is situated on the picturesque shores of City Island, near some of the finest stretches of water in the area. One of the advantages of this club is that their mooring areas are situated within the Eastchester Bay, which offers security against both high winds and rough seas. Aside from the usual benefits of most yacht clubs, The Harlem Yacht Club also arranges several social events for their members, where you're sure to meet other sailors, and make a few new friends.

37 West 44th St
Battery Park
Map 5-A4

New York Yacht Club
212 382 1000 | www.nyyc.org

With over 3,000 members, the New York Yacht Club is considered to be one of the leading yacht clubs in New York. Members can take part in numerous regattas throughout the year, and have access to two clubhouses, both of which offer a wide range of services. And since this club's history stretches back almost 200 years, you're sure to find quite a few old salts to swap sailing stories with.

Lincoln Harbor Marina

Sail NY
212 400 1668

If you're looking to sail through the scenic waters of New York Harbor, then you may want to contact Sail NY. This non-profit group provides sailing instruction, and organises races for members throughout the warmer months of the year. Since Sail NY is funded by grants and donations, you'll find that their membership rates are very reasonable, and that sailing through this busy urban waterway can be quite an experience.

Chelsea Piers
Chelsea
Map 6-C4

Steve and Doris Colgate's Offshore Sailing School
800 221 4326 | www.offshore-sailing.com

Whether you've never been aboard a sailboat, or you're an experienced sailor looking to sharpen your skills, the Offshore Sailing School has a course for you. Although this school offers courses for advanced sailors, such as performance sailing, they also offer a two-hour crash course to help you learn the basics of sailing within one intensive session. Corporate outings can also be arranged, and all sailors know that a day on the water is always better than a day in the office.

Salsa Dancing

Other options **Dance Classes** p.260

65-52 Myrtle Ave
Glendale
Queens

Lorenz Latin Dance Studio

718 418 5484 | www.lorenzdancestudio.com

This dance studio offers weekly classes in everything from salsa to ballroom. Group classes will teach you the basic steps, and are open to all levels of dancers, regardless of how clumsy you may be on the dancefloor. Intensive workshops are available at the studio, as well as children's programmes to help get the young ones moving their feet. The studio also hosts social events where you can meet other hip-shakers from the area, mid-dancefloor.

888 Broadway
Brooklyn

Salsa Salsa Dance Studio

718 602 1322 | www.salsasalsadancestudio.com

If you're interested in learning the various different styles of salsa, but not sure where to start, then you may want to stop by the Salsa Salsa Dance Studio for a lesson or two. Students of all abilities are welcome, and classes are split up based on each dancer's skill level, so that the proper instruction is given on an individual basis, without frustrating experienced dancers or embarrassing the newbies. Styling workshops are available for advanced students, and the instructors will show you how to pull off some of those fancy dance steps that you've always wanted to learn.

Skiing & Snowboarding

Catskill State Park
Nr Poughkeepsie

Belleayre Mountain

800 942 6904 | www.belleayre.com

Just less than two hours outside of Manhattan, Belleayre Mountain is a great place for that quick day trip, or weekend getaway. This mountain offers 47 trails, as well as terrain parks and a half-pipe for freestyle skiers and boarders. The trails at Belleayre are a mix of greens, blues, and blacks, so that skiers and boarders of all abilities will feel at home. Private and group lessons are available, so if you're feeling a little rusty you may want to sign up for one before hitting the slopes.

Northern Catskill Mntns

Hunter Mountain

800 486 8376 | www.huntermtn.com

With a 1,600 foot vertical drop, Hunter Mountain offers some of the steepest trails to be found in New York, but don't worry – there are also plenty of runs for beginners and intermediate skiers and boarders. A four-star resort can be found at the base of the mountain, and will give you ski-in, ski-out access to help you get on and off the slopes without having to fight your way through any crowds. Hunter Mountain also offers ski and ride programmes, and the instructors will do their best to have you carving through the snow in no time. With the varying terrain at this mountain, you're sure to find something suited to just about every age and ability.

Skydiving

45 Sand Hill Rd
Gardiner

Skydive The Ranch

845 255 4033 | www.skydivetheranch.com

For the ultimate adrenalin rush, head on over to The Ranch and let one of their fully licensed instructors give you a thrill like no other. The Ranch offers 'Instructor Assisted Freefall', also known as a tandem jump, so you don't have to worry about ripcords or altimeters, all you have to do is enjoy the jump! The price of your jump includes equipment rental and a quick briefing. For an added fee you can have your jump recorded and then transferred to either VHS or DVD so that you can watch your descent over and over again.

Soccer

332 Bleecker St
West Village
Map 8-D3

Downtown United Soccer Club

917 941 1480 | www.dusc.net

The Downtown United Soccer Club coordinates various different programmes for players between the ages of 5 and 19. This club is part of the Cosmopolitan Junior Soccer League, and teams take part in various local tournaments throughout the season. This soccer club also offers a travel league that gives players the opportunity to compete against other teams outside the New York area.

Park West Station
Wards Island
Upper West Side

Manhattan Soccer Club

212 502 3451 | www.manhattansc.org

The Manhattan Soccer Club is a youth organisation, and games are played on Wards Island. This club is made up of over 40 teams, so players of all skill levels are matched accordingly. A summer soccer camp is also available, and offers the right kind of training for strengthening those legs and sharpening your skills.

Various Locations

New York Ramblers

www.newyorkramblers.org

New York's first openly gay soccer club was formed in 1980 and is now affiliated to the successful International Gay and Lesbian Football Association (IGLFA). Membership is encouraged, and can be paid for online through their website (various options are available, including a financial hardship scheme). Non players can also take out membership, at a reduced rate. If you decide not to become a member, you can just pay $13 each time you attend a practice (members pay only $8). Everyone is welcome at the New York Ramblers, regardless of your age, skill level or sexual orientation, so why not go along? You can find out when the next practice is from the events calendar on their website. The venue changes, depending on the season (you play outside in summer and inside in winter). Your first two practices are free.

Do You Mean Football?

Most people may call it football (including the international governing body of the sport, the Fédération Internationale de Football Association, aka FIFA), but in the US it is known as soccer, to avoid confusion with American Football, p.253. Unless you want to end up wearing shoulder pads and clutching an oval-shaped ball, you should make the switch while in New York too!

Social Groups

Other options **Support Groups** p.162

Is it still possible to be lonely in a city of eight million people? Of course it is! But it is totally unnecessary to be so, especially since there is an unending list of social groups that have been set up just to help people meet each other. And that's not 'meet each other' in the dating sense (although there are plenty of online dating sites and singles' organisations in the city). Whether you are single or attached, straight or gay, male or female, or a new arrival or a native New Yorker, joining a social group can catupult your social life to new heights and land you right in the middle of a new circle of friends. If you're looking for people to join you in an activity (like running or cycling), try finding an activity parter on www.craigslist.com.

283

Various Locations

Eight at Eight Dinner Club
www.8at8.com

New York is home to some of the world's best, and most diverse, restaurants, but it's hard to make the most of them when you're always booking a table for one. Enter the Eight at Eight Dinner Club, a social organisation that facilitates dinner parties at some of the city's most interesting venues for a group of eight people (usually four guys and four girls). The group is not just eight names picked out at random: the clever folk at Eight match you to people based on your age, interests and background, so you should find yourself sitting at the fun table for a change.

Various Locations

The Lunch Club
212 477 3127 | www.thelunchclub.com

The Lunch Club began in 2001 when a freelancer living in the East Village got bored of always eating lunch by himself. He posted a message on a website, looking for total strangers who would be interested in getting together for lunch once a week. Three people attended the first lunch; today, the Lunch Club has 12,000 members, with an average of 300 new members joining each month. You don't have to pay a membership fee, although each Lunch Club activity involves a reasonable charge to cover the costs of that activity. And it has gone so much further than just lunch: Lunch Clubbers have bonded over movies, museum visits, rock climbing, dance classes and scavenger hunts in Central Park. There are a few simple rules: it is not a dating club, so don't come on the prowl; it is not a platform for free self-promotion, so leave your stash of flyers at home; RSVP and show up on time; and finally, have fun and make an effort to meet and mingle with as many people as you can! As soon as you sign up as a member (which you can do through the website), you will receive emails notifying you of upcoming events.

Surfing
Other options **Beaches** p.227

Check the Weather
If you surf in New York, you're obviously hard core. But no matter how tough you are, it's important to check the weather report and local tide chart before heading out to surf. This information, as well as other surfing news and articles, can be found online at www.newyorksurf.com.

Although you won't find giant swells or large tubes with curls, you can still catch plenty of waves at many of the beaches in New York. These beaches are mostly located on Long Island, and some of them are just over an hour's drive from Manhattan. The three main beaches for surfing on Long Island are Tobay, Gilgo, and Long Beach. Each of these beaches offers different riding conditions, and you shouldn't have any trouble finding other surfers to give you tips on how to ride each area. Since the water temperatures can get pretty low, make sure that you have a thick enough wetsuit to keep you warm. If you don't have a wetsuit, then you can pick one up in any of the surf shops found in New York. Apart from being an awesome sport, surfing often instils a certain social conscience among those who do it – perhaps it's the feeling of being so close to nature as you ride on the crest of a wave. Nevertheless, there are several organisations, inspired by surfing, that are dedicated to the preservation of the ocean. Have a browse around www.surfrider.org/nyc – they will get you involved in beach cleanups, public education, and some pretty cool surfing parties.

Swimming
Other options **Leisure Facilities** p.293, **Beaches** p.227

New York has plenty of places to go swimming. With the numerous beaches that can be found in New York, and since many gyms have pools that can be used by both members and non-members, you'll be able to swim year-round without having to join a polar bear club. There are also many Olympic-size pools to be found in Manhattan, and while the majority of them are open to the public, other pools are private and can only be used by club members. If you plan on swimming during the fall and winter, then it may be a good idea to join a gym or club that has an indoor pool, since the water can get pretty cold at these times of the year. There are also public swimming events, as well as swimming clinics, that are organised by The Manhattan Island Foundation. This organisation hosts several swimming races in the metropolitan area, and has helped to teach countless numbers of swimmers everything that they've needed to know.

A good all-round source for swimming information, whether you're looking for a coach, you want to become a coach, or you need to know where your nearest pool is, is Metropolitan Swimming (www.metroswimming.org).

Manhattan Island Foundation

Various Locations

888 692 7946 | www.swimnyc.org

This organisation promotes swimming with several big races throughout the year. But the biggest must be the Manhattan Island Marathon Swim – the brave competitors actually swim around the entire Island of Manhattan – that's an incredible 46.8km (28.5 miles). And not just any fool in a bathing suit can do it – to be accepted into the race you have to prove that you are medically fit and have completed a four-hour swim in temperatures of 18C (64F) or colder. And you're not allowed to use a wetsuit (brrrrr!).

Tennis

Other options **Leisure Facilities** p.293

Everyone for Tennis

Distract everyone from your awful backhand by looking cute in the latest tennis gear. See where you can buy it from on p.349 in the Shopping section.

The annual US Open, the final in the pro-tennis circuit's Grand Slam, fills Flushing Meadows' Corona Park in Queens with Tennis enthusiasts and celeb spotters (See Annual Events p.48). For two weeks at the end of every August the city goes tennis crazy. But aside from Grand Slamming in August, the sport happens to be mighty popular, with over 500 tennis courts serving the city throughout the year. You can play both indoors and out depending on the weather and where you go, with some courts based in gyms or health clubs and others in public parks. About 100 of these courts require that you get a permit to play, which costs about $100 for adults and covers the period of April to November (apart from that, it's free). For more information on getting your permit, click on to www.nyc.gov/parks or call 212 360 8133. Concessions are available for children and senior citizens. If you don't want or need a full permit, you can just as easily buy a day card for about $7 at the Central Park permit centre (East 65th and Fifth Avenue). Paragon Athletics, a retail outlet in the city, also sells permits to play. The permits or day tickets will allow you to enjoy public park facilities at the Central Park Tennis Center as well as Prospect Park's Tennis Center. A full permit will allow you to book a court in advance, whereas a day pass works on a first-come-first-serve basis, so best to pick a time not likely to be busy. You won't have a problem finding lessons with most courts having a list of recommended coaches.

Some clubs organise tennis leagues, while some have state-of-the-art training facilities to help sharpen your backhand, so shop around before joining somewhere full time.

The Midtown Tennis Club

341 Eighth Ave
Chelsea
Map 6-D3

212 989 8572 | www.midtowntennis.com

This club offers air-conditioned, Har-Tru courts for those hot summer days. Private and group lessons are available for all skill levels, as well as a Junior Programme, which is conducted by the Randy Mani Tennis Academy. Re-stringing and re-gripping rackets can be done onsite, and most jobs are guaranteed to be completed in less than a week. The Midtown Tennis Club can also host private tennis parties, as well as

285

corporate functions and tournaments. There are no membership fees at this club, so courts can be booked by anyone with a credit card.

New York Tennis Club

3081 Harding Ave
The Bronx

718 822 8854 | www.newyorktennisclub.com
'A haven within the city' – nearly literally since it's neatly hidden away in uptown NYC. There are six courts, indoor facilities, a clubhouse and parking facilities to keep members coming back for more, as well as patio areas beside the courts for you to watch games while enjoying refreshments. Programmes and tournaments are regularly organised, new members get introductory rates for the first season, and, unlike other New York clubs, you don't have to pay an additional fee every time you play there.

NY Junior Tennis League

58-12 Queens Blvd
59th St, Woodside
Queens

718 786 7110 | www.nyjtl.org
This is a non-profit organisation that has been encouraging youngsters since its inception in the early 70s. The folks at the JTL are very serious about developing your child's tennis skills, but are equally into reaching out to disadvantaged youth and instilling values of leadership, competition and fairness. There are various programmes and tournaments worth looking into, such as the Schoolyard Tennis Programme, which provides schools with free equipment, materials and even teacher training.

TennisNYC

Various Locations

www.tennisnyc.com
Touting itself as 'the number one tennis league' in the city, the group has an impressive array of programmes and cater for aficionados as well as first timers. They also have tennis workouts (otherwise known as Cadio Tennis Drills) and organise regular games and tournaments. Tennis is their lifeblood with events going on all year round, whether it's indoors during the winter or to the parks to enjoy some sunshine.

Watersports

New York is famous for big traffic jams on its roads, but its waterways can get pretty clogged up too. Watersports like wakeboarding, waterskiing, windsurfing and kayaking require plenty of open space and as little marine traffic as possible, so it's better to head over to the Long Island Sound – at least there you'll get your adrenaline rush from performing some gravity-defying tricks, and not from playing chicken with a commercial freighter. There are plenty of places along the Sound where you can hire a boat; it may be harder to find somewhere that rents out skiing or boarding equipment. There are regulations in place that require you to have at least three people aboard your boat at all times while wakeboarding or waterskiing.

Learn First

It is always sensible to take a lesson or two before you head out onto the open waters – there are numerous watersports schools that offer individual or group lessons, even if you're an absolute beginner.

Inverted Wakeboard & Waterski School

Loon Lake Marina
Marina Rd
Chestertown

518 744 9826 | www.invertedschool.com
This relaxed and friendly wakeboarding and waterskiing school is set right near a beautiful lake, so you are literally on the water's edge. They offer instruction for all ages and all levels, and are particularly well-known for their ability to instil confidence in children who wish to learn this adrenalin-filled sport. A one-hour lesson costs $95. Daily board rental costs $30.

Neptune Waterski Club

Centre St
Lewiston

866 464 2675 | www.neptunewaterski.com

No experience is necessary if you want to waterski at this popular and long-standing club – even if you've never tried waterskiing before, the patient and experienced teachers at Neptune will help you find your feet and make the most of this amazing sport. Once you've mastered the basics, you can move on to learning how to jump, slalom and even how to ski barefoot. The club has a membership scheme – annual membership costs $300 for the first year, and $250 for each subsequent year.

Western New York Windsurfing Association

Various Locations

www.wnywa.com

This small group of enthusiastic windsurfers get together regularly to windsurf and to talk about windsurfing. They organise races, picnics and windsurfing clinics, and welcome new additions to their club – even if you've never been on a board before. Their website provides a list of good launching sites, and perhaps one of their most important functions as a group is to lobby for better access to certain beaches and launching sites for windsurfers.

Windsurfing Hamptons

188 County Rd 39
South Hampton

800 830 6098

This full service wind and wave shop is centrally located around many of the best launch spots in New York, and they provide sales and rentals of top-brand watersport equipment. Their team of certified instructors give windsurfing and kiteboarding lessons for both individuals and groups. They also arrange events such as clinics, swap meets, and demo days that will allow you test out new equipment on the market.

Weightlifting

With so many different gyms and health facilities in New York, you shouldn't have any trouble finding the right place to work out. The majority of gyms will have exercise and resistance machines, as well as free weights and personal trainers to help you reach your goals. Some clubs will also offer nutritional counselling, helping you eat the right foods to help you meet your workout goals. There are also various weightlifting clubs in the area, and some of these clubs will organise competitions for both men and women throughout the year. If you're interested in competing, then it is probably best to join a real weightlifting club rather than just a gym – they will be more experienced in the technical aspects of the sport rather than just the kudos of being able to bench press twice your body weight. They will also keep you informed of upcoming competitions.

Lost Battalion Hall Weightlifting

93-29 Queens Blvd
Rego Park
Queens

www.lostbattalionhallweightlifting.org

This is not a club for those with just a mild interest in building some bulging muscles – this is for those who have a genuine interest in the sport of weightlifting, Olympic-style. Whether you're young, old or in between, the club's experienced (and super-strong) instructors can put you on a programme that will improve your results and encourage you to take your sport into the competitive realm.

Wine Tasting

Does your partner, mother or boss keep nagging at you to stay out of bars and get yourself a hobby? Wine tasting could be perfect for you! The delicate skill is harder to master than you might think, but even if you take a while to get the hang of it you should still enjoy tasting the various wines, learning about the regions where they are produced, and meeting fellow tasters.

NYC Wine Company

West 23rd St
Btn Sixth & Seventh Ave
Chelsea
Map 6-E4

212 647 1875 | www.nycwineclass.com

The art of wine tasting involves much more than holding your glass at the right angle and learning words like 'bouquet'. The NYC Wine Company holds some fascinating classes where you can learn about some of the finer points of wine tasting – like figuring out the difference between 'woody' and 'fruity'. They also host a series of regional wine classes, where you can taste wines from different countries around the world. Classes last around two hours, and usually cost $90.

Otto

1 Fifth Ave
West Village
Map 8-F3

212 995 9559 | www.ottopizzeria.com

Apart from organising wine tasting evenings in its enoteca (where you can taste up to five different wines during an hour's session), Otto also hosts some fairly involved wine classes where you can learn all about wines made in the various regions of Italy. Otto's wine director, Peter Jamros, takes the classes and imparts some of his expertise on Italian wines in a way that will explode the myth that wine tasters are a snooty bunch who speak a different language – his aim is to help you identify the wines you like, the reasons why you like it, and what other wines are similar.

Tasters Guild

230 West 79th St
Upper West Side
Map 2-F1

212 799 6311 | www.tastersguildny.com

The Tasters Guild in New York is a splinter group of the Tasters Guild International (www.tastersguild.com), which is known around the world for their wine tasting programmes. Membership is required if you are interested in taking part in the numerous tastings and wine related events that are held throughout the year. And if you are serious about wine, membership has some serious benefits: the NYTG organises tasting evenings, tours and cruises – not only will you be an expert in no time, but you'll get to meet loads of other wine tasters in the process. The Tasters Guild is one of the oldest, and most respected, wine tasting groups in the metropolitan area, so you'll certainly find plenty of experts here.

Need Some Direction?

The *Explorer Mini Maps* pack a whole city into your pocket and once unfolded are excellent navigational tools for exploring. Not only are they handy in size, with detailed information on the sights and sounds of the city, but also their fabulously affordable price mean they won't make a dent in your holiday fund. Wherever your travels take you, from the Middle East to Europe and beyond, grab a mini map and you'll never have to ask for directions.

The Wine Coach, LLC

19 West 72nd St
Upper West Side
Map 2-E3

212 874 0146 | www.winecoach.biz

Jim Greif knows his wines – and he's made it his mission to spread the knowledge. He can organise a customised wine tasting event for you and your friends, where you can learn about a specific selection of wines or various methods of making wine. He is also an expert in picking wines to complement various foods, so if you're hosting an important dinner, give Jim a call and he'll come round and tell you what wines to serve. Prices vary according to what wines you want to select for your tasting, how many people will be there, and what other special services you require. The standard package includes cheese and bread and all the equipment you'll need (Like spit buckets – you probably don't have a stack of those hiding out in your kitchen!), but Jim can also arrange for catering on request.

Spectator Sports

 sidebar **Jets or Giants?**
Although the Jets and the Giants don't get to play against one another that regularly, there is still plenty of healthy rivalry between their respective fans. If you're new to New York, finding out whether you are behind the Blues or the Greens may take a few games – but once you pick a team, you'll rarely go back.

Spectator Sports
If you're a sports fan, then you'll be glad to know that there various teams, stadiums, race tracks and tournaments that call New York their home town. Major sports like baseball and American football each have two separate teams that reside in New York, and each team has a large fan base. There are also two separate hockey teams in New York, along with one basketball team, and all this makes for year-round sports excitement. If you're more of a tennis fan, the USTA Billie Jean King National Tennis Center, hosts some of the game's most famous players and the annual US Open. Or if you'd rather spend a day watching the ponies, then you're sure to enjoy racetracks like Belmont Park, where you can catch two seasons of racing, along with the Belmont Stakes, which is the third leg of the Triple Crown. Tickets for sporting events can usually be purchased at stadiums, team websites, or through TicketMaster (www.ticketmaster.com), unless it's a major event that sells out quickly. Since New York is teeming with sports fans, you will find that this happens pretty often, so it's best to plan ahead, and to purchase tickets as early as possible. Don't buy tickets from scalpers on the street, no matter how tempting. It's illegal, the prices are inflated, and the chances of buying a fake ticket and being denied entry at the gate are high.

American Football
If you're reading this and you're American, you'll probably refer to this simply as 'football' – it's only in other parts of the world that it's called 'American football', so as not to confuse it with football, which Americans call soccer. Confused? Don't be – all you need to know is that this is a fast-moving, action-packed sport that involves plenty of bone-crunching pile-ups of grown men running towards each other at great speeds. It has its origins in the English game of rugby, although today the two sports look vastly different – not least because of the helmets and padding worn by American football players, a move that became necessary early last century after numerous players died on the field. It's a tough sport, and one that is not without its controversies (safety, pressure and steroids among them). But at professional level, it is safe to assume that close regulations keep controversy to a minimum so that you can just enjoy the thrill of each game.

New York Giants
Giants Stadium Meadowlands Sports Complex New Jersey

www.giants.com
The New York Giants play their home games in Giants Stadium, which is located in the Meadowlands Sports Complex. This team has won two Super Bowls, as well as numerous Division and Conference championships. The list of Giants Hall of Fame players includes football great Lawrence Taylor, along with many other notable athletes. Although the official team name is the Giants, New Yorkers have called them the 'Big Blue Wrecking Crew' for many years.

New York Jets
The Meadowlands 50 State Highway 120 East Rutherford

www.newyorkjets.com
The New York Jets are another football team that play out of New York, and like the Giants, they too use the Meadowlands Sports Complex as their home field. Although the Jets have only produced five Hall of Fame players in their franchise history, they have still managed to win one Super Bowl title, as well as four Division Championships.

Baseball
New Yorkers love their ball games. Baseball is big business in the Big Apple – it is home to Madison Square Garden, two teams with intense rivalry between them (the Mets and the Yankees), and one of the ultimate legends of the game – Babe Ruth.

289

The Complete **Residents'** Guide

Shea Stadium
123-01 Roosevelt Ave
Flushing
Queens

New York Mets

http://newyork.mets.mlb.com

'You Gotta Believe!' – the Mets are one of the best-loved sports teams in New York, and have played an important role in the history of the city: a Mets game was the first major sporting event to take place after the 9/11 attacks, and in an ending that would not be out of place in any Hollywood blockbuster, they came from behind to beat the Atlanta Braves in a much-needed, morale-boosting finale. The New York Mets play in the National League and their home stadium is located in Flushing, Queens. A new stadium is under construction, and is scheduled to open in 2009. In their league history, the Mets have won two World Series, along with four National League Pennants, and five Division Titles.

Yankee Stadium
161 St & River Ave
The Bronx

New York Yankees

718 293 4300 | http://newyork.yankees.mlb.com

Baseball greats such as Babe Ruth, Lou Gehrig, Joe DiMaggio, and others have played on the Yankees, which is considered to be one of the greatest teams in baseball history. This team is part of the American League, and in their 39 appearances, the Yankees have won a total of 26 World Series, while producing numerous Hall of Fame players. They have a huge fan base and some of the whackiest fans in the world – the 'Bleacher Creatures' are famous (or perhaps infamous) for their rowdy behaviour and characteristic chants, all done in the name of fun and love for the game, of course.

Basketball

Madison Sq Garden
4 Pennsylvania Plaza
Midtown

New York Knicks

www.nba.com/knicks

The Knicks are New York's home basketball team, and their home court can be found in Madison Square Garden. The Knicks have won a total of eight Division titles, eight Conference titles, and two Championship titles, and have also produced numerous players that have been inducted into the Basketball Hall of Fame. One of their most famous players is the legendary Walt Frazier, who eventually became one of the Knicks' most memorable commentators.

The Five Boro
The Five Boro Bike Tour is becoming one of the largest events in the city's cycling calendar. This 42 miler draws thousands upon thousands of people each year – not just the brave cyclists, but also the many supporters who line the streets. Find out more on www.bikenewyork.org.

Cycling

The New York Cycling Series, held in Prospect Park, consists of five different events, and draws participants of all ages and abilities. There is also the NYC Spring Bicycle Racing Series, which is held in both Prospect and Central Park, and consists of 10 races over an eight-week period. Each race offers some of the most exciting courses in the area, and will give you a chance to watch some great cyclists in action. Races are generally held during the spring and summer months, and since the venues may change for future races, it is always best to check with you local cycling organisation for the most up to date details.

Golf

The Oak Hill Country Club (www.oakhillcc.com) in Rochester has a long history of hosting major championships, including the US Open in 1989, the Ryder Cup in 1995 and the PGA Championship in 2003. Ben Hogan was one of the first big names to play there, and in 1942 he shot a round of 64, which remains the course record to this day. History was made in 2002 when the famous Black Course at Long Island's Bethpage State Park (www.bethpagecommunity.com) became the first public course ever to host a US Open. Tiger Woods got the trophy on that day, and in case you missed it, mark your diary for 2009, when Bethpage will once again host the Open.

Horse Racing

110-00 Rockaway Bld
Jamaica

Aqueduct Racetrack
718 641 4700 | www.nyra.com
Racing fans descend upon Acqueduct to watch the Wood Memorial, one of the introductory races to the Kentucky Derby. The course hosts thoroughbred racing throughout the year, no matter what the weather – there is a clubhouse on the premises to save you from the rain if necessary! If you get hungry then you can grab a bite at one of the concession stands, or treat yourself to a fancy meal in the chic Equestris Restaurant.

2150 Hempstead Tpke
Belmont

Belmont Park
516 488 6000 | www.nyra.com
Belmont Park is home to the world famous Belmont Stakes – along with other major events – and offers some of the most exciting horse racing in the country. This track is famous for its well-maintained grounds, and even if you couldn't care less about horse racing, it's a great place to spend an afternoon surround by beautiful green lawns and foliage. Belmont Park is also the only place where you can have a Belmont Breeze, which is the official cocktail of the Belmont Stakes.

Ice Hockey

1255 Hempstead Tpke
Uniondale

New York Islanders
516 501 6700 | www.newyorkislanders.com
If you're looking for some excitement on the ice, then you may want to check out the New York Islanders at their next home game. The New York Islanders are the only ice hockey team in the NHL that can boast at having won four successive Stanley Cup championships. This team's home arena is Nassau Coliseum on Long Island. The team has six players who have made their way into the Hockey Hall of Fame.

Madison Sq Garden
4 Pennsylvania Plaza
Midtown
Map 6-E3

New York Rangers
212 465 6000 | www.newyorkrangers.com
One name: Wayne Gretzky. Even if you live under a rock and know nothing about ice hockey, chances are you'll have heard of Wayne Gretzky, arguably one of the greatest players of all time and a Rangers team member from 1996 to 1999. This hockey team is regarded as one of the 'Original Six' NHL teams, and has won four Stanley Cup championships, but not consecutively. Dozens of Rangers players have been inducted into the Hockey Hall of Fame.

Tennis

The US Open
For more information on the 2007 Open and how you can get your tickets early, see www.usopen.org.

The Billie Jean King National Tennis Center is where you can watch some of the best players in the world as they compete in the United States Open tennis tournament at the USTA Billie Jean King National Tennis Center (www.usta.com). Attracting thousands of fans each year, and with millions of dollars in prize money, this tournament is surrounded by an atmosphere of excitement and anticipation, and is something that every tennis enthusiast should experience at least once in their lifetime. Tickets get snapped up very early, so keep an eye on the website (www.usopen.org) to find out when they go on sale. The 2006 Open was certainly a good one: Roger Federer took his third straight win; golden girl and undisputed tennis hottie Maria Sharapova wore a little black dress (how New York!) and proved that she wasn't just a pretty face; and the world bid an emotional farewell to Andre Agassi, one of the game's greatest.

Health Clubs

There are plenty of health clubs in New York, and each of them offer something different. Some health clubs are geared towards physical activities such as yoga and massage, while other facilities will delve into luxurious body treatments like aromatherapy and seaweed wraps. Membership will often include benefits such as reduced pricing, personal attention, and workshops or seminars which revolve around various health-related topics. It is also important that you choose a health club with an environment that is best suited to your personality and your goals. Some health clubs are very upscale, and offer an environment that is more like an expensive spa than an actual health club, while others are more low-key, and focus less on posing and more on getting results.

482 West 43rd St
West Village
Map 4-D4

Manhattan Plaza Health Club
212 563 7001 | www.mphc.com

There's no excuse for keeping those love handles at this temple of body sculpting: there's a whole mezzanine floor dedicated to cardiovascular equipment, a range of heart-pounding group fitness classes, and a 75 foot pool (with a sun deck, should you wish to get some colour on your newly toned pecs). If the thought of another mile on the treadmill leaves you feeling demotivated, sign up for a group fitness class. Choose from spinning, yoga, hip hop, Pilates, step and even belly dancing, for a new twist on working out. Nutritional experts are on hand to help you choose an eating plan to match your fitness regime, and there is also a team of personal trainers and massage therapists (handy for when you're muscles are aching after a heavy workout).

Sports Clubs

When it comes to sports clubs, you'll find that New York has a whole lot of facilities that offer everything from team activities to individual competitions. Some of these sports clubs will allow you to register as a team, and will then help to organise games against other teams in your area. Other clubs may simply provide an environment for games and leagues, but will leave the organisation up to its members. Many sports clubs offer a wide range of activities, and some clubs will even host excursions to other parts of New York for competitions or social outings.

Various Locations

The New York City Social Sports Club
646 383 8508 | www.nycssc.com

Do you want to have fun and meet new people, but you're tired of hanging around in bars? The New York City Social Sports Club is a friendly organisation that gets loads of people together in an environment that celebrates the active, fun side of life. Both guys and girls are welcome to participate in any of their activities, and winning your game should take a back seat to having fun. Many of the club members are sporty types, but there's no need to be shy about your throwing, catching or running abilities. Just do what everybody else is doing, and have a good time!

160 Columbus Ave
East Village
Map 2-E4

Reebok Sports Club
212 362 6800 | www.thesportsclubla.com

It doesn't matter what your preferred sport is – this club has dozens of sports and activities available to its members. Want to reach new heights? Try out their 40 foot climbing wall. Or take a two-legged spin around their rooftop athletics track. The club houses four different gyms, kitted out with top-of-the-range weight training equipment, as well as free weights and resistance machines. A bevy of personal trainers can help you improve your abilities in swimming, martial arts, and many other activities.

Gyms

Various Locations ◄

Bally Total Fitness

800 515 2582 | www.ballyfitness.com

Bally Total Fitness is one of the largest, and most progressive, fitness giants in the industry. With a total of 36 locations throughout New York, there's one near you. Facilities do vary from one club to another, but some of the things you can expect to find are play centres, swimming pools, juice bars, a massage station and a team of personal trainers. Their group fitness classes are amazing and include some very novel ways to get fit – try Kwando, a mix of kickboxing, tae kwon do and karate), or Boot Camp, which is a challenging, drill-based class that will give you the body of a marine!

Various Locations ◄

Crunch

888 227 8624 | www.crunch.com

If you are bored of the same old workouts, you're going to want to give Crunch a try. They have one of the largest ranges of group exercise classes available in New York (if not the world). All the favourites are there, but the range of unique classes is amazing. Some of the more unusual ones include their 'Bring It On!' class, which is a series of cheerleader-inspired fitness routines, and the super-sexy Cardio Striptease, where you'll use stripper moves to work your muscles. There are a few classes that have to be seen to be believed, like Cycle Karaoke, where you get to belt out your favourite songs while you (and your fellow class members) sweat buckets on a stationery bike, or Ruff Yoga, where you and your pooch can find inner peace together on a yoga mat.

Various Locations ◄

Dolphin Fitness

718 815 7900 | www.dolphinfitnessclubs.com

The equipment at Dolphin reads like a 'who's who' of fitness brands: Flexmaster, Cybex, Icarian, Streamline... they're all here to help you slim down, beef up or get fit. Nationally certified staff are on hand to help you find those long-lost abs and biceps, and they teach some pretty good group fitness classes too. Should you want to work out under the watchful eye of a trained expert, you can hire one of their personal trainers who can help you with everything from stretching to nutritional counselling (and making sure you don't lose count of how many reps you've done).

Various Locations ◄

Equinox Fitness Clubs

www.equinoxfitness.com

Equinox Fitness mixes all the benefits of a gym with the soothing amenities of a spa. Some of the features of the gym include group classes, personal trainers, and the latest in strength training equipment. The spa side of this club is where you can enjoy services like stone therapy and tropical body smoothies. Another feature of this club is what is known as Trip Equinox, which is a programme that arranges various activities around the world such as hiking in Ireland, or cycling in Italy.

Various Locations ◄

Gold's Gym

www.goldsgym.com

With over 600 facilities world wide, Gold's Gym is one of the largest chains in the industry. Their gyms offer the latest in exercise and cardiovascular training equipment, along with classes for spinning, Pilates and yoga. Although the gym has a tradition of weightlifting, you'll find that their facilities offer something for every type of exercise programme, and that their staff are knowledgeable and helpful. Recently, Gold's Gym has teamed up with The American Diabetes Association to initiate a programme known as Fight Diabetes with Fitness.

293

Well-Being

The flip side to New York's accelerated pace is its well-rounded world of well-being, with a plethora of possibilities to ease off the fast track, wind down and, if you so desire, be pampered to within an inch of your life (think luxuriating in a bath of rose petals while your shoulders are massaged with scented oils). New Yorkers are nothing if not driven, and looking good is a powerful motivator. For toned abs and torso – oh, and inner calm – many turn to pilates and yoga, among other core-strengthening exercises, which now often supplant more traditional workouts.

Hairdressers	
Hair Papillon	212 448 7383
J. F. Lazartigue	212 288 2250
Jean Louis David	212 808 9117
John Frieda	212 327 3400
Josephine	212 223 7157
K. E. Haas Hair Salon	212 228 2550
Linda Tam Salon	212 757 2555
Prive	212 274 8888
Rodolfo Valentin Salon	212 327 4227
Supercuts	212 447 0070
Vidal Sasoon	212 535 9200
Warren Tricomi	212 262 8899

Hairdressers

On the surface, it may seem as though fabulous shoes were the real co-stars of *Sex and the City*, but heavenly hairdos were also an important contender. New York has long been at the forefront of trendy tresses, and you'll find a slew of cutting-edge – quite literally – salons where stylists can give you hair just like, well, name your celebrity. Popular these days? The 'Jessica' (Simpson) – for those who want the Texas beauty queen look. Of course, the top-notch places will cost you top dollar – celeb stylists like Frederic Fekkai command $600 for a snip session. But that's just one end of the spectrum – you'll find an enormous range of salons where you can get an excellent cut and colour no matter what your budget.

Arrojo Studio

180 Varick St
Nr King St
West Village
Map 10-E1

212 242 7786 | www.arrojostudio.com

Walk into celebrity stylist Nick Arrojo's studio, and you'll dare to do something different with your hair. The hip, youthful staff – each with their own unique, spiky 'dos – snip, fluff, blow-dry and colour hair at their stainless steel workstations, humming along to the jaunty soundtrack. You'll be humming too, as your scalp is massaged and your hair lathered with fragrant shampoo, which is just the warm-up to the main act. The studio team trains for 18 months in Nick Arrojo's exclusive programme – put your hair in their hands, and you'll emerge with a style that's definitely a cut above.

When Nick himself wields the shears, it's pricey – about $400 – but otherwise you can get a cut for a very decent $80.

Bumble and bumble

415 West 13th St
Washington & 9th Ave
Chelsea
Map 5-C2

212 521 6500 | www.bumbleandbumble.com

Hair salons come and go in New York City, but the playful-meets-professional Bumble and bumble is here to stay. The salon's legions of silky-haired fans will make sure of that. Around since the 1970s, Bumble and bumble has managed, impressively, to not only survive in a cut-throat city like New York, but also to maintain its trend-setting status, from one decade to the next. The sassy salon is particularly popular with fashionistas and models, but its reasonable prices and anything-goes attitude also draw plenty of free-thinking gals on budget. And even if you're not in the market for a cut and colour, the top-notch Bb product line is reason enough to stop by. Try their super-rich conditioner for glossy locks, or go for a whole new hairdo with their thickening and styling sprays or 'Sumo wax'.

712 Fifth Ave
Midtown
Map 5-A2

Frederic Fekkai

212 753 9500 | www.fredericfekkai.com

Celebs and socialites flock to the dashing A-list stylist Frederic Fekkai, whose shrine to haute hair sits on the top floor of the posh Henri Bendel department store. The Fekkai experience begins in the luxurious waiting room, which is decked out in plush couches and animal rugs. Head into the sleek salon and you'll see gleaming rows of work stations, where Manhattan's upper crust – and anyone else who can fork out the dough – enjoys pampering from their follicles to their nails. While Fekkai only comes through several times a year to actually cut hair, his well-oiled team executes the master's style – sleek, modern cuts – with panache.

746 Madison Ave
Btn 64th & 65th Ave
Upper East Side
Map 5-B1

Oscar Blandi

212 988 9404 | www.oscarblandi.com

These days, the most coveted beauty appointment in town is with the dashing Italian stylist Oscar Blandi, who has created 'looks' for loads of stars, from Reese Witherspoon to Renee Zelwegger. Even with his off-the-charts celeb status, Blandi's Madison Avenue salon is refreshingly casual, drawing inspiration from his home country. Natural light floods the second-floor salon of exposed brick walls and colorful Tuscan mosaics. Blandi's recently unveiled line of products, from shampoos to gels, are equally homegrown, incorporating natural ingredients like wheat protein and sea algae.

342 West 14th St
Btn 8th & 9th Ave
Chelsea
Map 8-D2

XO Blow

212 989 6282 | www.xoblow.com

Having a bad hair day? Don't cancel your hot date yet – pop by XO Blow Styling Salon where the speciality of the house is, you guessed it, blow-outs. Walk in with limp locks, and walk out with a glam head of hair that'll blow your date away. The cheery, pink salon was created by three thirtysomething gal pals, who saw a need for affordable blow-outs and decided to do something about it. They also offer a flat iron treatment for slick, straight hair, rollers for bouncy curls, and retro 'dos like chignons or French twists. Plus, there are manicures for girls on the go, including a 'quick' change of polish for $8, and waxing from head to toe and 'everything in between'.

Health Spas

Other options Massage p.298

When the urban jungle is getting you down, you'll find that there's nothing a floral body wrap or champagne manicure can't cure. Disappear into the soothing sanctum of one of New York's select spas, and you'll emerge revitalised (and probably with the cleanest pores around). New York is no stranger to excess – and its spas certainly fit the bill, with a wide selection of pamper palaces where uniformed experts will cater to your every whim. Day spas are particularly popular in New York, catering to the legions of professionals who need to fit in a facial on their lunch hour. The latest trend is 'medispas', where clinical treatments (laser lifts, collagen, botox) are offered alongside the more pleasurable wraps and facials. Note that most spas offer packages where you can enjoy several treatments at a lower price. And, if you'd like to share the spa experience with your honey, bond over a couples' massage, offered by many spas.

295

Acqua Beauty Bar

7 East 14th St
Union Square
Flatiron District
Map 8-F2

212 620 4329 | www.acquabeautybar.com

For a taste of paradise, Asian style, head to the peaceful Acqua Beauty Bar and treat your face to a botanical purifying facial. Or, try the 'Garden of Eastern Delights', which includes a shiatsu massage and a mist facial. Top it off with an Indonesian 'ritual of beauty' where your skin is scrubbed with ground rice and kneaded with fragrant oils. Those with sensitive skin will love threading, a gentle and effective alternative to waxing, after which hair growth is much finer. And, if you want to look like you spent the summer in Saint Tropez, try the twinkle tan, which will leave you looking sun-kissed – with a sexy shimmer.

Affinia Wellness Spa

The Benjamin Hotel
125 East 50th St
Midtown
Map 5-C3

212 715 2517 | www.thebenjamin.com

The outside world fades away the moment you step into peaceful Affinia. Slip on a fluffy robe, slide your tired feet into soft slippers, sip a warm herbal tonic and then let the spa therapists work their magic. Affinia is all about relaxation and harmony, and the treatments are tailored to the New York demographic – pressed-for-time professionals – with such treatments as the 'shopper's relief' for weary feet and calves, with a rosemary tonic followed by exfoliation and hydration in heated booties. The massages are so dreamy that you may find it hard to stop at just one. The East meets West massage combines Shiatsu and acupressure, while the deep Swedish massage will leave your body tingling from your scalp to your toes.

Babor at Takashimaya

693 Fifth Ave
Btn 54th & 55th St
Midtown
Map 5-A2

212 350 0119

This small, sumptuous spa – with soft leather sofas in the flower-filled waiting room – sits on the sixth floor of the posh Takashimaya department store. Try the luxurious champagne manicure, where champagne yeast extracts are combined with Chinese herbs to strengthen nails and regenerate and plump up the skin. The facials are similarly decadent (and addictive). Treat yourself to the heavenly, 80 minute Sea Creation facial, which incorporates sea shells and fragrant lotions to invigorate cells – and turn back time for your skin. Extend your soothing spa experience with a warm herbal tea at Takashimaya's relaxing Teabox Café.

Bliss

568 Broadway
Soho
Map 10-F1

212 219 8970 | www.blissworld.com

Money may not buy happiness, but it can buy you bliss (for a couple of hours, anyway) at the soothing Bliss Soho. Saunter through the spa, done up in soft blues and greys, and pick your pampering, like a carrot and sesame body buff, a hot salt scrub or a super blissage, a full-body massage like no other. Bliss also offers 'groom service' for the guys, including the cheekily named 'homme improvement', an energising facial, including blackhead eliminations, for men. Tired of battling cellulite? Try the 'high thighs' treatment, which includes an orange peel rub to tackle toxins and a seaweed mask. Their manis and pedis are pure decadence: go for the hot milk and almond or double chocolate pedicure, and you'll skip out with the prettiest tootsies in town. You'll also find Bliss on 57th Street and on Lexington Avenue.

Cornelia Day Resort

663 Fifth Ave
Btn 52nd & 53rd St
Midtown
Map 5-A3

212 871 3050 | www.cornelia.com

The reigning queen of New York's day spas has set the bar – and high – for its competitors. Rising over Fifth Avenue, the swank resort boasts a relaxation 'library' with soft leather couches, champagne and nibbles like grapes on toothpicks, and a sun-kissed roof garden with soaking baths. The woman behind this lavish venture is the Romanian beauty expert Cornelia Zicu, known for her signature facials, among other treatments. Deep-cleansing facials – with exfoliations and extractions – are customised to suit your skin, and incorporate vitamins, plant proteins and antioxidants. While you receive your facial, another therapist massages the rest of your body from your arms down to your feet.

Four Seasons Hotel Spa

57 East 57th St
Midtown
Map 5-B1

212 758 5711 | www.fourseasons.com

The Four Seasons name is synonymous with luxury – and nowhere is this more evident than in the cool-toned hotel spa. The sleek, low-lit waiting room, with its crystal vases of fresh-cut flowers, offers a hint of what awaits within the plush treatment rooms. The massage menu, for starters, leaves you spoiled for choice, including the signature therapeutic massage – shiatsu, aromatherapy, Thai and reflexology. Or, indulge in a hot-stone massage, where a deft therapist places warmed lava stones on key points of your body while deep-kneading your muscles. Once pummelled into submission, try the 'Four Seasons in One' treatment, with four pamper cycles, each related to a season of the year, from winter's cooling scrub to spring's floral body wrap. Suffering from jet lag? Revive yourself with their jet lag special, with hydrating gels and an ayurvedic scalp massage.

Great Jones Spa

29 Great Jones St
Nolita
Map 9-A4

212 505 3185 | www.greatjonesspa.com

Who says the granola crowd doesn't need pampering? The haute-hippie Great Jones Spa, with its organic purifications, chakra-light steam room and raw-food cafe, appeals to the bohemian-chic brigade who may shudder at the thought of processed anything, but aren't opposed to a lavender footbath and pedicure (and make the polish vampire-red, please). The Nolita neighbourhood, with its funky boutiques and veggie-friendly eateries, fits the spa like a glove. After a splash in the cold plunge pools and a naturopathic river-rock facial, you can browse the nearby shops for patchouli incense and continue the crunchy theme at home.

Haven Spa

150 Mercer St
Soho
Map 10-F1

212 343 3515

After a hard day's shopping in Soho, rejuvenate at the soothing Haven. From the airy waiting area, with its long, squishy couches and dim lighting, to the hushed, gleaming treatment rooms, Haven feels worlds away from the downtown bustle. The creative spa menu includes the Body & Sol (exfoliation and sunless tanning), the Forbidden Fruit, a lemon scrub followed by a lather in fruity emollient cream, and the perennially popular Hot Chocolate, with a warm milk mask and a gentle application of chocolate hydrating cream. Hands and feet are particularly pampered at Haven. Indulge in the Haven Foot Renaissance, a foot facial extraordinaire of a luxurious hydrating wrap and a moisturising massage. After this, you'll be ready to pound the Soho cobblestones for round two of shopping.

The J Sisters

35 West 57th St
Midtown
Map 5-A2

212 750 2485 | www.jsisters.com

The perennially popular spa J Sisters is the brainchild of seven Brazilian-born sisters who have made their name with their excellent waxings, which are relatively pain free and long lasting. The full-leg wax brings new meaning to smooth, and when summer approaches, try the popular Brazilian wax, perfect for your itty-bitty bikini. Those with sensitive skin might try threading, a fast, effective method of hair removal, often used

297

for trimming and sculpting eyebrows. The J Sisters also offer superb facials, manicures and pedicures. Nothing's rushed around here – the sisters are known for taking time with, and loving care of, each client. If you're popping in for a pedi, expect to have your toes pampered for up to two hours, including a deep cuticle treatment with scented lotions. You'll float all the way home.

60 East 56th St ◀

Btn Park & Madison
Ave
Midtown
Map 5-B2

Juva MediSpa

212 688 5882 | www.juvaskin.com

The well-established Juva MediSpa – part clinic, part comfort zone – is serious about skincare. Under the guidance of distinguished Dr Bruce Katz, who is the Director of the Cosmetic Surgery and Laser Clinic at Mount Sinai Hospital, Juva offers a full range of physician-formulated treatments, including chemical peels, eyelifts and laser procedures for aging, sun-damaged and loose skin. A facial here is more than just pampering and pore-cleansing – it's a two-hour-plus ritual that includes careful extractions, a hydrating mask and a sonic brush scrub. Curious about Botox? This pioneering spot is the place to do it. An extensive consultation is the first step, and the injections are adjusted to fit the needs of the patient, so there's no danger of the 'frozen look'.

320 East 52nd St ◀

Midtown
Map 5-D3

Mario Badescu

212 758 1065 | www.mariobadescu.com

Celebrities from Antonio Banderas and Sharon Stone to Cher and Oprah adore super-stylist Mario Badescu, whose facials and body scrubs, made with fresh fruits like plump raspberries and strawberries, are as popular as his products, which make for great gifts – or for some home pampering. Badescu's potions blend medical properties with lavish lotions, like a creamy collagen cream or a hydro-moisturiser infused with Vitamin C. Before walking out with your beauty bounty, head into the relaxing salon and indulge in a reflexology massage. Steady pressure is applied to points in the feet that correspond to different body parts and organs, which facilitates flow of energy and relieves tension.

1 Park Ave ◀

Btn 32nd & 33rd St
Midtown
Map 7-B2

Oasis Day Spa

212 254 7722 | www.oasisdayspanyc.com

New Yorkers can't keep humming at high gear without recharging their batteries every once in a while – and for that, they turn to Oasis Day Spa, with such indulgent treatments as the Vichy shower, which improves circulation, revitalises skin and limbers up sore muscles. If you have sensitive skin, the citrus crystal scrub will do you right – soft exfoliation with orange and grapefruit citrus along with fine-grain mineral crystals leave your skin smooth and stimulated. Men deserve pampering too, and Oasis offers up a slew of services just for the guys, like the brown-sugar scrub, a muscle-meltdown massage and a gentleman's facial, which includes deep cleaning and exfoliation. Lovebirds will want to try the couple's massage, where you'll both receive an hour-long Swedish massage, after which the therapist which teach you now to massage each other at home.

Massage

Other options **Health Spas** p.295

Unwinding in the concrete jungle can be a challenge. When a hot bath and a glass of wine just isn't cutting it, take it up (or rather, down) a notch and indulge in a massage. Better yet, do a couples' massage with your honey. Most spas (p.295) include massages in their repertoire, while for a massage on the go, try the therapists who set up makeshift sidewalk chairs in areas with plenty of foot-traffic, like Chinatown and Soho. At spa salons, a full-body massage generally starts at around $60–80.

Essential Therapy

122 East 25th St
Btn Park & Lexington Ave
Gramercy Park
Map 7-B4

212 777 2325 | www.essentialtherapyny.com
Athletes, dancers and models – the Mets, the Rockettes and Linda Evangelista among them – swear by the massages at this colourful, Indian-themed bi-level studio. Thanks to owner Carlos Araque, a former dancer and massage therapist of the Mets, Essential Therapy boasts the finest massages in the city, designed to provide long-lasting therapeutic results. Alleviate chronic tension with the deep-tissue massage; feel the warmth from hot stones penetrate the entire curvature of your back; relieve your weary neck and back with a craniosacral therapy session; and increase flexibility and reduce pressure on joints with stretching sessions.

Graceful Services

1097 Second Ave
At 58th St
Midtown
Map 5-D2

212 593 9904 | www.gracefulservices.com
The sighs of pleasure emanating from the massage rooms at Graceful Services offer a tantalising hint of what awaits within. Forget rose petals and champagne – this spare but comfortable spot eschews spa add-ons, focusing instead on the art of massage, pure and simple. Give in to a 'four hands' session, when two deft therapists pummel your entire body into tingling submission, from your scalp to the balls of your feet; indulge in a deep-tissue massage – Chinese, Swedish or Shiatsu; or try the invigorating Guasha, where a piece of bull's horn is scraped along the spine to release tension. Thanks to their keep-it-simple credo, the price is right, at $50 for a 45 minute massage.

Nail Bars

Having fabulous nails is practically de rigeur in New York, and with a salon or nail bar on just about every street, there's no excuse for scruffy fingers and toes. You can go 'froofroo' in opulent surroundings with high-end interior design and well-dressed 'nail artistes', or you can go for straight-up, no-frills service in cheaper (but still good) nail bars. If you can find a good nail bar in your area, this obviously cuts the risk of nail polish mush, but don't be surprised when you find out that any true New Yorker dedicated to dreamy nails is quite prepared to go across town for a coveted appointment with a favourite nail technician.

Artisan Spa

143 Fourth Ave
East Village
Map 9-A2

212 260 1338 | www.artisanspa.com
It's so much more than just a nail bar, but the nail technicians at Artisan will have your fingertips looking super sexy in no time. With so many colours to choose from, and an interior that caters to pampering, it's no surprise that New York women line up to get their nails done here. Prices are surprisingly low – a manicure can be had for as little as $10, and if you want nails that are not just beautiful but unique, you can get special designs applied to them for just $3 per nail. Don't forget your nails further south – spa pedicures are a brilliant way to unwind, thanks to the bit of reflexology that is thrown in. Foot scrubs and relaxing soaks will undo all the damage those gorgeous-but-cruel Jimmy Choo sandals have inflicted throughout the day. Artisan offers regular special promotions, so keep your eyes peeled for good deals.

Dashing Diva

41 East 8th St
West Village
Map 8-F3

212 673 9000 | www.dashingdiva.com
A whirl at this salon (more of an emporium, actually) is a rite of passage rather than a quick two-stroke lacquer job. If your natural nails are nothing to be ashamed of, you

299

can opt for a basic manicure or pedicure to get them tidied up and painted in one of the season's hottest shades. But if your nails look like werewolves have been using them as toothpicks, then help is at hand in the form of 'Virtual Nails' – glamorous falsies that come in over 100 pre-decorated styles. Prices are reasonable: a basic manicure starts at around $10. The salon's bright pink decor is a haven of girliness, and you'll promise yourself that you'll return at least once a week to get in touch with your inner diva. But guys are not excluded totally: Dashing Diva does a great range of manly manicures to make sure your handshake is not just firm, but tidy too!

Pilates

Other options **Yoga** p.301

All you have to lose are those extra pounds. Move over Stairmaster – for a toned stomach, thighs and buttocks, Pilates is a proven way to go. Named after Joseph H. Pilates, a boxer and dancer who practiced yoga and meditation, Pilates incorporates precise movements to stretch and strengthen muscles, focusing on the body's energy core of the torso and abdomen. You'll find Pilates studios – for all levels – scattered throughout the city. Prices start at around $15–25 per class.

49 West 23rd St
Btn Fifth & Sixth Ave
Chelsea
Map 6-F4

Power Pilates

212 627 5852 | *www.powerpilates.com*

The success of this established Pilates programme, with studios throughout Manhattan, hinges on its top-notch, classically trained instructors. Power Pilates classes are centred on the principle that the body's core – or powerhouse – needs to be strong, steady and ready before the peripheral parts can be worked out. For a personalised introduction to Pilates, beginners are encouraged to try a private Pilates session, where they can learn the basics one-on-one with a teacher. After that, try a Tower class, which involves deep stretches while strengthening the abdomen. Keep it up and you'll have abs – and buns – of steel.

33 Bleecker St
Btn LaFayette & Bowery
Noho
Map 11-A1

re:AB

212 420 9111 | *www.reabnyc.com*

Whether a Pilates amateur or pro, you'll be warmly welcomed at this cheery, plant-filled studio owned by fitness diva Brook Siler, who authored the popular The Pilates Body. The beginner mat class teaches newcomers the basic principles of Joseph Pilates' system – abdominal control, breathing, centering, precision and posture, along with the use of arm weights. For a creative approach, try the Magic Circle class, which incorporates a resistance ring to challenge your strength and stability. And if you want to focus on stretching, go for the super stretch mat class, which will limber you up in no time.

Reiki

The ancient Japanese healing art of reiki involves a laying-on of hands technique to activate the 'rei', or spirit, and 'ki', a life force energy. After a session with a reiki practitioner, you're said to feel deeply relaxed and simultaneously recharged and aware. Reiki can aid in maintaining good health and also alleviate mental and emotional distress and chronic physical ailments. Sessions generally last from 30 to 60 minutes, and can cost anywhere from around $70 to $150 or more. You'll find

Reiki

Name	Address	Phone	Website	Area
New York Awareness Center	125 West 72nd St	866 522 5886	www.newyorkawareness.com	Upper West Side
Reiki Arts Continuum	59 West 19th St	212 570 1623	www.reikiartscontinuum.com	Chelsea
The Raising Waters Holistics Center	353 West 14th Street	718 981 2259	www.raisingwatersholistics.com	West Village

centres throughout New York where you can arrange for a reiki session. The established New York Awareness Center offers reiki, along with hypnosis and transformational workshops. The Reiki Arts Continuum has private reiki sessions, called 'Healing Journeys for your Heart, Mind and Body', offered by several long-time practitioners. You can also call to set up a reiki session at The Raising Waters Holistics Center for Energy Healing and Education.

Tai Chi

Channel your inner 'chi' – and hone your self-defence skills for the mean streets of New York – by practising Tai Chi, an ancient Chinese martial art. Sometimes referred to as 'moving meditation', Tai Chi promotes a harmonising integration of body, mind and emotions. As an 'internal' martial art, Tai Chi's emphasis is on strengthening muscles, tendons, bones and internal organs, and those who practise it regularly enjoy numerous health and emotional benefits. You'll find a variety of Tai Chi centres throughout New York, where classes last from a half hour to two hours; five classes usually start at around $100.

Chu Tai Chi

156 West 44th St
Midtown
Map 4-F4

212 221 6110 | www.chutaichi.com

At the top-notch Chu Tai Chi, you can train with none other than Master Chu, the martial arts emperor of New York. New students receive individual instruction from Chu, as they learn a series of defined movements known as the Tai Chi short form. And yes, it's all about practice, practice, practice. After about six months of twice-weekly classes, you can graduate to long form Tai Chi, and eventually begin learning techniques like the Push Hands, a relaxed sparring between two people, and street fighting and weapons forms, all of which highlight Tai Chi's powerful self-defence strategies. If you'd like to focus on healing, try the Eternal Spring Chi Kung and Tai Chi, which involves meditation and deep breathing, and improves balance and flexibility.

Yoga

Other options **Pilates** p.300

Millions of devotees can't be wrong. Yoga, born as a philosophy in India more than 5,000 years ago, gained popularity in the US in the 1960s, and has since been practised across the country. Yoga means 'to yoke or join', with the goal of bringing body and mind together into one harmonious experience through exercise, breathing and meditation. New York features an enormous array of yoga studios, big and small, that are open to yogis and yoginis (male and female) of all levels. Single classes, which are usually 90 minutes, start at $20, though many studios offer multi-class cards, which are more economical.

Everybody Say Ohmmm

For a calming respite from the hectic pace, many city dwellers turn to meditation, which is offered at centres throughout New York. You'll find quite a variety, from Buddhist meditation and chants to simple breathing practices, where all that's needed is a quiet space where you can sit comfortably. A number of yoga studios offer meditation, including Jivamukti Yoga (p.302).

Before you start a course of yoga classes, your studio should give you some guidelines on the correct yoga etiquette. Each studio will have its own set of rules, although there are some issues that are universal. One of the most important rules of yoga etiquette is to stick to the times of the class. Rushing in five minutes after the class has started is not only disrespectful to the instructor, it won't win you any points with your classmates who are trying hard to concentrate. Similarly, leaving before the end of the class is also frowned upon, not just because of the disruption, but because you will miss out on your Savasana – an essential part of the class.

Bikram Yoga NYC

182 Fifth Ave
Btn 22nd & 23rd St
Flatiron District
Map 6-F4

212 206 9400 | *www.bikramyoganyc.com*

The heat is on – literally – at Bikram Yoga NYC, where classes are conducted in a studio heated to 105 degrees. Bikram poses like 'the chair', where you squat as if sitting, and hold that pose for 10, 20, 30 and, if you're really good, up to 60 seconds, are challenging even at room temperature. Crank up the heat, though, and you'll really start to sweat. A lot (Bikram newbies have been known to mutter a string of non-Yoga-like curses under their breath when first starting out). Tough as it may be, the heat is in fact a bonus for your body: it speeds up the blood flow to the muscles and tendons, and limbers you up for deeper stretches. The spacious studio, equipped with whirring heat fans, feels like a sauna. But, say the long-timers, after a second or third session, you won't even notice the heat. That is, if you make it back for a second time…

Exhale Mind Body Spa

80 Madison Ave
Upper East Side
Map 3-B3

212 561 6400 | *www.exhalespa.com*

It's easier to contort your sweaty limbs when you're doing it in the light-flooded Exhale Mind Body Spa, with its high ceilings, billowing white linens and gleaming hard-wood floors. Journey into the Core, Ride the Vinyasa Wave and Dance into Trance at a variety of yoga sessions, the perfect antidote to Manhattan's pell-mell pace. And, if you think that yoga isn't enough of a workout, try the Core Fusion Power Pack Abs session – your rippled abs will be the envy of everyone.

Jivamukti Yoga

481 Broadway
Btn 13th & 14th St
Soho
Map 9-A2

212 353 0214 | *www.jivamuktiyoga.com*

Find your inner 'Om' at this venerable studio, credited with introducing yoga to a wider audience throughout New York and the US – and turning plenty of celebs into yoga afficionados along the way, including Christy Turlington and Sting. Jivamukti means 'liberations while living', a philosophy that forms the bedrock for every class, from the light-hearted family and kids sessions and classes 'en espanol' to the freewheeling open class, with Sanskrit chanting, deep breathing and backbends, all to the tunes of global trance, Gregorian chants and even Bob Dylan and Miles Davis. Harried New Yorkers are particularly grateful for the popular 45 minute yoga classes, which incorporate sweaty physical practice, meditation and relaxation – all within the lunch hour.

Laughing Lotus

55 Christopher St
West Village
Map 8-F1

212 414 2903 | *www.laughinglotus.com*

The name says it all: enjoying yoga is as important as benefitting from it at this communal, engaging studio with peach and pink walls. Yoga virgins are welcomed with open arms, and with a winning 'Absolute Beginner' series. Passionate co-owners Dana Flynn and Jasmine Tarkeshi celebrate, in their words, 'life in all its colours' with free-form Vinyasa Yoga classes where the mantra is 'be yourself'. Classes are offered throughout the day, from the Early Bird to a midnight Yoga Jam, when you can stretch into the night to live music tunes.

Small but indispensable…

Perfectly proportioned to fit in your pocket, these marvellous mini guidebooks make sure you don't just get the holiday you paid for, but rather the one that you dreamed of.

Explorer Mini Visitors' Guides
Maximising your holiday, minimising your hand luggage

BIGGEST CHOICE OF BOOKS

MAGIC CHOICE OF BOOKS

EXCITING CHOICE
OF *BOOKS*

Phenomenal choice of books

UNBEATABLE CHOICE OF BOOKS IN FULL COLOUR

SPECIAL CHOICE of books

 THRILLING CHOICE OF BOOKS

Encyclopedic choice of Books

 BALANCED CHOICE OF BOOKS

 **FANTASTIC
CHOICE OF BOOKS**

BORDERS.

BIGGEST CHOICE OF BOOKS, STATIONERY AND MAGAZINES

Shopping

Shopping

New York City is well-known for its love affair with fashion. It is here that fashion and art are interchangeable, and where clothing can appear more fit for a museum than your closet. New York Fashion Week (www.mbfashionweek.com/newyork) happens twice a year, and sees a flurry of famous designers gathering in Bryant Park to show off their new collections. New York is also the setting for *Project Runway*, a fashion reality TV show that harvests unknown designers and puts them to the test by getting them to create runway–worthy pieces under high pressure.

The city is ranked as one of the most expensive cities in the world to live in, with a special nod going to Manhattan. Rents soar every year, leaving more residents migrating to the boroughs. Happily, sales and bargains can always be found. Stores like Century 21 (p.360), Filene's Basement (p.360) or Loehmann's (p.322) may require time and dedication to find the best bargains, but they make designer creations a bit more attainable. Sample sales (see p.322) are fantastic resources for finding luxury items at a fraction of the cost. There are bargains on everything around the holidays, and with many stores extending their hours around

> ## Clothing Sizes
>
> Why, oh why do they make sizes different in Europe and the US? Never mind, figuring it out isn't rocket science. Firstly, check the label - international sizes are often printed on there. Secondly, check the store - they will often have a helpful conversion chart on display. And finally, do the sums yourself: A UK size is always two higher than a US size (so a UK 8 is actually a US 6), and a European size is always 30 more than a US size (so a European 38 is actually a US 8).

these dates you will have ample time to comparison shop. On Black Friday (the day after Thanksgiving) most retailers offer big discounts to encourage early Christmas shopping, so you can anticipate both deals and crowds on this day. New York is also home to many second-hand shops (although the Manhattan ones can still be pretty pricey). Vintage clothing shops (see p.317) offer a range of labels in varying conditions, but they are always worth a visit - nothing can beat the feeling of finding a gorgeous vintage handbag at a bargain price.

Fifth Ave window display

Fishs Eddy

What is New York's Best Shopping Area?

Ah, that's the million-dollar question. Many New Yorkers tend to shop in their home or work areas, but if you're serious about shopping you should definitely spread your wings. Soho is one of the most popular areas and has a huge variety of stores - it is also jam-packed on the weekends. Nearby in Nolita, speciality boutiques and eclectic shops are gaining ground. Browse Project 234 (212 334 6431) for funky female clothing, Area ID (212 219 9903) for home furnishings or VICE (212 219 7788) for streetwear. Tribeca has a modern, yet untouched, feel, and you might think you've strayed off course if it weren't for the excellent shopping. Steven Alan (212 343 0692) is a good destination stop for trendy men's and women's clothing, while Butter and Eggs (212 676 0235) offers chic home accessories. Designed by Frank Gehry, the interior space of the Tribeca Issey Miyake (212 226 0100) is equally as intriguing as the fashion it sells. Along Fifth Avenue, 50th Street and up, indulgent brands like Louis Vuitton share street occupancy with more affordable brands like Zara and Mexx.

There's More?

Oh, yes. While New York City can be most content with its range of consumer products, Woodbury Common offers exceptional outlet shopping for the diehard. Do not expect to conquer it in a day: there are over 200 shops and returning is almost mandatory. Chanel, Gucci, Cole Haan, Tahari, Crate & Barrel, Off 5th- Saks Fifth Avenue, Fendi and Burberry are just a few of its enticing attributes. Woodbury Common is located in Central Valley, New York, and is accessible by car, bus and train. Go to www.premiumoutlets.com/woodburycommon for details.

Buy American... It's Cheaper

Certain items are worth buying in the US, particularly those that have not been exported. Brands like Coach, Levi's and Nike are cheaper in the US, and certain electronic items such as MP3 players, laptops and cameras are also well priced. With the weak dollar and so many sales and promotions, shoppers should continue finding plenty of reasons to smile! There is no sales tax on clothing or footwear under $110, with normal tax in New York City standing at 8.375%.

Online Shopping

In response to the activity's heightened popularity, most stores offer online shopping services and deliver to almost anywhere in the US. Internet purchases of goods from outside the country will be stopped by US Customs and Border Protection for proper

Online Shopping Sites

www.amazon.com	Books, CDs, DVDs, clothes, food and much more
www.barnesandnoble.com	Books, CDs and DVDs; ships to numerous countries
www.craigslist.com	Second-hand items, jobs, services and apartments
www.deepdiscountdvd.com	Cheap DVDs, as well as movie posters and memorabilia
www.ebay.com	Everything and anything, and lots of weird stuff
www.findegifts.com	Discount source of electronics, games and gadgets
www.fragrance.net	Shop for fragrances in Euros, Pounds, US dollars
www.freshdirect.com	Yummy fresh food delivered right to your doorstep
www.netflix.com	Movie rentals
www.overstock.com	Furniture, electronics, apparel, entertainment and more
www.bluefly.com	Designer fashions up to 75% off
www.sephora.com	Beauty products; online sites available for other countries
www.shoebuy.com	Great source for men's, women's and children's shoes
www.fandango.com	Movie tickets

Times Square

inspection. Packages with a declared value of under $200, or $100 for a gift not sent to the purchaser, will generally sail by. If an item is less than $2,000 and is not a restricted or prohibited item, or in need of a quota, paperwork and duties will be appropriated and the item will have to be cleared. Any fees applied can be payable at the post office. Purchasing something online to be sent to your country of origin might not be as simple, as the international delivery services of department stores, some chain stores, and certain sites vary greatly, and stores like Bergdorf Goodman (p.344) and Bloomingdale's (p.359) require you to phone in your order on items intended to be delivered abroad, rather than place it in person, in the store.

Refunds & Exchanges

Store policies on refunds or exchanges can vary wildly from one shop to another. The best way to protect yourself against buying something and then living to regret it, is to find out what the refund and exchange policy is before you hand over your money. Many reputable shops will have their policy on display near the checkout counter, but if you don't see it there, be sure to ask the assistant.

If their policy isn't posted in the store, then technically you are allowed to return the item within 20 days, provided it is in the original condition. And save those receipts! If you spend more than $20, the retailer is legally obliged to give you a receipt automatically. If you spend less than $20, then you are well within your rights to request a receipt if one is not issued. Make sure your receipt lists the name of the store, the date and time of purchase, the amount, the tax amount, and a description of the item. In general, you will have to fight pretty hard, often to no avail, to get a refund on 'as-is' purchases (things that you knew were faulty when buying) or sale items.

Consumer Rights

If you are accosted in a shop by all means scream or call 911. Most stores have in-house security so screaming will generally get the job done. If an employee seems ill-versed in a store's policy or is mistreating you, request to see the manager. Businesses tend to operate under the mantra, 'the customer is always right', so you will typically be seen very promptly.

Should repeated requests for assistance prove futile, or if you encounter matters such as services not rendered, false advertising, or fraud, you can call 311 (New York City's 24 hour Citizen Service Center), and an operator will offer advice.

Shoppers are protected under the Consumer Protection Law and you can file a complaint to the Department of Consumer Affairs (www.nyc.gov/dca). Still steaming? The Better Business Bureau (www.bbb.org) is another site where you can file a report or view a company's reliability report.

Shipping

Many stores will warn you that the cost of shipping larger goods could sometimes exceed the cost of the item in question (especially if you bought that television for half price). And they are probably right. But some stores are very helpful when it comes to shipping, and will assist you with the arrangements. You can send

Shipping Companies		
DHL	800 225 5345	www.dhl.com
FedEx	800 463 3339	www.fedex.com
UPS	800 742 5877	www.ups.com
United States Postal Service	800 275 8777	www.usps.com

many items via the United States Postal Service, but shopping around could guarantee cheaper costs, more efficient tracking and quicker arrival time. FedEx and UPS offer international shipping and DHL lets you import from over 210 countries with an all-inclusive price and one predetermined currency. All three companies have comprehensive websites with easy guides to shipping internationally. The cost of shipping any item is usually determined by weight, time of arrival and destination. You can usually track items by simply entering your reference number on the company's website.

How to Pay

With so many stores vying for your rent money, paying for goods is easy. Debit cards and credit cards are widely used, with Mastercard, Visa, and American Express leading the pack. Diners Club, Discover, US Travellers' Cheques and personal cheques are another option, but their acceptance varies from store to store. Cash is worshipped at flea markets and on the rare occasion it is required in a shop, ATMs are in no short supply. Attempting to pay in foreign currency will produce quizzical looks so it's best to keep your yen at home.

Bargaining

Other options **Markets** p.363

Once you've ascertained that the coveted Gucci knock-off is spelt correctly, try bargaining for a few bucks less than the asking price. Most street merchants and flea market stall holders would rather close a sale than see you walk away empty handed, but the practice is rare in major retail stores, boutiques and independent shops. Bargaining at a farmers' market is unwise, as prices for fresh produce are not demanding and customers would be remiss to insult the hardworking vendor. Some stores that sell high-end merchandise, such as fine jewellery or electronics, might be slightly flexible with their prices, so asking if the going price is the final offer never hurts. Your luck will vary depending on the store. Advertisements for the same product sold cheaper at another store should be brought to the attention of a sales assistant or manager, as most companies will match the alternative offer so as not to lose business to a competitor.

Alcohol

Other options **Drinks** p.372, **On the Town** p.409

Between supermarkets, delis, happy hour at your favourite bar and various liquor stores, consuming alcohol could not be easier in New York – as long as you are over 21 (a law that is strictly enforced) and have valid ID. Supermarkets sell a bevy of beers where six bottles of Guinness cost about $9, while a no-frills bottle of pinot grigio costs $5.99. Selection and prices will depend on the supermarket or deli, and designated liquor stores are the best option for pickier palates.

Alcohol		
Acker Merrall & Condit Co.	Upper West Side	212 787 1700
Ambassador Wines & Spirits	Midtown	212 421 5078
The Bottle Shoppe	Brooklyn	718 388 4122
Bottlerocket Wine & Spirit	Flatiron District	212 929 2323
Chelsea Wine Vault	Chelsea	212 462 4244
Garnet Wines & Liquors	Upper East Side	212 772 3211
Grande Harvest Wines	Midtown	212 682 5855
Morrell & Company	Midtown	212 688 9370
September Wines & Spirits	Lower East Side	212 388 0770
Sherry-Lehmann	Upper East Side	212 838 7500
Sutton Wine Shop	Midtown	212 755 6626
Union Square Wines & Spirits	East Village	212 675 8100

399 Lafayette
At 4th Street
Noho
Map 9-A3

Astor Wines & Spirits

212 674 7500 | www.astoruncorked.com

Rookies and experts alike will find something at Astor Wines & Spirits. The space is large and inviting with signs for specific types of wine. Or maybe you prefer to go by a region, like northern Italy, France or Spain. The organic section boasts wine produced from four special winemaking practices: certified organic, practising organic, biodynamic, and natural. A chart explains the hardship. In the back, a roll call of every type of liquor is offered. Astor's 'Cool Room' contains 500 bottles of rare and vintage wines.

1291 Lexington Ave
Btn 86th & 87th St
Upper East Side
Map 3-D1

Best Cellars

212 426 4200 | www.bestcellars.com

Toast with a glass of chianti from a bottle that only cost $9. Most wines from Best Cellars hang out in the $12 range, making the vino very appealing. Bottles are grouped according to taste and style, with information cards flaunting witty titles, such as Nero Hero, Bada Bing, Three Way, Sip Sip Hooray! and Purple Rain. Choose from champagne, cabernet, merlot, sauvignon, pinot, chardonnay, zinfandel or riesling, with a 'Beyond the Best' section hovering around $30. Cheers!

482 Broome
At Wooster St
Soho
Map 10-F2

Vintage New York

212 226 9463 | www.vintagenewyork.com

Wine at Vintage hails from areas like the Finger Lakes, Hudson Valley and Lake Erie. Lower tier wines can be found in the $15 range. Cabernet sauvignons from Long Island can cost between $13.99 and $39.99. Both Vintage New York locations have wine tasting bars and charge a flat rate of $10 to sample five wines. Classes are also available for beginner winos. Other location: 2492 Broadway at 93rd Street (212 721 9999).

Art

Other options **Art Galleries** p.214, **Art Classes** p.254, **Art & Craft Supplies** p.311

Art Made Easy
The sheer number of galleries in New York City is staggering. That said, a great tool in finding one tailored to your taste is www.art-collecting.com. You can search a specific area of Manhattan and click a gallery's weblink to view its current and/or upcoming exhibits, even artist biographies where available. The website www.artupdate.com is also good for exhibition listings.

The city hosted a significant branch of the Dada movement, revealed the pop art creations of Andy Warhol and Roy Lichtenstein, and witnessed the raw talent of Jean-Michel Basquiat. New York thrives on fiercely subjective art. New and emerging artists arrive constantly and display every art concept imaginable. For the art connoisseur, this is great news and you'll find galleries throughout the city. In Chelsea, between 22nd and 25th streets, a number of galleries prevail, exhibiting flat, sculpture, photography and installation pieces. The Soho District and 57th Street are other hot gallery locales, while the converted warehouses of Brooklyn's DUMBO (Down Under Manhattan Bridge Underpass) are full of uber-hip paintbrush wielders.

Purchasing art is not an elitist hobby. In fact, there are several avenues to try to start your own personal collection. AAF Contemporary Art Fair exhibits art from many galleries, with a $100-$5,000 price range. Scope Art Fair showcases rising stars in the contemporary art world – its 2007 New York exhibition will take place at the Lincoln Center. TOAST, The Tribeca Open Artists Studio Tour, introduces you to over 100 local artists' work on a walking tour. See p.214 for more information on galleries.

Art		
AAF Contemporary Art Fair	Chelsea	212 255 2003
Art in General	Tribeca	212 219 0473
Frere Independent	Chelsea	212 604 0519
Reproductions	Midtown	212 382 3730
Scope Art Fair	Chelsea	212 268 1522

Portrait photography is quite common, with many aspiring actors and models heading to Reproductions, but services are not exclusive to getting headshots as several photographers offer additional portrait possibilities. If you just want an accurate artist's sketch or caricature of yourself in a jiffy, head to Times Square, where rows of easels are poised to bear your image for $20 or so.

Art & Craft Supplies

Other options **Art Classes** p.254, **Art** p.311, **Art Galleries** p.214

Aspiring Van Goghs shop at Kremer Pigments for quality raw materials, resins and ground pigments. Knitting nuts are fond of Knit-A-Way of Brooklyn, where staff can order yarn supplies and classes are taught to adults and children. Those with a flair for jewellery might try Beads of Paradise for semi-precious stones or Bruce Frank on the Upper West Side to purchase that rare glass bead. The School of Visual Arts (www.schoolofvisualarts.edu) keeps students shopping at inexpensive Pearl Paint, while there are plenty of other options to keep the artistically inclined happy, from the professionals to first time dabblers.

1-5 Bond Street
Noho
Map 11-C1

Blick Art Materials

212 533 2444 | *www.dickblick.com*

Airy and easy to navigate, this is an artist's paradise with a huge range of art supplies and materials. Choose from a colourful selection of oil and acrylic paints, pastels, charcoals, brushes, writing instruments, sculpture and graphic design tools, speciality paper, frame kits, scrapbooking supplies and photo albums. Ready made canvases are available, or they can be ordered by the yard for at-home stretching. The lower level features easels, light boxes, art kits for kids, sketch pads and portfolios. Teachers and students can join a loyalty programme for free which yields 10% off non-sale items (everyone else pays $10). When you're done shopping, take a left out of the store and head to the nearby cafe where you can sketch your masterpiece while sipping a latte.

311

12 West 20th Street
Btn Fifth and Sixth Ave
Flatiron District
Map 8-F1

Sam Flax

212 620 3000 | www.samflaxny.com

In 1920, Sam Flax sold art supplies out of a cart. Today, the stores relish their reputation as 'innovators' and continue to kick-start customers' careers by supplying superb quality products. Aside from paints, pastels, pads and paper, you'll find leather Filofax day planners and refills, Gravis backpacks (for around $85), computer cases (ranging from $83 to $260), furniture, and presentation portfolios. Custom framing and custom vinyl graphics are available, but the selection of modern frames and pre-cut pieces will spark do-it-yourself ideas.

Custom printing is offered at the flagship store on Third Avenue, but at both outlets, students with a valid ID receive 10% off on art supplies and portfolios. Other location: 900 Third Ave, between 54th and 55th Streets (212 813 6666).

Art & Craft Supplies		
A.I. Friedman	Flatiron District	212 243 9000
Beads of Paradise	Flatiron District	212 620 0642
Bruce Frank	Upper West Side	212 595 3746
DaVinci Artist Supplies	Chelsea	212 871 0220
Knit-A-Way of Brooklyn	Brooklyn	718 797 3305
Kremer Pigments	Chelsea	212 219 2394
Lee's Art Shop	Midtown	212 247 0110
Pearl Paint	Tribeca	212 431 7932

Baby Items

Congratulations! If you are about to be a parent or are celebrating the new existence of someone else's bundle of joy, you have some great choices in a city brimming with kids. For all things baby, shop at buybuy BABY. With departments specialising in feeding, nursing, bath, health and safety you'll find everything you could possibly need here. Sales associates are helpful and registry is available.

Takashimaya (p. 362) also offers unique gift ideas, such as decorative bibs and playful clothing. For definite pampering, try Calypso Enfant & Bebe where you can go gaga for leather Robeez booties or a cashmere sweater.

Many health-conscious moms-to-be are delighted over Giggle, relishing the stylish, carefully selected products including the modish bassinets or organic cotton diapers (nappies). And if you're shopping at the Soho locale, pop into Psny and pick up a hip baby sling in cotton or linen and check out the 'Mommy and Me' jewellery. Diapers, formulas, and trusted baby products by Johnson & Johnson can be picked up at supermarkets and most pharmacies for daily maintenance.

Two enterprising Brooklyn moms have developed a shopping blog dedicated entirely to finding, reviewing and sharing hot kiddie-related products. From kids' music to baby gear to art and gift ideas, no hip parent should shop until they have consulted www.coolmompicks.com, which features independent companies and non-mainstream items.

Once your bubba is more tyke than bundle-size, a good way to free up space in your shoebox apartment is by donating any baby paraphernalia you no longer need to the charity Baby Buggy. Serving over 60 social service programmes in the five boroughs, they collect and redistribute baby clothing and gear to families in need. Call 212 736 1777 to contribute, volunteer or find out more.

Baby Items		
Albee Baby Carriage Co.	Upper West Side	212 662 5740
Babies 'R' Us	Flatiron District	212 798 9905
	Brooklyn	718 277 3400
Baby Bird	Brooklyn	718 788 4506
Baby Chic	Brooklyn	718 953 8695
Babylicious	Tribeca	212 406 7440
Bu and the Duck	Tribeca	212 431 9226
buybuy BABY	Chelsea	917 344 1555
Cadeau	Nolita	212 674 5747
Calypso Enfant & Bebe	Soho	212 966 3234
Destination Maternity	Midtown	212 588 0220
Giggle	Upper East Side	212 249 4249
	Soho	212 334 5817
Jacadi	Upper East Side	212 717 9292
	Upper West Side	212 246 2753
	Brooklyn	718 871 9402
Liz Lange Maternity	Upper East Side	212 879 2191
Maternity Works	Midtown	212 399 9840
Psny	Soho	212 253 0630
Takasimaya	Midtown	212 350 0179
Veronique	Upper East Side	12 831 7800

Beachwear

Other options **Sporting Goods** p.349, **Clothes** p.315

Whether you're vacationing in Saint Tropez, or spending summer weekends at a nearby shore, you will need an outfit. Department stores like Macy's (p. 325), Lord & Taylor (p. 361) and Saks Fifth Avenue (p. 362) offer good seasonal options for beachwear during peak vacation months.

Those in need of year-round service might try the reasonably priced Paragon Sports, as shopping here will benefit serious swimmers and those in need of additional gear such as goggles, swimmies, or wetsuits. Style queens should try Canyon Beachwear or Eres, while boys and girls and the occasional thirtysomething will find Billabong and Quiksilver's board shorts and triangular bikini tops the stuff surfing dreams were made of. Prices and sales at these and other stores vary depending on the season.

Beachwear		
Azaleas	East Village	212 253 5484
Billabong	Midtown	212 840 0550
Calypso	Upper East Side	212 535 4100
Canyon Beachwear	Upper East Side	917 432 0732
Eres	Midtown	212 223 3550
	Soho	212 431 7300
Maila Mills Swimwear	Upper West Side	212 874 7200
Paragon Sporting Goods	Flatiron District	212 255 8036
Quiksilver	Soho	212 226 1193
Vilebrequin	Upper East Side	212 650 0353
	Soho	212 431 0673

Bicycles

Road Relations

When you're a cyclist, you will be annoyed by pedestrians and motorists – and when you're a pedestrian or motorist, you will loathe the cyclist. Don't be alarmed, this is just how things are. For help sharing the road with all types, go to www.dot.state.ny.us for cycling rules and tips.

Bicycle shops are plentiful in a city where few people own cars. The shops provide excellent gear for both the cycling pro and the casual park-bound biker. Bicycle Habitat carries the foldable Dahon, Specialized, Trek and Marin to name a few, and you can purchase a Mercian bike made to order. The repair service is reputable at Bicycle Habitat and walk-ins are welcome. If you choose your bike from Toga Bike Shop, a free lifetime service accompanies the purchase. Metro Bicycles has six locations in Manhattan and sells bikes from around $160 up into the thousands. Rentals here will cost $7 an hour or $35 for the day. For the avid cyclist, try NYC Velo for advice from pros and a lounge complete with bagels and coffee.

With bike theft hard to deter, you may not want to shell out too much on your two wheels, so many residents buy them second-hand. Once you've got your wheels, see p.259 for a list of cycling clubs that you can join group rides.

Bicycles		
Bicycle Habitat	Soho	212 431 3315
Bicycles Plus NYC	Upper East Side	212 794 2929
Bicycles-Metro Bicycle Stores	Upper East Side	212 427 4450
Bike Heaven	Upper East Side	212 230 1919
Bike Works	Lower East Side	212 388 1077
Champion Bicycles	Upper West Side	212 662 2690
Chelsea Bicycles	Chelsea	212 727 7278
City Bicycles	Hell's Kitchen	212 563 3373
Gotham Bikes	Tribeca	212 732 2453
Metro Bicycles	Various Locations	www.metrobicycles.com
NYC Velo	East Village	212 253 7771
Pedal Pusher Bike Shop	Upper East Side	212 288 5592
Toga Bike Shop	Upper West Side	212 799 9625

313

Books

Other options **Libraries** p.270, **Second-Hand Items** p.347

As the birthplace of Herman Melville and JD Salinger, New York City knows a thing or ten about books. Barnes & Noble will be an excellent resource, but for personal atmosphere and the occasional conversation with like-minded individuals, find an independent shop. Partners & Crime specialises in mysteries while St Mark's Bookshop provides the East Village with dependable stock of cultural theory, periodicals and small press publishers. Art fans should try the MoMA Design and Book Store as it carries 1,500 titles from around the world, while Shakespeare & Co. offers scripts and film criticism.

The New York Public Library is on a par with the British Library and the Library of Congress. Obtaining a New York Branch Library card is free to anyone who 'lives, works, pays property taxes' or studies here, and provides privileges to checkout books, CDs, and movies. Non-residents will pay an annual fee of $100, but if you just need to check your email on a computer, you can do that sans card. In addition to the Branch card, an 'ACCESS' card enables you to conduct research at one of the Research Libraries whether you are a resident or not. Free classes, including English classes for non-English speakers are also available. Check out www.NYPL.org for branch locations and hours. And don't miss the beautiful ceiling of the reading room.

Save Your Books

For book preservation and restoration supplies visit Talas in person, or online. If you're an expert or just starting out, www.talasonline.com has a comprehensive catalogue of assorted tools and kits for cleaning, bookbinding, storage and framing.

Various Locations

Barnes & Noble

www.barnesandnoble.com

During the Great Depression William Barnes and G. Clifford Noble opened a shop on Fifth Avenue and 18th Street. Today, it has become the 'go to' for students searching for textbooks, medical books, or any title academic in nature. The Union Square shop on East 17th is a superstore, spanning several floors and including, among other genres, biography, fiction, health, travel, science, history, nature, reference, games and puzzles, business and, America's most beloved, self-improvement. Fellow literary lovers sit at the cafe and tap on laptops or read from a heap of journals grabbed from the magazine area. Listening stations are provided in the music department which also sell videos and DVDs. Sales can be found daily on bestsellers while bargain-priced books reside on the second floor. Joining Barnes & Noble's Member Program for an annual fee of $25 entitles you to added savings. Check the website for the store's event schedule as current and well-known authors give readings.

18 West 18th Street
Btn 5th & 6th St
Flatiron District
Map 8-F1

Books of Wonder

212 989 3270 | www.booksofwonder.com

The bookshop Meg Ryan owned in the movie *You've Got Mail* is said to be based on Books of Wonder. It is the oldest and largest independent children's bookshop in New York City and home to an extensive collection of rare and new books. Many new books are signed by the authors as Books of Wonder hosts a couple of signings a week, along with a story hour every Sunday and a gallery that rotates artwork. Wide aisles provide areas to read from nursery books, modern picture books, pop-up books, poetry, folk and fairytales, or fiction. The original Winnie-the-Pooh volumes are behind glass, but a notable collection of Oz books, which Books of Wonder holds the exclusive rights to, are out on shelves. The bookshop shares a space with the Cupcake Café where tasty confections sweeten the deal for both kids and adults. The staff are attentive and caring to the pint-sized literati and can ship internationally from their shop, website or catalogue.

314

Strand Book Store

212 473 1452 | *www.strandbooks.com*

828 Broadway
At 12th St
East Village
Map 9-A2

You might need a ladder here. At Strand, explore towering stacks of every genre belonging to this independent second-hand shop of choice. Named in honour of an old literary magazine and the famous street in London, it has been a family business since 1927. Savings will make you look twice, with up to 50% off on hardcovers and paperbacks, and about 20% off 'front list' books. James Joyce's *Ulysses* may not be your idea of a beach read, but should your offspring require it through school, paperback classics start at $2.95. Dollar carts located outside the store are good to peruse; delve deeply and you might rustle up a John Grisham. The peaceful third floor contains the city's largest rare book collection and a water fountain (it gets dry up there), where a first edition of Don DeLillo's *Americana* sells for $450. Strand has another location on Fulton Street (212 732 6070), as well as various 'street market' locations throughout the city.

Books		
192 Books	Chelsea	212 255 4022
Forbidden Planet	West Village	212 475 6161
Mid-Manhattan Library	Midtown	212 340 0833
MoMA Design and Book Store	Midtow	212 708 9700
Partners & Crime	West Village	212 243 0440
Shakespeare & Co.	West Village	212 529 1330
St. Mark's Bookshop	East Village	212 260 7853
Talas	Flatiron District	212 219 0770

Clothes

Other options **Beachwear** p.313, **Lingerie** p.337, **Tailoring** p.352,
Sporting Goods p.349, **Shoes** p.347

Why Pay More?
Paying full price is never fun, especially if you are on a budget. When shopping in stores like Gap, Banana Republic, Club Monaco, Anthropologie and French Connection, check the sales racks first as these seem to be permanent fixtures. And if you spot a striking top but don't like what the tag reads, come back in a week or two and you might find it has been marked down.

Entire volumes could be written on the clothing in New York City. From time-sensitive trends (found most economically at stores like H&M) to the high art pieces of Comme des Garcons (212 604 9200), New York is a playground for those determined to look fabulous. Prevalent throughout the city, chain stores epitomise the offerings at most US malls. Designer fashions and new innovative labels are perhaps the most sought after, with many budget-conscious fashionistas turning to Century 21 (p.360), Loehmann's, and the hidden gems of Find Outlet and Gabay's Outlet for the discounted best. Vintage shopping still remains a desired device in spicing up the new, and the Manhattan Vintage Clothing Show (www.manhattanvintage.com) is worth the $20 admission. Parents will enjoy shopping at Daffy's (p.360) where the kids' clothing section is large and varied. Other department stores offer almost unlimited options as well.

Saks Fifth Avenue

Unusual Sizes

With the average size in America in flux, many more stores accommodate varying proportions. Ann Taylor, which sells contemporary business and dress wear for women, is available in petite sizes. Department stores like Macy's (p.361) and Lord & Taylor (p.361) carry both petite and plus sizes, and other department stores have similar size offerings. Rochester Big & Tall is a men's clothing store selling designer labels for the, ahem, big and tall.

Vintage Guru
Having been in
business for years and
discovered some
incredible pieces (like a
brand new Hermés bag
from the 60s) Stacey
Winnick carries high-
end clothing, jewellery
and accessories as far
back as the Victorian
period. Vintage by
Stacey Lee is located in
White Plains and is
available by
appointment only to
vintage groupies. Call
914 328 0788 or email
at vintagesl@aol.com.

Accessories

An outfit is not fully complete without the proper accessories, and with many designers and stores dipping their hands into fashion trimmings, there's no excuse for bad accessories. Department stores have some of the largest selections of handbags, jewellery, hats, scarves, socks, belts and gloves, where smaller boutiques and speciality shops usually deal in quirky, quality accessories. Kate Spade and her husband Jack Spade have made a valuable contribution to the market with their sleek utilitarian handbags, wallets, makeup cases, toiletry bags and even shoes and ties.

Urban Outfitters (www.urbanoutfitters.com) sells retro and modern clothing and accessories. From costume jewellery with hearts and crosses to aviator sunglasses, woolly scarves, funky hats, bags and gloves, this store offers a moderately priced way to keep hot and hip. Destination can transform the most stubborn of swine into a savvy vixen. Think European designers with an avant-garde flair in the trendiest of locales: the Meatpacking District (with prices to match). Verve is another great shop for girls interested in finding the newest in handbags, belts, scarves, and jewellery, with its hot collection of shoes shining at the Bleecker Street location.

When searching for the best for less, Century 21 (p.360) offers a myriad of accessories, including a selection of designer handbags. Loehmann's sells many accessory items at great prices. If you're feeling creative you can always have a go at making up your own jewellery. There are a strip of independent bead and button shops along Sixth Avenue in Midtown (just past Herald Square) where you can wander in and create your own jewellery (with assistance if necessary).

Know Your Areas
Manhattan may not be the biggest city, but it sure has a lot of shops. To get a better feel for what to find in particular areas, turn to p.364 and check out Streets & Areas

91 Greene Street
Btn Prince & Spring St
Soho
Map 10-F1

A Bathing Ape

212 925 0222 | www.bape.com

The Japanese cult invasion of DJ Nigo's flashy streetwear which could flip any B-boy out of his mind, with its hip hop infused denim, jackets, and accessories. BAPE, as it is known, sells limited edition items so while you may scoff at those jeans for $363, others may appreciate being one of the lucky few. Sneakers in bright colour combos (think neon and fluorescent) or primary hues reside on a carousel in the window and also in the shoe salon upstairs. Sneakers start at $180 and hoodies can range from $275-$313. Warning: ape images and camouflage are not uncommon and look even cuter on the kids' apparel.

720 Fifth Avenue
Midtown
Map 5-A2

Abercrombie & Fitch

212 381 0110 | www.abercrombie.com

This is preppy slacker wear with sex appeal. Every variation on fraternity clothing is available, from hoodies to cargo pants to sassy underwear – occasionally advertised by semi-clad models wandering around the store, bronzed, buff and happy to pose for photos. The label's street credibility does come at a slightly steeper price, although there are regular very reasonable sales. The store at South Street Seaport (199 Water Street, 212 809 9000) is the size of a small country house, making the whole shopping experience feel like a short break in the Catskills.

417 West 14th Street
Btn 9th & 10th Ave
Chelsea
Map 8-C1

Alexander McQueen

212 645 1797 | www.alexandermcqueen.com

It may take a while to work up the courage to walk into this store, but once you do, you can expect the unexpected and find some showy, futuristic tailored suits, women's

316

dresses, and just the right pair of shoes for him and her. These clothes are designed with a slight curve forward into the unknown, all meticulously crafted by a man many regard as the 'bad boy of fashion'.

Amarcord Vintage Fashion

252 Lafayette Street
Btn Prince & Spring St
Soho
Map 11-A1

212 431 4161 | *www.amarcordvintagefashion.com*
Owners Patti Bordoni and Marco Liotta search Italy and other parts of Europe for high-end clothing and accessories, and display these treasures in their showrooms for you to drool over (and buy, if you've got the money). Merchandise is in excellent condition and prices seem reasonable for designs by Gucci, Dior and YSL. A two-piece suit by Etro sells for $195 and is tailored outstandingly well for today's man. Fur coats and fancy frocks dresses are a bit pricier, like the black tulle dress with corset bodice for $475 or the green clutch Bottega Veneta purse for $300, both of which look like they have never been touched by human hands. Other locations: East Village (212 614 7133) and Brooklyn (718 963 4001).

Banana Republic

Various Locations

212 974 2350 | *www.bananarepublic.com*
Banana Republic designs respected and affordable clothing for the office and home. Men can shop for chinos, jeans, pants, suits, sweaters, shoes, as well as sharp-looking dress shirts for around $80. Women fare well with updated shirts, pleated and non-pleated skirts in contrasting fabrics and lengths, sweaters, pants, jeans, and blazers that can either be dressed up or dressed down. Jewellery, leather handbags and fragrance lines are indicative of the brand: clean, classic and contemporary. Banana Republic is a Gap Inc. brand and is more expensive than Gap itself, but worth every penny when John Varvatos and CELINE are out of your price range.

Beacon's Closet

88 North 11th St
Btn Berry & Wythe St
Williamsburg

718 486 0816 | *www.beaconscloset.com*
Familiarise yourself with this image: tired old trucker hat, unaffected demeanour, iPod blaring a song from some underground band. This has been New York City's hipster, referenced in articles, mentioned in passing, and spotted mainly in Brooklyn and the Lower East Side for a few years now. Beacon's Closet is their homeland. Check it out, either to trade in your own threads or pick up a Sergio Valente jean skirt for $24. Beacon's Closet is a must, with 5,500 square feet of modern and vintage clothing, accessories, shoes and novelties. Men and women can shop together and know they are getting a nod-worthy deal. Operating as a clothing exchange, Beacon's Closet 'selectively' buys, sells and trades items and yet donates a portion of its profits to charities, creating even more incentive to shop here. There is another location in Park Slope (718 230 1630).

Brooklyn Industries

Various Locations

212 219 0862 | *www.brooklynindustries.com*
Lexy Funk and Vahap Avsar co-founded a company based on the principle of being able to Live, Work and Create. It began with recycling a billboard scrap into a messenger bag and has quickly turned into one of the fastest-growing private companies. Designs of hoodies, graphic T-shirts, pants, outerwear, shirts, and sweaters for men and women seem to rotate frequently. The kid's clothing is great and sending a hoodie with 'Brooklyn' emblazoned on it will ensure that your baby cousin in Wales is keeping it real. Graphic T-shirts can sell around $28, hoodies around $64, and a fab hat a la Fidel Castro for $32. All bags are durable and industrial in appearance, and with fabric prints and styles are updated every season.

317

106 Franklin St
Tribeca
Map 10-E3

Bu and the Duck

212 431 9226 | *www.buandtheduck.com*

Located in Tribeca, this store may inspire you to start a family. Bu and the Duck has captured the heart of parents for its ability to outfit kids in sweet and unassuming apparel. Crochet sweaters, pastel coloured dresses, rainboots and leggings in pretty prints for girls, or handsome blazers for boys, are all lovely to look at in a store that resembles a bit of the French country. A striped jersey dress sells for $58, while a pair of overalls reminiscent of Huckleberry Finn sells for $65. Around the New Year a big sale prevails in the back room where Mary Jane shoes can go for $60.

Various Locations

Calypso Christiane Celle

www.calypso-celle.com

It does not matter if your trip to the Hamptons was suddenly postponed or your trip to Bermuda cancelled, Calypso can still inject tranquillity into any aspect of your life. The five-floor wonderland on Madison Avenue houses worldly treasures and includes beautiful apparel for women, personal and home accessories, children's clothes, toys, and gifts. Shopping at any one of the numerous Calypso stores is both inviting and a retreat onto itself, as the airy atmosphere and feel-good behaviour of the staff will tempt you to stay for hours.

Various Locations

Donna Karan New York

www.donnakaran.com

The muted and serene backdrop ensures nothing upstages the clothing. One of the quintessential designers of New York, Donna Karan's career began with a summer job at Anne Klein where three years as an associate designer followed. In 1984, she went solo and founded her own company with her late husband Stephan Weiss. The Madison Avenue flagship branch (212 861 1001), with its water rock garden and relaxing mood, houses classic contemporary wear that is timeless. DKNY (www.dkny.com) is Donna Karan's cheaper, sportier line where you can save a few bucks.

Various Locations

Express

www.express.com

If you have to get dressed for a third date and don't want a repeat performance of that gold halter top, go to Express, where you will be able to add a few stylish pieces to your wardrobe without suffering buyer's remorse. Women can find dresses under $100 as well as skirts and pretty blouses for the office. Men shopping at Express Men might have a harder time finding a sweater, jacket or shirt that suits their taste as merchandise tends to be hit and miss.

169 Spring Street
Soho
Map 10-F1

Flying A

212 965 9090 | *www.flyinga.net*

It began as a 'concept' store when it was founded in Denmark in 1994 by Glenn Gosling and Mia Berglund. Today, you cannot escape the store unscathed. A security guard is at the door and usually greets you upon arrival. Within minutes, you are cooing over vintage boots and your male companion is asking your opinion on a pair of Spitfire sunglasses for $25. The clothing is somewhat urban for men and occasionally feminine for women. Flying A has its own label while other brands include Modern Amusement, Nabi, Kobo, Sneaky Fox, Sophia Costas, G-Star and Jonathan Aston. Airline bags, leather handbags, watches, hats, hosiery, jewellery and belts are fashionable and fun to shop. The sales are always good and are usually on the bottom shelf for men or at the back of the store for women.

Various Locations

Gap

www.gap.com

You're never far away from a Gap store, and although it tries hard with ad campaigns featuring celebrities like Missy Elliot, Sarah Jessica Parker and Chris Rock, it is still regarded as a bit 'ho hum' by many New Yorkers. However, Gap is a safe and sure bet for reasonably priced staples like socks, T-shirts, cotton underwear and sometimes denim, depending on the fit you are looking for. Spurts of trend rarely occur but again, the shopper who can pick up a pair of straight leg jeans for $59.50 when most denim is selling for over $100 is hardly concerned. All major Gaps feature a men's and women's department and sometimes house a GapBody, a BabyGap, a GapKids or a GapMaternity.

111 Christopher St
Btn Bleecker & Hudson
West Village
Map 8-D3

The Leather Man

212 243 5339 | *www.theleatherman.com*

Seeking out The Leather Man can be as much fun as shopping in the store itself. Located in Greenwich Village, you will be tempted to go into other interesting stores along the way, before thrusting the door open to find everything that can possibly be made in leather – in leather. The Leather Man has been around since 1965, selling high quality leather fetish items, most of which are made in the store and can be customised. Leather pants, chaps, hats, cuffs, whips, jackets, and other accoutrements (insert your imagination here) are in abundance, along with rubber and latex goods. The home decor accessories market has not been ignored by The Leather Man – you can purchase a leather picture frame or a long stem leather rose for $20. Check your bags and get a 'Sassy Tart' ticket, then head down the winding staircase for other leather goods and items including videos, books, bondage and whips.

109 Thompson St
Btn Prince & Spring St
Soho
Map 10-E1

Legacy

21 296 6827 | *www.legacy-nyc.com*

You might walk by without even noticing it, but back up ladies, and hit this small boutique which gets it right every time. Rita Brookoff's original shop offered only vintage, but now she not only designs herself, but she works with small independents so that the names are fresh and sometimes obscure. Don't be surprised to find that vintage green leather coat in mint condition selling for $300 mingling with a 30s inspired dress designed by Rita. Jewellery, shoes, bags and hats are selective and can be either new or vintage. If you venture to her website you can view other vintage pieces up for sale, such as a Gucci handbag for $375 or the Hermés Kelly Bag for $2995. The key to shopping here is to mix and match. Rita Brookoff also teamed up with Joanna Baum to create Dear (212 226 3559), located on Broome Street in Nolita, offering even more possibilities for the female trendsetter. Legacy has other locations in Brooklyn (718 403 0090) and on Broome Street (212 226 3559).

319

232 Mulberry St
Btn Prince & Spring St
Nolita
Map 11-A1

Lisa Shaub Fine Millinery

212 965 9176 | *www.lisashaub.com*

Lisa Shaub is an innovative milliner who has been in the business for 20 years. She began as a wholesaler for places like Barneys (p.358) and Henri Bendel, but decided her one-of-a-kind pieces deserved an outlet and opened a boutique in Nolita. Appliqué and hand-knit berets, mods, striking fedoras, knit baby caps and men's cowboys prove Lisa Shaub can make style accessible to anyone. Hats range from $60-$250 and can be customised to fit any sized melon, guaranteeing a perfect and most comfortable fit. Scarves are also available with future sights set on expanding into handbags, jewellery and belts.

163 Mercer St
Btn Houston & Prince St
Soho
Map 10-F1

Marc Jacobs

212 343 1490 | *www.marcjacobs.com*

A native New Yorker, Marc Jacobs is responsible for kick-starting the concept of grunge back in the 90s. Today, in keeping with the spirit of the city his clothing is witty, satirical, inspiring, and yes, kind of expensive. Marc Jacobs marries many fabrics together creating looks that are distinct to him and both his labels. His store in Soho carries men's and women's and even a few children's items. A pair of shoes can sell for $1600. If that seems too indulgent, check out his occasionally kitsch Marc by Marc Jacobs line which sells for a tad less, or Century 21 (p360) for spill overs.

172 Ludlow Street
Houston & Stanton St
Lower East Side
Map 11-C1

Marmalade

212 473 8070 | *www.marmaladevintage.com*

Walking in and hearing Stevie Nicks singing overhead will only tempt you to try on a black fringed skirt or a pair of scrunchie suede boots even more. Marmalade has printed blouses and oversized sweaters nestling loudly between calmer, cooler frocks. If you are not sure if that belted dress is for you, try it on: vintage fabric sometimes looks better on you than on the hanger. Tank style dresses made by the owner from vintage scarves guarantee one-of-a-kind originality; once you succumb, throw in a pair of hoop earrings.

211 West 20th Street
Btn Seventh & Eighth Ave
Chelsea
Map 8-D1

Purple Passion

212 807 0486 | *www.purplepassion.com*

Purple walls and a smiling staff are concealed behind a curtain-covered door in Chelsea. Look closely or you might miss it. The store has an abundance of fetish items for men and women, including clothing, sex and electrical toys, videos, magazines, BDSM gear, boots and shoes. Women can check out a good selection of corsets, garters belts or costumes, or try on a pair of stilettos or platforms. Or even platform stilettos. You can order online if you blush easily!

Various Locations

Scoop NYC

www.scoopnyc.com

At Scoop, find the latest styles in jeans, sweaters, skirts, dresses, jewellery, handbags and shoes in prime labels like Katayone Adeli, Daslu, Alice & Olivia, Ella Moss and Diane von Furstenberg. Scoop Men's is equally in vogue in which a Fred Perry Track Jacket costs only $115. Scoop Kids will start them young in a pair of Chip & Pepper jeans and if fashion is your first priority, pick junior up a thermal with The Beatles on it for $70. Expect a sale twice a year when those AG cords you were pining for might get marked down to $100.

65 West Houston St
Cnr of Wooster St
Soho
Map 10-E1

Trico Field

212 358 8484 | *www.fith-usa.com*

This stocks what children's clothing should be: wearable, a bit rugged, and not the least bit pretentious or precious. The Trico Field kid likes to jump in puddles and get muddied up. Just a few months old, Trico Field has a general store atmosphere with tiny denim and corduroy pants hanging in a line as if on a door knob of a child's bedroom. Long sleeve and short sleeve cotton shirts (the cutest one with a detachable waist apron), plaid flannel shirts, knit sweaters and puffy vests suggest outdoor adventure and campfire songs. Fith, Denim Dungaree and Go to Hollywood are the sensible labels of choice. This kind of frolic does not come cheap however; a denim skirt might cost $135, while a pair of relaxed sweatpants might be $99.

290 Lafayette St
Btn Houston & Prince
Soho
Map 11-A1

Triple Five Soul

212 431 2404 | *www.triple5soul.com*

What does it say on your shirt? Wear the original designs and you'll always be ready for any spontaneous street party. Twills, cotton, denim, and cord abound, including rugged bags, streetwear accessories and winter bomber jackets for him and her. Merchandise tags suggest you 'beat' items 'on rocks' to enhance the distressed look, but clearly this is not necessary as some garments even appear unfinished. This is part of the charm. Triple Five Soul began in 1989 and continues to be a competitive provider of urbanwear, with its clothing and accessories sold at many outlets both nationally and internationally. Other location: Brooklyn (718 599 5971).

15 Gansevoort St
Hudson & West 4th St
West Village
Map 8-D2

Yoya Mart

212 242 5511 | *www.yoyashop.com*

The funky and urban Yoya Mart nabs kids from ages 2-12 and delivers funky clothing, footwear, and accessories that are as hip as the parents buying them. T-shirts with monkeys, wacky but plush toy characters, books, parent friendly CDs, and jewellery designed by Dinh Van leave no one questioning the taste of its celebrity clientele.

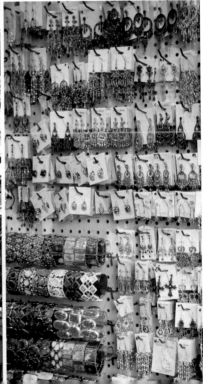

Clothes

A	Soho	212 941 8435
Add	Soho	212 539 1439
Ann Taylor	Various Locations	www.anntaylor.com
Artbag	Upper East Side	212 744 2720
Barneys Co-Op	Various Locations	www.barneys.com
Big Bag	East Village	212 353 3503
Bottega Veneta	Midtown	212 371 5511
Catherine Malandrino	Soho	212 925 6765
Dane 115	Soho	212 243 1295
delfino	Upper East Side	212 517 5391
Destination	Meatpacking District	212 727 2031
Eye Candy	Noho	212 343 4275
Find Outlet	Various Locations	www.www.findoutlet.com
Gabay's Outlet	East Village	212 254 3180
Gerry's	Chelsea	212 243 9141
Girlshop	Meatpacking District	212 255 4985
Hat Shop	Soho	212 219 1445
JJ Hat Center	Midtown	212 239 4368
Jack Spade	Soho	212 625 1820
Kangol	Upper West Side	212 724 1172
Kate Spade	Soho	212 274 1991
LaCrasia Gloves	Chelsea	212 803 1600
Loehmann's	Various Locations	www.loehmanns.com
Lucy Barnes	West Village	212 255 9148
Odin	East Village	212 475 0666
Paul Frank	Nolita	212 965 5079
Paul Smith	Flatiron District	212 627 9770
Rafe New York	Noho	212 780 9739
Rebecca Taylor	Nolita	212 966 0406
Roberto Vascon	Upper West Side	212 787 9050
Rochester Big & Tall	Midtown	212 247 7500
Tracy Feith	Nolita	212 334 3097
Urban Outfitters	Various Locations	www.urbanoutfitters.com
Verve	West Village	212 375 1277
Wink	Soho	212 334 3646

Bargain Hunting
Sample sales are frequent and signing up for sites like www.dailycandy.com and www.topbutton.com will alert you to their schedule. New York Magazine, *the Style Section in the* New York Post, *and* Time Out New York *are other great resources when trying to tap sample sales of designers. What can be better than paying $60 for a cashmere sweater normally priced at $180? Another goldmine is the Barneys Warehouse Sale which happens twice a year and where men's, women's and children's clothing and accessories can climb to 80% off. Check its website www.barneys.com or call 212 450 8400 for details.*

Computers

Other options **Electronics & Home Appliances** p323

Maybe you have not seen the commercials depicting the showdown between the Mac and PC user, but deciding which route to go will be your biggest challenge. The Apple Stores have drawn in both the diehard fan and disbeliever with friendly service and a vast array of flashy technology. Both locations in Manhattan are as slick as the laptops, with the store on Fifth Avenue open around the clock. The Apple Store in Soho boasts a state-of-the-art theatre where free workshops (and Wi-Fi) are bound to keep you occupied. Any Apple Store's Genius Bar is available for repairs and troubleshooting and with store locations across the world, your warranty can be honoured when you travel. Macs are also sold at CompUSA along with Sony, Toshiba, Compaq, and Samsung, among others, as well as a range of computer software, accessories and components. Computer deals happen often, with newspapers like *The New York Times* and *The Daily News* announcing sales. For comparison shopping try Staples (p.352), Best Buy (p.324), J&R Music & Computer World (p.323), or Target (p.323).

Mac CPR

Should your Mac come down with a cold or feel feverish for any length of time, Tekserve could be just what you need. Tekserve (212 929 3645) offers computer repair service, upgrades, rentals, even 10% off a new iPod if you recycle yours and purchase one at the same time. You won't even get penalised if it is inoperable.
www.tekserve.com

Computers			
Apple Store		Soho	212 226 3126
		Midtown	212 336 1440
CompUSA		Midtown	212 782 7798
		Hell's Kitchen	212 262 9711
J & R Music & Computer World		Financial District	212 238 9000

Electronics & Home Appliances

Other options **Computers** p.323

If you need to buy a trusty toaster for your Sunday bagels, Bed Bath & Beyond (p.329), Kmart (p.361) and Macy's (p.361) are ideal sources. Several shops selling electronics can be spotted throughout the city; however, it is usually advisable to buy large, more expensive, items from well-known and reputable outlets.

Electronics & Home Appliances		
Adorama	Chelsea	800 223 2500
Bang & Olufsen	Various Locations	www.bang-olufsen.com
Bloom & Krup	Hell's Kitchen	212 673 2760
Brookstone	Various Locations	www.brookstone.com
Calumet Photo	Chelsea	212 989 8500
Canal Hi-Fi	Soho	212 925 6575
Circuit City	Various Locations	www.circuitcity.com
DataVision	Midtown	212 689 1111
Drimmers	Brooklyn	212 995 0500
Gracious Home	Various Locations	www.gracioushome.com
Hammacher Schlemmer & Co	Midtown	212 421 9000
Harvey Home Entertainment	Various Locations	www.harveyonline.com
Home Depot	Various Locations	www.homedepot.com
In Living Stereo	Noho	212 979 1273
J & R Music & Computer World	Financial District	212 238 9000
Manhattan Center for Kitchen & Bath	Flatiron District	212 995 0500
PC Richard & Son	Various Locations	www.pcrichard.com
RadioShack	Midtown	212 953 6050
Sharper Image	Various Locations	www.sharperimage.com
Sony Style	Midtown	212 833 8800
Sur La Table	Soho	212 966 3375
Target	Various Locations	www.target.com

323

420 Ninth Ave
Btn 33rd & 34th St
Hell's Kitchen
Map 6-D2

B&H

212 444 6600 | *www.bhphotovideo.com*

An extensive gallery of photo, video and pro-audio equipment is housed in this superstore. B&H carries a remarkable stock, with in-store events showcasing new products from manufacturers. Digital cameras by Leica, Casio, Pentax, Olympus, Rollei and Nikon, among others, can be purchased from $50-$8,000. They stock studio, darkroom and lighting equipment, as well as a range of binoculars. There is an information desk for the confused and free parking for the first hour with a $100 purchase, or two hours if you spend $300. B&H also buys and sells used equipment and will ship to a US residential address or internationally.

Various Locations

Best Buy

www.bestbuy.com

Here you are free to roam and shop either unguided, or assisted by a knowledgeable associate equipped to handle all of your electronic needs. Choose from computers, printers, iPods, MP3 Players, VCRs, DVDs, appliances, cameras, camcorders, music, movies, games, even GPS navigation systems to help you get back home. Televisions can range from under $200 up to the thousands, depending on how pumped up you want your pad to be. Delivery service is available or you can take it with you to spare some cost. The website is comprehensive for online shoppers but it will deprive you the joy of publicly cooing over the flatscreens.

iKnow iPod

Nobody knows Apple better than Apple. And no other store can do up iPods like the Apple Store (p. 323). The two Manhattan stores carry the best stock of iPods and accessories. After you've purchased your pod, call up HungryPod who can pick up your music collection and load it in for you. They charge per CD with the price decreasing as your number albums increase. They will also make recommendations and legally download music for you.
www.hungrypod.com

Eyewear

Other options **Sporting Goods** p.349

There are numerous places to get eye exams or pick up a pair of shades. Macy's (p.361) has a Vision Express centre where exams cost $49. Cohen's Fashion Optical and Lens Crafters, two of the more recognised names in optometry and eyewear, can check your family as well, while Myoptics is favoured among more style conscious spec wearers. You'll find sunglasses everywhere from department stores to the street (for no names and knock offs). Century 21 (p.360), Loehmann's (p.322) and Filene's Basement (p.360) have a good selection of designer eyewear at a discount.

Fabulous Fanny's

335 East 9th St
Btn First & Second Ave
East Village
Map 9-B3

212 533 0637 | www.fabulousfannys.com
Fabulous Fanny's houses what has to be the finest vintage eyewear collection in the city, with some pieces dating back as far as the 1700s. A vintage pair can start as low as $40 with some antiques ranging from $1,000 to $2,000. They stock their own line, as well as 30 years of Dior, Versace and Givenchy. New frames from different designers are also included with an array from Corinne McCormack at $75-$145. For prescriptions, they will direct you to one of the six opticians they work with. Glasses can be customised and many have unique rhinestone detailing crafted in-store. Be sure to check out the glasses 'museum' case, which houses wacky eyewear from the past, and the attached men's and women's vintage clothing store.

Solstice

500 Fifth Avenue
On 42nd St
Midtown
Map 7-A1

212 730 2500 | www.solsticestores.com
Label junkies unite at this quintessential sunglasses hut where designer names take a stab at protecting your pupils. Chanel, Gucci, Tom Ford, Giorgio Armani, Marc Jacobs…it seems every fashion house is available. Try on a pair of Kate Spade sunglasses for $178, or an Oliver Peoples for $420, while Diesel stakes claim on the young urbanite. Prescription sunglasses are not available but the line of Maui Jim and Ray Ban offer a polarisation option for those more interested in preventing glaucoma than advertising for Juicy Couture. There is another location in the Time Warner Center (212 823 9590).

Eyewear		
Cohen's Fashion Optical	Various Locations	www.cohensfashionoptical.com
Lens Crafters	Various Locations	www.lenscrafters.com
Macy's Vision Express	Midtown	212 494 7300
Myoptics	Various Locations	www.myoptics.com
Nakedeye	Lower East Side	212 253 4935
Oakley	Soho	212 673 7700
Oculus 20/20	Brooklyn	718 666 0040
Oliver Peoples	Various Locations	www.oliverpeoples.com
Robert Marc	Various Locations	www.robertmarc.com
Selima Optique	Various Locations	www.selimaoptique.com
Sol Moscot	Various Locations	www.solmoscotopticians.com

Flowers

Other options **Gardens** p.329

A corner deli is perhaps one of the most convenient, and inexpesive, places to pick up a last minute token of affection. If you are looking for a wider selection, or just want to pick up something pretty and fragrant for your home, take a stroll down 28th Street

325

between Sixth and Seventh Avenues and you will be delighted by the range large and small interior plants, floral bouquets, silks, vases and pots. Starbright Floral Design has floral arrangement options for every occasion. To place an international order for

Flowers		
Flora New York	Soho	212 274 1887
Kampo Floral Design	West Village	212 206 0820
Katrina Parris Flowers	Upper West Side	212 222 7030
Lexington Gardens	Upper West Side	212 861 4390
Spruce	West Village	212 414 0588
Starbright Floral Design	Chelsea	212 229 2623
Takashimaya	Midtown	212 350 0100
United Wholesale Florist	Chelsea	212 929 8264
Wild Poppy	Upper East Side	212 717 5757

delivery throughout the US, you must call Starbright directly. Also on 28th Street is United Wholesale Florist, which specialises in exotics and tropicals from such countries as Holland, Ecuador, Thailand and Costa Rica. Spruce, in Greenwich Village, has some traditional arrangements with a twist, as well as some lovely contemporary bouquets.

Get creative and send something special – lab bottles as vases and shortened flowers in a glass cube offer a modern and minimalist approach. Flora New York carries many seasonal flowers and makes stunning floral presentations – their bridal bouquet filled with orchids and calla lilies is just breathtaking.

Food

Other options **Health Food** p.330

With its fabulous restaurants and market outlets, New York City can turn anyone into a foodie. Check the Health Food section on p.330, or visit one of the city's many outdoor greenmarkets, as buying straight from a farmer offers many advantages. The Amish Market and Garden of Eden Farmers' Market each sell fresh fruit and vegetables at affordable prices, in addition to speciality items. The Amish Market in particular has a wide selection of cheeses. If olives are your thing, Fairway imports 70% of those produced in Europe, and is great when scouting out that random mushroom. Alternatively, if you just feel like grabbing a reasonably priced bite, head to the upstairs cafe at its 74th Street location. Fancy feasts can be found at the famous Zabar's, a place famed for its smoked fish. In addition to the aesthetics in Balducci's, the prepared foods are quite savoury with contemporary, fusion, ethnic and vegetarian dishes on offer.

Delivery services and fees vary depending on each store, while the catering options at Dean & DeLuca, Balducci's, Zabar's and Fairway can come to your rescue if you're reknowned for burning your rump. Chocolate has come a long way since Hershey, with shops like Scharffen Berger and La Maison du Chocolat tantilising taste buds and offering sharp instore presentations. Dylan's Candy Bar is your dentist's worst nightmare, as liquorice, lollipops and chocolate bars are difficult to deny. For true

fanatics, make an appointment at Chocolat Michel Cluizel for an Introductory Tasting course. Priced at $35 per person, you can devour the history of chocolate and chow down your sickly fill of tasters during the 30 minute treat. Quel amusement!

When grocery shopping, you will notice that a Manhattan zip code is both a blessing and a curse: you may have more options than other boroughs, but your friends in Queens can always get their chicken three dollars cheaper than you. Key Food stores (www.keyfoodstores.com) can be found in all five boroughs, with Manhattan hosting other chain stores such as Gristedes (www.gristedes.com) and D'Agostino (www.dagnyc.com). New York, particularly Manhattan, does not tend to have supermarkets, but rather smaller grocery stores, with better quality food. If you have to survive on $10 a week, there are plenty of Jack's 99 Cent stores (the one at 110 W 32nd St is a big one – call 212 268 9962), dotted around the city. They're stuffed with cheap packets of noodles, soups, breads and frozen foods, as well as plastic jewellery and lovable junk, such as cow-shaped lighters.

Dean & DeLuca

560 Broadway
Cnr of Prince St
Soho
Map 10-F1

212 226 6800 | www.deananddeluca.com

These are the gourmet gladiators. It began in 1973 with Giorgio DeLuca's speciality cheeses. Four years later and with Joel Dean on board, the company branched into various gourmet offerings of the finest calibre. The list is long and includes a comprehensive selection of cheeses, packaged goods, olive oil, balsamic vinegar, farm-raised and wild fish, a chocolate area, cakes, cookies, pies, produce and more. Organic apples that appear to have just left a photo shoot cost about $2.50 a pound. There is also a kitchenware section with classic stemware and pots by Paderno. You can choose a pre-made customised gift basket or have one made up especially. For the holidays, say yuletide with a European Holiday Basket for $150. Expect prices to match its ultra chic address in Soho. Or just order a $3 latte from the swanky coffee bar, sip by the standing counters and people watch. Other location: Upper East Side (212 717 0800).

The Food Emporium

Various Locations

www.thefoodemporium.com

There are over 30 branches of the Food Emporium in Manhattan and chances are one will be near you. You can tell the organic produce from the conventional by the size and colour difference, but if you are looking for something truly gourmet, you might not find it. The selection of groceries will mirror the size of each store location with service being unpredictable at times. If leaving your apartment for a week's worth supplies is at all inconvenient, online shopping is available with free delivery on purchases over $40 (beer not included). Sign up for The Food Emporium Card for in-store and online savings.

Magnolia Bakery

401 Bleecker St
Cnr of West 11th St
West Village
Map 8-D3

212 462 2572

There is no place to sit or even loiter in this tiny sugar paradise, so it's best to buy your piece of ecstasy and leave shortly thereafter. Magnolia Bakery bakes everything from scratch in just a few ovens. People come at all hours for the cupcakes, which it is most noted for, and salivate in a self-serve line waiting to buy up to a dozen. Any more than that and an ambulance will have to follow you home. Chocolate or vanilla cost $1.75 while the coconut, german chocolate, red velvet and devil's food are $2.25. Other delicious bets include the banana pudding and the Snickers icebox pie. If it happens to be warm out, savour your cupcake in the public sitting area located diagonally across the street. For parties, order cakes a few weeks in advance.

142 East 14th St ◄
Btn Third Ave & Irving Pl
East Village
Map 9-B2

Trader Joe's

212 529 4612 | www.traderjoes.com

Long time fans and the newly converted are raving about Trader Joe's on 14th Street. The privately owned Californian grocery store has just one location in Manhattan and assures the city dweller via the website that they 'taste every product before we decide to sell it.' Some favourites include the healthy frozen meals, the cranberry goat's cheese, the dried fruit and nuts, the pre-made sandwiches and even the toothpaste. Prices are reasonable but the waiting can be lengthy, making many long for another outlet.

132 Spring Street ◄
Soho
Map 10-F1

Vosges Haut-Chocolat

212 625 2929 | www.vosgeschocolate.com

Sit at the marble tabletop under a crystal chandelier and sip an exotic bianca cocoa that has been infused with lemon myrtle imported from Australia. Those who love their chocolate with a surprise, say wasabi, will love the strange cocoa treats on offer here. Owner Katrina Markoff abides by the mantra that chocolate is not just an occasional indulgence, it is a way of life. The mouth-watering (and pricey) truffles are packed full of natural and exotic ingredients. The nine piece collezione Italiano sells for $37 and is comprised of taleggio cheese, Tuscan fennel pollen, olive oil, balsamic vinegar and Sicilian sea salt.

Various Locations ◄

Whole Foods Market

www.wholefoodsmarket.com

The 'Whole Philosophy' extends to providing incomparable service, excellent organic and natural products, and committing itself to the environment through reducing reusing and recycling (whenever possible), and sustainable agriculture. The produce is fresh, the meat comes minus the antibiotics and the chickens were free to roam about. Cereal starts around $2.49 with the Galaxy Granola is priced at $8.39. A half a gallon of milk ranges from $3.50-$4.50 in a sizeable selection of soy, rice and organic brands. The sushi is always fresh and great to grab when on the go, but if you happen to be at the Columbus Circle or Union Square locations you will want to dine from the buffets of salads or ethnic offerings. The food is priced according to weight, so a $7 lunch is not unusual.

Lazy Shopping

Why bother mulling over melons in the grocery store when Fresh Direct allows you to sit in your pyjamas all day? Order from www.freshdirect.com and pay $4.95 for deliveries to Manhattan, Brooklyn and Queens. Choose from conventional, organic, or Kosher, and rest assure that your groceries will be in fine form when they arrive.

Food

Amish Market	Midtown	212 370 1761
Balducci's	Various Locations	www.suttongourmet.com
Chocolat Michel Cluizel	Flatiron District	212 477 7335
Citarella	Various Locations	www.citarella.com
Dylan's Candy Bar	Upper East Side	646 735 0078
Eli's Manhattan	Upper East Side	212 717 8100
Fairway	Various Locations	www.fairwaymarket.com
Garden of Eden Farmers Market	Chelsea	212 675 6300
Gourmet Garage	Various Location	www.gourmetgarage.com
Han Ah Reum Market	Midtown	212 695 3283
Kalustyan's	Gramercy Park	212 685 3451
La Maison du Chocolat	Various Locations	www.lamaisonduchocolat.com
Little Pie Company	Meatpacking District	212 414 2324
Russ & Daughters	Lower East Side	212 475 4880
Sahadi's	Brooklyn	718 624 4550
Scharffen Berger	Upper West Side	212 362 9734
Zabar's	Upper West Side	212 787 2000

Gardens

Other options **Hardware & DIY** p.329, **Flowers** p.325

Dig It

If, like most New Yorkers, you don't have a garden, but you still possess green fingers, get involved with Green Guerillas (212 402 1121, www.greenguerillas.org). Since 1973, the group has been preserving community gardens, helping community garden groups grow more food to distribute in their neighbourhood, and organising fundraising events, such as mural painting. On the other hand, if you're lucky enough to require a gardener, check out www.nygardener.com for local companies.

Green pastures are a rare sight unless you are spending the day in Central Park. But for those who can make gardens grow in a limited space, GRDN Bklyn carries the basic necessities, such as tools, plants, seeds, bulbs and beautiful terracotta pots. It will be a much quainter shopping experience than going to the Home Depot (www.homedepot.com) or Kmart (www.kmart.com), and less limited than your loal supermarket. The Planter Resource has a range of pots and vases in glass, ceramic, aluminium and fibreglass, from tiny to gigantic. Stop in at a one of the neighbouring plant shops and you will undoubtedly find a match. Smith & Hawken aim to unleash your gardening potential by offering a range of garden equipment, furniture, fountains, even a bocce ball set, and while you might manage a gazebo in the near future, you might not be snapping up an ivy ball topiary any time soon. Just don't forget to add water.

Gardens		
Bed Bath & Beyond	Various Locations	www.bedbathandbeyond.com
Gracious Home	Upper West Side	212 231 7800
GRDN Bklyn	Brooklyn	718 797 3628
Mecox Gardens	Upper East Side	212 249 5301
Munder-Skiles	Upper East Side	212 717 0150
Planter Resource	Chelsea	212 206 7687
Sears	Various Locations	www.sears.com
Smith & Hawken	Soho	212 925 1190
Treillage	Upper East Side	212 535 2288

Hardware & DIY

Other options **Gardens** p.329, **Home Furnishings & Accessories** p.331

DIYers unite at the Home Depot. With stores in the Bronx, Queens, Brooklyn, Staten Island and two locations in Manhattan, you will find all you need to hammer to your heart's content. Prices here range from safe to splurge with an array of services for those in need of a helping hand, such as flooring installation, interior and exterior painting, custom organisation for the home and an in-store design centre for consultation. Kids' workshops and other clinics are also available for those who have yet to convert. Kmart (p.361) sells paint and painting supplies along with Janovic and Ben Franklin Paints. Name brands will depend on the store's individual preference. The Home Depot carries Ralph Lauren, among others, and Kmart will carry Martha Stewart. Some other good names to look for include Benjamin Moore, Pratt & Lambert and Sherwin-Williams. For lumber, New York City has several options including Metropolitan Lumber,

Hardware & DIY		
Ace Hardware	Tribeca	212 571 3788
Ben Franklin Paints	Upper West Side	212 595 3800
C & S Hardware Corp.	Upper West Side	212 222 8720
Dykes Lumber Co	Hell's Kitchen	212 246 6480
Great Jones Lumber Corp	Noho	212 254 5560
Home Depot	Various Locations	www.homedepot.com
Homefront Hardware & Lumber	Gramercy Park	212 545 1447
Janovic	Various Locations	www.janovic.com
Kraft Hardware	Upper East Side	212 838 2214
Lumberland Hardware	Gramercy Park	212 696 0022
Metropolitan Lumber	Various Locations	www.metrolumberco.com
Midtown Lumber	Chelsea	212 675 2230
Mike's Lumber	Upper West Side	212 595 8884
Scheman & Grant	Hell's Kitchen	212 947 7844
Simon's Hardware & Bath	Gramercy Park	212 532 9220
Thalco Maintenance Supply	Upper East Side	212 879 3396

Dykes Lumber, and the 24 hour Homefront Hardware & Lumber for those late night urges. Delivery services and pricing depends upon the store and your needs. Local hardware stores can be found throughout the city selling everything from basic hardware supplies to contact paper, with some even able to copy a set of keys for your out-of-town visitors.

> **Man With a Hammer**
>
> If you're after a custom-made garden shed or dog kennel, check out the skilled trade services section on Craig's List (http://newyork.craigslist.org). For larger jobs, such as kitchens and bathrooms, try www.findcontractor.org or www.manhattancarpentry.com.

Health Food

Other options **Food** p.326, **Health Clubs** p.292

With the increased popularity of yoga and meditation and the growing interest in Eastern philosophies, more and more residents are seeking out ways to enrich other aspects of their life. New York City is thriving with health food stores selling a range of vitamins, supplements, elixirs, powders, specific foods, protein and energy bars. Many stores cater to a range of dietary restrictions such as dairy, wheat, yeast or gluten allergies, and will have a wider selection of products targeting this niche than some supermarkets. Whole Foods Market (p.328) is perhaps a good exception – there you can find a slew of natural and organic foods.

Health Food

Back to the Land	Brooklyn	718 768 5654
Bell Bates Natural Food Market	Tribeca	212 267 4300
Commodities Natural Market	East Village	212 260 2600
Food for Health	Upper East Side	212 369 9202
Good N Natural	The Bronx	718 931 4335
The Health Nuts	Upper West Side	212 724 1972
Healthfully Organic Market	East Village	212 598 0777
Integral Yoga Natural Foods	West Village	212 243 2642
Jamba Juice	Various Locations	www.jambajuice.com
Lifethyme Natural Market	West Village	212 420 9099
Organic Market	Chelsea	212 243 9927
The Pump Energy Food	Various Locations	212 764 2100
Westerly Natural Market	Hell's Kitchen	212 586 5262

Some gyms offer healthy items pre or post-workout, while popular juice chains like Jamba Juice can blend fruit juices with optional powder boosters. You can even sidle up to the counter with a buddy and do wheat grass shots. Restaurants serving vegetarian cuisine are also available and places like The Pump Energy Food offers high-protein, low-sodium, sugar-free and vegetarian food options. Westerly Natural Market, a health food store located on the cusp of the Theatre District, has been servicing many from the Broadway community with healthy food. An expert associate can navigate anyone through the sea of vitamins, and although the aisles are cramped, people always return. Spas also offer nutritional services and holistic remedies.

Delicious Dubai

If you're lucky enough to visit Dubai then make sure you pick up a copy of the fabulous eating and drinking guide *Posh Nosh, Cheap Eats and Star Bars*. Not only is this coffee table style book full of stunning images of some of Dubai's most splendid establishments but it is also packed with over 350 impartially written reviews, detailed maps and fun directories.

Home Furnishings & Accessories
Other options **Hardware & DIY** p.329

Bed Bugs Bite
If possible, mattresses should be bought new as bed bugs do not make fun evening companions. Visit showrooms to try out mattresses and ensure that individual preferences are met. 1-800-Mattress and Sleepy's carry famous makes like Sealy, Serta and Simmons, and have showrooms throughout the city with delivery options. For futons, try Futonland or the Futon Furniture Center.

Go forth and decorate! Your options are limitless in a city that forgives you when carrying chump change and rewards you when bills are overflowing. Home furnishings abound everywhere as stores revel in selling designer sweaters on one side, and glass vases on another. Discount department stores like Marshalls (p.333), TJ Maxx (p.333) and Filene's Basement (p.360) have cornered the market in offering brand name linens, rugs, cookware and pillows at reduced prices.

Though the nearest IKEA is in Long Island (www.ikea.com), inexpensive home furnishings can be purchased at Target (p.323) stores located in Queens, Brooklyn, New Jersey and the Bronx. Major department stores like Macy's (p.361) and Bloomingdale's (p.359) carry quality furniture in prices that start out nice, than graduate to the overwhelming.

Tastes change and vary upon individual. Those looking and needing to purchase second hand cast-offs can do so at the Salvation Army or at the Spence-Chapin Thrift Shops. At the Housing Works Thrift Shop, prices are a bit steeper but the merchandise is more memorable (expect to participate in an auction for popular items).

A Renoir found in a barn? It could happen. Hunt antique shops for rare and unusual finds because New York City has some history. A Repeat Performance is great for period furniture and household accessories, while Hyde Park Antiques specialises in 17th to 19th century furniture as well as paintings, mirrors and porcelains. For the authority, go to the Lexington Avenue location of Agostino Antiques as it sells premium English and continental furnishings from the 18th and 19th centuries. Warning: it gets pricey.

The city has also become a playground for shoppers looking for the latest in innovation and design and if you stroll down Greene Street in Soho, you will be amazed by the number of modern furniture stores. Places like Modernica, specialising in funky chairs, and the couch crazed Nuovo Melodrom will make you stand out. Sure it will cost about $5,000 to swing from a plastic bubble chair from C.I.T.E, but cool doesn't come cheap. At Moss you can redecorate your kitchen, office, or bedroom in the freshest and hippest in home design.

Various Locations

ABC Carpet & Home
www.abchome.com

The Indian Ganesha statue outside indicates the vitality and spirit within the store. Once in, you'll be greeted by lush colours, heavenly scents and lavish goods with an Indian emphasis. Plush satin and silk pillows can range from $65 to $245 depending on detail, while linen ones can cushion your cheek for around $45. Meander through the maze of candles, chandeliers, handcrafted jewellery, stemware, porcelain tableware, funky Judith Leiber glasses, silk scarves and furniture that can be contemporary, traditional, vintage or antique. The socially conscious MISSIONmarket sells unique gifts. Upstairs, you'll find children's furniture and clothing where a basic wooden crib can sell for $900, while a painted Peter Rabbit one demands $2,550. Hastens Beds (212 219 4099) shares the space and sell top of the line mattresses made from natural materials (the King of Sweden sleeps on one!). ABC's carpet store is the largest single retailer of rugs in the world. Handmade, machine made, antique, modern, and oriental rugs comprise four floors with the basement housing a noteworthy clearance section. ABC Carpet & Home has a personal shopper service and can ship anything, anywhere!

48 West 17th St
Btn Fifth & Sixth Ave
Flatiron District
Map 8-F1

Apartment 48
212 807 1391 | www.apartment48.com

Though the store needs no further publicity (it was featured in *Elle Decor*), it has to be said that Rayman Boozer, the store owner, knows about details. Step down into what resembles someone's personal habitat and check out home decor accessories with character. Wooden chairs garnered from an estate sale, decorative throws and funky housewares are here to be perused in tight quarters. Influenced by his travels abroad to places like Prague and Morocco, Boozer is also an interior designer. Four times a year the store changes merchandise so it is worth coming back.

Various Locations

Bed Bath & Beyond

www.bedbathandbeyond.com

Behold, the store that will cater to your every need regarding home matters. Be it appliances, bath linens, bed linens, pillows, crockery, cutlery, picture frames, curtains, organisers, bathroom accoutrements, seasonal items, or comforters. Price ranges start from low end but climb. Employees are more than willing to direct you through aisles of dizzying goods you never knew you needed until you laid eyes on them. The bridal registry department is top notch. Although Bed Bath & Beyond does not currently accept credit card purchases online with international address locations, call 1 800 GO BEYOND and an associate will gladly take an order at the 24 hour eService Center. Shopping in the store has the added benefit of a staffed doorman who helps you to hail a cab.

629 Sixth Ave
Btn 18th & 19th St
Chelsea
Map 8-E1

The Container Store

212 366 4200 | www.containerstore.com

Contain yourself! And everything you own. Simplifying and organising closets, kitchens and offices since 1978, the container store takes the guesswork out of saving space. Shoe racks for $17.99, shower caddies as low as $12.99, this store stocks some 10,000 items to help you store your life. Shelving options, cabinet organisers, cute floral laundry hampers and canisters to hold everything from cereal to pasta. Your trash will look best concealed in a bamboo basket. Employees clad in blue aprons are interactive and able to give advice. Still stumped? Expert Help boxes on their website provide organising ideas, even tips on how to protect your clothing. Ranked high in *Fortune*'s list of '100 Best Companies To Work For' – who knew so much goodness could come from containers. There is another branch in Midtown (212 366 4200).

> ### Custom-Made Furniture
> Some choice carpenters in the city include Gothic Cabinet Craft (212 420 9556), Manhattan Cabinetry (212 750 9800), Pompanoosuc Mills (212 226 5960) and Tucker Robbins (212 355 3383).

611 Broadway
Cnr of Houston
Noho
Map 11-A1

Crate & Barrel

212 780 0004 | *www.crateandbarrel.com*

It prides itself on 'People. Product. Presentation.' But it is frequented by many international visitors and residents for its well-priced home furnishings. Purchase high quality classic furniture preassembled, or work up a sweat and do it yourself for less. A dining table from the Furniture Collection can cost $1,000, but one in need of your touch, from the Ready to Assemble category, can cost $500. Children's furniture and bedding is cheerful and will add sparkle to any nursery, playroom or bedroom. Flatware, dinnerware and drinkware lean towards contemporary and nondescript, with the exception of a few more original pieces. Quilts start at $149 and are trusted friends when nursing a hangover. Oh, and the Cuisinart coffee maker from the appliance section will help too. There is another branch on the Upper East Side (212 308 0011).

889 Broadway
At 19th Street
Flatiron District
Map 9-A1

Fishs Eddy

212 420 9020 | *www.fishseddy.com*

Fishs Eddy offers cheap and moderate dinnerware that is both kitsch, quirky and perhaps even a dinner party conversation piece. Items include glasses with cows on them and mugs trimmed with dogs, although there are also more bare everyday kitchen supplies, if you don't want to spice up your crockery too much. A plain dinner plate can sell for $4.95, or

one that is decorated can fetch $12.95. Hoola girl glasses make especially great gifts. There is another branch in Brooklyn (718 797 3990).

Home Furnishings & Accessories

1-800-Mattress	Various Locations	www.mattress.com
A Repeat Performance	East Village	212 529 0832
Agostino Antiques	Various Locations	www.agostinoantiques.com
C.I.T.E. Design	Soho	212 431 7272
Futon Furniture Center	Various Locations	www.futonfurniturecenter.com
Futonland	Various Locations	www.futonland.com
Gothic Cabinet Craft	Various Locations	www.gothiccabinetcraft.com
Housing Works Thrift Shop	Various Locations	www.housingworks.org
Hyde Park Antiques	East Village	212 477 0033
Manhattan Cabinetry	Midtown	212 750 9800
Marshalls	Harlem	212 866 3963
Modernica	Soho	212 219 1303
Moss	Soho	212 204 7100
Nuovo Melodrom	Soho	212 219 0013
Pompanoosuc Mills	Tribeca	212 226 5960
Salvation Army	Various locations	www.salvationarmyusa.org
The Silk Trading Co.	Flatiron District	212 966 5464
Sleepy's	Various Locations	www.sleepys.com
Spence-Chapin Thrift Shops	Various Locations	www.spence-chapin.org
TJ Maxx	Flatiron District	212 229 0875
Target	Brooklyn	718 290 1109
Tucker Robbins	Midtown	212 355 3383

353

1965 Broadway
At 67th St
Upper West Side
Map 2-E4

Pottery Barn

212 579 8477 | *www.potterybarn.com*

Pottery Barn assures us that though at first glance the store may appear exclusive, it's not. Coffee tables that will last can range from $399 to $899 depending on incorporated materials. Furnishings for your bedroom, kitchen, bathroom, and living room are simple and clean and though duplicates might show up at your friend's pad, yours will look better. Pottery Barn Kids is located on Second Avenue and offers a wide range of furniture and bedding. Kids' beds can start at $599. There are other locations in Soho (212 219 2420) and Midtown (917 369 0050), as well as a Pottery Barn Kids on the Upper East Side (212 879 4746).

112 West 18th St
Btn Sixth & Seventh Ave
Chelsea
Map 8-E1

West Elm

212 929 4464 | *www.westelm.com*

At West Elm, you can expect Asian-influenced furniture and home accessories that make you look like you know interior design. The low-platform beds, coffee tables and side tables trigger your inner zen, while the duvets and decorative pillows (starting at $9) add a fresh spin. A king-size metal canopy bed priced at $749 looks as though it might have cost more. In addition to furniture, West Elm sells contemporary rugs, tableware, lamps and some bedding. Because quality tends to match the affordable pricing scale, invest in something sturdier that won't collapse mid-lounge. There is another branch in Brooklyn (718 875 7757).

They Think of Everything

Accessed via ABC Carpet & Home is The Silk Trading Co. It sells silk lampshades, pillows, picture frames and bed frames. No curtains, but draperies reside; some around $500. The Drapery-by-Design service allows you to choose from a plethora of textiles (located on the lower level of ABC Carpet & Home) and have them custom made. Prices depend on fabric and design and can be calculated online or in-store. The re-upholstery service will pick up your piece of furniture for you once a fabric is selected then deliver it upon completion.

Jewellery, Watches & Gold

From wooden bracelets to layered beads, and nameplate necklaces to glass pendants, New York jewellery trends are constantly evolving. Commonly referred to as the Diamond District, 47th Street between Fifth and Sixth Avenues is home to many independent businesses selling diamonds and fine jewellery at relatively affordable and negotiable prices. Be prepared upon entering any one of these establishments for some pushy and eager behaviour from sellers. Jewelry 55 Exchange seems a bit old world, but it is vast and has an inexpensive repair shop downstairs, even a barber shop in case you grew a beard while procrastinating between a princess or an emerald cut. If you are at all doubtful of a diamond's quality, shop at an established store – or if you are interested in committing financial suicide, Harry Winston is renowned for beautiful diamonds, at gasp-inducing prices.

Cartier

Lighter wallets can relish in costume jewellery at Agatha Paris, or create trinkets from an array of materials at Femmegems which also hosts private parties and events complete with wine and food. Ten Thousand Things defines exceptional design and craftsmanship. In addition to the beautiful creations of Ron Anderson and David Rees, the store's layout also includes select designers like Cara Croninger who works with vintage pieces from the 60s and 70s. Oversized bangles and chunky necklaces from her collection balance the more delicate designs of others. Department stores are great for shopping for jewellery and watches, especially if you are unsure of your desires. You will also find that the level of quality and unique offerings tends to equal a department store's reputation.

Buying a watch at any one of the department stores is a good bet but if you are looking for a bona fide distinct dealer, Wempe has a great selection as well as a marvellous repair department.

465 Broome Street
Btn Greene & Mercer St
Soho
Map 10-F2

Alexis Bittar

212 625 8340 | www.alexisbittar.com

Think original and fun, like large plaid patterned Lucite bangles and jewelled brooches in the shape of an owl or a peacock. A native of Brooklyn, Alexis began by designing jewellery from 20s era depression glass and selling it as a street vendor in Soho. Stock in Saks Fifth Avenue, exports to London and Japan soon followed, along with designs for Burberry and the Cooper Hewitt Museum in New York City. He is internationally represented in department stores and boutiques with his own store in Soho just blocks away from his humble beginnings. Buy earrings with semi-precious stones, necklaces picturing butterfly wings from the Elements collection, sharp-looking belts or an eye-shaped Lucite pendant with a fake eyelash attached.

133 Spring St
Btn Greene & Wooster
Soho
Map 10-F1

Garrard

212 201 7346 | *www.garrard.com*

You will need to ring the buzzer and take an elevator up to this inventive jewellery boutique. Garrard is an English company which has been operating for eons. Past commissions span royalty and aristocrats alike, with pieces appearing in museums and gracing private collections. It was also appointed Crown Jeweller by Queen Victoria in 1843, and sales associates are still delighted to show common gentry the dazzling collection once you enter. Admire pave diamonds in the shape of wing pendants, drop earrings with rubies, or try on the white gold tiara ring with yes, more diamonds, for $3,600. Garrard can customise a piece for you in-house, and with the comfy couches and chic setting, you'll have no problem staying.

727 Fifth Ave
Cnr of 57th St
Midtown
Map 5-A4

Tiffany & Co.

212 755 8000 | *www.tiffany.com*

He said it with his heart and not a tiny blue box? Curses! Tiffany & Co. is not off limits to anyone – the secret is in the silver, such as the $175 butterfly pendant by Elsa Peretti or Tiffany's own mesh ring for an obtainable $150. Internationally known and revered for its watches, diamond encrusted baubles, exquisite tableware and accessories, this stalwart also carries engagement rings that can bring both men and women to their knees. See serious shoppers discussing the four Cs of a diamond or witness young girls crowding the popular Tiffany & Co. heart and logo chokers. Engraving is available, as well as a complimentary personal shopping service. For those in need of a quick rest before the big spend, the sixth floor has restrooms and a lounge area.

Various Locations

Tourneau

www.tourneau.com

It is the largest selection of fine watches anywhere, having established itself in 1900 and continuing today by selling every major brand of watch including Rado, TAG Heuer, Breitling, Cartier, Baume & Mercier, Movado, Ebel, among many others. Sales associates will not hound or pressure you while you deliberate and they can offer style recommendations along with information regarding the timepiece's background or most noted qualities. This will prove most helpful when dropping close to a $1,000 on a Raymond Weil. Tourneau can repair every watch it sells and offers an added warranty (along with the manufacturer's), totalling three years from the purchase date. You can also trade up later on, or get a free appraisal to trade-in a watch and put the credit towards something new.

Jewellery, Watches & Gold

Agatha Paris	Midtown	212 758 4301
Bulgari	Various Locations	www.bulgari.com
Cartier	Various Locations	www.cartier.com
Doyle and Doyle	Lower East Side	212 677 9991
Femmegems	Nolita	212 625 1611
Fragments	Various Locations	www.fragments.com
Fred Leighton	Upper East Side	212 288 1872
Harry Winston	Midtown	212 245 2000
Helen Ficalora	Nolita	212 219 3700
Jewelry 55 Exchange	Midtown	212 354 5200
Pearldaddy	Nolita	212 219 7727
Swarovski	Various Locations	www.swarovski.com
Ten Thousand Things	Meatpacking District	212 352 1333
Wempe	Midtown	212 397 9000
Wendy Mink	West Village	212 367 9137

Lingerie

Other options **Clothes** p.315

The English call them knickers. In Spanish, the translation is ropa interior. But for many American women it is simply underwear, a range of which can be purchased at department and discount stores across the city. Lingerie pieces can be lusted over at Mixona, and if you scour Century 21 (p.360) and Filene's Basement (p.360), designer sets like DKNY and Cosabella might appear for half the price. Whether they are cotton briefs or black lace panties so indulgent you will want to wear them over your trousers (rarely a positive fashion statement), lingerie has come a long way since the training bra your mother bought for you years ago.

Lingerie		
Catriona MacKechnie	Meatpacking District	212 242 3200
Isaac Sultan & Sons	Lower East Side	212 979 1645
Laina Jane	Upper West Side	212 875 9168
Mixona	Nolita	646 613 0100
Only Hearts	Upper West Side	212 724 5608

133 Mercer St
Btn Prince & Spring St
Soho
Map 10-F1

Agent Provocateur

212 965 0229 | www.agentprovocateur.com

The first store opened in London in 1994 and its creators Joseph Corré and Serena Rees were the first to merge lingerie with fashion and humour. And, quite frankly, women's undergarments have never looked more enticing. Pink and black fill the store's boudoir and plush fitting rooms invite you to try on feminine demis, seductive corsets, and sleek suspenders. A pleated tulle slip sells for $300, while a cupless bra with a large satin bow sells for $135. For the exhibitionist, a barbed wire choker, a set of sequined pasties, and a Swarovski encrusted whip will surely set your man stammering.

93 Greene St
Btn Prince & Spring St
Soho
Map 10-F1

La Perla

212 219 0999 | www.laperla.com

At La Perla, expect a warm reception to counteract the icy prices. If money is no object to you, then buying a bikini for $418 shouldn't hurt too much. Though La Perla began as a small corset laboratory in Bologna, it is now an international retailer offering a range of highbrow lingerie, pyjamas, beachwear and clothing. The woman who shops here is probably a vice president for a major network and checks the time on her Cartier. Yes, this is luxury. There are other branches in the Meatpacking District (212 242 6662) and on the Upper East Side (212 570 0050).

Various Locations

Victoria's Secret

www.victoriassecret.com

The Herald Square branch (212 356 8383) of this lingerie queen is part emporium and part disco. Cue infectious music, bright lights and men sitting on the sidelines as their significant others coo over lacy corsets, bow-adorned panties and ruffled bras. From the design collection, putter through creations by Dolce & Gabbana, Pleasure State and Andres Sarda, which are unique to this location and a few others. A Betsey Johnson pink floral slip can cost $58, while a French-inspired bra designed by Chantal Thomass can go for $108. The beauty department carries makeup lines Pout, Vincent Longo, and Very Sexy (in case the atmosphere did not imply this enough), along with Victoria's body care and fragrance lines. Check out the botox in a jar, Freeze 24•7, promising to diminish that number 11 between your eyebrows in no time.

Well Endowed?

Lucky you. Isaac Sultan & Sons carries 20% off trusted brands like Maidenform, Olga and Warner's, and carry hard-to-find bra sizes. Online shopping at www.isaacsultan.com guarantees a wider selection than going to the store.

Luggage & Leather

Other options **Shipping** p.308

You may be hanging your hat in Queens, but that doesn't mean you shouldn't look like a Manhattanite when you come to town. Department stores (p.358) will carry a range of sizes and styles, with Target (p.323) and Kmart (p.361) asking little of you financially. Be it carry-on, duffel, garment, or messenger, Innovation Luggage offers a spectrum of choices with names like Samsonite, Briggs & Riley, Kipling and Victorinox, where a travel tote (bag) can cost around $80. If your luggage never seems to return in its proper state, spend a little more at Tumi for something slightly sleeker, understated, and downright durable. Bored airport employees will appreciate the floral or

Luggage & Leather		
Altman Luggage	Lower East Side	212 254 7275
The Bag House	West Village	212 260 0940
Crouch & Fitzgerald	Midtown	212 755 5888
Flight 001	West Village	212 989 1001
Hans Koch	Soho	212 226 5385
Hunting World	Soho	212 431 0086
Innovation Luggage	Various Locations	www.innovationluggage.net
Jack Spade	Soho	212 625 1820
Jennifer Convertibles	Various Locations	www.jenniferfurniture.com
Jensen-Lewis	Chelsea	212 929 4880
Jutta Neumann	Lower East Side	212 982 7048
LeSportsac	Various Locations	212 988 6200
Levitz	Flatiron District	212 473 8157
Lexington Luggage	Upper East Side	212 223 0698
m0851	Various Locations	www.m0851.com
Mirti Leather	Upper East Side	212 774 1886
Swiss Army	Soho	212 965 5714
Tod's	Upper East Side	212 644 5945
Tumi	Various Locations	www.tumi.com
Tusk	Chelsea	888 438 8875

camouflaged trolley you purchased from Flight 001. This store sells everything you will possibly need for your trip, including special flight kits to freshen up or keep the kids entertained.

The popularity of leather clothing seems to arrive and depart depending on a designer's feel for the season. However, leather goods such as wallets, handbags, belts and shoes are mainstays, and several stores have established themselves in the hearts of shoppers. The Village Tannery on Bleecker Street has a great selection of well-priced items and you can also repair your split hide. Tusk sells modern leather bags and accessories which will not empty your snakeskin wallet. For heavenly skins, Jutta Neumann's handcrafted leather goods have been featured in Vogue, Elle and Madamoiselle, and include eye-popping handbags, wristbands, sandals and wallets in a spectrum of colours. m0851 in Soho sells classic outerwear and accessories year-round, where modern jackets and buttery bags live in harmony. Leather pricing remains solid unless on sale, but it can still be affordable. For inexpensive imitations look to street vendors; the quality will vary but a good find can be found. And if your love of leather extends into home furnishings, Jennifer Convertibles and Jensen-Lewis can hook you up with low to moderately priced sofas.

Designer Leather

If you like your cowhide super stylish, you're living in the right city. Slick designer labels are not hard to find - try the following luxury stores:

Coach in Midtown (212 599 4777)
Fendi in Midtown (212 759 4646)
Ghurka on the Upper East Side (212 826 8300)
Gucci in Midtown (212 826 2600)
Louis Vuitton in Midtown (212 758 8877)
T. Anthony Ltd in Midtown (212 750 9797)

Medicine
Other options **General Medical Care** p.146

Pharmacies are widespread in New York City and tend to operate independently of supermarkets, hospitals and some shopping centres. In fact, if you happen to visit the emergency room of a hospital and receive a prescription, you will get it filled at a pharmacy. There are a few pharmacies (located within drugstores) that stay open around the clock, but with many drugstores having later hours or 24 hour service you will still be able to purchase basic medicine.

Prescription medication is very costly without insurance and sometimes even with insurance. Almost everything is available with a doctor's prescription including a range of anti-depressants and anti-pain medications like Codeine and OxyContin. Certain over-the-counter medications containing pseudoephedrine now require ID and a signature when purchasing. This regulation is due to the growing epidemic of methamphetamine use in the US the drug relies on pseudoephedrine as a component. Meanwhile, the morning-after pill, called Plan B in the US, is now available over the counter to women 18 or older.

Although most prescriptions are accompanied by a sheet of information, pharmacists are also helpful when double checking side effects or drug interactions.

Pharmacy Locator
The following chains have multiple locations throughout the five boroughs of New York. Check their websites to find the closest one to you (and whether your local pharmacy is open 24 hours).

CVS	www.cvs.com
Duane Reade	www.duanereade.com
Eckerd	www.eckerd.com
Rite Aid	www.riteaid.com

Mobile Telephones
Other options **Telephone** p.142

Wait for the Apple
The iPhone is making waves in the cellular market. At time of going to print the phone was not available for sale, but you can bet that when it is first launched, there will be a rush to get this super-cool gadget that combines the technologies of a phone, an iPod, and the internet in one funky handset. See www.apple.com for more information.

Perhaps the only place you will not find someone on a mobile is underground. Handsets are such a common sight that some stores have gone as far as posting signs at checkouts telling costumers to turn off their phones as a courtesy. Because the malls in Manhattan are not major shopping targets, there are several mobile phone stores for clients to shop for comprehensive packages and phones - as well as the all-important Blackberry. Verizon Wireless, T-Mobile, Cingular and Sprint are the most popular carriers offering competitively priced packages, customer care and service.

Cingular and T-Mobile operate on the global GSM system, so providing your international phone has been 'unlocked' (an agreement put in place between you and your network provider) and you have a tri-band phone, you can purchase SIM cards here and they will be recognised. Buying a mobile second-hand seems unnecessary when prices start from free (inclusive in some packages), and go up to $300 for a PDA or smartphone. Contracts are offered at stores with proof of US residency, and if you don't have residency, 'pay as you go' cards are the next alternative.

Mobile Telephones

Cingular Wireless	Various Locations	www.cingular.com
Sprint	Various Locations	www.sprint.com
T-Mobile	Various Locations	www.t-mobile.com
Verizon Wireless	Various Locations	www.verizonwireless.com

Music, DVDs & Videos

New York City is home to such breakthrough artists as The Ramones, Madonna, The Beastie Boys and The Strokes. It is a city rich in music culture and history and remains an epicentre for both established artists, and those struggling to get signed by a label. Then, there are the fans: both the mainstream listeners and those who shudder at the mere mention of mainstream. There are those who proudly wave their Coldplay banner and those who prefer to keep their love of Neil Diamond hidden.

iTunes is a hugely popular resource for the legal purchase of music; it charges 99 cents a song and is available at any time once you create an account. The Virgin Megastore, located in Times Square, is a hotbed of possibly every musical genre ever thought up and has numerous listening stations where you can listen to them. It has a great offering of DVDs, books, games and videos, even a small cafe downstairs where you can sip coffee and read sleeve notes. New releases generally hover around $14.99 with bins for both discounted CDs and DVDs, providing ample opportunity to increase your library. In-store events or appearances from artists shooting the popular MTV Total Request Live show across the street can also occur.

As convenient as shopping at a chain or large outlet can be, independents cater more to an exclusive tastes or preferences. Finyl Vinyl and Vinylmania are two such stores, both with huge ranges. You can purchase vinyls of rap or hip hop at Fat Beats, which has become an ultimate resource in this genre and where buying the latest Jay Z album will only cost $14.99. Or, if domestic deep house or techno is your thing, you might want to check out the selection at Dance Tracks. Colony Music has a wonderful selection of sheet music for the crooner looking to belt out a Broadway showtune. Located in the Theatre District, you will also find piano, vocal, guitar, and sax books in large supply, as well as instructional videos, a selection of karaoke music and rock and pop culture memorabilia, such as an autographed Bee Gees guitar for $1,200. CDs are also available but tend to be pricier – around $23.

Film Buff?

Blockbuster Video (www.blockbuster.com) is located all over New York City and is one of the main stores for rentals of DVDs and video games. You can also buy movies here and throw in a tub of popcorn for your movie marathon. For the convenience of sending and receiving titles through the mail, Netflix is a popular online site with package choices to suit your viewing schedule. Go to www.netflix.com where you can begin a rental queue from a multi-genre selection. Purchasing DVDs online is easy and inexpensive through www.deepdiscount dvd.com. Although the wait may be longer than purchasing from a store, you'll have the film for the rest of your life.

Music, DVDs & Videos		
Barnes & Noble	Various Locations	www.barnesandnoble.com
Bleecker Street Records	West Village	212 255 7899
Colony Music	Midtown	212 265 2050
Dance Tracks	East Village	212 260 8729
Etherea	East Village	212 358 1126
Fat Beats	West Village	212 673 3883
Finyl Vinyl	Noho	212 533 8007
Future Legends	Hell's Kitchen	212 707 8180
Halcyon	Brooklyn	718 260 9299
Jazz Record Center	Chelsea	212 675 4480
Mondo Kim's	Various Locations	www.mondokims.com
Rockit Scientist	East Village	212 242 0066
St Marks Sounds	East Village	212 677 2727
Vinylmania	Midtown	212 924 7223
Virgin Megastore	Flatiron District	212 598 4666
Virgin Megastore Incredibly	Flatiron District	2125 984 666
World Music Institute	Chelsea	212 545 7536

Downtown boasts some cool independent shops with an interesting, if strange, selection. Venture to St Marks Place and you will find Mondo Kim's. Don't expect ambience in this haunt, but you will find a great range of CDs, DVDs and Videos. New and used CDs from around $6.99-$18.99 are laid out according to genres which include, among others, garage rock, US/UK prog rock and indie/new school. Two listening stations preside in the back. Music DVDs always have 15% off, and if you feel like a poster of The Arctic Monkeys or The Doors, you can browse the small print collection.

Even cheaper music discoveries can be found at St Marks Sounds, with some CDs starting at $3.99. However if you are looking for conversation with a knowledgeable and appreciative staff, head over to Rockit Scientist which offers incredibly eclectic merchandise of new and used music - peruse the outside vinyl bins and you might come across Barbara Streisand on one trip or Midnight Oil on another, each for $1. The store itself is small but well-stocked with classic rock, funk, soul, jazz, and other genres. Vinyls are in the back categorised by group or artist and represent an excellent selection considering the size of the store. A limited edition Gram Parsons costs $11.99.

Musical Instruments

Other options **Music, DVDs & Videos** p.340, **Music Lessons** p.274

With musical theatre pumping at the heart of the Broadway scene, it comes as no surprise that instrument shops are located nearby. Servicing all musicians, from 'pit' orchestra harpists to aspiring rock stars, 48th Street between Sixth and Seventh Avenues stocks a wide range of musical instruments in several stores. Sam Ash is a good stop whether you are a beginner or a pro looking to try out something new. There are a couple of Sam Ash stores on 48th Street specialising in strings, brass, woodwinds, keyboards, sheet music and audio equipment. Here you can purchase a basic clarinet for $249, or buy a popular French Buffet for $849. A five-piece drum set can sell for $600 at

Musical Instruments		
30th Street Guitars	Chelsea	212 868 2660
Drummers World	Midtown	212 840 3057
Manny's	Midtown	212 819 0576
Matt Umanov Guitars	West Village	212 675 2157
Morel & Gradoux-Matt	Midtown	212 582 8896
Rayburn Music	Upper West Side	212 541 6236
Rivington Guitars	Lower East Side	212 505 5313
Rudy's Music Stop	Midtown	212 391 1699
Sam Ash	Various Locations	www.samash.com

Drummers World; throw in a set of sticks for $6.50 and rock on!

Rudy's Music Stop on 48th Street sells more high-end guitars, including exclusive vintage that might have been plucked by some famous fingers. Guitar enthusiasts have a penchant for Rivington Guitars and 30th Street Guitars for the collections of new, used, and vintage acoustics, basses, electrics and amps. In the heart of the studio and rehearsal district, 30th Street Guitars carries brands such as Martin, Gibson, Fender and Les Paul, among many others. Considered an institution by many local musicians as well as a go-to for international collectors, the vintage market at 30th can run from $500-$50,000. The repair shop is excellent, offering one-week turnarounds and $75 for a guitar setup. Staff at both stores are extremely knowledgeable and helpful.

Rivington Guitars

Party Accessories

Other options **Party Organisers** p.434, **Parties at Home** p.434

Seasonal decorations, invitations and thank you notes can be found in various supermarkets and pharmacies, but stationery stores have a wider selection. For more specific partying supplies, Village Paper and Broadway Cards & Party Suppliers carry party trimmings like plates, decorations, birthday candles, and gift ideas. At Balloons To Go, a minimum of six mylar or 12 latex balloons can be delivered in Manhattan for $42.16. Here you can customise, order centre pieces, drops, bouquet arrangements or even a singing telegram. If you want to entertain the adult kids as well as the young ones, try Arnie Kolodner Magic; he will make both the children and parents laugh. Linda Kaye's Birthdaybakers, Partymakers (www.partymakers.com) focuses on themed birthday parties for children, while party trendsetters SWAG Events hosts memorable bashes for adults and the teen and 'tween' (between 9 and 14 years old) demographic. If you're looking to scare your friends come Halloween, the Abracadabra Superstore has an enormous stock of costumes, masks, wigs, props, special effects items and juggling supplies. For the next themed party you can dress up as Keith Richards and your child can be a pirate.

Party Accessories		
Abracadabra Superstore	Flatiron District	212 627 5194
Arnie Kolodner Magic	www.arniemagic.com	212 582 2633
Balloons To Go	Chelsea	212 989 9338
Broadway Cards & Party Suppliers	Upper West Side	212 866 9219
Company's Coming!	Various locations	212 260 3036
Daisy Doodle	www.daisydoodle.com	212 501 4828
E.A.T. Gifts	Upper East Side	212 861 2544
Hallmark Card & Party Basket	Midtown	212 838 0880
Havin' a Party	Brooklyn	718 251 0500
Linda Kaye's	Upper East Side	212 288 7112
Odds Costume Rental	Chelsea	212 268 6227
Party Poopers	Tribeca	212 274 9955
SWAG Events	Various locations	www.swagevents.com
Village Paper	West Village	212 675 9697

Perfumes & Cosmetics

Other options **Markets** p.363

Beauty is Cheap

Pharmacies make the acquisition of beauty products financially possible, carrying such makeup lines as L'Oréal Paris, CoverGirl and Revlon. Another line, Maybelline New York, sells some of the best mascara you will find anywhere for around $5.

Major fragrances and cosmetic lines such as Clinique, Estée Lauder, Shiseido and Lancôme can be purchased at many department stores, with Barneys (p.358), Bloomingdale's (p.359) and Saks Fifth Avenue offering a more unique selection of brands you might not have been privy to otherwise. For specific skin conditions, or if you are in need of a cosmetic line that caters to a certain skin shade, department stores can be a helpful resource in discovering the right product. M.A.C Cosmetics has a wonderful range of pigments for many skin types and continues to be quite popular. Men in need of grooming aids can seek solace in several lines including Kiehl's, which has been selling wonderful skincare and haircare products for over a hundred years. The steady trend of spas and salons also offer another alternative for purchasing beauty aids. Many sell products so that daily skin regimens and pampering can continue even after your treatment has ended; and, upon the completion of that hour long massage you'll be receptive to just about anything your aesthetician recommends.

Are you always taking the wrong turn?

Whether you're a map person or not, these pocket-sized marvels will help you get to know the city… and its limits.

Explorer Mini Maps
Putting the city in your pocket

9 Bond St ◀
Broadway & Lafayette
Noho
Map 9-A4

Bond No. 9

212 228 1732 | *www.bondno9.com*

Imagine smelling like the true essence of New York City, with a fragrance that mirrors the spirit of a particular district, such as Chinatown, Chelsea Flowers, Wall Street or Broadway Nite (minus the pungent sewer smell of course). Some are spicy, while others are clean or energetic – but all are original. Cleanse your olfactory sense by sniffing the coffee beans and continue on to the smelling stations of Gramercy Park, West Broadway and Park Avenue. The flagship store is very inviting, you can take your time inhaling and asking the staff questions. You can also concoct your own scent, or prolong your stay in the tea room at the back. The Scent of Peace is rather popular and sells for $125. Some fragrances can be purchased in ounces, in decorative bottles or special spray atomisers encased in leather. A travel spray sells for $40 and would make a great gift. Other locations on the Upper East Side (212 838 2780) and in the West Village (212 633 1641) spread the fragrance throughout the city.

110 Prince St ◀
Cnr of Greene St
Soho
Map 10-F1

Face Stockholm

212 966 9110 | *www.facestockholm.com*

Gun Nowak's quest for wild colours led her to establish her own makeup line in Sweden. Owned and operated by Gun and her daughter, Martina Arfwidson, Face Stockholm's wide spectrum of lipsticks, blushes, eye dusts and shimmering and matte shadows will tempt you to build an outfit around your face. Face Stockholm is noted for its hard-wearing nail polish: pastel, iridescent, bold or glittery, priced at $12 a bottle. Some other items that stand out include the Lip Exfoliator, for buffing those chapped lips, and the Lash Base, which pumps up whispy leyeashes. Professional brushes, makeup bags, and a skincare line which includes natural botanical ingredients are also available. There are other branches on the Upper West Side (212 769 1420) and in the Time Warner Center (212 823 9415).

Perfumes & Cosmetics

Alcone	Hell's Kitchen	212 633 0551
The Bathroom	West Village	212 929 1449
Bergdorf Goodman	Midtown	212 753 7300
Carol's Daughter	Various Locations	www.carolsdaughter.com
Caswell-Massey	Midtown	212 755 2254
CB I Hate Perfume	Brooklyn	718 384 6890
Clarins	Various Locations	http://us.clarins.com
Clyde's	Upper East Side	212 744 5050
Floris of London	Upper East Side	212 935 9100
Henri Bendel	Midtown	212 247 1100
Il Makiage	Midtown	212 371 0551
Jo Malone	Flatiron District	212 673 2220
Kiehl's	Various Locations	www.kiehls.com
L'Artisan Parfumeur	Soho	212 334 1500
L'Occitane	Various Locations	http://usa.loccitane.com
Luilei	Various Locations	www.luileiny.com
M.A.C Cosmetics	Various Locations	www.maccosmetics.com
Make Up For Ever	West Village	212 941 9337
Malin + Goetz	Chelsea	212 727 3777
Molton Brown	Various Locations	www.moltonbrown.com
Origins	Various Locations	www.origins.com
Pir Cosmetics	Nolita	212 219 1290
Shu Uemura	Soho	212 979 5500

Various Locations ◀ ## Fresh

212 477 1100 | *www.fresh.com*

The pleasant sales people here could sell you anything, but the pretty items, including ceramic dishes, scented soaps, makeup, and bodycare lines in soy, rice, milk or sugar, sell themselves anyway. The Index fragrance line comes in a variety of notes including the popular Fig Apricot and Redcurrant Basil. Testing is not only allowed, it is encouraged. Fresh's decadent sugar-based body polish can be applied at the in-store sink, or try out the sugar lip balm that melts on contact. Free gift wrapping is available year-round, but don't forget to pick up something for yourself.

Various Locations ◀ ## Ricky's

212 949 7230 | *www.rickys-nyc.com*

If you have a hankering for funky reading glasses, wigs, costumes for Halloween, a slew of beauty products and paraphernalia, or just the unusual, go to this trendy 'beauty shop' where haircare products include Biolage, KMS, Paul Mitchell, Aveda and more. Or perhaps your lame locks need the 'Manipulator' by Bed Head for $14. The 'Red Light District' near the back is where you can purchase items more risqué than the nearby incense. Ben Nye and Mattése dominate the makeup scene and if you need to purchase a gag gift, who wouldn't appreciate a whoopee cushion?

Various Locations ◀ ## Sephora

212 625 1309 | *www.sephora.com*

This is absolute heaven for the beauty obsessed. Originating in France in 1969, Sephora houses a massive selection of cosmetics, fragrances, skincare essentials and beauty tools, with trained staff who are eager to help locate the perfect shade or the proper skincare product for any troubled dermis. Sephora's walls are lined with fragrances for men and women, but the cosmetics are the most enticing aspect, as loud colour palettes by Urban Decay, Stila, Benefit, Smashbox and Hard Candy beg you to test them out. Skincare lines include, among others, Dr. Hauschka, Murad and MD Formulations. A Decleor cleansing gel sells for $30. Men can beautify too under the 'Men's Skincare' and 'Solutions for Men' section which includes a decent offering of products by Clinique, Lab Series, Anthony Logistics, and Zirh. Sephora sells its own makeup line for slightly less, along with numerous brushes, tools, assorted bags and travel cases.

Pets

Other options **Pets** p.137

New York City can make you feel both lonely and claustrophobic at the same time. For this reason among others, furry friends can be spotted and cooed over throughout. Dog runs at several parks in the five boroughs display the cutest breeds of dogs and spark many onlookers to consider getting an animal. Cats perched on window sills are another temptation for the individual debating whether to become a pet parent.

Exclusive Smells

Only in New York would you find a perfume boutique known to stock brands that most people have never even heard of, such as Cote Bastide and Hierbas de Ibiza. Industry folk, fashion models and celebrities including Gwen Stefani love Aedes de Venustas which translates to 'temple of beauty' in Latin. Owners Karl Bradl and Robert Gerstner are sensory experts who can help you pick out that perfect scent. Fragrant candles from the Mariage Fréres collection like Thé Rouge and Thé Dansant are not to be missed, and you cannot find scents like VIP Room, or such fine gift-wrapping, anywhere else. 9 Christopher Street (between Sixth and Seventh Avenues) 212 206 8674.

345

Broadway Barks
Actresses Bernadette Peters and Mary Tyler Moore started Broadway Barks to raise awareness for homeless animals and encourage adoption. Check out www.broadwaybarks.com for more information

Pet stores in general do not have the best of reputations when it comes to purchasing an animal; consequently, many prospective buyers seek out adoption. Stores like Pet Stop and Spoiled Brats not only offer premium pet products, but adoption services for kitties as well. Beasty Feast, which works in conjunction with The Renaissance Project, has placed cats and dogs in many homes. View kitties at the Washington Street location, inquire about available dogs, or, if you're already 'with pup', put it in for a Beasty groom.

Supermarkets sell pet supplies in limited amount and quality. IAMS, which is now sold at most supermarkets, is healthy pet cuisine. Petco is a large chain store which contains an abundance of supplies. For further pampering, try the dedicated staff at Whiskers or check out the awe-inspiring apparel at Canine Styles. If you want to extend your New York family an adopt a pet, there are several places you can try. Organisations include ASPCA (www.aspca.org, 212 876 7700 ext. 4162), Barc Shelter (www.barcshelter.org, 718 486 7489), Animal Haven www.animalhavenshelter.org, 718 886 3683), and Mayor's Alliance for NYC's Animals (www.animal alliancenyc.org, 212 252 2350).

21 Murray St
Tribeca
Map 10-E4

The Paw Stop
646 546 5171 | *www.thepawstop.com*

Dan Rubenstein opened this pet care centre in November 2006 with the aim to 'create a pet-loving community both physical and online, whereby pet parents can receive the best care, information, and education to strengthen the human-animal bond'. The service therefore provides everything from transportation, training, grooming, overnight boarding, products, and dog daycare at a state of

the art facility in Tribeca. Dog owners can even keep an eye on their fluffy friends from the office via live digital webcams.

Pets		
American Kennels	Upper East Side	212 838 8460
Beasty Feast	West Village	212 620 4055
Calling All Pets	Upper East Side	212 734 7051
Canine Styles	West Village	212 352 8591
Doggystyle	Soho	212 431 9200
Le Chien Pet Salon	Upper East Side	212 861 8100
Pet Stop	Upper West Side	212 580 2400
Petco	Various Locations	www.petco.com
Petland Discount	Hell's Kitchen	212 459 9562
Spoiled Brats	Hell's Kitchen	212 459 1615
Whiskers Holistic Petcare	East Village	212 979 2532

Second-Hand Items

Other options **Books** p.314

Second-hand items are easy to come by if you are willing to pay more for them. With stores' high rents, deals happen less often, leaving those searching for a coffee table for $80 a bit stressed. The Salvation Army on 46th Street has several floors of items including clothing, records, housewares, knickknacks and a large selection of furniture. There are several locations around the city that are good for browsing if luck failed you at a flea market. If you feel that $60 for a chipped end-table is not acceptable, try to bargain a bit. Just leave your Fendi bag at home. At Angel Street Thrift Shop you can mix with passers-by and those who have made bargain hunting a full-time

Second-Hand Items		
17 at 17 Thrift Shop	Flatiron District	212 727 7516
A Second Chance	Upper East Side	212 744 6041
Angel Street Thrift Shop	Chelsea	212 229 0546
Cancer Care Thrift Shop	Upper East Side	212 879 9868
Goodwill Industries	Various Locations	www.goodwillny.org
Housing Works Thrift Shop	Various Locations	www.housingworks.com
Memorial Sloan-Kettering Thrift Shop	Upper East Side	212 535 1250
Michael's, The Consignment Shop for Women	Upper East Side	212 737 7273
Salvation Army	Various locations	www.salvationarmy-newyor.org
Spence-Chapin Thrift Shops	Various Locations	www.spence-chapin.org
Vintage Thrift Shop	Gramercy Park	212 871 0777

job. The quality varies and if you try and bargain down a beaded necklace from $15, a sales person might just laugh. Finds can happen and prices tending to fluctuate, like a vintage bureau for $100 or a chaise for $650. Housing Works Thrift Shop sometimes has good merchandise and Vintage Thrift Shop carries some unusual items.

You can donate to any one of New York City's thrift shops and know that proceeds go to good causes. Items that you would rather see work for your own bank account can be posted on www.craigslist.com, www.ebay.com or www.amazon.com. There are also many consignment stores in New York who will resell your clothing and offer a certain percentage back – so before you chuck that Hermés scarf from '05, try A Second Chance or Michael's, The Consignment Shop for Women, who are happy to rid you of your high-end designers. Stores can be selective during the process, but don't take it personally – it's your goods, not you, they're assessing.

Shoes

Other options **Clothes** p.315, **Sporting Goods** p.349, **Beachwear** p.313

It's only fair that a city which demands so much walking should offer such an enviable shoe selection. Dare to walk the side streets in a pair of Christian Louboutin stilettos, or bounce comfortably in a pair of Tod's flats - some women swear by them. And no serious shopper in New York can utter the word 'shoe' and not think of Manolo Blahnik; the tiny sign outside the shop downplays the must-haves poised on pedestals – some for $649, some as high as $2,200. West 8th Street between Fifth and Sixth Avenues is sometimes referred to as shoe row, and while it is somewhat disappointing, there are a few stores worth walking into for trendier styles and fine Italian leather shoes. The shoe departments in Macy's (p.361), Bloomingdale's (p.359) and Lord & Taylor (p.361) have recognisable names and new names you'll want to get to know better, while Barneys New York (p.358) has shoes that deserve a round of applause. Kenneth Cole is a great stop for men's and women's casual or dressy footwear, and East Side Kids starts them young and continues even after they've outgrown Harry Potter. For the avant-garde, the

347

Canadian designed John Fluevog Shoes promise to set you apart – with wild colour schemes and distinct designs, these shoes are built to last.

And though you may start innocently enough at Payless Shoe Source, buying a cheap pair of boots or sandals for $20, a shoe addiction can quickly escalate into trips to high-street notables like Nine West, Steve Madden and Aldo until finally, you may find yourself at an ATM machine checking your balance so you can rush back to Sigerson Morrison and purchase those must-have purple pumps.

Sneaker Pimps

You might call them 'runners', 'trainers' or 'pumps'. But whatever they're called, they're available all over New York. Choose from Adidas (212 529 0081), Alife Rivington Club (212 375 8128), Classic Kicks (212 979 9514), Clientele (212 219 0531), David Z (www.davidz.com), and Puma (212 334 7861).

125 Prince Street
Cnr of Wooster
Soho

Camper

212 358 1841 | www.camper.com

After walking miles on the streets of Soho, your throbbing feet will rejoice in a pair of Spanish-made Campers. The term camper means peasant, and this shoe company offers an imaginative take on the comfortable shoe of yore. Forget convention, at Camper you can get modern Mary Jane flats and a pair of heels boasting detachable suede spats. A man's loafer sells for $185 while a pair of soft leather boots can go for $300. Benches with rubber seating discs offer respite and the chance to slip your feet into the familiar Pelotas, which some refer to as the bowling shoe.

Shoes

Aldo	Various Locations	www.aldoshoes.com
Christian Louboutin	West Village	212 255 1910
East Side Kids	Upper East Side	212 360 5000
Jimmy Choo	Various Locations	www.jimmychoo.com
John Fluevog Shoes	Nolita	212 431 4484
Kenneth Cole	Various Locations	www.kennethcole.com
Manolo Blahnik	Midtown	212 582 3007
Nine West	Various Locations	www.ninewest.com
Payless Shoe Source	Various Locations	www.payless.com
Sigerson Morrison	Nolita	212 219 3893
Steve Madden	Various Locations	www.stevemadden.com
Tod's	Upper East Side	212 644 5945

Souvenirs

You have probably already been bombarded with tiny Statue of Liberty pedestals, keychains, T-shirts, and umbrellas, before you even left the airport. If you have managed to leave the terminal without a trinket, set your mind at ease, there is plenty more where that came from. Tourist hotspots like South Street Seaport and inside the Empire State Building sell souvenirs. Step into Times Square and neon signs, billboard ads and a wealth of souvenir shops will compete for your attention. Some stores are standard in their offerings with the traditional phrase 'I love NY' emblazoned on many items. They sell ashtrays, snowglobes and sometimes even luggage in case you need an extra suitcase to take all your tack home. Canal Street, at the tip of Chinatown in downtown Manhattan, is another good option for souvenirs, as well as decent knockoff handbags for the ladies and watches for both him and her. Souvenirs are usually cheap, and for a couple of bucks, you can obtain lasting memories. Of course, if you really want something that best represents New York with a slice of Americana, buy a pair of jeans. New York City is the foremost authority.

Sports Goods

Various Locations

Blades Board & Skate
www.blades.com
Snowboarders, skateboarders and in-line skaters alike are catered to in this specialty store offering a selection of gear, apparel and footwear. Skateboarding enthusiasts can buy a collection of boards starting at $100 in some seriously trippy designs. Snowboards are not sold at the location in Manhattan Mall, but brands like Burton, Salomon and Never Summer are available at the uptown and downtown stores. Blades Board & Skate sell protective gear as well – always a good investment.

591 Broadway
Btn Prince & Houston St
Soho
Map 10-F1

EMS (Eastern Mountain Sports)
212 966 8730 | www.ems.com
Two rock climbers who had trouble locating a sizeable selection of rock climbing gear decided to open up their own store in Massachusetts in 1967. It is now one of the most recognised names in outdoor goods in the US, with over 80 stores nationwide. Whether your love is camping, hiking, or climbing, or you are just in need of some apparel, shopping at EMS is a treat. Sales associates are happy to assist and chances are they share a similar fondness for your activity. EMS has a 100% satisfaction guarantee on its products, so should you and your tent not make the best of companions, the store will gladly exchange it or offer cash back if you have a valid receipt.

40 East 52nd St
Btn Madison & Park Ave
Midtown
Map 5-B3

Gym Source
212 688 4222 | www.gymsource.com
Gym Source is the largest commercial fitness provider in America with clients including the Armed Forces, the Federal Reserve, celebrities and US presidents. It caters to the not-so-famous too with steppers, treadmills, ellipticals, free weights and home gym equipment by such brands as HOIST and Tuff Stuff. Stationary bikes can start at $700. Gym Source will deliver and help you get started.

117 East 24th St
Btn Lexington & Park Ave
Gramercy Park
Map 7-A4

Manhattan Saddlery
212 673 1400 | www.manhattansaddlery.com
Believe it or not there are equestrians in New York City, and whether you are a beginner or a pro, shopping at Manhattan Saddlery is very beneficial. You can choose from quality jodhpurs, bridles, tack or clothing, purchase a plastic helmet for $64 or check out the velvets which run from $105 to $400. Once you've outfitted yourself, prepare to blaze a trail on one of the bridle paths in Central Park. The nearby Claremont Stables rents horses out for $55 an hour.

349

Various Locations

Modell's Sporting Goods

www.modells.com

The first store popped up on Cortlandt Street in lower Manhattan and has since spanned four generations of the Modell family. Today, it is a go-to for athletic enthusiasts or sports fans interested in shopping from a large pool of team jerseys and hats. Here you can support the Yankees or look like you belong on a basketball court. Modell's sells balls for all types of sports, and footwear includes work boots, cleats and sneakers, dumbbells, some racquets and a better selection of men's apparel than women's. Go Knicks!

Fifth Ave at 52nd St
Midtown
Map 5-A3

NBA Store

212 515 6221 | *www.nba.com/nycstore*

Sort of shaped like a giant basketball, this is where shoppers come to worship the game – or at least all the merchandise and sports wear that comes with it. The 35,000 square foot store spreads over two floors, packed with all the basketball photography, gifts, NBA-branded sportswear, personalised authentic jerseys and Reebok apparel and footwear you can possibly want. There's also a half-court shooting area with basketball hoop, a range of multimedia-driven attractions, such as an interactive player video wall, and regular in-store player appearances – check their website for a schedule. You can even host an NBA Store All-Star birthday party.

867 Broadway
At 18th St
Flatiron District
Map 9-A1

Paragon Sporting Goods

212 255 8036 | *www.paragonsports.com*

The directory at Paragon will be your best friend when trying to steer your way around this sporting goods staple. In operation since 1908, Paragon carries a great selection of equipment for golfing, tennis, scuba diving, snowboarding, skiing, cycling and more. The backpacking section carries major brands like The North Face, Kelty, Marmot, Victorinox and Osprey. For major exercise buffs Paragon also sells home gym equipment including free weights, and treadmills which range from about $1,500-$3,000. Accessories worth checking out include the 'techie' watches and stylish sunglasses. The wall of sneakers is no joke either but the lack of service may leave you grumbling.

Sporting Goods		
Bicycle Habitat	Soho	212 431 3315
Burton Store	Soho	212 966 8068
Capitol Fishing Tackle Co.	Midtown	212 929 6132
Champs	Midtown	212 354 2009
City Sports	Midtown	212 317 0541
Gerry Cosby & Co.	Midtown	212 563 6464
Grand Central Racquet	Midtown	212 292 8851
New York Golf Center	Various Locations	www.nygolfcenter.com
Orvis	Midtown	212 827 0698
Pan Aqua Diving	Hell's Kitchen	212 736 3483
Princeton Ski Shop	Flatiron	212 228 4400
Scandinavian Ski & Sport	Midtown	212 757 8524
Sports Authority	Various Locations	www.sportsauthority.com
Supreme	Soho	212 966 7799
SwimBikeRun	Midtown	212 399 3999
Tent and Trails	Financial District	212 227 1760
Urban Angler	Gramercy Park	212 689 6400
Vespa	Soho	212 226 4410

655 Sixth Ave
Btn 20th & 21st St
Chelsea
Map 8-F1

Scuba Network

212 243 2988 | *www.scubanetwork.com*

Deep sea diving for buried treasure requires some durable gear. Purchase fins, booties, masks, snorkels, regulators, gauges, dive lights and bags – the only thing you will be missing is a map. Lessons in a classroom or pool are offered year-round in Manhattan, with travel trips available for you to hone in on your skills, or complete the certification process. The friendly in-store staff will help you suss out the details. There is another location in Midtown (212 750 9160).

Stationery

It seems simple. Buy some envelopes from a pharmacy, scrawl Happy Birthday inside, slap on a stamp and mail out. Not so fast. Check out the extensive line of MikWright cards sold at Ricky's (p.345) which will have you laughing so hard, you will want to send one to yourself. If you want to make your own card, or just need some extra marker pens, check out the other find stationery stores in New York.

219A Mulberry St
Btn Prince & Spring St
Nolita
Map 11-A1

Cat Fish Greetings

212 625 1800 | *www.catfishgreetings.com*

At Cat Fish Greetings on Mulberry Street, you can pick up a handmade card whatever the occasion, or a special infant T-shirt for $22 with a pumpkin or cupcake emblazoned across it - enough to make any naughty little tyke appear sweet.

91 Crosby St
Btn Prince & Spring St
Soho
Map 11-A1

IS INDUSTRIES Stationery

212 334 4447 | *www.industriesstationery.com*

For minimalism and a modernistic approach to organising one's life, look no further. The design of the store is chic, as are the 'couture' notecard sets, of which 50 can be monogrammed for $195. The small store is split between INDUSTRIES Stationery's own line of contemporary style notebooks and date books, and Italian designed Nava products such as the Settegiorni diary by Bob Noorda (previously featured at the MoMa). Other Nava products include briefcases, computer bags, and backpacks, all refreshingly understated and moderately priced. Products change seasonally to assure variety.

Various Locations

Kate's Paperie

www.katespaperie.com

Leonard Flax and Joe Barriero want to get you jazzed about paper, and so do their staff. Offering over 4,000 exotic and gorgeous papers from such countries as Nepal, Egypt, and France, they are suitable for gift wrapping, shelf lining, and even as creative window decoration. Paper pricing can range from $3 for a 22x30 sized modern print to as high as $39 for a Basho Natural woven piece, worthy of being framed. Kate's also offers an array of accoutrements and services like packaged and custom designed invitations and cards, photo albums, dayplanners, Mont Blanc and Caran D'Ache pens, and a vast selection of blank and decorative boxes. Staff trained in the Japanese art of tsutsumi ensure your gift gets wrapped most impressively. Kate's At Home on Spring Street has a seasonal section, Company C furniture, and colourful rugs.

23 West 18th St
Btn Fifth & Sixth Ave
Flatiron District
Map 8-F1

Paper Presentation

212 463 7035 | *www.paperpresentation.com*

Punch the hole, lace the ribbon and add annoying confetti - you will be inspired to do it all yourself. An extensive craft department has been added to Paper Presentation's already large and looming stationery section which sells singular and packaged paper and envelopes. You can pay $12 for a box of Crane's resume paper, then be lured by every sticker ever dreamed of and an assortment of rubber stamps ideal for personalising a letter. Party items, picture frames, and gift ideas can also be found.

776 Eighth Ave
Btn 47th & 48th St
Midtown
Map 4-E3

Staples

212 265 4550 | www.staples.com

This office supply mainstay services businesses and the odd individual looking to shred incriminating documents. Staples offers a cornucopia of telephones, printers, faxes, and all-in-ones for the home and office. Buying their own brand is cheaper, with products returnable at anytime if you are not satisfied. Furniture is available through the catalogue, website and also at the 40th Street location. Staples advertise store specials in *The Daily News* and through their website. If an item is out of stock they can ship it from another store location to you, or to your nearest store so you can pick it up. Self-serve copy machines are downstairs and recommended as the copy centre focuses on bigger jobs and is less prone to assist you with reproducing that photograph of your cat. There are other locations on Water Street (212 785 9521) and in Midtown (212 997 4446).

Tailoring

Other options **Clothes** p.315, **Souvenirs** p.348, **Textiles** p.353

Getting a garment tailored to your personal specs can be a tricky task, especially if you are unsure of where to go. Purchasing from a department store often has the added bonus of a tailor on the premises, and with the heavy volume of shoppers you can be sure they know their trade. Many dry cleaners in the city also offer tailoring services, but trusting a random person with your precious pants may require too much faith; consequently, it is always advisable to go with a recommendation. When this is not an option and you have to take a chance, start small, with hemming, before hiring anyone to create your ensemble for the Academy Awards. Pricing will depend on the job. In addition to alterations for men and women, Bermini Custom Tailors & Designers use the finest fabrics to build custom-fitted suits and shirts. Lifetime alterations are also available should your weight fluctuate. A custom-made shirt ranges from $125-$400. Bhambi's Custom Tailors has received favourable reviews for reliability, craftsmanship and customising. Alterations and handmade suits are services that might be pricier, but the quality is clear. Guillermo Couture is known to duplicate anything from a photograph or sketch, including that Chanel you saw on Nicole Kidman in *Us Weekly*. Its owner, William Molina, has been featured in many magazines and offers free estimates.

Customise!

Whether you bring in your own fabric or choose from its brilliant selection, Beckenstein Fabrics & Interiors can make custom draperies, linens and reupholster furniture. It even sells furniture with the intent of it being slipcovered, like headboards, chairs and loveseats. Shelia's Decorating and Martin Albert Interiors also offer custom-made services.

Tailoring

Beckenstein Fabrics & Interiors	Flatiron District	212 366 5142
Bermini Custom Tailors & Designers	Midtown	212 551 7835
Guillermo Couture	Midtown	212 366 6965
Martin Albert Interiors	Flatiron District	212 673 8000
Mohan's Custom Tailors	Midtown	212 697 0050
Sheila's Decorating	Lower East Side	212 777 3767
St Laurie Merchant Tailors	Midtown	212 643 1916

352

You can make or break an outfit with those little details. For those extra pretty bits, head to M&J Trimming (1008 Sixth Avenue, between 37th and 38th Sts, 212 204 9595), Daytona Trimming (251 West 39th St, between Seventh and Eighth Aves, 212 354 1713), or Tender Buttons (143 East 62nd St, between Lexington and 3rd Aves, 212 758 7004).

Textiles

Other options **Tailoring** p.352, **Souvenirs** p.348

New York City is considered by most to be a pre-eminent force in fashion, so when it comes to designing from scratch, many still head to the Garment District. For runways, Broadway, or for creative types in need of fabric, there are fabulous choices prevail. Between 37th to 40th Streets and between Seventh and Eighth Avenues, you will encounter reputable textile stores like Mood Fabrics which was named 'Best Fabric Store' in New York by both *The Daily News* and *The New York Press*. Filled with designer and one-of-a-kind fabrics, it includes an inventory picked out by such fashion pillars as Donna Karan and Calvin Klein. These are not your average brocades, chenilles or sateens, but that is nothing to be intimidated by, as a helpful staff is here to assist. It sells

Textiles		
B&J Fabrics	Midtown	212 354 8150
Beckenstein Fabrics & Interiors	Gramercy Park	212 366 5142
The City Quilter	Chelsea	212 807 0390
Mood Fabrics	Midtown	212 730 5003
Paron Fabrics	Midtown	212 768 3266

wholesale and retail with a minimum purchase of a quarter of a yard and can ship all over the world. B&J Fabrics specialises in natural fibre, European and bridal fabrics and are noted for carrying some of the best and equally some of the more expensive. Paron Fabrics starts moderately with a good-sized selection of linens, synthetics, jerseys, velvets, novelties and more. Solid silks can start at $6 a yard and go up to $48 a yard. A range of patterns including Vogue, Burda, Butterick and McCalls are also available to get you started.

Toys, Games & Gifts

Toys R Us is a special wonderland and sound resource come Christmas time or any special occasion. However, if you intend on winning the prize for best gift at a birthday party, try giving a robot kit from Robot Village which can start at $14.95. If the parents are socially conscious, win extra points by giving a Fair Trade Jamtown music kit from Sons + Daughters. Gepetto's Toy Box is a favourite for toys that are educational and entertaining. For adults, popular games like Cranium and Scrabble are purchasable at stores like Barnes & Noble (p.314), and promise an evening of camaraderie with your chums. FAO Schwarz remains to be one of the biggest draws for visitors when it comes to toys, while American Girl Place has created quite a craze among young girls in the US.

Toys R Us

Disney Store

609 Fifth Avenue
At 49th Street
Midtown
Map 5-A3

American Girl Place

212 371 2220 | *www.americangirl.com*

See the red bags, witness the jubilant faces…your daughter will love you until she turns into a teenager. American Girl Place is a four-storey heaven dedicated entirely to American Girl dolls and accompanying accessories for ages 3 to 12. Haven't heard? These dolls are coveted and collected and can go for about $87 a pop. A sparkly tunic ensemble for Emily sells for $26; get the coordinating outfit for your daughter for around $60. Try the hair salon where store attendants style your doll's hair, complete with a tiny cape and chair, or the hospital, where you can admit your doll for such emergencies as an eye replacement. Oh, and the Photo Studio, where the classic package yields you a framed glossy photo of you and your doll. Needless to say, use the coat check at the store, because you will probably be staying for a while.

767 Fifth Avenue
At 58th St
Midtown
Map 5-B2

FAO Schwarz

212 644 9400 | *www.fao.com*

In 1870, an immigrant from Germany named Frederick August Otto Schwarz opened a speciality toy store in lower Manhattan. With a keen eye for quality, innovation and fun, his store is now a 50,000 square foot menagerie of toys located in the landmark General Motors Building. It is the oldest toy store in the US and is visited by wide-eyed children and adults alike. Barbie, LEGO, plush toys, classic toys and games are just a few of the products to be found. The lower level centres on baby through to preschool products and sells items by such brands as Maclaren, Kate Spade and Neurosmith. A colourful playset by Melissa & Doug can fetch $15. There is also a nursing area for mothers which provides an escape from the main level, housing an icecream parlour and bouncy kids high on sugar from the candy area. On the second floor, the 'dance-on piano' (featured in the famous 1988 movie *Big*) allows you to tap out Chopsticks after being taught by an instructor. Boys can construct cars in the Hot Wheels Factory, girls can make dolls in the Madame Alexander Doll Factory, and parents can pay prices that echo standard retail for toys and upwards (and upwards still).

Need Some Direction?

The *Explorer Mini Maps* pack a whole city into your pocket and once unfolded are excellent navigational tools for exploring. Not only are they handy in size, with detailed information on the sights and sounds of the city, but also their fabulously affordable price mean they won't make a dent in your holiday fund. Wherever your travels take you, from the Middle East to Europe and beyond, grab a mini map and you'll never have to ask for directions.

Toys, Games & Gifts

Acorn	Brooklyn	718 522 3760
Alphabets	East Village	212 475 7250
Build-A-Bear Workshop	Midtown	212 871 7080
Citibabes	Soho	212 334 5440
Dinosaur Hill	East Village	212 473 5850
Geppetto's Toy Box	West Village	212 620 7511
KB Toys	Various Locations	www.kbtoys.com
Kidding Around	Flatiron District	212 645 6337
La Brea	Midtown	212 371 1482
Le Sabon	Upper East Side	212 319 4225
Nintendo World	Midtown	646 459 0800
Pearl River Mart	Soho	212 431 4770
Robot Village	Upper West Side	212 799 7626
Romp	Brooklyn	718 230 4373
The Scholastic Store	Soho	212 343 6166
Sons + Daughters	East Village	212 253 7797
Toys R Us	Midtown	646 366 8800
Virgin Megastore Incredibly	Flatiron District	212 598 4666
World of Disney	Midtown	212 702 0702
Zitomer	Upper East Side	212 737 5560

Wedding Items

For those who can't afford to go Vera Wang, the famed bridal dress designer, David's Bridal in Queens and RK Bridal in Manhattan will be the least expensive route to go. Both offer one-stop shopping for the bride, her party and even her mother, complete with accessories. You need to make an appointment for some stores, so call ahead. Wedding Atelier is by appointment only but is another full-service store where gowns generally range from $2000 to $4000. Mom's Night Out caters for pregnant brides and has gowns from $425.

If you're not paying, take your benefactor to Saks Fifth Avenue where you can find gowns by Badgley Mischka and Carolina Herrera, among others. When you're done, skip down to My Glass Slipper where affordable designer shoes in labels like Stuart Weitzman, Anne Klein and Cynthia Rowley will add the perfect touch. Should you love your bridesmaids, they will appreciate a gown from Vera Wang Maids or from the Thread Bridesmaid line featured at the Wedding Library. The Wedding Library also offers a primo planning service, right down to the invitations. Kate's Paperie (p.351) and Papyrus (p.355) produce gorgeous invitations too. Attendees of a wedding can find appropriate party garb at various department stores, as fancy attire tends to be seasonless. Filene's Basement (p.360) has a famous annual wedding gown sale where you can pick up designer gowns at a fraction of the cost - just don't forget to take your 'mean girl' attitude with you because you'll be up against crowds of bridezillas. If you don't mind wearing somebody else's dress, The Bridal Garden stocks a range of sample dresses and dresses that have only been worn once. Think about it - you're the only one who will know you're wearing a pre-worn dress, and you could pick up a stunning designer gown for $300.

If you're out of inspiration and you need some good gift ideas, have a browse around the following stores: Barneys (p.358), Bed Bath and Beyond (www.bedbathandbeyond.com), Bergdorf Goodman (p.358), Bloomingdale's (p.359), Clio (www.clio-home.com), Gracious Home (www.gracious home.com), Macy's (p.361), Moss (www.mossonline.com), Pier 1 Imports (www.pier1.com), Restoration Hardware (www.restorationhardware.com), or Williams-Sonoma (www.williams-sonoma.com).

Wedding Items		
Adriennes Bridesmaid	Lower East Side	212 475 4206
Amsale	Midtown	212 583 1700
Annique Couture Bridal	Midtown	212 840 9535
Bed Bath & Beyond	Flatiron District	212 255 3550
Bergdorf Goodman	Midtown	212 872 8957
Beverly Feldman	Midtown	212 484 0000
Birnbaum & Bullock	Chelsea	212 242 2914
The Bridal Garden	Flatiron District	212 252 0661
Carolina Herrera	Upper East Side	212 249 6552
Clifford Michael Design	Upper East Side	212 888 7665
Clio	Soho	212 966 8991
David's Bridal	Queens	718 784 8200
Designer Loft	Midtown	212 944 9013
Gallery of Wearable Art	Upper East Side	212 570 2252
Galo Shoes	Various Locations	www.galoshoes.com
Kleinfeld	Flatiron District	212 229 0203
Macy's East	Midtown	2126 954 400
Mom's Night Out	Upper East Side	212 744 6667
Moss	Soho	212 204 7100
My Glass Slipper	Flatiron District	212 627 0231
Papyrus	Various Locations	www.papyrusonline.com
Peter Fox	Soho	212 431 7426
Pier 1 Imports	Flatiron District	212 206 1911
Restoration Hardware	Flatiron District	212 260 9479
RK Bridal	Hell's Kitchen	212 947 1155
Saks Fifth Avenue	Midtown	212 753 4000
Vanessa Noel	Upper East Side	212 906 0054
VeKa	Nolita	212 925 9044
Vera Wang	Upper East Side	212 628 3400
Vera Wang Maids	Upper East Side	212 628 9898
Wedding Atelier	Flatiron District	646 638 3263
Wedding Library	Upper East Side	212 327 0100
Williams-Sonoma	Midtown	212 823 9750

355

Places to Shop

Not only is New York home to just about every international consumer brand in the world, but it is also a place where you can choose from several shopping environments. Love malls? It's got them. Hate malls? Head for some amazing streetside shopping (Fifth Avenue, anyone?), markets, independent shops, and of course, department stores (any shopaholic's best friend). And if you simply can't be bothered to run a comb through your hair and step outside, then just press the power button on your laptop and shop online. As long as you've got money in your pocket, or space on your credit card, you've got plenty of places to get rid of it!

Shopping Malls

It is strange that one would need to seek a collective arena of shopping stores when the island of Manhattan seems to embody one giant mall. Space, having been in short supply for both the resident and commercial occupant,

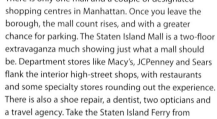

does not allow for too many chances to shop in a mall, with department stores having a stranglehold on the shopping scene.

There is only one mall and a couple of designated shopping centres in Manhattan. Once you leave the borough, the mall count rises, and with a greater chance for parking. The Staten Island Mall is a two-floor extravaganza much showing just what a mall should be. Department stores like Macy's, JCPenney and Sears flank the interior high-street shops, with restaurants and some specialty stores rounding out the experience. There is also a shoe repair, a dentist, two opticians and a travel agency. Take the Staten Island Ferry from

Queens Center (p.129)

Whitehall Terminal at Whitehall and South Streets, then board the S44, S61, or S91 bus to the mall (open Mon-Sat 10:00-21:30; Sun 11:00-18:00).

The newly expanded and improved Queens Center is accessible from major boulevards and highway routes and is a modern shopping environment complete with amenities like a play area for children and additional parking. Trendier stores like Urban Outfitters, A/X Armani Exchange, Club Monaco and H&M are an added bonus. (G/R/V train to Woodhaven Boulevard, open Mon-Sat 10:00-21:30; Sun, 11:00-20:00)

Take a train out to Brooklyn to shop at the esteemed Target store located at Atlantic Terminal. The massive superstore carries everything from home furnishings to clothing to electronics to toys, and has become a reason for many to venture out to one of the boroughs housing this delight. With convenient subway access at Atlantic Terminal, you can stockpile on things like low-priced linens and head back home. There is also a DSW shoe store, a Daffy's, and a nearby Old Navy for those fleece jackets and cargo pants you cannot live without.

Shopping Malls

Sixth Avenue
At 33rd Street
Midtown
Map 6-F2

Manhattan Mall

212 465 0500 | *www.manhattanmallny.com*

If you are absolutely desperate for a fix, and if no other district seems to satiate your inner mallrat, then you might try Manhattan Mall in Herald Square. Good luck. Sometimes, you can judge the clientele of a mall by its restaurants, and at Manhattan Mall there is a McDonald's, a Sbarro (for pizza), a Subway (for sandwiches), and an Arby's (better off at Sbarro). The stores volley between decent (Express, Brookstone, Foot Locker, The Body Shop) and the mediocre (most of the rest). Kiosks selling Proactiv

Solution for the acne ridden and digital pictures shot instantly are among the distractions. And even though there is a huge Victoria's Secret up the block, another one triumphs here. The Children's Place has cute clothes for kids good enough to justify a trip inside the mall. An outfit can cost $35. The subway can be accessed directly from the lower level and offers a quick escape.
Subway: B/V/D/F/Q/N/R/W trains to 34th Street – Herald Square

South Street Seaport
Fulton & South St
Financial District
Map 13-B2

Pier 17
212 732 7678

Once you get down to lower Manhattan and witness the Seaport, the last place you might want to be is cooped up in a mall. However, with more novelty shops than the familiar, shopping here can be fun. Civilised and clean and catering mainly to tourists, Pier 17 houses a large Express store for women, one for men, a Victoria's Secret, and a Sharper Image where you can play with gadgets. Pricing here is on par with other stores, but prices at the kiosks and trinket shops seem a bit steep. A mug for $8 and five M&Ms for 50 cents from the candy machine hardly seem fair.

The Mariposa Gallery is a must see where you can purchase the gorgeous artwork of Marshall Hill who works with real butterflies and Lucite. The Bonsai Gallery houses beautiful creations and the Van der Plas Gallery sells fine art, prints and postcards. Go into the As Seen On TV store where you might feel compelled to buy a $39.99 Sauna Belt for your abs, or step out onto the pier and see the spectacular views of Brooklyn Bridge and New York Harbour. Dining here is pricey, so if you have to, try Sequoia (212 732 9090) for the seafood.
Subway: 2/3/4/5/J/M/Z train to Fulton Street; A/C train to Broadway-Nassau

10 Columbus Circle
At Broadway & 59th St
Midtown
Map 4-E1

Time Warner Center
212 823 6300 | *www.shopsatcolumbuscircle.com*

Central Park, and the now diminutive statue of Christopher Columbus, lend a picturesque backdrop to the colossal glass building that is the Time Warner Center. Gracefully curved at the base with two looming towers jutting out, it is comprised of CNN offices, condominiums, a jazz centre, a five-star Mandarin Hotel, a Whole Foods Market (p.328), and an Equinox Fitness Club. The Shops at Columbus Circle are immediately accessible upon entering, and offer a tame and more upscale shopping environment than that of Manhattan Mall. Stores like Coach, Cole Haan, Hugo Boss and Thomas Pink set the tone for high-end style and sophistication. For beauty, try the FACE make-up line or L'Occitane for bodycare. The modern design of the Samsung store beckons you to browse the latest in laptops, phones and electronic gadgets, while the Bouchon Bakery offers wine and lunch with a skyline view.
Subway: 1/A/C/B/D trains to Columbus Circle

Department Stores

Steeped in retail history, New York City proudly boasts the flagship stores of Macy's, Bloomingdale's, Barneys, and Saks Fifth Avenue; and despite what some analysts predict as the decline of the department store, these tend to be the most popular attractions to tour after the Statue of Liberty and the Empire State Building.

Opening Hours

Hours for department stores may fluctuate around holidays and sales. Macy's and Kmart in particular are inclined to open stores earlier and close later to accommodate the weeks of Thanksgiving and Christmas. Check department store websites or call ahead to verify any changes.

Bergdorf Goodman is special to New York City and Henri Bendel has just one other store in the country; both present aesthetically intriguing shopping experiences and merit at least one visit. Large and at times exhausting, the behemoths provide most of the benefits of one-stop shopping, dressing you from head to toe and sometimes flaunting a furnishings department that would ignite any latent passion for home-owning. Complementary personal shoppers, a tailor on premise (except at Takashimaya), restrooms that range from the bearable (Macy's) to the decadent (Saks Fifth Avenue), an info desk and at some, a full-service concierge can be anticipated. At Christmas time the window displays remain a tradition; Lord & Taylor prefers convention while Barneys likes to provoke thought.

All major and upscale department stores can be accessed via street level, some with multiple entrances. At Bloomingdale's, you can even enter from the Lexington Avenue subway station directly. Parents and children are easily accommodated within spacious department stores. For shoppers at higher-end department stores, spa services will soothe your shopping limbs. The Chantecaille Energy Spa at Barneys is particularly good. If upscale department store prices are too high, bargain shopping will sustain you in a city that epitomises style. And, with the cost of living in New York City showing no sign of ebbing, discount department stores are reliable allies in obtaining luxury. Kmart sells current and personal brand clothes and furnishings, while off-price stores such as Century 21, Daffy's, and Filene's Basement, sell overstock and closeout merchandise, enabling you to buy that Versace tie without sacrificing your savings. Off-price discount stores carry merchandise of varying quality, in correspondence to the reputation of its zip code. Inspect items before purchasing and be sure to try on the clothing before you start fantasising about its future in your wardrobe. There is also no prestige in giving a gift from a discount department store, and unlike major and upscale department stores who offer basic and signature gift wrapping, you have to be inventive yourself.

660 Madison Ave
At 61st St
Upper East Side
Map 5-B1

Barneys

212 826 8900 | *www.barneys.com*

It takes just one visit to see why this store is considered an underground institution and why it was one of Carrie Bradshaw's favourite stores in *Sex and the City*. Barneys makes you feel as if you have landed on a fabulous planet with only the finest merchandise, all a couple of hundred dollars away from being yours. Designer monikers are significant, especially for men's and women's clothing and perhaps a wiser indulgence come bonus time. Mix among label-conscious women and the occasional celebrity as they purchase beauty products from D. Sebagh, Sco, and Serge Lutens. Smelling booths are located in the fragrance department on the lower level and feature Frederic Malle's infamous Editions de Parfums. An offshoot of Barneys is Barneys Co-Op, where the flagship's seventh and eighth floors have expanded into three separate store locations, attracting shoppers to its edgy trends. Barneys Co-Ops can be found in Chelsea (212 593 7800), Soho (212 965 9964), and on the Upper West Side (646 335 0978).

754 Fifth Ave
Btn 57th & 58th St
Midtown
Map 5-A2

Bergdorf Goodman

212 753 7300 | *www.bergdorfgoodman.com*

Haute fashion for an elite clientele. If your rich aunt is treating, take her here. Unfortunately, sales racks are lacking. The women's store spans seven floors while the men's store, across the street, sums it up in three. Both make you feel as if you have entered a private home. Labels for men include Adam Kimmel, Thom Browne, Etro, Charvet, and Alexander McQueen, among others. At the men's store you have the option of a tourist-free lunch at Café 745. At the women's store, encounter swoon-worthy stellar clothing, decadent home goods, and $2,000 Burberry coats. You might get immediate service from the staff at either location if you don't dress the part and if you're attempting a monetary conversion, don't bother – it equals a lot! Use the in-house credit card to accumulate a point for every dollar spent, part of the store's InCircle rewards programme; and with most purchases starting in the hundreds, it's certainly wise to join. Bergdorf Goodman Men is located on Fifth Avenue at 58th Street.

1000 Third Ave
Btn 59th & 60th St
Upper East Side
Map 5-C2

Bloomingdale's

212 705 2000 | www.bloomingdales.com

It's hard to believe this marvel resulted from the hoop skirt fad of the 19th century. What began as a small women's speciality shop on the lower east side in Manhattan is now synonymous with the city itself, with over 30 locations nationwide. 'Bloomie's' sells fine men's, women's, and children's clothing, a vast array of accessories, shoes, housewares, furniture and a cosmetics department that prides itself on offering obscure brands. Committed and approachable salespeople abound and if you are working within the confines of a budget, they are still eager to help. There is an elaborate visitor centre on the first-floor balcony catering to out-of-state and international visitors, complete with translators, an accommodating concierge, and a coupon with which to shop for that day. A smaller store location in Soho (212 729 5900) is good if you are stuck downtown, but, compared to the other store, somehow you feel cheated.

22 Cortland St
Btn Broadway & Churc h
Financial District
Map 12-E1

Century 21

212 227 9092 | *www.c21stores.com*

If you saw a Gucci skirt a while back but shuddered at the price, this shopper's goldmine offers you a second chance. Top American and European fashions for the family and home can be found 25% to 75% off, with the location on Cortland Street in lower Manhattan offering the largest selection. Sectioned off primarily by brand, there is little elbow room to scour the packed racks so weekdays are best, and, since it opens at 07:45, you can start early. The shoe department is a bit tricky to find, but follow the permanent footprints on the second floor and you won't wander aimlessly. Century 21 tenders gift cards that never expire. It also guarantees a ten-dollar gift certificate if no receipt is issued at the time of purchase. And, if they forget to ring up an item entirely, they will go as far as giving it to you for free, with an additional $25 gift certificate. Cellphone service is shoddy and fitting room lines are long on weekends, but stay strong and stay to witness why this store is considered the apex of bargain shopping. There is another branch in Brooklyn (718 748 3266).

1311 Broadway
At 34th St
Midtown
Map 6-F2

Daffy's

212 736 4477 | *www.daffys.com*

The chief location is in Herald Square, across the street from Macy's through the Herald Center building. There is an adjacent Staples office store and a Department of Motor Vehicles (may you never have to incur the wrath) that share the space. Express elevators let you out on the seventh men's floor, descending escalators take you through an enormous amount of inexpensive, sometimes designer, collection of clothing, shoes, lingerie, home decor accessories and incidentals. Seasonal outerwear is decent, and cute clothing and footwear for kids can stock a closet until the not-so-little ones outgrow it the following month. Semi-disgruntled employees serve you at Daffy's, but this doesn't seem to matter when a Calvin Klein underwear set is selling for less than $25. Other Daffy's branches can be found Midtown on Madison Ave (212 557 4422), in the Financial District (212 422 4477), in Atlantic Terminal, Brooklyn (718 7894477), and in Queens (718 760 7787).

4 Union Sq South
At 14th St
Upper West Side
Map 9-A2

Filene's Basement

212 358 0169 | *www.filenesbasement.com*

It's the oldest off-price department store selling a range of medium to high-end products to the urban professional. Macy's acquired its main department store, Filene's, but the Basement survived untouched much to the merriment of many Americans. The Union Square store is located above a DSW shoe store, accessible through the building. Merchandise rotates frequently with fresh truck deliveries arriving three times a week. Discover designer jeans like True Religion, Joe's, Blue Cult and J & Company, some starting as low as $49.99. Bridal gown sales have been transpiring at various Filene's Basements throughout the country since 1947, and now in New York. Dresses originally priced at $800 to $9,000 dollars are discounted drastically, then sold to the bevy of frantic and sometimes tearful national and international brides-to-be who camp out and rush the store to try on and swap gowns. Call ahead for the event date and location and get your tent ready. Other stores are located in the Flatiron District (212 620 3100), on the Upper West Side (212 873 8000), and in Queens (718 479 7711).

712 Fifth Ave
Btn 55th & 56th St
Midtown
Map 5-A2

Henri Bendel

212 247 1100 | *www.henribendel.com*

Devoted to women, well, girls really, Henri Bendel caters to the fashionably committed wealthy set (and their mothers). Made up of two landmark buildings: the Rizzoli and the Coty, it also has historic Lalique windows spanning the second to fourth floors. The latest trends, reasonably and frighteningly priced, mingle in a giant walk-in closet. Boutiques flank the store's interior, including such treats as designer lingerie, Chanel, and signature Bendel cashmere sweaters that will make you wish you were back in college. Semi-annual 'Open See' events cast new designers to showcase their merchandise. Past success stories have included Anna Sui and Todd Oldham. There are no escalators, just elevators, and a spiral staircase to ensure that no aspect of this picturesque store is overlooked. The famed Federic Fekkai hair salon is on the fourth floor and services men, women and children.

Kmart

250 West 34th St
Btn Broadway & 8th St
Midtown
Map 6-E2

212 760 1188 | www.kmart.com

Made famous in the past for holding spontaneous 'blue light specials' and for the catch phrase 'attention Kmart shoppers,' this discounter allows you to buy big, even when your budget's small. Offering clothing, bedding, furniture, jewellery, beauty products, grocery products, electronics and housewares, you can justly furnish your apartment and not be ashamed to say that your curtains are made by Martha Stewart for Kmart. In fact, it is best to save on things like plastic organisers, socks, or wall paint, and have more to splurge on classier clothing at the major department stores. Both Manhattan Kmarts have a pharmacy and a portrait studio. The 34th Street location is just north of the entertainment arena, Madison Square Garden. Exit through the main entrance on 34th Street and walk east, where you'll eventually hit Herald Square and then Macy's, Gap, Victoria's Secret and Payless Shoe Source. Don't load up on beverages though – Kmart has no bathroom. Other Kmart stores can be found in the West Village (212 673 1540), on Bruckner Boulevard (718 430 9439) and on Baychester Avenue (718 671 5377), both in The Bronx.

Lord & Taylor

424 Fifth Ave
Btn 38th & 39th St
Midtown
Map 7-A1

212 391 3344 | www.lordandtaylor.com

Your mother's store. Known for playing the national anthem at the start of each day, you may soon forget about this sleepy retailer after visiting its flashier comrades. However, if you want to avoid the crowds, it will become one of your favourite hidden gems. There is only one store in the city and unfortunately this one does not include a furniture department. The Larry Forgione Signature Café, located on the sixth floor, offers cheap fare for children and the customer service in the shoe department is excellent. If the attractive Christmas decorations do not entice you during the holiday season, perhaps the frequent sales throughout the year will.

Macy's

151 West 34th St
Btn Broadway &
Seventh Ave
Midtown
Map 6-F2

212 695 4400 | www.macys.com

Take two aspirin and prepare to be inundated with stimuli. This tourists' favourite occupies most of Herald Square in Midtown. Macy's is as famous for its annual Thanksgiving Day parade as it is for its endless sales. You can expect a full range of everything from inexpensive to designer for the whole family, including a furniture department and a 'Cellar' containing homewares and gourmet food. Shops on the mezzanine level offer a reprieve from the crowds, where you can browse a wide hosiery selection or purchase something distinctive from the Metropolitan Museum of Art gift shop. An American Express currency exchange counter offering currency exchange is also located on the mezzanine, tucked behind a tiny lounge area belonging to Starbucks. If you have a teenage daughter she will love the loud juniors department, or the icecream from the oddly placed Ben & Jerry's vendor. Macy's By Appointment is a complementary shopping service that can also ship items internationally (Japan wins for being one of the most expensive countries to ship to).

361

Sales people are less than thrilled to assist on all but the bridal registry floor, and busy weekends are a shopper's nightmare, so weekdays or off-peak hours are best. There is another Macy's on Fulton Street in Brooklyn (718 875 7200)

Saks Fifth Avenue

611 Fifth Ave
At 50th St
Midtown
Map 5-A3

212 753 4000 | *www.saksfifthavenue.com*

There are international locations in China, Saudi Arabia and Dubai, and in Midtown Manhattan, this shopping haven is a welcome retreat from the stream of storefronts that line Fifth Avenue. Saks is considered the big sister to Bloomingdale's and pampers the sophisticated shopper who prefers to do damage in a quieter environment. The sixth and seventh floors are devoted to men, so women – drop them off and hit the designer shoe salons. Café SFA on the eighth floor delivers moderate fare and views of Rockefeller Center and St Patrick's Cathedral. Whether you go for the Elizabeth Arden Red Door Signature Facial at the spa, or visit the celebrated perfume department, you will always want to return.

Takashimaya

693 Fifth Ave
Btn 54th & 55th St
Midtown
Map 5-A2

212 350 0100 | *www.ny-takashimaya.com*

There is only one Takashimaya in the United States, so great care and consideration have gone into making this Japanese store a calming haven for the avid shopper. This is most evident in the level of quality and craftsmanship in the items offered for purchase and the feeling of tranquility you experience when buying them. Its mission statement, located on the back of take-away directories by the elevators, is to cross Eastern philosophy with a Western practicality. This is reflected in the exquisite jewellery made by local and foreign artisans, men's and women's loungewear, tea shop, and floral boutique. World-renowned Santa Maria Novella skin care products and colognes made from formulas that are centuries old are exclusively available here – the soap is reportedly the best in the world. The Home Collection warrants a jaunt to the third floor as truly unique tableware and lacquered chopsticks make original gifts for any occasion.

Macy's

Macy's

Saks Fifth Avenue

Hypermarkets

Hypermarket is not a term traditionally used in the US. The American equivalents to huge French stores such as Carrefour are Kmart, Target or Wal-Mart, and they are more commonly referred to as a superstore or a big box store. Kmart (p.361) has two locations in Manhattan, and Target (p.323) is available in the Bronx, Brooklyn and Queens. They sell mainstream goods at lower prices. Famous designers like Martha Stewart and Isaac Mizrahi have graced the shelves and racks of Kmart and Target respectively, enhancing the image of each store. Both are ideal when you need to completely overhaul your home or are looking to buy in bulk.

Independent Shops

A moment of silence should be observed in respect for all of the past, present and future independent shops that have kept and keep New York City free from total gentrification and conformity. Their struggle to stay afloat amid rent hikes and evolving tastes are a testament to their dedication to protect New York's position as one of the world's fashion capitals.

35 Howard St
Btn Broadway & Crosby
Soho
Map 10-F2

Opening Ceremony

212 219 2688 | *www.openingceremony.us*

Let fashion ring at this boutique where it is all about the clothing and accessories and less about the store's interior. Established in 2002, Opening Ceremony has graduated from word of mouth to preferred pit stop on the shopping trail. Owners Carol Lim and Humberto Leon travel the globe to get a feel for the energy of a particular country, eventually choosing designers they have personally gravitated towards. The store is loft-like with racks of forward-thinking and sometimes out-there clothing which would be difficult to find elsewhere. Jeans by Acne, Rag & Bone, and Cheap Monday are beyond cool, and don't even bring up jewellery – it is fabulous too. Labels rotate, with the top-shelf designs of Top Shop currently inhabiting the upstairs, where styles seem more accessible for the less adventurous. This place is irresistible – so be prepared to spend.

17 West 18th St
Btn Fifth & Sixth Ave
Flatiron District
Map 8-F1

UTOWA

212 929 4800 | *www.utowa.com*

Fresh and invigorating, UTOWA captures the essence of fashion and art in its clothing, accessories and cosmetics. Vivid hues from the floral gallery pop up against stark white walls transforming a retail experience into a private Zen moment. Everything has been carefully thought out by its founder, Hiroshi Uemura, son of the famous makeup and cosmetic artist Shu Uemura. This is apparent in the select pieces by such designers as Sergio Davila, Vivienne Westwood, Keita Maruyama and Mel en Stel. The Helen Wang dresses are stunning, in taffeta, chiffon or knit, and with one price tag set at $350, it seems just about obtainable. There is an ML makeup line, beautifully crafted jewellery and fragrances by Montgomery Taylor. Take a whiff of Ambra di Venezia and be transported to a sunset in Venice, the inspiration behind the scent. UTOWA means a unity of the five elements of fire, water, air, earth and spirit, and when you leave you too will feel like some sort of harmonising has occurred.

Markets

If you prefer to shop in the open air than pound the malls, New York has plenty of markets to choose from. For local produce, check out the Essex Street Market (120 Essex Street btwn Delancy & Rivington Streets, www.essexstreetmarket.com, Mon-Sat 08:00-18:00), which is 60 years old and especially great for wines and breads. The farmers' market at Union Square (held every day except Sunday and Tuesday) and Chelsea Market (75 Ninth Avenue, between 15th and 16th Streets, www.chelseamarket.com, Mon-Sat 07:00-09:00; Sun 10:00-20:00), a city block chock full of gourmet food shops ripe with meats, wine, cheese, bread, and flowers, as well as cosy cafes to stop off and refuel, are both choice destinations. If you have a spare few minutes before your train at Grand Central, browse the beautiful terminal's bustling indoor market (www.grandcentralsquare.com). Located at the east end of the main floor, you'll find tasty produce and, come the festive season, quaint Christmas stalls. The Garage (112 West 25th Street, between Sixth and Seventh Avenues, 212 647 0707) attracts fashionistas and designers to its flea market, where stalls simply overflow with vintage clothes, art and jewellery. Or, if you want a sprinkling of history with your haggling, the Malcolm Shabazz Harlem Market (52 West 116th St, between Malcolm X Blvd and Fifth Avenue, 212 987 8131, 10:00-17:00) is run by the neighbouring Malcolm Shabazz mosque, which houses the former pulpit of assassinated Muslim orator, Malcolm X. The Harlem market offers African craft, such as tribal masks and drums, as well as bargain clothing, music and films.

Streets/Areas to Shop

Conveniently laid out in a grid, Manhattan streets and districts are easily reached by buses and subways. Where it gets tricky is downtown, mainly below 13th Street, as many numbered streets switch to named streets and it becomes easy to get lost. Downtown is a hotbed of burgeoning boutiques and independent shops, where merchandise and atmosphere are

Buy in Brooklyn

Brooklyn has become a beloved borough for shoppers and renters alike. Certain stores in the hipster haven of Williamsburg or in the blooming area of Park Slope have become worth the train ride out. Smith Street, running through Cobble Hill and Carroll Gardens, is one of the cooler places to shop in the city. Area Kids sells the cutest clothes for children aged 1 to 8. Bird, Flirt, or Dear Fieldbinder for the ladies and Watts on Smith for the men guarantee everyone stays happy and hip. Afterward, enjoy a romantic Italian meal at Panino'teca.

among the most unique offered in the city. Greenwich Village, Nolita, Tribeca and Noho are just some of the downtown districts that will send you into a shopper's delirium. Uptown (on Madison Avenue from 57th to 79th Street) boasts exclusive shopping stores like Calvin Klein, Lana Marks, Roberto Cavalli and Giorgio Armani where credit cards are constantly unleashed by the 'ladies who lunch'.

South of East 14th St
North of East Houston
East of Broadway
Map 9

East Village

It has been said that much of the grit and grim of New York City has departed, making way for Disney ventures, large corporate chain stores and rainbows. The East Village is one district clinging tightly to its cool vibe, determined not to lose its individuality and position as a surviving emblem of the city's distinct history. St Marks Place is home to alternative, punk and goth fashions where you can pick up something in mesh at Trash & Vaudeville (212 982 3590), but then dine at the quaint Café Orlin (212 777 1447). Many fresh independent shops line 7th and 9th Streets. Women will love to stroll down 7th Street between First Avenue and Avenue A and hit Sophie Roan (212 529 0085). Once you find your groove, head south for a community feel in the Lower East Side where the young minded hunt for new designers in shops like TG-170 (212 995 8660) on Ludlow, or for glam rock jewellery at Exhibitionist (212 375 1530) on Orchard Street. The Sugar Sweet Sunshine bakery (212 995 1960) nearby is great if you need to refuel. For more information on living, eating, shopping and exploring the East Village, see Exploring (p.178) and Residents (p.56)
Subway: 6 train Astor Place; F train to Second Avenue

365

Fifth Avenue

From Central Park
South to the Flatiron
District
Maps 5, 7 & 8

If you shop around the Flatiron District on Fifth Avenue, take a moment to admire the impressive architecture of the Flatiron Building at 23rd Street, before walking down to a range of chain and boutique-style shops. This district is great for leisurely perusals, with prices that range from the moderately trendy stores, such as Zara and Club Monaco, to the sky-high designer labels at Searle and Intermix. If you have yet to be introduced to Anthropologie, it is a must for feminine clothing, accessories, and rustic homeware. Going up Fifth Avenue into Midtown also has its advantages with high-end stores like Ermenegildo Zegna, Gucci and Van Cleef & Arpels servicing bigger budgets. Sports enthusiasts looking for a customised basketball jersey can shop at the NBA Store (p.350), while the college sect will love the beachy feel of Abercrombie & Fitch (p.316), where a pair of men's jeans cost around $80.

Subway: R/W train to 23rd Street (Flatiron District); E/F train to Fifth Avenue/53rd Street (Midtown)

Meatpacking District

Bordered by Chelsea
& the West Village
Map 8

Her daddy was a Beatle and her late mum, a photographer, but in the Meatpacking District Stella McCartney's stellar clothing sets the tone for this offbeat, high style, scene-stealing area of Manhattan. Frequented by New Yorkers and fashionistas looking for a shopping environment not laden with tourists, the Meatpacking District delivers a powerful one-two punch of expensive goods. Shop in Diane von Furstenberg, Elizabeth Charles, or Jeffrey New York, the latter of which contains selected pieces by labels such as DSquared2 and Gucci. At Jean Shop, men, women and kids can choose washing treatments for their one-of-a-kind jeans cut from Japanese fabric. Dining in the Meatpacking District can be pricey, with delicious restaurants like FIG & OLIVE (212 207 4555) charging around $14 for a salad. The disposition of shoppers and sales associates may gravitate toward 'too cool', so if you find yourself questioning your own adequacy, just remember, this place is named after meat.

Subway: A/C/E/L train to 14th Street

Soho

South of Houston St
North of Canal St
West of Lafayette St
Map 10

Expect street vendors selling 'hot' items with questionable origins amid artists hawking original wares on cobbled streets. Or at least, that's the way it used to be. Soho's image has changed over the years causing many shoppers to seek out its adjoining district neighbours, Nolita and Noho, where the smallish niche shops that have recently been shut out of Soho due to high rents have relocated. Broadway has instead become a hub for chain stores like H&M, Guess and Foot Locker, causing some residents to long for Soho's heyday of artistic endeavours. But don't fear, streets like Wooster, Greene, Grand and West Broadway are still ripe with designer boutiques, art galleries and innovative home furnishing stores. Some fantastic shops for clothing and accessories include Ted Baker, Anna Sui, and IF. Soho remains a popular shopping spot with weekday outings offering a more pleasurable experience (you don't have to dodge the determined weekend consumer crowds). Lunching at Kelley & Ping (212 228 1212) for inexpensive Asian fare is a must.

Subway: C/E or 6 train to Spring Street; R train to Prince Street

The world has much to offer.
It's just knowing where to find it.

If you're an American Express® Cardmember, simply visit
americanexpress.com/selects or visit your local homepage, and click on
'offers'. You'll find great offers wherever you are today, all in one place.

selects.

THE WORLD OFFERS. WE SELECT. YOU ENJOY.

Going Out

Going Out

Spend one night out on the buzzing streets of New York and you'll understand why it's called the city that never sleeps. Come sunset, the restaurants swell with dressy diners and the bars and lounges spill over with revellers knocking back warm-up cocktails. After that, it's time to hit the clubs, for some grooving – and flirting – on the dancefloor until the wee hours. Evenings in the city start late, and go even later, with many of the thumping clubs hitting their stride after midnight. As for sampling the latest, trendiest, hottest, you name it – New York is it. New nightclubs are unveiled on a monthly basis, with celebs, club kids, and models, their friends and their friends' friends descending on the city for glittering opening night galas. Of course, what's hot and what's not changes with alarming regularity, which keeps nightclub promoters on their toes and ensures an ever-changing after-dark scene. The velvet ropes and premium vodka cocktails of the Meatpacking District clubs are just one face of a New York night – you'll find a bar to match every mood, from rumpled pubs and basement dives in the East Village where the drink specials are scrawled on a blackboard, to candlelit lounges with white-leather banquettes in Soho and Tribeca, to Midtown's rooftop bars, where you can gaze out at the sparkling skyline of Manhattan, while sipping a cocktail of the same name.

Local Cuisine

If America is a melting pot, then New York's culinary diversity is one of its finest manifestations. The city's Jewish heritage introduced such favourites as bagels with cream cheese that have become synonymous with New York cuisine, and you'll find old-world delis across town, particularly on the Lower East Side, where you can delve into all manner of Jewish specialities, including warmed blintzes (crepes filled with soft cheese). New York-style pizza – usually thin-crusted – is a city obsession, and a gooey slice, best when wolfed down while on the run, is the ultimate carb-rich energy booster. As for who makes it best? That's a big point of contention – shout 'who makes the best pizza?' into a crowded subway car and everyone will give you a different answer. Brooklynites claim they make the greatest pies, Staten Islanders vigorously dispute that and say they do while Manhattanites don't even deign to respond. The city also boasts top-notch Asian fare – head to cacophonous Chinatown to sample fragrant dim sum dumplings, China's answer to brunch, at one of the neighborhood's massive, aeroplane hangar-sized dim sum restaurants, or tuck into steaming platters of wok-fried chicken and pork at a cosy Cantonese eatery. For rib-sticking soul food – fried chicken, succulent ribs, collard greens, and cornbread – make your way to the superb Southern-style eateries in Harlem. And when it comes to dessert, don't miss a creamy wedge of New York cheesecake, which makes for a sweet finale to any meal.

Restaurant Week

Foodies, mark your calendars: twice a year, usually in January and June, New York celebrates Restaurant Week, when the city's finest restaurants serve three-course prix-fixe meals – for a mere $24.07 for lunch and, occasionally, $35 for dinner. The price goes up incrementally every year. It's a wonderful opportunity to dine at a restaurant that might normally be out of your price range, or to go on a culinary adventure and sample new restaurants without having to fork out top dollar at each one. Over 150 restaurants generally participate including, in previous years, Bouley (p.387), Union Square Café (p.397), River Café (p.378) and Tocqueville (p.390). Look out for Restaurant Week ads in the local newspapers and magazines, including the New York Times, and make reservations as soon as possible.

Smoking in the City

In July 2003, smoking in most businesses, including restaurants, bars, bowling alleys, dance clubs and pool halls, was banned across New York State, backed by hefty fines. But that doesn't mean smokers now hide at home, yellow-fingered and ashamed. Smoking is still permitted in 'cigar bars' across New York City (only cigars, mind - no cigarettes), personal cars, Indian casinos and private residences (smoking has been known to go on at certain 'members' bars', but whether this is absolutely legal is hazy). The 'smoker's break' is now common NY practice, when the nicotine-addicted pop outside of the bar or restaurant to get their fix (even in sub-zero temperatures).

Eating Out

Few cities equal New York's world-class and marvellously diverse culinary offerings. Here in the foodie capital of America it's not so much a question of finding a cuisine, but rather choosing from the plethora of options when you do. The city boasts walnut-panelled French restaurants that rival those in Paris; boisterous Italian trattorias serving up robust sauces that hark back to grandma's kitchen in Naples; cacophonous Chinese banquet halls filled with the smoky tang of crackling peking duck; Middle Eastern mezze feasts of hummus and lamb kebabs followed by apple tobacco hookahs; and of course plenty of American comfort food, from gooey 'mac and cheese' to giant steaks and thick-cut french fries. As for costs, while New York has long been known (and often derided) for its $300 martini lunches and truffle hamburgers, in fact you can dine out – and well – no matter what your budget. Note that it's a good idea to make reservations, especially on the weekends, except for at the more basic, casual spots.

Cuisine List – Quick Reference

American	p.375	International	p.391
Brunch	p.380	Italian	p.392
Chinese	p.381	Japanese	p.395
Deli	p.381	Latin American	p.396
Dinner Cruises	p.382	Pizzerias	p.397
European	p.383	Seafood	p.397
Far Eastern	p.385	Spanish	p.398
French	p.386	Vegetarian	p.399
Indian	p.391		

While you'll find restaurants of all stripes throughout the five boroughs, certain neighbourhoods have their specialities: Little Italy and parts of Brooklyn, the Bronx and Staten Island serve up the best Italian; the Upper East Side features the finest French restaurants; the no-nonsense Korean eateries clustered on and around West 32nd Street dole out superb Korean eats; fans of Chinese need look no further than the thronged eateries of Chinatown; for hearty soul food, head up to Harlem, while you can dig into fiery Mexican, Caribbean and Latin American at the convivial taquerias of Spanish Harlem; the Greek tradition lives on in the bustling Greek eateries of Astoria in Queens; and for a filling Russian feast, make your way to Brighton Beach in Brooklyn.

Discount Dining

You'll find a slew of dining discounts in NYC, though keep in mind that many are targeted towards groups – and the best offers are usually for restaurants of the chain variety. That said, investing in discount coupons can save money in the long run, especially if you dine out frequently. You can occasionally find offers and coupons in the city's mags, such as New York Magazine, and dining websites like Dining Fever (www.diningfever.com), which offers deals across New York, from casual eateries to fine dining, and the Entertainment book (http://new-york.entertainment.com/discount/home), where you can 'savour good deals' – sometimes up to 50% off – at a host of restaurants and takeaway joints.

Earth NYC

Daniel

Hidden Charges

Most restaurants are upfront about their charges, but occasionally you'll find that the bread you've been happily munching on is costing extra. It's therefore always best to ask at the beginning, rather than waiting for the bill to arrive. Perhaps the most common addition to a restaurant bill is the bottled water, so if you're on a budget, it pays to ask for tap water which is surprisingly good in New York.

Restaurant Timings

Restaurants are generally open for breakfast from 07:00 or 08:00 to around 11:00, for lunch from about 11:30 to around 14:30 and for dinner from 17:30 onward. The most popular time for dinner is generally from 18:30 to 20:00. Closing times vary: most restaurants serve food until at least 23:00, although increasingly you'll find many kitchens continue serving until midnight or shortly thereafter. A handful of restaurants, like Pastis (p.389x) and Balthazar (p.387), which serve a limited menu until 01:30, and Coffee Shop (p.397), offering food until 05:30, cater to the late-night crowd and sometimes other chefs who come by after their shifts end. And then there are the 24 hour eateries, which New York boasts plenty of – this is the city that never sleeps, after all. Most are diners, serving simple American fare like burgers and salads, and you'll find them across the five boroughs. As for holidays, most restaurants are open throughout the year, although some do close on Thanksgiving and Christmas.

Delivery

The mantra in New York City is what can't be delivered? Seemingly nothing, judging from the reams of delivery menus that paper the city on a daily basis. The city's hectic pace of life makes the delivery option hugely popular, especially among young professionals. Restaurants and eateries across the city will cater to every whim, delivering everything from smoked salmon, profiteroles and organic vodka, to pizza and the ubiquitous Chinese. Increasingly, many supermarkets, particularly of the upscale and gourmet variety, deliver groceries, including Fairway (www.fairway.com) and Whole Foods (www.wholefoods.com). The New York-based FreshDirect (www.freshdirect.com), one of the first successful online stores, has gained in popularity over the last few years, and delivers organic and local produce and ready-to-cook meals such as kabobs and stir-fries.

Drinks

Other options **Alcohol** p.310

As long as you are at least 21 years of age, alcohol flows freely (though, not free, unfortunately) in New York City. From cans of Pabst Blue Ribbon to high-end scotch, from potent shots to wine flights, and from $300+ bottles of champagne to exquisitely prepared speciality cocktails, bars cater to literally every taste and budget. In terms of drink prices, expect to pay $4-$7 average for a beer, $6-$12 for a glass of wine, and $8-$20 for a fancy cocktail. Soft drinks like Coca-Cola and 7-Up are usually around $2. Beer can also be purchased at grocery stores, and there is a wealth of liquor and wine stores that sell the 'harder stuff'.

It's All in the Water

It's a question that pops up nearly every time you dine: 'sparkling or still?' Or, as some waitstaff put it, '...or New York?' As in New York water, which is not only good - but good for you. Unless you have a real aversion to tap water, it's worth giving New York's H20 a swallow - it's known for its quality taste (in fact, it's said that the city's famed bagels are so tasty because they're boiled in the local water). Fluoride has also been added to the city's water, for maintenance of healthy teeth. And, it is of course free, so if you dine out frequently, you can save a pretty penny if you just tell your server, 'I'll have the New York water, please'.

Hygiene

The vast majority of the city's restaurants are clean and hygienic. The New York City Department of Health inspects all 20,000 food service establishments, including restaurants, bakeries and 'take outs', evaluating the way that food is received, stored and processed, and also the temperatures at which it is cooked. A full list of the inspection results is posted on the Department of Health's extensive, helpful website (www.nyc.gov/html/doh), where you can search restaurants by neighbourhood. You can also call the NYC Citizen Service Center at 311, and they'll send the inspection report in the mail. Note that street vendors are also regulated by the department of health, and to sell food on the street they need both a Department of Health licence and a permit for a food cart. That said, some food vendors may be operating illegally, so if you're concerned, and don't see their licence displayed – or suspect that they may not have one – then you should ask before ordering (or live to regret it!).

Prix Fixe?

Prix Fixe is the fancy term for 'fixed price', and you can find this at many New York restaurants, even the posh ones. Often the Prix Fixe menu will include several courses (sometimes with choices), and it can be a great way to eat out at a top venue without having to endure the end-of-meal palpitations when you get a hefty bill.

Special Deals & Theme Nights

When holidays roll around, many restaurants get into the spirit by offering themed, prix-fixe menus and drink specials. As you might expect, Irish pubs and restaurants celebrate St Patrick's day with gusto, serving nicely priced Paddy's Day dishes, which you can wash down with the obligatory green beer. Thanksgiving is another big day for restaurants, and especially in New York, where trying to shove a big bird into your economy-sized oven at home can be a thankless – and impossible – task. Many restaurants will advertise weeks in advance for their Thanksgiving meal, and it's a good idea to make reservations.

Tax & Service Charges

New York City sales tax of 8.625% will be added to your restaurant bill. This tax does not include service, but it can be helpful in calculating how much you should leave for a tip (see below and p.409), which is roughly double the tax amount.

Tipping

Tipping is an expected practice across the US. Tipping hovers in the range of 15% to 20%; at casual spots, 15% is acceptable, while at the more upscale restaurants, where sometimes you'll have a small army of people catering to your needs, 20% is the norm. When paying with a credit card, most people will add the tip to their credit card bill. Note that a simple way to calculate the tip is to double the sales tax of 8.625%. Though in theory a tip is given for service – with the amount being directly proportionate to the quality of the service – in practice, a 15%–20% tip has become the standard. In the eyes of many, it's unacceptable not to tip, in part because the service industry – from waiters to coat-check staff – rely on tips, which make up a sizeable portion of their salary.

Independent Reviews

All of the outlets in this book have been independently reviewed by a team of food and nightlife experts who are based in New York. Their aim is to give clear, realistic and, as far as possible, unbiased views of each venue, without back-handers, hand-me-downs or underhandedness on the part of any restaurant owner, nightclub promoter, crafty PR guru or persuasive barista.

373

Restaurant Listing Structure

With so many restaurants gracing the streets of New York, choosing the perfect place to eat out can be an arduous task. Reviewing every single restaurant, bar, nightclub and coffee shop would fill an entire book in itself (probably several, in fact), so this section of the New York Explorer features just under 200 outlets that have been carefully selected by a team of food and nightlife experts who live and breathe New York's social scene.

Each review attempts to give an idea of the food, service, decor and ambience, while those venues that are particularly brilliant earn the coveted 'Explorer Recommended' big yellow star.

Primarily the restaurants have been categorised according to cuisine (in alphabetical order), but if you want to go out for a special occasion, such as to watch the match, eat outdoors, impress a date, get sozzled on cocktails or eat on a budget, see 'Get Some Fresh Air' (p.374), 'Cheap Eats' (p.380), 'Happy Hours' (p.422), and 'Always Ace That First Date' (p.410).

Get Some Fresh Air

When the weather is gorgeous, eating outdoors or sipping a cocktail on a fairy-lit terrace adds a dash of summer pizzazz to your night out. Try AVA Lounge (p.411), Sushi Samba 7 (p.397), River Café (p.378) or Employees Only (p.380), all of which are great alfresco venues.

Vegetarian Food

Vegetarians can dine well in New York. The city's well-known culinary creativity also applies to vegetarian restaurants, and many feature surprisingly imaginative menus. As is often the case, it's the neighbourhoods with a large student and youthful population that sprout the most veggie spots: Greenwich Village, the East Village and Soho feature a bevy of eateries, including Sacred Chow (p.399), Angelica Kitchen (212 228 2909) and Spring Street Natural (p.380). Increasingly, many of the city's restaurants offer vegetarian options on their regular menus – Daniel (p.388), for example, features a splendid vegetarian tasting menu. Indian, Middle Eastern and Kosher restaurants often feature largely vegetarian menus. Stroll through Murray Hill, or 'Curry Hill', roughly around the 20s and 30s between Madison and Third Avenues, and you'll come upon a number of veggie-friendly eateries, including Mavalli Palace (46 East 29th, between Park and Madison, 212 679 5535) which serves spicy south Indian vegetarian fare. Other outlets to try if you believe 'Meat is Murder' (or you just don't like the taste of the red stuff), include Teany (p.405), Jackson Diner (p.391), Union Square Cafe (p.379) and Zen Palate (p.399).

New York also features numerous farmers' markets, including the Union Square Farmers' Market (p.328), generally held four days a week, where you can browse fragrant stalls of fresh produce from local purveyors and farms. The city is also sprinkled with many top-notch health shops and grocery stores, such as Health & Harmony (470 Hudson Street, 212 691 3036). The non-profit Vegetarian Center of New York City (call for an appointment: 212 242 0011, www.vivavegie.org) hosts lectures and discussion groups and offers a referral service to vegetarian restaurants and stores around New York City.

The Yellow Star

This pretty yellow star is our way of highlighting places that we think merit extra praise. It could be the atmosphere, the food, the cocktails, the music or the crowd – but whatever the reason, any review that you see with the star attached is somewhere that we think is a bit special.

American

34 East 61st St
Upper East Side
Map 5-B1

Aureole

212 319 1660 | www.charliepalmer.com

The elegant, hushed Aureole, awash in romantic details from fresh flowers to ornate silver cutlery, has become the ultimate 'special occasion' restaurant, with a menu that lives up to every celebration. Aureole is revered chef Charlie Palmer's baby, his first restaurant in what is now an award-winning empire that spans the country, and Palmer's signature, daring culinary style emerges in every dish, from delectable thyme-scented veal sweetbreads with cepes to monkfish braised in persimmon and lobster salad drizzled in a ginger vinaigrette, with the added kick of wasabi.

308 Lenox Ave
Nr 125th St
Harlem

Bayou

212 426 3800

For a taste of the Big Easy in the heart of Harlem, make your way to the welcoming Bayou, which serves up New Orleans cuisine in all its incarnations. Try Voodoo shrimp enveloped in a spicy black bean sauce with hearty sides of hush puppies and french fries; turtle soup scented with sherry; cornmeal-fried catfish; and a classic crawfish etoufee. Black and white photos of Louisiana lend a genteel touch to the spare but comfortable dining room. Save room for dessert – the lemon icebox pie is divine, as is the pecan brownie topped with peppermint icecream and drizzled in chocolate sauce.

120 Hudson St
At North Moore St
Tribeca
Map 10-E3

Bubby's Pie Company

212 219 0666 | www.bubbys.com

For comfort food amid a homey, Mom's-kitchen decor in the heart of Tribeca, come on by to Bubby's where you can fill up on American favourites like a sticky 'mac and cheese', buttermilk fried chicken and meatloaf and gravy. Save room for dessert: the mouthwatering pies are made from scratch using recipes culled from kitchens throughout the Midwest (and Brooklyn). The challenge here is in choosing your pie – selections include a tart sour cherry pie, a banana cream pie, the decadent chocolate peanut butter pie and, last but not least, the mile-high apple pie. Bubby's is, not surprisingly, a hit with youngsters, with a creative and nicely priced kid's menu.

507 Third Ave
At 34th St
Midtown
Map 7-B2

Carl's Steaks

212 696 5336 | www.carlsteaks.com

Skip the drive to Philly. This Murray Hill favourite serves up the juiciest cheesesteaks in New York. Owner Carl Provenzano knows his cheesesteak commandments and follows them with zeal: a proper cheesesteak should be made with sliced or chopped beef, melted cheese (provolone or Cheez Whiz) and grilled onions. Then, you need the perfect Italian roll, which, in Carl's words, should be 'soft enough to soak up the grease, but with a little crunch'. Carl's delivers on all the above and, most importantly, has won the endorsement of native Philadelphians. The cheese fries and chili are also crowd pleasers. Another branch has opened downtown (79 Chambers Street).

Corner Bistro

331 West 4th St
West Village
Map 8-D2

212 242 9502

Ask any local where to find the best burger in NYC and chances are they'll point you to this West Village institution. Oh, and they'll also tell you how cheap it is. They're right on both counts. For four bucks – yes, four – you can sink your teeth into a juicy meaty eight-ouncer. Add bacon, melted American cheese and a thick-cut round of onion, and it's a buck more. The bar itself is nothing to write home about – worn wooden booths, regulars knocking back pints, a TV blaring sports in the corner and no-nonsense service – but let's face it: you're here for the burgers. There's a line on the weekends, but a couple of tall cold ones at the bar makes time fly.

District

130 West 46 St
Midtown
Map 4-F2

212 485 2999 | www.district-musehotel.com

It used to be that theatre district restaurants could get away with serving mediocre food because of a captive audience of show-goers. In this foodie-inspired age, however, where arugula has replaced iceberg, and everyone has their favourite brand of virgin olive oil, uninspired dishes are shunned like saturated fat. The 85 seat District, with a Broadway-esque decor of spotlights and woven steel curtains pulled back as if for a performance, is one of a new wave of theatre restaurants that are aiming higher. The menu caters to the theatre crowd, with a 'short pour' of select wines to accompany your pre-show meal, which includes pan-roasted salmon with asparagus and grilled veal with a port wine syrup. They even offer a goodie bag of tootsie rolls and gummy bears that you can bring along to nibble during the show. After the performance, stop by and play critic over a steaming espresso and cheesecake or apple cobbler.

Empire Diner

210 10th Ave
At 22nd St
Chelsea
Map 6-C4

212 243 2736

A slice of Americana in Chelsea, this 24 hour classic chrome hangout – with a replica Empire State Building perched atop the roof – is one of New York's finest diners. Slide into a vinyl booth and forget about your diet for the night. Retro starters like pigs in a blanket – sausages swathed in biscuit dough – are followed by such comfort fare as a juicy steak sandwich, fried eggs on a roll with crunchy strips of bacon or a big ol' bowl of beef-studded chili. Between bites, look around: whether you're inside or out, at one of the sun-speckled sidewalk tables, the eclectic crowd might include decked-out pre- and post-clubbers, gay couples, newspaper-reading locals, black-clad art gallery folks and insomniacs, all of whom seem to lose any pretense when dessert arrives – sucking on a Hot Fudge Sundae will do that to you.

Gallagher's Steak House

228 West 52nd St
Hell's Kitchen
Map 4-F3

212 245 5336 | www.gallaghersnysteakhouse.com

Gallagher's blends history and gastronomy into one meaty package: when it opened in 1927 it was one of prohibition's first 'speakeasies', and it was also the first kitchen to introduce the 'New York Strip'. Today, it is well worth a visit, although make sure you pass the ATM on your way - 80 years of historical importance, celebrity guests and rave reviews do not come cheap. But the menu is satisfying and meaty, with macho-sounding entrees like Prime Rib, Chopped Steak and Jumbo Lump Crab Cakes - it's not going to make any Vegetarian top 10 lists, but if you are a veggie and you've been dragged along by your carnivorous friends, there is a Seasonal Vegetable Plate to munch on. The decor is pretty macho too, with plenty of dark-wood panelling and non-frilly wall decorations. Gallagher's is now spreading the joy of meat through its online store, should you want to send a gift package of prime beef home to Dad.

Hudson Cafeteria

356 West 58th St
Btn Eighth & Ninth Ave
Hell's Kitchen
Map 4-E1

212 554 6500 | *www.hudsonhotel.com*

When the designer-restaurateur dream team of Ian Schrager and Jeffrey Chodorow opened Hudson Cafeteria, its stringent door policy was as elitist as the admissions board of the Ivy League prep school it was modelled after. This didn't go over well with New Yorkers, and the 'cafeteria' limped through its first year. These days, it's a different story. The gleaming mahogany and dark-wood decor is still reminiscent of a prep school dining hall – think *Dead Poet's Society* – but other than that it's refreshingly free of pretensions, especially once you're comfortably ensconced at one of the communal, candlelit tables looking onto the open kitchen where white-clad chefs bustle around a fire-dancing stove. Taking a page from the cafeterias of yesteryear, the kitchen turns out comfort food – with a twist. The retro allure of 'mac and cheese' is hard to resist, and here you can have it topped with foie gras or succulent shrimp, while classic spaghetti is accompanied by surprisingly meaty tuna balls.

Junior's

386 Flatbush Ave
Brooklyn

718 852 5257 | *www.juniorscheesecake.com*

While cheesecake may not have been invented in New York, it was certainly perfected here. One bite into a creamy wedge of Junior's famous cheesecake and you'll no doubt agree with their longtime boast that 'You haven't really lived until you've had cheesecake at Junior's'. This cheery Brooklyn institution doesn't just ooze cheesecake, but history as well. The family-style diner has been serving up slices since 1950 to a parade of visitors from long-time Brooklynites to movie stars and politicians, including one Bill Clinton, who popped in while on the campaign trail. New York cheesecake is made, quite simply, with cream cheese, cream, eggs and sugar. Traditionalists go for Junior's plain cheesecake, but choices abound, from the brownie marble swirl to cherry crumb.

Nathan's Famous Hot Dogs

1310 Surf Ave
Coney Island
Brooklyn

718 946 2202 | *www.nathansfamous.com*

For the ultimate New York hot dog, head to Nathan's Famous Hot Dogs in Coney Island, which doles out the hugest, juiciest dogs in town – and slathered in sauerkraut and relish, if you so desire. Nathan's began as a nickel hot dog stand in Coney Island in 1916, and has since grown into dozens of stands throughout the United States. The hot dogs may be the most popular eats, but the big burgers and sausage sandwiches washed down with root beer are equally tasty. If you're around in the summer, check out the mildly nauseating – but loads of fun – Fourth of July annual Nathan's Famous hot dog eating contest. In 2006, Takeru Kobayashi of Japan won again, stuffing 53 and 3/4 hot dogs and buns into his mouth in just 12 minutes. His mum must be so proud!

Norma's

118 West 57th St
Btn Sixth & Seventh Ave
Midtown
Map 5-A2

212 708 7460 | *www.parkermeridien.com*

For the ultimate brunch, head to the classy Norma's in Le Parker Meridien Hotel, where you can settle into soft leather banquettes and feast on such artery-chokers as the house eggs benedict served with a buttermilk pancake layered in bacon, and the rock lobster and asparagus omelette. Most guests, though, go the sweet route, opting for chocolate French toast, heaped with strawberries and pistachios, and lemony griddle cakes topped with thick Devonshire cream. Do yourself a favour, and don't count the calories. For a vitamin boost, order the freshly squeezed orange juice, served in lovely Italian glassware.

45 East 18th St
Flatiron District
Map 9-B3

Old Town Bar & Restaurant
212 529 6732

Old-world New York doesn't get much better than this: a tin ceiling, dark booths and a crowd of crusty regulars, college jocks and trendsters jostling for space at the long bar. The kitchen turns out juicy burgers, crispy onion rings, tangy BBQ wings and giant salads, all of which are sent up to the bar via dumbwaiter. Wash it all down with a frothy beer or two – sampling your way through the suds on offer should keep you busy until the wee hours.

178 Broadway
Brooklyn

Peter Luger Steak House
718 387 7400 | *www.peterluger.com*

Steak battles are being fought across New York, with new steakhouses continually opening up and claiming to serve the juiciest slabs in town. Even so, Peter Luger, which was one of the first, is still unsurpassed – it's been voted the best steak in New York for 20 years in a row. Since 1887, the venerable Brooklyn steakhouse has been serving up huge steaks, all of which come from hand-selected sides of beef that are dry-aged and then broiled in the restaurant's kitchen. This kind of meat-and-potatoes meal calls for a classic ambience, and Peter Luger's dark-wood panelling and heavy tables fit the bill. As for what to drink? Finish off the night with an aged scotch or whiskey.

54 East First St
Btn First & Second Ave
East Village
Map 5-D3

Prune
212 677 6221

A tempting pocket of country chic in the East Village, Prune warms the heart as much as it does the belly. Chef Gabrielle Hamilton's homegrown menu is nostalgic, with a twist: For the splendid brunch, a traditional Monte Cristo triple-decker of ham, turkey and swiss cheese is battered in custard and fried; bacon and eggs are served with a tangle of peppery spaghetti; and a toasted caraway seed omelette oozes sour cream. Dinner brings forth manila clams with hominy and smoked paprika butter, and suckling pig with pickled tomatoes and chipotle mayonnaise. Wooden tables, tiled floors and hand-picked flowers complete the snug scene – as do classic cocktails like Pimms Cup and Rose's Gimlett, and no less than 25 kinds of Bloody Mary.

1 Water St
Brooklyn

River Café
718 522 5200 | *www.rivercafe.com*

It is a New York maxim that for the best Manhattan views, you need to leave the island. The River Café, on the Brooklyn waterfront, boasts one of the most romantic vistas of the city, particularly come nightfall, when the skyline shimmers under the dark sky. There isn't a bad seat in the house: whether you're in the ample dining room or on the breezy terrace, you're treated to full-on cityscape view. While the River Café sees a stream of tourists most nights of the week, the cuisine hasn't suffered an iota because of it: start off with scallop ceviche chilled on the half shell with coriander, and follow with the duck breast draped in a fresh pomegranate sauce with yellow green beans. Top it off with their most popular dessert, a mini chocolate replica of the Brooklyn Bridge with toasted hazelnuts and vanilla icecream.

225 Liberty St
2 World Financial Ctr
Financial District
Map 12-D2

SouthWest NY
212 945 0538 | *www.southwestny.com*

When Wall Streeters are in need of some south-of-the-border escapism – and potent shots of tequila – they sprawl out on SouthWest NY's ample waterfront deck and feast on cheesy quesadillas, tasty lobster clubs, barbecued pulled pork sandwiches and hefty burgers in between rounds of margaritas, Coronas, and hell, another shot of tequila. Downtown clears out on the weekends, but Southwest NY doesn't, when locals plus financial guys pulling a long weekend at work come here to kick back and soak in the rays and the liquor. After a few margaritas, even the polluted Hudson starts looking like Biarritz.

Sylvia's

328 Lenox Ave
Btn 126th & 127th St
Harlem

212 996 0660 | www.sylviassoulfood.com

It's easy to be smitten by Sylvia's, a family-owned soul food joint in Harlem. Come for the stick-to-your-ribs Southern eats – and stay for the friendly, down-home ambience. Tuck into BBQ ribs slathered in Sylvia's 'sassy sauce', fried chicken, macaroni and cheese and candied yams. Sylvia's does a brisk business throughout the week, but especially during the Gospel Sunday Brunch when the wait can be excessive – but then so are the generous servings of such favourites as corn meal-fried catfish with grits, homemade biscuits and eggs – plus warm waffles and hotcakes, if you still have an appetite. Best of all, you can take Sylvia's with you – pick from an array of homemade products like the 'Kicking Hot Hot Sauce' and the sweet potato pie mix, and make your own soul food spread at home.

Tavern on the Green

Central Park
At West 67th St
Upper West Side
Map 2-D4

212 873 3200 | www.tavernonthegreen.com

From its humble beginnings in 1870 as a sheepfold, when it housed 200 sheep that grazed in the park, to its emergence as one of Manhattan's signature restaurants, the Tavern on the Green has gamely evolved with the times, which explains its perennial popularity with both locals and visitors. The contemporary American cuisine (grilled salmon, juicy steaks, salads and the like) is rather pricey for what you get, but then that's not really the draw. Rather, it's the chance to experience a New York icon. Over the years, Tavern on the Green has hosted countless politicians, movie stars and opening night receptions for Broadway shows and movies, from *Cat on a Hot Tin Roof* to Woody Allen's *Crimes and Misdemeanors*. When the sun's out, you can kick back on the outdoor garden terrace amid bright bouquets of flowers. Come cooler evenings, enjoy your meal in the fin-de-siecle dining room with crystal chandeliers and stained glass windows. If you're on a budget, go for the Garden Bar menu (service starts at 5pm), with tasty appetisers like grilled chicken quesadilla heaped with avocado or a crispy bruschetta, for around $9–12, that you can wash down with a cocktail or two.

TribeCa Grill

375 Greenwich St
At Franklin St
Tribeca
Map 10-E3

212 941 3900 | www.myriadrestaurantgroup.com

There may be no other celebrity who has been as instrumental as Robert DeNiro in putting Tribeca on the map. Thanks to his efforts, especially after 9/11, the neighbourhood has emerged to become one of the hippest enclaves in the city. One of DeNiro's earlier projects was the spacious TribeCa Grill, which he opened along with restaurateur Drew Nieporent in 1990. The modern restaurant has been a roaring success since its first day, drawing a mix of Upper East Siders and downtown trendsters who come to feast on grilled meats and seafood, including short ribs with foie gras ravioli and halibut drizzled in sage butter. The cuisine is rivalled by the people-watching, and on any given night you may spot anyone from Uma Thurman to DeNiro himself.

Union Square Cafe

21 East 16th St
Btn Fifth Ave & Union
Square West
Flatiron District
Map 8-F2

212 243 4020 | www.unionsquarecafe.com

The perennial success of Danny Meyer's Union Square Cafe – which graces the top 10 lists of the city's food magazines year after year – hinges on a simple concept: contemporary Italian-influenced American fare made with the freshest local ingredients, bought from right around the corner at the Union Square Greenmarket. The vibe is equally casual – Meyer has smartly avoided the snooty route, instead offering a pretension-free dining experience, starting with the chatty, amiable staff. Colourful paintings adorn the walls, and the long bar does a roaring trade throughout the day and night. As for the eats, you'll find everything from a classic, juicy burger on a poppy-seed bun to semolina dumplings with baby potatoes and pesto cream and polenta infused with gorgonzola. The terrific wine list – most offered by the glass – features excellent California vintages, among others. For a sweet finale, dig into the berry pie topped with home-made vanilla bean icecream.

50 Clinton St
Lower East Side
Map 11-D1

wd~50

212 477 2900 | www.wd-50.com

The LES, once populated mainly by dive bars and old-world delis, has come into its culinary own over the last decade – and the modern, airy wd~50 is a prime example. The stripped-down name (the initials of the chef, Wylie Dufresne, and the street address) belies the inspired New American cuisine created within. To describe Dufresne's dishes as unusual might be an understatement. He pairs seemingly disparate ingredients and flavours, and the result is magic in the mouth – well, most of the time. When a chef takes these kinds of chances, dishes can sometimes be hit or miss, but here it's well worth the adventure. Mediterranean bass is served with artichokes, cocoa nibs and brittle peanut; a pinenut cassoulet envelops rabbit sausage and smoked octopus; and a rack of lamb is flavoured with banana consomme and served with broccoli and black olives. At $105, the nine-course tasting menu is, for New York, a great deal.

Cheap Eats

It's tough living in New York sometimes, unless you have a trust fund or you're married to a billionaire. Fortunately there are some excellent venues where you can fill up on good grub without going broke. Give your wallet a break at Gorilla Coffee (p.402), Back Fence (p.412), Alligator Lounge (p.411), Moustache (p.391), Jing Fong (p.381) or Corner Bistro (p.414).

Brunch

New York abounds with cheery brunch spots where you can ease into the day over eggs prepared every which way, fluffy pancakes drizzled with maple syrup, French toast heaped with whipped cream and healthful options like steel-cut granola and fresh fruit. Most brunch spots serve a la carte and are busiest on weekends. Prices are generally reasonable, making this a prime way to fill up for relatively cheap, especially if you have kids in tow. And many places are quite family-friendly, with creative kids' menus and, occasionally, a jar of crayons so that the little ones can scribble between bites.

Brunch

Balthazar	Soho	212 965 1785	p.387
Bubby's Pie Company	Tribeca	212 219 0666	p.375
Empire Diner	Chelsea	212 243 2736	p.376
Employees Only	West Village	212 242 3021	p.415
Jing Fong	Chinatown	212 964 5256	p.381
Norma's	Midtown	212 708 7460	p.377
Pastis	Meatpacking District	212 929 4844	p.389
Prune	East Village	212 677 6221	p.378
Spring Street Natural	Soho	212 966 0290	p.399
Sylvia's	Harlem	212 996 0660	p.379

Chinese
Other options **Far Eastern** p.385

19 Elizabeth St
At Canal St
Chinatown
Map 11-A3

Jing Fong
212 964 5256

Like all good dim sum halls, Jim Fong is loud and lively, and occasionally even physical – that is, when you have to chase down that dim sum cart with your favourite pork dumplings that just whizzed by. But even if you don't manage to catch it, no worries – just keep your eyes peeled and fingers at the ready. Dozens more carts will be wheeled by soon enough, from which you can pluck such tasty morsels as Ha Gow (shrimp dumplings), Cha Su Bao (pork buns), crisp vegetable egg rolls and, for the brave, chicken feet. Dim sum is the Chinese answer to brunch, so it's best to hit Jing Fong by mid-morning for the freshest selections. The prices are nice too, at $3–5 per plate. You'll have plenty left over to pick up a fake Gucci around the corner on Canal.

22 Mott St
Chinatown
Map 11-A4

Ping's Seafood
212 602 9988

Bug-eyed fish with rippling fins, sinewy eels unfurling languidly and pale-pink prawns waving their pincers greet you upon entering Ping's – say hello to your dinner. Settle in with a hot tea at this spirited Chinatown favourite, and before long deft waiters are whisking out fish so fresh it's practically flopping on your plate. Chef and owner Chung Ping Hui wisely eschews any fancy preparation, instead trusting the fruits of the sea to shine on their own. In the Hong Kong tradition, the seafood is lightly steamed and served with simple sauces, such as garlic-ginger, which adds a subtle kick to sweet white prawn meat. The decor is typical Chinatown – a showy sign out front and a slightly faded and functional interior, but then so is the lively crowd of Asian families who pack the place nightly – the best proof that Ping's is the real deal.

Deli

854 Seventh Ave
At 55th St
Midtown
Map 4-F2

Carnegie Deli
212 757 2245 | *www.carnegiedeli.com*

The quintessential New York deli has it all: monster corned beef and pastrami sandwiches, old-timer staff cracking jokes behind the counter, celebrity headshots plastering the 'wall of fame', sour pickles on every table and a line out the door, especially around lunch. Size matters at Carnegie Deli: The turkey, corned beef and swiss cheese sandwich weighs in at a whopping three pounds, while the 'Broadway Danny Rose' combo of pastrami and corned beef arrives teetering on the plate, daring you to try and eat the whole thing. And if you can't, that's what the doggie bags are for. Don't miss a wedge of creamy cheesecake, among the best in NYC.

205 East Houston St
At Ludlow St
Lower East Side
Map 11-C1

Katz's Deli
212 254 2246 | *www.katzdeli.com*

There are sandwiches, and then there are sandwiches. For the latter, make for Katz's Deli, the renowned Jewish deli established in 1888 in the Lower East Side. Here, pastrami comes towering on rye, layers upon layers of hot corned beef are slathered with mustard and steaming, giant knoblewurst – garlic beef sausage – dwarfs the bread it sits on. If Katz's wasn't in the public consciousness before, it certainly was after the movie *When Harry Met Sally* came out. The famous 'I'll have

what she's having' scene – yes, that one – was filmed right here. You can't miss the table where it happened – a hanging sign marks the spot. Kudos to those who can finish their giant sandwich – otherwise, do like everyone else, and have them wrap it up for you. For dessert, try an egg cream, a uniquely New York concoction of milk, chocolate syrup and carbonated water.

601 Sixth Ave
Chelsea
Map 8-F1

Pick a Bagel
212 924 4999 | *www.pickabageltogo.com*

Pick a bagel... or salad, pasta, knish or any combo sandwich at this crowd-pleasing bagel shop with multiple Manhattan locations. Go for a bagel spread with a rich lox spread, or try the tofu cream cheese with scallions. While the plump bagels are the best-sellers, the menu is packed with a plethora of tasty options: Make your own salad, try a Cajun or sesame chicken sandwich or sink your teeth into a potato, mushroom or spinach knish. For an afternoon energy boost, sip a savoury fruit smoothie, made fresh on the premises.

Dinner Cruises
Other options **Boat & Yacht Charters** p.236

New York has one of the most famous skylines in the world. It is also home to some of the most exciting culinary temptations. So it seems only natural that you can combine the two by taking a dinner cruise along one of the city's waterways, where you can enjoy a unique vantage point of the beautiful skyline, and some fine dining too. Cruise timings and routes vary from company to company, and of course bad weather may affect the schedule. It is always sensible to book in advance, and call on the day of your booking to confirm that the cruise will go ahead.

Pier 62
Chelsea Piers
West 23rd St
Chelsea
Map 6-C4

Bateaux New York
212 727 2789 | *www.bateauxnewyork.com*

The all-glass vessel means that you won't miss anything from the second you step on a New York Harbour cruise. There are four main cruises to choose from: lunch cruises, afternoon sightseeing cruises, dinner cruises and themed cruises. No matter which you choose, you can tuck in to gourmet cuisine, washed down with fine wine from a fully comprehensive menu, to the soundtrack of a baby grand

and classic jazz. Over a couple of hours, you get to indulge in the fabulous views of the New York skyline and then be pampered and entertained by the friendly staff. A dress code is enforced and jeans and trainers (sneakers) are an absolute no-no. This is a very popular cruise so be sure to book well in advance to avoid disappointment.

East 23rd St
At FDR Drive, Astoria
Queens

Marco Polo Cruises
212 691 6693 | *www.marcopolocruises.com*

The Marco Polo group has three boats and yachts perfect for any occasion or special event. You can charter your own private yacht and bring in your own caterers or allow the folks at Marco Polo to spoil you rotten with incredible service, food and a festive party atmosphere. Sailing the New York Harbour, you can soak up the awesome views while you boogie on down to the on-board DJ. The group provides special cruises aimed at the kids, surreptitiously slipping in some landmark learning into pizza party fun.

Skyline Cruises

Pier 1
World's Fair Marina
Flushing
Queens

718 446 1100 | *www.skylinecruises.com*

The Skyline Princess is certainly a bit of royalty on water, all 120 feet and three tiers. Offering a host of services, from land-based catering to weddings and Bar Mitzvahs, the Princess will make magic of your night out on the waters of New York. The experience extends to the tri-state area with cruises operating around the Long Island area, Connecticut Harbour and as far afield as New Jersey and Westchester.

Spirit Cruises

Pier 62
Chelsea Piers
West 23rd St
Chelsea
Map 6-B4

212 727 7735 | *www.spiritcitycruises.com*

New York is only one of the cities served by this luxurious boat and yacht group. Offering lunch, dinner and themed cruises, the company has two pick-up points, one in Manhattan and one in New Jersey. The event cruises are good fun and there seems to be something on all the time, be it Jim Kerr's Love Boat Cruise (the DJ from Q104.3 spins classic rock over a delicious meal while couples get to gaze into each other's eyes) or the Christian singles cruise (touted as match-making for all denominations). Check the website for a full list of events and prices, and be sure to book in advance to avoid disappointment.

World Yacht

World Yacht Marina
81 N, River Piers
Hell's Kitchen
Map 4-B4

212 630 8100 | *www.worldyacht.com*

Tuck in to good American fare as you glide around the Hudson. The luxury yachts at World Yacht offer the ultimate chic experience while celebrating the city's culture and history at sunset. Anything from a romantic dinner for two to a full on corporate event can be taken care of over the two-level dining room and outdoor sundeck with music playing softly in the background. The dinner cruises typically take about three hours and allow you to enjoy the breathtaking views of the Manhattan skyline, as well as the serene waterfront of neighbouring New Jersey. Special events like Valentines Day and Thanksgiving, among others, are taken care of and provide for an interesting change to the regular humdrum of the celebration of land lovers.

European

Other options **Italian** p.392, **Pizzerias** p.397, **Spanish** p.398, **French** p.386

Agnanti

10-06 Ditmars Blvd
Astoria
Queens

718 545 4554 | *www.agnantimeze.com*

The rustic Agnanti celebrates – with gusto – Astoria's long-standing Greek heritage. One glance at the appetiser menu – 'Tastes of Constantinople' – and you may decide to make your meal out of them. That's what most of the regulars do – and you'd do well to follow suit. Start off with plump grape leaves stuffed with aromatic rice and herbs followed by fried cod with garlic mashed potatoes and phyllo filled with dried beef and cheese. In the cooler months, you can cosy up around the fireplace. When the balmy weather arrives, enjoy your Greek goodies on the breezy outdoor patio, where if you crane your neck, you can catch a glimpse of the Manhattan skyline in the distance. For once, you won't be in any hurry to get back.

47 Bond St
Btn Lafayette & Bowery
Noho
Map 9-A4

Il Buco

212 533 1932 | *www.ilbuco.com*

Ah, the countryside. Charming European scenery and luscious Mediterranean fare made from the freshest market ingredients... hold on a second, can this really be Manhattan? It is - Il Buco is possibly the most rustic retreat you'll find in the city, with wooden floorboards, copper pots hanging from the ceiling, and a range of market produce on display. The food is masterful, with a selection of seasonal Mediterranean appetisers and main courses such as tuna crusted in wild fennel pollen, pan-fried king prawns in a sea-salt crust, and even the miraculously simple plate of olives marinated in fennel flowers and rosemary (you can almost taste the sunshine). The award-winning wine list is hard to resist. Stock up your kitchen on your way out with their lip-smacking range of products like aged balsamic vinegar, rich olive oil, and sundried peppers.

One Beacon Court
151 East 58th St
Midtown
Map 5-C2

Le Cirque

212 644 0202 | *www.lecirque.com*

Few restaurants capture New York's joie de vivre – and ego – like the lavish Le Cirque, which reopened amid much fanfare in 2006 in the Bloomberg Tower in Midtown. Le Cirque wouldn't be what it is without Sirio Maccioni, the savvy, gregarious owner who has hosted high society in his sumptuous restaurants for over three decades. This latest incarnation boasts another dazzling blend of haute decor and cuisine. Saunter into the semi-circular dining room panelled in ebony and look up: soaring ceilings rise to a colossal 'big top' light shade. Then, look around: ringing the room are crystal-laden tables where, on most nights of the week, you'll spot plenty of famous faces. If that looks like Bill Clinton in the corner, it probably is. The food, when it comes, seems almost like an afterthought – but it's as bold and flavourful as the rest of the place. The Italian-French offerings include Mozambique langoustine scented with red curry and ginger and cashew-crusted red snapper topped with green tomato chutney.

130 East 57th St
Midtown
Map 5-C2

Opia

212 688 3939 | *www.opiarestaurant.com*

Striking the perfect balance between haute and hip, the plush Opia brings some welcome zing to Midtown's dining scene. Whether you have a hankering for cocktails or fine cuisine (or both), Opia serves it up with Mediterranean flair. The main lounge and bar, with plump sofas, fat pillars and blonde-wood floors, is an inviting spot to chill out over a cocktail – try the Orange Blossom, with vodka, crisp white wine and a splash of orange juice – or enjoy lunch at tables flanked by arched, floor-to-ceiling windows. For a more formal meal, head to the second-floor red-walled dining room, and tuck into entrees like seared salmon with tabouleh and roasted cod and white beans. Soccer fans take note: Opia features World Cup and Champions League matches at the bar. They also serve a weekend brunch – try the omelette oozing with asparagus and gruyere cheese.

Employees Only

This hip hangout could easily be classified as a bar or a restaurant: you'll find more information under Bars on p.411, but don't think that means you'd better catch a bite to eat before you go. Apart from a staggering range of cocktails, EO also serves up some pretty good grub. Their brunch is particularly recommended.

282 Brighton Beach Ave
Brooklyn

Primorski

718 368 9637 | *www.primorski.net*

The Russian restaurants of Brighton Beach Boardwalk, or 'Little Odessa', are known as much for their kitschy decor – think velvet paintings and fake flowers – as for their cheap, free-flowing vodka and hefty servings of borscht, beef stroganoff and the like. Primorski cheerfully upholds this Brighton Beach tradition – and then some. Here you can also feast on Georgian specialities, including dumplings and lavash bread. Once satiated, turn your sights to the dancefloor, above which hangs a sparkling disco ball (nothing's done in moderation around here). The live bands are usually no more than a couple of old locals on keyboard and guitar, but they know their rousing 80s hits, and all it takes is a couple of Wham and Phil Collins numbers – and another vodka or two – to bring diners to their feet to boogie down.

Far Eastern

Other options **Japanese** p.395, **Chinese** p.381

60 Thompson St
Soho
Map 10-E2

Kittichai
212 219 2000

The savvy owners of Kittichai, who also manage several other Asian hotspots in Manhattan, know their Soho demographic well. Kittichai may serve Thai, but it's the kind of fusion, trendy Thai that would probably go unrecognised in its native country. That's not to say that it falls short. In fact, Kittichai's delectable, inventive cuisine - along with its orchid-strewn, Asian-inspired interior - has earned it heaps of well-deserved accolades. At the helm is Bangkok chef Ian Chalermkittichai, who creates bold Thai dishes with European and American influences. The menu skews towards little dishes - Thai 'tapas' - so you have the chance to try out the wide array of sweet, sour, and spicy concoctions, from marinated monkfish in pandan leaves to crispy chicken 'lollipops' in a tamarind-palm sugar. The waitstaff all look like models, but they're also consummate professionals, guiding you knowledgeably through the menu. Don't leave without sampling the Kittichai Lychee martini, made with lychee, fresh coconut and lime juice.

1 Little West 12th St
Meatpacking District
Map 8-C2

One Little West Twelfth
212 255 9717 | www.onelw12.com

Once the rough domain of butchers hacking at swinging sides of beef, these days (and particularly nights) the Meatpacking District is a whole different animal. The trendy One Little West Twelfth, with its exposed brick walls, high ceilings, flickering candles and top-shelf (and top-price) liquors, could be the poster child for the neighbourhood. Come sunset, the Kettle One and Veuve Cliquot are lined up behind the bar, the mood lighting switched on and the beautiful people start piling in, eager to get buzzed on fusion cocktails while tasting their way through the global tapas menu of crunchy shrimp tempura and paper-thin slivers of Kobe beef, before hitting the clubs.

240 Columbus Ave
At 71st St
Upper West Side
Map 2-E3

Penang
212 769 8889

Fusion cuisine can be hit or miss, but the casual Penang, overlooking Columbus Avenue, has struck a fine balance with its Malay and Pan Asian dishes. The chefs at

Penang draw inspiration from a variety of Asian cuisines, including Indian, Malaysian, Thai and Chinese – and the result is a flavourful lineup of Chinese dishes liberally laced with Indian and Thai spices. The champ of appetisers is the Roti Canai, a crispy Indian pancake with curry chicken dipping sauce. Vegetarians can indulge as freely as meat-eaters; a favourite is Buddhist delight, a generous platter of vegetables and glass noodles sauteed in garlic. What's for dessert? How can you pass up pancake stuffed with ground peanuts, aptly described on the menu as 'crispy outside, moist inside'.

403 West 13th St
Meatpacking District
Map 8-C2

Spice Market

212 675 2322 | www.jean-georges.com

Spice up your night at this sumptuous, spacious spot, helmed by celebrity restaurateurs Jean-Georges Vongerichten and Gray Kunz. In a city where space is at a premium, the whopping 12,000 square-foot interior is particularly impressive. They've also done a top-notch job at dressing it up, with wooden arches, cosy nooks hung with paper-thin curtains and antique South Asian artefacts. Try the grilled chicken with kumquats, mussels dunked in a lemongrass sauce, short ribs brushed with a tangy chili-and-onion sauce and thick coconut sticky rice. If there's a wait – or even if there isn't – sample one of their Asian-accented cocktails, which are as pricey as they are potent.

148 Mercer St
Btn Prince & Houston St
Soho
Map 10-F1

Woo Lae Oak

212 925 8200 | www.woolaeoaksoho.com

Woo Lae Oak's menu features the same Korean favourites of fiery kimchi and grilled short ribs as its no-nonsense Koreatown cousins, but the sleek decor – and dashing waitstaff – is all very Soho. So is the clientele, who often pop in after a day of shopping to relax over martinis and potent fruity cocktails while digging in to Bi Bim Bop (cold veggies over rice) and Dae Ji (grilled pork). You can also Korean-barbecue your meal: Choose anything from black tiger prawns and tuna loins to filet mignon and sliced beef tongue, and then cook it over the grills embedded in the tables.

French

2 Park Ave, at 32nd St
Midtown
Map 7-B3

Artisanal

212 725 8585 | www.artisanalcheese.com

When in Manhattan, cheese connoisseurs make a beeline for Chef Terrance Brennan's Artisanal, The Big Cheese of the city's fromageries. You're greeted at the front door with pungent wafts of cheeses from around the globe, including dry Spanish Manchego, tangy Bucheron goat cheese and marbled, crumbly Bleu d'Auvergne. The bustling bistro, with wooden tables set closely together family-style, features a menu that's a true 'homage to fromage'. Dip warm hunks of bread into a steaming fondue of stilton and sauternes; savour a buckwheat crepe oozing emmenthal; or try the myriad of sandwiches, including meaty Portobello with melted fontina. Top it off with a robust French red and finish off with - what else? - a creamy wedge of cheesecake.

Balthazar

80 Spring St
Btn Broadway &
Crosby St
Soho
Map 11-A1

212 965 1785 | www.balthazarny.com

It could be the multi-tiered silver trays laden with oysters being whisked through the dining room amid popping champagne corks. Or maybe it's the trio of smartly attired bartenders pouring, mixing, shaking and stirring top-shelf spirits behind the long, burnished bar. Whichever it is, New Yorkers can't get enough of Balthazar, and on every night of the week, you'll see well-heeled, cocktail-clutching revellers laughing it up – at the candle-topped tables, between the tables, around the bar and spilling out onto Spring Street. New York's answer to a Paris brasserie, Balthazar serves up splendid spreads, no matter what time of day. Brunch brings forth dishes like Eggs Norwegian, poached eggs and smoked salmon topped with hollandaise, while for dinner you can tuck into steak frite and sauteed black cod.

Bouley

120 W Broadway
Btn Duane & Reade St
Tribeca
Map 10-E4

212 964 2525 | www.davidbouley.com

When conversation turns to New York's creme de la creme restaurants, Bouley always comes up – as well it should. Daniel Bouley's superb French-American cuisine is a testament to his mastery in the kitchen – and his classical training at the Sorbonne in Paris and at acclaimed restaurants throughout Europe and the US. The dishes, presented with flourish, include organic lamb baked in a black truffle crust with jumbo white asparagus; duckling with wheat berries, vanilla glazed turnip and roasted chestnuts, and delicate squab and a rich foie gras wrapped in cabbage. The impeccable service is among the finest in the city, and you feel graciously cared for from the moment you step in to the low-lit elegant dining rooms until you're spooning up your last mouthful of dessert. And the sweet side of the menu is not to be missed – try the chocolate banana tart topped with ethereal hot chocolate foam, pecan nuts and nutmeg.

Café Boulud

20 East 76th St
Btn Fifth & Madison Ave
Upper East Side
Map 3-B2

212 772 2600 | www.danielnyc.com

The younger, but no less impressive, sibling to Daniel Boulud's grande-dame restaurant Daniel, Café Boulud offers up the same exquisite French fare – at more affordable prices – in an intimate dining room awash in earthy hues. Burnished mahogany-lined walls and cream curtains give way to rich brown banquettes and carved dark-wood chairs, while elegant lamps with rice-paper shades cast a buttery glow onto the crystal-laden tables. With award-winning Daniel Boulud at the helm, the talented team of chefs delight the palate with four different menus: seasonal, global, traditional and vegetarian. The La Tradition menu reveals Boulud's classical training, with such marvels as tender beef with black truffle, leeks and poached foie gras. Le Voyage takes your tastebuds globe-hopping, offering up dishes like the Mediterranean-inspired grilled octopus 'La Rioja', enveloped in spicy chorizo and peppers.

Cafe Pierre

Pierre Hotel
2 East 61st St
Upper East Side
Map 5-B1

212 940 8195 | www.tajhotels.com

Housed in the classic 1930 Pierre Hotel, this genteel restaurant exudes an old-world European flavour, offering a welcome retreat from the go-go-go of everyday Manhattan. For a quiet evening, this is the spot: enjoy your dinner in the hushed dining room, crisp linen napkin across your lap, with just the sounds of heavy silverware clinking and the low murmurs of the smartly attired staff presenting the day's specials. Chef Julian Bompard's creative twists on French fare include black bass drizzled in a fragrant artichoke sauce, silky salmon topped with creme fraiche and roast chicken

with organic potatoes and green beans. Cafe Pierre is also open for breakfast, where you can wake up over a freshly baked scone washed down with a fragrant tea.

Daniel

60 East 65th St
Upper East Side
Map 5-B1

212 288 0033 | www.danielnyc.com

Competition is fierce in the culinary capital of America, but time and again Daniel is ranked as the finest haute restaurant in the city – a position it richly deserves. The regal dining room sets the tone for the feast to follow: pillars rise to lofty ceilings amid an Italian Renaissance decor of mosaics, detailed moldings and plush red chairs. Award-winning chef Daniel Boulud, managing a gifted team of 40 cooks, wows the palate with a menu that showcases every season of the year. Spring introduces asparagus, lobster and artichoke salad with hearts of palm; summer brings forth a chilled tomato gelee sprinkled with basil; and in the fall, you can feast on jumbo mushrooms in a white truffle sauce and braised turnips stuffed with pigs' feet. If you'd like to soak up the luxurious atmosphere without breaking the bank, head to the adjoining bar and lounge, where you can recline at lacquer tables with flickering candles and sip exotic cocktails, like a honeydew martini with ginger.

DB Bistro Moderne

55 West 44th St
Midtown
Map 5-A4

212 391 2400 | www.danielnyc.com

Lucky for foodies on a budget, chef Daniel Boulud opened DB Bistro Moderne, a bustling bistro where you can enjoy his renowned cuisine without quite the same pinch on the wallet as at his signature Daniel (p.388). In the spacious dining room, traditional European decor meets modern Manhattan, with tiled floors, a wood-panelled ceiling, swirling floral photographs and chairs carved with African motifs. The menu stars French classics that have been creatively fine-tuned for the American palate, like Moroccan tuna tartare with chickpeas and oversized shrimp with squash-arugula risotto and toasted pumpkin seeds. Entrees start at around $20. If you want to splurge, try the justifiably famous DB burger, stuffed with foie gras and black truffles. It's the most expensive burger in New York City – but you won't soon forget it.

Jean Georges

Trump Intl Hotel
One Central Park West
Upper West Side
Map 4-E1

212 299 3900 | www.jean-georges.com

The sleek interior at Jean Georges, with soaring windows overlooking Central Park, is the perfect backdrop for the phenomenal French dishes, which epitomise chef Jean

Georges Vongerichten's philosophy in the kitchen. He keeps it refreshingly simple – meats and fish are often cooked whole and on the bone to maintain their juices – while introducing vibrant new flavours, many of which have emerged from his experiments with wild edible plants including nettles, chickweed and garlic mustard. Vongerichten's expanding culinary empire includes a range of other top-notch spots across the city, including Mercer Kitchen in Soho (212 966 5454) and Spice Market in the Meatpacking District (p.386).

MoMA
9 West 53rd St
Midtown
Map 5-A3

The Modern
212 333 1220 | *www.themodernnyc.com*

In the months leading up to the MoMA reopening in 2004, it wasn't just the chance to see the gleaming new space with all its Picassos and Van Goghs that had everyone salivating. It was also the food. And chef Gabriel Kreuther didn't disappoint – his exquisite contemporary French fare at the sleek, light-flooded The Modern includes pork tenderloin marinated in wheat beer with a barley risotto and turnips, juicy beef poached in an earthy cabernet, chorizo-crusted cod, and veal sweetbreads drizzled in wild mushroom jus. Kreuther also takes olive oil to new levels, using it to poach salmon and flavour icecream (really, it's delicious). There are over 900 vintage wines on offer – and, thankfully, a sommelier to guide you through the list. The three-course prix-fixe menu is $82.

9 Ninth Ave
Meatpacking District
Map 8-C2

Pastis
212 929 4844 | *www.pastisny.com*

Amid the velvet ropes of the Meatpacking District sits Pastis, a lively bistro with aged mirrors and colourfully tiled floors, reasonably priced brasserie cuisine and a charged, flirty vibe – all the hallmarks of a Keith McNally restaurant. New York restaurateur McNally has repeated this popular formula across Manhattan, from Balthazar in Soho to Schillers in the East Village, and his magic works particularly well here in the Meatpacking District. The clubby neighbourhood – and its Jimmy Choo-sporting demographic – is a perfect match for Pastis, and the enormous space, from its long bustling bar to the breezy sidewalk tables, fill to capacity day and night. The classic bistro fare includes a sliced steak sandwich topped with onions and gruyere cheese and an herb omelette with pommes frites. Wash it down with a hearty French red or two and then prepare to hit the nightclubs.

10 Columbus Circle
At 60th St
Hell's Kitchen
Map 4-E1

Per Se
212 823 9335 | *www.frenchlaundry.com*

Chef Thomas Keller's seminal restaurant French Laundry, in California's Napa Valley, has been called nothing less than the best restaurant in the United States. In 2004, Keller took on Manhattan with the opening of the stellar Per Se, which resides in the enormous Time Warner Center on Columbus Circle. The elegant dining room, awash in detailed fabrics, walnut-panelled walls and elegant furnishings, offers leafy vistas of Central Park. Even so, the cuisine takes centre stage. Keller's creative adaptation of French fare

includes the exquisitely presented 'oysters and pearls' (oysters, tapioca and caviar), foie gras with white peaches and succulent duck with sweet plums. The nine-course Chef's Tasting Menu is $150.

180 Prince St
Btn Sullivan &
Thompson St
Soho
Map 10-E1

Raoul's
212 966 3518 | www.raouls.com

Amid the ever-changing culinary landscape of trendy Soho, the venerable Raoul's has become something of a neighbourhood institution. Since 1975 this bohemian-chic haunt with dark-wood tables, honey lighting and oil paintings (look for the one of the reclining nude) has been drawing an eclectic mix of artsy locals and well-heeled urbanites. When discerning celebs descend on Soho, they come to this discreet sanctum where plenty of hidden nooks provide an escape from prying eyes, while solo diners will enjoy sitting at the long, burnished bar where the chatty bartenders include you as one of the family. In the best bistro tradition, Raoul's is more familial than formal, with simple, superb French fare. The perfectly charred hanger steak is served with roasted tomatoes in a red wine sauce, and the fragrant chicken paillard topped with basil and goat cheese. Near the bar, a circular staircase leads to a dim loft where a shawled fortune teller dispenses her predictions.

1 East 15th St
Btn Fifth Ave & Union
Square West
Flatiron District
Map 8-F2

Tocqueville
212 647 1515 | www.tocquevillerestaurant.com

New York City has no shortage of upscale French restaurants, but the intimate Tocqueville, near Union Square, has long occupied a special spot in the heart of many a New Yorker. From the flickering candles on the linen-covered tables to the thick carpeting and plush chairs, Tocqueville is a parfait blend of romantic and classy. The seasonal menu abounds with market-fresh entrees, like chilled green and white asparagus drizzled in black truffle vinaigrette and seared scallops with artichokes, forest mushrooms and fava beans. Top it off with a glass or two of bordeaux. One look at the dessert list is enough to kill any diet: Try the apple tart topped with chai icecream and citrus vanilla sauce.

49 West 44th St
Midtown
Map 5-A4

Triomphe
212 453 4233

The lovely, understated restaurant Triomphe serves up simply prepared French fare like seared filet mignon with creamed spinach and ricotta gnocchi, and plump chicken breast drizzled in a cranberry puree with warm bread dumplings. Though small, Triomphe makes the most of the space it has, with an elegant dining room of dark-wood tables and white walls that look freshly painted. As for romantic, it's the ideal date place, either before or after the theatre. Chances are you'll be back soon – Triomphe fills nightly with regulars who know this is Midtown's best-kept secret.

Indian

34-47 74th St
Jackson Heights
Queens

Jackson Diner
718 672 1232 | www.jacksondiner.com

Delhi meets Queens at this boisterous buffet palace where you can feast on steaming samosas, fragrant curries and tender chicken tikka, sopping it all up with warmed naan. It takes a special spot to lure Manhattanites off the island, and here at Jackson Diner you'll see droves of them, heaping their plates alongside locals at the generous – and nicely priced – lunch buffet (available daily between 11:30 and 16:00), which is replenished as soon as it's picked clean. The chefs certainly don't skimp on the spices – when they say hot, they mean it – but that's where the chilled Indian Kingfisher beer and smooth mango lassis come in. Cool your throat, and then go for seconds.

18 Murray St
Financial District
Map 12-E1

Spice Grill
212 791 3511

If your idea of Indian food is curry and… more curry, spice it up at this casual restaurant where the dishes are a refreshing departure from typical Indian fare: The fried Banarsi Samosa, for example, is crammed with potatoes, crumbled feta cheese and tangy pomegranate seeds, while the naan is enhanced with pesto. Shrimp are tossed in a delicate sauce of basil, cilantro and coconut milk. Top off your meal with a creamy lassi ice milk drink. Convenient to Wall Street and downtown, Spice Grill draws a lively lunch crowd, although business slows down considerably come nightfall when all the Wall Street 'suits' head home.

International

242 Mott St
Btn Prince & Houston St
Nolita
Map 11-A1

Café Gitane
212 334 9552

A petite slice of French Morocco in the heart of Nolita, this is the kind of casual little bistro where you could see Graham Greene kicking back, stiff drink in hand. Its ongoing appeal might well be proof that behind many a New Yorker there's a Francophile who just wants to smoke Gitanes and slouch around in a beret. The itty-bitty outdoor cocktail tables are 'parfait' for channelling your inner European and ogling the passing trendsters. Or, stake out a cosy nook in the small, eavesdrop-friendly dining room with a smattering of tables and a counter with a few stools. Tuck into Moroccan-influenced nibbles, like spicy olives and tart oranges or a terrific combo of gorgonzola, walnut and honey, and wash it all down with a French red or an imported beer - the Belgian Leffe Blonde and Bavarian Ayinger are tasty, sudsy bets.

90 Bedford St
Btn Barrow & Grove St
West Village
Map 8-D4

Moustache
212 229 2220

For a taste of the Middle East in the West Village, duck into the comfy Moustache where you can graze on smooth hummus with a hint of lemon, rich babaganoush spiked with garlic, and spicy lamb sausage with onions and tahini. The signature 'pitzas' come piping hot out of the brick oven, and include such toppings as marinated chicken, garlic, bell peppers and scallions. What draws the crowds isn't just the great eats, but the great prices: with the average cost of an entree coming in under 10 bucks, you'll have plenty left over for dessert – try the saffron rice pudding and, oh why not, a tasty baklava or two.

1576 Third Ave
At 88th St
Upper East Side

Uptown Lounge

212 828 1388 | *www.uptownloungenyc.com*

The stylish Uptown Lounge, with a skylight bar and circular booths, hums nightly with a glossy crowd. The ample, group-friendly tables make it a popular gathering spot for the post-work crowd, but there are plenty of intimate nooks for romancing couples. The lively speciality nights include Sangria Sundays, with $6 pitchers keeping everyone well-lubricated, and Tuesday Jazz nights, when you can relax with a date over a fine selection of wines. The global menu offers up Thai chicken skewers, nachos topped with grilled chicken, fried calamari and coconut shrimp. If you'd like a more substantial meal, feast on the grilled steak or duck breast in plum sauce.

Italian

Other options **Pizzerias** p.397

110 Waverly Place
At north-west cnr of
Washington Sq
West Village
Map 8-E3

Babbo

212 777 0303 | *www.babbonyc.com*

The acclaimed, two-floor restaurant sits mere paces from Washington Square Park, and not too far from Little Italy, but the cuisine couldn't be more different than the touristy trattorias along Mulberry. In chef Mario Batali's world, it's all about simplicity and freshness, and each of his inspired creations are based on seasonal produce, much of it from local farms, and the finest seafood, meat and game. It's Batali's boldness in the kitchen – pairing ingredients that would seem to have nothing to do with each other – that makes each dish such a pleasure to eat. Menu highlights include the mint love letters with spicy lamb sausage, succulent rabbit with red cabbage, and the spicy two-minute calamari.

260 Sixth Ave
West Village
Map 8-E4

Da Silvano

212 982 2343 | *www.dasilvano.com*

Believe the hype: Da Silvano offers Cucina Toscana as tasty as the beautiful eye-candy crowd that struts in every night. 'Yummy, yummy', gushed Madonna about Da Silvano's dishes and it appears that most of New York agrees. The larger-than-life owner, Silvano Marchetto, has a lot to do with it, presiding over his cosy, eclectically furnished restaurant with panache – and a careful eye and hand – almost every day of the week. The robust, earthy Tuscan fare includes Silvano's famous panzanella, bread pudding seasoned with sea salt and tangy red vinegar; juicy pepper tuna steaks; mussels dunked in garlic, olive oil and white wine, and all kinds of housemade pastas. Come summer, the outdoor tables overflow with diners enjoying their Tuscan specialities, wine and grappa 'al aire libre'.

524 Port Richmond Ave
Staten Island

Denino's

718 442 9401

New York's pizza wars go way back, with plenty of sauce-slinging from all sides. Most pizza nuts are loyal to their borough – Brooklynites in particular stick to their turf – but sometimes an exception will be made. Denino's is that kind of a place. Those who know their pizza will make the ferry trip to Staten Island for the express purpose of chowing on a Denino's pie, which achieves the perfect balance of the pizza holy trinity of crust, sauce and cheese. History has a lot to do with it: The family-run Denino's has been around since 1937, and they've learned a thing or two in their seven decades of making pizza. Their motto? 'In crust we trust'. And what crust – whisked piping hot out of the brick oven, the crust is thin yet holds its own no matter how heavy the toppings. Traditionalists opt for the cheese and tomato, while meat lovers go for the signature 'MOR' – meatballs, onions and ricotta. Denino's decor is spare and practical –

neon beer signs in the window, sports TV, basic tables with lots of elbow room – but all that becomes moot after the first bite. In the spirit of fairness, two other Staten Island contenders deserve mention (and, in the minds of some, deserve the ferry ride too): Nunzio's (2155 Hylan Blvd, 718 667 9647) and Joe and Pat's (1758 Victory Blvd, 718 981 0887).

206 Spring St
Btn Sullivan St &
Sixth Ave
Soho
Map 10-E1

Fiamma Osteria
212 653 0100 | www.brguestrestaurants.com

The glass elevator at the triplex Fiamma travels all of three floors, but still, ascending in hushed comfort to the dining room (or even down to the bathrooms) lends a certain cachet to the evening – as does the attentive staff, who are knowledgeable about the nuovo Italian cuisine. Delve into a delectable appetiser of braised octopus, olives and roasted red peppers, and move on to the grilled sea bream with fingerling potatoes and string beans topped with capers and basil. Tasty cocktails include the signature Fiamma, a tart concoction of raspberry Stoli, white cranberry and lime, or the memorable Manhattan Below Houston, a mix of Maker's Mark, amaretto, vermouth and grappa-drunk cherries. The impressive wine list is also worth a gander, and the chatty, knowledgable sommelier steers you, rightly, past the usual suspects – chardonnay, pinot noir – to more sacred Italian offerings, such as the Lacryma Christi (Tears of Christ) from Campania or the Brunello di Montalcino from Toscana. There's no better spot to enjoy your buzz than in the lovely lounge, done up in inviting reds and oranges, with flickering candles and orchids floating in crystal vases of water. Fiamma's dessert menu is hard to resist, especially the melt-in-your-mouth semifreddo, with praline parfait, vanilla souffle and sour cherry marmalade.

19 Old Fulton St
Under Brooklyn Bridge
Brooklyn

Grimaldi's Pizzeria
718 858 4300 | www.grimaldis.com

When you have a hankering for Brooklyn-style pizza – and for many purists, there's just no other kind – hightail it to Grimaldi's. Appropriately enough, it sits right under the borough's most famous icon – the Brooklyn Bridge. Courtesy of the coal ovens, the divine pies boast a thin, smoky crust – and are topped with a rich tomato sauce and gooey rounds of mozzarella. A cheery mix of locals and visitors gather round tables covered in red checked tablecloths while Sinatra croons from the jukebox – it just doesn't get more Italian than this.

781 5th Ave
Btn 59th & 60th St
Upper East Side
Map 5-B1

Harry Cipriani
212 753 5566 | www.cipriani.com

Even in a city saturated with swank celebrity hotspots, Harry Cipriani gleams like a well-cut diamond. History has a lot to do with it: The rustic-chic restaurant can trace its roots to the legendary Harry's Bar in Venice. In the 1980s, the Cipriani clan looked to America, with the idea of opening a swish yet welcoming slice of Venice on the other side of the Atlantic. The big-city sibling – at the enviable perch of 58th and Fifth – got off to a roaring start, and shows no signs of slowing down. Smitten celebs, the moneyed set and anybody who thinks they're somebody flock here nightly to tuck into northern Italian fare – such as calamari risotto – and sip sweet bellinis (Cipriani's signature peach 'n wine cocktail) but most of all to see and be seen. For all the stars that strut in and out, the interior is refreshingly casual, with mustard walls, hardwood floors and a welcoming bar. If you're in the mood for a quintessential New York evening to tell your friends about, hang your hat at Harry's.

393

32 Spring St
Btn Mulberry & Mott St
Nolita
Map 11-A2

Lombardi's
212 941 7994 | *www.firstpizza.com*

For over 100 years, this Little Italy landmark has been serving up some of the best pizza in New York. Lombardi's opened as a family grocery in 1897, and started dishing out pies in 1905, making it one of the oldest pizzerias in the country. Here it's all about the crust – baked in a coal-fired oven, it emerges perfectly charred on the outside and warm and doughy on the inside. Purists can opt for the margarita, with mozzarella, chunky tomato sauce and fresh basil. Or, take it up a notch with meaty toppings like meatballs, pancetta and sweet Italian sausage. The justly famous clam pie, made with garlic-infused olive oil, is topped with clams, romano cheese and black pepper. While some recent renovations have left parts of Lombardi's interior a bit antiseptic, there are still enough original nooks that recall the good old days – and a long-time staff that can be as crusty as the pies they serve.

Flatotel
135 West 52nd St
Midtown
Map 8-F3

Moda Restaurant & Lounge
212 887 9400 | *www.flatotel.com*

Midtown's dapper post-work crowd descends on Moda, a swank Italian restaurant in the lobby of the Flatotel. Though Moda sometimes tries too hard to live up to its name ('fashion' in Italian), with all-black furniture and recessed lights, the food, thankfully, does not. Chef Frank Whittaker's rustic Italian fare includes lobster with cannellini beans and roasted duck with apples and gnocchi. Later in the evening, a lounge vibe pervades, and the low, leather ottomans fill with flirting hipsters. Moda's real draw, though, is the vaulted, plant-strewn outdoor patio, dubbed Moda Outdoors. You'd be hard pressed to find a more inviting outdoor Midtown cocktail spot than here, where you can kick back under the evening sky and enjoy beer and barbecue on Tuesdays and Absolut cocktails on Wednesdays.

1 Fifth Ave
At 8th St
West Village
Map 11-A1

Otto
212 995 9559 | *www.ottopizzeria.com*

Chef Mario Batali, who turned the city's Italian cuisine scene on its head with his seminal restaurant Babbo (p.392), expands his culinary empire with the casual 'pizzeria and enoteca' Otto (the name means 'eight' in Italian, in a nod to its perch on 8th Street in the West Village). Batali knows his pork, and here it makes a unforgettable appearance in the Lardo pizza, which is topped with melting strips of smoky pork fat. At the other end of the spectrum is the exquisitely simple Bianco, drizzled in nothing more than virgin olive oil and sea salt. Batali's inspired touch extends to the Italian train station decor, with high marble tables where you can stand and sip wine en route to your next destination (the table). As an enoteca, Otto rivals any you'd find in Italia, with over 400 choices, most of which you can order by the glass at prices that are easy to swallow. And how many Italian joints boast a chef dedicated to making gelato? Otto's Meredith Kurzman concocts it fresh on the premises, and it's best savoured in the simplest of flavours, like lemon or chocolate.

194 Elizabeth St
Btn Prince & Spring St
West Village

Peasant
212 965 9511 | *www.peasantnyc.com*

Indulge in Italian fare born of peasant roots at the charming-but-chic spot Peasant, including plump gnocchi with wild mushrooms, paper-thin prosciutto with melon and 'asparagi e uovo' - crisp asparagus and grapes. You could be in a well-appointed country manor, with the communal wooden tables and an open kitchen fronted by brick arches with hanging copper pots. If you're opting for liquid sustenance, park yourself at the festive bar or head downstairs to the wine lounge, with low ceilings, low lighting and, happily, low prices on selected wines.

Roberto Restaurant
718 733 9503

When you're in the mood for an Old-World Italian spread, head to Roberto's in the Bronx, where you can feast on homemade pasta, from farfalle (bowtie) to long, thick bucatini, heaped with such fragrant sauces as pureed tomato studded with clams, mussels, shrimp and cannelloni beans. The inviting dining room is both cosy and classy, with heavy farmhouse tables, velvet curtains and a massive shelf of gleaming wine bottles. Yes, Roberto's is quite a trek from Manhattan, but perhaps the greatest proof of its success is that it's packed nightly with diners from all five boroughs, most of whom became regulars after their first visit.

Japanese
Other options **Far Eastern** p.385

Blue Ribbon Sushi
212 343 0404 | *www.blueribbonrestaurants.com*

Blue Ribbon Sushi makes the short list for most sushi lovers in Manhattan – which accounts for the long wait on many nights. Stick it out, though, and a fresh, flavourful sushi feast is your reward. Try the tuna with tempura flakes, Hamachi yellowtail with straw mushrooms or the house special roll of lobster, shiso and black caviar. If you'd like to watch the slick sushi chefs in action, pull up to the bar at the front; otherwise, retreat to the romantic back room, where you can suckle fresh fish and sake surrounded by a stylish Soho crowd doing the same.

Hatsuhana
212 661 3400

For a Midtown lunch that's miles better than a bland sandwich, try Hatsuhana, a sushi stalwart that's been around since 1976. Sushi restaurants can live or die alone on the quality of their tuna – Hatsuhana's freshly delivered slabs of tuna are as red and meaty as beef, and taste superb when finely sliced and draped over vinegared sushi rice. Stand-out appetisers include an ostrich carpaccio and red snapper, while sushi favourites are the spicy yellowtail, California salmon and eel. The lunch menu includes the pricey but worth it $24 sushi special: 10 pieces of sushi and one roll and a choice of salad or Miso soup – go for the latter, as the warm, earthy soup made with fermented soybean paste, diced bonito shavings and konbu seaweed is the perfect accompaniment.

Nobu
212 219 0500 | *www.myriadrestaurantgroup.com*

Getting a reservation at Nobu is like trying to hail a cab during rush hour – in the rain. Nearly impossible, but what sweet victory when you do. Chef Nobuyuki Matsuhisa takes sushi to a high art, incorporating Latin American and European influences to emerge with such concoctions as black cod with miso, mussels livened up with a spicy salsa and yellowtail sashimi topped with jalapenos. With co-owners like restaurateur Drew Nieporent and actor Robert De Niro, it's no surprise that Nobu is a celeb magnet, and between bites you'll no doubt spot plenty of recognisable faces amid the sleek Japanese decor of river-stone walls and elegant birch trees. If you can't score a table at Nobu, try the sister restaurant Nobu Next Door, where you don't need a reservation to enjoy the same splendid Japanese fare, from sea urchin and soft shell crab to skewers of Kobe beef and monkfish pate with caviar. If you show up early – before 18:00 – you'll usually be seated within a half hour; the later you arrive, the longer the wait, though a glass or two of chilled sake helps pass the time.

Gansevoort Hotel
18 Ninth Ave at 13th St
Meatpacking District
Map 8-C2

Ono

212 206 6766 | *www.hotelgansevoort.com*

As one might expect from the uber-hip and prolific restaurateur Jeffrey Chodorow, his latest venture – the high-profile Ono – spills over with beautiful people. Join them in swilling sake and sampling sushi rolls and other Japanese fare, like rock shrimp and calamari tempura topped with a garlic chili sauce and fragrant steamed dumplings. The soothing, multi-level interior flickers with lanterns, while ample windows offer soothing views of bamboo gardens, where you can dine

alfresco in warm weather and knock back yummy fusion cocktails. The playful menu also offers, for those who are anti-carbs, 'O No rice rolls', smoked salmon and tuna rolls with no rice, and 'O Yes rice rolls', made the traditional way. Ono's speciality is robatayaki (robata for short), meats and vegetables grilled over an open flame, including skewered king crabs, scallops, clams, shiitake mushrooms and juicy cuts of Kobe beef, chicken livers and quail.

205 East 45th St
Midtown
Map 7-C1

Riingo

212 867 4200 | *www.riingo.com*

Flickering candles cast a golden glow onto the ebony tables and bamboo plank floors of Riingo, the sophisticated American-Japanese restaurant in The Alex Hotel. By day, Riingo fills with suited guys and gals negotiating deals over business lunches of sushi and steaming bowls of miso soup. By night, the stylish post-work crowd comes to sip sake and tuck into the creative fusion cuisine. With celeb chef Marcus Samuelsson at the helm, the kitchen turns out inventive, memorable entrees like plump chicken dumplings topped with scallions, tuna Caesar salad drizzled in a sea urchin vinaigrette, foie gras rice balls with pickled daikon and rare tuna topped with black endamame. Save room for the desserts – the coconut pudding with mango sorbet and donuts with green tea icecream are out of this world.

Latin American

324 Bowery St
At Bleecker St
Noho
Map 9-A4

Agozar

212 677 6773 | *www.agozarnyc.com*

Come for the mouthwatering mojitos, and stay 'a gozar!' – to enjoy! – the robust Cuban menu of Churrasco skirt steak and roast pork drizzled in a mojo criolla sauce. An island atmosphere pervades, in decor and in spirit. The lively entrance that opens onto Bowery Street gives way to green palms fronting bright yellow walls, and come dusk, Agozar becomes a hotbed for flirting – it's no surprise that many a 'summer romance' has been sparked by the smouldering glances exchanged here. Gracias to its Latin roots, Agozar is not an early-to-bed spot. Once the dinner plates are whisked off, the tables are pushed together and dancing – plus more imbibing – is heartily encouraged until about 01:00 or later, depending on how many are left standing. The welcoming brother-and-sister co-owners Gerardo and Diana, along with the attractive, alcohol-fuelled crowd, ensure a sassy night out.

29 Union Sq West
At 16th St
Flatiron District
Map 9-A2

Coffee Shop
212 243 7969

While the name conjures up formica counters and bottomless cups of coffee, this lively, late-night eatery is anything but. The waitstaff, for starters, aren't Flo with a beehive but rather aspiring models and actors – easy on the eyes though also with the requisite snooty attitude. The food is Brazilian meets American, including sopa de peixa bahia, a flavourful Brazilian seafood chowder, plantain chips with black bean dip and corn salsa, fried calamari, spaghetti and meatballs and the 'classic' meatloaf with gravy. Best of all, they serve until 05:30 every day except Sunday, so you can fill up after a night out on the town amid a cocktail-fuelled social scene that buzzes into the wee hours.

87 Seventh Ave
West Village
Map 8-E3

Sushi Samba 7
212 212 691 7885 | *www.sushisamba.com*

Leave it to the *Sex and the City* gals to make sushi sexy. After appearing in an episode of the hit TV show, the fusion hotspot Sushi Samba 7 became a de rigueur destination for show groupies. It continues to draw trendy crowds who flock here for the loungey vibe, tropical cocktails like potent caipirinhas, mojitos and all sorts of delicious rum concoctions, and the 'Latinese' cuisine of fresh ceviche, miso soup, grilled shrimp and sushi rolls with salmon, tuna and other fresh fish. Come summer, revellers take to the splashy roof garden, sipping fruity drinks under the stars. On the weekends, Sushi Samba 7 serves up a Brazilian brunch, complete with samba music.

Pizzerias
Other options **Italian** p.392

You can get a slice of pizza anywhere in the world these days, but despite other cities' best intentions, the only place to get a true New York slice is, in fact, New York. The thing that sets New York pizza apart is the crust: ever since Lombardi's (p.394) opened its doors in 1905, New Yorkers have enjoyed their pizza with a crust that is ever so thin and yet, miraculously, still doughy on the inside. It's a science. Even more of a science though, is learning how to eat it properly - eating with two hands is for tourists, so fold that humungous slice of pizza lengthways and wolf it down one-handed (while walking, for real NY street cred). It would be pointless (and much less fun) to try to provide you with a list of great New York pizza parlours - you'll find one every few blocks and within time you'll have found your favourite. Do a survey among a group of New Yorkers though, and many will direct you to Grimaldi's (p.393) just over the Brooklyn Bridge. If the walk over doesn't give you a voracious appetite, standing in the queue for an hour certainly will. Is it worth the wait? Of course it is! Alternatively, try Two Boots (various locations), where the pizzas are named after famous people and you'll find some of the most inventive toppings in town. And just try to finish the calzone in one sitting (www.twoboots.com).

Seafood

W Hotel Times Sq
1567 Broadway
At 47th St
Midtown
Map 4-F4

Blue Fin
212 918 1400 | *www.brguestrestaurants.com*

Finding a decent meal in Times Square can be a challenge, what with all the bland chain restaurants and touristy, price-gouging eateries flashing their neon. Enter Blue Fin, an upscale sushi and seafood restaurant in the W Hotel. Chic and spacious, Blue Fin serves up arguably one of the best seafood menus in Times Square, including sushi rolls of lobster, mandarin oranges and bibb lettuce, oven-roasted halibut with goat cheese gnocchi, and grilled black bass. You'll find oyster lovers happily slurping from half-shells at the premium raw oyster bar. Afterwards, head upstairs to the alcove bar and enjoy some smooth jazz.

Looking After the Little Ones
Take your kids where they will be treated as valued customers rather than unwelcome guests. New York has plenty of kid-friendly places, like Bubby's Pie Company (p.375), City Bakery (p.401), Café Lalo (p.401), Full City Coffee (p.402) and Café Edison (p.400).

397

Grand Central Stn
42nd St
At Lexington Ave
Midtown
Map 7-B1

Grand Central Oyster Bar

212 490 6650 | *www.oysterbarny.com*

You go to Grand Central Station to catch the dozens of trains and subways that rumble through daily, and to bask in the splendid historic architecture. But oysters? Yep, that too. The Grand Central Oyster Bar, which opened in 1913 when the terminal first started operating, sits in the gorgeous vaulted underground of the station. They serve up oysters prepared in every manner imaginable – but best slurped down raw and sprinkled simply with lemon juice. If oysters aren't your thing, try the rest of the seafood menu, including fresh salmon, sea bass, trout and swordfish. Wash down the fruits of the sea with fruits of the vine – the impressive wine list showcases prime reds and whites from around the world.

155 West 51st St
Midtown
Map 4-F3

Le Bernardin

212 489 1515 | *www.le-bernardin.com*

This handsome temple to fresh fish harks back to Paris in the early 70s, when Maguy and Gilbert Le Coze opened the first Le Bernardin, a restaurant dedicated to fish and seafood. In 1986, they set their sights on the US, and opened up a Le Bernardin in New York, where they've continued the family tradition of serving up the freshest seafood, prepared as simply as possible. The menu is divided up by 'Almost Raw', including four different ceviches and scallops in lemon and olive oil; 'Barely Touched', such as warm spicy octopus with black olives and sherry vinegar; and 'Lightly Cooked', featuring poached halibut with clam juice and roasted garlic.

19 West 49th St
Midtown
Map 4-F3

The Sea Grill

212 332 7610 | *www.rapatina.com*

New York City is awash in iconic images, among them the famed Prometheus sculpture rising over the Rockefeller Center skating rink. Nearly every seat at the modern, cool-toned Sea Grill offers vistas of the rink, making for a particularly memorable experience during winter, when swarms of skaters pass by the windows. The menu boasts fresh fruits of the sea, and most are lightly grilled and simply dressed, all the better to savour the natural flavours and juices. The seared yellowfish tuna exudes just a hint of rosemary oil while the grilled scallops are spiked with a dash of orange miso vinaigrette. Due to its central location, plenty of tourists come through, but that doesn't detract from the sophisticated ambience and top-notch service. Shellfish fans will swoon at the raw bar, where you can suckle on a wide variety of oysters and clams along with enormous shrimp.

Spanish

64 West 10th St
At Sixth Ave
West Village
Map 8-F3

Alta

212 505 7777

The aptly named Alta ('high') takes a lofty approach to Spanish tapas, or 'little plates', and the result is a daring nouveau Mediterranean menu that has New York's gourmands gushing. The two-tiered dining room, with its ochre walls and candlelit honey glow, is a comforting counterbalance to the impish creations whisked out from the bustling kitchen, such as peekytoe crab enveloped in white polenta, fried goat cheese squiggled with lavender-infused honey, Danish pork ribs brushed with kecap manis, a sweet Southeast Asian soy sauce, and lamb meatballs studded with dates and pine nuts that fill the mouth with a nutty warmth. As for wine, the choice is clear: Try one of Spain's earthy Riojan reds.

52 Irving Place
Btn 17th & 18th St
Flatiron District
Map 9-A2

Casa Mono

212 253 2773 | *www.mariobatali.com*

Gleaming wine bottles line the bar and wooden tables fill the snug dining room of Casa Mono, where chef Mario Batali – of Babbo fame (p.392) – and his partner Joe Bastianich, serve up their creative takes on Spanish cuisine. Croquettes are flavoured with pumpkin and goat cheese - creamy with just a hint of sweetness – while the patatas bravas are liberally spiced with onions and cayenne pepper. Seafood lovers are also spoiled for choice: try mussels steamed in sparkling cava, squid, dorada (sea bream) and salted cod. Daring diners can opt for innards and offal, including tripe, sweetbreads and cocks' combs. The menu may be adventurous, but the ambience is rustic Spain, with an open kitchen and tables set close together.

Vegetarian

227 Sullivan St
Btn West 3rd Ave &
Bleecker St
West Village
Map 8-F4

Sacred Chow
212 337 0863 | www.sacredchow.com

This is not your mother's vegetarian cuisine. Sacred Chow's cheeky logo – a meditating cartoon cow, complete with thick eyelashes – and cheery red walls set the stage for what's whisked to your table: playful plant-based cuisine like protein-rich tapas of tofu in sunflower pesto and hefty soy meatballs; the jaw-stretching Hot Diggity Soy Dog; and Italian frittata, a tofu omelette stuffed with tomato sauce and vegan mozzarella. Top it off with a Sinner Bar, coconut caramel dipped in chocolate. Need a natural energy boost? Look no further than the 'Powerations, Libations & Stimulations' menu, including Very Berry and Gym Body (bananas, toasted almonds, cinnamon and soy milk) smoothies. And now off to the gym...

62 Spring St
At Lafayette St
Soho
Map 11-A2

Spring Street Natural
212 966 0290 | www.springstreetnatural.com

This Soho stalwart, blessed with a prime corner perch at Spring and Lafayette, is among the finest – and longest-running – vegetarian restaurants in New York. Sunlight streams in through large windows, illuminating the spacious dining room with exposed brick walls hung with modern paintings. The wide-ranging menu has something for everyone, appealing as much to vegetarians as to those craving organic, healthful fare. For four decades and counting, Spring Street Natural has upheld their noble philosophy of using all-natural foods that are minimally processed. The result is a stellar lineup that includes corn-crusted tofu with miso-jalapeno sauce and spaghetti squash to yellowfin tuna steak with a soy glaze and wasabi mashed potatoes. This being Soho, what's doubly impressive is that they've kept their prices low – for under $10, you can feast on a breakfast special of eggs with chicken apple sausages, oven-roasted potatoes and organic coffee, or stuffed sandwiches like an almond veggie burger with white cheddar on a sesame bun.

34 East Union Sq
Btn 15th & 16th St
Flatiron District
Map 9-A2

Zen Palate
212 614 9345 | www.zenpalate.com

The path to enlightenment may well be through the inspired vegetarian fare at Zen Palate. It's not your conventional green cuisine – Zen Palate doles out veggie specialities with a kick, like eggplant and bok choy enveloped in a spicy garlic sauce, sweet yam fries, pan-fried green-tea vegetable dumplings, scallion pancakes and Shredded Heaven, a heaping plate of chives, bean sprouts, three kinds of shredded soy, taro spring rolls and brown rice. Wooden screens and wicker chairs offer an earthy backdrop to the cuisine, though the Union Square crowds that pile in keep it loud and lively. For dessert, it's hard to resist the Tofu Honey Pie, before cleansing your palate with a sparkling flavoured iced tea. The other branch is on Ninth Avenue (212 582 1669).

Cafes & Coffee Shops

Other options **Afternoon Tea** p.405

Anyone who's seen an episode of Friends knows that New Yorkers love their coffee shops. And while Central Perk may only exist in TV Land, there are hundreds of real cafes and coffee shops that New Yorkers can call home, from mom-and-pop hideaways to urban teahouses to well-known chains like Starbucks (p.404) and Le Pain Quotidien (p.403). While these establishments are busiest during the day and on weekends, it's possible to find cafes that keep late hours; some even switch into bar mode at night, serving beer and wine along with espressos. Sustenance often comes in the form of pastries, sandwiches, and salads. And while cafes like Tea Lounge (p.404) are great for families, that's not always the case; many are better-suited to those who need a quiet place to work, or just want a relaxing brunch with friends.

71 Irving Place
Gramercy Park
Map 9-A1

71 Irving Pl.

212 995 5252 | *www.irvingfarm.com*

Claustrophobes beware: personal space is hard to come by in this bustling cafe, but there's a good reason why caffeine junkies squeeze into this cosy, den-like space. Clusters of small round tables fill the front of the room (there are also two outdoor tables in the front of this slightly-below-street-level, mocha-brown lair), which boasts a cocoon-like vibe thanks to exposed brick and dim lighting. A coffee bar in the rear of the space serves up a lengthy menu that runs the gamut from coffee ($1.48 for a small) and coffee floats to beer and wine; all of the coffee is roasted in small batches by the Irving Farm Coffee Company in the Hudson Valley region (www.irvingfarm.com). Hungry? Sandwiches, panini, homemade waffles, and pastries are all on offer. 71 Irving Place also keeps late hours, proving it's never too late to indulge in a coffee fix.

68 Bleecker St
Noho
Map 11-A1

Cafe Angelique

212 475 3500 | *www.cafeangelique.com*

Couldn't get away to Provence this summer? A European getaway - or a taste of it, at least - may be closer than you think. With two Manhattan locations (the other is at 49 Grove Street - 212 414 1400) and one in Edison, New Jersey (201 541 1010), Cafe Angelique charms with its provincial French country cafe vibe. Cafe tables pepper the sidewalk, and the interior is cosy. An impressive selection of hearty soups, gourmet sandwiches, salads, pastries, and breakfast dishes like a mushroom omelette sandwich are on offer. The flavourful house coffee has lots of fans, but one can't go wrong with an iced Americano or cinnamoccino. The quaint farmhouse atmosphere and ambient music make this an ideal destination for relaxing with an engrossing novel and something warm.

228 West 47th St
Midtown
Map 4-E3

Cafe Edison

212 840 5000

The chaos of Times Square gets tuned out – sort of – at the unique Cafe Edison, located in the Hotel Edison. Inside, it's common to hear servers frantically shout out orders, but overall the large diner-like cafe (also called the Polish Tea Room) is a great place to hide, or perhaps rub elbows with some theatre professionals after curtain call. Be assured that the ornate ceilings and chandeliers are the fanciest things in this joint, which is no-frills to say the least. Food is cheap and filling, and includes exotic gems like cold borscht, gefilte fish, and blintzes; coffee is of course served, but don't get cute and order anything fancy like an espresso. Eccentric, entertaining, and economical, Cafe Edison is a must-see.

201 West 83rd St
Upper West Side
Map 2-E1

Cafe Lalo

212 496 6031 | www.cafelalo.com

Movie buffs may recognise Cafe Lalo from the Tom Hanks and Meg Ryan film *You've Got Mail*, and in case they don't, there are film stills in the window to refresh one's memory. In reality, this colourful cafe is much better suited for treating the kids to some Linzer cookies than planning a romantic rendezvous with an online suitor. The spacious but very crowded brick-and-tile interior boasts floor-to-ceiling windows and vintage French posters. Attractive waitresses in tank tops run back and forth with orders, and upbeat European pop music plays, creating a somewhat frenzied atmosphere. Packed or not, there's no denying that Cafe Lalo is a picturesque, whimsical spot for dessert, espresso, or wine – they're open until 04:00 on Friday and Saturday and until 02:00 the rest of the week.

3 West 18th St
Union Square
Flatiron District
Map 8-F1

City Bakery

212 366 1414 | www.thecitybakery.com

Two words: hot chocolate. The chocolate goodness served here is so rich and thick it could almost be classified as soup, and the kicker is the enormous square marshmallow that accompanies it. What else can you expect from this massive and bustling bi-level cafe where even Carrie and Samantha came in for a sugar fix in one *Sex and the City* episode? An area at the back boasts fruit and yogurt and salad bars, although everything from couscous to catfish can be found. A large island in the middle of the space is where customers pay, order their hot chocolate (seriously, don't leave without getting one) or coffee, and ogle baked goods like croissants, cookies, and tarts. City Bakery's popularity may make it difficult to snag one of the banquette seats that line the walls, and the semi-loud noise level reveals a social environment better suited to chattering small groups than solitary newspaper readers.

4 Clinton St
Lower East Side
Map 11-D1

Clinton St. Baking Co.

646 602 6263 | www.clintonstreetbaking.com

In the mood for buttermilk biscuits, blueberry pancakes, and a steaming-hot cup of cafe con leche? Unfortunately, so is everyone else, as evidenced by the large cluster of young hipsters waiting outside Clinton St.'s red entrance. But good things come to those who wait: Dishes like the crab cake sandwich and Southern breakfast are winners, and drinks like hot apple cider and Harney & Sons' passion plum tea are a nice way to wash it down. Though Clinton St. keeps late hours Monday through Saturday, the bustling weekend crowds make it better for eating and catching up with friends – then getting out of there so the next group can sit down - rather than lingering with a book and a coffee.

75 University Pl
West Village
Map 8-F3

Dean & DeLuca

212 473 1908 | www.deandeluca.com

A person isn't a New Yorker until they've stepped inside a Dean & DeLuca. And with two stores and six cafes throughout the city, that's easy enough to do. At the University Place branch of this minimalist-but-hip New York City chain - which has been featured in film and on TV - urbanites from textbook-toting students to senior citizens reading the paper jockey for space around a horseshoe-shaped common table. The sparse, all-white room also holds several small, and usually occupied, tables and a counter along one wall where laptops

401

are put to good use. An adjacent room is where customers can order lemon bars, bagel sandwiches, coffee (up to $4.75 for an iced latte), and the like. From the barely audible piped-in music to the simple slate-gray coffee cups, everything is understated - which is a welcome thing in this loud, boisterous town.

17 Perry St
West Village
Map 8-D3

Doma Cafe & Gallery
212 929 4339

A sense of community pervades this open space of white exposed brick, tasteful art, and wall-length windows that give passersby an enticing peek inside. Customers can grab a book off the bookshelf to read while they sip their coffee or wine, and it's not unusual for departing patrons to leave their newspaper behind for someone else to enjoy. An extensive menu includes pate and artichoke sandwiches. A primarily brainy crowd gathers at the sometimes-difficult-to-procure tables up front after ordering at the counter in the back of the space, while their furry friends can make use of the dog bowls left outside by the sidewalk benches. Doma is also open until midnight each night, providing plenty of time to swing by and soak in the homely atmosphere.

409 Grand St
At Clinton St
Lower East Side
Map 11-D2

Full City Coffee
212 260 2363

This diamond-in-the-rough coffee shop is surrounded by a bank and a supermarket, but its artsy vibe and strong drink selection belie its strip mall-like location. Past a smattering of outdoor cafe tables, Full City Coffee's long space reveals small tables, some wicker furniture, a very worn couch, and artwork for sale. It's reminiscent of a grandmother's den, and, sure enough, many of the customers are over 60. Funk-jazz music plays, there's a collection of books for adults and kids alike, and dishes like sandwiches, buttery scones, and enormous Crumbs cupcakes are served on dainty china plates. Full City prides itself on its Arabica beans and small-batch roasting; an extensive array of beverages and flavoured syrups like cinnamon and gingerbread will also tempt any coffee lover.

97 Fifth Ave
Park Slope
Brooklyn

Gorilla Coffee
718 230 3243 | www.gorillacoffee.com

Is your coffee habit a monkey on your back? Don't fight it - put some hair on your chest with the freshly roasted brew at Park Slope's Gorilla Coffee, an independent coffeehouse that prides itself on its organic, Fair Trade-certified coffee (take that, Starbucks!) Red Formica tables and black plastic chairs play host to caffeine addicts who are more often than not doing work on laptops. The daily roast is $1.50, and special orders like a tasty Honey Almond Latte, Iced White Mocha, or Caramel Apple Cider tend to stay in the $3-$4 range. A small selection of treats, like cookies and Rice Krispies bars, is available to accompany your coffee fix, and Gorilla Coffee can be purchased for at-home roasting as well.

33 Carmine St
West Village
Map 8-E4

Grey Dog Coffee
212 462 0041 | www.thegreydog.com

A colourful country-style cafe in the middle of New York City? What's not to like? Grey Dog, with its red exterior and assortment of paintings of dogs (what else?), sees a predominantly late 20s crowd that lines up for fresh coffee and hot cider. A menu above the counter is written in coloured chalk and includes comfort food gems like pancakes, banana bread and matzoh ball soup, in addition to gourmet salads and sandwiches. A sophisticated soundtrack of jazz keeps things mellow. Grey Dog is open late, when flickering candlelight at each table provides an almost romantic vibe.

138 West 10th St
West Village
Map 8-E3

Jack's Stir Brew Coffee
212 929 0821 | www.jacksstirbrew.com

Jack's has the charm of a mountain cabin (brick walls, a cramped but homey space) that's still undeniably New York (Bob Dylan tunes, black and white photos of locals). It also has a hippie streak: The coffee is organic and fair trade, and vegan pastries make an appearance. Patrons can also dine on sandwiches from Salt restaurant, or bite into a crispy upstate apple while sitting at one of the wooden tables up front or on the outside bench. The din of conversation blends with the whirr of the espresso machine in the back, live music is offered on Tuesdays (along with beer and wine), and customers do their best to obey the no cellphones rule.

822 Madison Ave
Upper East Side
Map 3-B4

KAI Restaurant
212 988 7111 | www.itoen.com

There are teahouses, and then there's KAI. This sleek, pristine restaurant and teahouse is perched above the immaculate ITO EN shop, which sells the Japanese brand's line of teas and accessories. Of course it's ITO EN tea that takes centre stage at KAI, where the ancient art of formal tea ceremonies is brought to life. For a truly unique, memorable experience, come in for the afternoon tea service, where fragrant brews are paired with delicate Japanese pastries. Open for lunch and dinner Tuesday through Saturday, KAI is undeniably pricey, but then again, it is on the Upper East Side. The dark-wood space exudes a calming Zen atmosphere, and the menu, while limited to a handful of sushi and omakase dishes, demonstrates the highest quality and the freshest fish. Don't leave without picking something up from the shop downstairs.

1270 First Ave
Upper East Side
Map 3-E4

Le Pain Quotidien
212 255 2777 | www.lepainquotidien.com

Le Pain Quotidien has locations all over the world - there are several in New York City alone - and it's easy to see why it's so popular. Proving that a franchise doesn't have to feel impersonal, this rustic cafe provides a soothing, quaint atmosphere thanks to large communal tables (there are also smaller tables if customers want a little privacy); a simple, French countryside decor; and calming classical music. Everything seems surprisingly subdued, except when it comes to the very ornate, very tempting pastries, including a pistachio marzipan tart. Mint lemonade, Belgian hot chocolate, and a slew of coffee drinks are on hand, and customers can even purchase gourmet treats like jars of capers and olive spread to give as gifts.

841 Broadway
Nr 13th St
Flatiron District
Map 9-A2

Max Brenner, Chocolate by the Bald Man
212 388 0030 | www.maxbrenner.com

'I invite you to watch, smell, taste, and feel my love story', a sign at the entrance to Max Brenner reads. If you can get past that and the strange name, you're in for a chocolate experience of epic proportions. This seemingly always packed cafe, bakery, and shop is overwhelming in its possibilities: To the right of the entrance, whimsically designed chocolate squares and chocolate waffle balls can be purchased for at-home enjoyment; to the left, a bakery counter dishes out chocolate-topped waffles, chocolate pizza - you get the idea. The rest of this brown (what else?) space is a cafe - beware the long line of waiting customers - where fudge fanatics can dig into chocolate soup or non-chocolate dishes like salmon quiche. To drink, there's everything from chocolate chai to frozen 'choctails' to 'Hug Mugs' filled with Mexican spicy hot chocolate, chocolate with orange zest, and endless other options.

Roebling Tea Room

143 Roebling St
Brooklyn

718 963 0760 | *www.roeblingtearoom.com*

Looking for something more exciting than Earl Grey? You've hit the tea jackpot. The Mad Hatters at this tea party are more often than not boasting tattoos and asymmetrical haircuts, and they're drinking just about every tea imaginable. There are your basic greens, blacks, whites, oolongs, and herbal and fruit infusions, but it's flavoured teas like the Almond Cookie and Moon Pie that really stand out. Teas are served in steins and help wash down plates of chocolate sandwiches, baked brie and frittatas. Come nightfall, this large and laidback teahouse and restaurant - featuring tables up front, limited bar seating, and cosy couches in the back - replaces caffeine with alcohol for happy hour. Prices are very reasonable, but since service is usually lethargic, Roebling Tea Room is best for a leisurely weekend brunch when you have time to kill.

Starbucks

Various Locations

www.starbucks.com

As much as New Yorkers rant and rave about their preference for mom-and-pop businesses over global chains, it's nearly impossible to find an empty seat at any of the countless Starbucks on a weekend afternoon. Indeed, many of the city's freelancers and writers have adopted Starbucks as their 'office', thanks to the free wireless internet and all the Sumatra blends and Mocha Frappucinos (with extra whipped cream, please) one can drink before the jitteriness sets in. Throw in pastries, light menu items like breakfast sandwiches, in-store events, and seasonal favourites like the gingerbread latte, and it's easy to see why people can't get enough of this Seattle import. Yes, it can get very crowded, but there's always a hot, steaming cup of goodness waiting at the end of the line.

Sweet Melissa Patisserie

175 Seventh Ave
Brooklyn

718 502 9153 | *www.sweetmelissapatisserie.com*

Desserts are the main attraction at this petite Park Slope cafe, where bakery cases full of tarts and florentines draw plenty of drooling customers. Space is at a premium in this cosy, orange-hued room, where singles can grab a seat at the small porcelain counter up front or sit with friends in one of the snug tables in the back. In addition to the beloved pastries, the slightly older crowd can feast on cheese plates, quiches, and roasted vegetable sandwiches, or indulge in the afternoon tea service: small pot of tea, scones, finger sandwiches, and petits fours for $19.95 per adult. This is a great spot to linger over pastries and a cappuccino with your friends or parents. Look for another Sweet Melissa location in Carroll Gardens at 276 Court Street (718 855 3410).

Tea Lounge

837 Union St
Park Slope
Brooklyn

718 789 2762 | *www.tealoungeny.com*

You might feel out of place at this popular Park Slope hangout if you're not packing a laptop or a book. In addition to strollers and some youngsters who make use of the two video games while Mom catches up with friends, a predominantly intellectual crowd in

404

its mid-to-late 20s packs every worn couch and chair as they sip Nutella Breves and Red Eyes and type away (there's free wireless internet). Gooey cupcakes, salads, smoothies, and the requisite coffees and teas ($5 for a pot of tea for two people) are all on offer, as are beer, wine, and cocktails. A laidback, community vibe is present, as Morrissey plays in the background and flyers and local freebie magazines line a wall up front. Tea Lounge has additional locations in Park Slope at 350 7th Avenue and in Cobble Hill at 254 Court Street.

90 Rivington St
Lower East Side
Map 11-C1

Teany
212 475 9190 | www.teany.com

Musician Moby opened this socially conscious teahouse and cafe with his former girlfriend Kelly Tisdale in 2002. Now Teany has spawned its own cookbook, a line of refrigerated flavoured tea beverages and tea accessories, and a Teany To Go takeout space. While the selection of teas is staggering - there are 98 to choose from - most of the scruffy-hip twenty- and thirtysomethings who squeeze into the small, minimalist space and its outdoor tables are drawn to Teany's reasonably priced baked goods and vegan and vegetarian items like an incredible goat cheese and artichoke salad. The space can get crowded quickly, so either arrive early to stake out a spot to enjoy your paper - and maybe even get a glimpse of Moby doing the same - or prepare to wait outside for a table if you're with a group. If you're keen to branch out from the normal cup of English Breakfast tea, be sure to ask about the daily tea recommendations.

Afternoon Tea
Other options **Cafes & Coffee Shops** p.400

Spending a leisurely afternoon sipping tea and gorging on a silver platter of delicious treats is as British as Queen Elizabeth, rainy summers and stiff upper lips, and definitely something you should try at least once. There are several venues offering traditional afternoon teas, as well as some that offer more modern twists on the original (try Moby's shrine to tea, Teany (see review, above), where you can tuck into a plate of goodies and one of the 98 teas on offer).

The Inn At Irving Pl
56 Irving Place
Map 9-A2

Lady Mendl's Tea Salon
212 533 4466 | www.ladymendls.com

If Her Majesty the Queen of England did a whirlwind tour of New York, the chances are that she would pop into Lady Mendl's for her afternoon tea, and give it her royal stamp of approval. This is how the English Lords and Ladies must have taken their tea in times gone by - relaxing, but with a tangible air of formality and properness. The rules are clear at Lady Mendl's: you can partake of your tea at two specific seating times. From Wednesday to Friday, those times are 15:00 and 17:00, and on Saturdays and Sundays, they are 14:00 and 16:30. Get this right, and your reward is a five-course tea consisting of a salad, a selection of sandwiches (usually salmon, cucumber, goat cheese and turkey), scones with clotted cream and preserves (jam not fancy enough!), cake with fresh berries, and finally, assorted biscuits and strawberries dipped in chocolate. It costs $35 per person, plus tax and a 20% gratuity. But it's worth it.

The Rotunda at The Pierre

The Pierre Hotel
Fifth Ave at 61st St
Upper East Side
Map 5-B1

212 838 8000 | www.tajhotels.com

This grand lounge features some of the most distinctive trompe l'oiel murals you'll ever see - squint up at the ceiling and you may even be able to trick yourself for a moment that you are enjoying your tea alfresco. Before you enjoy your tea though, you'll have to make a few important choices - the Rotunda has a staggering range of teas from black to green and everything in between; but a safe tip is to try the famous 'Royal Rotunda', which is a blend of berries, vanilla and Earl Grey. Then you need to choose the decadence level of your calorie intake: the light tea includes scones and a choice of finger sandwiches or cakes, while the full tea has all of these piled up on the classic three-tiered silver tray. If you're really pushing your indulgence to the limit, have the Royal Tea, which includes a glass of sparkling wine or port (all the better for squinting at the trompe l'oiel).

Tea and Sympathy

108 Greenwich Ave
West Village
Map 8-D2

212 989 9735 | www.teaandsympathynewyork.com

This is the place to be if you're a homesick Brit hankering for a taste of the motherland, or even if you're a born-and-bred American who wants to know whether it's worth booking that holiday to London. It's a little slice of the UK tucked away on Greenwich Avenue, and is just about as close to an authentic British experience as you can get without crossing the Atlantic. Apart from the afternoon tea, Tea and Sympathy also serves up some brilliant English specialities (think fish and chips, steak and kidney pie, bangers and mash and roast dinners) that will make you wonder why Her Majesty's island has such a poor reputation for its cuisine. It's the ultimate comfort food - but don't miss out on the afternoon tea, which includes finger sandwiches, scones with clotted cream and jam (raspberry or strawberry), a selection of cakes, and a great big pot of tea.

TY at the Four Seasons

Four Seasons Hotel
57 East 57th St
Midtown
Map 5-B2

212 758 5700 | www.fourseasons.com

This is a smartish tea venue, situated just off the main lobby of the grand Four Seasons. The tea service comes with a great big pot of tea (it may take you a few moments to pick one from the list of 20 teas) and some fresh-from-the-oven scones (either apple cinnamon - yum! - or traditional) served with jam and that ultimate guilty pleasure: clotted cream. Then you get to choose three savoury items and three sweet items too. The savoury items are mostly finger sandwiches with a selection of delectable fillings, and the sweet items include some mouthwatering cakes and biscuits. When the weather is cold outside try to get a sofa near the huge fireplace and snuggle down for a leisurely few hours. Don't get too comfy though, otherwise your afternoon tea may turn into an afternoon sleep.

Internet Cafes

Have laptop, will travel. Internet access is very easy to come by in this city, with many cafes and even some bars offering wireless access for free (buy a latte for good karma points). The city also has internet cafes that provide computers and a quiet space to check email. At Cybercafe (250 W. 49th Street, 212 333 4109; www.cyber-cafe.com) a prepaid hour of internet use is $11.52 plus tax. But if it's size you're after, head to the massive easyInternetcafe (234 West 42nd Street; www.easyinternetcafe.com), which boasts over 600 PCs and is the largest internet cafe in the world.

Fashion Boutiques p.123
Financial Advisors p.95

Written by residents, the Sydney Explorer is packed with insider info, from arriving in a new destination to making it your home and everything in between.

Sydney Explorer Residents' Guide
We Know Where You Live

Fruit Juices

Other options **Cafes & Coffee Shops** p.400

History for Lunch
Culture for Dinner
You could spend days
on end learning about
New York's fascinating
history, but you've got
to stop to eat now and
then. Fortunately there
are several venues that
are as much part of the
history and culture of
the city as the Statue of
Liberty or the
Guggenheim. Learn
more at Fraunces
Tavern (p.416), Lenox
Lounge (p.417), Katz's
Deli (p.381), the Apollo
Theater (p.436) and
The Modern (p.389).

Juice bars don't have the popularity in New York City that they do in Los Angeles, but that's not to say the lines at Jamba Juice, the biggest of the bunch, aren't insanely long. Jamba's range includes fruit, green tea and milk-based smoothies, as well as a selection of light smoothies for those watching their weight. Their functional smoothies aim to help with specific health requirements, so if you have a cold or you need an energy boost, this is the section of the menu you need to concentrate on. Jamba Juice has branches throughout the country, with over 20 locations in New York alone (www.jambajuice.com).

Street Food

Ever heard the expression 'in a New York minute'? It's another way of saying fast, which aptly sums up the city's pace of life. Enter street food, the ultimate urban fuel for those on the go. Hot dogs head the list, and you'll find vendors selling them across the city, from Battery Park to Times Square. At a buck fifty for a dog slathered in condiments, it's one of the best deals in New York. Vendors also sell chewy pretzels and roasted chestnuts (a warm bag of which is heaven in the winter), and ethnic fare, from spicy kebabs and falafel to pita sandwiches. Even a hearty breakfast can be bought streetside: around Midtown and Wall Street, you'll spy plenty of hungry suits lining up to buy egg and ham on a roll – with a coffee, make that a large – to start off the day.

Need Some Direction?
The *Explorer Mini Maps* pack a whole city into your pocket and once unfolded are excellent navigational tools for exploring. Not only are they handy in size, with detailed information on the sights and sounds of the city, but also their fabulously affordable price mean they won't make a dent in your holiday fund. Wherever your travels take you, from the Middle East to Europe and beyond, grab a mini map and you'll never have to ask for directions.

On the Town

Welcome to the city that never sleeps. With many bars keeping the party going until 04:00 and some opening their doors again as early as 08:00 - not to mention the 24-hour cafes - the nightlife really doesn't just apply to the night. There are also widely different scenes here, from the dingy hipster rock dens of the East Village and Lower East Side, to the too-cool-for-school Meatpacking District and Chelsea clubs, to the gay and lesbian hangouts of the West Village, to Murray Hill and the Upper East Side's stretch of Irish pubs and sports bars, to the ritzy martinis-and-mergers lounges of the Financial District and Midtown.

The bar scene in New York City picks up in the after-work hours - around 17:00 - when the corporate crowd comes out to enjoy cheap happy hour prices and take the edge off a long day. People tend to eat dinner around 20:00 or 21:00, and then head out to bars again for a little more drinking action. With clubs, the party doesn't usually get going until 23:00 or midnight. Thank goodness for Red Bull and vodka! While the boroughs of Queens, Staten Island, The Bronx, and especially Brooklyn have a number of standout bars, the heart of New York City's nightlife is firmly planted in Manhattan. Weekends, of course, are the busiest going out times, though here 'weekends' translates to Thursday through Sunday. Many die-hard clubbers also prefer to go out earlier in the week to avoid the weekend crowds of 'Bridge and Tunnelers', the Manhattan term for residents of New Jersey, Long Island, and other boroughs.

The great thing about New York City nightlife is that there is literally something for everyone. Live music of every genre - jazz, rock, country-western, blues, folk, salsa - plays every night in the town that launched Charlie 'Bird' Parker, Bob Dylan, The Ramones, Blondie, and, most recently, The Strokes. Studio 54 may be long gone, but the city's dance clubs - despite a stringent cabaret licence policy - are considered the best in the country, with big-name DJs spinning for huge crowds. There are home-away-from-home neighbourhood bars filled with enough characters to give *Cheers* a run for its money. Sports fanatics can catch any game their heart desires on thousands of flat-screen TVs; karaoke buffs can sing any song in any language; pool sharks can rack 'em up on a sea of green felt; outdoor bars provide a natural refuge and, oftentimes, incredible views of that famous city skyline; and oenophiles can soak in the world's finest vintages. There are bars with bowling alleys, bars with ice skating rinks, bars with bocce courts, you name it. The possibilities are endless, and the energy is unrivalled.

Door Policy

Nightclub doormen get bad press for being pretty strict when it comes to letting the average Joe into their venues - not always undeserved. To stand in line for hours at the newest hotspot only to be denied entry when you get to the front is almost enough to make you give up the nightlife altogether and spend your evenings watching TV. There are some

Ladies' Nights

The city isn't that big on freebies so when Happy Hour rolls around or a bar or club happens to have a Ladies Night, you can imagine the popularity. Said to have the best Margarita's in town, ACME Bar & Grill (www.acmebarandgrill.com) has some pretty sweet deals on all week with 2-4-1 for the gals every Wednesday night. In fact, Wednesdays happen to be particularly good for ladies who want to get tipsy for not very much. Bar None (212 777 6663) knock their drink prices down to a buck each. Down The Hatch (p.415) has the same deal for the ladies on Tuesday nights instead. For a comprehensive list of drinking establishments and the great deals that they offer, click on to www.drinkdeal.com.

409

ways to improve your chances of getting in though. Firstly, you've got to look cool, so brush up on your fashion sense and your 'I'm too bored to care' expression. Secondly, attitude is everything – don't beg, cry, act drunk, argue or offer bribes - be cool. If looking cool and acting cool isn't getting you anywhere, try to fake a celebrity connection, or take your custom to one of the less pretentious venues in town – they're usually more fun anyway!

Dress Code

Many places in New York have some kind of dress code: some require you to dress in the latest threads, and others may have strange dress codes (take The Eagle (p.430), where on certain nights you can't get in if you're not wearing leather). To make sure you don't make a dress faux pas, always try to check the venue's website for some guidelines - most will offer some kind of clue regarding what's acceptable.

Special Nights

New Yorkers are always looking for an excuse to party, especially when discounted drinks are involved. While most bars offer some sort of happy hour after-work promotion with drink specials, the budget-conscious should also be on the lookout for specials tied to sporting events, particularly on Sundays during the football season. As far as holidays, it can be a crapshoot: There's always a party, but cheap drinks may not be part of the deal. For instance, bar owners know that they're guaranteed to be packed on St. Patrick's Day, and therefore may charge a cover and not reduce drinks in order to rake in more money. It's always best to call ahead, but don't worry - between happy hour, ladies' nights, and game day discounts, a cheap drink is always close at hand.

Always Ace that First Date
It can be hard to get a date in New York. If you do find someone who is normal enough to take out for the evening, make sure you treat them right by taking them to one of the city's most romantic spots. Try Shalel Lounge (p.420), Morrell Wine Bar (p.418), Flatiron Lounge (p.415), Butter (p.424), Daniel (p.388), Peasant (p.394) or Bin 71 (p.412).

Taxes & Service Charges
While food is taxed at bars, alcohol thankfully is not: If a beer costs $5, you pay $5 (plus tip, of course). If you're enjoying bottle service at a nightclub, however, expect a 20% service charge to be tacked onto the bill (never assume the server is going to tell you that you've already tipped him or her). Some bars may also charge extra or incur a drink minimum if you're paying a bar tab by credit card, so ask before you hand the Visa over. And if you're visiting a live music or comedy venue, be aware that a drink minimum (often in addition to a cover charge) is par for the course.

Bars & Pubs

Bars

Other options **Nightclubs** p.423

Between a smoking ban, hard-to-procure cabaret licences, and constant battles over noise violations, New York City bars have taken a beating lately, but for the most part they've rolled with the punches. This is still the ultimate city to experience nightlife in its many forms, from elegant wine bars to retro speakeasies that specialise in immaculate cocktails to unruly dive bars to modest neighbourhood pubs. It's impossible to lump this diverse city into any one category, and that's the beauty of it all. All ages, all nationalities, all personalities, all genders, and all interests have a home here, and that's something that no legal restriction can take away.

---

600 Metropolitan Ave
Williamsburg
Brooklyn

Alligator Lounge

718 599 4440 | www.alligatorlounge.com

Beer. Food. Beer. Food. When you're down to your last few dollars, it's nice to know that there's at least one place where you can go and not have to serve as a mediator between your stomach and your liver. At this ultra-casual neighbourhood hangout, every drink comes with a free brick-oven cheese pizza (toppings are extra). And since most beers cost just $5, you'll still have money left over for a game of pool, a few Galaga plays, a rock song or two on the digital jukebox, and a tip for your charismatic bartender. Regulars rule the roost in this kitschy den, though karaoke and hip-hop nights in the back room draw a mixed bag. The same-owned Capone's (Williamsburg) and Crocodile Lounge (East Village) also offer the free pizza deal, but nothing beats the energy of this original.

---

95 Stanton St
Lower East Side
Map 11-C2

Arlene's Grocery

212 995 1652 | www.arlenesgrocery.net

Downtown rock bars come and go, and even the venerable CBGB's has bit the dust, but Arlene's Grocery is still going strong after more than a decade. Sure, the bands - many of them unknowns - can be hit or miss, but the cover's cheap and, with bands playing nightly, the odds of witnessing next year's MTV rock darling before they hit it big are good. Beyond its musical roster, Arlene's is best known for its insanely popular Monday night Rock and Roll Karaoke, where aspiring rockers can screech their lungs out to their favorite Guns N' Roses and Led Zeppelin hits while backed by a live band. On Sunday nights though, the raw space hears more hollers than howls when Kuntry Karaoke takes over. Arlene's Butcher Bar provides a chill escape from the mayhem, especially when the monthly Amateur Female Jell-O Wrestling is in session.

---

210 West 55th St
Midtown
Map 4-F2

AVA Lounge

212 956 7020 | www.avaloungenyc.com

Modern-day hepcats can gaze out at Times Square, Columbus Circle, and the Hudson River from their lofty perch atop the Dream Hotel, where AVA Lounge takes up the penthouse floor. Named for Ava Gardner, the lounge's colour palette of white and cool soft blues and greens, mod furnishings, and panoramic views of the city fittingly capture a Rat Pack ambience. In the summer, the outdoor space transforms into a lush English-garden-inspired wonderland where Manhattan's movers and shakers sip martinis as they take in the stunning view. AVA is an appropriately stylish apex for this dazzling hotel, where exotic statues fill the lobby and the downstairs DREAM Lounge - which shares owners with AVA – presents a vivid pinstriped cocktail playground.

AVA Lounge

155 Bleecker St
West Village
Map 8-F4

Back Fence

212 475 9221 | *www.thebackfenceonline.com*

The Lower East Side may have all the rock cred now, but not so long ago Greenwich Village was where legends like Bob Dylan cut their musical teeth. The Back Fence - established in 1945 - was there to see it all. Though today this area teems with more tourists than Beat poets, it's still worth paying homage to rock history by checking out the earnest singer-songwriters and bands that play everything from folk to R&B to country. This no-frills - unless sawdust floors and free peanuts count as frills - joint hosts two to three musicians per night in addition to a Sunday afternoon open poetry reading. Leave your expectations - and pretension - at the door and you might be pleasantly surprised by this no-fuss blast from the past.

175 Second Ave
Bt 11th & 12th St
East Village
Map 7-B3

Bar Veloce

212 260 3200 | *www.barveloce.com*

You might need to suck in your stomach to fit into this very slim Italian wine bar, where a staggering selection of moderately priced vino and grappa is accompanied by small plates of panini and bruschetta. Though a newer Bar Veloce location in Chelsea has more space, this narrow hideaway - holding just a bar on one side and an itsy-bitsy counter-top with chairs on the other - is big on charm. The dapper servers behind the brushed metal bar are extremely polished and professional, and most of all, accommodating when patrons can't decide on a wine. Ambient music plays, an old-school, European vibe pervades, and a chill, 30 something crowd soaks it all in.

388 Union Ave
Brooklyn

Barcade

718 302 6464 | *www.barcadebrooklyn.com*

This arcade-meets-bar has seen more quarters than the NFL. Boasting over 20 vintage videogames - including Tetris, Frogger, Galaga, and Super Mario Bros. - the warehouse-like Barcade is the hipster alternative to playing PlayStation 3 at home with your bros. Game play tends to take precedence over socialising ('Dude! You made me get hit by that fireball!'), but a pool table, a smoking area out front, and a formidable selection of reasonably priced, hard-to-find brews aims to level the playing field for non-gamers. Top players get their name on a chalk board, there's a change machine, and beer nuts can be purchased at the bar. Judging by the hoodie-wearing guys and gals in their 20s and 30s, there's no such thing as saying 'game over' to your inner child.

237 Columbus Ave
Upper West Side
Map 2-E3

Bin 71

212 362 5446

When the evening calls for sophistication, look no further than Bin 71. This cosy, dimly lit wine bar oozes with maturity, and that's not just a reference to the aged wines it serves. An older, intellectual crowd clusters around the petite room's few small tables, countertop, and large horseshoe-shaped marble slab bar, nibbling on crostini, panini, and desserts as they savour their glasses of reds and whites. Jazzy tunes add to the elegant scene. But although Bin 71 is a wonderful setting for a romantic date - provided you don't mind having an audience - it manages to retain an air of unpretentiousness that is fitting for casual get-togethers with friends too.

Bohemian Beer Hall

29-19 24th Ave
Astoria
Queens

718 274 4925 | *www.bohemianhall.com*

Even die-hard Manhattan elitists can't resist making a pilgrimage to this Astoria, Queens institution. At over 90 years old, Bohemian Hall & Beer Garden is the last of the city's original beer gardens, and each summer hordes of drinkers come to pay tribute, soak up some sun in the outdoor garden, raise mugs of unpronounceable beers like Staropramen and Brouczech to their lips, and dig into hearty plates of kielbasa, goulash, and potato pancakes. There's an indoor bar and restaurant as well, so visitors can get their fix year-round. This place takes its Czech heritage seriously, offering a society for those of Czech or Slovak descent as well as a Czech school for children 13 and under.

Bondi Road

153 Rivington St
Lower East Side
Map 11-D1

212 253 5311 | *www.bondiroad.com*

Every day - and night - is a g'day at this Aussie addition to the Lower East Side. Named for Sydney's famed Bondi (pronounced 'Bond-eye') Beach, this laid-back hangout pays tribute with beachy wall murals of its namesake and an overhead screen that plays surfing footage. Seafood from Down Under is flown in to create the Aussie and Kiwi dishes, and culinary risk-takers can wash down their kangaroo with a spicy oyster shooter. A late-night menu offers $6 bites and drinks, including fruity cocktails and barramundi. On weekends this narrow space - which has a bar in the back, a handful of tall bar tables in front, and booth-like seating on the side - gets packed with yuppie types and the girls who love them. Come during the week to chat up the Aussie bartender and really savour the relaxed atmosphere.

Bounce

1403 2nd Ave
Upper East Side
Map 3-D3

212 535 2183 | *www.bounceny.com*

He wants to watch the game. She'd rather die than eat nachos. Can this relationship be saved? Yes, if they head to Bounce, a sports bar that understands that sometimes jocks would rather nibble on roasted garlic hummus, lobster rolls, and veggie burgers than shovel Buffalo wings down their throat. But let's not get crazy here - men are men, so the requisite guilty pleasure bar food, hot waitresses, sports memorabilia, and, most importantly, multiple plasma screens are present and accounted for. High table seating and a separate, semi-dressed-up dining area separates Bounce and its downtown brother, Bounce Deuce, from the city's rough-around-the-edges sports bars. Dirt-cheap drink specials and weekend DJs keep everybody happy.

Brandy Library Lounge

25 North Moore St
Tribeca
Map 10-E3

212 226 5545 | *www.brandylibrary.com*

Welcome to the best library ever. Okay, so there aren't that many books - and the ones that are here are all about alcohol - but the shelves of almost every brandy, whiskey, and rum known to man will provide plenty of education. The upscale lounge glows with a warm amber light; the patrons' cheeks, meanwhile, glow with the warmth of an elusive French cognac. Jazz plays in the background as Financial

413

District heavyweights settle into their leather chairs and sample steak tartare to accompany the exquisite single-malt scotch recommended by the in-house spirit sommelier. Cocktails like the Sun of Normandy and Hot Brandy Alexander showcase the best of the bottles that line the walls. The bar also hosts frequent tastings and a Spirit School which explores a particular spirit in-depth.

1485 Second Ave
Upper East Side
Map 3-D2

Brother Jimmy's

212 288 0999 | www.brotherjimmys.com

Anyone who thinks Manhattan bars are all about expensive cocktails, snobby doormen, and ear-assaulting house music obviously hasn't been to Brother Jimmy's three saloons. The pretension-free college crowd at this original location probably thinks Jimmy Choo is a sneeze and they'd rather spend their hard-earned money on fried pickles, all-you-can-eat ribs, and $1 ladies' night margaritas than bottle service. The rustic decor could best be described as 'trailer park after a tornado' chic, with checkered tablecloths, beer signs, and lots of pigs. A Southern Appreciation Day on Wednesdays gives a 25% food discount to patrons with a valid Southern ID, but let's be honest: Every day is Southern Appreciation Day in this endearing country honkeytonk.

331 West 4th St
West Village
Map 8-D2

Corner Bistro

212 242 9502

Some bars warm you up the instant you step inside. Corner Bistro is one of those bars. This neighbourhood veteran is low on frills: The brick-walled front room holds some tables, sports-playing TVs, and a long L-shaped wooden bar packed with bottles and assorted items like an encyclopaedia; the back dining room has more tables, which are in high demand thanks to what is generally regarded as the city's best burger. Plastic ketchup and mustard bottles and the red neon sign outside are just about the only dashes of colour in this dimly lit, comfortably shabby hangout, unless you count the colourful old-timer patrons who elbow past the post-college crowd to snag a stool and a $2.50 McSorley's and yuk it up with the bartender.

228 Thompson St
West Village
Map 8-F4

Dove

212 254 1435

In a neighbourhood better known for loud-and-proud NYU student bars and dingy live music institutions, The Dove flies solo as a drinking den for sophisticated scenesters. With its red velvet-flocked wallpaper, roaring fireplace, and intimate candlelit seating, The Dove teems with the sexy vibe of a retro speakeasy. A glance at the cocktail menu reveals old-fashioned indulgences like sidecars, grasshoppers, and french lavender martinis, while late 20 something guys and dames can soak in Billie Holiday tunes in the early hours. The vibe picks up as the evening progresses, with Billie being replaced by The Smiths and birthday parties crowding out the canoodling couples. There's no food menu served, but the cheese crackers put out on the bar are addictive, and the extremely friendly bar staff encourages ordering in. Just leave the Buffalo wings to the frat boys across the street.

414

Down the Hatch

179 West 4th St
Btn Sixth & Seventh Ave
West Village
Map 8-E3

212 627 9747 | *www.nycbestbars.com/DTH*

Say what you like about frat boys and testosterone, but when it comes to sports, beer, and raunchy good times, nobody does it better than Down the Hatch. A short flight of

stairs leads to this underground alpha-male den where the game is always on, the Atomic wings are always hot, and the foosball, darts, and beer pong competitions are always in progress. Drink specials are too good to pass up, but the best deal may be the $19 wings-and-pitchers special on the weekends, when the two-room dive fills to capacity with jersey-wearing fans coming to watch the big game. Down the Hatch is the epitome of a lowbrow hangout where fart jokes and grunts serve as pick-up lines, but sometimes you just need a little rowdy, down-and-dirty drinking experience.

Employees Only

510 Hudson St
Btn Christopher
& West St
West Village
Map 8-D3

212 242 3021 | *www.employeesonlynyc.com*

Not sure if you'll like Employees Only? Just ask the fortune teller parked up front, one of this retro joint's many endearing quirks. This old-school wedge of the Village, home to beery taverns and mom-and-pop shops, got a welcome shot in the arm with the arrival of this stylish speakeasy-style bar and restaurant. Perhaps a better name would be Hipster Employees Only, as this sexy spot has been pulling in a cool crowd since opening night. The slick crew behind the venture were, in fact, once employees (waiters, bartenders) at some of Manhattan's trendiest nightspots and restaurants, and here they've managed to create an ambience that's both timeless and very 'now'. Once you're inside, a handlebar-mustachioed bartender will mix you a $12 Pimm's Cup or Pisco Sour cocktail, or fetch you a glass of wine (beers are few, but they are of the hard-to-find variety). Once you get past the bar you'll find an all-ages collection of hip urbanites and local characters in the dining area or in the airy courtyard, tucking into some delicious bistro fare. If a bar could make you cool by osmosis, it'd be this place.

Flatiron Lounge

37 West 19th St
Flatiron District
Map 8-F1

212 727 7741 | *www.flatironlounge.com*

There are those for whom going out isn't about downing shots of whiskey or singing Bon Jovi at the top of their lungs, and Flatiron Lounge is their Mecca. A black cocktail dress-clad hostess greets you at the mirrored entrance of this retro-chic den, where soft lighting, cool piped-in jazz, and a womblike arched pathway leading to the bar signal a sophisticated evening ahead. Cocktails like the $12 Martinez and New York Sour are

paramount here, and the well-heeled, older-skewing crowd knows better than to order a beer (though it's available, at $7-$11). Though the long bar is polished and adorned with lovely blue glass overhead lamps, you'll really feel lucky if you can snag one of the curved booths in the rear, which boasts a breathtaking dark blue cut-glass mosaic wall. Life is good.

54 Pearl St
Financial District
Map 12-F3

Fraunces Tavern

212 968 1776 | www.frauncestavern.com

George Washington may not have been able to tell a lie, but he had no qualms about enjoying a pint at this historic restaurant and watering hole, which dates back to 1762 and has its own museum. Today it's captains of industry and Wall Street wheelers and dealers who frequent this colonial relic, sealing deals over lunches of beef Wellington and rack of lamb in the quaint dining room. The classic menu is a bit bland but plentiful – if you've got an appetite, go for the New York strip steak and chicken with a garlic glaze. After work, it's back to the bar for a few beers - and, on Wednesday nights, live classical guitar - before heading home. Dinner is also available, but things wind up early in these parts; last call is at 22:50.

355 West 14th St
Meatpacking District
Map 8-C1

Gin Lane

212 691 0555 | www.ginlanenyc.com

Paying $14 a pop for cocktails may sound hard to swallow, but the carefully crafted libations at Gin Lane go down surprisingly easy. Cocktail guru Dale DeGroff designed the speciality cocktail list, which includes flavourful hits like a Tea Time Martini and includes complex ingredients. It's best to make a reservation if one wants to dine in this retro hotspot, which is guarded by a quaint white picket fence. Inside, singles mingle at the oak bar and settle into leather chairs, while couples on the make head to the romantic back dining area for steak, fancy salads, and gourmet macaroni and cheese. The sophisticated decor evokes speakeasies from eras past with staples like chandeliers, mahogany walls, pristine leather booths, Victorian wallpaper, and a well-dressed, formal wait staff.

11 East 36th St
Midtown
Map 7-A2

The Ginger Man

212 532 3740 | www.gingerman-ny.com

Got beer? The Ginger Man does - over 60 draughts and 130 bottles, to be precise. Beer aficionados will drool over the arsenal of bocks, ciders, ambers, seasonals, barley wines, stouts, organics, and more, spanning the globe from Sri Lanka's Lion Stout to Scotland's Orkney Skullsplitter. Wine and liquor, including a nice offering of single-malt Scotch, are also present, with Guinness stew and bratwurst plates on hand to line the stomach. Ginger Man's huge, warm space includes a mile-long bar on one side that's perpetually packed with a jovial corporate crowd after work, as well as a quieter den-like room in the back. Expect lots of wood, worn couches, and cosy nooks where one can contemplate which beer to try next.

106 Kenmare St
Btn Lafayette St &
Cleveland Pl
Nolita
Map 11-A2

La Esquina

646 613 7100 | www.esquinanyc.com

When this place first opened, the city's scenesters congratulated themselves on knowing the hush-hush address. Today, the cat's out of the bag, but that doesn't mean getting a table is easy. Reservations are a must if one wants to experience this Mexican hotspot that lurks underneath a seemingly innocent taco shack. Don't worry - it's worth it. Diners can't help but feel smug as a host checks their name against the list and whisks them through a door, down a flight of steps, through the kitchen, and to another host, who will verify the reservation a second time before escorting them to the lounge. An air of intrigue permeates this glam grotto, which features dark lighting, candelabras, dungeon-like railings, and a bar area where puddles of candle wax line the counter. Couples and small groups pack the tiny tables, and a wayward elbow could land in a neighbour's ceviche. Tequila connoisseurs will marvel at the outstanding selection, which pairs nicely with the seafood specialities.

783 Eighth Ave
Hell's Kitchen
Map 4-E3

Latitude

212 245 3034 | *www.latitudebarnyc.com*

If bigger is better, then this massive Hell's Kitchen bar and lounge is the cream of the crop. Top 40 tunes blare, sports are broadcast on the many TVs, and an after-work crowd of flirty singles make themselves at home on the three roomy floors, which include a swanky upstairs lounge, a billiards area, and a casual, wood-heavy downstairs dining space with a fireplace. Drink specials make Latitude easy on the wallet, and the menu runs the gamut from Buffalo wings to coconut shrimp. Just don't overindulge - climbing the stairs is a lot tougher when you're full of beer and burgers.

288 Lenox Ave
Malcolm X Blvd
Harlem

Lenox Lounge

212 427 0253 | *www.lenoxlounge.com*

Billie Holiday and Miles Davis performed here, and Malcolm X and writer Langston Hughes were regulars. Opened in 1939, this Harlem institution holds a place of honour in not just the city's history but the history of modern music as well. A major renovation has restored this club's original Art-Deco glory, and nightly jazz performances whisk patrons back in time. That's not to say this swanky zebra-striped legend can't keep up with the times: Twisted Tuesdays feature live DJs spinning hip hop, soul, and R&B. Cover can run anywhere from nothing to $25, and a two-drink minimum is usually required. Arrive early to enjoy a proper soul food meal before the show.

20 Seventh Ave
At Leroy St
West Village
Map 8-E2

Little Branch

212 929 4360

And then there were three. Little Branch is the youngest of cocktail wunderkind Sasha Petraske's cocktail triumvirate, joining the cloak-and-dagger Milk & Honey (134 Eldridge St) and the obscure East Side Company Bar (212 614 7408). The old-fashioned, dark yellow-hued jazzy lounge looks like it came right out of a James Cagney film, and the tie-wearing bartenders - er, mixologists - do too. Armed with enough cocktail recipes to fill a book, these guys know their stuff, so don't insult them by ordering a beer. Cocktails go for $12, but anyone with a true appreciation for fresh, exotic ingredients and an excruciating attention to detail (like using blocks of ice so drinks aren't quickly watered down) won't mind one bit. Just be sure to heed the house rules (no hats, no fighting, no name-dropping, etc.).

24 First Ave
Btn 1st & 2nd St
East Village
Map 11-C1

Lucky Cheng's

212 995 5500 | *www.planetluckychengs.com*

The dolled-up waitresses at Lucky Cheng's sure are pretty. And suddenly, after a few of the potent 'orgy bowls', one notices a husky voice here and an unusually large hand there, and the realisation comes: these waitresses are waiters. Drag queens are all part of this kitschy Asian-themed restaurant and lounge's charm, whether they're emceeing the after-dinner karaoke action downstairs, sassing diners as they serve $8 cocktails like Jocelyn's Luscious Lips and Dirty Delta's Nasty Lemonade, or working giggly bachelorette parties into a frenzy with the saucy cabaret show, which is included with the cost of a prix fixe Asian Feast dinner. This is an experience best enjoyed intoxicated.

417

15 East 7th St
East Village
Map 9-B3

McSorley's

212 473 9148 | www.mcsorleysnewyork.com

Old, kind of cranky, and cheap: McSorley's Old Ale House is the grandpa of New York City bars. Established in 1854, and looking every day of it, this blast from the past should be on any visitor's to-do list, if only to take advantage of the $2.25 mugs of McSorley's Ale, light or dark (yes, it's the only beer available, and there's a minimum of two mugs per order). The old-school (and short-tempered) bartenders wear white collared shirts and throw bills into a box that's presided over by a bust of John F. Kennedy. Old newspapers line the walls, sawdust cakes the wooden floors, and everyone from college students to old men squeezes in as best they can. In addition to a few tables up front, a back dining room hosts groups feasting on fish and chips, clam chowder, and the cheese plate, which, according to the chalkboard menu, features a choice of 'cheddar or American'. Drinking songs may break out, the men's bathroom door isn't exactly opaque, drinkers blocking the server's way might get kicked, and women weren't allowed inside until the 1970s. They just don't make them like this anymore.

217 East Houston St
Lower East Side
Map 11-C1

Mercury Lounge

212 260 4700 | www.mercuryloungenyc.com

Any indie band worth its salt has played this live music venue, which insiders say has one of the best sound systems in the city. The standing-room-only performance space in the back of this dark (and pretty dingy) club isn't big when compared to local live music venues like Bowery Ballroom or Irving Plaza, but the presence of a large, wider-than-normal stage has earned the respect of musicians. This is a musicians' rock club, but the fans are happy campers too thanks to low ticket prices and excellent acoustics. A front bar hosts the pre-show crowd, and Mercury Lounge claims to have a tombstone embedded in its bar countertop. Fortunately, the only things haunting the club are the ghosts of the rock legends who've played here.

34 Ave A
East Village
Map 9-C4

Mo Pitkin's House of Satisfaction

212 777 5660 | www.mopitkins.com

Only in New York, kids, only in New York. Take some Jewish heritage, throw in a dash of down-home comfort food, add a pinch of Latin flair, and stir in an exuberant helping of comedy, live music, and performance art, and the result is Mo Pitkin's House of Satisfaction. Diners wash down Jewish- and Latin-inspired dishes like the Cuban Reuben, potato latkes, and deep-fried mac 'n' cheese with He'brew beers and cocktails like Mo's Famous Orange Julius in the booth-lined downstairs space. The three performance spaces - one upstairs, one downstairs, and Sadie's Lounge - offer some of the most eclectic acts in town, including everything from drag king Murray Hill (find out more at www.mrmurrayhill.com) to the Jewish comics of the Borscht Belt Brunch on Sundays. Everything comes with a side of kitsch.

1 Rockefeller Plaza
Midtown
Map 5-A4

Morrell Wine Bar & Cafe

212 262 7700 | www.morrellwinebar.com

Pinot Noir, Zinfandel, Merlot, Syrah… so many wines, so little time. That's especially true given this wine behemoth's list of - gulp - 2,000 bottles, with over 150 wines available by the glass. That list is easier to navigate thanks to the smart, less overwhelming breakdown

418

Morrell provides: The Market List features the best bottles currently on the market; 100 rarer labels can be found on the Reserve List; and the By-the-Glass List is a short sampling of rotating wines to encourage experimentation. Located adjacent to Morrell & Company's massive wine store, this airy bar and restaurant is a nice place to try before you buy, enjoy American dishes in the dining room, and pick the brain of a 'Resident Wine Geek'.

Nancy Whiskey Pub

1 Lispenard St
Tribeca
Map 10-E3

212 226 9943 | *www.nancywhiskeypub.com*

They don't make them much divier than this. Pretty much the only frill in this joint - open since 1967 - is the shuffleboard table up front, which hosts tournaments. A ragtag assortment of young adults with an appreciation for irony and cheap beer, blue-collar types, and the occasional crazy lady who'll try to steal your drink take over the downstairs bar stools and the small upstairs seating area. Drink specials like $7.50 Bud pitchers Monday through Thursday are too good to pass up, especially on Saturdays, when sports fans can catch college football on the six TVs and enjoy two deluxe burgers with a pitcher of beer for just $15. This come-as-you-are neighbourhood bar wouldn't know pretension if it bit it in the you-know-what, and that's hard to come by in this town.

Nevada Smith's

74 Third Ave
Btn 11th & 12th St
East Village
Map 9-B3

212 982 2591 | *www.nevadasmiths.net*

When Nevada Smith's says it's where 'football is religion', they're not talking about touchdowns and Giants fans. The 'football' here is the kind Americans like to call soccer, and it comes in the form of the English Premier League and other European matches that are broadcast live on the many TVs - even if that means opening the bar early in the mornings. Naturally this spacious wooden den welcomes a lot of (mostly male) homesick expatriates, and the fact that Guinness, Carlsberg, and Boddingtons are all on tap is the icing on the cake. Football jerseys and sports memorabilia line the walls as bands like Red Hot Chili Peppers play in the background; a karaoke night and the more dressed-up downstairs lounge, Chrissy Mac's, do their best to lure the ladies. Sports like basketball also get their dues, and when the World Cup and St. Patrick's Day come around, watch out. This place turns into a madhouse.

The Park

118 Tenth Ave
Chelsea
Map 8-C1

212 352 3313 | *www.theparknyc.com*

The Park's huge, elegantly wasted interior is a glitzy expanse of eye candy, but it doesn't hold a candle to the enchanting backyard garden, a ripped-from-the-fairy-tales haven of stone tables, patio tables, and trees with twinkling lights. If the garden's full - and it often is - or the weather's too cold, one should explore the sweeping dining room specialising in Mediterranean dishes, the ornate Asian-flavoured Red Room lounge, the sexy glass-walled upstairs lounge, and the uber-hip rooftop bar. Come nightfall, this former garage teems with exclusivity. Wear something designer, be prepared to shell out some major dough for cocktails, and give a little attitude if you want to fit in with this scorching-hot scene.

Pete's Candy Store

709 Lorimer St
Williamsburg
Brooklyn

718 302 3770 | *www.petescandystore.com*

Bored? Not anymore. There's always something going on at this former candy shop, and that 'something' includes adult spelling bees, trivia, Bingo, nightly live music, and readings. Groups of laid-back hipsters fill the no-frills front room where Dark & Stormy cocktails can be enjoyed with a sandwich (prices are a tad high for this neighbourhood, but there's no charge for the music). Further back is the modest performance space, where up-and-coming but decent bands of the indie-rock-folk persuasion play on the

419

small stage. A narrow hallway leads to an outdoor space, where summertime barbecues are hosted. In a neighbourhood that teems with too-cool-for-school attitude, Pete's is a refuge for those who just want to hear a band, chill, and maybe spell a word or two.

129 East 18th St
Union Square
Gramercy Park
Map 9-B1

Pete's Tavern

212 474 7676 | *www.petestavern.com*

Talk about a golden oldie. Established in 1864, Pete's Tavern has the distinction of being the oldest continuously operating bar and restaurant in the city, and it was in one of the former speakeasy's wooden booths that O. Henry wrote *The Gift of the Magi*. Fittingly, oldies tunes pour out of the speakers and the original 30 foot rosewood bar sees college students making new friends with the old-timers seated on the next stool. Decked out in wood, with dozens of liquor bottles gleaming on shelves behind the bar, this neighbourhood hangout has a little bit of something for everyone: Families with strollers crowd the dining room in the back where Italian-American staples like baked clams oreganata and burgers are served; sports fans can catch the game on three TVs in the front room; and solitary drinkers can order up the signature 1864 Pete's House Ale and read the paper in peace. Come by during the holidays, when things get festive with eggnog and wall-to-wall coloured lights.

281 Lafayette St
Soho
Map 11-A1

Pravda

212 226 4696 | *www.pravdany.com*

The prolific restaurateur Keith McNally is behind this Russian caviar bar and vodka lounge, but it's more fun to pretend that this is a secret KGB hideaway. Given the hush-hush vibe and Iron-Curtain-chic metal tables, that's not hard to do. Frosty thoughts of the Cold War are banished by the stylish subterranean bar's warm glow and the belly-warming vodka martinis, which come in flavours as diverse as coconut, sake, and pear. Purists can wash down their blinis and borscht with straight

shots of more than 70 vodkas, including infusions like fig, blackcurrant, spiced cranberry, and chili and horseradish (aspirin and breath mint not included). The clandestine booths and vaulted ceilings make this Russkie a great date spot - but bring lots of rubles!

65 West 70th St
Btn Columbus Ave &
Central Park West
Upper West Side
Map 2-E3

Shalel Lounge

212 873 2300

If romance doesn't ignite at Shalel Lounge, it clearly wasn't meant to be. Walk down a candlelit flight of stairs to uncover this semi-hidden subterranean den, which calls to mind both Casablanca and Indiana Jones. It's hard not to get lost in this maze-like arrangement of intimate nooks filled with low-slung upholstered couches upon which drooling lovebirds inch closer and closer towards one another. Shalel's dark Moroccan-inspired grottos create a fantasy world thanks to global beats and exotic fixtures like hanging lanterns, curtains, a trickling stone fountain in the back, mirrors, floor pillows, and knick-knacks from faraway lands. The long bar serves a respectable list of beers, wines, and somewhat pricey speciality cocktails, along with dishes like couscous.

1590 Second Ave
Upper East Side
Map 3-D1

Ship of Fools

212 570 2651 | *www.shipoffoolsnyc.com*

If it involves a ball, kicking, swinging, short shorts, tight pants, or basically anything that breaks a sweat, the 40 plus TVs at Ship of Fools will be airing it. Welcome to the sports headquarters of Manhattan. During the football season, Ship of Fools has more guys wearing jerseys than the Super Bowl. Who can blame them, given the bar's satellite dish, several big-screen TVs, menu of game-day stomach-lining staples like mozzarella sticks and burgers, and unbeatable drink specials, which range from $4 margaritas and $2 Miller and Miller Lite pints during the week to the $30 Bucket and Bucket wings and beer deal? And unlike sports bars that turn the game on but leave the sound off, Ship of Fools knows that its patrons aren't looking for conversation, and has set up five sound zones so every play-by-play is heard.

10 Columbus Circle
At Eighth Ave
Hell's Kitchen
Map 4-E1

Stone Rose
212 823 9770 | *www.midnightoilbars.com*

It's safe to assume that a guy married to a supermodel (Cindy Crawford, in this case) knows what he's doing. And Rande Gerber, who has nearly two dozen hotspots under his belt, definitely knows what he's doing. His decadent Stone Rose lounge in the Time Warner Center personifies upscale cocktailing, from the model-look-alike waitresses to the tasteful but modern furniture to the wallet-gouging cocktails. There's plenty of seating in this 5,500 square-foot space, which is always a good thing. The view of Central Park competes for attention with the good-looking patrons, which sometimes include Gerber's movie star buddies like George Clooney, who, like Stone Rose itself, is rich, handsome, and effortlessly cool.

767 Washington St
West Village
Map 8-C3

Tortilla Flats
212 243 1053

With its colourful tinselled ceiling, coloured lights, beer signs, Mexican art, and a Virgin Mary beaded curtain, Tortilla Flats looks like a pinata exploded inside it. This bar and restaurant takes 'fiesta' to a new level, hosting raucous events that encourage the youngish crowd to get loco. That includes trivia, Bingo, and even hula-hoop competitions, and when the crowd's fueled up on Corona and the legendary margaritas, anything can happen. A bar sits to one side, but most of the space is packed with diner-style booths and tables where guests wolf down Tex-Mex food. Sidewalk seating is available during the warmer months.

702 Union St
Brooklyn

Union Hall
718 638 4400 | *www.unionhallny.com*

Imagine the best, coolest, cosiest library in the world, and you've got Union Hall. Of course, books have nothing to do with it, though the walls of bookshelves are filled with them. This enormous bi-level space boasts a grandfather's-study-meets-the-Elk-Lodge decor: think old-fashioned couches, leather chairs, a globe, a roaring fireplace

with seating on either side (the best seats in the house), rich wooden floors and a long matching bar, portraits of fez-wearing Shriners, and, the piece de resistance, two indoor bocce courts. Downstairs is home to a live music space and one of the nicest bathrooms in the city. The drink selection runs the gamut from $3 Pabst Blue Ribbon and $6 Guinness (more obscure options are

available as well) to $7 hot toddies and $10 bellinis; a modest menu includes $11 Triple Threat mini burgers. All types congregate here, and all seem right at home.

211 West Broadway
At Franklin St
Tribeca
Map 10-E3

Vino Vino

212 925 8510 | www.vinovino.net

In case there was any doubt, this captivating enoteca is all about the vino - so much so that the space also includes a wine store. Rustic exposed brick walls and sleek leather couches host oenophiles who come to sip 20 plus wines by the glass, experiment with a wine flight, and nibble on cheese plates and cured meats. Free champagne and wine tastings occur weekly, and frequent live jazz and bossa nova performances create an intimate and sophisticated warmth.

Vino Vino's wine shop carries over 200 labels, with an emphasis placed on artisanals. And what could be better than discovering a particularly delicious wine and being able to immediately buy a bottle to enjoy at home?

123 Rivington St
Lower East Side
Map 11-C1

Welcome to the Johnsons

212 420 9911

Two words: cheap beer. In a city of $14 martinis, it's comforting to know that there are still places where one can find three beers for $10. As for frills, who needs 'em? This divey den - inspired by run-down rec rooms of decades past - boasts little more than a jukebox, a pool table, and two scary, but functioning, bathrooms, but that and the cheap shots are all the motivation this laid-back yuppie-meets-hipster-meets-NYU-student crowd needs. Seating on the torn booth by the pool table or at the tables up front can be limited on the weekends, so be prepared to throw a few elbows. It is the Lower East Side, after all - a little bad behaviour is par for the course.

Quiz Nights

Fancy putting your general knowledge smarts to the test as you swill on beer and munch on non-pretentious fodder? Ah well, you're in luck, because quiz nights are quite the trend for a lazy night out of drinking with a purpose. Reading and re-reading the Trivial Pursuit cards will put you in good stead, or of course you could do it New York style and just wing it and have some fun. Some places offer computer-screened personal play, where you compete against the rest of the pub and then pubs nationwide, since they're all linked up. Alternatively leave the gadgets behind and do it 'old school' on Wednesday nights in Saints and Sinners in Queens (718 396 3268), and on Monday nights at the highly recommended Cherry Tree in Brooklyn (718 399 1353). You could also try the Slipper Room on alternate Monday nights (p.428) or Fiddlesticks on the last Tuesday in the month (212 463 0516). Neighbourhood locals offer great ambience and by getting into teams, it's also a fantastic way of getting to know people while having a good time. The Big Quiz Thing (www.bigquizthing.com) is a touring trivia event bought to audiences live at various locations. With random prizes, even more random question categories and Elvis thrown in for extra giggles, you can hire the folks from BQT to entertain you wherever you happen to be or catch them at their next stop (see website for more details).

Happy Hours

Everybody loves a bargain, especially when you're out drinking. The following places all have excellent happy hour offers: Bohemian Beer Hall (p.413), Bondi Road (p.413), Bounce (p.413), Down the Hatch (p.415), Duvet (p.25), Henrietta Hudson (p.431), Latitude (p.417), Roebling Tea Room (p.404), Therapy (p.433), Tortilla Flats (p.421) and Welcome to the Johnsons (p.422). Bottoms up!

422

Nightclubs

The ultra-decadent days of Studio 54 may be long gone, but the atmosphere of excess, attitude, partying like a rock star, and dancing until the sun comes up is still alive and well in New York City. Trendy neighbourhoods like the Meatpacking District and West Chelsea have seen a huge concentration of nightclubs in recent years, creating a sort of Pleasure Island on the weekends where well-dressed revellers can visit several hot spots without leaving the block. Here, it's all about being the hippest and sleekest, and to that effect clubs bring out the big guns, whether it's extravagant – and insanely expensive – bottle service, an A-list guest list, superstar DJs (all of the big names play here), multimillion-dollar designs, or bells and whistles like scent machines, live dancers, and concierge service. The drama at the door can rival the drama happening inside, so be prepared for cover charges (usually in the $20 bracket) and picky, prickly door people who don't care whether or not you're on the list. Dress to kill, bring lots of cash, and know that anything can – and often does – happen.

49 Grove St
Btn Christopher St &
Seventh Ave
West Village
Map 8-D3

49 Grove
212 727 1100 | *www.49grove.com*

Are you ready to go down? 49 Grove's subterranean lounge is a chic purplish-blue lair of plush velvet couches, a fireplace, bottle service, and an aura of snug intimacy. The four-room club is no stranger to celebrity sightings, but one doesn't need a movie deal to feel like a star. In addition to having a VIP room, the club will also accommodate the most decadent of requests, including access to a fleet of luxury vehicles. Hip hop, funk, and house tunes encourage dancing, but it's hard for the trendy crowd to resist the lure of cooling their heels with a cocktail while nestled on one of the inviting couches. 49 Grove is a popular choice for private parties – just remember the platinum credit card.

419 West 13th St
At Ninth Ave
Meatpacking District
Map 8-C2

APT
212 414 4245 | *www.aptwebsite.com*

Let the trendy club kids have their Lotus and their Aer. At the still-going-strong APT, the scene is more about having a good time with a come-as-you-are crowd than spending your paycheck on bottle service and wearing Jimmy Choos. That's not to say that the door at this Meatpacking District club can't be strict; it's just that here, personality goes further than designer labels. Striped wallpaper greets revellers to this apartment-themed lounge. A narrow flight of stairs leads to a long bar where an artsy, indie, mixed race crowd dances up against each other (call ahead or check the website for a weekly DJ and event lineup). Upstairs is all about lounging on sofas and admiring the homey details (photos, books) that might just make you want to move in.

423

515 West 27th St
Chelsea
Map 6-C4

Bungalow 8
212 629 3333

You know a club is high profile when its owner (Amy Sacco) becomes a bold-faced name. You know a club is really high-profile when even its doorman (Armin) makes the local gossip columns. Those who don't know somebody (like, say, George Clooney) will have a difficult time making it past these pearly gates, but those who do will be treated to a tropical wonderland of models, bottles, and lots of celebrities. The space, with its chic tiki-lite decor, is small, creating an intimate vibe where anything can happen. Think Olsen twins dancing on banquettes, gossip reporters taking notes, and a cluster of desperate clubbers begging to get in and see it all.

415 Lafayette St
Btn East 4th St & Astor Pl
Noho
Map 9-A4

Butter
212 253 2828 | *www.butterrestaurant.com*

Termites would have a field day in this wood-heavy lounge and restaurant, which looks like the most luxurious log cabin one can imagine. Celebrities regularly make appearances at this downtown hotspot, whether it's to nibble on high-end American cuisine in the vaulted-ceiling dining room (check out the gorgeous birch forest mural), sip a speciality cocktail at the bar, or groove downstairs in the lounge where a DJ spins and the pretty people perch on cedar seats. Butter's greatest asset is its warm wood decor, and its beauty can get lost on the weekends, when the place fills up with trendy folks making the scene. It's better to come during the week to fully appreciate the chic factor without too many distractions.

544 West 27th St
Btn 10th & 11th Ave
Chelsea
Map 6-C3

Cain
212 947 8000 | *www.cainnyc.com*

Who's the king of the Chelsea nightlife jungle? Cain, that's who. This safari-inspired nightspot is owned by South African native Jamie Mulholland, and has a second summertime location in the Hamptons. Hottie servers in revealing khaki uniforms bring pricey libations to a crowd that's likely to include a few celebs. Exotic African decorative touches like zebra skin abound, while the natives get restless to the beats of the DJ, who spins from a boulder-like DJ booth and is often accompanied by a live bongo drummer. Cain's door is tough (buying a bottle helps), but once inside one feels like they're part of something special.

285 West Broadway
At Canal St
Tribeca
Map 10-E2

Canal Room
212 941 8100 | *www.canalroom.com*

Part swanky downtown spot, part cool (and cheap) live music joint, Canal Room is an interesting hybrid. A hugely varied lineup of performers has included everyone from reggae to folksy singer-songwriters to tribute bands to blast-from-the-past 80s one-hit-wonders to impressive big names like Toots & the Mayhals, with cover charges rarely rising above $20. The standing-room-only concert space is large but retains intimacy, with a bar to one side where fans can grab a beer and an empanada. When a band's not playing, the space transforms into a sleek Eurasian-inspired nightclub, complete with DJs, modern furniture, and a glass-enclosed VIP room where the occasional superstar might drop in.

248 West 14th St
Btn Seventh &
Eighth Ave
West Village
Map 8-D2

Dirty Disco
212 488 2525

Located on the outskirts of the ultra-trendy Meatpacking District madness, the recently opened Dirty Disco brings the dancing minus the drama. Working its hip but not snobby crowd into a frenzy with 80s, rock, and hip hop tunes on the petite dancefloor, the bi-level club is known for its powerful sound system and 70s-disco-

424

inspired decorating scheme of disco balls, funky wallpaper, sleek low banquettes, and black and white photos of naked women. Surprisingly, it all comes off as stylish, not cheesy. Drink prices are high, but standard for the neighbourhood. What's not standard for the neighbourhood is Dirty Disco's intimate space and cool cat vibe, features that entice partiers who are burnt out on the Meatpacking velvet rope scene.

Duvet Restaurant and Lounge

45 West 21st St
Flatiron District
Map 8-F1

212 989 2121 | www.duvetny.com

Mattresses take centre stage at this Flatiron restaurant and lounge. A Monday-Friday happy hour gives Duvet an after-work scene that few clubs have, with diners staking claim on the welcoming beige and gold beds to feast on steak tartar rolls and pork tenderloin; customers are provided with comfy slippers to wear for added relaxation. Things get livelier as the evening progresses, with the house-y music growing in intensity as a twentysomething crowd huddles around the 'Ice Bar' to order cocktails like the White Satin Mojito. While the colour-changing lighting scheme – think purples and aqua blues – will dazzle the eyes, it's nothing compared to the jellyfish tank behind the bar. The unisex downstairs bathroom is also a must-see (the bathroom stall doors are translucent from the inside).

Element

225 East Houston St
Lower East Side
Map 11-C1

212 254 2200 | www.elementny.com

A mega-club on the Lower East Side? The neighbourhood of dive bars, derelicts, and small rock clubs welcomed the three-level danceteria Element in 2006, and, thanks to a steady lineup of respectable DJs and promoters, it hasn't looked back. The massive former bank greets clubbers with a long line and an intimidating door, but inside it's an all-out dance party as bodies groove in the vibrant disco-like main room to throbbing tunes (bring your own glow sticks). A more intimate and swankier brick-walled downstairs space is well-suited to private parties, while the top floor, which overlooks the dancefloor below, has a VIP space, sleek lounging areas, and the all-important DJ booth. This club oozes energy, and it's all dictated by whatever DJ happens to be at the decks. Saturday night's Bank party is especially popular.

The Grand

41 East 58th St
Midtown
Map 5-B2

212 308 9455 | www.thegrandnyc.com

Grand indeed. This opulent nightclub has brought new energy to a neighbourhood more commonly known for its luxury department stores than its nightlife. Modern red couches and a glamorous chandelier adorn a dark-wood main room. Through a translucent wall with a mod-circular cut-out entrance is a yellow-walled nook where partiers reclining on velvet settees and a long banquette empty bottles of vodka and champagne. Dancing is, of course, the order of the day at this James Bond-reminiscent lounge where DJs spin mainstream and hip hop hits. Speaking of mainstream… though The Grand's been graced by film and music heavyweights, its core clientele is a more down-to-earth, young professional crowd than one might see at the super-trendy downtown clubs.

Guest House

542 West 27th St
Btn 10th & 11th Ave
Chelsea
Map 6-C3

212 273 3700 | www.homeguesthouse.com

Where else would you expect to find house music than at a club called Guest House? This spin-off of Home (p.426), which resides in the same building, upholds the original's high standards in terms of a see-and-be-seen crowd and a seductive

425

ambience. Here dancers undulate to hypnotic beats amidst a decorating scheme of hardwood floors, candles, damask wall coverings, exposed brick, and leather wall panels. Big-spenders can unwind with bottle service in the VIP room, or just mingle with the energetic, flirtatious crowd at the bar over specialty cocktails like the Dreamsicle. Keep in mind that not all visitors are welcome: Like Home, Guest House has an exclusive door policy that keeps out unwanted (read: un-hip) houseguests.

Home

542 West 27th St
Btn 10th & 11th Ave
Chelsea
Map 6-C3

212 273 3700 | www.homeguesthouse.com

There's no place like Home, there's no place like Home. And with this Chelsea nightclub's uber-hip Steve-Lewis-and-Antonio-Di-Oronzo-designed interior of leather ceilings and a sensual red decor accented with candles, mirrors, and chandeliers, that statement couldn't be truer. Hollywood starlets can often be spied perched on one of the banquettes, though the DJs pack some star power of their own. The club's blend of pop, rock, and hip hop keeps the dancefloor full, but those looking for more beats and fewer lyrics can slip down the hallway to Guest House (p.425), the house-fuelled sister bar.

Marquee

289 Tenth Ave
Nr 26th St
Chelsea
Map 6-C3

646 473 0202 | www.marqueeny.com

In a city where one-word clubs open and close in the blink of an eye, Marquee is a true veteran. Still at the top of its game after three years in business – a lifetime in this town – Marquee's swanky bi-level, three-room space is still Plan A for most clubbers and celebrities. Weeknights are the best time to really savour the club's energy: star-watch upstairs, enjoy a bottle in the hip downstairs Red Room, and dance to the hip hop-heavy grooves up front. A sweeping staircase is the club's focal point, but don't worry – the good-looking crowd will cause plenty of whiplash too. If you can get past the discerning doormen, of course.

Movida

28 Seventh Ave
At Leroy St
West Village
Map 8-D4

212 206 9600 | www.movidanyc.com

It's rare to find a downtown club that can compete with the Meatpacking District and Chelsea heavyweights, but Movida does it with ease. The greatest asset of this three-level West Village hotspot is its Saturday night Robot Rock party, a high-energy mix of new wave, dance rock, electronic, and other synthesiser-heavy tunes that keep the crowd on its feet. The club has a slight cruise ship inspiration going on, from the portholes and blue couches in the subterranean Aqua Room, to the Titanic-worthy chandelier in the Main Deck, to the ship-like railings in the all-white Mezzanine. The downtown-cool crowd is more likely to be wearing vintage sneakers than just-off-the-runway stilettos, which is another bonus. The club is popular with music industry types, and hosts the occasional record release party.

151 East 50th St
Midtown
Map 5-C3

Nikki Beach

212 753 1144 | *www.nikkibeach.com*

Miami may be thousands of miles away, but an evening at Nikki Midtown comes pretty close to the real thing. The Manhattan offshoot of the internationally famous Nikki Beach club chain is a stylish oasis featuring an all-white, beach-inspired decor, seafood dishes like lobster beignets and Florida mahi mahi, and gorgeous cocktail waitresses wearing revealing dresses that are probably illegal in some states. Visitors can enjoy bottle service and soak in the sexy ambience (and those waitresses!) from the comfort of a pillow-lined banquette, hop on the long wooden table to show off their dance moves, or head upstairs for a little more privacy in one of the curtained-off VIP cabanas. Dance and house tunes add to the party.

618 West 46th St
Hell's Kitchen
Map 4-C3

Pacha

212 209 7500 | *www.pachanyc.com*

When a club co-owner is one of the top DJs in the world, it's safe to assume that the music will be good. DJ and producer Erick Morillo is one of the heavyweights behind this international brand, which boasts mega-clubs in 25 cities around the world – the New York City club is the first North American branch. So what should you expect? Lots of space, for one thing – as in four levels, and 30,000 square feet. Still, when major DJs like Morillo or Jonathan Peters take over the black-mirrored DJ booth, the crowds may make it hard to find ample dancing space. In fact, everything about Pacha is over-the-top and jaw-dropping, from the shower-encased go-go dancers to the celebrity sightings to the stellar sound system to the top floor Pachita VIP lounge, a sleek, more intimate space featuring a smoking deck. VIPs can also purchase a Pacha Passport, which entitles them to perks like an on-site liquor locker.

246 West 14th St
Chelsea
Map 8-D2

The Plumm

212 675 1567 | *www.theplumm.com*

Just east of the Meatpacking District – and next door to Dirty Disco (p.424) – The Plumm holds court in a space formerly occupied by the legendary nightclub Nell's. Celebrity investors like actor Chris 'Mr. Big' Noth and hip hop mogul Damon Dash, along with nightlife guru Noel Ashman, have helped breathe new life into this address, and the famous friends they've brought along for the ride certainly don't hurt. The bi-level club features a bar on each floor and a tasteful decor of wooden walls, plants, inviting couches, artwork, and amber lighting; imagine a hip version of your living room. Nightly events ensure a long line outside the (semi-strict) door, and the music flows from house to alternative to hip hop, rock, and 80s, with the beats varying on the two floors.

50 Gansevoort St
Meatpacking District
Map 8-C2

PM Lounge

212 255 6676 | *www.pmloungenyc.com*

PM may be located in the hauter-than-hot industrial-chic Meatpacking District, but inside it's a Caribbean paradise of palm trees, high ceilings, bright colours, and coconut-scented air. Escape the island of Manhattan and head to the islands, where celebrities are a guarantee and the energy is almost tangible. The island theme makes its way to the menu as well, where dishes like coconut shrimp purses and spiny lobster rolls are washed down with pricey bottles of Patron Silver. The club often hosts special events and private parties in its large space, which can hold up to 450 people. If you'd like to be one of those 450, dress sharp and be prepared to splurge on bottle service.

35 East 21st St
Flatiron District
Map 9-A1

Room Service
212 254 5709

Bottle service is just the tip of the iceberg at Room Service, the hotel-themed nightclub that's recently checked into the Flatiron neighbourhood. A provocative, Victorian-lite space of chandeliers, upholstered walls, and floral ceiling accents welcomes guests, but the piece de resistance are the club's nine semi-private rooms, which can be rented for $350-$800 (sleepovers not included). It's in these rooms where partiers can recline on leather couches while indulging their every whim, thanks to a personal mixologist, a masseuse, plasma TV and DVD player, fully stocked mini-bar, a toiletry drawer packed with mouthwash and condoms (one never knows), and a concierge service that's only too happy to fetch food from the kitchen. It's the ultimate extravagance. A central dancefloor lined with ottomans and access to the neighbouring Tens strip club take Room Service to a whole new level.

167 Orchard St
At Stanton St
Lower East Side
Map 11-C1

The Slipper Room
212 253 7246 | *www.slipperroom.com*

This place is sexy with a capital sizzle! With a whole host of special events and theme nights, from classy Burlesque to side-splitting comedy nights, and even the Big Quiz Thing showing up every other week (on Monday nights) for some head scratching trivia and nifty little giveaways. There's a Victorian stage for performances, comedy acts and DJs, and delicious cocktails to get you wobbly enough to perhaps even have a go yourself or just dance around your handbag. Consider the Slipper Room a fabulously down-to-earth slice of decadence – with extra sequins. Tip: Look out for Scotty the Blue Bunny - tres cute.

26 Little West 12th St
Meatpacking District
Map 8-C2

Tenjune
646 624 2410 | *www.tenjunenyc.com*

This Meatpacking District hotspot was visited by just about every major celebrity (Beyonce, Joaquin Phoenix, and Penelope Cruz, to name a few) before it even opened, in early Autumn 2006, and things haven't slowed down any. The city's newest place to see and be seen is a swanky conglomeration of three unique partying spaces. Sip delicious libations like the Pure Chocolate at the sexy black bar accented with streaming light, or take a seat on one of the velvet banquettes. Next, follow the beats to the dance room, where a dancefloor is bordered by a DJ booth and modern lounging areas. VIPs, meanwhile, can relax in a dark purple semi-private lounge decked out with padded walls and an inviting fireplace. Naturally, a luxurious den like this is very exclusive, but it's worth it.

Cattyshack

Pieces

Gay & Lesbian

Boys Vs Girls

There are plenty of venues all over the island worth checking out. As in most cities, gay men and lesbians rarely mix and there's much more variety for men; however, lesbians will find a thriving scene in Brooklyn's Park Slope neighbourhood. Furthermore, recent times have seen the closing and opening (and sometimes closing again) of a number of places. For the most current listings, check out the city's two main weekly gay party rags, HX and Next, which are free in most gay venues. A city teeming with gaiety awaits!

The gay scene in New York is as eclectic as the city's residents. Hipster bars, leather nightspots, throbbing dance clubs, fashionable restaurants – it's all here and terrifically queer. While gay hotspots exist in all five boroughs, the vast majority of fun awaits in Manhattan, where you'll find you can easily stroll from venue to venue in a particular neighbourhood. And while light public displays of affection on the street are generally acceptable, as New York is the nation's safest large city, occasional hate crimes against gays do take place.

Having a good time should be your number one priority, and there's no better place to start than Chelsea, the city's main 'gaybourhood'. It's hard to walk a few blocks here without spotting a rainbow flag, especially along the area's main catwalk, Eighth Avenue between 14th Street and 23rd Street, which boasts tons of bars, restaurants, clothing stores, and gays and lesbians strutting along. The area is also home to some of the most popular gay spots, from mega-club Roxy to mega-bar Splash, the only place featuring dancing each night of the week. When you're done exploring Chelsea, you can go to Hell – Hell's Kitchen, that is. Sometimes dubbed 'Hellsea' or 'Chelsea North', due to the increasing popularity and number of trendy gay establishments popping up here, Hell's Kitchen brims with a hot after-work crowd that only gets spicier as the night goes on.

If you crave a scene that isn't, well, so much of a scene, then head to the East Village, where you'll discover a more low-key vibe along with guys whose primary focus isn't how many reps they've done at the gym. Whereas some places here cater to alternative guys and gals, others ooze with scandalous sleaze. For a campier feel, there's always the West Village, whose main artery is Christopher Street. You'll be able to step back in time – and not just because patrons here tend to be older – as this is where the gay movement began, with the 1969 riots outside the historic Stonewall Inn. Today, you don't have to fight for your right to party at one of the street's numerous flaming bars. Actually, the only struggles still going on here involve fitting into the tight shirts and trousers in the various colourful apparel shops dotting the area.

Barracuda

275 West 22nd St
Chelsea
Map 6-D4

212 645 8613

Drag yourself along to Barracuda for some of the hottest drag shows in town - they happen nightly here at this popular gay bar. 'Star Search' on Thursdays (hosted by the inimitable dragster Shequida) pulls a crowd - amateur drag queens (some good, some bad) take to the stage to sing for the $100 prize. Other nights are also good, and not just for the acts: Barracuda is famous for being friendly - men will actually smile back at you here! So if you're looking for a place where you can just be yourself and have a great time, here's where you'll find your team mates. Just remember - leave your attitude at the door or you won't fit in. To help things along, a cute and attentive team of waiters makes sure that getting a drink here is as easy as getting a guy.

Cattyshack

249 4th Ave
Brooklyn

718 230 5740 | www.cattyshackbklyn.com

With a name like Cattyshack, you'd think the gays and lesbians who frequent this joint would have their claws out ready to start all sorts of drama. Luckily, that's not the case at this pleasant Park Slope bar. While most nights attract locals, Fridays reel in ladies from all over for one of the city's most happening lesbian nights. Wednesday's Oink party, meanwhile, is for the boys, who come for a karaoke contest hosted by drag diva Sherry Vine; the winner receives a $50 bar tab. But it's Sunday's outdoor BBQ party, where $15 buys all the food and beer you can drink, that really draws a crowd. More of a neighbourhood bar than a destination hangout, Cattyshack nonetheless offers a great escape from Manhattan.

61 Christopher St
West Village
Map 8-E3

The Duplex

212 255 5438 | *www.theduplex.com*

The Duplex may be located nowhere near the theatre district, but that doesn't stop gays and lesbians from belting out their favourite show tunes at this friendly West Village piano bar. Open mic starts at 21:00, so you've got plenty of time to work up some Dutch courage at the bar. Even if singing is not your thing, it's great fun to watch – and make fun of – those who slur off-key. The cabaret room often hosts some real talent, in case your ears need a break, and the games room is the one to head for if you're just not feeling the music at all (although they do have a stomping sound system in there!). But perhaps one of the best features about the Duplex is its terrace overlooking the West Village's cruisiest intersection - perfect for settling down to gaze at the gays passing by.

554 West 28th St
Chelsea
Map 6-C3

The Eagle

647 473 1866 | *www.eaglenyc.com*

Chelsea's Eagle is really a bear. The slightly older leather-and-denim men who flock to this mothertrucker of a bar are anything but the fashionistas, twinks, and reality TV stars who populate other hotspots. Instead, you'll find plenty of daddies eager to teach you all sorts of lessons. Thursday night's Code party is especially popular among the leather crowd. A dress code is enforced, but don't fret if you've come in your chinos – the bar houses a Leather Man store where you can pick up a harness and some chaps. The legendary outdoor roof deck is always packed (when the weather is warmer of course - a harness doesn't provide much protection against the elements!) partly thanks to the low-key but much-needed food served up there.

156 Seventh Ave
Chelsea
Map 8-E1

Elmo

212 337 8000 | *www.elmorestaurant.com*

At this gay-friendly restaurant there's never any shortage of scenesters. Whether at night or during a weekend brunch, the club vibe is definitely stronger than the restaurant vibe here, thanks in part to the loud (and oh so hip) music. With its chic decor and hot waiters, you'll begin to think you came here to go out rather than simply eat out. In fact, for those who prefer to drink their meals, a highlight on the menu is the raspberry lemonade (with lots of vodka). But the food should not be ignored: sesame-crusted tuna and the fried chicken, along with a wide assortment of typical diner, comfort, and slightly more upscale American entrees will keep your energy levels high. However, what Elmo serves up best is 'cool', so if you've ever wondered – or want to relive – what it's like to sit at the popular kids' table in grade school, then this is the place to pull up a chair.

149 Eighth Ave
Chelsea
Map 8-D1

Food Bar

212 243 2020

This restaurant knows all the right ingredients to serve to its predominantly gay clientele. By starting with some friendly locals, adding some fun music, stirring in what must be the cutest wait staff in all of New York, and, of course, mixing in enough tasty dishes, Food Bar cooks up a terrific dining experience. In fact, judging by the nightly boisterous scene inside and how some tables are 'thisclose' to each other, it's easy to mistake Food Bar for an actual bar. Then again, real bars usually don't have such tempting dishes on their menus. And they certainly don't usually serve up the perfect meal for those on a low-carb regime: the Chelsea Boy Special is a muscle-building combo of grilled chicken breast, scrambled egg whites and spinach. So it would seem that Food Bar is almost certainly a restaurant then. But on the other hand, real restaurants don't usually have such an amazing bar. There's only one thing for it: to work out whether this is a restaurant that serves drinks, or a bar that serves (delicious) food, you'll just have to head down there to solve the riddle yourself.

g Lounge

225 West 19th St
Meatpacking District
Map 8-D1

212 929 1085 | www.glounge.com

This perennially popular bar may be a bit pretentious and haughty at first glance, but where else are you going to wear your new Prada pants? Though the men may initially seem stand-offish, a few of the bar's famous cocktails (Appletini, anyone?) will do wonders to help lubricate conversation. Cosy couches await at the front of this drinkery, but g's best part is its shapely rear, where a circular bar makes for a loopy cruising experience. And while your wallet may suffer as much as your liver here, since drinks can be slightly costly (many are $8 and up), g remains an ideal place to hang out before heading out for some further debauchery.

Gym Sportsbar

167 Eighth Ave
Chelsea
Map 8-D1

212 337 2439 | www.gymsportsbar.com

This Gym is definitely worth joining if you're eager to score home runs with some laid-back, jeans-and-T-shirt-type men. Surprisingly, there's no Fashion TV or E! here - instead the several big-screen televisions show all the big games. Most of the patrons are not there to simply spectate of course, and would rather get in on the biggest game of all: checking out the tight ends in the bar itself. Or if all the sporting action gives you a testosterone headache, you can always saunter out onto the outdoor terrace overlooking 'Hot Homo Highway' (that's Eighth Avenue) and check out the passing scene. There's a much-used pool table at the back - handy for making 'sticks and balls' innuendos more than anything else. You don't want to miss $5 Svedka Tuesdays and $5 Absolut Thursdays because, after all, every athlete needs to stay hydrated.

Henrietta Hudson

438 Hudson St
West Village
Map 8-D4

212 924 3347 | www.henriettahudson.com

This West Village lesbian hotspot is all about girl-on-girl action, just for the girls. On weekends it is packed tighter than a subway car during rush hour (but much more pleasant), although drinks specials and theme nights keep the weekday trade brisk as well. Come on Mondays for $3 draft beer, or revel in the decadence of the monthly singles night (on the last Thursday of the month). Other nights feature eye-popping delights like Jell-O wrestling, thong-athons and go-go girls aplenty. Two full-size bars and an early-evening happy hour keeps things well lubricated. Whether you take your chances and arrive late when the queues might be long, or come early when the cover charge is usually lower, the crowd at Henrietta Hudson is always loud, proud and rowdy.

Metropolitan

559 Lorimer St
Brooklyn

718 599 4444 | www.gaybarsnyc.com

There's nothing really special about Metropolitan – and that's exactly what makes it special. Sometimes it's refreshing to actually be underwhelmed and step into a bar that doesn't boast its fabulousness. There's more than just geography separating this local watering hole from your typical Manhattan bar. With no overpriced drinks and no attitude, this Brooklyn bar is for the big-town dude with a small-city attitude. Average

431

gays and lesbians in their 20s and 30s for whom 'average' isn't a four-letter word come here to enjoy cheap drinks, a pool table, two fireplaces in the winter, and an excellent jukebox. The outdoor patio is particularly popular, especially in the summer when Metropolitan hosts a lively BBQ on Sundays. Yet regardless of the day, you're always guaranteed to find a friendly face to talk to about something other than the gym, protein supplements, and whatever else is being discussed at more fancy-shmancy gay venues.

mr. BLACK

643 Broadway
West Village
Map 9-A4

212 253 2560 | *www.mrblacknyc.com*

mr. BLACK describes itself as 'a quirky music savvy dancebar' that is 'neither too big to lose yourself nor too small that you can't dance in'. As such, this dark, cavernous venue attracts a young, energetic crowd nightly. The only thing easier than getting swept up in the music here are the patrons themselves. As the dancefloor fills with a sea of bodies, sex is definitely in the air, though in a playful, mischievous way. The sleazefest gets even wilder as waiters periodically walk around offering free shots, which helps compensate for the $10 cover charge on Fridays and Saturdays. Best of all, this is one of the few venues where dressing in outrageous attire is as common as the standard gay uniform of a t-shirt and jeans. From the music to the eclectic men that come here to the clothes, at mr. BLACK, anything goes.

Phoenix

447 East 13th St
East Village
Map 9-C3

212 477 9979 | *www.gaybarsnyc.com*

You'd think you were in a straight Upper East Side bar rather than a gay East Village one after stepping into this place. Surrounded by a plain, nondescript decor, with beer in hand and wearing baseball caps, the patrons here are some of the straightest gay boys you'll find. But rest assured, your favorite Cher song will come on the jukebox in no time. A low-key vibe is matched by low-priced drinks, from $1 Buds on Wednesdays to $2 domestic beers on Sundays. While a pinball machine, video games, and a pool table help draw in a decent number of patrons during the week, Phoenix really takes flight on weekends, when it seems every guy here has his gears set to major cruise control. All of which makes Phoenix the ideal antidote when you get tired of bar-hopping in Chelsea.

Pieces

8 Christopher St
West Village
Map 8-E3

212 929 9291 | *www.piecesbar.com*

You definitely can't mistake this place for a straight bar. An abundance of rainbow decorations helps to ensure that Pieces reigns as Christopher Street's most flaming bar, which also means that it's also one of the area's most popular. Tuesday's karaoke party draws an especially raucous crowd as gays and lesbians who really should know better eagerly take the stage to embarrass themselves in front of gay New York. Pieces also has something going on during other nights, from drag acts to games, where you can win anything from a penny to $500. Meanwhile, friendly staff contribute to a lively atmosphere, ensuring big fun at this little nightspot. It's the kind of place where you might need a friend to be your designated memory: particularly if you partake of the daily happy 'hour' (14:00-20:00), which might just wipe your slate clean.

Roxy

515 West 18th St
Chelsea
Map 8-C1

212 645 5156 | *www.roxynyc.com*

Roxy is a gay institution that ranks right up there with Madonna. In fact, Madonna has even performed here a couple of times. Talk about homo-nirvana! Every Saturday night, this mega-club lures a super-sized crowd of chiselled gym queens, as well as tons of twinks with drinks, happy hipsters, and everyone in between. Dollar drinks from 23:00 to midnight intoxicate the crowd for a night of shirtless dancing to techno and house sounds on the main floor. Meanwhile, the DJ upstairs gets everyone into the groove by spinning pop music that includes – shockingly! – plenty of Madonna. Though general admission is usually $30, a voucher printed out from www.jblair.com will get you a $10 discount. The club also hosts a roller-skating night on Wednesdays. While the event isn't exclusively gay, you still shouldn't have any problems 'inadvertently' colliding with a fellow hot homo in the roller rink.

50 West 17th St
Chelsea
Map 8-F1

Splash
212 691 0073 | www.splashbar.com

Cute guys LOVE Splash, probably because they usually pay less to get in. But with all the eye candy guaranteed to be inside, you won't hear the ugly guys complaining as they fork out extra dollar. And once you're in, who cares who's cute and who's rich? Splash is the kind of place where you'll create your own legends - it's all about having fun, from the hotties dancing under showers to the see-through bathroom doors - and your mission is clear: set your cruise control to full throttle and make the most of it. If the watery theme starts to go soggy on you, be sure to check out their other theme nights: frat-style parties on Thursdays (including a 'Stud Search' competition), 'Full-Frontal' Fridays, and Karaoke on Tuesdays keep Splash ahead of the party pack and you in the good times. And if that doesn't do it for you, the amazing happy hour (16:00-21:00) certainly will.

348 West 52nd St
Hell's Kitchen
Map 4-E3

Therapy
212 397 1700 | www.therapy-nyc.com

Do your parents worry that you're acting crazy? Make them feel better by telling them you're in Therapy. They don't need to know that it's actually one of the hottest gay hotspots and that the 'medication' is actually a mind-expanding selection of raunchy cocktails. And definitely don't tell them that this is where the 'nice' boys go wild, thanks to Thursday night keg parties, super-lengthy happy hours (17:00-20:00), or Wednesday night's 'Cattle Call' talent contest, where you're invited to 'sing, dance or show off your underpants' to win the grand prize of $100. Telling them about the raucous dance nights involving swarms of sexy men will only upset them and cause them more worry. So just tell them that you're in Therapy on a regular basis, and that you've never been happier.

331 West 51st St
Hell's Kitchen
Map 4-E3

Vlada
212 974 8030 | www.vladabar.com

It's hard to tell what makes this purportedly Russian-style bar Russian – that is, until you look at the drinks menu. 15 infused vodkas remind you how much fun Russia's number one export can be, even when you don't know exactly what's in them to make them taste so good - that information is known only by the KGB, if the menu is to be believed. To ensure you drink your vodka like a true Russian (very, VERY cold!), the folks at Vlada have thoughtfully slapped a thick layer of ice down on the bar. If that leaves you feeling chilly, a weekly schedule of DJs, Broadway stars and drag artistes will heat up your night, as will the happy fact that Vlada seems to attract a very sexy crowd of clubbers.

433

Party Organisers

Other options **Party Accessories** p.342

Unless you're lucky or have great connections (or both), chances are your apartment is the typical New York size – small. This can make it tricky to entertain at home, and many people often throw parties, from birthdays to bridal showers, at restaurants or other venues. For help in finding a prime party space in New York, try Successful Affairs (212 684 6402, www.successfulaffairs.com), a company that specialises in 'locating the perfect location' for your event. That said, with a little creativity – and the help of party

Reservations

It's true that there are hundreds of great eateries in New York, but there are also eight million people to compete with for a table at your favourite restaurant. If you're planning to eat out at Bouley (p.387), Da Silvano (p.392), Jean Georges (p.389), Nobu (p.395), Per Se (p.389), Tocqueville (p.390) or Woo Lae Oak (p.386), you'll need to make a reservation, often weeks in advance.

professionals – hosting a dinner soiree at home can make for a memorable evening. You'll find many caterers that can provide everything from party platters to drinks, while a top-notch event planner like Qevents (718 268 4196, www.qevents.com) will plan the entire evening, down to the professional waitstaff. As for throwing a party for the little ones, New York abounds with children's party planners, like the community-oriented Kid Parties NYC (www.kidpartiesnyc.com), which offers fun suggestions on where to celebrate birthday parties in New York, and has lots of links to resources for parents. Focus on Fun Entertainers (212 874 0533, www.focusonfunentertainers.com) provides, as you guessed, fun entertainers for toddlers and kids, from magicians and puppet shows to cuddly clowns.

Caterers

You'll find a wide range of caterers in New York, from high-end, haute cuisine services to casual, no-party-is-too-small outfits. A company like Steven Brown Caterers (www.stevenbrowncaterers.com) focuses more on corporate and larger events, while the city's many gourmet markets, such as the New York-based Dean and DeLuca (www.deandeluca.com), caters parties of all sizes, and features an international menu of full spreads with such themes as Pan-Asian, Tangier and Provencal. The online food shop FreshDirect (www.freshdirect.com) also offers catering services, with party platters that incorporate fresh, local produce. Many upscale restaurants, like Bouley Restaurant and Bakery (p.387), also do a roaring trade in catering, as do casual spots like a number of Little Italy restaurants, many of which have affordable prices. As for party cheer, plan on having top-notch wine and spirits on hand, which you can order from Sherry-Lehmann Wines and Spirits on Madison Avenue (212-838-7500, www.sherrylehmann.com). For something a little different, you can also have a professional chef come to your home to teach you and a small group of your friends how to cook a delicious meal (see Cookery Classes, p.259).

Cabaret & Strip Shows

Things can get steamy in this city, and as such, there are several strip clubs to help New Yorkers indulge their fantasies. For the most part, it's pretty much harmless fun: a $20 lap dance here, a few gyrating topless dancers there. But what happens behind closed doors is, well, anybody's guess. What one doesn't have to guess about is the cost: strip clubs are very expensive. Between the cover, pricey drinks, tips, and whatever is spent on 'special services', customers drop dollars as quickly as the dancers drop their clothes. Also note that while there are several clubs showcasing female dancers, male strip clubs exist primarily in the form of revues that set up shop at nightclubs on certain nights; visit Hunk-O-Mania (www.usahunk.com) and HunkMania (www.hunkmania.com) for more information.

In-your-face sex is so passe, but neo-Burlesque has taken the city by storm and continues to titillate without cliche. The risque but beautiful shows are scheduled in random bars around the city or can be found regularly at venues specialising in the glamorous and chic style of 'tease to please' raunchiness. Before you start tutting and crossing it off as demoralising to women, this isn't your average strip show: it's more like deliciously classy women (and men) strutting their feather fans and nearly bare booties; a throwback to the 20s and 30s. The clothes come off slower, the sultry moves are white-hot, and the scene is fuelling a burlesque revival in the city. The annual New York Burlesque Festival (www.thenewyorkburlesquefestival.com) was so popular last year that people were turned away. Check out Galapagos (718 782 5188) for a heady mix of professional exotic dancers and the odd oddity. The Va Va Voom Room at Fez (212 579 5100), is a weekly neck-craning riot and touted as New York's best, with tickets starting at $15, with a two drink minimum. Le Scandal at The Cutting Room (212 6911900), takes centre stage every Saturday night from 22:00, and is a great spot to experience a cabaret of classy classical Burlesque, including a lineup of exotic performers from around the world.

Other places to try if you like your nudie thrills with less of the mystery include Larry Flynt's Hustler Club (641 W. 51st Street, 212 247 2460, www.hustlerclubs.com), Penthouse Executive Club (603 W. 45th Street, 212 245 0002, www.penthouseexecutiveclub.com), or Scores West Side (536 W. 28th Street, 212 868 4900, www.scoresny.com).

Casinos

Going Gambling

For a weekend of gambling, head to Atlantic City or Foxwoods, each about a two and a half hour drive from Manhattan. Find out more on p.243.

The only gambling done in New York City is deciding whether or not to risk using a dive bar's bathroom. But if blackjack is calling your name, Atlantic City, New Jersey is just a two-and-a-half-hour Greyhound bus ride away, and bus passengers are even given a cash-back bonus to gamble with when they arrive at the casino. You must be at least 21 years of age to gamble; that's partly due to the free cocktails that are given to gamblers. The new Borgata Hotel Casino & Spa (www.theborgata.com) is easily the flashiest of all the casinos, and even has swanky nightclubs and fine restaurants under its roof.

Cinemas

New York – a city that has starred in scores of movies – is a boon for film fans. Most Hollywood movies celebrate their East Coast premieres in New York, when the stars sashay down the red carpet with all their handlers in tow. Films often open here before the rest of the country, which gives New Yorkers a leg up in catching flicks first. Movie theatres run the gamut from the glittering Ziegfeld, an old-world theatre that seats over a thousand, to multiplex palaces with stadium seating, monster screens and gourmet snack bars where you're lucky if you can buy nibbles for less than a tenner. Tickets, too, hit the $10 mark a while back, and the average price is about $11, with

435

some posh spots charging up to $13. Matinees (generally before 16:00) are $3–4 dollars less, as are tickets for seniors and children. New York also boasts a well-oiled indie and foreign film scene, with several venerable movie houses, such as the Angelika and the Film Forum, dedicated to showing independent and global flicks. The city's longest-running film fest is the prestigious New York Film Festival, which will celebrate 45 years in 2007. The two-week fall festival, which takes place at theatres around Lincoln Center, showcases new films from around the globe. An up-and-coming contender is the Tribeca Film Festival, spearheaded by Robert DeNiro to revitalize Lower Manhattan after September 11. The festival features a huge range of new films, both local and international, plus musical concerts, street fairs and film lectures.

Cinemas

AMC Empire 25	Midtown	212 398 3939	www.amctheatres.com
Angelika Film Center	Soho	212 995 2000	www.angelikafilmcenter.com
BAM Rose Cinemas	Brooklyn	718 636 4100	www.bam.org
Cinema Village	West Village	212 924 3363	www.cinemavillage.com
Film Forum	West Village	212 727 8110	www.filmforum.com
Landmark Sunshine Cinema	Lower East Side	212 330 8182	www.landmarktheaters.com
Lincoln Plaza Cinemas	Upper West Side	212 757 2280	www.lincolnplazacinema.com
Loews 42nd St E-Walk	Midtown	212 505 6397	www.enjoytheshow.com
Loews Lincoln Square	Upper West Side	212 336 5000	www.enjoytheshow.com

Comedy

This is one city that takes its comedy seriously. Though the jokes themselves can be hit or miss, the variety of talent, both in stand-up and sketch comedy, that New York City offers is unparalleled. Because performers and showtimes can vary widely, it's best to contact comedy clubs directly to see what's on the schedule. Note that a cover charge and drink minimum is almost always in effect.

253 West 125th St
Harlem

The Apollo Theater
212 531 5300 | www.apollotheater.com

Famous for the Amateur Night contests which started back in 1934 and gave all who braved the stage their 15 minutes worth of fame and glory. The venue has played host to many other events and is considered the major player in the inception, emergence and development of musical genres including jazz, swing, bebop, R&B, gospel, blues, soul and hip-hop with the likes of Ella Fitzgerald, Billie Holiday, Sammy Davis Jnr, James Brown, Bill Cosby – the list is endless – all treading the boards at some stage in their careers, and for many, more than the once. Many an artist has claimed their fame after an appearance at the Apollo which still has a massive fan base, whether for its historical significance, its cultural legacy, its architectural importance or just its guaranteed good nights out. A definite must-see.

Comedy

Name	Address	Phone	Website	Minimum Spend
Carolines on Broadway	1626 Broadway	212 757 4100	www.carolines.com	Drink minimum
Comedy Cellar	117 MacDougal Street	212 254 3480		Food or drink minimum
Comix	353 W. 14th Street	212 524 2500	www.comixny.com	No drink minimum
Gotham Comedy Club	208 W. 23rd Street	212 367 9000	www.gothamcomedyclub.com	Drink minimum
New York Comedy Club	241 E. 24th Street	212 696 5233	www.newyorkcomedyclub.com	Drink minimum
Upright Citizens Brigade	307 W. 26th Street	212 366 9176	www.ucbtheatre.com	No drink minimum

436

Entertainment

'Come On Now Toots'

Started by three friends with a passion for music, the Music Slut (musicslut.blogspot.com) is fast becoming a much-loved phenomenon on New York's music scene. Apart from reviews on new releases and profiles on new bands, the Music Slut trio attend all the city's concerts and club performances to give you the lowdown on up and coming acts. If you're serious about your music, both mainstream and off the beaten track, give the Music Slut a gander.

Concerts

Live music is a huge part of the New York City scene. Mega-bands like U2 and the Rolling Stones have recently played to sold-out crowds at Madison Square Garden, while more alternative and up-and-coming bands play more intimate venues like Irving Plaza and Bowery Ballroom. The Blue Note, Birdland, and Dizzy's Club Coca-Cola are popular jazz haunts, while Lincoln Center is home to the esteemed New York Philharmonic. Come summer, festivals like Central Park SummerStage (www.summerstage.org), Siren Music Festival (www.villagevoice.com/siren), and Celebrate Brooklyn (www.celebratebrooklyn.org) offer free concerts.

Fashion Shows

Every February and September, Manhattan is bursting with skinny models, fabulously dressed fashion editors, and parties galore. It's Olympus Fashion Week (www.olympusfashionweek.com), when elite designers like Donna Karan and Calvin Klein showcase their spring and fall collections. Besides the fashion shows, much of the excitement of Fashion Week is provided by the nightclub openings that generally coincide with it. It's a heady, exhausting week of parties, models, bottles, and excellent celebrity sightings.

Theatre

One word: Broadway. The Great White Way is home to some of the world's finest theatrical productions, from musicals like *Les Miserables* and *Hairspray* to dramas like the recent *History Boys*. Theatres are clustered around Times Square, with performances generally running Tuesday through Sunday, with matinees on Wednesday and Sunday. Expect to pay anywhere from $60-$110 for a decent seat, although purchasing tickets via www.playbill.com or waiting on line at the TKTS booth in Times Square (www.tdf.org/tkts) can fetch better deals on select shows. Off-Broadway and Off-Off-Broadway shows are less expensive and oftentimes more avant-garde alternatives. Visit www.nytheatre.com for updated show listings.

Hot Tip for Tickets

There is a lesser-known alternative to the TKTS booth in Times Square, where the queues are usually much shorter. Head for the corner of Front and John Streets at South Street Seaport (you can take the M15 bus all the way down Second Avenue). See www.tdf.org/tkts for more info on opening times.

437

The Complete **Residents'** Guide

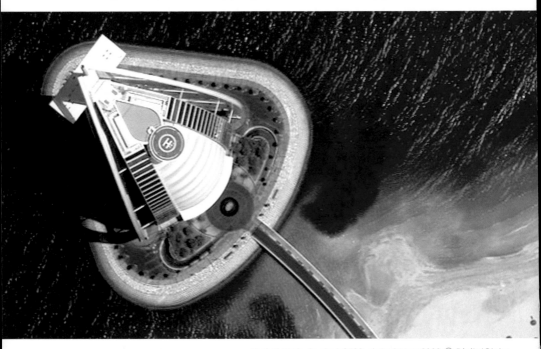

Maps

Maps

User's Guide

This section has 13 detailed maps of Manhattan, split into its various neighbourhoods. They are intended to help you get your bearings when you first arrive, and give you an idea of where some of the attractions and venues listed in the main chapters of the book can be found.

The Manhattan overview map (facing page) shows where these areas are. They are blown up at a scale of 1:7,500 (1cm=100m). Some of the things you can find marked on the map are main hotels, shopping areas and malls, hospitals, heritage sites and parks. See the legend below for an idea of which is which. You'll also find the major subway stations, but if you need more help navigating the comprehensive underground network, you can take a look at the map on the inside back cover.

Street Index

Manhattan is one of the easiest major cities in the world to navigate , thanks to the grid system. However, once you get below 14th Street, things get a bit more random and it can be difficult to find your bearings. Turn to the street index on p.470 for a listing of all street names and their corresponding map reference.

More Maps

Beyond these maps and the very nifty New York Mini Map, there are a number of detailed street directories to be found in New York's bookshops and newsagents. In addition, most New York guide books have pullout maps in them, and of course you'll find numerous free maps being distributed at tourist centres, heritage sites and at major subway stations

Throughout the book, you'll see map references listed next to various locations in the following format: 4-A5. The first number is the map number, and the other two digits refer to the grid location on the map. To get the bigger picture, the pullout map gives an overview of Manhattan in relation to its neighbouring boroughs, to help you get your bearings when you are heading further afield. There's even a map of the whole of the USA on p.442.

Need More?

This is a pretty big book – it needs to be to pack in all the information you need when you live in a city like New York. But unless you've got huge pockets, it's not the ideal size for carrying around with you when you're out and about. With this in mind, Explorer has created the New York Mini Map as a more manageable alternative. This handy little fold-out map packs the whole city into your pocket, and is an excellent navigational tool. It is part of a series of Mini Maps that includes cities as diverse as London, Dublin, Sydney and Paris. To find out more about Explorer's nifty range of visitor's and residents' guides, log on to www.explorerpublishing. com, or nip into any good bookshop.

Online Maps

There are a few websites that have searchable maps of New York: www.ny.com/maps and www.mapquest.com are both useful, and Schmap maps (see www.schmap.com and download New York) are also pretty good. Hardcore map fans tend to like Google Earth (download from http://earth.google.com) for its satellite images, powerful search facility and incredibly detailed views, but the street directory isn't very detailed. However, Google also has some excellent online street maps.

Map Legend

Hotel		Main Highway	
Water Text		Major Road	
Park		Secondary Road	
Hospital		Other Road or Track	
Shopping		State Border	
Museum		Country Border	
Education		Underway	
Built-up Area		59th St	Metro Station
		New Zealand	Embassy/Consulate
		SOHO	Area Name

New York Explorer 1st Edition

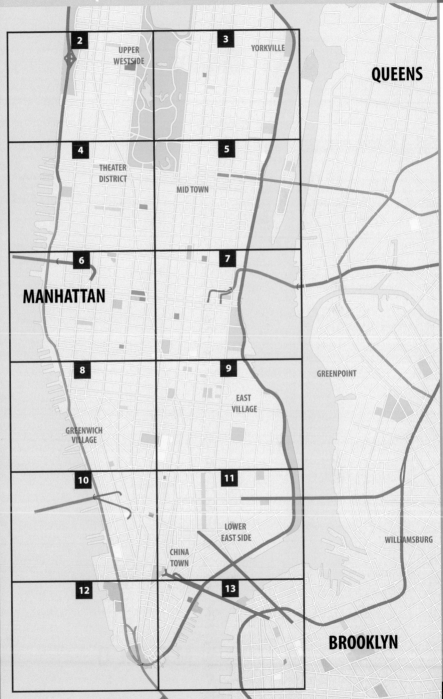

N

A   B   C

Edmonton ○

CANADA

Vancouver ○

Regina ○

1

○ Seattle

Olympia ○

Washington

Montana

Salem ○   Helena ○   **North Dakota**

Bismarck ○

Oregon   **Idaho**

Boise ○   **South Dakota**

Pierre ○

2   **Wyoming**

Sacramento ○   ○ Carson City   Salt Lake City ○   Cheyenne   **Nebraska**
                                                            ○
San Francisco ○   **Nevada**   **Utah**   Denver ○

California   **Colorado**

                                                            Kansas

Las Vegas
○

3   Los Angeles ○   Santa Fe   **Oklahoma**
                                    ○   Oklahoma City ○
                        Arizona
                        Phoenix ○   **New Mexico**
Mexicali ○

Texas

Austin ○

North
Pacific
Ocean   Hermosillo ○

Chihuahua ○

4

MEXICO

A   B   C

New York Explorer 1st Edition

CANADA

Winnipeg

Québec

Maine

Montréal   Augusta

OTTAWA   Montpelier

Minnesota   New Hamshire

Vermont   Concord

St. Paul   Albany   Boston

Wisconsin   Massachusetts

Providence

Madison   Toronto   New York   Connecticut   Rhonde

Island

Lansing   Detroit

Iowa   Chicago   Pennsylvania

New York

Des Moines   Indiana   Philadelphia   Trenton

Harrisburg   New Jersey

Lincoln   Ohio   Dover

Indianapolis   Columbus   Maryland   Delaware

Illinois   Annapolis

Springfield   West

Virginia   • WASHINGTON, D.C.

Topeka   Charleston   Richmond

Jefferson City   St. Louis   Virginia

Frankfort

Missouri   Kentucky   Raleigh

North

Nashville   Carolina

Tennessee

Arkansas   Memphis   Columbia

Little Rock   Atlanta   South

Carolina

Alabama   Georgia

Mississippi

Dallas   Montgomery

Jackson   North

Louisiana   Atlantic

Tallahassee   Ocean

Baton

Rouge

Houston   New Orleans

Florida

THE BAHAMAS

Miami

Gulf of Mexico   Nassau

175km

The Complete **Residents'** Guide

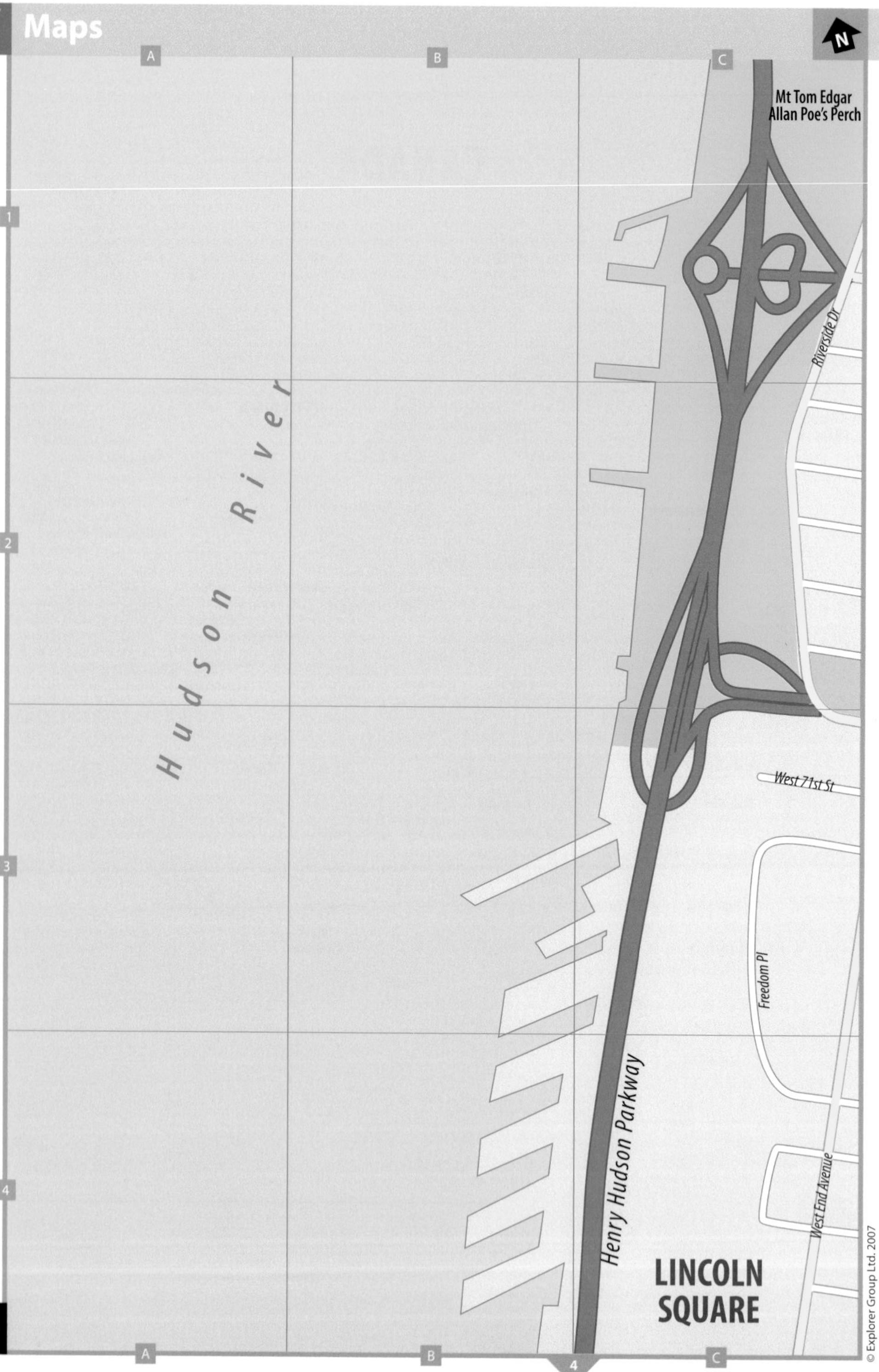

N

Mt Tom Edgar
Allan Poe's Perch

Riverside Dr

Hudson River

West 71st St

Freedom Pl

Henry Hudson Parkway

West End Avenue

**LINCOLN
SQUARE**

© Explorer Group Ltd. 2007

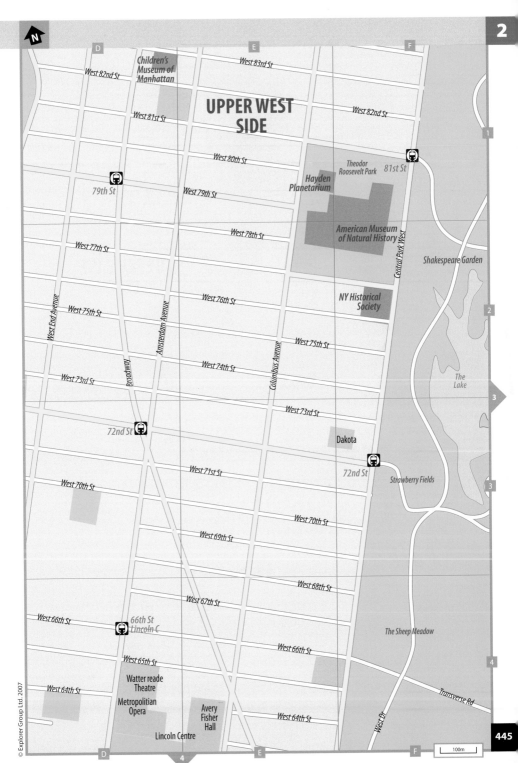

N

D — Children's Museum of Manhattan

West 82nd St

West 83rd St

E

F

UPPER WEST SIDE

West 82nd St

West 81st St

1

Theodor Roosevelt Park

West 80th St

81st St

Hayden Planetarium

79th St

West 79th St

American Museum of Natural History

Central Park West

Shakespeare Garden

West 78th St

West 77th St

NY Historical Society

2

West End Avenue

West 75th St

West 76th St

Amsterdam Avenue

Columbus Avenue

West 75th St

Broadway

West 74th St

The Lake

West 73rd St

3

West 73rd St

72nd St

Dakota

72nd St

West 71st St

Strawberry Fields

3

West 70th St

West 70th St

West 69th St

West 68th St

West 67th St

West 66th St

66th St Lincoln C

The Sheep Meadow

West 66th St

4

West 65th St

Watter reade Theatre

Metropolitian Opera

West 64th St

Avery Fisher Hall

West 64th St

Transverse Rd

West Dr

Lincoln Centre

D

4

E

F

445

100m

© Explorer Group Ltd. 2007

N

The Great Lawn

Cleopatra's
Needle

Metropolitian
Museum of Art

Turtle Pond

79th St Transverse Rd

Ukrainian Inst
of America

France

The Mark

Yivo Inst for
Jewish Research

Fifth Avenue

Madison Ave

Park Avenue

East 81st St

**UPPER EAST
SIDE**

East 79th St

East 77th St

77th St

The Carlyle

Lenox
Hill Hospital

Statue of Alice
in Wonderland

The
Lake

Statue of H Ch
Andersen

Conservatory
Water

Whitney Museum
of American Art

East 75th St

East 74th St

East 73rd St

Lexington Ave

East 72nd St

Park

Frick
Collection

East 71st St

Austria

Bridle Path

East Green

Fifth Avenue

Madison Ave

Park Avenue

Italy

CUNY Hunter
College

East 69th St

68th St
Hunter College

East 67th St

Temple
Emanu-El

East 66th St

446

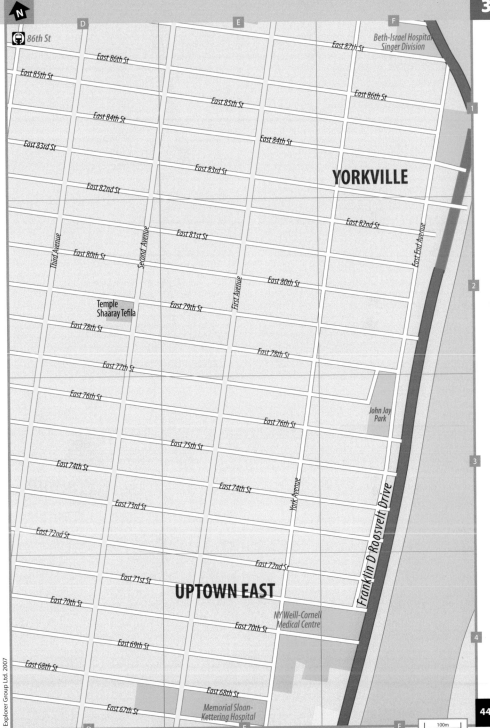

N

86th St

East 86th St

East 85th St

East 84th St

East 83rd St

East 82nd St

East 85th St

Beth-Israel Hospital
Singer Division

East 87th St

East 86th St

East 84th St

East 83rd St

YORKVILLE

Third Avenue

Second Avenue

East 81st St

East 80th St

East 79th St

First Avenue

East 82nd St

East 81st St

East 80th St

East End Avenue

Temple
Shaaray Tefila

East 78th St

East 77th St

East 76th St

East 78th St

East 75th St

East 74th St

East 73rd St

East 72nd St

East 76th St

York Avenue

John Jay
Park

East 74th St

East 72nd St

Franklin D Roosvelt Drive

East 71st St

UPTOWN EAST

East 70th St

East 69th St

East 68th St

East 67th St

East 70th St

East 68th St

NY Weill-Cornell
Medical Centre

Memorial Sloan-
Kettering Hospital

© Explorer Group Ltd. 2007

100m

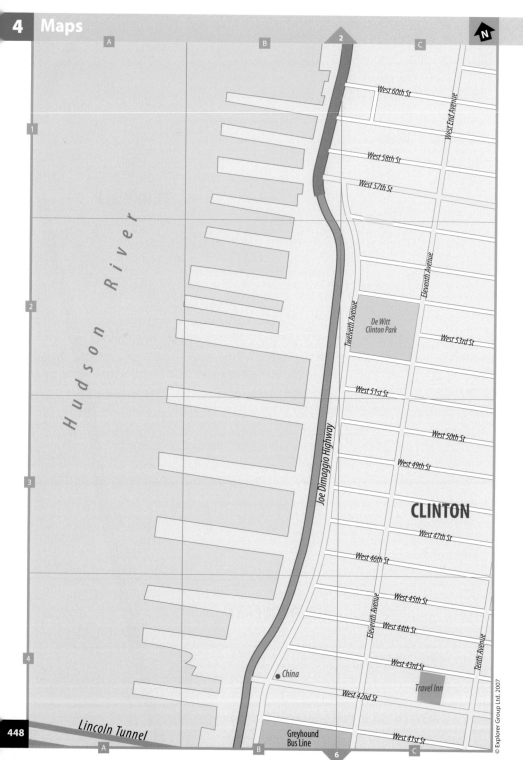

N

A B 2 C

1

Hudson River

2

West 60th St

West End Avenue

West 58th St

West 57th St

Eleventh Avenue

Twelveth Avenue

De Witt
Clinton Park

West 53rd St

West 51st St

3

West 50th St

West 49th St

CLINTON

Joe Dimaggio Highway

West 47th St

West 46th St

Eleventh Avenue

West 45th St

West 44th St

Tenth Avenue

West 43rd St

4

● *China*

Travel Inn

West 42nd St

West 41st St

Lincoln Tunnel

A B 6 C

Greyhound
Bus Line

© Explorer Group Ltd. 2007

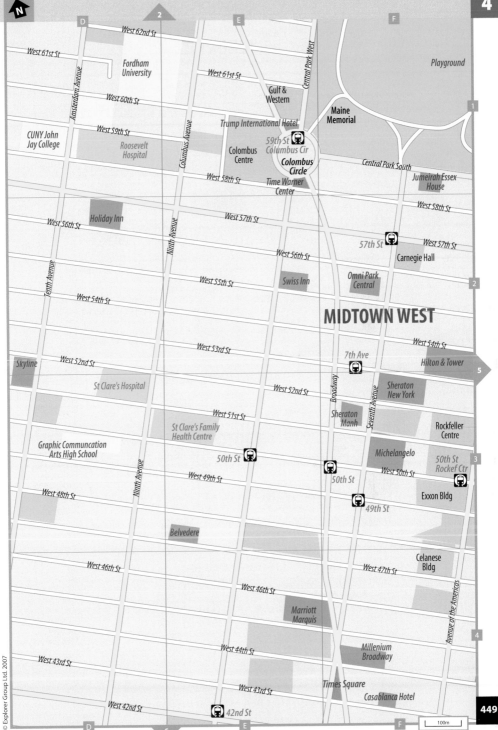

West 62nd St
West 61st St
Fordham University
West 61st St
Gulf & Western
Central Park West
Playground
West 60th St
Trump International Hotel
Maine Memorial
Amsterdam Avenue
West 59th St
CUNY John Jay College
Columbus Avenue
Colombus Centre
59th St Columbus Cir
Colombus Circle
Roosevelt Hospital
West 58th St
Time Warner Center
Central Park South
Jumeirah Essex House
West 58th St
Holiday Inn
West 57th St
West 56th St
Ninth Avenue
57th St
West 57th St
West 56th St
Carnegie Hall
Tenth Avenue
West 55th St
Swiss Inn
Omni Park Central
West 54th St

MIDTOWN WEST

West 53rd St
West 54th St
Skyline
West 52nd St
7th Ave
Hilton & Tower
St Clare's Hospital
West 52nd St
Broadway
Sheraton New York
West 51st St
Seventh Avenue
Sheraton Manh
St Clare's Family Health Centre
Rockfeller Centre
Graphic Communcation Arts High School
Ninth Avenue
50th St
Michelangelo
50th St Rockef Ctr
West 49th St
50th St
West 50th St
West 48th St
49th St
Exxon Bldg
Belvedere
Celanese Bldg
West 46th St
West 47th St
West 46th St
Avenue of the Americas
Marriott Marquis
West 44th St
Millenium Broadway
West 43rd St
West 43rd St
Times Square
Casablanca Hotel
West 42nd St
42nd St
100m

N

● India

LENOX HILL

East 65th St

Wollman Skating
Rink

East 64th St

**Central Park Wildlife Center &
Tisch Children's Zoo**

Fifth Ave
Synagogue

East 63rd St

63rd St
Lexington Ave

Barbizon

East 62nd St

The
Pond

Regency

Pierre

East 61st St

Central Park South

5th Ave

Sherry
Netherland

Ritz Carlton

Barneys

Bloomingdale's

Medical Arts
Centre

General Motors Bldg

59th St

East 59th St

Solow Bldg

Bergdorf
Goodman

East 58th St

57th St

Four Seasons

Ritz
Tower

Spain

Germany

West 56th St

Trump
Tower

IBM Bldg

East 57th St

West 55th St

Sony Bldg

East 56th St

Warwick

St Regis

American Folk
Art Museum

Museum of
Modern Art

East 55th St

Hong Kong

Lever Bldg

Citibank
Bldg

East 54th St

909 Third Ave

Mus of
Television
& Radio

5th Ave

West 53rd St

MIDTOWN

Lexington
Ave

East 53rd St

Rockefeller
Plaza

Olympic
Tower

Ireland

East 52nd St

Nikon
Hse Mus

St Patrick's
Cathedral

New York
Palace

Grolier Bldg

United Kingdom

East 51st St

GE Bldg

Saks Fifth
Avenue

● Canada

51st St

East 50th St

Waldorf=Astoria

Dahesh
Museum

270 Park

Westvaco Bldg

East 49th St

Chem
Bank Bldg

East 48th St

Hammarskjold
Plaza

East 47th St

French Bldg

Roosevelt

The Algonquin

East 46th St

Met
Life Bldg

Grand
Central Terminal

East 44th St

East 45th St

© Explorer Group Ltd. 2007

New York Explorer 1st Edition

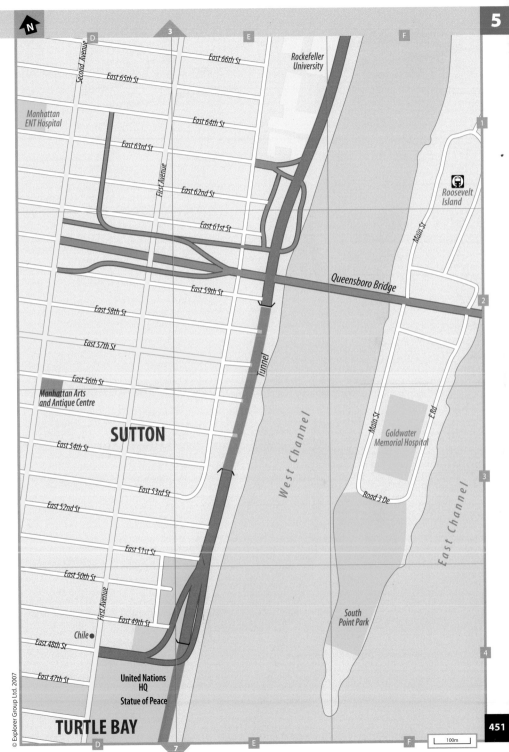

N

East 66th St

Rockefeller
University

Second Avenue

East 65th St

Manhattan
ENT Hospital

East 64th St

East 63rd St

Roosevelt
Island

First Avenue

East 62nd St

Main St

East 61st St

East 59th St

Queensboro Bridge

East 58th St

Tunnel

East 57th St

East 56th St

Manhattan Arts
and Antique Centre

SUTTON

West Channel

Main St

Goldwater
Memorial Hospital

E Rd

East 54th St

East 53rd St

Road 3 De

East 52nd St

East 51st St

East 50th St

First Avenue

East 49th St

South
Point Park

Chile ●

East 48th St

East 47th St

**United Nations
HQ**

Statue of Peace

TURTLE BAY

East Channel

100m

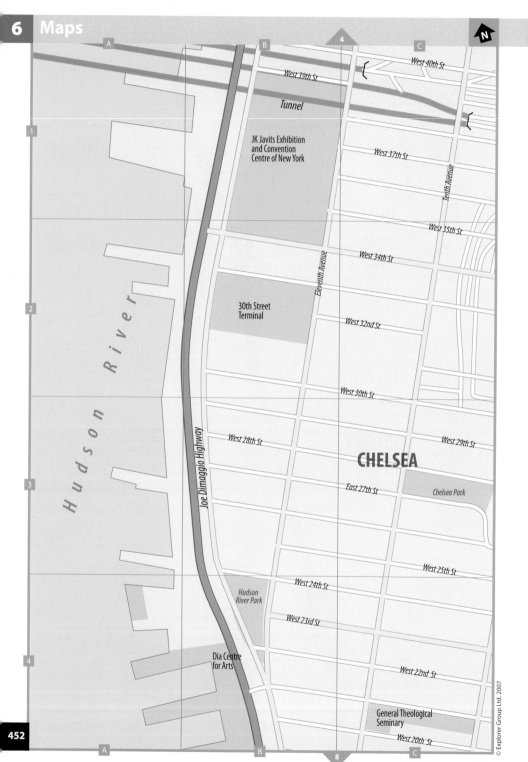

West 40th St

West 39th St

Tunnel

JK Javits Exhibition
and Convention
Centre of New York

West 37th St

Tenth Avenue

West 35th St

West 34th St

Eleventh Avenue

30th Street
Terminal

West 32nd St

West 30th St

West 28th St

West 29th St

CHELSEA

East 27th St

Chelsea Park

West 25th St

Hudson
River Park

West 24th St

West 23rd St

Dia Centre
for Arts

West 22nd St

General Theological
Seminary

West 20th St

Joe Dimaggio Highway

H u d s o n   R i v e r

N

Port Authority
Bus Terminal

Madame Tussaud's

Hilton Times Square

Times Sq 42nd St

East 42nd St

42nd St

NY Telephone Bldg

East 41st St

Bryant Park

JAVITS CENTRE

West 40th St

West 39th St

Avenue of the Americas

FASHION CENTRE

East 39th St

Empire State Building

West 38th St

West 37th St

East 37th St

Navarre Bldg

Ninth Avenue

West 36th St

West 35th St

Eighth Avenue

West 36th St

West 34th St

34th St Penn Station

Nelson Tower

Macy's

East 35th St

34th St

West 33rd St

1 Penn Plaza

34th St

34th St

East 34th St

General Post Office

New York Penn Station

Madison Square Garden

New York Pennsylvania

Manhattan Mall

East 32nd St

7

West 31st St

West 30th St

West 30th St

East 30th St

West 29th St

28th St

3

28th St

Fashion Institute of Technology

West 28th St

28th St

West 26th St

MANHATTAN

Seventh Avenue

West 25th St

West 26th St

Broadway

4

West 24th St

The Hotel Chelsea

Avenue of the Americas (Sixth Ave)

West 24th St

23rd St

23rd St

23rd St

West 23rd St

23rd St

West 21st St

West 22nd St

100m

N

East 44th St

East 43rd St

Grand
Central Terminal

42nd St
Grand Central

5th Ave

Grand
Hyatt

Australia

East 42nd St

Israel

Ford Found
Bldg

New York
Public Library

Lincoln Bldg

Chanin
Bldg

Mobil Bldg

Former Daily
News Bldg

American
Standard Bldg

East 41st St

Switzerland

New Zealand

East 41st St

East 39th St

Mexico

Redford

Lexington Ave

East 40th St

Lord & Taylor

MURRAY HILL

East 39th St

Madison Ave

East 38th St

East 37th St

East 37th St

Pierpont
Morgan Library

Lexington Ave

East 36th St

East 35th St

East 35th St

Empire State
Bldg

East 34th St

St Gabriel's Park

East 35th St

East 32nd St

33rd St

East 33rd St

East 34th St

MIDTOWN SOUTH

East 32nd St

East 33rd St

KIPS BAY

East 31st St

New York University
Hospitalls Center –
Tisch Hospital

Carlton

East 30th St

Kips Bay Plaza
Apartments

Fifth Avenue

East 29th St

Gershwin Hotel

28th St

East 29th St

East 28th St

New York Life
Insurance Bldg

Hotel
Giraffe

East 27th St

East 27th St

Phipps
Plaza

Lexington Ave

Third Avenue

Madison Sq Park

East 25th St

East 26th St

Madison Ave

Park Avenue South

East 24th St

CUNY

Second Avenue

East 25th St

Metropolitian
Life Insurance
Bldg

East 23rd St

23rd St

East 24th St

East Midtown
Plaza

Veterans
Administration
Hospital

© Explorer Group Ltd. 2007

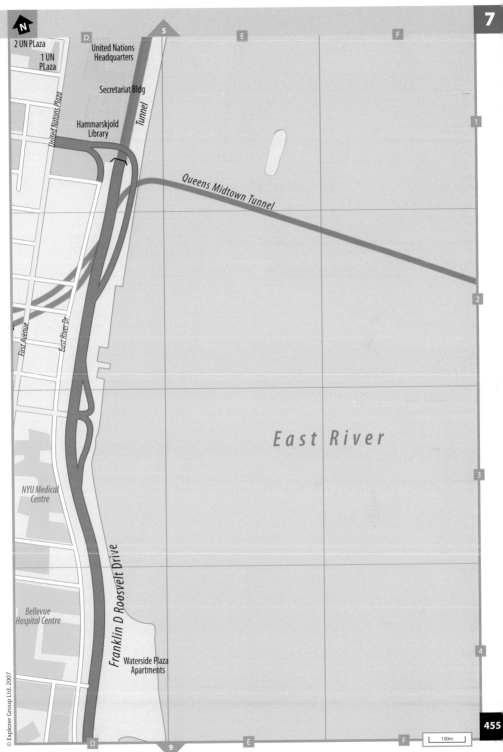

2 UN PLaza

1 UN PLaza

D

United Nations Headquarters

5

E

F

United Nations Plaza

Secretariat Bldg

Tunnel

Hammarskjold Library

1

Queens Midtown Tunnel

First Avenue

East River Dr

2

East River

NYU Medical Centre

3

Franklin D Roosevelt Drive

Bellevue Hospital Centre

4

Waterside Plaza Apartments

© Explorer Group Ltd. 2007

D

9

E

F

100m

The Complete **Residents'** Guide

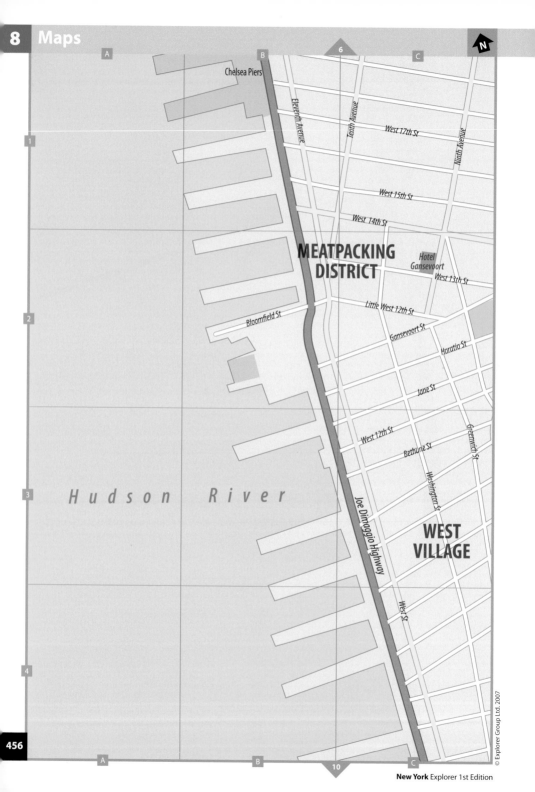

Chelsea Piers

Eleventh Avenue

Tenth Avenue

West 17th St

Ninth Avenue

West 15th St

West 14th St

MEATPACKING DISTRICT

Hotel Gansevoort

West 13th St

Little West 12th St

Bloomfield St

Gansevoort St

Horatio St

Jane St

West 12th St

Bethune St

Greenwich St

H u d s o n   R i v e r

Joe Dimaggio Highway

Washington St

WEST VILLAGE

West St

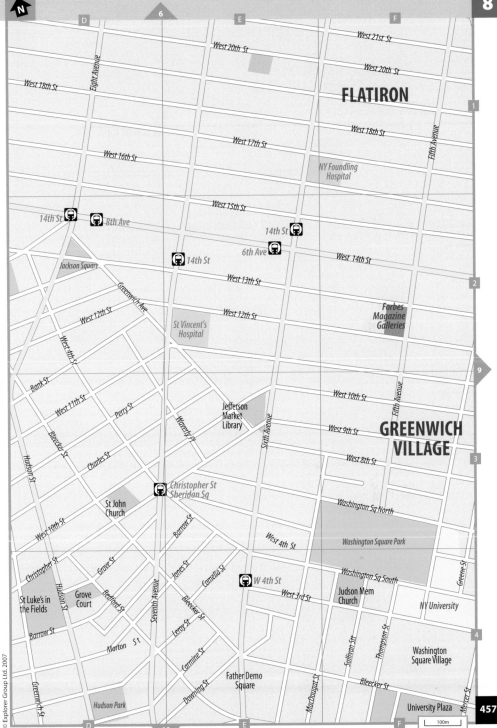

FLATIRON

GREENWICH VILLAGE

West 21st St
West 20th St
West 20th St
West 18th St
West 18th St
West 17th St
West 16th St
West 15th St
NY Foundling Hospital
14th St
8th Ave
14th St
6th Ave
14th St
West 14th St
West 13th St
Jackson Square
West 12th St
West 12th St
Greenwich Ave
St Vincent's Hospital
Forbes Magazine Galleries
Bank St
West 11th St
Perry St
West 12th St
West 4th St
Waverly Pl
Jefferson Market Library
West 10th St
West 9th St
Fifth Avenue
Sixth Avenue
West 8th St
Christopher St Sheridan Sq
St John Church
Washington Sq North
Washington Square Park
West 10th St
Christopher St
Grove St
Barrow St
Jones St
Camelia St
W 4th St
West 4th St
West 3rd St
Washington Sq South
Greene St
St Luke's in the Fields
Grove Court
Bedford St
Seventh Avenue
Bleecker St
Leroy St
Judson Mem Church
NY University
Barrow St
Morton St
Carmine St
Downing St
Sullivan St
Thompson St
MacDougal St
Washington Square Village
Father Demo Square
Bleecker St
Hudson Park
University Plaza
Mercer St

© Explorer Group Ltd. 2007

100m

N

East 22nd St

CYNY Boruch College

East 23rd St

Gramercy Park Hotel

East 21st St

East 22nd St

Gramercy Park

East 20th St

Police Academy Museum

Th Roosevelt Birthplace

East 19th St

Cabrini Medical Centre

GRAMERCY

East 19th St

East 18th St

1st Ave

East 17th St

East 17th St

Union Sq Park

East 16th St

Irving Pl

Stuyvesant Sq

Beth-Israel Medical Centre

East 15th St

Con Edison Bldg

East 15th St

Loop

East 14th St

14th St

3rd Ave

East 14th St

East 15th St

1st Ave

New York Eye & Ear Hospital

East 13th St

East 12th St

Broadway

Fourth Avenue

East 12th St

East 11th St

East 10th St

East 11th St

West 9th St

Third Avenue

East 10th St

West 8th St

8th St

Second Avenue

East 10th St

Astor Pl

East 9th St

Waverly Pl

Marks Pl

Mercer St

NOHO

East 7th St

Merchant's House Museum

First Avenue

Avenue A

East 5th St

Village View Houses

East 4th St

East 3rd St

East 4th St

East 2nd St

East 3rd St

© Explorer Group Ltd. 2007

New York Explorer 1st Edition

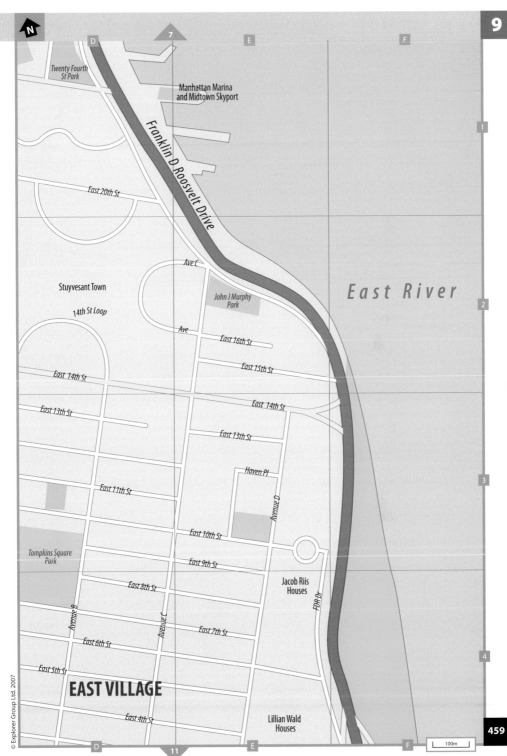

Twenty Fourth St Park

Manhattan Marina and Midtown Skyport

Franklin D Roosevelt Drive

East 20th St

Ave C

Stuyvesant Town

John J Murphy Park

14th St Loop

Ave

East 16th St

East 15th St

East 14th St

East 14th St

East 13th St

East 13th St

Haven Pl

Avenue D

East 11th St

East 10th St

Tompkins Square Park

East 9th St

East 8th St

Jacob Riis Houses

Avenue B

Avenue C

FDR Dr

East 7th St

East 6th St

East 5th St

EAST VILLAGE

East 4th St

Lillian Wald Houses

East River

100m

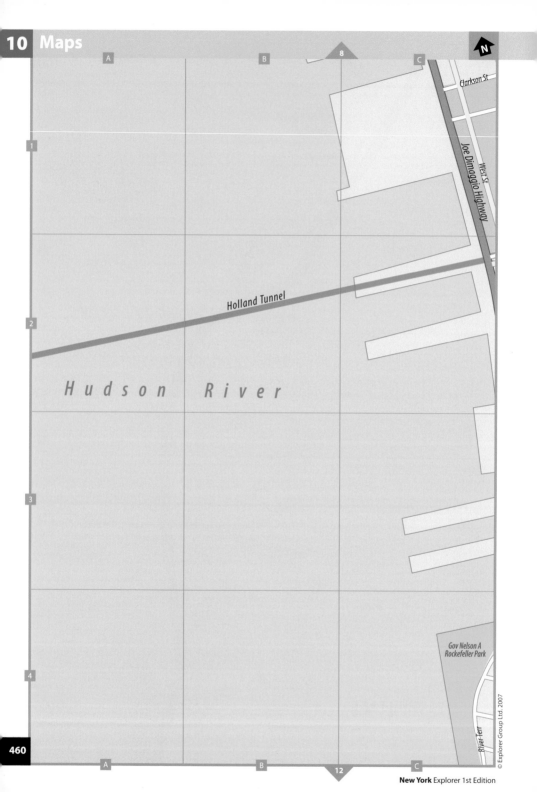

Clarkson St

West St

Joe Dimaggio Highway

Holland Tunnel

H u d s o n   R i v e r

Gov Nelson A
Rockefeller Park

River Terr

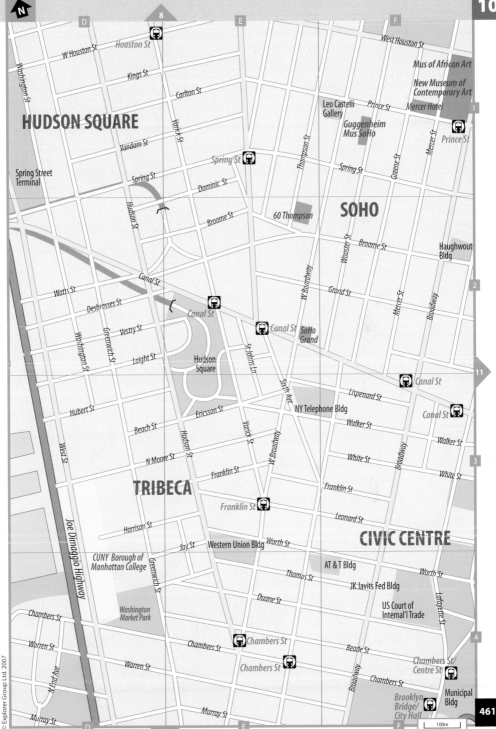

N

D 8 E F

West Houston St

W Houston St
Houston St

Mus of African Art

New Museum of
Contemporary Art

Kings St

Leo Castelli
Gallery

Carlton St

Prince St
Mercer Hotel

1

Guggenheim
Mus SoHo

Prince St

HUDSON SQUARE

Vandam St

Spring St

Spring St

Spring St

Mercer St
Greene St
Thompson St

Spring Street
Terminal

Dominic St

SOHO

Hudson St

Broome St

60 Thompson

Broome St

Wooster St

Haughwout
Bldg

Canal St

Watts St

Grand St

2

Desbrosses St

Vestry St

Canal St

Mercer St
Broadway
W Broadway

Washington St
Greenwich St

Laight St

Hudson
Square

Canal St

SoHo
Grand

St Johns Ln

11

Canal St

Hubert St

Ericsson St

Sixth Ave

Lispenard St

NY Telephone Bldg

Canal St

Beach St

Walker St

N Moore St

White St

Walker St

Hudson St
Varick St
W Broadway

3

West St

Franklin St

White St

TRIBECA

Franklin St

Franklin St

Franklin St

Leonard St

Joe Dimaggio Highway

Harrison St

CIVIC CENTRE

Jay St

Western Union Bldg

Worth St

CUNY Borough of
Manhattan College

Greenwich St

AT & T Bldg

Worth St

Thomas St

JK Javits Fed Bldg

Broadway
Lafayette St

Duane St

US Court of
Internat'l Trade

Washington
Market Park

Chambers St

4

Warren St

Chambers St

Chambers St

Reade St

Chambers St/
Centre St

Warren St

Chambers St

Broadway

Chambers St

Brooklyn
Bridge/
City Hall

Municipal
Bldg

Murray St

Murray St

N End Ave

100m

The Complete **Residents'** Guide

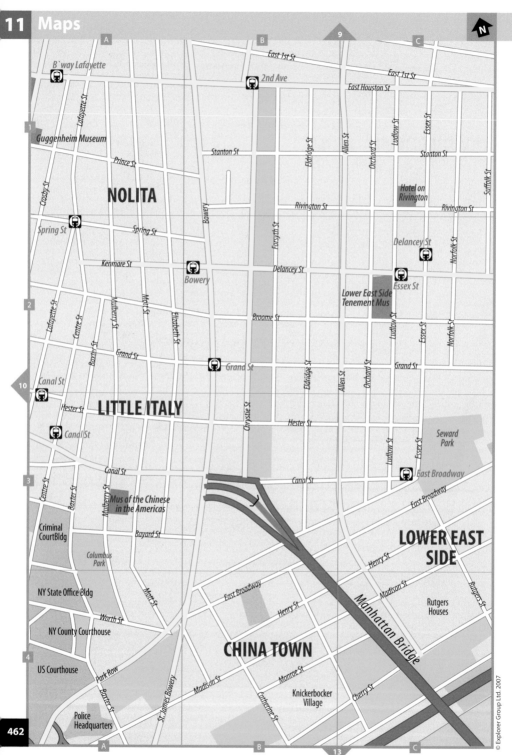

N

A | B | 9 | C

East 1st St

B`way Lafayette

2nd Ave

East 1st St

East Houston St

1

Guggenheim Museum

Stanton St

Prince St

Ludlow St
Essex St

Eldridge St
Allen St
Orchard St

Stanton St

NOLITA

Bowery

Rivington St

Hotel on Rivington

Suffolk St

Rivington St

Spring St

Spring St

Forsyth St

Delancey St

Norfolk St

Delancey St

Kenmare St

Bowery

Delancey St

Essex St

Essex St

2

Lafayette St
Centre St
Baxter St

Mulberry St
Mott St

Elizabeth St

Broome St

Lower East Side Tenement Mus

Ludlow St

Norfolk St

Grand St

Grand St

Grand St

Eldridge St
Allen St
Orchard St

Grand St

10

Canal St

Canal St

Hester St

LITTLE ITALY

Chrystie St

Hester St

Essex St

Ludlow St

Seward Park

Canal St

Canal St

East Broadway

Canal St

3

Centre St
Baxter St

Mulberry St

Mus of the Chinese in the Americas

East Broadway

Criminal Court Bldg

Bayard St

Columbus Park

LOWER EAST SIDE

NY State Office Bldg

Mott St

East Broadway

Henry St

Madison St

Rutgers St

Worth St

Henry St

Rutgers Houses

NY County Courthouse

CHINA TOWN

Manhattan Bridge

4

US Courthouse

Park Row

Madison St

Monroe St

Knickerbocker Village

Cherry St

Police Headquarters

Baxter St

St. James Bowery

Catherine St

© Explorer Group Ltd. 2007

East 3rd St
East 2nd St

Avenue D

Attorney St
Clinton St

Hamilton
Fish Park

East River

1

Ridge St

Columbia St

Baruch
Houses

Baruch Dr

Gompers
Houses

Franklin D Roosevelt Drive

East
River
Park

Attorney St
Pitt St

FDR Dr

FDR Dr

FDR Dr

Williamsburg Bridge

2

Broome St
Clinton St

Pitt St

Hillman
Houses

Lewis St

Carlears
Hook

Grand St

Steward
Park Houses

Henry St

East Broadway

Madison St

Jackson St

Cherry St

3

Gouverneur
Hospital

Montgomery St
Gouverneur St

Vladeck House

Water St

Corlears
Hook Park

La Guardia
Houses

Clinton St

Cherry St

Franklin D Roosevelt Drive

W a l l a b o u t   B a y

4

© Explorer Group Ltd. 2007

100m

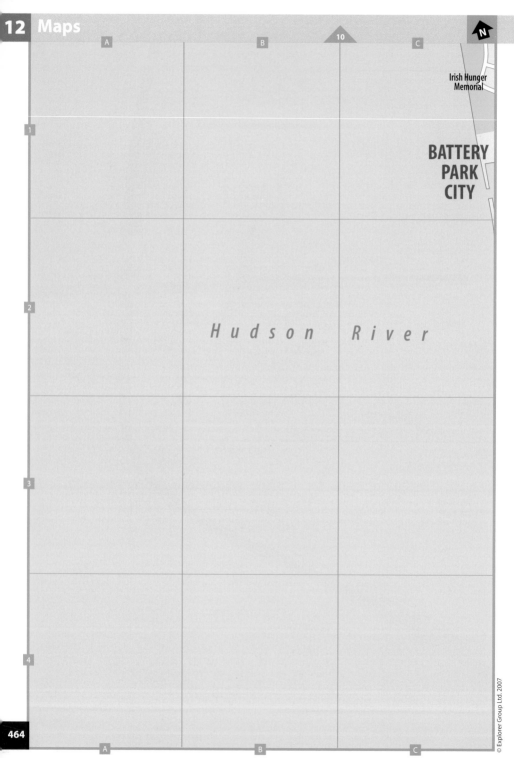

Irish Hunger
Memorial

**BATTERY
PARK
CITY**

Hudson River

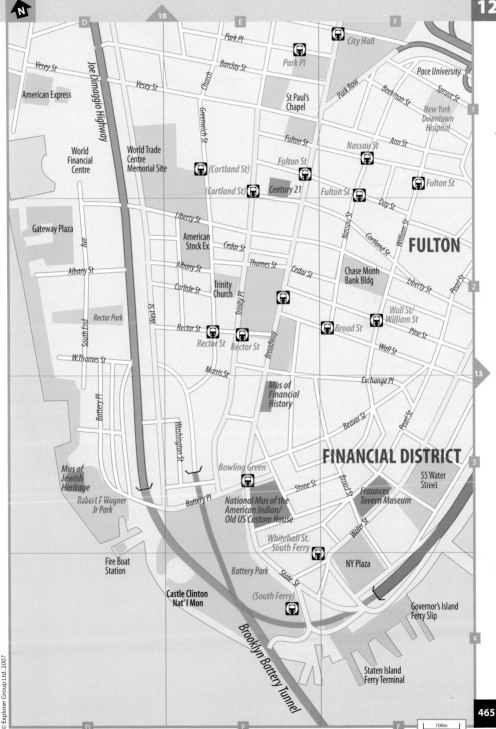

© Explorer Group Ltd. 2007

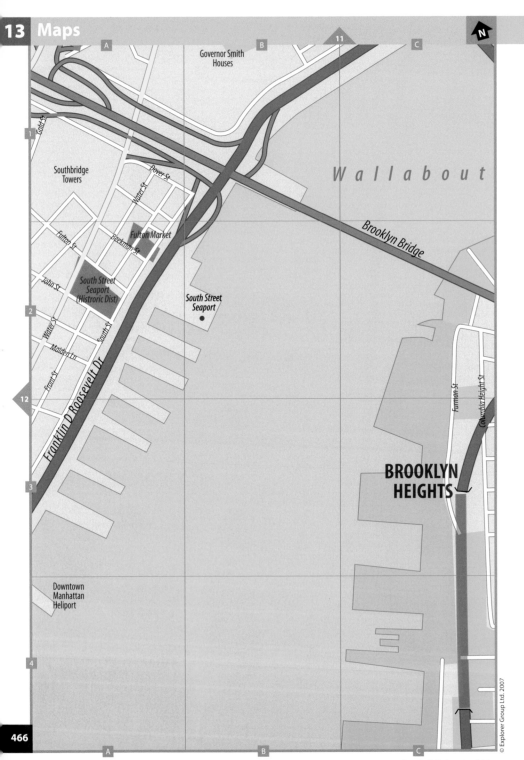

Governor Smith
Houses

11

Wallabout

Southbridge
Towers

Dover St

Water St

Brooklyn Bridge

Fulton Market

Fulton St

Beekman St

John St

South Street
Seaport
(Histroric Dist)

South Street
Seaport

Water St

South St

Malden Ln

Front St

12

Furman St

Columbia Height St

Franklin D. Roosevelt Dr

**BROOKLYN
HEIGHTS**

Downtown
Manhattan
Heliport

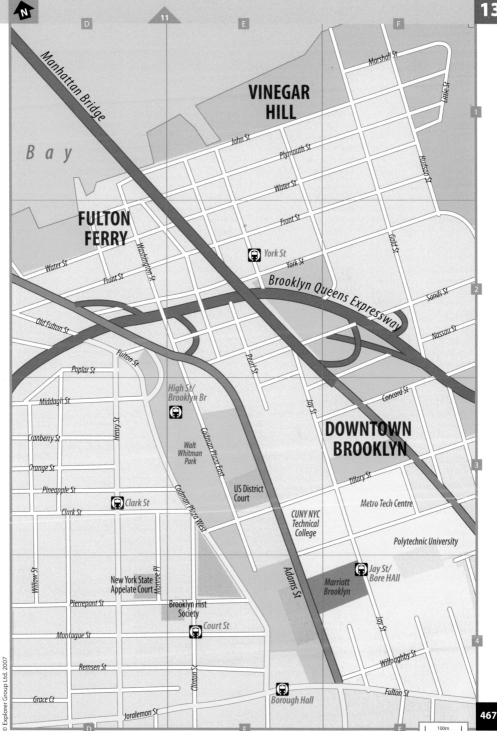

The Complete **Residents'** Guide

© Explorer Group Ltd. 2007

Index

Index

Index

477

Index

481

The *New York Explorer* Team
Lead Editor Jane Roberts
Deputy Editors Becky Lucas, Helen Spearman
Editorial Assistants Mimi Stankova, Ingrid Cupido
Lead Designer Rafi Pullat
Cartographers Sunitha Lakhiani, Zain Madathil & Noushad Madathil
Photographers Pamela Grist, Jane Roberts, Tom Jordan,
Louise Denly, Tilo Richter
Proofreader Audrey Lee

Publisher
Alistair MacKenzie

Editorial
Managing Editor Claire England
Lead Editors David Quinn, Jane Roberts, Matt Farquharson,
Sean Kearns, Tim Binks
Deputy Editors Helen Spearman, Katie Drynan, Tom Jordan
Editorial Assistants Ingrid Cupido, Mimi Stankova

Design
Creative Director Pete Maloney
Art Director Ieyad Charaf
Senior Designers Alex Jeffries, Motaz Al Bunai
Layout Manager Jayde Fernandes
Designers Hashim Moideen, Rafi Pullat,
Shefeeq Marakkatepurath, Sunita Lakhiani
Cartography Manager Zainudheen Madathil
Cartographer Noushad Madathil
Design Admin Manager Shyrell Tamayo
Production Coordinator Maricar Ong

Photography
Photography Manager Pamela Grist
Photographer Victor Romero
Image Editor Henry Hilos

Sales and Marketing
Area Sales Managers Laura Zuffa, Stephen Jones
Marketing Manager Kate Fox
Retail Sales Manager Ivan Rodrigues
Retail Sales Coordinator Kiran Melwani
Distribution Executives Abdul Gafoor, Ahmed Mainodin,
Firos Khan, Mannie Lugtu
Warehouse Assistant Mohammed Kunjaymo
Drivers Mohammed Sameer, Shabsir Madathil

Finance and Administration
Administration Manager Andrea Fust
Accounts Assistant Cherry Enriquez
Administrator Enrico Maullon
Driver Rafi Jamal

IT
IT Administrator Ajay Krishnan R.
Software Engineers Roshni Ahuja, Tissy Varghese

Explorer Publishing & Distribution
Office 51B, Zomorrodah Building, Za'abeel Road
PO Box 34275, Dubai, United Arab Emirates
Phone: +971 (0)4 335 3520, **Fax:** +971 (0)4 335 3529
info@explorerpublishing.com
www.explorerpublishing.com

Contact Us
Reader Response
If you have any comments and suggestions, fill out
our online reader response form and you could win prizes.
Log on to **www.explorerpublishing.com**

General Enquiries
We'd love to hear your thoughts and answer any questions
you have about this book or any other Explorer product.
Contact us at **info@explorerpublishing.com**

Careers
If you fancy yourself as an Explorer, send your CV (stating
the position you're interested in) to
jobs@explorerpublishing.com

Designlab and Contract Publishing
For enquiries about Explorer's Contract Publishing arm
and design services contact
designlab@explorerpublishing.com

PR and Marketing
For PR and marketing enquries contact
marketing@explorerpublishing.com
pr@explorerpublishing.com

Corporate Sales
For bulk sales and customisation options, for this book or
any Explorer product, contact
sales@explorerpublishing.com

Advertising and Sponsorship
For advertising and sponsorship, contact
media@explorerpublishing.com

Main Hotels

60 Thompson	877 431 0400
The Algonquin	212 840 6800
Casablanca Hotel	212 869 1212
Gershwin Hotel	212 545 8000
Gramercy Park Hotel	212 920 3300
The Hotel Chelsea	212 243 3700
Hotel Gansevoort	212 206 6700
Hotel Giraffe	212 685 7700
Hotel on Rivington	212 475 2600
Jumeirah Essex House	212 247 0300
Mercer Hotel	212 966 6060
Morgans Hotel	212 686 0300
Roosevelt Hotel	212 661 9600
Soho Grand	212 965 3000
Trump International Hotel	212 299 1000
Waldorf=Astoria	212 355 3000

Airport Information

JFK International Airport:

Lost Luggage	718 244 4224
Airport Information	718 244 4444

LaGuardia Airport:

Lost & Found	718 533 3988
Airport Information	718 533 3400

Newark Airport:

Lost & Found	973 961 6230
Airport Information	973 961 6000

Useful Numbers

Ambulance	911
Animal Emergency Clinic	212 924 3311
Babysitters' Guild	212 682 0227
Con Edison	800 752 6633
Crime Victims' Hotline	212 577 7777
Fire	911
General City Information	311
Missing Persons	212 473 2042
Operator	0
Police (Emergency)	911
Police (Information)	646 610 5000
Subway Information	718 330 4847
Terrorism Hotline	888 692 7233

Hospitals with Emergency Rooms

Bellevue Hospital Center	212 562 4141
Beth Israel Medical Center	212 420 2000
Cabrini Medical Center	212 995 6000
Harlem Hospital Center	212 939 1000
Lenox Hill Hospital	212 434 2000
Mount Sinai Hospital	212 241 6500
Weill Cornell Medical Center	212 746 5454
NYU Downtown	212 312 5000
NYU Medical Center (Tisch)	212 263 7300
St Luke's – Roosevelt Hospital	212 523 4000
St Vincents	212 604 7000

Tourist Information

Big Apple Visitors' Center	212 879 8905
Bronx Tourism Council	718 590 3518
Brooklyn Information & Culture	718 855 7882
Intours	718 888 1717
NYC and Co	212 484 1222
Staten Island Tourism Council	800 573 7469

Public Holidays

New Year's Day	January 1
Martin Luther King's Day	3rd Monday in January
President's Day	3rd Monday in February
Memorial Day	Last Monday in May
Independence Day	July 4
Labor Day	1st Monday in September
Columbus Day	2nd Monday in May
Veterans Day	November 11
Thanksgiving	4th Thursday in November
Christmas Day	December 25

Consulates

Australia	212 351 6500	7-B1
Austria	212 737 6400	3-B4
Bahamas	212 421 6420	5-C4
Bangladesh	212 599 6767	7-C1
Belgium	212 586 5110	5-A2
Brazil	212 827 0976	4-F4
Canada	212 596 1628	5-A3
Chile	212 980 3707	5-D4
China	212 244 9456	4-B4
Czech Republic	212 717 5643	3-C1
Denmark	212 223 4545	5-C4
Egypt	212 759 7120	na
France	212 606 3688	3-B2
Germany	212 610 9700	5-B2
India	212 774 0600	5-B1
Ireland	212 319 2562	5-B3
Israel	212 499 5610	7-C1
Italy	212 737 9100	3-C4
Jamaica	212 935 9000	na
Japan	212 371 8222	5-B4
Malaysia	212 490 2722	7-C1
Mexico	212 217 6400	7-A1
Netherlands	212 246 1430	5-A3
New Zealand	212 832 4038	7-C1
Norway	212 421 7333	5-C3
Peru	212 481 7410	5-C4
Philippines	212 764 1330	5-A3
Russia	212 348 0626	na
Saudi Arabia	212 752 2740	5-D4
South Africa	212 213 4880	5-C2
Spain	212 355 4080	5-C2
Sweden	212 563 2550	5-C4
Switzerland	212 599 5700	7-C1
Thailand	212 754 1770	5-D3
United Kingdom	212 745 0200	5-C3